STATISTICS FOR HEALTH SCIENCES

Online Lessons

▶ Contain highly engaging and interactive videos that use cutting-edge Cloud Learning technologies.

▶ Break down statistical concepts into logical and intuitive steps that enhance the learning process.

▶ Prepare students for upcoming classes, labs, and quizzes through self-study lessons.

▶ Contain lessons that are self-paced and are excellent for visual learners.

Online Labs

▶ Contain a comprehensive test-bank of real-world problems, which may be used as an assessment tool.

▶ Break down every answer into dynamic, step-by-step solutions.

▶ Provide unlimited amount of practice through algorithmically generated problems.

▶ Contain numerous statistical tools to analyze students' strengths and weaknesses.

Vretta

STATISTICS FOR HEALTH SCIENCES

First Edition

Authors

Sean Saunders, *Sheridan College*

Thambyrajah Kugathasan, *Seneca College*

Irene Lee, *Humber College*

Copyright © 2017 by Vretta Inc.

ISBN: 978-1-927737-24-8

Statistics for Health Sciences, First Edition

Textbook printed in Canada

Authors: Sean Saunders, Thambyrajah Kugathasan, Irene Lee

Textbook Editor: Lakshmi Kugathasan
Developmental Editor: Arbana Miftari
Copy Editor: Connor Peebles
Art Director: Aleksandar Vozarevic
Assistant Editors: Erika De Vega, Bukelwa Nkungu

PowerPoint Presentations: Ali Alavi, Uma Kalkar
Instructional Design: Charles Anifowose, Elisa Romeo, Danny Panche Barrios
Interactive Technology & Data Solutions: Taylor Anderson, Zach Williams, Nabil Fannoush
Marketing: Harsha Varlani, James Howell

Expert Advice: TK Academic Consulting Inc.
Online Resources Management System: Intromath.ca

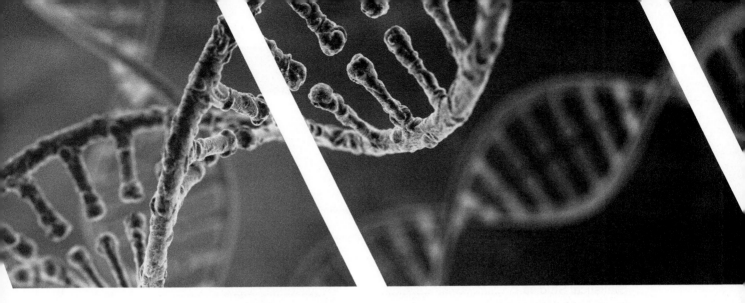

STATISTICS FOR HEALTH SCIENCES

Brief Contents

Contents

Chapter 3
Measures of Dispersion 84

Chapter 4
Linear Correlation and Regression 114

Chapter 5
Elementary Probability Theory 152

Chapter 6
Discrete Probability Distributions 200

Chapter 7
Continuous Probability Distributions

Chapter 8
Sampling Distributions and the Central Limit Theorem..................................268

Chapter 9
Estimation and Confidence Intervals...294

Chapter 10

x

List of Exhibits and Tables

Exhibits

Tables

Preface

Greetings! Thanks for choosing this resource to learn about statistics for health sciences. This book is aimed specifically at providing post-secondary students who are entering the health sciences field with an understanding of the statistical tools that they will need to know in the field. **Statistics for Health Sciences** has many unique features, a few of which we have highlighted below:

Practical Problems

In this book, you will find that the main concepts and ideas are presented with a health science motivation, right from the start. Throughout each section, examples are provided that relate to the health sciences and reinforce the statistical concept being explained. At the end of each section, there are dozens of exercises to practice and master the concepts, with most or even all of the examples connecting directly to practical scenarios and situations that arise in the health sciences field, whether in nursing, pharmacy, athletic therapy, kinesiology, or in paramedical services.

Detailed Descriptions

Unlike many applied statistics textbooks in a particular field that expect prerequisite statistical knowledge and experience, this book builds up from scratch the statistical concepts that are presented and used within. As new ideas and concepts are introduced, a thorough overview and explanation of each is provided, along with a discussion as to why it should matter to students, and examples to clarify the main ideas. The more challenging concepts are given more time and emphasis, with the examples provided being broken down into smaller pieces along the way, so students can see how each individual statistical concept relates to the larger practical scenario being analyzed. When formulas are introduced, they are accompanied by a brief explanation or simple proof to provide a better understanding of not only how to use the formula to solve a problem, but why a particular formula is used in each situation.

88%   91%   96%   80%   79%

Creating Connections

One of the most important distinguishing features of this textbook is the connections that are created between the concepts introduced within. Throughout the book, references are made back to previous concepts, examples, and scenarios, as well as forward to future ones, in order to help students understand the deep and intricate connections that exist within statistics, as well as foster a motivation and desire to learn new approaches to analyzing problems that arise in the health sciences. And while this book is an "introductory" book, it goes beyond the basics by introducing students to more advanced, related concepts that build upon the basics quite naturally, and are very useful in the health sciences field.

"Why the Vretta Hybrid Learning Platform?"

This book is only "one side of the equation" when it comes to ensuring student success. To optimize the learning experience, we have leveraged the cutting-edge technologies available to us to provide students with a highly immersive and engaging learning experience. Realizing that every student learns differently, students are given access to innovative online tools, tailored to each individual student's personal strengths and areas that need development. These tools are designed to help them master the concepts using diverse methods of learning, such as interactive online lessons which provide an understanding of the concepts before class, and our online lab system which tests all the core concepts covered throughout the course, so students will know how well they're doing **before** they write the test! Our aim in building the hybrid tools that accompany this book was to help overcome the negative perceptions associated with statistics, and to help students create those connections between the course material and their professional field.

Whether you are a professor or a student, we trust that you will find **Statistics for Health Sciences** and the online resources that accompany it to be useful and beneficial in the learning experience in your course. Because at Vretta, we believe that if you learn math, you will live smarter. And we truly believe that this hybrid resource will help students to develop an appreciation for the mathematical concepts taught within, and discover the deep, relevant connections that exist between statistics and the health sciences, which will, ultimately, lead to a more enriching and satisfying experience, both in their professions and in their lives!

Sean Saunders, Thambyrajah Kugathasan, and Irene Lee

Resources

Textbook

Language

The language used in this textbook is simple and straight-forward, while maintaining the levels of sophistication required to thoroughly prepare students for the next stage in their academic and professional careers.

Pedagogies and Learning Methods

Numerous pedagogies and learning methods that have been developed and proven over 60 years are incorporated into the textbook. These pedagogies have succeeded in simplifying critical mathematical concepts and significantly improving retention of concepts. The different learning methods to solve problems have also proven to cater to the varied student learning styles.

Exercises

The textbook has 1272 exercises, review exercises, and self-test exercises, as well as 161 solved examples. Problems are designed to test students on real-world, practical applications and are presented in increasing levels of difficulty. The problems are categorized into pairs of similar questions to provide professors with an opportunity to solve the even-numbered problems in class and assign the odd-numbered problems as homework.

Solution Manual

All problems in the end-of-section exercises, review exercises, self-test exercises, and cases have been solved using detailed step-by-step methods, as demonstrated in the solved examples. The solution manual is available online.

PowerPoint Presentations

The animated PowerPoint presentations are available for professors to use in class. The PowerPoint presentations are designed to work with clickers in class to gauge student understanding of concepts.

Test Bank

A comprehensive test bank, of 1000+ problems in varying levels of difficulty, that covers all concepts in the textbook is provided for professors to use as a database for exercises, quizzes, cases, group projects, or assignments.

Online Lessons

The online lessons are created as a pre-study component for students. They contain pedagogies that are highly interactive and engaging, and which teach concepts in a very logical and intuitive way. These lessons are not PowerPoint presentations but are interactive videos that have been created to enrich and enhance the learning experience. Every frame is locked to ensure that students go through the lessons sequentially as they are designed to build on learning concepts in succession. The system automatically records students' progress and performance. Once students complete a lesson, the frame unlocks itself, allowing students to navigate back and forth through the lesson. Professors, on the other hand, have administrative access which allows them to navigate through the online lessons without any restrictions.

Online Labs

The online lab assessment system contains a rich comprehensive test-bank of real-world problems that are algorithmically generated and that provide students with dynamic feedback on their responses. The labs can also be customized based on course requirements. A few of the customizable features include: previewing and selecting questions, setting the number of questions, setting and modifying start and due dates, opening, closing and re-opening labs, creating new labs and quizzes, and determining the weighting and number of attempts for each question.

Administrative Tools

The following administrative tools will provide professors with the ability to monitor overall class performance and individual student performance on online lessons and labs.

Performance Dashboard for Professors

The lesson performance dashboard provides professors with the average completion percentage per chapter, including a lesson-by-lesson percentage completed visualization for the entire class. The lab performance dashboard provides them with the average percentage mark on each lab for the class. Professors can also download or export individual grades for lessons and labs to a spreadsheet or to the college's course management system.

Performance Dashboard for Students

The lesson performance dashboard provides students with their chapter completion mark, including a lesson-by-lesson percentage completed visualization. The lab performance dashboard provides them with their lab percentage marks.

Chapter 3

88%

Chapter 4

76%

Lab Management System The lab management system is provided for administrators or subject leaders to create new labs, quizzes and case studies, preview and select questions, set the number of questions, set and modify start and due dates, open, close and re-open labs, and determine the weighting and number of attempts for each question.

STATISTICS FOR HEALTH SCIENCES

First Edition

Authors

Sean Saunders, *Sheridan College*

Thambyrajah Kugathasan, *Seneca College*

Irene Lee, *Humber College*

1 INTRODUCTION TO STATISTICS

LEARNING OBJECTIVES

- Define terms used in statistics and distinguish between descriptive and inferential statistics, as well as populations and samples.
- Identify the benefits and drawbacks of the various sampling methods used in statistics, including simple random, stratified random, systematic, cluster, and multi-stage random sampling, along with when to use each of them.
- Distinguish among the types of studies used in statistics, including experimental studies, observational studies, and surveys and censuses.
- Differentiate among qualitative, continuous quantitative, and discrete quantitative variables, as well as nominal, ordinal, interval, and ratio levels of measurements.
- Organize and present qualitative data using tools, including tally charts, frequency distribution tables, pie charts, and bar charts.
- Organize and present quantitative data using tools, including stem-and-leaf plots, tally charts, frequency tables, histograms, frequency polygons, ogives, and line graphs.

CHAPTER OUTLINE

1.1 Overview of Data and Data Collection

1.2 Organizing and Presenting Qualitative Data

1.3 Organizing and Presenting Quantitative Data

Introduction

Statistics is a branch of both mathematics and science that helps researchers to develop a set of procedures to collect, organize, present, analyze, and interpret data for the purposes of drawing conclusions and/or making decisions.

Statistics is an essential discipline in the health sciences, as it relates either directly or indirectly to almost every fact cited and decision made by health-care professionals - this is why statistics is required in just about every post-secondary health sciences program! The following are just a few examples of how statistics is used by professionals in the health sciences:

- To learn about the overall health trends and patterns of the population.

- To provide important information to patients about medical procedures.

- To determine when public health intervention may be necessary.

- To assess the efficacy of specific health-related programs, treatments, or drugs.

- To weigh the potential risks and benefits of a particular medical treatment.

- To analyze costs associated with health-care and preparing a budget.

However, while statistics is very useful, it can also be easily abused. Hence, it is important to ensure a proper understanding of what statistics can and cannot do (i.e., its purposes and limitations), including knowing how to define appropriate goals and establish proper procedures when employing statistics.

In this chapter, we will learn the various sampling methods and types of studies used in statistics, as well as techniques to organize and present data using tables and charts to summarize data in a meaningful way.

1.1 | Overview of Data and Data Collection

In order to understand how to properly use statistics, it is important to distinguish between two sub-categories of statistics, based on two very different goals: **descriptive statistics** and **inferential statistics**.

Descriptive Statistics	Inferential Statistics
• deals with the organizing, presenting, and summarizing of raw data to provide meaningful information about the data and the group from which it was collected	• deals with the analysis of a smaller sample drawn from a larger population to develop meaningful conclusions about the population based on sample results
• i.e., *descriptive* statistics serve to *describe*	• i.e., *inferential* statistics serve to *infer*

Populations and Samples

In the definition for inferential statistics, two new terms were introduced: **population** and **sample**.

Population	Sample
• refers to a set of all possible individuals, objects, or measurements of items of interest	• refers to a subset drawn from the population, meaning a portion or part of the population
• the size of a population is usually very large, or even infinite	• the size of a sample is usually much smaller and more manageable than the size of the population from which it is drawn
• e.g., all students enrolled in a post-secondary health sciences program in Canada	• e.g., 200 students drawn from the post-secondary health sciences student population previously mentioned

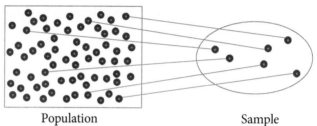

Population   Sample

There are a few more basic terms that need to be defined:

Attribute	Variable
• a characteristic of the data that can be observed, measured, or categorized	• represents the value of an attribute
• it is also known as a data item	• the value may *vary* from one data value to another
• e.g., age, income, gender, blood type, etc.	• e.g., the numerical value of the attribute *'a'* may be different for each data

Variables are used to measure or quantify the attributes of data. Often, we are most interested in the summary values of variables for an entire set of data, rather than individual values of specific data.

Parameter	Statistic
• a value that summarizes a certain variable for an entire population	• a value that summarizes a certain variable for a sample
• usually represented by letters from the Greek alphabet	• usually represented by lowercase letters from the Latin (common) alphabet
• e.g., mean: μ, standard deviation: σ	• e.g., mean: $\bar{x}$, standard deviation: s

---

Example 1.1-a   Identifying Population Parameter and Sample Statistic

A researcher is interested in determining the average annual income of family physicians in the city of Toronto. She does this by randomly selecting 50 family physicians from the Toronto area and using the data gathered to estimate the average annual income for all family physicians in Toronto. Identify the population parameter of interest in this study and the sample statistic collected to estimate it.

Solution

Population parameter of interest: The average annual income of **all** family physicians in Toronto.

Sample statistic: The average annual income of the **50** family physicians **selected**.

Normally, we will not have access to the whole population we are interested in investigating. Therefore, population parameters are often estimated from the sample statistics. Sample statistics are calculated from the actual data observed or measured from the sample.

For example, assume that there are 40 students in a particular college statistics class, and 80% of those students passed the final exam. This 80% pass-rate could be either a population parameter or a sample statistic, depending on which group of data we are interested in:

- If we are only trying to summarize the results of this particular class (descriptive statistics), the 80% pass rate would be a *parameter*, as the population we are interested in is the group of students in this particular class.

- However, if this class is selected as the representative statistics class of all the statistics classes in the college (inferential statistics), then the 80% pass rate is a *statistic*, because it represents only a sample of the population.

Sampling Methods

One of the most important, and often one of the most overlooked, aspects of inferential statistics is drawing a sample from the population that is representative of the entire population. In order to do this, it is important for a researcher to eliminate any bias he/she may have. It is important to note that we all have biases: some might be prejudicial (e.g., only selecting people of a certain culture/colour/creed), while others arise out of good intentions (e.g., wanting to be inclusive to all). However, both kinds of bias can result in a sample being chosen that does not reflect the population. As such, it is important for researchers to identify their biases and not allow them to influence how a sample is selected. In order to ensure personal biases do not impact the sample, researchers need to employ **randomization**:

A sampling method is randomized if every element in the population has an equal chance of being selected for the sample.

Achieving true randomness is often very difficult, if not impossible. However, there are several different methods researchers can use in order to ensure a sufficient degree of randomness in their sampling:

- Simple Random Sampling

- Stratified Random Sampling

- Systematic Sampling

- Cluster Sampling

- Multi-stage Random Sampling

- Convenience Sampling

Simple Random Sampling

This is the truest form of randomization, as every element in the population truly has an equal chance of being selected. Listed below are some examples of simple random sampling:

- Drawing numbers or names from a bin.

- Assigning values to every element in the population and using a computerized random number generator to select the values for the sample.

- Using a Random Number Table and a thumb-tack to select numbers corresponding to identification numbers of elements in the population.

Stratified Random Sampling

In certain populations, where a particular attribute of the data (e.g., gender) will potentially strongly impact the value of the variable being analyzed (e.g., weight), it may be considered desirable to have a sample that reflects the proportionate diversity of the population with respect to that attribute. For example, if half a population is composed of males and the other half females, it may be desirable to have a sample where half the sample is also composed of males and the other half females.

Stratified random samples can be selected by following these steps:

Step 1:	Identify the particular attribute to be isolated (e.g., gender, age, income, etc.).
Step 2:	Divide (or **stratify**) the population into groups (or **strata**) based on this attribute (e.g., male/female; under 20/between 20 and 40/between 41 and 60/over 60; etc.).
Step 3:	Select a random sample from each stratum that is proportionate in size to the original population.

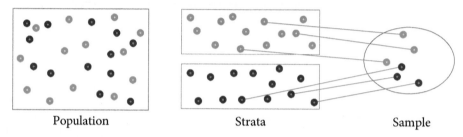

Population   Strata   Sample

Systematic Sampling

If making use of one of the simple random sampling methods above is infeasible or impractical, it is possible to achieve a seemingly randomized result without actually using randomization - this is called a systematic approach:

Step 1:	Create an ordered (i.e., numbered) list of all elements in the population, in any order.
Step 2:	Divide the size of the population by the size of the sample to get the **interval value**: k. *Note: Ignore any decimal places by rounding k **down** to the nearest whole number below.*
Step 3:	Randomly select a starting value between 1 and k, and choose the element of the population that corresponds with that value.
Step 4:	Choose the element corresponding to every k^{th} value from your starting value (i.e., add k to the starting value and choose the element that corresponds with that value, and repeat until the entire sample is selected).

Population

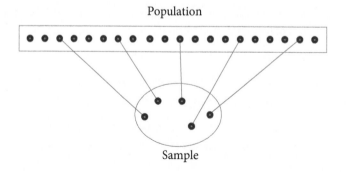

Sample

For example, to select a systematic sample of 30 from a population of 1,000, we calculate

$k = \dfrac{1,000}{30} \approx 33$. Then we randomly select a value between 1 and 33 for a starting point: e.g., 27.

Then we select every 33rd element in the population, starting at element #27, until we have our sample of size 30:

#27	#60	#93	#126	#159	#192	#225	#258	#291	#324
#357	#390	#423	#456	#489	#522	#555	#588	#621	#654
#687	#720	#753	#786	#819	#852	#885	#918	#951	#984

Cluster Sampling

In some populations, it is very convenient to break the population up into **clusters** that reasonably reflect the population (or at least with no discernable reason why they would not reflect the population). These clusters can be thought of as "mini-populations", and so selecting a sample requires only randomly selecting a sufficient number of these clusters and then sampling *every element* of the selected clusters.

For example, in order to get a sense of patient satisfaction with the level of care in a regional hospital, a few wards from the hospital may be randomly selected and then all patients from each of those wards would be included in the sample.

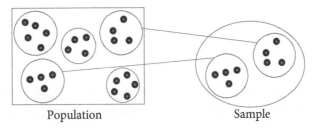

Population   Sample

Multi-stage Random Sampling

Often, when a population is very large, it may be difficult to list out every element in the population in order to perform any of the above sampling methods. In these cases, it is necessary to first "narrow down" the population into smaller and smaller groups before finally employing one of the above sampling techniques (usually cluster sampling) to select the actual sample.

For example, in order to determine the public's approval rating of the government's new budget, communities and then neighbourhoods are selected according to a stratified sample, based on ethnic and other demographic factors. Finally, specific blocks (clusters) within those neighbourhoods are selected randomly from the stratified population, and all residents living on those blocks are sampled.

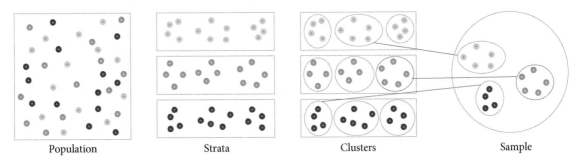

Population   Strata   Clusters   Sample

Convenience Sampling

Convenience sampling is a method that is sometimes used to collect a sample by selecting elements of the population who are readily available and willing to participate. While this is an easy and cost-effective method for collecting a sample, it does not generally produce a random sample and is often very biased, sometimes to the point where the sample is useless for drawing any inferences about the population. Convenience sampling should only be used when no other sampling method is feasible, and even then, should be done with extreme caution!

For example, a professor wishes to know what students think of the cafeteria food on campus, and so she distributes a survey to students in the cafeteria during lunch, asking them to rank the cafeteria food from 1 (poor) to 5 (excellent) based on a variety of different criteria. Students are then asked to submit their ballot before the end of lunch for the chance to win a prize. Since there is no reason to assume these students would have a specific bias toward the cafeteria food one way or the other, it seems reasonable to expect that this convenience sample could reasonably approximate the population of the entire student body. However, if the professor wants to ensure a better sample, she should use one of the randomized sampling methods previously discussed.

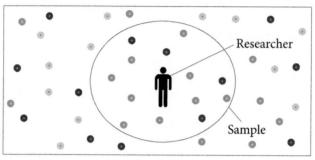

Population

Note: In the previous diagram, the 'green' population is being overrepresented in the sample, and the 'orange' population is not being represented at all!

| Table 1.1-a | **Sampling Methods - Benefits and Drawbacks** |

Sampling method	Benefits	Drawbacks
Simple Random Sampling	• Only true random sample • Every element has the same chance of being selected • Good for small populations or numbered ballots/tickets	• Need a list of the whole population • Difficult for large, non-numerical populations (e.g., people) • Labour intensive, time-consuming, and expensive
Stratified Random Sampling	• Useful when a particular trait in the population affects the result • Proportionate samples • Cheaper, easier, and quicker than Simple Random Sampling	• Can be difficult to sort by certain traits (e.g., race, ethnicity, etc.) • May be based on incorrect estimates of population proportions
Systematic Sampling	• Eliminates researcher bias • Pseudo-random sample when Simple Random Sampling is not feasible	• Elements close together in the population cannot be chosen (may cause pattern bias in the sample)
Cluster Sampling	• Useful when the population is naturally divided into sub-groups that reflect the entire population	• Requires a list of all sub-groups • Possible bias from sub-groups that are dissimilar to the population
Multi-stage Random Sampling	• Useful for very large populations • Cost-effective and accurate	• Possible bias/error from leaving out entire geographical areas/groups
Convenience Sampling	• Cheap, easy, and quick • Results may be used if sample has no inherent bias to the study • May be good as a preliminary study	• Very high probability of bias/error • Most likely that results cannot be used to make inferences about the population

Example 1.1-b	Identifying Sampling Methods

Identify the sampling methods used in the following studies: simple random, stratified random, systematic, cluster, multi-stage random, or convenience.

(handwritten: convient?)

(i) A dietician would like to explore the relationship between the fat percentage in a patient's diet and coronary heart disease. To obtain data for this study, the dietician solicits volunteers from the clients of her practice.

(handwritten: simple Random sampling)

(ii) A student is interested in estimating the proportion of students who are left-handed. A list of names of all 1,500 students enrolled during the current semester is available. 150 students are randomly selected from the list, using a random number generator.

(handwritten: systematic)

(iii) A pharmaceutical company wants to estimate the mean dollar revenue per sale during the past month. It finds that 200 sales invoices were recorded and decides to select 10 invoices to do the estimate. Selecting every 20th invoice from all 200 invoices forms the sample of 10.

(handwritten: stratified)

(iv) A sample of households is selected from a city to provide feedback on the current health care system. First, the city population was divided into three groups based on income level: low-, medium-, and high-income households. A random sample from each group is taken, proportional to the size of the individual groups. The collection of all three samples selected from the three groups gives the required sample.

(handwritten: Cluster)

(v) A survey is conducted by randomly selecting five health clinics and interviewing all employees working at each selected clinic to provide feedback on the working environment of clinics in the region.

(handwritten: Muti-stage)

(vi) A college wants to study the effectiveness of reading week on students' academic success. First, the population of the students in the college is divided by faculty; from each faculty, the population is divided by program. Specific programs are randomly selected from each faculty, proportional to the overall size of each faculty within the college, and every student from these programs are sampled.

Solution

(i) Only volunteers who are readily available to the dietician are being sampled. Therefore, **convenience sampling** is being used.

(ii) By using a random number generator, every student has an equal chance of being selected. Therefore, **simple random sampling** is being used.

(iii) Every 20th invoice from the population of invoices is selected. Therefore, **systematic sampling** is being used.

(iv) The population of households is first divided into groups based on a particular attribute: income level; each group is then proportionally represented in the sample. Therefore, **stratified random sampling** is being used.

(v) Every employee working at the five health clinics (i.e., "clusters") is sampled to reflect the employees of all health clinics in the region. Therefore, **cluster sampling** is being used.

(vi) The population of students is first divided into groups based on a particular attribute: faculty (stratified sampling); from each faculty, every student within specific programs is sampled (cluster sampling). Therefore, **multi-stage random sampling** is being used.

Statistical Studies

When researchers desire to know the value of a particular variable in a population, they make use of a **study**. There are three different kinds of studies that researchers use:

- Experimental studies
- Observational studies
- Surveys and Censuses

Experimental Studies

Experimental studies, or simply **experiments**, involve manipulating the value of a particular variable - called a **treatment** - to determine the impact on another variable - called the **response**. An example of an experimental study would be a clinical drug trial in which the efficacy of a new drug is tested on participants against a specific disease (e.g., cancer), condition (e.g., insomnia), or symptom (e.g., dry skin).

Experiments are conducted by taking a sample of the population being studied (e.g., Stage III lung cancer patients) and dividing it into an **experimental group** and a **control group**; members of the experimental group receive the treatment, while members of the control group do not. This sorting of the sample into experimental and control groups is typically performed by a random process. The results of the variable being measured in each group are recorded, tabulated, and analyzed using statistical methods discussed later in this book, and then compared to each other to determine if the treatment was effective or not.

It is important that every element in the sample be as similar as possible and that all other possible variables that could affect the response (e.g., diet, exercise, environmental factors, etc.) are controlled - that is, kept the same for each member within the sample. Otherwise, variables other than the treatment, called **confounding variables**, might be responsible for the change in response. By controlling the possible confounding variables as much as possible, researchers can better understand the effect of the treatment.

However, even in controlled experiments, a strange phenomenon has been known to take place called the **placebo effect**, in which patients seem to experience improvement, despite the treatment actually having no effect. To combat this, most scientific experiments involving human participants are **blinded**, meaning that patients do not know whether they belong to the experimental group or control group. This may mean that treatments are performed while the patient is under anesthesia or, in the case of drug trials, that patients in the control group are given sugar pills (called **placebos**) instead of the drug.

Note: Before participating, all patients would be made aware of this process and would have to consent to the possibility of being in either the experimental or control group.

Finally, in order to ensure that researchers do not introduce their own bias into the results (e.g., looking for more improvements from the experimental group), experiments are often **double-blinded**, where the researchers recording the results remain unaware of the groups to which patients are assigned. In these cases, patients would be assigned into groups by one researcher (A), and another researcher (B) with no knowledge of the group assignments would record the results for each patient. The results for each patient compiled by researcher B would then be compared to the list by the researcher A for analysis.

Observational Studies

Another type of study is an **observational study**, in which researchers observe and measure the results of a particular variable in a sample of the population, without attempting to influence or manipulate the variable in any way. An example of an observational study would be the effects on babies of mothers who smoke during pregnancy. Since it would be considered grossly unethical to actually ask pregnant mothers to start or even continue smoking, researchers would instead observe the health of babies born to mothers who chose of their own accord to smoke during their pregnancy and compare to the health of babies born to mothers who did not smoke during pregnancy.

The benefits of observational studies over experiments are that they are easier to conduct than experiments and have significantly fewer ethical concerns. However, the main drawback is that the results from observational studies are typically less scientifically valid than those obtained from experiments, as it is much harder to control the confounding variables in observational studies than in experiments.

Surveys and Censuses

The third main type of statistical study is called a **survey** (when conducted from a sample) or a **census** (when conducted from the entire population). In a survey, respondents are asked questions and they are responsible for providing the information about themselves to researchers through their answers. In most surveys, researchers are not able to verify the correctness or accuracy of the information. As such, surveys are not useful to learn about issues in which individuals would tend to have a biased view of themselves (e.g., personal health, driving habits, etc.).

However, there are two instances when surveys and censuses are very effective:

- In obtaining basic demographic information (e.g., gender, age, etc.)

- In learning about opinions held by individuals in the population (e.g., political views)

The Government of Canada, for example, administered a census in 2016 in which all households in Canada were required to provide basic demographic information about the people living there, such as age, gender, marital status, etc.

As well, polling companies like to administer surveys to samples of typically around 1,000 voters, leading up to federal and provincial elections, in order to determine the political party with the highest chance of being elected and whether there will be enough support to form a majority or minority government.

Table 1.1-b   **Responsibilities of the Researcher in Statistical Studies**

Type of Study	Responsibility of the Researcher		
	Design the Study and Select a Sample	Observe & Record Results	Apply a Treatment
Experiment	Yes	Yes	Yes
Observational Study	Yes	Yes	No
Survey/Census	Yes	No	No

Example 1.1-c   **Identifying Statistical Studies**

Identify the type of study being used in the following scenarios: experiment, observational study, or survey.

(i)   To test the effect of regular exercise on diabetes, a researcher takes a sample of 100 diabetic adults who volunteered for the study. Over the course of three months, the amount of exercise performed and the blood sugar levels of each volunteer is monitored and recorded by the researcher.

(ii)   Statistics Canada wishes to determine labour market information regarding Canada's working-age population, such as hours of work, industry, occupation, wages, etc. Questionnaires are mailed out to randomly selected Canadian households.

(iii)   Two diets are being promoted by two different companies, with each company claiming their diet is the best for losing weight. A researcher divides a sample of overweight adults randomly into two groups, and assigns each group to one of the two diets. The weight-loss results of the two groups are then compared.

(iv)   The Canadian Cancer Society wants to find out the most common forms of cancer that resulted in deaths in the last year in Canada.

(v)   To determine the impact of smoking on lung capacity, a researcher randomly selects 50 participants who are smokers and 50 participants who are non-smokers and tests their lung capacities by measuring the maximum amount each person can exhale in one breath. The researcher records the results for each person and compares the results for the two groups.

(vi)   A pharmaceutical company wants to find out how a new drug affects blood pressure. The dosage level of the new drug is controlled, with different groups of consenting individuals in the study being given different dosage levels. Data on blood pressure is then collected from each group.

(i) Since the researcher is monitoring and recording the data, but not manipulating the amount of exercise each volunteer performs, this is an **observational study**.

(ii) Since the households are to answer questions about themselves, this is a **survey**.

(iii) Since the researcher is controlling which participant goes on which diet, this is an **experiment**.

(iv) Since the society is collecting information from a past event (i.e., cannot be manipulated/observed), this is a **survey**.

(v) Since the researcher is recording and comparing the data, but not manipulating who is in the smoking group and who is in the non-smoking group (i.e., the participants decided for themselves which group they were a part of), this is an **observational study**.

(vi) Since the dosage amount received by each participant is being controlled by the researcher, this is an **experiment**.

Errors

Regardless of the type of sampling method chosen, or how diligent researchers are in eliminating bias, results from statistical studies that are performed on a sample are unlikely to exactly reflect the results of the entire population. Such a difference between an observed sample statistic and the actual population parameter is known as a **sampling error**. Note that sampling errors are not "mistakes" - they simply represent a discrepancy between the population and the sample selected. For example, if 1,000 people were randomly selected from the population of the planet, we would expect approximately half to be male and half to be female. However, it is not reasonable to anticipate selecting exactly 500 individuals from each gender if the sample is selected randomly (as a matter of fact, that result would probably imply a bias or a stratified sample). Hence, sampling errors are the result of the **randomness** of a sample.

However, there is another kind of error called a **non-sampling error**, which is the result of an error in the study, such as poor sampling or data collection techniques, incorrect measurements or calculations, or researcher bias in the study. Some common non-sampling errors are listed below:

Table 1.1-c **Non-sampling Errors**

Self-selected Sample	• respondents get to decide for themselves who will participate in a study • often only people with strong opinions will elect to participate
Small Sample	• small samples have a very low likelihood of representing the entire population and, as such, the results are untrustworthy to use to make inferences • much more likely to be biased, as certain groups in the population (especially small groups) will either be over- or under-represented in a small sample
Unverified Response	• researchers cannot verify the truth/correctness of a response given by a respondent • as such, there is a possibility that the response is untrue/incorrect, whether intentionally or unintentionally
Poor Wording	• surveys that use words that are vague or questions that are **loaded** (i.e., asked in a biased way to solicit a certain response) • results from these surveys are most often useless
Incorrect Conclusion	• researchers may have entirely valid data, collected from a valid sample, and still draw incorrect conclusions or present misleading information from the study • some examples of this type of error would be exaggerating results, omitting important information, or making unsubstantiated claims about causation (discussed more in Chapter 4)

Types of Variables

In order to calculate the value of a parameter or statistic, a researcher must first assign a variable to the attribute of interest. Different attributes (e.g., age, income, gender, etc.) will have different values that the corresponding variable can take on. Variables can be classified primarily into two categories: **quantitative variables** and **qualitative variables**.

Quantitative Variables

Quantitative variables represent numeric data that can be measured or counted. Quantitative data take on values that are expressed using numbers. However, these numbers must represent a measurement or quantity, and not simply be numbers assigned to a non-numeric value (e.g., 1 = "yes", 2 = "no"), or strings of digits that have no numeric meaning (e.g., phone numbers, identification numbers, etc.).

Furthermore, quantitative variables can then be further sub-categorized into **continuous variables** and **discrete variables**.

Continuous Variables	Discrete Variables
• represent data that are obtained by measuring, such as measurements of length, weight, time, temperature, etc.	• represent data that are either obtained by counting or that can only take on specific values, such as the number of students in a class, the year an event took place, the number on a die roll, etc.
• the values that these variables take on can be expressed as whole numbers, fractions, or decimals, with any pre-defined level of precision (i.e., number of decimal places)	• the values that these variables take on are usually whole numbers
• continuous variables do not have a "smallest increment" - i.e., between any two values a continuous variable can take on, there is another value in between the variable could take on	• discrete variables can also be fractions or decimals with a "smallest increment" - e.g., in Canadian currency, there is nothing smaller than $0.01, and so there would be no currency values between $5.00 and $5.01

It can sometimes be challenging to determine whether a variable is discrete or continuous, in which case we must look at the context of the data that is being analyzed, as in the following examples:

- **Money:** While currency is discrete (i.e., has a smallest increment, such as $0.01 in Canada), money in general is continuous, since there is no limit to the number of decimal places possible (e.g., currency exchange rates or stock prices).

- **Age:** The age of an adult person is discrete, since it is always expressed as a whole number of years; however, age in general is continuous, since time progresses without a smallest increment (e.g., the age of a cell or radioactive isotope).

Qualitative Variables

Qualitative variables represent non-numeric data that can neither be measured nor counted. In most cases, qualitative data take on values that cannot be expressed using numbers, and are otherwise known as categorical data, such as gender and nationality of people, make and model of cars, colour and texture of objects, feelings and perspectives of customers, etc. However, in order to make data collection and analysis easier, numbers are often assigned to these values; it is important not to confuse qualitative data that has been given a numeric assignment with actual quantitative data.

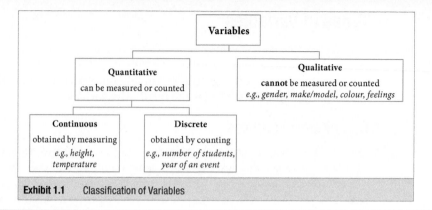

Exhibit 1.1   Classification of Variables

| Example 1.1-d | Identifying Types of Variables |

Identify each of the following variables as quantitative or qualitative. If quantitative, further classify as continuous or discrete.

(i)   A person's blood type

(ii)   The number of people who visited a walk-in clinic last week

(iii)   Burn classification (1 = Slight; 2 = Moderate; 3 = Intense; 4 = Severe)

(iv)   The amount of time a surgeon spent performing a heart surgery

(v)   The average annual salary of a family physician

(vi)   The number of emergency calls received by a dispatch centre in a day

Solution

(i)   Qualitative

(ii)   Discrete quantitative

(iii)   Qualitative

(iv)   Continuous quantitative

(v)   Continuous quantitative

(vi)   Discrete quantitative

Levels of Measurement

As previously stated, one of the most important disciplines to learn about interpreting data values is to know what the limitations of the data are. Consider the following three examples for patients that are admitted to the E.R.:

1.   Patients are assigned a triage number from 1 to 5, with 1 representing the highest level of urgency, 2 representing a high level of urgency, 3 representing a moderate level of urgency, 4 representing a low level of urgency, and 5 representing the lowest level of urgency.

2.   The number of hours that patients were required to wait in the E.R. before being seen by a doctor is recorded, rounded to the nearest whole hour. Results range from 1 to 5 hours.

3.   The primary language of patients admitted to the E.R. is recorded: 1 represents English, 2 represents French, 3 represents Spanish, 4 represents Punjabi, and 5 represents Mandarin.

In all three examples above, the data is recorded and an average is taken, with the following results:

2.7, 3.2, and 1.6, respectively. How would these averages be interpreted?

1.   The first average of 2.7 seems to indicate that the average triage level is a slightly higher than moderate level of urgency, but we cannot determine exactly what it means.

2.   The second average of 3.2 would be interpreted as follows: the average length of time a patient was required to wait in the E.R. before seeing a doctor was 3.2 hours.

3.   The third average of 1.6 is completely nonsensical.

Why are there three entirely different interpretations of three similar situations? The answer has to do with the **level of measurement** for each of the three different variables analyzed.

The level of measurement of a variable indicates what limitations (if any) exist in how the variable can be analyzed. There are four levels of measurement that are used to categorize data: Nominal, Ordinal, Interval, and Ratio. These four levels of measurement are summarized in the following two tables:

Table 1.1-d **Properties and Examples of Levels of Measurement**

Levels of Measurement	Properties	Examples
Nominal	• Have no order, but numbers may be assigned for referencing and differentiating purposes using codes. • The interval between measurements is not meaningful. • No meaningful zero point. • Qualitative data and usually classified using letters, symbols, or names.	• Gender • Religion • Country of birth • Colour
Ordinal	• Have order by their relative position. • The interval between measurements is not meaningful. • No meaningful zero point. • Qualitative data and usually classified using letters, symbols, or numbers.	• Level of satisfaction • Rating of movies • GPA (A = 4, B = 3, C = 2, ...) • shoe/clothing size
Interval	• Have order by their relative position. • Meaningful intervals between measurements. • No meaningful zero point (the zero point is located arbitrarily.) • Quantitative data but measurements cannot be multiplied or divided.	• Temperature • Dates • Calendar years • IQ score
Ratio	• Have order by their relative position. • Meaningful intervals between measurements. • Meaningful zero point. • Quantitative data and measurements can be multiplied or divided.	• Percent • Age • Weight • Speed

In the example above, the first scenario, where patients receive a triage number, would be an example of ordinal data, since the triage numbers indicate a ranking, but there are no meaningful differences between the numbers. The second scenario, where the length of time spent in the E.R. is recorded, would be an example of ratio data, since the data is time which is quantitative and can be compared using a ratio (for example, 6 hours is twice as long as 3 hours). The third scenario, where the primary language is recorded, would be an example of nominal data. Though a numerical value is assigned, the numbers have no meaning and no inherent ranking can be established.

Table 1.1-e **Summary of Levels of Measurement**

Levels of Measurement	Order (Rank)	Meaningful Difference	Meaningful Zero
Nominal	No	No	No
Ordinal	Yes	No	No
Interval	Yes	Yes	No
Ratio	Yes	Yes	Yes

Example 1.1-e   Identifying Level of Measurement

The placement office at a college regularly surveys the diploma graduates. For each of the following questions, determine the type of data in terms of the level of measurement: nominal, ordinal, interval, or ratio.

qualitative (i)   Are you employed now?

qualitative (ii)   What is your occupation (i.e., field of occupation)?

qualitative (iii)   What is your position in the company?

quantitative (iv)   What is your annual salary?

quantitative (v)   What diploma did you obtain?

quantitative (vi)   How would you rate the quality of instruction in your college on a scale from 1 to 5?

quantitative (vii)   What was your GPA when you graduated?

quantitative (viii) What was your year of graduation?

quantitative (ix)   How many years of post-secondary schooling have you completed in total?

Solution

(i)   Answers can be "Yes" or "No", which have no order: **nominal**.

(ii)   Occupations (e.g., registered nurse, family doctor, surgeon, physiotherapist, etc.) have no order: **nominal**.

(iii)   There is a hierarchy among positions (e.g., head nurse > charge nurse > staff nurse): **ordinal**.

(iv)   Amounts of money can be ranked, have a meaningful difference, and have a meaningful zero point (i.e., a $0 salary means that you do not make a salary): **ratio**.

(v)   Diplomas (e.g., Bachelor of Nursing, Occupational Therapist, Radiation Technician, etc.) have no order: **nominal**.

(vi)   Answers have an order (e.g., a response of 4 indicates a higher quality than a response of 2), but the difference between two ratings does not mean anything: **ordinal**.

(vii)   Answers have an order (e.g., a GPA of 3.5 > 3.0), but the difference between two GPA's does not mean anything: **ordinal**.

(viii) Calendar years can be ordered and the difference between two calendar years is meaningful (e.g., 2017 – 2015 = 2-year difference), but year "0" is arbitrary: **interval**.

(ix)   Number of years can be ranked, have a meaningful difference, and a meaningful zero point (i.e., 0 years means you have completed no years of post-secondary schooling): **ratio**.

1.1 | Exercises

Answers to odd-numbered problems are available at the end of the textbook.

1.   Identify which sampling method would be most appropriate for the following studies:

   a.   Opinions about workplace harassment protocols and procedures from flight attendants, approximately 75% of whom are female and 25% of whom are male

   b.   Approval rating for new Transport Canada airport security measures from all Canadians

   c.   Passenger satisfaction with the new tiered cabin configurations on an airline's planes

   d.   An airport security checkpoint's random bag-check for restricted items/substances

2.   Identify which sampling method would be most appropriate for the following studies:

   a.   The average wait in an E.R. in a hospital in Ontario

   b.   Examining pay equity between physicians in different provinces in Canada

   c.   Overall patient satisfaction for the out-patients seen at a particular hospital in a month

   d.   Selecting 250 of the 500 participants in a clinical drug trial to receive the treatment

3. Identify which type of study (experiment, observational study, or survey) should be used in the following examples:
   a. Comparing the length of recovery times from a surgery with or without physiotherapy
   b. Calculating the average total physiotherapy cost for post-operative patients
   c. Determining the effectiveness of a particular physiotherapy exercise in rehabilitation
   d. Determining public support for OHIP-coverage of physiotherapy fees

4. Identify which type of study (experiment, observational study, or survey) should be used in the following examples:
   a. Determining which type of pain-relief medication is most effective
   b. Determining which type of pain-relief medication is most-frequently purchased
   c. Determining which type of pain-relief medication is most well-known
   d. Determining which type of pain-relief medication has the most side effects

5. Identify the following variables as either quantitative or qualitative:
   a. Percent grade on a final exam
   b. Ward in a hospital
   c. Amount of drug to administer
   d. Treatment options available

6. Identify the following variables as either quantitative or qualitative:
   a. Letter grade on a final exam
   b. Height of a patient
   c. Vertebrae injured in a fall
   d. Ontario health card number

7. Identify the following variables as either discrete or continuous:
   a. Weight of a patient
   b. Number of surgeries performed in a month by a surgeon
   c. Time of birth of a baby born in the hospital
   d. Age of a patient in years

8. Identify the following variables as either discrete or continuous:
   a. Number of patients assigned to each nurse
   b. Treatment cost not covered by OHIP
   c. Position of a patient on an organ-transplant waiting list
   d. Duration (i.e., length of time) of an operation

9. Identify the level of measurement (nominal, ordinal, interval, or ratio) for the following:
   a. Professional credentials held by a medical practitioner
   b. Annual salaries of nurses in different parts of Canada
   c. The year in which a medical practice first opened
   d. The pain experienced by a physiotherapy patient on a scale of 1 to 10

10. Identify the level of measurement (nominal, ordinal, interval, or ratio) for the following:
    a. The volume of chemical solution needed in a laboratory experiment
    b. The GPA of a student graduating from a Pre-Health Sciences program
    c. The temperature set in a resident's room in a nursing home
    d. Type of animal brought into a veterinarian's office

1.2 | Organizing and Presenting Qualitative Data

Once data has been collected, the next step is for it to be organized and presented visually, most commonly using tables and charts.

A **table** is a method of displaying data in a 2-dimensional grid, organized into rows and columns.

A **chart** is a method of displaying data in a graph, constructed of plotted points, lines, bars, or slices.

Test #	Student 1 Grade	Student 2 Grade	Student 3 Grade	Student 4 Grade
1	C	A	A+	A
2	D	B	A+	A
3	B	C	A+	B
4	F	A	A	A
5	B	A	A+	A+
6	B	B	A+	A

Exhibit 1.2-a   Table showing the grades received by 4 students on 6 different tests

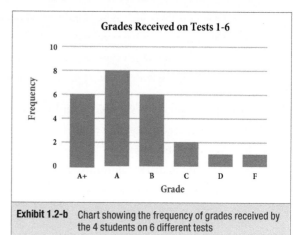

Exhibit 1.2-b   Chart showing the frequency of grades received by the 4 students on 6 different tests

We will now examine some common tables and charts used to organize and present qualitative data (recall that qualitative data is non-numerical data that can neither be measured nor counted - it relates to a *quality* or characteristic of the data collected).

Tally Charts and Frequency Distribution Tables

A **tally chart** organizes qualitative data by displaying how many pieces of data fall into each of a specified set of categories (e.g., for car data, the categories may be colour, make, model, etc.). Although it is called a tally *chart*, it is actually a *table*. The categories are organized by row in the first column of the table, and the data count in each category is represented using tally marks in the second column, organized into multiples of five: vertical lines "|" are used for the first to fourth tally marks in each group, and a horizontal (or diagonal) line "——" across the four vertical tally marks is used for the fifth tally mark in the group. This helps to quickly and accurately count the data in multiples of five.

For example, 12 counts of the same item is shown as ||||| ||||| || - two groups of five and two single tally marks = 12.

Once the tally chart is completed, the tally marks in each category are tabulated and summarized in a third column, called the **frequency** (*f*) column. Once the frequency column has been added, the tally chart has become a **frequency distribution table** (or simply a **frequency table**).

Example 1.2-a   Constructing a Tally Chart and Frequency Table

A class of 40 students enrolled in a Statistics for Health Sciences class are surveyed about their field of interest (**N**ursing, **P**harmacy, **A**thletic Therapy/**K**inesiology, **V**eterinary Services, Para**M**edicine, or **O**ther), and the results are recorded as follows:

N	P	N	A/K	P	V	O	A/K	N	N
P	A/K	V	N	A/K	M	N	P	P	V
N	P	M	P	M	N	V	N	A/K	N
P	N	O	V	A/K	P	N	A/K	M	O

Organize and present the above data using a tally chart and frequency table.

Solution

Step 1: Draw 3 columns to represent Field of Interest, Tally, and Frequency (f).

Step 2: List the fields of interest in any order (e.g., alphabetical order) in 6 rows in Column 1.

Note: Regardless of the order chosen, if there is any kind of "Other" category, it is placed in the last row.

Step 3: Starting from the first data value, use tally marks in Column 2 to count the occurrences of each field of interest in the data set.

Step 4: Total the tally marks in each row to get the frequency distribution of the fields in Column 3.

Field of Interest	Tally	Frequency (f)
A/K (Athletic Therapy/Kinesiology)	卌 ‖	7
M (Paramedicine)	‖‖	4
N (Nursing)	卌 卌 ‖	12
P (Pharmacy)	卌 ‖‖‖	9
V (Veterinary Services)	卌	5
O (Other)	‖‖	3

Example 1.2-b **Interpreting a Tally Chart**

A veterinarian records the types of animals brought into her practice over the course of one month and displays the data in a tally chart as follows:

Type of Animal	Tally	Frequency (f)
Bird	卌 卌 卌 ‖	16
Cat	卌 卌 卌 卌 卌 卌 卌 卌 ‖‖	43
Dog	卌 卌 卌 卌 卌 卌 卌 卌 卌 卌 卌 卌	60
Horse	‖‖	3
Rabbit	卌 ‖‖‖	9
Reptile (snake, lizard, turtle, etc.)	卌 ‖‖	7
Rodent (guinea pig, hamster, gerbil, mouse, rat, etc.)	卌 卌 卌 ‖‖	18
Other	‖‖	4

(i) Construct a frequency distribution from the tally chart by filling in the Frequency column.

(ii) Which type of animal was seen most frequently and which type was seen least frequently?

(iii) What was the total number of animals seen at this vet's practice during the month?

(iv) Determine what percent of the vet's time was spent on cats and dogs during the month.

Solution

(i)

Type of Animal	Tally	Frequency (f)
Bird	||||| ||||| |||||		16
Cat	||||| ||||| ||||| ||||| ||||| ||||| ||||| ||||| |||	43
Dog	||||| ||||| ||||| ||||| ||||| ||||| ||||| ||||| ||||| ||||| ||||| |||||	60
Horse	|||	3
Rabbit	||||| ||||	9
Reptile (snake, lizard, turtle, etc.)	||||| ||	7
Rodent (guinea pig, hamster, gerbil, mouse, rat, etc.)	||||| ||||| ||||| |||	18
Other	||||	4

(ii) Dogs were most frequent at the practice, with a frequency value of 60, and horses were least frequent, with a frequency value of 3.

(iii) Adding up all the frequency values: $16 + 43 + 60 + 3 + 9 + 7 + 18 + 4 = 160$

Therefore, the vet saw a total of 160 animals over the month.

(iv) % Time spent on cats and dogs: $\dfrac{43 + 60}{160} \times 100\% \approx 64.4\%$

Relative-Frequency Distributions

Part (iv) of Example 1.2-b introduces the concept of **relative frequency**. A **Relative-Frequency Distribution** expresses the frequency of occurrence in each category as a percent of the total frequency. Relative frequencies can also be expressed as a decimal value between 0 and 1, though this is less common than as a percent. As such, the sum of all relative frequencies in the relative frequency distribution should always be 100% (or 1), with the possible exception of a small discrepancy caused by rounding (as shown in Example 1.2-c below).

Example 1.2-c	Constructing a Relative-Frequency Distribution Table

Construct a relative-frequency distribution from the frequency table constructed in Example 1.2-b.

Solution

Type of Animal	Tally	Frequency (f)	Relative Frequency
Bird	||||| ||||| |||||		16	$\dfrac{16}{160} = 10.0\%$
Cat	||||| ||||| ||||| ||||| ||||| ||||| ||||| ||||| |||	43	$\dfrac{43}{160} \approx 26.9\%$
Dog	||||| ||||| ||||| ||||| ||||| ||||| ||||| ||||| ||||| ||||| ||||| |||||	60	$\dfrac{60}{160} = 37.5\%$
Horse	|||	3	$\dfrac{3}{160} \approx 1.9\%$
Rabbit	||||| ||||	9	$\dfrac{9}{160} \approx 5.6\%$
Reptile (snake, lizard, turtle, etc.)	||||| ||	7	$\dfrac{7}{160} \approx 4.4\%$
Rodent (guinea pig, hamster, gerbil, mouse, rat, etc.)	||||| ||||| ||||| |||	18	$\dfrac{18}{160} \approx 11.3\%$
Other	||||	4	$\dfrac{4}{160} = 2.5\%$
		Total = 160	***100.1%**

*discrepancy due to rounding

Pie Charts

Pie charts are used to summarize and show classes or groups of data in proportion to the whole dataset. The whole pie (circle) represents the total of all the values in the dataset, which is 100%, and is equal to 360 degrees.

The size of each sector represents the percent portion (or fraction) of each category of data. Pie charts are very often used in presenting poll results, expenditures, etc.

The pie chart is constructed by first converting each category or group into a percent of the whole and then multiplying this by 360 degrees to determine the number of degrees for the sector of the category being represented in the pie chart.

For example, 15% of the data is represented by a sector with an angle of 54° (0.15 × 360° = 54°).

The interpretation of a pie chart is based on the fact that the largest "slice of pie" relates to the largest proportion of the data and the smallest "slice" to the smallest proportion. It is therefore easy to make comparisons between the relative sizes of data items.

Example 1.2-d	Constructing a Pie Chart

The following data represents the monthly expenses for a senior citizen living on a fixed income in an assisted living facility:

Item	Expense
Housing	$2,000
Meals	$1,200
Health Care	$800
Taxes	$500
Transportation	$300
Miscellaneous	$200
Total	**$5,000**

Based on this table, draw a pie chart and label the percent and sector angle allocated to each sector.

Solution

The total monthly expenses of $5,000 represent 100% of the pie chart, so the entire 360° of the circle.

First, we calculate each listed expense as a percent of the total by finding the ratio of each individual expense to the total monthly expense and multiplying by 100%: e.g., Housing $= \dfrac{2,000}{5,000} \times 100\% = 40\%$

Next, we calculate the angle that corresponds to each sector by multiplying the calculated percent for each of the expense items by 360°: e.g., Housing = 0.40 × 360° = 144°

We do this for each item in the table above, adding two additional columns (one for Percent and one for Sector Angle) and filling them in with our calculations:

Item	Expense	Percent	Sector Angle
Housing	$2,000	40%	144.0°
Meals	$1,200	24%	86.4°
Health Care	$800	16%	57.6°
Taxes	$500	10%	36.0°
Transportation	$300	6%	21.6°
Miscellaneous	$200	4%	14.4°
Total	**$5,000**	**100%**	**360.0°**

Now we can construct a pie chart using the appropriate sector angles, being sure to label both the percent and the angles for each sector:

Solution
continued

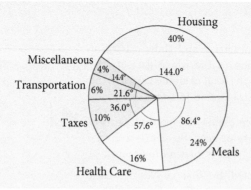

Example 1.2-e   Interpreting a Pie Chart

The final grades of 40 students who passed a math exam are represented in the pie chart below. Use the pie chart to complete the table.

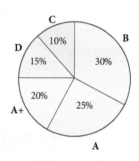

Grade	Number of Students	Percent	Sector Angle
A+			
A			
B			
C			
D			
Total	40	100%	360°

Solution

Grade	Number of Students	Percent	Sector Angle
A+	20% of 40 = 8	20%	20% of 360° = 72°
A	25% of 40 = 10	25%	25% of 360° = 90°
B	30% of 40 = 12	30%	30% of 360° = 108°
C	10% of 40 = 4	10%	10% of 360° = 36°
D	15% of 40 = 6	15%	15% of 360° = 54°
Total	40	100%	360°

Bar Charts

A **bar chart** is a graph that uses vertical (or horizontal) bars to show comparisons among categories or class intervals of grouped data. The categories or class intervals are plotted on the horizontal X-axis. The distribution of the data in these categories or the frequencies associated with the class intervals is plotted on the vertical Y-axis.

The width of the base of the rectangle for each category or class interval should be equal.

Classes should be set up without any overlap in the data.

Bar charts are easy to produce and easy to interpret. The heights (or lengths) of the bars show the quantity of the data in that category or the frequency of that class interval. These are represented by a rectangle with a base that corresponds to a category or class interval and a height (or length) that is proportional to the values that they represent.

A bar chart is also used to represent two or more sets of data having the same class interval, side-by-side, on one graph. This allows for the data values in these sets to be compared easily.

Example 1.2-f — Constructing a Bar Chart

Draw a vertical bar chart for the frequencies of grades obtained by students in a math exam, and use the chart to calculate the following:

(i)   Total number of students graded

(ii) Number of students obtaining a B grade or better

Grade	Number of Students
A+	8
A	10
B	12
C	4
D	6

Solution

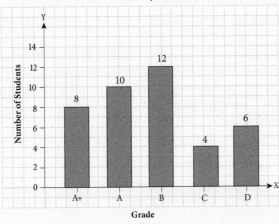

Bar Chart of Grades Obtained by Students on a Math Exam

(i)   Total number of students graded = 8 + 10 + 12 + 4 + 6 = 40

(ii) Number of students obtaining a B grade or better = 12 + 10 + 8 = 30

Example 1.2-g — Interpreting a Bar Chart

The following bar chart shows the number of males and females who were treated at a Physiotherapy and Wellness Clinic during the months of January to June.

Bar Chart of Number of Males and Females Treated at a Physiotherapy and Wellness Clinic from January to June

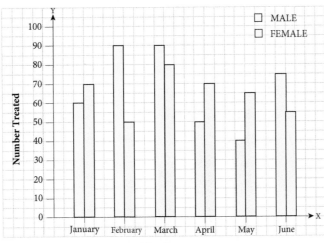

Use the bar chart above to answer the following questions:

(i)   How many males and how many females were treated in total at the clinic over the course of the 6-month period recorded?

(ii)   In which months were more females treated at the clinic than males?

(iii) In which month was there the greatest difference between the number of males treated and the number of females treated at the clinic?

Solution

(i)   Total number of males treated = 60 + 90 + 90 + 50 + 40 + 75 = 405
       Total number of females treated = 70 + 50 + 80 + 70 + 65 + 55 = 390

(ii)   In January, April, and May, more females were treated at the clinic than males.

(iii) In February, there were 90 males treated and only 50 females - a difference of 40.

Pareto Charts

In the above examples of bar charts, the qualitative data being represented was ordinal-level data - i.e., there was an inherent order present in the data. As such, there was an obvious way to arrange the categories on the horizontal axis of the bar graph.

However, for nominal data, there is no such inherent order, so a special kind of bar chart known as a **Pareto chart** is commonly used. In a Pareto chart, the categories are arranged along the horizontal axis by the frequency in each category, from greatest (left-most category) to least (right-most category).

Example 1.2-h | **Constructing a Pareto Chart**

Recall the field of interest frequency table from Example 1.2-a:

Field of Interest	Number of Students
A/K (Athletic Therapy/Kinesiology)	7
M (Paramedicine)	4
N (Nursing)	12
P (Pharmacy)	9
V (Veterinary Services)	5
O (Other)	3

Construct a Pareto chart from this frequency table.

Solution

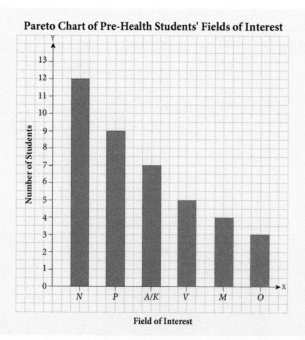

1.2 | Exercises

1. The following data was collected from a sample survey of 40 first-year students in a Pre-Health Sciences program who were asked to indicate their favourite subject among the following four subjects: Math (M), Biology (B), Chemistry (C) and Physics (P).

C	M	B	B	M	B	C	M	M	C
B	B	M	P	C	B	B	M	M	C
M	P	M	B	C	M	P	B	B	M
B	C	M	M	C	P	C	P	M	P

   Organize the data in a frequency table using a tally chart.

2. The following data was collected from a sample survey of 40 students who were asked to indicate the mode of transportation that they normally use to get to college during the summer term. Their choices were walking (W), bicycling (B), taking public transportation (P), and driving a car (C).

C	B	C	B	C	B	P	W	P	C
W	B	P	P	B	P	C	W	W	P
W	W	P	C	B	W	W	C	C	B
P	C	P	W	B	W	B	C	P	B

   Organize the data in a frequency table using a tally chart.

3. A hospital cafeteria uses a questionnaire to ask a sample of their customers how they rate the food quality. The rating is on a scale of outstanding (O), very good (V), good (G), average (A), and poor (P).

G	O	V	G	A	O	V	O	V	G	O	A
V	O	P	V	O	G	A	O	O	O	G	V
V	A	G	O	V	P	V	O	O	G	O	V
O	G	A	O	V	O	P	G	V	A	G	P

   a. Organize the data in a frequency table using a tally chart.
   b. What is the total number of responses acquired?
   c. What was the most commonly given rating?

4. The following data give the six most frequent types of cancer-related deaths in a hospital in the past three months. They are lung (L), breast (B), colorectal (C), pancreas (P), liver (LV), and stomach (S).

B	L	L	C	P	LV	LV	L	B	B	S	P
P	L	B	B	P	L	S	S	LV	P	P	S
C	C	L	L	P	LV	S	P	LV	L	L	B
S	S	B	C	C	P	C	S	C	L	B	P
C	P	B	L	L	C	C					

   a. Organize the data in a frequency table using a tally chart.
   b. What is the total number of cancer-related deaths recorded in the past three months in this hospital?
   c. Which of these cancers has contributed to the most deaths?
   d. Which of these cancers has contributed to the least deaths?

5. Construct a relative frequency distribution based on the frequency table constructed in Problem 1.

6. Construct a relative frequency distribution based on the frequency table constructed in Problem 2.

7. a. Construct a relative frequency distribution based on the frequency table constructed in Problem 3.
   b. What percent of the customers rated the food quality better than "good"?
   c. What is the ratio of "outstanding" to "poor" ratings?

8. a. Construct a relative frequency distribution based on the frequency table constructed in Problem 4.

    b. What percent of deaths were due to pancreas cancer?

    c. What is the ratio of breast cancer-related to colorectal cancer-related deaths?

9. The following are the letter grades obtained by 200 students in statistics, in a Pre-Health Sciences program of a college:

Grade	Number of Students	Percent	Angle
A+	24		
A	30		
B	36		
C	52		
D	42		
F	16		
Total	200		

    a. Complete the above table for percent and angle.

    b. Draw a pie chart using either the percent or the angle measure.

10. Victoria kept a record of the average number of hours she spent on different activities during the weekdays. The information is provided below:

Activity	Number of Hours	Percent	Angle
School	7.0		
Meals	1.0		
Homework	2.0		
Travel	2.5		
Sleep	8.0		
Other	3.5		
Total	24		

    a. Complete the above table for percent and angle.

    b. Draw a pie chart using either the percent or the angle measure.

11. The following pie chart illustrates the age groups of a sample of homeless people living in shelters: Youth (under 18), Young Adults (18 to 30), Middle-Aged Adults (31 to 50), Older Adults (51 to 60), and Senior Citizens (over 60).

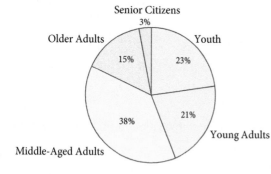

    a. What age group represents the largest segment of the sheltered homeless population?

    b. What is the ratio of the number of the sheltered homeless who are young adults to the number who are older adults?

    c. What percent of the sheltered homeless population is under the age of 51?

    d. On average, how many of every 10,000 homeless people living in shelters are senior citizens?

12. The following pie chart shows the number of blood donors of each blood type who participated in the previous blood drive at a college:

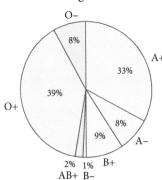

a. Which blood type has the least amount of donors?

b. What is the ratio of donors with type O+ blood to those with type O– blood?

c. What percent of donors have an A-type (i.e., A+ or A–) of blood?

d. If there were a total of 150 donors, how many donors had blood type AB+?

13. The flextime system at a local hospital allows volunteers to begin their working day at 7:00, 7:30, 8:00, 8:30, or 9:00 AM. The following data represent a sample of the starting times of 30 volunteers:

7:00	8:30	9:00	8:00	7:30	7:30	8:30	8:30	7:30	7:00
8:30	8:30	8:00	8:00	7:30	8:30	7:00	9:00	8:30	8:00
8:30	8:00	9:00	7:30	7:30	8:30	7:00	7:00	8:30	7:30

Construct a vertical bar chart for the frequencies of starting times of volunteers.

14. A physiologist suspects that the reason elementary students have neck pain is from carrying their heavy school bags. He surveyed 50 students, enquiring whether they ever experience neck pain, and the data are shown below. The responses can be never (N), sometimes (S), often (O), very often (VO) and always (A).

N	A	S	VO	N	O	O	N	S	N	N	A	S
VO	N	S	N	O	VO	A	N	N	S	S	A	S
N	N	O	VO	A	N	N	A	S	S	N	S	
O	O	VO	N	N	S	O	O	N	N	S	A	

Construct a vertical bar chart for the frequencies of responses of the students.

15. a. Construct a Pareto chart for the data in Problem 13.

b. What is the most popular start time for the volunteers?

c. Does it make sense to put this set of data in a Pareto chart? Why?

16. a. Construct a Pareto chart for the data in Problem 14.

b. Which response was mentioned the most often?

c. Does it make sense to put this set of data in a Pareto chart? Why?

17. The following data was collected from the Canadian Vital Statistics Death Database at Statistics Canada. It shows the number of deaths for selected cancers by sex in Canada for year 2015.

Type of Cancer Death	Male	Female
Lung	10,900	11,080
Colorectal	5,100	4,655
Pancreas	2,300	2,550
Leukemia	1,550	1,275
Non-Hodgkin Lymphoma	1,450	1,330
Stomach	1,300	865
Kidney	1,150	730
Oral	810	435
Brain/CNS	1,250	775

a. Create a multi-bar chart for the above data.

b. Which type of cancer has the biggest difference between male and female deaths?

c. What is the ratio of the number of deaths in males to females due to oral cancer?

18. The following table compares the Age Standardized Incidence Rate (per 100,000) between prostate cancer and breast cancer in Canada, for the years 2011 to 2016.

Year	Prostate Cancer	Breast Cancer
2011	147.7	130.8
2012	128.8	127.2
2013	117.2	126.9
2014	117.7	129.7
2015	115.1	129.9
2016	112.7	130.0

a. Create a multi-bar chart for the above data.

b. Which year has the biggest difference in incidence rates between the two types of cancer?

c. What is the percent of change in incidence of prostate cancer from year 2011 to year 2016?

19. Use the multi-bar chart below to answer the following questions:

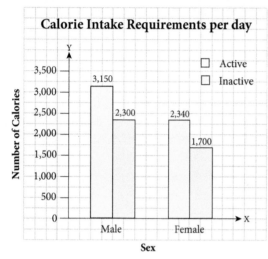

a. What is the difference in calorie intake requirements per day between an active male and an active female?

b. What is the ratio of the calorie intake requirements per day of an active male to an inactive male?

c. What is the ratio of the calorie intake requirements per day of an active female to an inactive female?

20. Use the multi-bar chart below to answer the following questions:

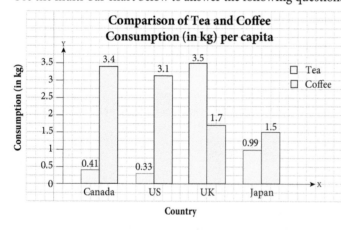

a. Which country has the biggest difference in their tea and coffee consumption?

b. What is the difference between the amounts of tea and coffee consumed in the UK per capita?

c. What is the ratio of tea to coffee consumption per capita in the US?

1.3 | Organizing and Presenting Quantitative Data

The previous section of this chapter examined methods of organizing and presenting qualitative data that has been collected and recorded. This section will examine several more methods that can be used for quantitative data. Before these methods are examined, however, it is important to reiterate the difference between discrete data and continuous data:

Discrete Data	Continuous Data
• obtained by counting	• obtained by measuring
• can only take on specific (usually integer) values	• can take on any (real-number) value within a range of values (usually rounded to a desired degree of precision)

Stem-and-Leaf Plots

A **stem-and-leaf plot** is one method of displaying data to show the spread of data and the location of where most of the data points lie. The method is simply a sorting technique to arrange the data from the lowest to the highest value, which is known as an **array**.

In this display, the set of numbers is re-written so that the last digit (unit or ones digit) becomes the leaf and the other digits become the stem. The stems are written vertically and the leaves are written horizontally. A stem-and-leaf plot shows the exact values of individual data values.

For example, for a two digit number, 38, the stem is the tens digit number, 3 (written on the left side), and the leaf is the unit digit number, 8 (written on the right side), as shown on the stem-and-leaf plot below.

For a three digit number, 156, the stem is 15 and the leaf is 6.

For a one digit number 8, the stem is 0 and the leaf is 8.

For decimal numbers, all the digits including the decimal point will be the stem and all the decimal values will be the leaves.

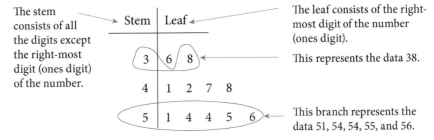

The stem consists of all the digits except the right-most digit (ones digit) of the number.

The leaf consists of the right-most digit of the number (ones digit).

This represents the data 38.

This branch represents the data 51, 54, 54, 55, and 56.

The following example illustrates the procedure for constructing a stem-and-leaf plot.

Example 1.3-a | **Constructing a Stem-and-Leaf Plot**

The marks on a statistics exam for a sample of 40 students are as follows:

63	74	42	65	51	54	36	56	68	57
62	64	76	67	79	61	81	77	59	38
84	68	71	94	71	86	69	75	97	55
48	82	83	54	79	62	68	58	41	47

(i) Construct a stem-and-leaf plot to display the data in an array.

(ii) Use the stem-and-leaf plot to determine the number of students who scored:

   (a) 70 marks or more.

   (b) less than 50 marks.

Solution

(i) Construct a stem-and-leaf plot to display the data in an array.

Step 1: Identify the lowest and highest stems of the data.
Looking at the data, the lowest stem is 3 and the highest stem is 9.

Step 2: Use Step 1 to identify the range in the stem. The stem will have the digits 3, 4, 5, 6, 7, 8, and 9. Draw a vertical line and write out the stem in this order to the left of the line.

Step 3: Starting from the 1st data, place each leaf of the number to the right of the vertical line on the corresponding stem, until the last data is recorded. There is no need to use commas on the leaf side.

For example,

- The first data value is 63. Therefore, the stem is 6 and the leaf is 3.

- The second data value is 74. Therefore, the stem is 7 and the leaf is 4.

- Continue until the last data, 47, where the stem is 4 and the leaf is 7.

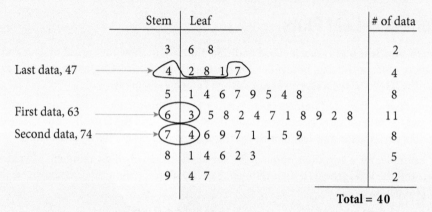

Stem	Leaf	# of data
3	6 8	2
4	2 8 1 7	4
5	1 4 6 7 9 5 4 8	8
6	3 5 8 2 4 7 1 8 9 2 8	11
7	4 6 9 7 1 1 5 9	8
8	1 4 6 2 3	5
9	4 7	2

Last data, 47 → (4 | 2 8 1 7)
First data, 63 → (6 | 3) 5 8 2 4 7 1 8 9 2 8
Second data, 74 → (7 | 4) 6 9 7 1 1 5 9

Total = 40

Step 4: Rearrange the leaves against each stem, from the smallest to the largest number, to have the numbers displayed in an array.

Stem	Leaf	# of data
3	6 8	2
4	1 2 7 8	4
5	1 4 4 5 6 7 8 9	8
6	1 2 2 3 4 5 7 8 8 8 9	11
7	1 1 4 5 6 7 9 9	8
8	1 2 3 4 6	5
9	4 7	2

Number of data less than 50 is 2 + 4 = 6.

Number of data 70 and above is 8 + 5 + 2 = 15.

Total = 40

(ii) The number of leaves against stem 7 is 8, against stem 8 is 5, and against stem 9 is 2.
Therefore, the number of students who scored 70 marks or more is 8 + 5 + 2 = 15.

The number of leaves against stem 4 is 4 and against stem 3 is 2.
Therefore, the number of students who scored less than 50 marks is 4 + 2 = 6.

Example 1.3-b	Interpreting a Stem-and-Leaf Plot

The data regarding the number of prescriptions filled in each of the 15 hours that a certain pharmacy was open is collected at the end of the day and summarized in the following stem-and-leaf plot:

Stem	Leaf
0	6 8
1	0 1 3 4
2	6 8 9
3	0 3 8 9
4	1 4

Based on the above data, calculate the following:

(i)   The total number of prescriptions filled over the course of the day.

(ii) The highest and the lowest number of prescriptions filled in a given hour.

(iii) The number of "high-workload" hours for the pharmacists (a "high-workload" hour is defined as one in which 30 or more prescriptions are filled).

Solution

(i)   Adding all the data values in each row of the stem and leaf plot,

Sum of 1st row data:	6 + 8	=	14
Sum of 2nd row data:	10 + 11 + 13 + 14	=	48
Sum of 3rd row data:	26 + 28 + 29	=	83
Sum of 4th row data:	30 + 33 + 38 + 39	=	140
Sum of 5th row data:	41 + 44	=	85
	Total	**=**	**370**

Therefore, the number of prescriptions filled over the course of the day was 370.

(ii) The highest number of prescriptions filled in a given hour was 44 and the lowest number of prescriptions filled in a given hour was 6.

(iii) To determine the number of hours in which 30 or more prescriptions were filled, simply count the number of leaves in the rows with the stem of 3 and 4.

There are 4 leaves in the row with the stem of 3 and 2 leaves in the row with the stem of 4.

Therefore, the number of high-workload hours is 4 + 2 = 6.

Tally Charts and Frequency Tables

We have already been introduced to the use of tally charts and frequency tables for qualitative data in Section 1.2. These methods of organizing and presenting data can also be used for quantitative data. However, the categories used in the tally chart will depend on the nature of the quantitative data:

- If the quantitative data is discrete and all the values are fairly close together, the categories in the tally chart can simply be the individual data values (see Example 1.3-c).

- If the quantitative data is continuous, or if the data is discrete but the values are very spread out, the categories in the tally chart will be intervals of values, called **classes** (see Examples 1.3-d, 1.3-e).

| Example 1.3-c | Constructing a Tally Chart and Frequency Table for Discrete Quantitative Data |

The ages of 35 randomly-selected high-school students were recorded as follows:

14	15	14	16	15	13	14	14	16	15
17	16	13	15	16	14	15	13	15	17
15	16	15	14	16	18	15	17	15	16
15	17	15	17	18					

Display the data using a tally chart and then construct a frequency distribution for the students' ages.

Solution

Step 1: Draw 3 columns to represent Age, Tally, and Frequency (*f*).

Step 2: Identify the lowest and highest data.

13 is the lowest and 18 is the highest. Therefore, the first column will have 6 entries displaying ages from 13 to 18.

Step 3: Starting from the first data, use tally marks in Column 2 to count the frequencies of the ages in the dataset.

Step 4: Total the tally marks in each row to get the frequency distribution of the ages and enter it in Column 3.

Age	Tally	Frequency (*f*)
13					3
14	JHT	6
15	JHT JHT ||	12
16	JHT ||	7
17	JHT	5
18				2

Total = 35

Frequency and Relative Frequency Distributions with Class Intervals

In situations where the data collected is discrete but quite spread out and without many duplications, it would not be appropriate to list the individual data values as the categories in the tally chart, as there would only be one or two tally marks in each category and a lot of empty categories in between data values. In situations where the data collected is continuous, it becomes impossible to list out all the possible data values as categories. As such, these situations require the use of intervals of values, called **classes**, as the categories for the tally chart:

- The lower number on the interval is called the **Lower Class Limit (LCL)**.

- The upper number on the interval is called the **Upper Class Limit (UCL)**.

- The size of the interval is called the **Class Width**.

While there are no specific rules to determine what the ideal class width should be, a number of factors need to be considered:

- The class width should be a convenient counting number.

- There should always be between 5 and 20 classes, and the number of classes should follow the 2^k rule:

  - Given *n* data points, choose a value of *k*, the number of classes, so that $2^k \geq n$

  - For example, if there are 100 data points, we need at least 7 classes, since $2^7 = 128 \geq 100$

- All data, from the minimum value to the maximum value, must fall into exactly one class.

- There should be minimal empty classes (i.e., intervals of values in which no data falls).

According to these principles, we can determine an appropriate class width using the following steps:

Step 1:	Calculate the **range** by subtracting the minimum value from the maximum value.
Step 2:	Determine a value of *k* for the number of classes so that $2^k \geq n$, the number of data points. • Ensure that your value for *k* is somewhere between 5 and 20.

Step 3:	Calculate the class width by dividing the range by *k* classes and choosing the *next largest integer*.
	• e.g., regardless of whether the result is 6.28, 6.91, or 6 exactly, choose a class width of 7.

Step 4:	Set your first LCL to be the minimum value in the data set (in the case of discrete data), or a convenient number just *below* the minimum value in the data (in the case of continuous data).

Step 5:	Establish the remaining LCLs by starting with the first LCL and adding the class width to it for as many classes as needed.
	• e.g., if the first LCL is 0 and the class width is 10, then the LCLs would be 0, 10, 20, 30, etc.

Step 6:	To set the UCLs, first determine if the data is discrete or continuous:
	• If the data is discrete, set the UCL of each class to be one value below the LCL of the subsequent class (e.g., 0 - 9, 10 - 19, 20 - 29, 30 - 39, etc.)
	• If the data is continuous, set the UCL to be the same as the LCL of the subsequent class, with the word "under" in front (e.g., 0 to under 10, 10 to under 20, 20 to under 30, etc.)

Note: *In some cases, it may be desirable to use a more convenient counting number than the class width established in Step 3 (e.g., if the result of the calculation is 28.6, it may be better to choose a class width of 30 instead of 29). However, the principle of **rounding up** always applies, so if the calculation in Step 3 reveals a value of 30.8, it is not appropriate to select a class width of 30; instead, use 35.*

Example 1.3-d **Constructing a Frequency Distribution for Highly-Variating Discrete Data**

A statistics professor records the data for the number of correct answers on his 55-question multiple-choice midterm exam for each of his 36 students. The results are as follows:

38	42	31	36	45	27	19	24	37	37	41	12
26	31	38	43	51	8	16	29	36	49	47	15
41	50	22	10	33	40	52	32	29	34	35	48

Construct a tally chart and frequency distribution for this data. Use 8 different classes and use the lowest mark as the LCL of the first class.

Solution

Step 1:	The minimum value is 8 and the maximum value is 52.
	Range = 52 – 8 = 44

Correct Answers	Tally	Frequency (*f*)
8 - 13	|||	3
14 - 19	|||	3
20 - 25	||	2
26 - 31	JHT|	6
32 - 37	JHT|||	8
38 - 43	JHT||	7
44 - 49	||||	4
50 - 55	|||	3
	Total = 36	

Step 2:	We are told that we must use 8 classes, which satisfies the 2^k rule, since $2^8 = 256 \geq 36$.

Step 3:	If 8 classes are used, the class width $= \dfrac{44}{8} = 5.5 \approx 6.$

Step 4:	We are told to use the minimum value as the LCL of the first class, which is 8.

Step 5:	The LCLs of the classes will therefore be 8, 14, 20, 26, 32, 38, 44, and 50.

Step 6:	Since the data is discrete, our class intervals will be 8 - 13, 14 - 19, 20 - 25, 26 - 31, 32 - 37, 38 - 43, 44 - 49, and 50 - 55.

(handwritten: for discrete data)
(handwritten: class width)

| Example 1.3-e | Constructing a Frequency Distribution for Continuous Data |

The triage nurse at an E.R. records the weights (in kg) of the 24 patients seen during her shift as follows:

| 62.4 | 51.6 | 98.6 | 75.2 | 57.0 | 68.2 | 84.8 | 109.6 | 76.4 | 81.0 | 93.2 | 61.8 |
| 55.2 | 77.8 | 72.0 | 86.4 | 95.8 | 105.2 | 78.4 | 69.0 | 123.2 | 65.8 | 73.6 | 89.4 |

Construct a tally chart and frequency distribution for this data.

Solution

Step 1: The minimum value in the data is 51.6 kg and the maximum value is 123.2 kg.

Range = 123.2 − 51.6 = 71.6

Step 2: Since there are 24 pieces of data, we need at least $k = 5$ classes, since $2^5 = 32 \geq 24$.

Step 3: If 5 classes are used,

the class width $= \dfrac{71.6}{5} = 14.32 \approx 15$.

Step 4: The minimum data value is 51.6, so the lowest class will start at 50.

Step 5: The LCLs of the classes will therefore be 50, 65, 80, 95, and 110.

Step 6: Since the data is continuous, our class intervals will be 50 to under 65, 65 to under 80, 80 to under 95, 95 to under 110, and 110 to under 125.

Weight (kg)	Tally	Frequency (f)
50 to under 65	IIII I	5
65 to under 80	IIII IIII	9
80 to under 95	IIII	5
95 to under 110	IIII	4
110 to under 125	I	1
	Total = 24	

| Example 1.3-f | Interpreting a Tally Chart for Continuous Data |

A laser sensor at a science museum can measure the height of a person that steps into the beam. The heights of a sample of 50 adults recorded by the laser sensor are summarized in the following tally chart:

Height (cm)	Tally
140 to under 150	III
150 to under 160	IIII IIII
160 to under 170	IIII IIII IIII
170 to under 180	IIII IIII III
180 to under 190	IIII III
190 to under 200	II

(i) Construct a frequency distribution from the tally chart by adding in a Frequency (f) column, as well as a Relative Frequency column.

(ii) Identify the interval of values with the highest frequency (called the **modal class**) and the number of data values in that class.

(iii) What percent of the adults sampled have a height of at least 180 cm?

Solution

(i)

Height (cm)	Tally	Frequency (f)	Relative Frequency
140 to under 150	|||	3	$\frac{3}{50} = 6\%$
150 to under 160	ЖЖ ||||	9	$\frac{9}{50} = 18\%$
160 to under 170	ЖЖ ЖЖ ЖЖ	15	$\frac{15}{50} = 30\%$
170 to under 180	ЖЖ ЖЖ |||	13	$\frac{13}{50} = 26\%$
180 to under 190	ЖЖ |||	8	$\frac{8}{50} = 16\%$
190 to under 200	||	2	$\frac{2}{50} = 4\%$
	Total = 50		**100%**

(ii) The interval of values with the highest frequency (i.e., the modal class) is "160 to under 170 cm" and the number of data values in that class is 15.

(iii) The data values in the last two classes ("180 to under 190 cm" and "190 to under 200 cm") represent adults who have heights of at least 180 cm. There are 8 + 2 = 10 data values in these two classes combined, which represents 16% + 4% = 20% of the adults sampled.

Graphs of Frequency Distributions for Quantitative Data

For graphs of frequency distributions of quantitative data, unlike with qualitative data, the horizontal axis usually represents a continuous number line. However, recall that the class limits in a frequency distribution are the upper and lower data values that could fall into each of the classes, and for discrete data, there are apparent gaps between the UCL of one class and the LCL of the subsequent class. As such, we need to establish **class boundaries** - i.e., real-numbered values that separate adjacent classes:

- For continuous data, the class boundaries are the same as the class limits.

  - e.g., Class Intervals: 0 to under 10, 10 to under 20, 20 to under 30, 30 to under 40, …

  - Class boundaries are the same as the class limits: 0, 10, 20, 30, 40, …

- For discrete data, the class boundaries are halfway between the UCL and subsequent LCL of two adjacent classes.

  - e.g., Class Intervals: 0 - 9, 10 - 19, 20 - 29, 30 - 39, …

  - The size of the "gap" is 1, so halfway is 0.5

  - Class boundaries are 0.5 on either side of the class limits: –0.5, 9.5, 19.5, 29.5, 39.5, …

The final important piece of information in a frequency distribution is the **midpoint** of each class - i.e., the value that is exactly halfway between the upper and lower class boundaries:

- For the continuous example above, the class midpoints would be 5, 15, 25, 35, …

- For the discrete example above, the class midpoints would be 4.5, 14.5, 24.5, 34.5, …

We will discuss and use the class midpoints of a frequency distribution further in Chapter 2.

Example 1.3-g **Identifying Class Boundaries and Midpoints in a Frequency Distribution**

Identify the class boundaries and midpoints for the frequency distributions in Examples 1.3-d and 1.3-e.

Solution

1.3-d

Class Intervals	Class Boundaries	Class Midpoints
8 - 13	7.5	10.5
	13.5	
14 - 19		16.5
	19.5	
20 - 25		22.5
	25.5	
26 - 31		28.5
	31.5	
32 - 37		34.5
	37.5	
38 - 43		40.5
	43.5	
44 – 49		46.5
	49.5	
50 – 55		52.5
	55.5	

1.3-e

Class Intervals	Class Boundaries	Class Midpoints
50 to under 65	50	57.5
	65	
65 to under 80		72.5
	80	
80 to under 95		87.5
	95	
95 to under 110		102.5
	110	
110 to under 125		117.5
	125	

Histogram

A **histogram** is a specific type of vertical bar chart that is used to visually represent the summary data from a frequency table for quantitative data. To construct a histogram, the class intervals are marked on the horizontal axis and the class frequencies are represented by the heights of the bars on the vertical axis. However, in histograms, unlike with bar charts for qualitative data, there should be no space between the bars of adjoining class intervals - i.e., the bars are drawn immediately adjacent to each other without any gaps. This demonstrates visually that all possible values along the horizontal axis have been grouped into exactly one of the classes.

Frequency Polygon

The **frequency polygon** is the line joining the midpoints of the bars of a histogram - i.e., the points whose horizontal coordinates are the midpoints of the class intervals and whose vertical coordinates are the frequencies of the respective class intervals. Typically, an additional class interval (with a frequency of 0) is added on both ends of the histogram so that the frequency polygon begins and ends directly on the X-axis (at the midpoints of those additional empty classes).

Example 1.3-h **Constructing a Histogram and Frequency Polygon**

Draw a histogram and a frequency polygon for the distribution of age groups of 200 employees in a company as shown below.

Age (Class Intervals)	Number of Employees (Frequency)
20 to under 30	35
30 to under 40	42
40 to under 50	64
50 to under 60	30
60 to under 70	24
70 to under 80	5
Total	**200**

Solution

Histogram and Frequency Polygon of Number of Employees vs. Age

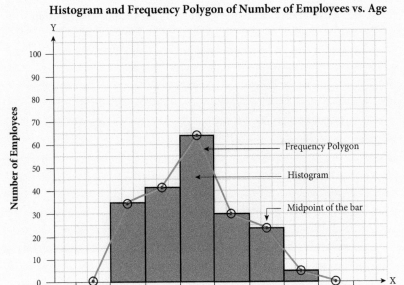

Note: Labels on the X-axis representing the class interval can be in any of the following formats: 20 to under 30, 30 to under 40, 40 to under 50, ... ; or 20-30, 30-40, 40-50, ... ; or as mid-points of class intervals (25, 35, 45, ...).

Outliers

Sometimes, there are **outliers** in the data set - that is, very high or very low values that are far removed from the other values in the data set. In these cases, it may be challenging to set appropriate class intervals and widths. As such, it is sometimes appropriate to modify the first or last class to say "Below [...]" or "[...] and above", respectively, to account for these outliers. However, this should be done only when absolutely necessary, as a lot of information can be lost by doing this.

Note: When constructing a frequency polygon for a frequency distribution with a modified first class ("Below [...]") and/or last class ("[...] and above"), no additional classes should be added to the ends of the histogram - instead, the frequency polygon should end on the modified classes.

Example 1.3-i	**Constructing a Histogram and Frequency Polygon with Modified First and Last Classes**

Data is collected from a sample of 200 households regarding their gross annual household income. The results are summarized in the following table:

Household Income	Frequency
Below $25,000	17
$25,000 to under $50,000	35
$50,000 to under $75,000	48
$75,000 to under $100,000	41
$100,000 to under $125,000	23
$125,000 to under $150,000	14
$150,000 to under $175,000	11
$175,000 to under $200,000	7
$200,000 and above	4
Total	**200**

Construct a histogram and a frequency polygon for this data.

Solution

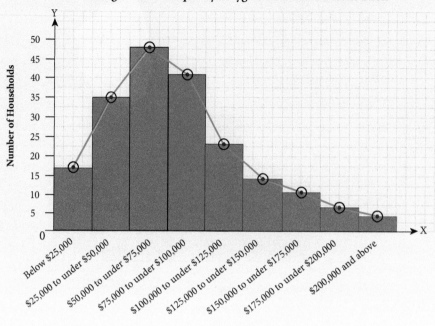

Histogram and Frequency Polygon for Income Distribution

Household Income

Cumulative Frequency Distributions and Cumulative Frequency Curves (Ogives)

The **cumulative frequency distribution** value at a given class interval is calculated by adding the frequency at that class interval to the frequencies of all the preceding class intervals - i.e., the sum of the frequencies of all the class intervals up to and including the given class interval. Simply put, it is the running total of the frequencies.

A **relative cumulative frequency distribution** is the cumulative frequency distribution expressed as a percent of the total number of data values - i.e., it is the percent of the data that falls into or below the given class interval. As such, the relative cumulative frequency value in the highest class will always be 100%. Simply put, it is the running total of all of the relative frequencies.

A curve showing the cumulative frequency plotted against the upper class boundary of the class interval is called a cumulative frequency curve or **ogive** (pronounced "oh-jive").

| Example 1.3-j | Constructing a Cumulative and Relative Cumulative Frequency Distribution |

Use the frequency distribution for the statistics exam marks of a class of 40 students given below to create the cumulative frequency distribution and the relative cumulative frequency distribution. Also, draw the cumulative frequency curve (ogive).

Class Interval	Frequency
30 to under 40	2
40 to under 50	4
50 to under 60	8
60 to under 70	11
70 to under 80	8
80 to under 90	5
90 to under 100	2
Total	**40**

Solution

Add two columns to the frequency table: one for the cumulative frequency distribution and one for the relative cumulative frequency distribution, as shown below.

Class Interval	Frequency	Cumulative Frequency	Relative Cumulative Frequency
30 to under 40	2	2	5.0%
40 to under 50	4	6	15.0%
50 to under 60	8	14	35.0%
60 to under 70	11	25	62.5%
70 to under 80	8	33	82.5%
80 to under 90	5	38	95.0%
90 to under 100	2	40	100.0%
Total	**40**		

The cumulative frequency of any class is computed by using the total value of the frequency up to and including that class.

For example, the cumulative frequency of class "50 to under 60" is 2 + 4 + 8 = 14.

The relative cumulative frequency is computed by dividing the cumulative frequency distribution of that class by the total number of observations and converting the answer to a percent.

For example, the relative cumulative frequency of class "50 to under 60" is $\frac{14}{40} \times 100\% = 35\%$.

When drawing the cumulative frequency curve (or ogive), recall that it is plotted against the upper class boundary of the class interval.

For example, the cumulative frequency of class "50 to under 60" (14) is plotted against 60 (the upper class boundary), as shown below.

Cumulative Frequency and Relative Cumulative Frequency vs. Marks

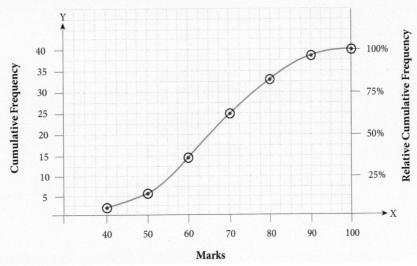

Time-Series Data and Line Graphs

When continuous data is collected from the same source(s) at several different points in time over the course of a fixed period of time, the resulting paired data values (a time value with a measurement value) is called **time-series data**. This data is often plotted on a **line graph**, which is a graph that has the following features:

- Title of the graph, describing the purpose.
- Labelled axes, with the horizontal axis representing time and the vertical axis representing the measurement of the continuous data.

- Interval scales on both axes - i.e., the differences between values on the scale must remain constant, but there does not need to be an "absolute zero" plotted at the origin.
- Plotted points whose coordinates correspond to the paired data values.
- Straight line segments connecting the points chronologically - i.e., sequentially from left to right (along the horizontal axis), representing the change in measurements over time.
- When multiple measurements are taken at each point in time, the various time-series data measurements are plotted on the same set of axes, each represented by their own data markers and line graph, indicated on the legend (not necessary for only one set of time-series data).

| Example 1.3-k | Constructing a Multiple-Line Graph |

A patient with high blood pressure (i.e., hypertension) is put on a medication to help bring his blood pressure down. His blood pressure is monitored and recorded daily for 10 days as follows:

Blood Pressure (mmHg)	Day 1	Day 2	Day 3	Day 4	Day 5	Day 6	Day 7	Day 8	Day 9	Day 10
Systolic	165	160	156	162	153	145	148	140	135	142
Diastolic	100	94	95	92	90	85	88	84	80	82

Draw a multiple-line graph to visually represent the systolic and diastolic blood pressure values recorded over the 10-day period.

Solution

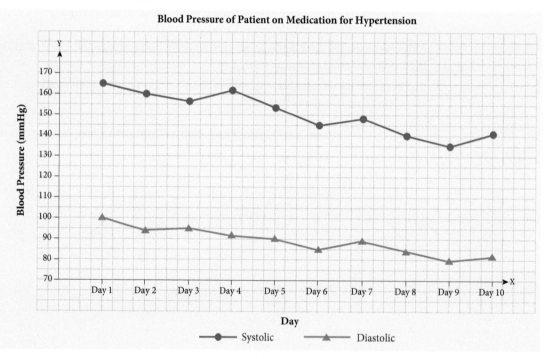

Example 1.3-I **Interpreting a Line Graph**

The following line graph shows the number of emergency calls that paramedics responded to each month over the course of the year:

Paramedic Responses to Emergency Calls by Month

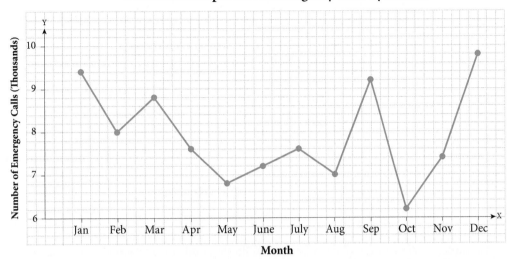

(i) Calculate the total number of emergency calls responded to by paramedics over the summer months (considered to be May through August).

(ii) What was the fewest number of emergency calls that paramedics responded to in one month, and in which month did that number occur?

(iii) What was the greatest number of emergency calls that paramedics responded to in one month, and in which month did that number occur?

(iv) Between which two months did the greatest change in number of emergency calls occur, and what was the difference between the number of calls in those two months?

Solution

(i)
Emergency Calls in May:	6,800
Emergency Calls in June:	7,200
Emergency Calls in July:	7,600
Emergency Calls in August:	7,000

TOTAL = 28,600

(ii) The fewest number of emergency calls that paramedics responded to was 6,200, which occurred in the month of October.

(iii) The greatest number of emergency calls that paramedics responded to was 9,800, which occurred in the month of December.

(iv) The greatest change in the number of emergency calls that paramedics responded to between two consecutive months occurred between September (9,200) and October (6,200), a decrease of 3,000 emergency calls.

1.3 | Exercises

1. Construct a stem-and-leaf plot to display the following data in an array:

39	32	44	13	29	38
31	18	19	37	25	27
34	31	19	43	21	28

2. Construct a stem-and-leaf plot to display the following data in an array:

7	16	19	5	37	25
22	18	26	20	32	11
17	31	9	16	13	35

3. Construct a stem-and-leaf plot to display the following students' heights data (in cm) in an array:

165	177	181	155	151	145	185	182
175	178	148	192	152	169	184	170
195	180	173	181	159	188	164	197

4. Construct a stem-and-leaf plot to display the following students' final grades data in an array:

76	95	77	75	78	66	97	71
72	84	88	62	58	52	92	91
89	83	85	59	97	87	80	65

5. A psychologist developed a test for measuring patient anxiety when going into a doctor's office. The test was administered to a group of patients, and the following stem-and-leaf plot was obtained; the maximum score is 100 and higher scores represent greater anxiety.

Stem	Leaf							
3	4							
4	1	2						
5	0	1	1	8				
6	1	2	2	2	4			
7	0	0	2	4	6	6	7	8
8	2	3	5	5	5	9		
9	3	8	8	9				

   a. How many patients participated in this test?

   b. What is the highest score and the lowest score?

   c. How many patients scored below 75?

6. The price-per-share data for a sample of 26 pharmaceutical companies is arranged in a stem-and-leaf plot below:

Stem	Leaf						
6	3						
7	2	4	5	6			
8	1	3	4	5	8		
9	0	1	4	7	9		
10	0	4	5	5	7	8	9
11	3	5	6	7			

   a. What are the highest and the lowest prices-per-share?

   b. How many companies have a price-per-share of $100 or more?

   c. Do any companies have the same price-per-share? If yes, list any repeating prices.

7. The number of babies delivered in a hospital per day for the past 30 days are recorded below:

4	2	1	0	6	3	2	3	5	6
3	4	5	3	4	2	1	0	1	2
3	5	5	4	3	2	0	6	1	3

a. Construct a tally chart and frequency distribution for the number of babies delivered in the hospital for the past 30 days.

b. What is the most frequent number of deliveries per day? How many days does it occur?

c. How many days were more than three babies delivered?

d. How many days were no babies delivered?

8. The data for the number of hospital beds available at a small local hospital for the past 20 days are shown below:

2	5	8	7	4	5	6	5	5	8
8	6	8	4	3	2	2	2	8	5

a. Construct a tally chart and frequency distribution for the number of hospital beds available at the hospital for the past 20 days.

b. How many days did the hospital have less than 5 beds available?

c. How many days did the hospital have 5 or more beds available?

9. Use the data from Problem 1 to construct a frequency distribution with 5 classes. The LCL of the first class should be the minimum value in the data set.

10. Use the data from Problem 2 to construct a frequency distribution with 7 classes. The LCL of the first class should be the minimum value in the data set.

11. Use the data from Problem 3 to construct a frequency distribution. Choose an appropriate number of classes using the techniques described in this chapter.

12. Use the data from Problem 4 to construct a frequency distribution. Choose an appropriate number of classes using the techniques described in this chapter.

13. The data for the number of I.V. tubes produced by a production line during the past 20 days are shown below:

160	162	170	156	181	179	156	142	176	150
148	157	189	154	179	179	162	178	151	156

a. Construct a frequency distribution with 6 classes, with the lower limit of the first class being 140.

b. Construct a histogram and frequency polygon for this set of data.

14. The following data were obtained for the number of minutes spent in an E.R. room before seeing the doctor for a sample of 30 patients.

88	34	50	35	94	45	12	96	100	53
29	35	70	99	40	64	85	24	68	28
47	28	53	29	99	136	30	82	65	65

a. Construct a frequency distribution with 5 classes, with the lower limit of the first class being 10.

b. Construct a histogram and frequency polygon for this set of data.

15. The frequency distribution below was constructed from data collected from a sample of 120 professors at a college.

Years of Teaching	Frequency
0 to under 5	10
5 to under 10	25
10 to under 15	39
15 to under 20	24
20 to under 25	13
25 to under 30	7
30 to under 35	2

a. Construct a histogram and a frequency polygon for the data.

b. Determine the class boundaries and class midpoints for the frequency distribution.

16. The frequency distribution below was constructed from data collected from a sample of 30 students at a college.

Height (cm)	Frequency
155 to under 160	2
160 to under 165	5
165 to under 170	9
170 to under 175	7
175 to under 180	4
180 to under 185	3

a. Construct a histogram and a frequency polygon for the data.

b. Determine the class boundaries and class midpoints for the frequency distribution.

17. The frequency distribution below was constructed from a sample of 48 male clients at a weight-loss clinic. Construct a histogram and frequency polygon for the data:

Weight (kg)	Frequency
Below 80	2
80 to under 90	5
90 to under 100	13
100 to under 110	16
110 to under 120	8
120 or above	4

18. The frequency distribution below gives the age distribution of patients who visited the E.R. during a long weekend at a hospital. Construct a histogram and frequency polygon for the data:

Age	Frequency
Below 20	7
20 to under 30	10
30 to under 40	16
40 to under 50	14
50 to under 60	30
60 and above	28

19. Use the frequency distribution from Problem 13 to construct the following:
    a.   Relative Frequency Distribution
    b.   Cumulative Frequency Distribution
    c.   Relative Cumulative Frequency Distribution
    d.   Cumulative Frequency Curve (Ogive)

20. Use the frequency distribution from Problem 14 to construct the following:
    a.   Relative Frequency Distribution
    b.   Cumulative Frequency Distribution
    c.   Relative Cumulative Frequency Distribution
    d.   Cumulative Frequency Curve (Ogive)

21. Use the frequency distribution from Problem 15 to construct the following:
    a.   Relative Frequency Distribution
    b.   Cumulative Frequency Distribution
    c.   Relative Cumulative Frequency Distribution
    d.   Cumulative Frequency Curve (Ogive)

22. Use the frequency distribution from Problem 16 to construct the following:
    a. Relative Frequency Distribution
    b. Cumulative Frequency Distribution
    c. Relative Cumulative Frequency Distribution
    d. Cumulative Frequency Curve (Ogive)

23. A store's monthly sales (in thousands of dollars) for last year were as follows:

Month	Jan.	Feb.	Mar.	Apr.	May	Jun.	Jul.	Aug.	Sep.	Oct.	Nov.	Dec.
Sales ($ Thousands)	45	52	74	78	70	95	98	120	105	89	80	92

Draw a line graph representing the data.

24. The average number of days a patient needed to wait for reconstructive shoulder surgery for the period from 2006 to 2014 is provided below:

Year	2006	2007	2008	2009	2010	2011	2012	2013	2014
Number of days	82	110	130	145	90	75	128	160	180

Draw a line graph representing the data.

25. The following data are the Age Standardized Incidence Rates (per 100,000) for prostate and breast cancers in Canada from the years 2007 to 2016:

Year	2007	2008	2009	2010	2011	2012	2013	2014	2015	2016
Prostate Cancer	168	155	151	146	148	129	117	118	115	113
Breast Cancer	128	126	129	130	130	127	126	130	130	131

Create a multi-line graph for the above data set.

26. The following data are the average weights and cholesterol levels of a patient per month over one calendar year.

Month	Jan.	Feb.	Mar.	Apr.	May	Jun.	Jul.	Aug.	Sep.	Oct.	Nov.	Dec.
Weight (lb)	285	273	264	259	245	251	242	247	240	232	221	225
Cholesterol level (mg/dL)	256	245	239	242	235	236	233	230	228	225	211	215

Create a multi-line graph for the above data set.

27. Based on the multi-line graph in Problem 25:
    a. Comment on the trend of prostate cancer incidence.
    b. Comment on the trend of breast cancer incidence.
    c. What is the percent increase in incidence of breast cancer from 2007 to 2016?
    d. What is the percent decrease in incidence of prostate cancer from 2007 to 2016?

28. Based on the multi-line graph in Problem 26:
    a. Comment on the trend of the patient's weight over the year.
    b. Comment on the trend of the patient's cholesterol level over the year.
    c. What is the percent decrease in the patient's weight from the beginning of the year to the end?
    d. What is the percent decrease in the patient's cholesterol level from the beginning of the year to the end?

1 | Review Exercises

1. Identify which sampling methods are being implemented in the following studies:

   a. A doctor selects a sample from volunteering patients in the waiting room.

   b. A survey is conducted by randomly selecting five nursing homes and interviewing all employees at the selected nursing homes.

   c. Selecting every 20th name from a registration list for an interview.

   d. Selecting random samples of patients from each ward in a hospital.

2. Identify which sampling methods are being implemented in the following studies:

   a. 10 raffle ticket winners are randomly selected from a box for a hospital fundraising event.

   b. A forensic scientist collected blood samples at every 15 cm interval of the blood trial at the crime scene.

   c. A chef collected responses to the new menu from the first 25 customers who visited the hospital cafeteria on Wednesday lunch hour.

   d. Listing all physiotherapy programs in a rehab center and randomly selecting three of them for an in-depth study.

3. Identify the following variables as qualitative, quantitative discrete, or quantitative continuous:

   a. Different types of surgery procedures administered at a hospital.

   b. The number of paramedics hired at a hospital.

   c. Pain classification (0 = slight, 1 = moderate, 2 = intense).

   d. The average daily parking fee at a hospital.

4. Identify the following variables as qualitative, quantitative discrete, or quantitative continuous:

   a. The amount of saturated fat (oz) in a grilled cheese sandwich.

   b. Different types of fruits sold in a grocery store.

   c. Number of recipes offered in a cookbook.

   d. The amount of sugar found in a cranberry cocktail.

5. Identify the level of measurement (nominal, ordinal, interval, or ratio) for the following:

   a. Your grade-point-average (GPA).

   b. The number of years since you graduated from college.

   c. Your occupation.

   d. The position you hold in your company.

6. Identify the level of measurement (nominal, ordinal, interval, or ratio) for the following:

   a. Voting preference: Conservative, Liberal, NDP, or Independent.

   b. Hospital funding (in millions of dollars) provided by the federal government every year.

   c. Types of rooms a patient stayed in: private, semi-private, or standard ward.

   d. Temperature set in a semi-private room.

7. The following data represents the financial stress-level of a group of 90 fulltime students:

Financial Stress-Level	Number of Responses
No financial stress	24
Some financial stress	38
High financial stress	20
Overwhelming financial stress	8

   a. Draw a pie chart and label the percent allocated to each level.

   b. What is the percent of students that have no financial stress?

   c. What is the ratio of students with high financial stress to students with overwhelming financial stress?

8. The following data represents 50 people's views on their favorite types of donuts:

Types of Donuts	Number of Responses
Glazed	15
Frosted	12
Filled	10
Plain	5
Sprinkled	8

a. Draw a pie chart and label the percent allocated to each type.

b. What is the percent of people who prefer filled donuts?

c. What is the ratio of preference of glazed to frosted donuts?

9. Patients are referred to a Fracture and Orthopaedic Clinic either through the emergency room (*ER*), an inpatient department (*I*), by an orthopaedic surgeon (*OS*), or by a family physician (*FP*). The following data shows 18 referrals on a particular day:

OS	ER	I	FP	ER	I
ER	FP	OS	ER	OS	FP
OS	I	ER	OS	I	ER

a. Organize the data in a frequency table using a tally chart.

b. Construct a Pareto chart using the data.

c. What is the most common form of referral at this clinic?

d. What percent of referrals are through an orthopaedic surgeon or a family physician?

10. Given the Pareto chart below:

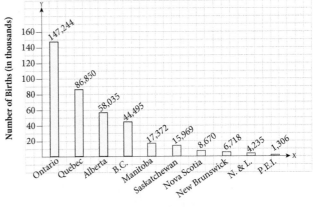

Number of births in Canada in 2016, by Province

a. What was the total number of births in all ten provinces of Canada in 2016?

b. Which provinces had the most and least numbers of births in Canada in 2016?

c. What was the number of births in the Eastern Provinces (which include New Brunswick, Nova Scotia, Newfoundland & Labrador, and P.E.I.)?

d. What is the ratio of number of births in Ontario to the Eastern Provinces?

11. The following are the scores of 30 college students on a statistics test.

90	52	80	96	65	79	71	87
93	95	89	72	81	76	99	86
81	68	50	93	81	80	71	60
77	85	71	92	47	98		

a. Construct a stem-and-leaf plot to display the data.

b. How many students scored below 60 on this test?

c. How many students scored 85 or above on this test?

12. The following stem-and-leaf plot represents the number of hours that 26 students spent working on a computer during the past month.

Stem	Leaf
0	7
1	1 2 9
2	0 8
3	2 4 7 8
4	1 3 6 8 8
5	2 5 7
6	3 6 6 7 9
7	
8	6 9
9	0

a. How many students worked below 35 hours during the past month?

b. How many students worked above 55 hours during the past month?

13. The following data give the number of orders of flyers received for a sample of 30 days at a Pharmaceutical Marketing Company:

34	28	30	44	20	27	31	46
45	52	41	38	41	49	34	47
53	46	38	57	33	35	36	30
47	32	25	39	37	50		

a. Construct a tally chart and frequency distribution table for this data. Use 4 classes and use the lowest value as the LCL of the first class.

b. What is the modal class?

c. What percent of days sampled have at least 40 orders?

14. The following data give the number of text messages sent on 20 randomly selected school days by a college student:

62	43	33	54	70	37	67	36
45	59	71	68	41	58	34	47
53	46	28	57				

a. Construct a tally chart and frequency distribution table for this data. Use 4 classes and use the lowest value as the LCL of the first class.

b. What is the modal class?

c. What percent of days sampled did the student send less than 50 messages?

15. The following data represent the years of service of a sample of nurses at a hospital:

17.5	30	28	22	11	19.5	15	15
26	20	15	12	13	15.5	10	7.5
12	8.5	9.5	22.5	17	18	23.5	6

a. Is this data qualitative, quantitative discrete, or quantitative continuous?

b. Construct a frequency distribution table with 5 classes, using the lowest value as the LCL of the first class.

c. Construct a relative frequency distribution.

d. Construct a cumulative frequency distribution.

e. Construct a relative cumulative frequency distribution.

f. Create a histogram and frequency polygon for this set of data.

g. Create a cumulative frequency curve (ogive curve) for this set of data.

h. Based on the ogive curve, estimate:
   (i) How many nurses have 12 or fewer years of service?
   (ii) How many nurses have more than 12 but 24 or fewer years of service?
   (iii) How many nurses have more than 20 years of service?

16. The following data represent the weight (in pounds) of 20 third grade boys at an elementary school during a recent school health fair:

45.1 52.8 66.2 70.0 84.9 82.1 76.2 53.9
63.2 48.6 62.3 78.2 55.2 68.5 67.1 73.0
81.2 47.3 64.5 65.4

a. Is this data qualitative, quantitative discrete, or quantitative continuous?

b. Construct a frequency distribution table with 5 classes, using 40 as the LCL of the first class.

c. Construct a relative frequency distribution.

d. Construct a cumulative frequency distribution.

e. Construct a relative cumulative frequency distribution.

f. Create a histogram and frequency polygon for this set of data.

g. Create a cumulative frequency curve (ogive curve) for this set of data.

h. Based on the ogive curve, estimate:
   (i) What percent of the boys weigh 50 or fewer pounds?
   (ii) What percent of the boys weigh more than 50 but 70 or fewer pounds?
   (iii) What percent of the boys weigh more than 75 pounds?

17. The following data give the time (in minutes) taken by 25 students to complete a statistics test.

Time (in minutes)	No. of Students
Below 30	2
30 to under 40	4
40 to under 50	3
50 to under 60	10
60 and above	6

a. Construct a relative frequency distribution.

b. Construct a cumulative frequency distribution.

c. Construct a relative cumulative frequency distribution.

d. Create a histogram and frequency polygon for this set of data.

18. A health clinic has 80 employees. Their hourly wages are recorded in the following frequency distribution.

Hourly Wages ($)	No. of Employees
Below 20	2
20 to under 22	6
22 to under 24	15
24 to under 26	17
26 to under 28	20
28 to under 30	12
30 and above	8

a. Construct a relative frequency distribution.

b. Construct a cumulative frequency distribution.

c. Construct a relative cumulative frequency distribution.

d. Create a histogram and frequency polygon for this set of data.

19. The number of teenagers in Canada who received the meningitis vaccine in years 2009 to 2015 are as follows:

Year	2009	2010	2011	2012	2013	2014	2015
Number (in thousands)	29	30	22	27	28	30	35

a. Draw a line graph representing the data.

b. Between what two consecutive years was there a decrease in the number of teenagers receiving the meningitis vaccine?

c. What was the percent increase in number of teenagers taking the meningitis vaccine from 2011 to 2012?

20. A nurse monitors the temperature levels of a patient for two days. The line graph below shows the readings during the two day period:

Temperature of a Patient

a. What was the patient's highest temperature and at what time?

b. Find the difference in temperature at midnight (12:00 AM) on day 1 and day 2.

c. At what time does the temperature seem to spike up?

21. The average monthly amounts of rainfall, in millimetres (mm), from January to June of 2014, for Edmonton, Alberta and Vancouver, British Columbia are listed below.

Months	Edmonton	Vancouver
Jan	20	25
Feb	9	18
Mar	26	30
Apr	36	25
May	57	50
Jun	88	95

a. Construct a multi-line graph to show the amounts of rainfall between the two cities.

b. Which month showed the biggest difference in rainfall between the two cities?

c. In general, which city had more rain?

d. In Edmonton, what was the biggest increase in rain between two consecutive months, and in what months did it occur?

e. In Vancouver, what was the biggest decrease in rain between two consecutive months, and in what months did it occur?

22. The following multi-line graph represents the smoking rate of Canadians aged 15 and older, male and female, from 1965 to 2010.

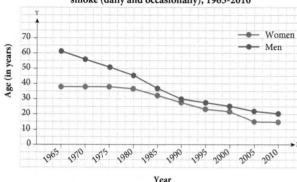

Percentage of Canadians aged 15 and older who smoke (daily and occasionally), 1965-2010

a. Between what five-year-span was the biggest decrease in the percent of smokers in the male group?

b. Between what five-year-span was the biggest decrease in the percent of smokers in the female group?

1 | Self-Test Exercises

1. A researcher believes that women whose mothers took a specific drug during pregnancy are twice as likely to develop health problems than those whose mothers did not. A sample of 3,800 women were interviewed and it was found that 120 women have developed tissue abnormalities.

   a. What are the populations involved in this study?

   b. Were the data obtained by a survey, an observational study, or an experiment?

2. Identify which sampling methods are being used for the following studies:

   a. Determining the cleanliness of the rooms in a senior home by selecting random hallways in the home and then observing all the rooms that connect to those hallways.

   b. Determining the average length of time that patrons spend waiting for wheelchair transit by recording the wait times of every 10th person who calls to request transit.

   c. Determining people's opinions on the pricing of parking at a hospital by asking people as they leave the parking lot.

   d. Determining patients' opinions on the hospital food by randomly sampling patients from each ward of the hospital, proportionate to the number of patients in each ward.

3. Identify the following variables as qualitative, quantitative discrete, or quantitative continuous.

   a. Number of deaths due to brain cancer.

   b. Annual budget of a hospital.

   c. Sex of a baby.

   d. Weight of a patient.

   e. Triage number assigned.

4. Identify the level of measurement (nominal, ordinal, interval, or ratio) for the following:

   a. Temperature in a mortuary.

   b. Patient identification number.

   c. Cleanliness index of a surgery room.

   d. Number of nurses attending the E.R.

   e. Room number on a hospital floor.

5. The following pie chart outlines causes of deaths in Canada in 2012:

   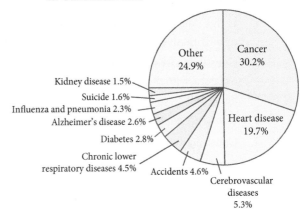

   a. Which was the biggest cause of death in Canada in 2012?

   b. What was the ratio of cancer to heart disease deaths in 2012?

   c. The 2016 Canadian census counted a total population of 35,151,728; if the percentages remain relatively stable, approximately how many deaths would be expected to be due to cancer? Round your answer to the nearest 1,000.

6. In a study of job satisfaction, a series of tests was administered to 30 nurses. The following data were obtained; higher scores represent greater satisfaction.

87	76	67	58	92	59	41	50
90	75	80	81	70	33	61	88
46	97	50	77	82	71	46	66
78	67	81	55	65	78		

   a. Construct a stem-and-leaf plot for the data.

   b. What is the lowest score in this study?

   c. How many nurses gave a score below 60?

   d. How many nurses gave a score of 80 or above?

7. Twenty patients had their cholesterol levels tested. Their results are given below in units of mg per dL.

142   156   240   143   179   233   220   195

168   200   248   158   205   197   150   181

215   198   166   232

a. Is this data qualitative, quantitative discrete, or quantitative continuous?

b. Construct a frequency distribution table with 6 classes, with the lower limit of the first class being 140.

c. Construct a relative frequency distribution.

d. Construct a cumulative frequency distribution.

e. Construct a relative cumulative frequency distribution.

f. Create a histogram and frequency polygon for this set of data.

g. Create a cumulative frequency curve (ogive curve) for this set of data.

h. Based on the ogive curve, estimate:

(i) How many patients have cholesterol levels below or equal to 190?

(ii) How many patients have cholesterol levels above 180 but below or equal to 220?

(iii) How many patients have cholesterol levels above 230?

8. The following data indicate the geographic location of top 20 medical schools based on continent: Asia (*A*), Europe (*E*), North America (*NA*), and South America (*SA*). The ranks are based on the amount of research funding the school received.

E	SA	A	NA	E
A	E	A	SA	NA
A	SA	E	NA	A
A	E	NA	NA	NA

a. Tally and construct a frequency distribution.

b. Construct a Pareto chart of the data.

c. Where are most of the top medical schools located?

d. What percent of the top medical schools are located in Asia?

9. The following data was collected by Canadian Vital Statistics Death Database at Statistics Canada. It shows the attributable risk, expressed as a percent, of various risk factors for pancreatic cancer for men and women.

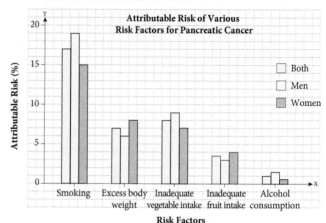

a. Overall, which factor has the biggest impact on pancreatic cancer risk, regardless of gender?

b. Which factors seem to have more impact on men than on women in pancreatic cancer risk?

c. Approximately what percent attributable risk are women with excess body weight?

d. Approximately what percent attributable risk are men with inadequate vegetable intake?

e. What is the difference in percent attributable risk between men and women in terms of the smoking factor?

10. The following multi-line graph shows Age Standardized Incidence Rates (ASIR) of males with selected cancers in five-year intervals from 1992 to 2017.

Age Standardized Incidence Rates (ASIR) for selected cancers in males in Canada

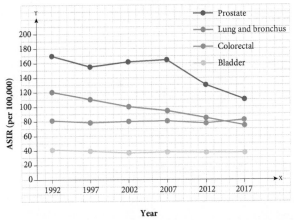

a. Which type of cancer has the most stable ASIR?

b. Which type of cancer has the most volatile ASIR?

c. Which type of cancer displays a consistently decreasing trend in ASIR over the 25-year period?

d. In which year did prostate cancer have the highest ASIR?

2

MEASURES OF CENTRAL TENDENCY

LEARNING OBJECTIVES

- Define and calculate various measures of central tendency for ungrouped data, including mean, median, and mode.
- State the advantages and disadvantages of the various measures of central tendency and indications for the use of each.
- Identify outliers and describe their effect on the arithmetic mean and compute the mean of a trimmed data set.
- Calculate the weighted arithmetic mean and various non-arithmetic means, including the geometric mean and the harmonic mean.
- Calculate the value of the mean, median, and mode for grouped data with unique classes or class intervals.
- Identify the relationships between mean, median, and mode for symmetrical and skewed distributions.

CHAPTER OUTLINE

2.1 Mean, Median, and Mode

2.2 Arithmetic and Non-Arithmetic Means

2.3 Measures of Central Tendency for Grouped Data

2.4 Skewness and Interpreting Measures of Central Tendency

Introduction

In Chapter 1, we examined proper methods of collecting, organizing, and presenting data. We will now shift our focus to analyzing and interpreting the data. In order to do this, we need to take the raw data and condense it to a handful of **summary statistics** - that is, values that tell us about certain characteristics of the data, including where the centre of the data is, what the shape of the data is, how spread out the data is, etc. In this chapter, we will look at the first two characteristics: the centre of the data and the shape of the data.

Measures of central tendency are numerical values that represent the **central position** of the data set (**mean**), the central location - or **middle value** - of the data set (**median**), or the data value with the **greatest frequency (mode)**. That is, a measure of central tendency is a single number that represents a "typical" value of a data set. This single value is useful to compare different data sets of the same type.

This section introduces three summarizing numbers (typical values) that describe the centre of the data set: the mean, the median, and the mode.

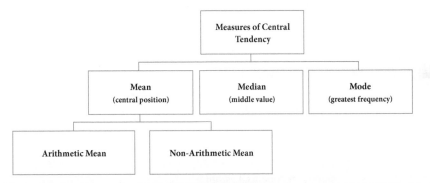

2.1 | Mean, Median, and Mode

Mean

The **mean** is a measure of central tendency that uses all the data and indicates the central position of the frequency distribution; in other words, it is the **average** of the values in the data set, meaning that if all the values in the data set were replaced with one single value, without changing the total, that single value would be the mean. The terms "mean" and "average" have the same meaning and are used interchangeably; however, "mean" is the more formal term used in statistics.

Arithmetic Mean

Mean is the ratio of all the values of the terms to the number of terms.

The most common mean is the **arithmetic mean** (or **simple arithmetic mean**), which is calculated by dividing the sum of the values of all the terms by the number of terms. If all the data values were plotted on a number line, the arithmetic mean would be the point where the number line is equally balanced on both sides - that is, the sum of the distances from the mean to each point above the mean would be exactly equal to the sum of the distances from the mean to each point below the mean. In other words, if the number line was a giant teeter-totter and the data values were all 1 kg weights placed at their respective positions on the number line, the arithmetic mean would be the "fulcrum," or balancing point, of the teeter-totter.

The arithmetic mean also represents the expected value - that is, if one piece of data was selected at random, the arithmetic mean would be the best guess for the value of that piece of data.

The arithmetic mean is the most commonly used measure of central tendency because of its mathematical qualities, and as such, it is usually referred to simply as the "mean." For the remainder of this chapter and throughout the rest of the text, every reference to the "mean" will be assumed to refer to the arithmetic mean (other types of means will be discussed in the next section and will always be referred to specifically by name).

Calculating the Mean of a Data Set

As mentioned previously, the mean of a data set is calculated by taking the sum of all the values in the data set (typically represented by the variable x) and dividing by the number of data values (represented by the letter n). The symbol used for the mean of a sample data set is $\bar{x}$, pronounced "x-bar" (x refers to the variable used to represent the data, and the bar above x indicates the sample mean of that data set):

Formula 2.1-a	**Mean of a Sample**

$$\bar{x} = \frac{\textit{Sum of All the Values of the Terms}}{\textit{Number of Terms}} = \frac{\Sigma x}{n}$$

The capital Greek letter Sigma 'Σ' represents the "sum of" a set of values.

In other words, the sample mean satisfies the following formula:

$$\Sigma x = n \cdot \bar{x}$$

This formula indicates that adding all the n individual data values in a sample is equivalent to adding the mean n times.

The formula for calculating the mean of a population is the same, but the population mean is represented by the symbol μ, pronounced "mew", while the number of terms in a population is represented by N.

Formula 2.1-b	**Mean of a Population**

$$\mu = \frac{\textit{Sum of All the Values of the Terms}}{\textit{Number of Terms}} = \frac{\Sigma x}{N}$$

Note: Unless the question explicitly states that the data set is a population, we will always assume that the data set represents a sample.

Example 2.1-a	Calculating the Mean

The number of patients seen by a nurse each day this week (Mon to Fri) is: {8, 15, 7, 11, 9}.

(i)   Determine the mean number of patients seen per day by the nurse this week.

(ii) Explain, on a number line, what this number represents in relation to the given values.

Solution

(i)   {8, 15, 7, 11, 9}   There are 5 terms.

To determine the mean, add all the terms then divide by the number of terms.

$$Mean = \frac{\textit{Sum of All the Values of the Terms}}{\textit{Number of Terms}} = \frac{(8 + 15 + 7 + 11 + 9)}{5} = \frac{50}{5} = 10$$

Therefore, the mean (or average) number of patients seen by the nurse per day this week is 10.

(ii) If we plot these values on a number line, the number 10 represents the centre of these values.

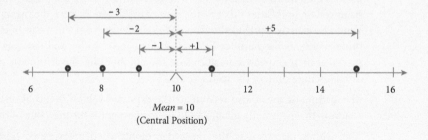

Mean = 10
(Central Position)

Example 2.1-b | **Calculating the Mean with New Data**

The mean of 6 observations is 70. If another observation with a value of 98 is added to the above data, calculate the mean of the 7 observations.

Solution

The mean of 6 observations (terms) is 70.

$$\text{Mean} = \frac{\textit{Sum of All the Values of the Terms}}{\textit{Number of Terms}}$$ Substituting values,

$$70 = \frac{\text{The sum of 6 terms}}{6}$$ Rearranging,

The sum of 6 terms $= 70 \times 6 = 420$

Therefore, the sum of the 6 observations (terms) is 420. When a new term with a value of 98 is added,

The sum of 7 terms $= 420 + 98 = 518$

The mean of 7 terms $= \dfrac{518}{7} = 74$

Therefore, the mean of the 7 observations (terms) is 74.

Example 2.1-c | **Solving for an Unknown Data Value**

The mean age of four patients seen by a pediatrician is 7. The ages of the first three patients are 3, 5, and 8. Determine the age of the fourth patient.

Solution

To solve for an unknown value, we make use of the rearrangement of the formula for the mean:

$$\sum x = n \cdot \bar{x}$$

Let x represent the unknown age of the fourth patient and substitute in all remaining known values:

$$3 + 5 + 8 + x = 4(7)$$
$$16 + x = 28$$
$$x = 28 - 16$$
$$x = 12$$

Therefore, the age of the fourth patient is 12.

Median

Median is the middle value when the data is in an array.

The **median** is the value of the middle term when the terms are in an array, arranged in ascending order (lowest to highest value) or in descending order (highest to lowest value). That is, half of the values are below the median and the other half of the values are above the median.

The location of the median in an array is determined by the following formula:

Formula 2.1-c | **Location of the Median**

$$L_m = \frac{(n + 1)}{2}$$

where n is the number of terms in the data set.

- If the number of terms in the data set is odd, this formula will result in a whole number, representing the location of the middle value in the list.

  - E.g., if $n = 19$, then $L_m = \dfrac{(19 + 1)}{2} = \dfrac{20}{2} = 10$; i.e., the median is the 10th term in the data set.

- If the number of terms in the data set is even, this formula will result in a number with a decimal of .5. In this case, the median is determined by calculating the average of the two middle values in the list.

  - E.g., if $n = 20$, then $L_m = \dfrac{(20 + 1)}{2} = \dfrac{21}{2} = 10.5$; i.e., the median is halfway between the 10th and 11th terms in the data and is calculated by averaging these two terms.

Since the median is the middle value in the list, it is not affected by extreme values (outliers), making it the preferred measure of central tendency when there are values in the data set that are not representative of the data set as a whole.

Example 2.1-d	**Determining the Median of a Data Set with an Odd Number of Terms**

The heights (in cm) of a sample group of students are:

{198, 168, 175, 180, 171, 179, 177}

Calculate the median height for this group of students.

Solution

Arrange the data in ascending order as follows:

> 168   171   175   177   179   180   198

There are 7 terms in the data set.

$$L_m = \frac{(n + 1)}{2} = \frac{(7 + 1)}{2} = \frac{8}{2} = 4$$

The 4th term in the array is 177.

Therefore, the median height for this group of students is 177 cm.

Example 2.1-e	**Determining the Median of a Data Set with an Even Number of Terms**

The costs for a two-week stay in a private hospital room at a sample of 6 different provincial hospitals are:

{2,700; 2,650; 2,925; 1,550; 3,050; 2,850}

Calculate the median cost for a two-week stay in a private hospital room in the province.

Solution

Arrange the data in ascending order as follows:

> 1,550   2,650   2,700   2,850   2,925   3,050

There are 6 terms in the data set.

$$L_m = \frac{(n + 1)}{2} = \frac{(6 + 1)}{2} = \frac{7}{2} = 3.5$$

Therefore, the median is located between the 3rd and 4th terms.

3rd term = 2,700

4th term = 2,850

Average of 3rd and 4th terms = $\dfrac{(2,700 + 2,850)}{2} = 2,775$

Therefore, the median cost for a two-week stay in a private hospital room in the province is $2,775.

Mode

Mode is the most frequently observed value in a data set.

The **mode** of a set of observations is the specific value that occurs with the most frequency (i.e., occurs most often). For non-numeric data (e.g., colour), or for numeric data where the frequency is more important than the value (e.g., shoe size), the mode is the preferred measure of central tendency.

If all the observations occur with the same frequency (i.e., there is no "most frequent" measurement in the data set), then there is no mode.

There may be more than one mode in a set of observations if there are several values that all occur with the greatest frequency (i.e., there is a "tie" for most frequent). A data set with two modes is described as **bi-modal** and a data set with more than two modes is described as **multi-modal**.

- In the data set {1, 3, 6, 7, 12, 15, 17}, there is no mode.

- In the data set {11, 13, **16, 16, 16**, 17, 17, 22, 22, 27}, the mode is 16 and it is unique.

- In the data set {10, **11, 11**, 12, 13, 14, **15, 15**}, the mode is not unique. There are two modes: 11 and 15. Therefore, the data is bi-modal.

Example 2.1-f	Calculating Measures of Central Tendency for a Data Set

Given the following set of data, calculate the (i) mean, (ii) median, and (iii) mode.

{14, 28, 17, 40, 26, 21, 36, 26, 27, 31}

Arrange the data in ascending order as follows:

14   17   21   26   26   27   28   31   36   40

(i) Using $Mean = \dfrac{\sum x}{n}$,

$$Mean = \frac{(14 + 17 + 21 + 26 + 26 + 27 + 28 + 31 + 36 + 40)}{10} = \frac{266}{10} = 26.6$$

Therefore, the mean is 26.6.

(ii) The median position is determined by using the formula $L_m = \dfrac{(n + 1)}{2}$.

There are 10 terms. Therefore, $L_m = \dfrac{(10 + 1)}{2} = 5.5$

The median is located between the 5th and 6th terms.

$$Median = \frac{(5^{th} \text{ term} + 6^{th} \text{ term})}{2} = \frac{(26 + 27)}{2} = 26.5$$

Therefore, the median is 26.5.

(iii) The value that occurs most frequently is 26. It occurs two times in the data set.

Therefore, the mode is 26.

Advantages and Disadvantages of the Mean, Median, and Mode

Table 2.1-a **Advantages and Disadvantages of the Mean**

Mean	
Advantages	Disadvantages
It is defined by an algebraic formula.	It cannot be determined by inspecting the data.
It is based on all values of the given data.	It cannot be computed for qualitative data.
It has a unique value and is useful in comparing sets of data.	Its value may not be equal to any of the data values.
It is used algebraically in further statistical calculations.	It is affected by extremely large or small values in the data.
It is used in calculating the sum of the values of the data by multiplying with the number of items.	It cannot be computed when class intervals have open ends.

Table 2.1-b **Advantages and Disadvantages of the Median**

Median	
Advantages	Disadvantages
It is easy to identify by knowing the number of items and the middle item in the data.	It is not a representative measure when the values of the data are far apart from each other.
It can be estimated through the graphical presentation of the data.	It is not based on all the items in the data.
It is not affected by extremely large or small values in the data.	It is an approximate measure when located between the two middle values.
It has a unique value and is useful in comparing sets of data.	It is not used in further statistical calculations.
It is a good measure of central tendency for data with a skewed distribution.	It is not useful to calculate the sum of the values of the data.

Table 2.1-c **Advantages and Disadvantages of the Mode**

Mode	
Advantages	Disadvantages
It is easy to locate in the data set without requiring a calculation that involves all of the data values.	It is not a representative value of all the items in the data.
It is not affected by extremely large or small values in the data.	It is not possible to identify when frequencies of all items are identical.
It is a very popular measure for qualitative data.	It may have more than one value which may make it difficult to interpret or compare.
It can be located graphically with the help of bar charts/histograms.	It may not reflect the centre of the distribution.
It will always be equal to a value in the data set.	It is not used in further statistical calculations.

Table 2.1-d	When to Use the Mean, Median, and Mode

Measure of Central Tendency	When to Use
Mean	Best used when the data is symmetrical or after outliers have been removed.
Median	Best used when the data is skewed (left or right) or when there are outliers in the data.
Mode	Best used when the frequency of observations is more important than the value of the observations or with qualitative data.

We will learn about skewed data in Section 2.4.

2.1 | Exercises

Answers to odd-numbered problems are available at the end of the textbook.

1. The final marks of a student in six subjects were 89, 95, 68, 86, 91, and 78. Calculate the average (arithmetic mean) mark.

2. The weights (in kilograms) of seven students were 62, 68, 65, 69, 73, 58, and 64. Calculate the average (arithmetic mean) weight.

3. Henry received the following marks on his first three math tests: 85, 94, and 89. What mark must he receive on his fourth test to have an average of exactly 90 on the four tests?

4. Giang received the following marks on her first four math tests: 87, 93, 89, and 88. What mark must she receive on her fifth test to have an average of exactly 90 on the five tests?

5. The mean of ten observations is 20 and that of another fifteen observations is 16. Calculate the mean of all 25 observations.

6. A class of 25 students took a science test. Ten students had an average (arithmetic mean) score of 80. The other fifteen students had an average score of 60. What is the average score of the whole class?

7. The mean of six numbers is 50. If one of the numbers is excluded, the mean gets reduced by 5. Determine the excluded number.

8. The mean of five numbers is 27. If one of the numbers is excluded, the mean gets reduced by 2. Determine the excluded number.

9. The average monthly salary of 50 people was $4,220. The average monthly salary of 42 of them was $3,500. Calculate the average monthly salary of the remaining eight people.

10. The average mark for a class of 40 students was 74. The fifteen male students in the class had an average mark of 70. Calculate the average mark of the female students in the class.

11. In a survey, ten people were found to have an average weight of 72 kg. When another person joined the survey, the average of the eleven people dropped by 2 kg. Calculate the weight of the eleventh person.

12. The average mark of fourteen students in a class was 75. Another student took a make-up test and the class average dropped by 1 mark. What was the mark of the fifteenth student?

13. Determine the median for the following data sets:

    a. {51, 56, 63, 46, 48}

    b. {26, 24, 29, 24, 25, 28, 23}

    c. {28, 24, 22, 24, 26, 26, 22, 28, 27}

14. Determine the median for the following data sets:

    a. {14, 11, 19, 17, 15}

    b. {30, 27, 29, 24, 22, 31, 25}

    c. {93, 90, 62, 44, 75, 89, 74, 78, 72}

15. Determine the median for the following data sets:

a. {41, 44, 37, 39, 27, 35, 42, 40}

b. {18, 13, 5, 14, 18, 14, 19, 17, 15, 10}

c. {74, 100, 78, 61, 78, 81, 67, 93, 90, 62, 75, 89}

16. Determine the median for the following data sets:

a. {75, 78, 92, 69, 84, 70, 75, 89}

b. {74, 99, 78, 61, 78, 81, 67, 93, 90, 62}

c. {52, 57, 61, 64, 70, 72, 78, 79, 79, 80, 80, 81}

17. The results on a recent class test out of 30 are: {30, 27, 19, 24, 22, 31, 25, 28, 26}.

a. Determine the median mark.

b. If a mark of 24, achieved by another student, is included in the test scores, determine the new median mark.

18. The test results on a recent exam out of 100 were: {67, 62, 70, 68, 90, 84, 94}.

a. Determine the median mark.

b. If a mark of 75, achieved by another student, is included in the exam scores, determine the new median mark.

19. Determine the mode for the following data sets:

a. {5, 6, 7, 10, 11, 12, 13, 15, 16}

b. {14, 16, 16, 27, 31, 31, 31, 35, 37}

c. {34, 36, 36, 36, 37, 41, 41, 41, 42}

20. Determine the mode for the following data sets:

a. {6, 7, 8, 11, 13, 14, 16, 17}

b. {15, 15, 17, 25,28, 29, 32, 34, 35}

c. {29, 30, 32, 34, 35, 37, 42, 42, 42}

2.2 | Arithmetic and Non-Arithmetic Means

As discussed in the previous section, a simple arithmetic mean is not always the best way to calculate the average of a set of data. Consider the following situations:

- Marks from six different evaluations, each weighted differently, that form a student's final grade.

- Figure skating scores from ten judges, with an extremely low or extremely high score due to bias.

- Five consecutive annual rates of growth on an investment.

- The rates of speed of a triathlete in each of the three different events.

In all of the above situations, the simple arithmetic mean examined in the last section would not provide a true "average".

In the first two scenarios, the contributions from each evaluation/score are not valued equally. Therefore, an arithmetic mean may still be calculated, but using a modified formula.

In the last two scenarios, the overall "total" value (e.g., overall rate of growth or overall speed) is not determined by adding together the individual values, but by using another mathematical approach. These situations require calculating a non-arithmetic mean, of which there are several different kinds.

This is summarized in the following diagram:

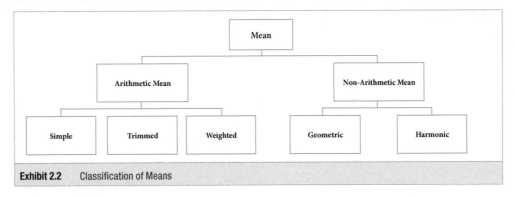

Exhibit 2.2 Classification of Means

Arithmetic Means

First, we will examine scenarios where an arithmetic (or additive) mean beyond the scope of the simple arithmetic mean is used to compute the average.

Outliers and the Trimmed Arithmetic Mean

Outliers

We will learn a specific method for identifying outliers in Chapter 3.

An **outlier** is a number that is very different from the rest of the group. If the data set includes outliers, these will strongly affect the value of the typical arithmetic mean. As such, it may be helpful to remove the outliers from the data set before calculating the mean of a data set, or to calculate the mean twice - once with the outliers included, once with the outliers removed - and compare the results in order to understand the effect of the outliers on the mean.

Example 2.2-a   Showing the Effect of Extreme Values (Outliers) on the Mean

Calculate the mean (i) using all values, and (ii) after removing the outlier(s) in the data set:

{3, 40, 45, 52, 60, 66, 70}

Solution

(i) Mean of all seven values in the data set:

$$\bar{x} = \frac{\sum x}{n} = \frac{(3 + 40 + 45 + 52 + 60 + 66 + 70)}{7} = \frac{336}{7} = 48$$

(ii) Except for the value 3, the other values are reasonably close to each other. Therefore, 3 is an outlier. After removing the value 3 from this data set, the mean of the remaining six values of the data set:

$$\bar{x} = \frac{\sum x}{n} = \frac{(40 + 45 + 52 + 60 + 66 + 70)}{6} = \frac{333}{6} = 55.5$$

Therefore, the mean is greatly affected by the extreme value (or outlier) of 3, which is very different from the rest of the values in the data set.

Trimmed Mean

A **trimmed mean** is a simple arithmetic mean of the middle values in the data set after a certain percent (usually 10%) of the highest and lowest values are removed from the data set. It is used in cases where it is important that outliers never affect the outcome.

To compute a trimmed mean, the following steps are taken:

Step 1: Arrange the data into an array.

Step 2: Identify the number of data points to be removed by multiplying the size of the data set by the percent to be trimmed and rounding to the nearest whole number.

Step 3: Remove the number of data points from Step 2 from the top and bottom of the array.

Step 4: Compute a simple arithmetic mean of the remaining values.

Example 2.2-b **Calculating a 10% Trimmed Mean**

A competitor in a judged sport is given the following ten marks (out of 10):
{8.6, 8.2, 7.8, 8.4, 9.0, 6.8, 8.2, 8.6, 8.0, 8.6}
Determine the competitor's final score by calculating a 10% trimmed mean of the given marks.

Solution

Step 1:   First arrange the data into an array:
{6.8, 7.8, 8.0, 8.2, 8.2, 8.4, 8.6, 8.6, 8.6, 9.0}

Step 2:   Next, calculate 10% of the data set. Since there are ten data values, 10% of the data is represented by one data value.

Step 3:   Remove the lowest and highest data value (i.e., 10%) from the array:
{~~6.8~~, 7.8, 8.0, 8.2, 8.2, 8.4, 8.6, 8.6, 8.6, ~~9.0~~}

Step 4:   Finally, compute the simple arithmetic mean of the remaining eight values:
$$\bar{x} = \frac{(7.8 + 8.0 + 8.2 + 8.2 + 8.4 + 8.6 + 8.6 + 8.6)}{8} = \frac{66.4}{8} = 8.3$$

Therefore, the competitor's final score, based on the 10% trimmed mean, is 8.3.

Weighted Arithmetic Mean

The **weighted arithmetic mean** is also known as the weighted average. It is similar to the simple arithmetic mean, but instead of each term contributing an equal weight in the average calculation, now each of the terms may contribute a different weight than the other terms.

When the degrees of importance of the terms are not equal, the value of each term to be averaged is assigned a different weight; the weightings determine the relative importance of each term. The weighted mean is then calculated by dividing the total of the weighted values by the total of the weights. If all the weightings are equal, then the weighted mean is the same as the simple arithmetic mean.

A common example of a weighted mean is a final grade calculation for a course in which the various assignments, projects, quizzes, tests, and exams have different weights (e.g., four quizzes each worth 5%, two projects each worth 20%, and a final exam worth 40%). In this example, the marks obtained on each evaluation will not contribute equally to the final grade, and so a weighted mean calculation must be used.

The formula for the weighted mean is as follows:

Formula 2.2-a   **Weighted Arithmetic Mean**

$$\bar{x} = \frac{\textit{Sum of All the Weighted Data Values}}{\textit{Sum of All the Weights}} = \frac{\Sigma\,(w \cdot x)}{\Sigma\,w}$$

Example 2.2-c   **Calculating a Weighted Mean**

In a math course, there are four assignments, each worth 5%; two midterm exams, each worth 20%; and a final exam, worth 40%. A student receives the following grades on each of the evaluations:

Assignment #1 – 80%   Midterm #1 – 63%

Assignment #2 – 75%   Midterm #2 – 82%

Assignment #3 – 90%   Final Exam – 70%

Assignment #4 – 95%

Calculate the student's overall final (weighted) grade.

Solution

Evaluation	Grade (x)	Weight (w)	Weighted Grade ($w \cdot x$)
Assignment #1	80%	5%	$0.05 \times 80\% = 4\%$
Assignment #2	75%	5%	$0.05 \times 75\% = 3.75\%$
Assignment #3	90%	5%	$0.05 \times 90\% = 4.50\%$
Assignment #4	95%	5%	$0.05 \times 95\% = 4.75\%$
Midterm #1	63%	20%	$0.20 \times 63\% = 12.60\%$
Midterm #2	82%	20%	$0.20 \times 82\% = 16.40\%$
Final Exam	70%	40%	$0.40 \times 70\% = 28\%$
		$\Sigma w = 100\%$	$\Sigma(w \cdot x) = 74\%$

Use the weighted arithmetic mean formula to determine the student's overall final grade:

$$\bar{x} = \frac{\Sigma (w \cdot x)}{\Sigma w} = \frac{74\%}{100\%} = 74\%$$

Therefore, the student's final grade in the course is 74%.

Non-Arithmetic Means

We will now examine some situations where using an arithmetic (or additive) mean is not an appropriate method for computing the average.

Geometric Mean

When it comes to calculating the average rate at which a quantity grows or decays over a time period, the arithmetic mean is not a good measure. This is because rates of growth are multiplicative rather than additive (that is, they are multiplied together, not added together). As such, we need a different type of mean, known as the geometric mean, to handle these situations.

The **geometric mean** (G) allows for the calculation of the average rate of growth over a period of time. It is a very useful measure in accounting and finance for processes involving compound interest, and in the sciences for processes involving exponential growth (e.g., bacteria cultures) or exponential decay (e.g., radioactive isotopes).

The geometric mean is calculated by multiplying all the values of the terms together and then taking the nth root of the product, or by raising the product to the exponent $\frac{1}{n}$ (recall this is the same as taking the nth root), where n is the total number of terms in the data set. Whereas the capital Greek letter Sigma (Σ) is used to represent the sum (Σ is the Greek letter S for Sum), the capital Greek letter Pi (Π) is used to represent the product (Π is the Greek letter P for Product). Hence, the formula for the geometric mean is as follows:

Formula 2.2-b	**Geometric Mean**

$$G = \sqrt[n]{\prod x} = \left(\prod x \right)^{\frac{1}{n}}$$

The capital Greek letter Pi 'Π' represents the "product of" a set of values.

In other words, the geometric mean satisfies the following formula:

$$\prod x = G^n$$

This formula says that multiplying all the n individual rates of growth together is equivalent to multiplying the geometric mean by itself n times (i.e., raising it to the nth power).

Example 2.2-d   Calculating and Comparing the Arithmetic and Geometric Means

Calculate and compare the arithmetic and geometric means for the following data set: {3, 4, 6, 9, 14}.

Solution

Arithmetic Mean: $\bar{x} = \dfrac{(3 + 4 + 6 + 9 + 14)}{5} = \dfrac{36}{5} = 7.2$

Geometric Mean: $G = \sqrt[5]{(3 \cdot 4 \cdot 6 \cdot 9 \cdot 14)} = \sqrt[5]{9{,}072} \approx 6.19$

Therefore, the arithmetic and geometric means are 7.2 and 6.19, respectively, which are considerably different.

In the previous example, the calculated arithmetic mean is higher than the calculated geometric mean. In fact, this will always be the case, except for when all the values being averaged are equal, in which case the arithmetic mean and geometric mean will be equal.

In summary, we can state as a fact: $\bar{x} \geq G$, and $\bar{x} = G$ if and only if all the data values are identical.

Note: The proof of this fact is quite difficult and well beyond the scope of this textbook. Simply put, it relates to how a square always has a lesser perimeter than any rectangle with the same area.

Example 2.2-e   Calculating the Average Annual Rate of Growth

Sam invested $100 for four years. If the growth rate for each year was 10%, 14%, 17%, and 18%, respectively, what was the average annual growth rate?

Solution

The average growth rate using arithmetic mean $= \dfrac{(10\% + 14\% + 17\% + 18\%)}{4} = 14.75\%$

However, since rates of growth are multiplicative rather than additive, this is not the correct calculation in this case. The correct calculation is to determine the geometric mean, as explained below:

End of the first year, the value $= 100(1 + 0.10)$

End of the second year, the value $= 100(1 + 0.10)(1 + 0.14)$

End of the third year, the value $= 100(1 + 0.10)(1 + 0.14)(1 + 0.17)$

End of the fourth year, the value $= 100(1 + 0.10)(1 + 0.14)(1 + 0.17)(1 + 0.18)$

If 'G' is the average annual growth rate over the four-year period, then,

$100(1 + G)^4 = 100(1 + 0.10)(1 + 0.14)(1 + 0.17)(1 + 0.18)$

$\qquad\qquad = 100(1.10)(1.14)(1.17)(1.18)$

Dividing both sides by 100 and taking the 4th root, we obtain the following:

$(1 + G) = [(1.10)\,(1.14)\,(1.17)\,(1.18)]^{\frac{1}{4}}$

$\qquad = 1.147073...$

$\quad G = 0.147073... = 14.71\%$

Therefore, the average annual growth rate was 14.71%.

Harmonic Mean

Just as computing average rates of growth requires a non-arithmetic mean, so does computing average rates of change, like rates of speed (i.e., the rate of change of distance over time). Consider the following example:

A runner runs for an hour at a constant speed of 15 km/h, and then turns around and walks home at a constant speed of 5 km/h. What is the runner's average rate of speed?

Intuitively, we want to say the answer is 10 km/h. However, upon analysis, we can that see this is incorrect:

- If the runner runs for an hour at 15 km/h, he has run a total distance of 15 km from his home.

- At a return speed of 5 km/h, he will take 3 hours to walk home.

- Thus, he has travelled a total of 30 km over the course of 4 hours, making his overall average $speed = \dfrac{30 \text{ km}}{4 \text{ hours}} = 7.5$ km/h.

This example differs from previous examples in that while the distance at both speeds is constant, the **time** is not, and it is the time spent at each speed that determines the average. In this scenario, the runner ran at 15 km/h for one hour, but walked at 5 km/h for three hours. As such, if we had used a weighted average, assigning a weight of 1 to the 15 km/h speed and a weight of 3 to the 5 km/h speed, we would've correctly calculated 7.5 km/h as the true average speed.

However, there is a more direct method to calculate this kind of average, known as the harmonic mean. The **harmonic mean** (*H*) takes the reciprocal average of the reciprocal values, as follows:

Formula 2.2-c	**Harmonic Mean**
	$$H = \dfrac{n}{\sum \left(\dfrac{1}{x}\right)}$$

Note: In the calculation of the harmonic mean, each x refers to a rate of speed over a fixed distance, and as such, no data value can be 0.

In the example above,

$$H = \dfrac{2}{\dfrac{1}{15} + \dfrac{1}{5}} = \dfrac{2}{\dfrac{4}{15}} = 2 \times \dfrac{15}{4} = 7.5 \text{ km/h}$$

Example 2.2-f	**Calculating Average Speed using the Harmonic Mean**

A personal fitness trainer recorded the average speed (in km/h) of her client running 10 laps of a 1-km track:

{10.4, 9.8, 9.2, 8.6, 8.8, 8.4, 7.8, 8.6, 9.0, 12.8}

Determine the client's average speed over the entire 10-km run.

Solution

Since the data values in question are rates of speed, the most appropriate average to use is the harmonic mean.

$$H = \dfrac{10}{\dfrac{1}{10.4} + \dfrac{1}{9.8} + \dfrac{1}{9.2} + \dfrac{1}{8.6} + \dfrac{1}{8.8} + \dfrac{1}{8.4} + \dfrac{1}{7.8} + \dfrac{1}{8.6} + \dfrac{1}{9.0} + \dfrac{1}{12.8}} = \dfrac{10}{1.089573...} \approx 9.2$$

Therefore, the client's average speed was 9.2 km/h.

2.2 | Exercises

Answers to odd-numbered problems are available at the end of the textbook.

1. The following data indicate the number of cell phone minutes used last month by twelve randomly selected students.

   230   160   397   410   380   236   3,846   184   201   327   225   198

   a. Calculate the mean using all the values.

   b. Calculate the mean after removing the outlier(s) in the data set.

2. The table below provides starting salary estimates for a number of health sciences occupations in Canada.

Occupation	Salary ($)
Dietitian	50,000
Medical Technologist	48,000
EMT/Paramedic	53,000
Radiologic Technician	51,000
Dental Hygienist	56,000
Orthodontist	97,000
Optician	41,000
Radiation Therapist	55,000
Midwife	57,000
Massage Therapist	38,000

a. Calculate the mean salary using all the values.

b. Calculate the mean after removing the outlier(s) in the data set.

3. The following data indicate the money spent (in dollars) on books during 2015 by 10 college students.

890   754   611   987   87   629   773   845   1,143   728

a. Calculate the mean using all the values.

b. Calculate the 10% trimmed mean.

4. The following indicate the number of patients who visited a walk-in clinic on each of 20 randomly selected days.

23   28   37   32   26   37   19   29   33   38
24   30   35   42   20   24   34   26   38   22

a. Calculate the mean using all the values.

b. Calculate the 15% trimmed mean for these data.

5. A class is given a quiz with five questions. 20% of the students got all five correct, 30% got four correct, 25% got three correct, 10% got two correct, 5% got one correct, and the remaining students got them all wrong. If there are 40 students in the class, what is the mean mark on the quiz?

6. A class is given a test with five questions. 15% of the students got all five correct, 25% got four correct, 40% got three correct, 5% got two correct, 10% got one correct, and the remaining students got them all wrong. If there are 40 students in the class, what is the mean mark on the test?

7. A student obtained marks of 75, 85, 60, 65, and 50 in the subjects of Finance, Statistics, Accounting, Marketing, and English, respectively. Assuming weights of 5, 4, 3, 2, and 1, respectively, for the above subjects, determine the weighted arithmetic mean mark for the subjects.

8. A student took five courses this term. His transcript showed a C in a four-credit course, a D in a two-credit course, an A in a three-credit course, an F in a four-credit course, and a B in a three-credit course. Grade points are assigned as follows: A = 4, B = 3, C = 2, D = 1 and F = 0. If grade points are weighted according to the number of credit hours, calculate the grade point average.

9. In a survey of 100 people, 75 have an average salary of $2,500 a month, and the other 25 have an average salary of $8,000 a month. What is the average monthly salary of all 100 people surveyed?

10. For the past month, Irene kept a record of the prices at which she purchased gas for her car. She bought 25 litres at $0.96 per litre; 39 litres at $0.86 per litre; 30 litres at $0.90 per litre; and 20 litres at $1.05 per litre. What is the average price-per-litre that Irene paid for gas over the past month?

11. Calculate the geometric mean for the following data sets:

a. 4, 36   b. 2, 4, 8   c. 1.10, 1.16, 1.13, 1.18

12. Calculate the geometric mean for the following data sets:

a. 9, 25   b. 4, 6, 8   c. 1.08, 1.09, 1.05, 1.12

13. The inflation rates for 5 consecutive years are 4%, 3%, 5%, 6%, and 8%, respectively. Thus, at the end of the first year, the price index will be 1.04 times the price index at the beginning of the year, and so on. Find the mean rate of inflation over the 5-year period.

14. The rates of return on investment earned by a pharmaceutical company for four successive years were 30%, 20%, −10%, and 80%. Thus, 1.30 represents the 30% rate of return on investment, which is 1.30 times of the original investment, and so on. What is the geometric mean rate of return on the investment by this company?

15. On a trip, Mary drives at 60 km/h for the first half of her journey and 120 km/h for the second half of the journey. What is her average speed?

16. A nurse is completing paperwork on his patients at a speed of 15 patients/hour. Halfway through his stack, he speeds up and begins completing paperwork at a speed of 20 patients/hour. What is the average speed at which he completes his paperwork?

2.3 | Measures of Central Tendency for Grouped Data

In many circumstances - such as for large studies performed by a third party, historical government records, or surveys where those surveyed respond by selecting a category or range of values as opposed to providing exact values - it is practically infeasible (or even impossible) to access the raw data values in order to determine the exact values of the measures of central tendency. In these situations, the values of the measures of central tendency must be estimated using the summarized values of the **grouped data**, which is usually displayed in a frequency table.

Frequency Tables with Unique Class Values

The calculation of mean, median, and mode for grouped data is different from that used for ungrouped data. However, in some cases, if the data is displayed in a frequency table with unique class values, the raw data can be reconstructed from the frequency table (similar to a stem-and-leaf plot). Consider the following example of the birth lengths of 100 newborn babies:

Lengths of Babies Born (in cm)	Frequency (f)
44	1
45	3
46	6
47	9
48	13
49	18
50	20
51	12
52	7
53	5
54	4
55	2

Since the exact values are known, the raw data can be reconstructed by listing out the length of each baby, according to the frequency for each category:

44, 45, 45, 45, 46, 46, 46, 46, 46, 46, 47, 47, 47, 47, 47, 47, 47, 47, 47, ...

As such, we can calculate the measures of central tendency as follows:

- **Mean:** use a weighted mean, with the frequency of each class value representing the weight for that value: $\bar{x} = \dfrac{\Sigma\,(f \cdot x)}{\Sigma f}$

- **Median:** construct a cumulative frequency table and use the location calculation $L_m = \dfrac{(n + 1)}{2}$ to determine the class value representing the median

- **Mode:** the class value with the greatest frequency is the mode

Example 2.3-a	Calculating the Mean, Median, and Mode for Grouped Data with Unique Class Values

Find the (i) mean, (ii) median, and (iii) mode of the birth lengths given in the table above.

Solution

(i) To calculate the mean birth length, use a weighted average:

$$\bar{x} = \frac{1(44) + 3(45) + 6(46) + 9(47) + \ldots + 2(55)}{1 + 3 + 6 + 9 + \ldots + 2} = \frac{4{,}951}{100} = 49.51$$

Therefore, the mean birth length is 49.51 cm.

(ii) To calculate the median birth length, first construct a cumulative frequency table:

Lengths of Babies Born (in cm)	Frequency (f)	Cumulative Frequency
44	1	1
45	3	4
46	6	10
47	9	19
48	13	32
49	18	50
50	20	70
51	12	82
52	7	89
53	5	94
54	4	98
55	2	100

Now, determine the location of the median: $L_m = \dfrac{100 + 1}{2} = \dfrac{101}{2} = 50.5$.

Therefore, the median is halfway between (i.e., the average of) the 50th and 51st values.

- 50th value: 49 cm
- 51st value: 50 cm
- Median: $\dfrac{49 + 50}{2} = 49.5$ cm

Therefore, the median birth length is 49.5 cm.

(iii) The value that occurs most frequently is 50 cm, with a frequency of 20 babies.

Therefore, the mode birth length is 50 cm.

Frequency Tables with Class Intervals

In most cases, grouped data is organised into a frequency table with class intervals and frequencies, with no way of knowing the exact values of the data (raw data) that lie within each class interval. Therefore, the best we can do is to use the **midpoints** of the class intervals to estimate values for the measures of central tendency as follows:

- **Mean:** use a weighted mean, with the midpoint of the class interval as the approximate class value and the frequency of each class representing the weight for that value: $\bar{x} = \dfrac{\Sigma (f \cdot x)}{\Sigma f}$

- **Median:** construct a cumulative frequency table and use the location calculation $L_m = \dfrac{(n+1)}{2}$ to determine which class represents the median class; then, use the midpoint of that class as an estimate for the median

- **Modal Class:** the class with the greatest frequency is known as the modal class

Note: With grouped data, it is more common to refer to the modal class than the specific mode.

Example 2.3-b	Calculating the Mean, Median, and Modal Class for Grouped Data with Class Intervals

The distribution of marks (out of 100) following a statistics exam for a sample of 50 students, grouped in a frequency distribution, is provided below. (i) Estimate the mean, (ii) estimate the median, and (iii) determine the modal class for the statistics exam marks:

Class interval (Exam marks)	Frequency (f) (Number of students)
40 to under 50	4
50 to under 60	5
60 to under 70	18
70 to under 80	10
80 to under 90	6
90 to under 100	7

Solution

(i)

Class interval	Frequency (f)	Class Midpoint (x)	Weighted Class Midpoint ($f \cdot x$)
40 to under 50	4	45	180
50 to under 60	5	55	275
60 to under 70	18	65	1,170
70 to under 80	10	75	750
80 to under 90	6	85	510
90 to under 100	7	95	665
Totals	$\Sigma f = n = 50$		$\Sigma (f \cdot x) = 3,550$

The third column (x) represents the class midpoints, and the value of x for each class is computed by finding the average of the lowest and highest class limit in each class interval.

For example, for the 1st class interval, the class midpoint is $\dfrac{40 + 50}{2} = 45$.

The last column ($f \cdot x$) represents the weighted class midpoint.

For example, for the 1st class interval, $f \cdot x = 4 \times 45 = 180$.

$$\bar{x} = \frac{\Sigma (f \cdot x)}{\Sigma f} = \frac{3,550}{50} = 71$$

Therefore, the mean exam mark is 71.

Solution
continued

(ii) Compute a cumulative frequency table:

Class interval	Frequency (f)	Class Midpoint (x)	Cumulative Frequency
40 to under 50	4	45	4
50 to under 60	5	55	9
60 to under 70	18	65	27
70 to under 80	10	75	37
80 to under 90	6	85	43
90 to under 100	7	95	50

$$L_m = \frac{n+1}{2} = \frac{50+1}{2} = 25.5$$

Therefore, the median is halfway between the 25th and 26th terms.

From the Cumulative Frequency column, both the 25th and 26th terms fall in the class interval '60 to under 70'. Therefore, this is the median class.

Using the midpoint value of that class, the median for the data is 65.

Therefore, the median exam mark is 65.

(iii) The modal class is the class interval with the highest frequency.

The class having the class interval '60 to under 70' contains the highest frequency of 18. Therefore, the modal class is '60 to under 70'.

2.3 | Exercises

Answers to odd-numbered problems are available at the end of the textbook.

1. The following table shows the number of TVs per household in a sample of 50 households. Compute the mean, median, and mode.

Number of TVs in household	0	1	2	3	4	5	6
Number of households	0	5	19	16	6	3	1

2. The following table shows the number of hours per day a sample of 60 people spend watching TV. Compute the mean, median, and mode.

Number of hours	0	1	2	3	4	5	6	7
Number of people	0	1	8	16	14	12	5	4

3. The following table shows the marks for a ten-mark, multiple choice quiz in Professor Smith's class of 30 students. Compute the mean, median, and mode.

Quiz mark	10	9	8	7	6	5	4	3	2	1
Number of students	2	5	8	9	3	1	0	2	0	0

4. In a survey of subscribers to a Canadian lifestyle magazine, the following question was asked: "How many of the last four issues have you read?" The following table summarizes 200 responses. Compute the mean, median, and mode.

Number of issues read	4	3	2	1	0
Number of people	125	20	37	15	3

5. The hourly wages for a sample of 45 students during their summer employment were grouped into the following frequency distribution. Estimate the mean and median, and determine the modal class.

Hourly Wages	Frequency (f)
$10 to under $12	3
$12 to under $14	6
$14 to under $16	12
$16 to under $18	15
$18 to under $20	7
$20 to under $22	2

6. The ages of a sample of 40 applicants for a training program are grouped into the following frequency distribution. Estimate the mean and median, and determine the modal class.

Age	Frequency (f)
20 to under 22	4
22 to under 24	7
24 to under 26	10
26 to under 28	14
28 to under 30	3
30 to under 32	2

7. A manager is evaluating the cost of the company's medical insurance plan. A survey of 150 random claims made within the company and their respective costs are reported. Estimate the mean and median, and determine the modal class.

Cost of Insurance Claims	Number of Claims
$0 to under $100	14
$100 to under $200	32
$200 to under $300	48
$300 to under $400	24
$400 to under $500	32

8. The following table lists the weights of 100 babies born at a hospital last month. Estimate the mean and median, and determine the modal class.

Weight (pounds)	Number of Babies
3 to under 5	9
5 to under 7	36
7 to under 9	40
9 to under 11	12
11 to under 13	3

9. The following table lists blood glucose levels for 30 diabetic and non-diabetic participants at a health fair.

Blood Glucose Level (mg/dL)	Diabetic		Non-Diabetic	
80 to under 90	3		6	
90 to under 100	2	5	5	11
100 to under 110	5	10	6	17
110 to under 120	5	15	4	21
120 to under 130	7	22	3	24
130 to under 140	5	27	4	28
140 to under 150	3	30	2	30

Estimate the mean and median, and determine the modal class for:

a. all 60 participants.

b. the groups of diabetic and non-diabetic participants. Compare your results.

10. The following table lists the weights in pounds for 30 male and female participants at a health fair.

Weight (pounds)	Male	Female
100 to under 150	7	12
150 to under 200	7	5
200 to under 250	13	10
250 to under 300	3	3

Estimate the mean and median, and determine the modal class for:

a. all 60 participants.

b. the male and female participants. Compare your results.

2.4 | Skewness and Interpreting Measures of Central Tendency

What do the measures of central tendency tell us about the data? The mean, median, and mode give us a variety of ways of interpreting where the centre of the data is, but beyond that, together they can tell us something about the shape of the distribution of the data:

- The mode typically presents itself as the highest peak in the distribution.

- The median is the middle value in the data distribution, with an equal number of data values above and below.

- The mean is the "balancing point" of the data distribution (see the discussion of Arithmetic Mean in Section 2.1 for more information).

Symmetry, Skewness, and Shape of a Distribution

A distribution of data that is balanced on both sides of the median is said to be **symmetrical**. For symmetrically-distributed data (zero skewness), the mean and median will be roughly equal. If the data has one mode, it will be roughly equal to the mean and median, and the distribution will appear "mound"-shaped. If the data is bimodal (i.e., has two modes), the two modes will be roughly equally spaced on either side of the mean and median, and the distribution will appear "camel hump"-shaped.

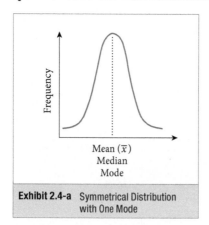

Exhibit 2.4-a Symmetrical Distribution with One Mode

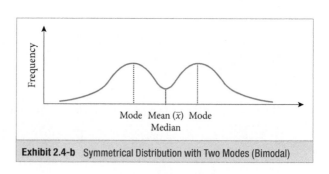

Exhibit 2.4-b Symmetrical Distribution with Two Modes (Bimodal)

For asymmetrical (non-symmetrical) data distributions, the mean, median, and/or mode will differ from each other, and the data is said to be **skewed**. There are two main cases for skewed data:

If the mean > median, then the data is **positively skewed** (since mean – median > 0). In this case, the mean will be drawn to the right of the median by the presence of high-valued outliers. The data will appear to have a longer tail to the right - hence the distribution is also said to be **skewed to the right**.

If the mean < median, then the data is **negatively skewed** (since mean – median < 0). In this case, the mean will be drawn to the left of the median by the presence of low-valued outliers. The data will appear to have a longer tail to the left - hence the distribution is also said to be **skewed to the left**.

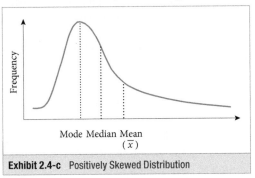

Exhibit 2.4-c   Positively Skewed Distribution

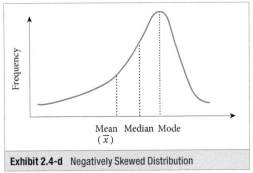

Exhibit 2.4-d   Negatively Skewed Distribution

When the data is skewed significantly, either to the right or to the left, the median tends to be a better measure of central tendency than the mean. However, it is still important to know both, as that gives us a better idea of how the data is distributed, as summarized in the following diagram:

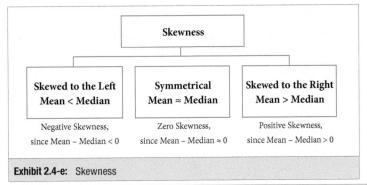

Exhibit 2.4-e: Skewness

Example 2.4-a   Determining the Skewness and Shape of a Distribution from Raw Data

Recall the baby birth length data from Example 2.3-a:

Lengths of Babies Born (in cm)	Frequency (f)
44	1
45	3
46	6
47	9
48	13
49	18
50	20
51	12
52	7
53	5
54	4
55	2

Using the mean, median, and mode of the data set, determine (i) the skewness and shape of the data distribution, and (ii) which is the best measure of central tendency to use to summarize the data.

Solution

(i) Recall the values of the mean, median, and mode from the solution of Example 2.3-a:

Mean = 49.51

Median = 49.5

Mode = 50

Since the mean and median are approximately equal, the data is roughly symmetrical (i.e., zero skewness). Since there is only one mode and it is approximately equal to the mean and median as well, we can infer that the distribution will be "mound"-shaped.

(ii) Since the data is relatively symmetrical, without any outliers, the mean is likely the most appropriate measure of central tendency to use to summarize the data.

Example 2.4-b   Determining the Skewness and Shape of a Distribution from Summary Data

For a given group of students working together on a project, the average age is 22 years old, the median is 19, and the mode is 18. Based on the given measures of central tendency, determine the skewness and shape of the distribution of the students' ages.

Solution

Mean = 22

Median = 19

Mode = 18

The difference between the mean and the median is positive (i.e., Mean > Median), which suggests that there are unusually high values (i.e., outliers) in the data set that have altered the symmetry.

Therefore, the distribution is "mound"-shaped and skewed to the right, with a long right tail (distribution is positively skewed).

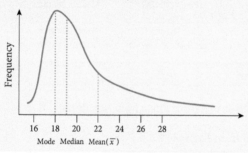

Example 2.4-c   Determining the Skewness and Shape of a Distribution from Grouped Data

The table below summarizes the results of a statistics exam given to a class of 60 students:

Students' Marks	Frequency (f)
20 to under 30	3
30 to under 40	5
40 to under 50	8
50 to under 60	12
60 to under 70	8
70 to under 80	13
80 to under 90	9
90 to under 100	2

(i) Estimate the mean and median, and determine the modal class(es) of the grouped data.

(ii) Use the information from (i) to determine the skewness and shape of the distribution.

Solution (i) First, establish a cumulative frequency table using class midpoints as the values for each class:

Students' Marks	Midpoint	Frequency (f)	Cumulative Frequency
20 to under 30	25	3	3
30 to under 40	35	5	8
40 to under 50	45	8	16
50 to under 60	55	12	28
60 to under 70	65	8	36
70 to under 80	75	13	49
80 to under 90	85	9	58
90 to under 100	95	2	60

Using the formula for a weighted mean, from a frequency table with class intervals as discussed in Section 2.3, we estimate the mean:

$$\bar{x} = \frac{(3 \cdot 25) + (5 \cdot 35) + (8 \cdot 45) + (12 \cdot 55) + (8 \cdot 65) + (13 \cdot 75) + (9 \cdot 85) + (2 \cdot 95)}{60}$$

$$= \frac{3{,}720}{60} = 62$$

Next, to calculate the median, $L_m = \dfrac{60 + 1}{2} = 30.5$, so we locate the 30th and 31st data values; both fall in the "60 to under 70" category, so the best estimate for the median is 65.

Finally, the modal class is "70 to under 80", as it has the highest frequency with 13 data values. However, since there is another class with almost as many data values - "50 to under 60" has 12 data values - it is fair to state that there are two modal classes. As such, this data set is best described as being **bimodal**.

(ii) Since the mean is 62, which is less than the median of 65, this data set is skewed to the left, or **negatively skewed**. Since there are (essentially) two modal classes, the distribution of this data will appear to be "camel hump"-shaped, with two mounds at 55 and 75, the midpoints of the two modal classes

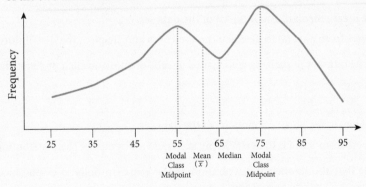

Empirical Relationship between Mean, Median, and Mode

There is a relationship between the mean, median, and mode of a given data set that is derived empirically (i.e., calculated from observations of these values for many different sets of data). The relationship that is most commonly observed is that the difference between the mean and the mode is approximately three times the difference between the mean and the median:

Mean – Mode = 3 · (Mean – Median)

Rearranging this formula gives us a convenient "1 + 2 = 3" version of the formula:

$$(1 \cdot) \, Mode + 2 \cdot Mean = 3 \cdot Median$$

Note: This formula only works for data sets that have one unique mode.

Since the median and mode are often easier to determine than the mean, we can use this formula to estimate the mean, given the median and mode.

Example 2.4-d	Estimating the Mean, given the Median and Mode

In a sample of patients seen in the E.R. of a hospital, the median height, according to the patients' driver's licences, was 169 cm, and the most common height recorded was 165 cm.

(i)   Estimate the average (mean) height for the sample of patients.

(ii) Use this information to determine the skewness of the data.

Solution

(i)   Using the formula $Mode + 2 \cdot Mean = 3 \cdot Median$, we substitute in the known values and solve for the Mean ($\bar{x}$):

$$165 + 2(\bar{x}) = 3(169)$$

$$2(\bar{x}) = 507 - 165$$

$$\bar{x} = \frac{342}{2} = 171$$

Therefore, the mean height of the sample of patients is estimated to be 171 cm.

(ii)   Since the mean is greater than the median, the distribution of the data is skewed to the right (positively skewed).

2.4 | Exercises

Answers to odd-numbered problems are available at the end of the textbook.

1.   The following are the annual salaries (in thousands of dollars) of 20 randomly selected health care workers.

35	38	39	40	44	45	50	53	55	57
58	59	61	62	64	64	67	71	74	77

a.   Determine the mean, median, and mode(s) of the data set.

b.   Use your answers from part (a) to describe the skewness and shape of the distribution.

2.   The following are the number of patients who visited a walk-in clinic on each of 20 randomly selected days.

19	20	22	23	23	24	24	26	26	26
30	30	30	30	35	36	37	38	39	40

a.   Determine the mean, median, and mode(s) of the data set.

b.   Use your answers from part (a) to describe the skewness and shape of the distribution.

3.   The following table lists the frequency distribution of the costs (in dollars) of purchasing medical supplies in a hospital for a sample of 50 purchasing orders.

Cost ($)	Frequency
0 to under 60	5
60 to under 120	21
120 to under 180	10
180 to under 240	8
240 to under 300	6

a.   Estimate the mean and median, and determine the modal class(es) of the grouped data.

b.   Use your answers from part (a) to describe the skewness and shape of the distribution.

4. The following table lists the frequency distribution of the number of days that 90 patients spent in a hospital.

Number of Days	Frequency
0 to under 7	5
7 to under 14	25
14 to under 21	30
21 to under 28	22
28 to under 35	8

   a. Estimate the mean and median, and determine the modal class(es) of the grouped data.

   b. Use your answers from part (a) to describe the skewness and shape of the distribution.

5. Using the empirical relationship among mean, median, and mode, estimate the mode if the mean is 17 and the median is 16 for a given statistical observation, and comment on the skewness of the distribution.

6. The average amount of weight loss, in pounds, by 10 participants in a six-month weight-reduction program is 21.6 pounds. The median weight loss for these participants is 24.5 pounds. Using the empirical relationship among mean, median, and mode, estimate the mode and comment on the skewness of the distribution.

7. Using the empirical relationship among mean, median, and mode, estimate the mean if the median is 22 and the mode is 30 for a given statistical observation, and comment on the skewness of the distribution.

8. A patient's blood sugar readings were recorded during a recent stay in the hospital. The median shows 150.5 mg/dL and the mode is 151 mg/dL. Using the empirical relationship among mean, median, and mode, estimate the mean and comment on the skewness of the distribution.

9. Using the empirical relationship among mean, median, and mode, estimate the median if the mean is 41.25 and the mode is 37 for a given statistical observation, and comment on the skewness of the distribution.

10. A consumer research group purchased identical items in eight drugstores. The mean cost for the purchased items was $85.62. The mode was $85. Using the empirical relationship among mean, median, and mode, estimate the median and comment on the skewness of the distribution.

2 | Review Exercises

Answers to odd-numbered problems are available at the end of the textbook.

1. The average daily sodium intake of a group of nurses is calculated and recorded. The amounts are 2,120 mg; 2,932 mg; 1,856 mg; 3,688 mg; 853 mg; 3,421 mg; and 1,479 mg.

   a. What is the average (arithmetic mean) daily sodium intake?

   b. If the recommended normal sodium intake is 1,100 mg to 3,300 mg per day, does the average fall within the normal limits?

2. A diabetic checks his blood glucose level q.i.d. (four times a day) and the following readings are recorded: 92 mg/dL, 123 mg/dL, 123 mg/dL, and 137 mg/dL.

   a. What is the average (arithmetic mean) reading for blood glucose?

   b. If the normal range for blood glucose is 70 to 100 mg/dL, does the average fall within the normal limits?

3. The recommended room temperature in long-term care facilities is 24 °C. After two readings of 22 °C and 27 °C in one day, what must be the third required reading to average 24 °C?

4. The average mark of four tests for a student is 75. The marks for the first three tests are 77, 92, and 80. What must be the mark for the last test in order to obtain this average?

5. In a survey, eight people were found to have an average weight of 75 kg. When another person joined the survey, the average weight of the nine people dropped by 2.5 kg. Calculate the weight of the ninth person.

6. In a survey, five people were found to have an average weight of 60.8 kg. When another person joined the survey, the average weight of the six people increased by 1.75 kg. Calculate the weight of the sixth person.

7. A student has obtained the following marks on six math tests: 62, 72, 69, 70, 60, 64.

   a. Calculate the mean, median, and mode.

   b. Which measure of central tendency would be the best measure for this data?

8. A student has obtained the following marks on seven math quizzes: 82, 82, 79, 89, 90, 86, 44.

   a. Calculate the mean, median, and mode.

   b. Which measure of central tendency would be the best measure for this data?

9. The amounts of weight lost, in pounds, by ten participants in a three-month weight-reduction program were: 19, 27, 18, 63, 19, 24, 21, 34, 8, 25.

   a. Calculate the 10% trimmed mean.

   b. Calculate the mean using all the values.

10. A pediatric nurse recorded the weights of infants, in ounces, born on New Year's Day in a local hospital. They were: 68, 92, 99, 140, 105, 110, 120, 115, 95, 112, 50, 102, 110, 144, and 92.

    a. Calculate the 20% trimmed mean.

    b. Calculate the mean using all the values.

11. A nursing student is taking a math course and has had two tests with grades of 87% and 92%, each worth 25% of her final grade. She still has to take the final exam, which is worth 50% of her final grade. What grade must she receive on her final exam in order to receive a final grade of 93%?

12. Consider the assessment in a math course that has two tests, one midterm, and one final exam. The tests are worth 15% each, the midterm is worth 30%, and the comprehensive final exam is worth 40%. If a student receives 78% and 62% on the two tests and 82% on the midterm, what grade must the student receive on the comprehensive final exam to receive a final grade of 80% in the course?

13. The inflation rates for four consecutive years are 8%, 6%, 4%, and 3%, respectively. Thus, at the end of the first year, the price index will be 1.08 times the price index at the beginning of the year, and so on. Calculate the mean rate of inflation over the four-year period.

14. The rates of return on investment earned by a pharmaceutical company for five successive years were 30%, 20%, –10%, 10%, and 50%. What is the geometric mean rate of return on the investment by this company?

15. A swimming coach recorded the average speed (in m/s) of her student doing the 400 m Women Medley: {freestyle: 1.62; butterfly: 1.35; backstroke: 1.45; breaststroke: 1.12}. Determine this student's average speed over the entire 400 m Medley.

16. A swimming coach recorded the average speed (in m/s) of his student doing the 400 m Men Medley: {freestyle: 1.75; butterfly: 1.61; backstroke: 1.53; breaststroke: 1.32}. Determine this student's average speed over the entire 400 m Medley.

17. The following table lists the frequency distribution of the time spent per patient in a doctor's office by a sample of 50 patients.

Times (minutes)	Number of Patients
0 to under 5	28
5 to under 10	10
10 to under 15	8
15 to under 20	4

   a. Estimate the mean and median, and determine the modal class.

   b. Comment on the skewness and the shape of the distribution.

18. The following table lists the frequency distribution of the number of hours spent per week on sports or exercising by a sample of 200 Canadians.

Hours per Week	Number of People
0 to under 5	25
5 to under 10	42
10 to under 15	64
15 to under 20	41
20 to under 25	28

   a. Estimate the mean and median, and determine the modal class.

   b. Comment on the skewness and the shape of the distribution.

19. A hospital information desk staff recorded the numbers of requests for information for the past month. The median was 126 requests and the mode was 130. Using the empirical relationship among mean, median, and mode, estimate the mean and comment on the skewness of the distribution.

20. The test scores for students taking a nursing exam were recorded. The mean was 86.2% and the mode was 75%. Using the empirical relationship among mean, median, and mode, estimate the median and comment on the skewness of the distribution.

2 | Self-Test Exercises

1. A dental office is doing an inventory of the number of pairs of latex gloves used by hygienists over the past six months. The amounts were 272, 246, 216, 298, 301, and 245.

   a. What is the average monthly usage (arithmetic mean) of pairs of latex gloves?

   b. If each pair of latex gloves costs $0.85, what is the estimated monthly cost for the latex gloves used per hygienist?

2. The mean price that five passengers paid for a domestic flight is $420 per ticket. The first three passengers paid $485, $530, and $333 from various sources. If the fourth and fifth passengers paid the same amount, what was the price of each of their tickets?

3. The average mark of 25 students in a class was 82. Another student took a make-up test and the class average dropped by 2 marks. What was the mark of that student who took the make-up test?

4. The following data represent the systolic blood pressure reading in mmHg for each of 10 randomly selected middle-aged males who were taking a blood pressure medication:

   130 144 127 169 127 121 144 149 125 148

   a. Calculate the mean, median, and mode for the data.

   b. Calculate the 10% trimmed mean for the data.

5. A statistics professor based her final grades on quizzes, in-class groupwork, a midterm exam, and a final exam. However, not all the assignments contributed equally to the final grade. The following table lists the scores a student received and the weights for each assignment. Calculate this student's final grade.

Assignment	Weights	Scores (out of 100)
Quizzes	20	75
In Class Group Work	15	85
Midterm Exam	25	70
Final Exam	40	62

6. The rates of return on investment earned by a pharmaceutical company for four successive years were 15%, –10%, 20%, and 35%. What is the geometric mean rate of return on the investment by this company?

7. A personal trainer recorded the average speed (in km/h) of his client running 5 laps of a 1-km track: {9.8, 11.1, 9.2, 10.3, 9.7}. Determine the client's average speed over the 5-km run.

8. The following table shows the frequency distribution of the number of hours spent per week on cell phones by a sample of 100 college students.

Hours per Week	Number of Students
0 to under 10	9
10 to under 20	20
20 to under 30	36
30 to under 40	25
40 to under 50	10

   a. Estimate the mean and median, and determine the modal class.

   b. Comment on the skewness and the shape of the distribution.

9. A class of pre-health students received the following test scores on an anatomy test.

Test Score	Number of Students
55	1
60	3
65	2
70	0
75	5
80	4
85	7
90	4
95	2
100	2

   a. Compute the mean, median, and mode.

   b. Comment on the skewness and the shape of the distribution.

10. A medical accountant checks the electric bills for a medical clinic for a six-month period. The mean is $375.89 and the mode is $374.50. Using the empirical relationship among mean, median, and mode, estimate the median and comment on the skewness of the distribution.

2 | Summary of Notation and Formulas

NOTATION

n = total number of data values in a sample

N = total number of data values in a population

$\bar{x}$ = sample mean

μ = population mean

w = weight of a data value

f = frequency

G = Geometric mean

H = Harmonic mean

FORMULAS

Mean of a Sample | 2.1-a

$$\bar{x} = \frac{\text{Sum of All the Values of the Terms}}{\text{Number of Terms}} = \frac{\Sigma x}{n}$$

Mean of a Population | 2.1-b

$$\mu = \frac{\text{Sum of All the Values of the Terms}}{\text{Number of Terms}} = \frac{\Sigma x}{N}$$

Location of the Median | 2.1-c

$$L_m = \frac{(n+1)}{2}$$

Weighted Arithmetic Mean | 2.2-a

$$\bar{x} = \frac{\text{Sum of All the Weighted Data Values}}{\text{Sum of All the Weights}} = \frac{\Sigma(w \cdot x)}{\Sigma w}$$

Geometric Mean | 2.2-b

$$G = \sqrt[n]{\prod x} = \left(\prod x\right)^{\frac{1}{n}}$$

Harmonic Mean | 2.2-c

$$H = \frac{n}{\Sigma\left(\frac{1}{x}\right)}$$

3

MEASURES OF DISPERSION

LEARNING OBJECTIVES

- Describe data using various measures of position, including quartiles, percentiles, range, and interquartile range (IQR).
- Construct and interpret a box-and-whisker plot and use it to identify outliers.
- Calculate and interpret various measures of dispersion, including the mean absolute deviation (MAD), variance, and standard deviation.
- Compare the standard deviations of two or more data sets to identify the set with greater dispersion.
- Interpret the standard deviation of a data set using the Empirical rule and Chebyshev's theorem, and how they relate to the shape of a distribution.
- Calculate the coefficient of variation and use it to compare the variation of two or more data sets.

CHAPTER OUTLINE

3.1 Measures of Position and Range

3.2 Measures of Deviation

Introduction

In Chapter 2, we examined methods for analyzing the centre of a data set. We will now examine methods for determining the rest of the data set, including how spread out the data is and the relative positions of certain values within the data set.

As a motivating example, consider the following two data sets:

Data Set A: {40, 42, 44, 46, 48, 50, 52, 54, 56, 58, 60}

Data Set B: {0, 10, 20, 30, 40, 50, 60, 70, 80, 90, 100}

You will notice that for both data sets A and B above, the mean and the median are the same and equal to 50. However, the spread of data in set A, which varies from 40 to 60, is very different from that in set B, which varies from 0 to 100.

To describe this spread, there are numerical measures known as **Measures of Dispersion (or Variation)**, which provide information on how the data in the set vary from each other and/or from the central number. There are two main sub-categories of measures of dispersion: **Measures of Position and Range** (which analyze the relative position of data values in the set and the spread between those values) and **Measures of Deviation** (which analyze the spread between data values in the set and the centre value, usually the mean).

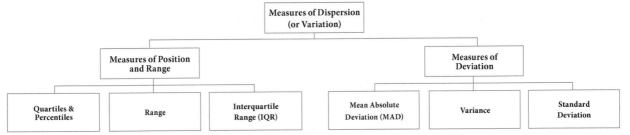

In this chapter, we will examine both measures of position and range (Section 3.1), and measures of deviation (Section 3.2).

3.1 | Measures of Position and Range

Quartiles and Percentiles

We learned in the previous chapter that the median is the data value below which one-half of the ranked data values lie. In a similar way, we define the **first quartile (Q_1)**, or **lower quartile**, as the point below which the first quarter (or lowest 25%) of the ranked data values lie, and the **third quartile (Q_3)**, or **upper quartile**, as the point above which the last quarter (or greatest 25%) of the ranked data values lie. Using that definition, the **second quartile (Q_2)**, or **middle quartile**, would be exactly the median.

Another way of describing these values is by using the term **percentiles**, which are the data values below which a certain percentage of the ranked data values lie:

- The **25th percentile (P_{25})** is the same as the first quartile, with 25% of the ranked data values lying below it.

- The **50th percentile (P_{50})** is the same as the second quartile (i.e., median), with 50% of the ranked data values lying below it.

- The **75th percentile (P_{75})** is the same as the third quartile, with 75% of the ranked data values lying below it.

Note: When a quartile or percentile falls between two values in a data set, we average them, just as we did when calculating the median for a data set with an even number of data values in Chapter 2.

Identifying the Quartiles in a Data Set

Step 1: Sort the data into an increasing array.

Step 2: Determine the median (Q_2).

Step 3: Using the median, divide the data set into two equal-sized groups: a lower and an upper group.

Note: If there are an odd number of data values, first remove the median, then divide the remaining data values into two equal-sized groups.

Step 4: Determine the median of each of the two separate groups: the median of the lower group is the first quartile (Q_1) and the median of the upper group is the third quartile (Q_3).

Step 5: Finally, identify the lowest and highest values in the data set, referred to as L and H, respectively.

Example 3.1-a Identifying Quartiles in a Data Set with an Even Number of Data Values

Calculate the quartiles of the following data set: {77, 65, 60, 68, 64, 80, 75, 70, 62, 68, 60, 63}

Solution

First, sort the data into an array as follows:

{60, 60, 62, 63, 64, 65, 68, 68, 70, 75, 77, 80}

Since there are 12 data values (an even number), the position of the median is $\frac{12+1}{2} = 6.5$, i.e., halfway between the 6th and 7th data values in the array.

$$\text{Median } (Q_2) = \frac{65+68}{2} = 66.5$$

Next, divide the data set into two groups, each with 6 data values:

Lower group: {60, 60, 62, 63, 64, 65}   Upper group: {68, 68, 70, 75, 77, 80}

Finally, calculate the median of the lower group and upper group to determine Q_1 and Q_3, respectively.

Q_1 = median of lower group

Position of $Q_1 = \frac{6+1}{2} = 3.5$, i.e., halfway between the 3rd and 4th data values.

$$Q_1 = \frac{62+63}{2} = 62.5$$

Q_3 = median of upper group

Position of $Q_3 = \frac{6+1}{2} = 3.5$, i.e., halfway between the 3rd and 4th data values.

$$Q_3 = \frac{70+75}{2} = 72.5$$

Therefore, the lowest value $L = 60$, the first (i.e., lower) quartile $Q_1 = 62.5$, the second (i.e., middle) quartile (median) $Q_2 = 66.5$, the third (i.e., upper) quartile $Q_3 = 72.5$, and the highest value $H = 80$.

Example 3.1-b Identifying Quartiles in a Data Set with an Odd Number of Data Values

Calculate the quartiles of the following data set: {30, 28, 38, 35, 42, 26, 40, 32, 21, 23, 33}

Solution

First, sort the data into an array as follows:

{21, 23, 26, 28, 30, 32, 33, 35, 38, 40, 42}

Since there are 11 data values (an odd number), the position of the median is $\frac{11+1}{2} = 6$, i.e., the 6th data value in the array.

Median (Q_2) = 32

Next, remove the median and divide the remaining values into two groups, each with 5 data values:

Lower group: {21, 23, 26, 28, 30}   Upper group: {33, 35, 38, 40, 42}

Finally, calculate the median of the lower group and upper group to determine Q_1 and Q_3, respectively.

Solution
continued

Q_1 = median of lower group

Position of $Q_1 = \dfrac{5+1}{2} = 3$, i.e., the 3rd data value.

$$Q_1 = 26$$

Q_3 = median of upper group

Position of $Q_3 = \dfrac{5+1}{2} = 3$, i.e., the 3rd data value.

$$Q_3 = 38$$

Therefore, the lowest value $L = 21$, the first (i.e., lower) quartile $Q_1 = 26$, the second (i.e., middle) quartile (median) $Q_2 = 32$, the third (i.e., upper) quartile $Q_3 = 38$, and the highest value $H = 42$.

Note: As demonstrated in the previous two examples, the position of Q_1 in the lower group is equal to the position of Q_3 in the upper group.

Identifying Percentiles in a Data Set

In order to identify other percentiles in a data set (e.g., P_{10} - the 10th percentile, or P_{90} - the 90th percentile), we make use of a "locator value", as we did when calculating the median, to first determine its position in the array:

Formula 3.1-a

Location of the kth Percentile

$$L_k = \frac{k}{100} \cdot (n+1)$$

L_k is the location or position of the corresponding data value in the array, k is the desired percentile, and n is the total number of data values in the data set.

- If L_k is a whole number, or less than .1 away from a whole number, then that whole number is the position of the corresponding data value in the array.

The formula for the location of the 50th percentile gives the same value as the formula for the location of the median in Chapter 2.

- If L_k is a decimal number between .1 and .9 inclusive, take the average of the data values that correspond to the whole-value positions above and below L_k in the array.

  E.g., if $L_k = 12.4$, take the average of the 12th and 13th data values in the array.

Note: There are several slightly different approaches to calculating percentiles, but the method above is chosen because it always yields the same results as the method described to find quartiles.

Example 3.1-c | **Identifying Percentiles in a Data Set**

Using the data sets provided in Examples 3.1-a and 3.1-b, determine P_{10}, P_{25}, P_{67}, and P_{90}.

Solution

Recall the data sets (sorted into arrays), as follows:

Data Set A

$\{60, 60, 62, 63, 64, 65, 68, 68, 70, 75, 77, 80\}$

Location of $P_{10} = \dfrac{10}{100}(12+1) = 1.3$

$$P_{10} = \frac{60+60}{2} = 60$$

Therefore, approximately 10% of the data values fall below 60.

Location of $P_{25} = \dfrac{25}{100}(12+1) = 3.25$

$$P_{25} = \frac{62+63}{2} = 62.5 \ (= Q_1)$$

Therefore, approximately 25% of the data values fall below 62.5.

Data Set B

$\{21, 23, 26, 28, 30, 32, 33, 35, 38, 40, 42\}$

Location of $P_{10} = \dfrac{10}{100}(11+1) = 1.2$

$$P_{10} = \frac{21+23}{2} = 22$$

Therefore, approximately 10% of the data values fall below 22.

Location of $P_{25} = \dfrac{25}{100}(11+1) = 3$

$$P_{25} = 26 \ (= Q_1)$$

Therefore, approximately 25% of the data values fall below 26.

$$\text{Location of } P_{67} = \frac{67}{100}(12 + 1) = 8.71$$

$$P_{67} = \frac{68 + 70}{2} = 69$$

Therefore, approximately 67% of the data values fall below 69.

$$\text{Location of } P_{90} = \frac{90}{100}(12 + 1) = 11.7$$

$$P_{90} = \frac{77 + 80}{2} = 78.5$$

Therefore, approximately 90% of the data values fall below 78.5.

$$\text{Location of } P_{67} = \frac{67}{100}(11 + 1) = 8.04 \approx 8$$

$$P_{67} = 35$$

> Since 8.04 is less than .1 away from 8, P_{67} is simply the 8th data value in the array.

Therefore, approximately 67% of the data values fall below 35.

$$\text{Location of } P_{90} = \frac{90}{100}(11 + 1) = 10.8$$

$$P_{90} = \frac{40 + 42}{2} = 41$$

Therefore, approximately 90% of the data values fall below 41.

Range

The **range** is the difference between the maximum (highest) value and the minimum (lowest) value in a data set. It provides information on the number of units between the maximum and minimum value between the data.

Formula 3.1-b

Range

Range = Maximum Value – Minimum Value

Example 3.1-d

Calculating the Range of a Data Set

Calculate the ranges of the data sets presented in Examples 3.1-a and 3.1-b.

Solution

Recall the data sets (sorted into arrays), as follows:

Data Set A	Data Set B
{60, 60, 62, 63, 64, 65, 68, 68, 70, 75, 77, 80}	{21, 23, 26, 28, 30, 32, 33, 35, 38, 40, 42}
Minimum value = 60	Minimum value = 21
Maximum value = 80	Maximum value = 42
Range = 80 – 60 = 20	**Range = 42 – 21 = 21**

Interquartile Range (IQR)

Since the range *only* uses the extreme values and does not take into consideration any of the other data, it is easily biased and distorted. As such, another type of range, known as the **interquartile range** (IQR), is used to understand the spread of the middle 50% of the data set. The interquartile range is the difference between the upper quartile (Q_3) and the lower quartile (Q_1). It is not affected by the extreme values of the data.

Formula 3.1-c

Interquartile Range

Interquartile Range (IQR) = Upper Quartile (Q_3) – Lower Quartile (Q_1)

Example 3.1-e **Calculating the IQR of a Data Set**

Find the IQR of the data sets presented in Examples 3.1-a and 3.1-b.

Solution

Recall the data sets (sorted into arrays), as follows:

Data Set A	Data Set B
$\{60, 60, 62, 63, 64, 65, 68, 68, 70, 75, 77, 80\}$	$\{21, 23, 26, 28, 30, 32, 33, 35, 38, 40, 42\}$
$Q_1 = 62.5, Q_3 = 72.5$	$Q_1 = 26, Q_3 = 38$
IQR = 72.5 – 62.5 = 10	**IQR = 38 – 26 = 12**

Another type of "middle of the data set" range measure, which is less-commonly used, is called the **10-90 Percentile Range**. It measures the spread of the middle 80% of the data set (trimming off the top and bottom 10% of the data set), and is calculated as follows:

$$\text{10-90 Percentile Range} = 90^{\text{th}} \text{ Percentile } (P_{90}) - 10^{\text{th}} \text{ Percentile } (P_{10})$$

Despite its infrequent use, the 10-90 Percentile Range is a good compromise between the range and IQR, and is often used in conjunction with the trimmed mean (from Section 2.2).

Box-and-Whisker Plots

A box-and-whisker plot is a visual way of summarizing and presenting the quartile and range information calculated for a data set. It quickly and clearly displays all five quartile values, including the range and IQR.

The steps to construct a box-and-whisker plot are outlined below:

Step 1: Draw a number line that starts below the lowest value and ends above the highest value.

Step 2: Draw a "box" from the lower quartile (Q_1) to the upper quartile (Q_3); the length of the box is the IQR.

Step 3: Split the box into two pieces with a line down the middle at the median (Q_2).

Step 4: Construct the "whiskers" by drawing one line from the lower quartile (Q_1) to the lowest value (L), and another line from the upper quartile (Q_3) to the highest value (H); the length of the entire box-and-whisker plot is the range.

Example 3.1-f **Constructing a Box-and-Whisker Plot for a Data Set**

Construct a box-and-whisker plot for the following data array, labelling all 5 points of the box-and-whisker plot, as well as the IQR: $\{7, 8, 13, 16, 16, 17, 17, 18, 18, 19, 19, 20, 20, 21, 26, 30, 32\}$

Solution

There are 17 data (odd number of data), already arranged in an array.

$$\text{Median Position} = \frac{17 + 1}{2} = 9$$

Median (Q_2) = 18

Divide the data into two groups of 8 data - a lower group and an upper group - excluding the median data.

Find Q_1 and Q_3 by finding the median in the lower and upper groups of data.

$$Q_1 \text{ and } Q_3 \text{ Position} = \frac{8 + 1}{2} = 4.5$$

$$Q_1 = \frac{16 + 16}{2} = 16, \quad Q_3 = \frac{20 + 21}{2} = 20.5$$

Range = 32 – 7 = 25,   *IQR* = 20.5 – 16 = 4.5

Solution
continued

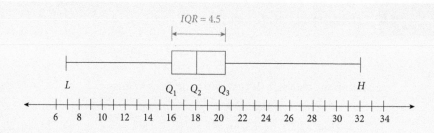

Outliers and Modified Box-and-Whisker Plots

Outliers are points that lie more than 1.5 times the IQR below Q_1 or above Q_3. When outliers are present in our data, we modify our box-and-whisker plots, as outlined in the following steps:

Step 1: Find Q_1 and Q_3 and use them to calculate $IQR = Q_3 - Q_1$.

Step 2: Multiply the IQR calculated in Step 1 by 1.5.

Step 3: Identify, as outliers, the points that are more than 1.5 times the IQR below Q_1 or above Q_3.

Step 4: Remove the outliers found in Step 3, and identify the new lowest and highest values remaining in the data set.

Step 5: Draw a modified box-and-whisker plot using the new lowest and highest values identified in Step 4 as L and H, respectively.

Step 6: Plot the outliers on the modified box-and-whisker plot as open dots.

Example 3.1-g | Identifying Outliers and Modifying a Box-and-Whisker Plot

For the data set given in Example 3.1-f, identify any outliers and draw a modified box-and-whisker plot to accommodate this new information.

Solution

Recall the data from Example 3.1-f: {7, 8, 13, 16, 16, 17, 17, 18, 18, 19, 19, 20, 20, 21, 26, 30, 32}

$Q_1 = 16$, $Q_3 = 20.5$, $IQR = 20.5 - 16 = 4.5$

$1.5 \times IQR = 1.5 \times 4.5 = 6.75$

Outliers are data below $(Q_1 - 1.5 \times IQR)$ or above $(Q_3 + 1.5 \times IQR)$,

i.e., outliers are data below $16 - 6.75 = 9.25$, or above $20.5 + 6.75 = 27.25$.

Therefore, in the data set {⑦, ⑧, 13, 16, 16, 17, 17, 18, 18, 19, 19, 20, 20, 21, 26, ㉚, ㉜},

7, 8, 30, and 32 are outliers.

After removing the outliers, the lowest value (L) in the data set is 13 and the highest value (H) in the data set is 26.

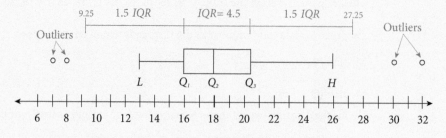

Relating Shape and Skewness to Box-and-Whisker Plots

In the previous chapter, we saw how to identify the shape and skewness of the distribution of a data set using the mean, median, and mode. We can also use the box-and-whisker plot to give us some information about the shape and skewness of the distribution.

Note: These are guidelines only and do not guarantee the shape or skewness of the data set. This analysis should be paired with a study of the mean, median, and mode, as well as an examination of the distribution of the data through the use of one or more histograms.

Skewness:

- If the median is in the middle of the box and the whiskers are roughly the same length, then the distribution is most likely **symmetrical**.
- If the median is closer to the left side of the box (i.e., Q_1) and/or the left whisker is significantly shorter than the right whisker, then the data is likely clustered to the left, making the distribution **positively-skewed**.
- If the median is closer to the right side of the box (i.e., Q_3) and/or the right whisker is significantly shorter than the left whisker, then the data is likely clustered to the right, making the distribution **negatively-skewed**.

Shape:

- If the box is roughly the same width as the two whiskers combined, then the data is likely **uniform** or approximately uniform.
- If the box is considerably shorter than the two whiskers combined, then the data is likely **mound-shaped**.
- If the box is considerably longer than the two whiskers combined, then the data is likely **bi-modal**.

Example 3.1-h	Identifying Shape and Skewness Using a Box-and-Whisker Plot

Consider the following data set:

{17, 17, 18, 18, 18, 18, 19, 19, 19, 20, 20, 21, 22, 22, 23, 25, 25, 28, 32, 37, 45}

(i) Calculate the quartiles and IQR for this data set and construct a box-and-whisker plot.

(ii) Use the box-and-whisker plot to identify any outliers in the data set.

(iii) Discuss the shape and skewness of the data set using the box-and-whisker plots.

(iv) Calculate the mean, median, and mode of the data set.

(v) Discuss the shape and skewness of the data set using the measures of central tendency calculated in part (iv) and compare your answer to part (iii).

Solution

(i) $L = 17$, $Q_1 = 18$, $Q_2 = 20$, $Q_3 = 25$, $H = 45$

$IQR = Q_3 - Q_1 = 25 - 18 = 7$

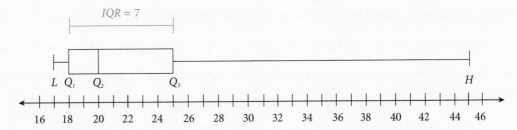

(ii) $1.5 \times IQR = 1.5 \times 7 = 10.5$

The length of the left whisker is $Q_1 - L = 18 - 17 = 1$, which is considerably less than 10.5, so the data does not contain low-value outliers.

However, the length of the right whisker is $H - Q_3 = 45 - 25 = 20$, which is greater than 10.5, so the data contains high-value outliers.

Outliers are data above $(Q_3 + 1.5 \times IQR) = 25 + 10.5 = 35.5$.

Therefore, in the data set given, 37 and 45 are outliers.

(iii) Based on the fact that the median is closer to the left-side of the box, and that the left whisker is significantly shorter than the right whisker, we can conclude that the distribution is highly positively-skewed.

Since the box is somewhat shorter than the two whiskers combined, the data is most likely mound-shaped.

(iv) Mean $= \dfrac{\sum x}{n} = \dfrac{483}{21} = 23$, Median $= Q_2 = 20$, Mode $= 18$

(v) Based on the fact that the mode < median < mean, we can conclude that the distribution of data is positively-skewed (see Section 2.4 for more information). This lines up with our assessment of skewness using the box-and-whisker plot.

Also, there is only one mode, and the data clusters around that mode, which indicates that the distribution is likely mound-shaped. This also lines up with our assessment of shape using the box-and-whisker plot.

3.1 | Exercises

Answers to odd-numbered problems are available at the end of the textbook.

1. Find the range for the following data sets:
   a. {56, 72, 98, 64, 87, 91, 22, 45}
   b. {3, 13, 6, 12, 9, 8, 16, 15, 11, 10}
   c. {72.9, 75.6, 74.3, 86.1, 80.5, 82.7}

2. Find the range for the following data sets:
   a. {24, 15, 19, 29, 24, 22, 23, 20}
   b. {113, 98, 107, 102, 123, 110}
   c. {0.8, 1.3, 1.7, 2.1, 2.5, 2.8, 3.2, 3.5}

3. Calculate the 1st and 3rd quartiles for the following data sets:
   a. {2, 3, 5, 7, 9, 13, 15, 18, 19, 20, 22, 23}
   b. {98, 109, 123, 126, 127, 139, 139, 143, 147, 151, 175}

4. Calculate the 1st and 3rd quartiles for the following data sets:
   a. {6, 7, 13, 17, 20, 25, 39, 41, 43, 49, 51, 62}
   b. {50, 60, 73, 77, 80, 81, 82, 83, 84, 84, 84, 85, 88, 95, 100}

5. Determine the interquartile range and identify the outliers, if any, for the data sets in Problem 3.

6. Determine the interquartile range and identify the outliers, if any, for the data sets in Problem 4.

7. Calculate P_{10} and P_{90} and determine the 10-90 percentile range for the data sets in Problem 3.

8. Calculate P_{10} and P_{90} and determine the 10-90 percentile range for the data sets in Problem 4.

9. In a data set, $Q_1 = 44$, median $= 48$, and $Q_3 = 58$.
   a. A value greater than what number would be an outlier?
   b. A value less than what number would be an outlier?

10. In a data set, $Q_1 = 75$, median $= 80$, and $Q_3 = 85$.
   a. A value greater than what number would be an outlier?
   b. A value less than what number would be an outlier?

11. The following are the ages (in years) of 15 employees at an insurance company:

24	33	59	62	28	39	31	46
47	51	30	37	42	26	57	

   a. Determine the values of L, Q_1, Q_2, Q_3, and H.

   b. Where does the age of 42 years fall in relation to these quartiles?

   c. Determine the IQR.

12. The following are the number of hours worked last week by 10 employees at an insurance company:

40	56	49	45	52	66	42	79	54	50

   a. Determine the values of L, Q_1, Q_2, Q_3, and H.

   b. Where does 50 hours of work fall in relation to these quartiles?

   c. Determine the IQR.

13. Determine the value of P_{70} for the data in Problem 11. Provide a brief interpretation of the 70th percentile.

14. Determine the value of P_{15} for the data in Problem 12. Provide a brief interpretation of the 15th percentile.

15. If Mary scores in the 80th percentile on her biology test, explain what this means. Did she do well on her biology test compared to her class?

16. If Brian scores in the 20th percentile on his chemistry test, explain what this means. Did he do well on his chemistry test compared to his class?

17. Explain how receiving a grade of 60% on a test is different than scoring in the 60th percentile on a test.

18. Explain how receiving a grade of 95% on a test is different than scoring in the 95th percentile on a test.

19. Given the following information for a data set, draw a box-and-whisker plot:

Lowest value	82
1st quartile	94
Median	95
3rd quartile	102
Highest value	110

20. Given the following information for a data set, draw a box-and-whisker plot:

Lowest value	2
1st quartile	6
Median	11.5
3rd quartile	16
Highest value	30

21. For the data set {76, 98, 102, 104, 76, 96, 57, 97, 99}, compute the following:

   a. Median

   b. 1st and 3rd quartiles

   c. Interquartile range

   d. Outliers, if any

22. For the data set {104, 139, 123, 142, 57, 104, 153, 105, 139}, compute the following:

   a. Median

   b. 1st and 3rd quartiles

   c. Interquartile range

   d. Outliers, if any

23. Draw a box-and-whisker plot for the data in Problem 21.

24. Draw a box-and-whisker plot for the data in Problem 22.

25. The following data are the times (in minutes) that each of 20 students waited in line at the bookstore to pay for their textbooks at the beginning of the semester:

15	18	23	21	5	17	25	22	34	19
14	20	16	19	30	3	30	45	25	20

a. Draw a box-and-whisker plot for the data.

b. Identify the outliers, if any.

26. The following data are the number of patients who visited a walk-in clinic before noon on each of 15 randomly selected days:

23	36	26	38	28	16	33	22	30	20
37	29	42	24	8					

a. Draw a box-and-whisker plot for the data.

b. Identify the outliers, if any.

27. Ten different brands of cereal have the following number of calories per serving:

92	70	105	50	83	90	75	65	83	95

a. Draw a box-and-whisker plot for the data.

b. Comment on the skewness and shape of the data.

28. The number of days that 12 patients stayed in a hospital after hip replacement surgery was recorded and are shown below:

5	3	4	4	3	6	4	7	5	5	3	4

a. Draw a box-and-whisker plot for the data.

b. Comment on the skewness and shape of the data.

29. The cholesterol levels for 60 adults (in mg/dL) were recorded and then displayed on the following box-and-whisker plot:

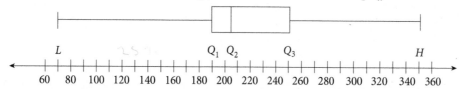

a. Approximately how many adults had a cholesterol level above 205 mg/dL?

b. Approximately how many adults had a cholesterol level below 250 mg/dL?

c. Approximately what percent of the adults had a cholesterol level of at most 190 mg/dL?

30. The body temperatures of 20 healthy adults (in °F) in a clinical drug trial were measured and recorded. The box-and-whisker plot of the data is displayed below:

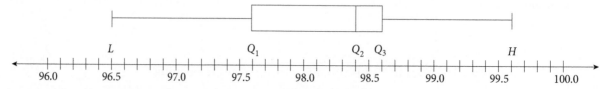

a. Approximately how many adults had a temperature above 98.4 °F?

b. Approximately how many adults had a temperature below 97.6 °F?

c. Approximately what percent of the adults had a temperature of at least 97.6 °F?

3.2 | Measures of Deviation

Given two different sets of data, it is possible that the sets have the same measures of centre, and even similar ranges and measures of position (e.g., quartiles), but very different distributions. As an example, consider the following two data sets:

Data Set A: {10, 33, 34, 35, 52, 53, 54, 55, 56, 57, 58, 75, 76, 77, 100}

Data Set B: {10, 20, 30, 35, 40, 45, 50, 55, 60, 65, 70, 75, 80, 90, 100}

Some quick calculations reveal the following summary statistics for **both** data sets:

Mean = 55	$Q_1 = 35$	Range = 90
Median = 55	$Q_3 = 75$	IQR = 40
Mode = N/A		

This seems to imply that the data sets are identical (since their summary statistics are identical). However, we know that this is incorrect, as data set A is more "clustered" than data set B. How then do we distinguish between the two data sets?

One way to measure the differences present in the two data sets is to calculate a **measure of deviation**, which analyzes the spread between individual data values in the data set and the centre of the data set (as determined by the mean).

$$Deviation\ from\ the\ Mean = x - \bar{x}$$

Example 3.2-a	Calculating the Total Deviation in a Data Set

Calculate the deviation from the mean in the sample data set: {55, 65, 70, 72, 78}.

Solution

First, calculate the mean.

$$Mean,\ \bar{x} = \frac{(55 + 65 + 70 + 72 + 78)}{5} = \frac{340}{5} = 68$$

The deviation of the 1st data in the data set from the mean = $x - \bar{x}$ = 55 − 68 = −13

Therefore, the 1st data in the data set is 13 units below the mean.

Calculate the deviation of each data from the mean by subtracting the mean from each data and tabulate as follows:

x	$\bar{x}$	$(x - \bar{x})$
55	68	−13
65	68	−3
70	68	2
72	68	4
78	68	10
		$\sum(x - \bar{x}) = 0$

Mean Absolute Deviation (MAD)

As we can see from the example above, the sum of the deviation from the mean will always be zero - i.e., the total deviation above the mean will exactly equal the total deviation below the mean (which makes sense, given that this is essentially the definition of the mean).

Therefore, to learn anything about the total deviation present in a data set, we need to use the **absolute deviation** - i.e., the amount by which a value in a data set differs from the mean, irrespective of its sign (positive or negative):

$$Absolute\ Deviation\ from\ the\ Mean = |x - \bar{x}|$$

Using this approach, we can calculate the **Mean Absolute Deviation** from the mean (**MAD**), by summing the absolute deviations for each data value and dividing by the number of data values:

Formula 3.2-a

Mean Absolute Deviation from the Mean

$$\text{Mean Absolute Deviation from the Mean } (MAD) = \frac{\sum |x - \bar{x}|}{n}$$

Similar to the range and IQR, the more spread out the values are in the data set, the larger the MAD will be. However, measures of deviation like the MAD tend to be better measures of dispersion than values like the range or IQR, as both of those values use only two data values, while deviation calculations use every value in the data set.

Example 3.2-b

Calculating the Mean Absolute Deviation in a Data Set

For the data set in Example 3.2-a, {55, 65, 70, 72, 78}, calculate the mean absolute deviation from the mean.

Solution

Using $\bar{x} = \dfrac{\sum x}{n} = 68$, calculate the absolute deviation of each data from the mean, $|(x - \bar{x})|$, then calculate $\sum |x - \bar{x}|$, as shown below:

x	$\bar{x}$	$(x - \bar{x})$	$|(x - \bar{x})|$
55	68	−13	13
65	68	−3	3
70	68	2	2
72	68	4	4
78	68	10	10
$n = 5$		$\sum(x - \bar{x}) = 0$	$\sum|x - \bar{x}| = 32$

$$\text{Mean Absolute Deviation from the Mean } (MAD) = \frac{\sum |x - \bar{x}|}{n} = \frac{32}{5} = 6.4$$

Therefore, the mean absolute deviation of the data from the mean is 6.4.

Variance

Another way to adjust for the positive and negative deviations, instead of using the MAD, is to calculate the **variance** of the data set. The variance is the mean of the squared deviations from each data value to the mean. Squaring makes all the deviation values positive and is a convenient way of overcoming the cancelling out effect, and is more commonly used in statistics than the MAD.

Like the MAD, variance increases the more spread out the data values are in the data set, and is a better measure of dispersion than either the range or IQR as it uses every value in the data set.

However, unlike the MAD, which is a descriptive statistic used for sample data sets, the variance is more of an inferential statistic by nature, and so the method of calculating it depends on whether the data set constitutes a population or a sample. The variance of a *population* is represented by the symbol σ^2 (i.e., the lowercase Greek letter sigma, squared), while the variance of a *sample* is represented by the symbol s^2 (lowercase *s*, squared) - this is similar to the convention used for the population mean (μ) and sample mean ($\bar{x}$).

Formula 3.2-b	**Variance of a Population**

$$\sigma^2 = \frac{\sum (x - \mu)^2}{N}$$

Where,

- μ is the population mean, and
- N is the number of elements in the population.

Formula 3.2-c	**Variance of a Sample**

$$s^2 = \frac{\sum (x - \bar{x})^2}{n - 1}$$

Where,

- $\bar{x}$ is the sample mean, and
- n is the number of elements in the sample.

In the above formulas, you will note that in calculating the population variance (σ^2), the sum of squares of the deviations is divided by N, whereas in the sample variance, (s^2), it is divided by ($n - 1$).

This is because of **Bessel's Correction**, which can be intuitively explained using the concept of **degrees of freedom** - that is, the number of independent variables in a statistical distribution.

In a population, the mean is based on all the values in the population, with every deviation value ($x - \mu$) being independent. That is, these values all "freely" (i.e., independently) add up to 0, and so the formula for population variance divides by N.

This is not the case with a sample, however. The sample mean, $\bar{x}$, is assumed to estimate the population mean, μ. Here, only the first ($n - 1$) deviation values ($x - \bar{x}$) are "free" (i.e., independent), as one of the values is dependent on the other ($n - 1$) values in order to make the total deviation equal to 0. Thus, the formula for sample variance divides by ($n - 1$).

Note: For the remainder of this chapter, we shall focus on the calculation of sample variance only.

Follow these steps to calculate the variance of a sample:

Step 1: Find the deviation for each data value by subtracting it from the mean: ($x - \bar{x}$).

Note: The sum of the deviations $\sum (x - \bar{x})$ should always equal zero.

Step 2: Square each deviation: ($x - \bar{x}$)^2. The squared deviations should all be positive (or zero).

Step 3: Find the sum of the squared deviations: $\sum (x - \bar{x})^2$

Step 4: Divide the sum of the squared deviations in Step 3 by one less than the number of data values: $n - 1$

The result is the (sample) variance: $s^2 = \frac{\sum (x - \bar{x})^2}{n - 1}$

| Example 3.2-c | Calculating the Sample Variance of a Data Set |

Calculate the variance of the sample data set in Example 3.2-a: {55, 65, 70, 72, 78}.

Solution

Using $\bar{x} = \dfrac{\sum x}{n} = 68$, calculate the squared deviation of each data from the mean, $(x - \bar{x})^2$, then calculate $\sum(x - \bar{x})^2$, as shown below:

x	$\bar{x}$	$(x - \bar{x})$	$(x - \bar{x})^2$
55	68	−13	169
65	68	−3	9
70	68	2	4
72	68	4	16
78	68	10	100
$n = 5$		$\sum(x - \bar{x}) = 0$	$\sum(x - \bar{x})^2 = 298$

Variance, $s^2 = \dfrac{\sum(x - \bar{x})^2}{n - 1} = \dfrac{298}{5 - 1} = 74.5$

Therefore, the variance of the sample data is 74.5.

Alternate Formula for the Sample Variance

Sometimes, if the sample mean is rounded, using the above formula to calculate variance can cause rounding errors, or require computations involving many decimal places. In order to avoid this, the following equivalent formula, which does not rely on the sample mean, may be used:

$$s^2 = \frac{n \cdot \left(\sum x^2\right) - \left(\sum x\right)^2}{n(n - 1)}$$

Standard Deviation

As previously mentioned, it is far more common to use the variance (square values) than the MAD (absolute values) as a measure of deviation. However, the problem with the variance is that the units are squared (e.g., if the data values represent heights in cm, the variance will be measured in cm², which is a measure of area!). To correct for this, the square root of the variance is calculated to arrive at the original units of the data set. The resulting value is known as the "standard deviation from the mean" or simply the **standard deviation** for short.

| Formula 3.2-d | Standard Deviation of a Population |

$$\sigma = \sqrt{\frac{\sum(x - \mu)^2}{N}}$$

| Formula 3.2-e | Standard Deviation of a Sample |

$$s = \sqrt{\frac{\sum(x - \bar{x})^2}{n - 1}}$$

The standard deviation is the most common and most often preferred statistical measure of dispersion. It measures the extent to which scores deviate from the mean, similar to the MAD (though it does not produce the same value); the smaller the standard deviation, the closer the data values are to each other. This also indicates that the data is more uniform and consistent. The frequency distribution curve will be narrower for data sets with smaller standard deviations and wider for sets with larger standard deviations.

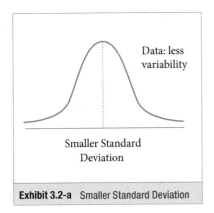

Exhibit 3.2-a Smaller Standard Deviation

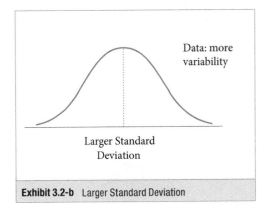

Exhibit 3.2-b Larger Standard Deviation

Example 3.2-d   Calculating the Standard Deviation of a Sample

Calculate the standard deviation of the sample data set in Example 3.2-a: {55, 65, 70, 72, 78}.

Solution

The variance of the sample set as calculated in Example 3.2-c is 74.5 (i.e., $s^2 = 74.5$).

$$s = \sqrt{s^2} = \sqrt{74.5} \approx 8.63$$

Therefore, the standard deviation of the sample data set is 8.63.

Example 3.2-e   Calculating the Sample Variance of Two Data Sets

Recall the two data sets A and B from the beginning of the section:

Data Set A: {10, 33, 34, 35, 52, 53, 54, 55, 56, 57, 58, 75, 76, 77, 100}

Data Set B: {10, 20, 30, 35, 40, 45, 50, 55, 60, 65, 70, 75, 80, 90, 100}

Calculate and compare the sample standard deviations of the two data sets to determine which set has a greater dispersion.

Solution

First, calculate the mean for both data sets:

Data Set A   **Data Set B**

$$\overline{x}_A = \frac{\sum x}{n} = \frac{825}{15} = 55 \qquad\qquad \overline{x}_B = \frac{\sum x}{n} = \frac{825}{15} = 55$$

Solution
continued

Next, use the mean to calculate the standard deviation for each data set:

Data Set A

x	$(x - \bar{x})$	$(x - \bar{x})^2$
10	−45	2,025
33	−22	484
34	−21	441
35	−20	400
52	−3	9
53	−2	4
54	−1	1
55	0	0
56	1	1
57	2	4
58	3	9
75	20	400
76	21	441
77	22	484
100	45	2,025
	$\sum (x - \bar{x})^2 =$	6,728

Data Set B

x	$(x - \bar{x})$	$(x - \bar{x})^2$
10	−45	2,025
20	−35	1,225
30	−25	625
35	−20	400
40	−15	225
45	−10	100
50	−5	25
55	0	0
60	5	25
65	10	100
70	15	225
75	20	400
80	25	625
90	35	1,225
100	45	2,025
	$\sum (x - \bar{x})^2 =$	9,250

$$s_A = \sqrt{\frac{\sum (x - \bar{x})^2}{n - 1}} = \sqrt{\frac{6{,}728}{15 - 1}}$$

$$= \sqrt{480.571428\ldots} \approx 21.92$$

$$s_B = \sqrt{\frac{\sum (x - \bar{x})^2}{n - 1}} = \sqrt{\frac{9{,}250}{15 - 1}}$$

$$= \sqrt{660.714285\ldots} \approx 25.70$$

Therefore, the standard deviation proves that Data Set B is more dispersed than Data Set A, as expected.

Alternate Formula for the Sample Standard Deviation

Just as with the sample variance, there is an equivalent formula for the sample standard deviation that does not rely on the sample mean. Use this when the sample mean must be rounded:

$$s = \sqrt{\frac{n \cdot \left(\sum x^2 \right) - \left(\sum x \right)^2}{n(n - 1)}}$$

Interpreting the Standard Deviation

A common question that is asked about the standard deviation is "What does it represent?" The other measures of variation, like range, quartiles, and MAD have a more obvious interpretation; for example, a MAD of 5.2 tells us that the average distance between a data value and the mean is 5.2 units. However, the standard deviation does not have such a simple interpretation.

The easiest way to understand the standard deviation is to understand some of its helpful mathematical properties, which will be demonstrated below.

Range Rule of Thumb

The first and simplest property of the standard deviation is its approximate relationship to the range. In most typical situations, where the data set is not extraordinarily large and does not contain outliers, the standard deviation is approximately one-fourth of the range:

$$Range \approx 4 \cdot s$$

*Note: This is a **rough** approximation and generally will not be true if the data set has outliers. In such cases, it is more accurate to first remove the outliers from the data set and calculate the range of the "typical" (i.e., non-outlier) values.*

The range rule of thumb can be used in two ways:

1. To quickly approximate the standard deviation of an array of data without involving tedious calculations:

$$s \approx \frac{Range}{4}$$

2. To approximate the minimum and maximum values of the "typical" data in a data set in which we only know the mean and standard deviation.

$$Minimum\ Value \approx \bar{x} - 2 \cdot s$$

$$Maximum\ Value \approx \bar{x} + 2 \cdot s$$

Example 3.2-f	Approximating the Standard Deviation using the Range Rule of Thumb

Approximate the standard deviation of Data Set A in Example 3.2-e using the Range Rule of Thumb:

{10, 33, 34, 35, 52, 53, 54, 55, 56, 57, 58, 75, 76, 77, 100}

Solution

First, calculate the range of the data: Range = 100 – 10 = 90

Next, divide by four to get an estimate for the standard deviation: $s \approx \dfrac{90}{4} = 22.5$

Therefore, the standard deviation is approximately 22.5, which is a close approximation to the actual value of 21.92 that was calculated in Example 3.2-e.

Example 3.2-g	Approximating the Minimum and Maximum Values of a Data Set using the Range Rule of Thumb

The average hourly wage for a registered nurse is $36.79/hour, with a standard deviation of $3.46. Using this information, find the minimum and maximum "typical" wages for registered nurses.

Solution

The Range Rule of Thumb tells us that the minimum value is approximately the mean minus 2 standard deviations, and the maximum value is approximately the mean plus 2 standard deviations:

Minimum Value ≈ $36.79 – 2($3.46) = $29.87

Maximum Value ≈ $36.79 + 2($3.46) = $43.71

Therefore, the "typical" wages of registered nurses fall between $29.87 and $43.71/hour.

The Empirical Rule

The Range Rule of Thumb provides a quick and convenient relationship between the standard deviation and the range, but it is not very accurate, as it does not take any other factors into consideration, such as the shape of the distribution or the size of the data set. Another property of the standard deviation that incorporates more information about the data set is the **Empirical Rule**:

The "bell-curve" is a special type of symmetrical "mound"-shaped distribution, that will be discussed in depth in Chapter 7.

For a data set that has a distribution that is symmetrical and roughly "bell-curved", the following holds true:

- Approximately 68% of all data values fall within ±1 standard deviation of the mean.

- Approximately 95% of all data values fall within ±2 standard deviations of the mean.

- Approximately 99.7% of all data values fall within ±3 standard deviations of the mean.

The empirical rule allows more precise information to be drawn about the distribution of the data and the percent of the data that falls within certain intervals around the mean. However, it only works for distributions that are symmetrical and roughly "bell-curved" - such distributions are referred to as being "normal" (we will discuss this further in later chapters).

Using the symmetry of the distribution, we can summarize this rule in the following diagram:

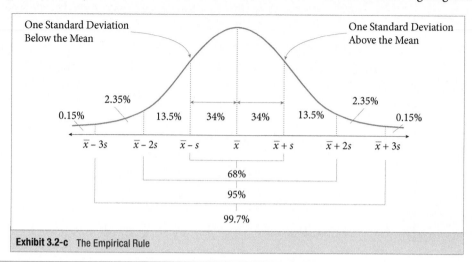

Exhibit 3.2-c   The Empirical Rule

Example 3.2-h	**Using the Empirical Rule**

In a college statistics class, the mean final exam mark is typically 70 with a standard deviation of around 10. Use the empirical rule (and the summary diagram above) to answer the following questions for a statistics class of 200 students:

(i)   How many students are expected to score between 60 and 80?

(ii)   How many students are expected to pass the exam (i.e., score greater than 50)?

(iii) What mark would the top five students in the class be expected to score above?

Note: Assume the distribution is symmetrical and roughly "bell-curved".

Solution

Since the we know that the mean $\bar{x} = 70$ and the standard deviation $s = 10$, we can label the diagram from Exhibit 3.2-c as follows:

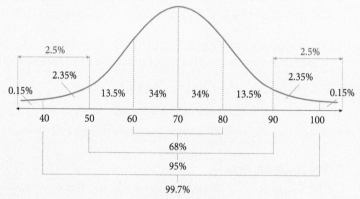

(i)   The empirical rule states that approximately 68% of the 200 students, or roughly 136 students, will score between 60 and 80 on the exam.

(ii)   Again, we can quickly see from the above diagram that approximately the top 97.5% (100% − 2.5%) of students, or roughly 195 students, will score above 50 - i.e., they will pass the exam.

(iii) To determine this, we first need to calculate what percent of the data five students represents:

$$\frac{5}{200} \times 100\% = 2.5\%$$

Since we are looking for the mark the *top* 2.5% of students will score above, we find the score that separates the right-most (or upper-most) 2.5% of students on our diagram, which is 90. Therefore, the top five students in the class are all expected to score above 90.

Chebyshev's Theorem

While the empirical rule is useful for understanding the standard deviation, it has two main disadvantages: first, it only applies to distributions that are approximately normal; and second, that despite being more accurate than the Range Rule of Thumb, it is not always accurate either. As such, we now look at a third way to interpret and use the standard deviation, which involves getting a *guaranteed* lower bound on the proportion of data within a certain interval of the mean, *for any distribution*. The following is known as Chebyshev's Theorem (named after the Russian mathematician Pafnuty Chebyshev who proved it):

For any given distribution of values of a random variable, a minimum proportion of $1 - \dfrac{1}{k^2}$ of the values must fall within k standard deviations of the mean, where $k > 1$.

For example, if $k = 2$, the theorem tells us that a minimum of $1 - \dfrac{1}{2^2} = \dfrac{3}{4}$ (or 75%) of the data must fall within two standard deviations of the mean. Similarly, if $k = 3$, the theorem tells us that a minimum of $1 - \dfrac{1}{3^2} = \dfrac{8}{9}$ (or approximately 89%) of the data must fall within three standard deviations of the mean.

Example 3.2-i | **Using Chebyshev's Theorem**

Determine the proportion of the data that Chebyshev's theorem will guarantee to fall within 1.6 standard deviations of the mean. Demonstrate that this holds true for both data sets A and B from Example 3.2-e.

Solution

If $k = 1.6$, then according to Chebyshev's theorem, a minimum of $1 - \dfrac{1}{1.6^2} = 1 - \dfrac{1}{2.56} \approx 1 - 0.39 = 61\%$ of the data must fall within 1.6 standard deviations of the mean.

Data Set A: {10, 33, 34, 35, 52, 53, 54, 55, 56, 57, 58, 75, 76, 77, 100}

- The data set has a mean of 55 and a standard deviation of 21.92.
- 1.6 standard deviations are equal to approximately 35.
- Therefore, 1.6 standard deviations on either side of the mean is a range of values from 20 to 90.
- 13 out of 15 pieces of data fall within that range, which represents approximately 87% of the data, which is more than the guaranteed 61%.

Data Set B: {10, 20, 30, 35, 40, 45, 50, 55, 60, 65, 70, 75, 80, 90, 100}

- The data set has a mean of 55 and a standard deviation of 25.70.
- 1.6 standard deviations are equal to approximately 41.
- Therefore, 1.6 standard deviations on either side of the mean is a range of values from 14 to 96.
- Again, 13 out of 15 pieces of data fall within that range, which represents approximately 87% of the data, which is more than the guaranteed 61%.

Coefficient of Variation

Finally, in order to fully appreciate the interpretation of the standard deviation, we need to understand that a smaller standard deviation does not always mean more consistency. Consider the following two scenarios:

1. The distribution of wait times for patients to get an appointment with a certain specialist has a mean of 16 weeks with a standard deviation of 2 weeks.

2. The distribution of wait times for results from a certain lab has a mean of 16 days with a standard deviation of 6 days.

Clearly, the second set of data has a lower standard deviation (since 6 days < 2 weeks); however, when viewed proportionally, we get a different picture: both have a mean of 16 units, but the first set has a standard deviation of 2 respective units, while the second set has a standard deviation of 6 respective units. The first set of data is more consistent, as the Range Rule of Thumb shows that most patients are seen within 12 to 20 weeks, while the second set of data is less consistent, with patients waiting anywhere between 4 and 28 days for their results.

In order to fully appreciate whether the standard deviation indicates high or low variation in the data set, we need to consider it in proportion to the mean. This is called the **coefficient of variation (CV)**.

Formula 3.2-f | **Coefficient of Variation**

$$CV_{population} = \frac{\sigma}{\mu} \times 100\% \qquad \text{or} \qquad CV_{sample} = \frac{s}{\bar{x}} \times 100\%$$

Example 3.2-j | **Comparing Variation of Data Sets Using the Coefficient of Variation**

Determine which of the following two sample data sets is more consistent and which has more variation:

Data Set A: {58, 69, 74, 65, 53, 62, 59, 68, 62, 70}

Data Set B: {14, 24, 25, 11, 26, 19, 31, 16, 24, 20}

Solution

First, calculate the mean for both data sets:

Data Set A

$$\bar{x}_A = \frac{\sum x}{n} = \frac{640}{10} = 64$$

Data Set B

$$\bar{x}_B = \frac{\sum x}{n} = \frac{210}{10} = 21$$

Next, use the mean to calculate the standard deviation for each data set:

Data Set A

x	$(x - \bar{x})$	$(x - \bar{x})^2$
58	−6	36
69	5	25
74	10	100
65	1	1
53	−11	121
62	−2	4
59	−5	25
68	4	16
62	−2	4
70	6	36
	$\sum (x - \bar{x})^2 =$	368

Data Set B

x	$(x - \bar{x})$	$(x - \bar{x})^2$
14	−7	49
24	3	9
25	4	16
11	−10	100
26	5	25
19	−2	4
31	10	100
16	−5	25
24	3	9
20	−1	1
	$\sum (x - \bar{x})^2 =$	338

$$s_A = \sqrt{\frac{\sum (x - \bar{x})^2}{n - 1}} = \sqrt{\frac{368}{10 - 1}}$$

$$= \sqrt{40.8} \approx 6.39$$

$$s_B = \sqrt{\frac{\sum (x - \bar{x})^2}{n - 1}} = \sqrt{\frac{338}{10 - 1}}$$

$$= \sqrt{37.5} \approx 6.13$$

Finally, use the standard deviation and mean to calculate the coefficient of variation for each data set:

$$CV_A = \frac{s}{\bar{x}} \times 100\% = \frac{6.39}{64} \times 100\% \approx 10\%$$

$$CV_B = \frac{s}{\bar{x}} \times 100\% = \frac{6.13}{21} \times 100\% \approx 29\%$$

Therefore, the coefficients of variation indicate that the data in Data Set A is more consistent, with the standard deviation representing only 10% of the mean, while the data in Data Set B has more variation, with the standard deviation representing approximately 29% of the mean.

3.2 | Exercises

1. Find the mean absolute deviation for the data set: {92, 75, 95, 90, 98}.

2. Find the mean absolute deviation for the data set: {26, 87, 34, 21, 67, 92, 74}.

3. Which of the following data sets has the bigger mean absolute deviation?
   a. {1, 2, 3, 4, 5}   b. {1, 4, 9, 12, 15}

4. Which of the following data sets has the bigger mean absolute deviation?
   a. {3, 9, 15, 21, 27}   b. {3, 5, 9, 12, 18}

5. Calculate the variance and standard deviation of the sample data sets in Problem 3.

6. Calculate the variance and standard deviation of the sample data sets in Problem 4.

7. Given the following information of a sample data, calculate the variance and standard deviation:
   $n = 10$, *sum of the squared deviation* = 40, and *the sum of the data* = 610.

8. Given the following information of a sample data, calculate the variance and standard deviation:
   $n = 5$, *sum of the squared deviation* = 46, and *the sum of the data* = 40.

9. The weights (in kilograms) of a group of ten randomly selected men are as follows:
   | 82 | 79 | 80 | 80 | 72 | 74 | 88 | 82 | 92 | 83 |

   Calculate: a. mean   81.2   b. standard deviation

10. The marks of a group of ten students are as follows:
    | 77 | 82 | 43 | 63 | 59 | 61 | 66 | 61 | 76 | 54 |

    Calculate: a. mean   b. standard deviation

11. The following are the annual incomes of five randomly selected professors of a college:
    $75,000, $78,000, $72,000, $83,000, and $90,000.
    Compute the following:
    a. Mean   b. Mean absolute deviation
    c. Variance   d. Standard deviation

12. The following are the weekly incomes for a group of seven randomly selected employees:
    $875, $945, $905, $885, $910, $820, and $841.
    Compute the following:
    a. Mean   b. Mean absolute deviation
    c. Variance   d. Standard deviation

13. Approximate the standard deviation of the data in Problem 11 using the Range Rule of Thumb, and compare the approximation to the calculated standard deviation value from Problem 11.

14. Approximate the standard deviation of the data in Problem 12 using the Range Rule of Thumb, and compare the approximation to the calculated standard deviation value from Problem 12.

15. The average annual salary of a pharmacist is $102,972 with a standard deviation of $15,086. Using this information and the Range Rule of Thumb, determine the minimum and maximum "typical" wages for pharmacists.

16. The average hourly wage for a certified dental assistant is $17.01 per hour, with a standard deviation of $2.34. Using this information and the Range Rule of Thumb, determine the minimum and maximum "typical" hourly wages for certified dental assistants.

17. An aptitude test is normally distributed with a mean of 500 and a standard deviation of 100. Use the empirical rule to answer the following:

    a. Approximately what percent of the students will have a score between 400 and 600?

    b. Randomly selected students will have a 95% chance of having scores fall between what values?

    c. Randomly selected students will have a 99.7% chance of having scores fall between what values?

18. A bell-shaped distribution has a mean of 550 and a standard deviation of 150. Use the empirical rule to answer the following:

    a. What percent of the data will fall between 400 and 700?

    b. Randomly selected data will have a 95% chance of falling between what values?

    c. Randomly selected data will have a 99.7% chance of falling between what values?

19. Out of a sample of 100 boxes of cereal, 95 boxes weigh between 780 and 820 grams. Use the empirical rule to estimate the average weight (in grams) of the cereal box and the standard deviation in weight of the sample.

20. Out of a sample of 100 juice bottles, 68 bottles contain between 975 and 1,025 litres of juice. Use the empirical rule to estimate the average quantity (in litres) in the juice bottles and the standard deviation in volume of the sample.

21. On average, a college test center can accommodate 350 students per day with a standard deviation of 75 students. Use the empirical rule to estimate the minimum and maximum number of students that the test center can expect in a day.

22. On average, a flight reservation center can handle 200 customer calls per day with a standard deviation of 35 calls. Use the empirical rule to estimate the minimum and maximum number of calls that the flight reservation center can handle in a day.

23. For a set of 4,000 insulin measurements, the mean was found to be 75mg/100mL with a standard deviation of 4.5mg/100mL. Assuming that the distribution is approximately bell-shaped, determine:

    a. The percentage of the 4,000 measurements that will fall within 2 standard deviations of the mean.

    b. The number of measurements that will be above 88.5mg/100mL.

    c. The number of measurements that will be above 70.5mg/100mL.

24. For a set of 200 urine protein measurements, the mean was found to be 60.8 mg/day with a standard deviation of 7.5 mg/day. Assuming that the distribution is approximately bell-shaped, determine:

    a. The percentage of the 200 measurements that will fall within 3 standard deviations of the mean.

    b. The number of measurements that will be below 75.8 mg/day.

    c. The number of measurements that will be below 45.8 mg/day.

25. According to a survey, students spend an average of 152 hours per month using the computer for their studies. Assume a bell-shaped distribution applies and that the standard deviation is 28 hours. A student is classified as a light user if he/she is in the bottom 16% in terms of hours of usage. How many hours per month must a student use the computer in order to be classified as a light user?

26. A person must score in the upper 0.15% of admission test scores in order to qualify for a very competitive nursing program. If the admission test scores are bell-shaped with a mean of 250 and a standard deviation of 15, what is the minimum score that a person must achieve in order to qualify for this program?

27. The following are the ages (in years) of 10 employees of an insurance company:

47	28	39	51	33	37	46	55	34	33

    a. Calculate the mean age and the standard deviation of the data set.

    b. Using Chebyshev's theorem, determine the minimum percentage of employees who will fall within 1.5 standard deviations of the mean age.

    c. Demonstrate that this holds true for the above data set.

28. The following are the one-way commuting times (in minutes) from home to college of 12 students.

55	24	18	29	14	39	17	5	45	63	37	40

    a. Calculate the mean commuting time and the standard deviation of the data set.

    b. Using Chebyshev's theorem, determine the minimum percentage of students who will fall within 1.25 standard deviations of the mean commuting time.

    c. Demonstrate that this holds true for the above data set.

29. The average systolic blood pressure for 1,000 women who were screened for high blood pressure was found to be 187 mmHg with a standard deviation of 22 mmHg. Using Chebyshev's theorem, determine the minimum percentage of women in this group who have a systolic blood pressure between 132 and 242 mmHg.

30. The average diastolic blood pressure for the 1,000 women in Problem 29 who were screened for high blood pressure was found to be 109 mmHg with a standard deviation of 15 mmHg. Using Chebyshev's theorem, determine the minimum percentage of women in this group who have a diastolic blood pressure between 82.75 and 135.25 mmHg.

31. The result of a survey of 1,200 adults showed that on average, adults sleep 5.9 hours per day during the workweek. The standard deviation is found to be 1.2 hours.

    a. Using Chebyshev's theorem, calculate the minimum percent of individuals who sleep between 2.3 and 9.5 hours per day.

    b. Assume that the number of hours of sleep follows a bell-shaped distribution. Using the empirical rule, calculate the percent of individuals who sleep between 2.3 and 9.5 hours per day.

    c. Compare your results from parts (a) and (b). Why are they different?

32. The result of a survey showed that the average cost of books and supplies per semester for students in college was $434 with a standard deviation of $140.

    a. Using Chebyshev's theorem, calculate the minimum percent of students who spend between $154 and $714 for books and supplies in college.

    b. Assume that the costs for books and supplies follow a bell-shaped distribution. Using the empirical rule, calculate the percent of students who spent between $154 and $714 for books and supplies in college.

    c. Compare your results from parts (a) and (b). Why are they different?

33. The test scores for a large statistics class have an unknown distribution with a mean of 72 and a standard deviation of 10. Find k such that a minimum of 50% of the scores are within k standard deviations of the mean. What is the range of values within k standard deviations of the mean?

34. Using the test-score data from Problem 33, find k such that a minimum of 82.6% of the scores are within k standard deviations of the mean. What is the range of values within k standard deviations of the mean?

35. For a sample of students in a college pre-health program, the mean grade point average is 3.10 with a standard deviation of 0.25. Calculate the coefficient of variation and interpret its meaning.

36. For the sample of students in Problem 35, the mean age is 22.4 with a standard deviation of 2.7. Calculate the coefficient of variation and interpret its meaning.

37. The resting heart rates for two patients involved in a clinical trial of a new drug were recorded at five different intervals. The results in beats per minute were as follows:

Patient I	62	66	68	73	78
Patient II	78	90	85	88	95

    a. Calculate the mean and standard deviation of the heart rates for each patient.

    b. Compare the standard deviations. Which patient has a smaller deviation?

    c. Calculate the coefficient of variation for each patient.

    d. Compare the coefficient of variations. Which patient has a more consistent resting heart rate?

38. Police records indicate the following numbers of daily crime reports for a particular week during the summer and winter months:

Summer	28	28	24	32	28	29	30
Winter	18	16	20	18	15	18	14

a. Calculate the mean and standard deviation of the crime reports for the summer and winter months.

b. Compare the standard deviations. Which month had a smaller deviation?

c. Calculate the coefficient of variation for the summer and winter months.

d. Compare the coefficient of variations. Which month had a more consistent number of crime reports?

39. Nurse A is employed by a government-funded hospital, where the distribution of weekly pay has a mean of $365 with a standard deviation of $98. The privately-owned hospital at which Nurse B works has a weekly pay distribution with a mean of $158 and a standard deviation of $69. Which hospital is more consistent in their weekly pay scale?

40. A city's records indicate the following statistics on the temperature for a sample of days during the summer months and a sample of the same number of days during the winter months:

	Summer	**Winter**
Mean	26.6	10.7
Standard deviation	4.67	3.86

Based on the coefficient of variation, which season has more variation in temperature?

3 | Review Exercises

Answers to odd-numbered problems are available at the end of the textbook.

1. The following are the number of hours worked last week by 18 randomly selected employees working at a hospital:

45 54 63 79 48 50 49 52 74
55 61 56 58 56 77 66 64 70

a. Compute the 1st, 2nd, and 3rd quartiles.
b. Compute the interquartile range (IQR).
c. A value greater than what number would be an outlier?
d. A value less than what number would be an outlier?
e. Are there any outliers in this set of data? If yes, list them.

2. The following are the dollar amounts spent on massage therapy by nine individuals in the past month:

315 220 225 580 190 250 210 90 285

a. Compute the 1st, 2nd, and 3rd quartiles.
b. Compute the interquartile range (IQR).
c. A value greater than what number would be an outlier?
d. A value less than what number would be an outlier?
e. Are there any outliers in this set of data? If yes, list them.

3. The commuting distances, in kilometres, of 12 students attending college for the first year are recorded as follows:

4.6 4.6 8.2 7.8 9.5 9.3
9.4 5.3 5.5 5.4 6.8 5.2

a. Calculate P_{10} and P_{90}.
b. Determine the 10-90 percentile range.

4. The following are the number of orders received for a sample of 15 days at a pharmaceutical company:

34 44 31 52 41 47 38 42
18 24 57 39 45 39 46

a. Calculate P_{10} and P_{90}.
b. Determine the 10-90 percentile range.

5. The following are the times (in minutes) of 15 patients waiting to be seen in an Emergency Room:

75 62 84 73 107 81 93 72
67 90 83 112 135 77 85

a. Prepare a box-and-whisker plot for the data.
b. Identify the outliers, if any.
c. Comment on the skewness and shape of the distribution, based on your box-and-whisker plot.

6. The following are the total number of students 15 professors in a university have in all their classes combined, during the winter semester:

105   124   175   90   55   361   68   258

60   780   136   200   390   245   71

  a. Prepare a box-and-whisker plot for the data.

  b. Identify the outliers, if any.

  c. Comment on the skewness and shape of the distribution, based on your box-and-whisker plot.

7. If Connor scores in the 68th percentile on the weight-scale for men in his age group, what can you conclude about his weight?

8. If Irene scores in the 98th percentile on her math final exam, explain what this means. Did she do well on her math final exam, compared to her class?

9. Determine the mean, mean absolute deviation, and standard deviation of the test scores for each of the following two students:

Student A:	89	69	78	82	75
Student B:	64	70	69	80	72

Based on the standard deviation, which student shows more variation in his/her performance?

10. Determine the mean, mean absolute deviation, and standard deviation of the time spent (in minutes) on five quizzes for each of the following two students:

Student A:	24	20	22	28	32
Student B:	16	10	18	12	25

Based on the standard deviation, which student shows more variation in terms of time spent on quizzes?

11. 25 college students were surveyed on the number of hours per week spent on exercise.

The answers given by 12 first-year students were as follows: 6, 5, 3, 6, 12, 8, 8, 4, 12, 4, 9, 18

The answers given by 13 fourth-year students were as follows: 5, 6, 3, 2, 6, 4, 3, 1, 3, 2, 3, 8, 4

  a. Calculate the range for each group.

  b. Calculate the mean for each group. Which group (first-year or fourth-year students) exercises more on average?

  c. Calculate the standard deviation for each group.

  d. Calculate the coefficient of variation for each group.

  e. Which group is more consistent based on the coefficient of variation?

12. Two patients' body temperatures are recorded as follows:

Patient 1 (°C):	37.0	36.8	37.2	37.8	38	36.9
Patient 2 (°F):	98.6	101	100.8	97.5	97.8	98.6

  a. Calculate the range of body temperatures for each patient.

  b. Calculate the mean body temperature for each patient.

  c. Calculate the standard deviation for each patient's body temperature.

  d. Calculate the coefficient of variation for each patient's body temperature.

  e. Which patient's body temperature is more consistent based on the coefficient of variation?

13. The average number of days it takes to fill a job posting is 20 days with a standard deviation of 3.5 days. Using the Range Rule of Thumb, determine the minimum and maximum "typical" number of days it takes to fill a job posting.

14. The average height of a human skeleton in the biology department of a college is 66 inches with a standard deviation of 2 inches. Using the Range Rule of Thumb, determine the minimum and maximum "typical" height of a human skeleton.

15. The age distribution of female patients diagnosed with breast cancer follows a bell-shaped distribution with a mean of 47 years and a standard deviation of 9 years. Using the empirical rule, approximately 95% of the female patients are within what range of ages?

16. The one-way commuting time from home to work for a sample of 200 employees working at a downtown hospital have a bell-shaped curve with a mean of 40.8 minutes and a standard deviation of 12.7 minutes. Using the empirical rule, approximately how many employees in this hospital have a one-way commuting time between 28.1 and 53.5 minutes?

17. The average amount of precipitation in Toronto during the month of March is 3.5 inches. Assume that the precipitation follows a bell-shaped curve with a standard deviation of 0.8 inches.

  a. What percent of the time is the amount of precipitation in March less than 4.3 inches?

  b. A month is classified to have "very heavy" precipitation if the amount of precipitation is in the upper 2.5% for that month. How much precipitation must fall in the month of March to be classified "very heavy"?

18. The time needed to complete a math final examination is bell-shaped with a mean of 80 minutes and a standard deviation of 10 minutes.

    a. What percentage of students will complete the exam in one hour or less?

    b. Assume that the class has 200 students and that the examination period is 90 minutes in length. How many students do you expect will be unable to complete the exam in the allotted time?

19. The amounts of time members spent at a health club were observed for a week. It was found that members spent an average of 90.5 minutes at the club with a standard deviation of 15.5 minutes. Using Chebyshev's theorem:

    a. Determine the interval of time that at least 89% of members spent at the club.

    b. Determine the minimum percentage of the members who spent between 63.4 minutes and 117.6 minutes at the club.

20. The mean time taken by all participants to run a road race was found to be 210 minutes with a standard deviation of 16 minutes. Using Chebyshev's theorem:

    a. Determine the interval of time in which at least 93.75% of runners took to complete the race.

    b. Determine the minimum percentage of runners who completed the race in 186 to 234 minutes.

21. A city's records indicate the following statistics on the temperatures for a sample of days during the winter months and a sample of the same number of days during the summer months:

	Summer	Winter
Mean	27.5	14.2
Standard deviation	4.1	4.1

    a. Based on the standard deviation, which season has more variation in temperature?

    b. Based on the coefficient of variation, which season is more consistent in temperature?

22. A study on the amount of monthly bonus paid to sales employees at a company and the years of service at the company indicated the following: the mean bonus paid was $180 with a standard deviation of $30; the mean number of years of service was 10 years with a standard deviation of 1 year. Calculate the coefficients of variation for the amount of monthly bonus paid and the number of years of service, and interpret the meaning.

3 | Self-Test Exercises

1. The amounts of weight lost, in kg, by 10 participants in a six-month weight reduction program were: 10, 8, 14, 7, 11, 8, 12, 12, 17, and 5.

    a. Compute the 1st, 2nd, and 3rd quartiles.

    b. Compute the interquartile range (IQR).

    c. A value greater than what number would be an outlier?

    d. A value less than what number would be an outlier?

    e. Are there any outliers in this set of data? If yes, list them.

2. There are 15 students in a Practical Nursing class at a college. Their ages are as follows:

21	25	28	31	40	27	23	21
35	36	28	21	20	45	42

    Calculate P_{10} and P_{90} and determine the 10-90 percentile range.

3. If Angelica scored in the 92nd percentile on her chemistry test, explain what this means. Did Angelica do well on her chemistry test, compared to her class?

4. One of the gases that contribute to global warming is carbon dioxide. The world's 10 biggest emitters of carbon dioxide are listed below (in millions of metric tons per year):

0.64	1.26	1.52	0.47	0.59
6.05	5.01	0.81	1.34	0.45

    a. Prepare a box-and-whisker plot for the data.

    b. Identify the outliers, if any.

5. A pharmacy offers free drug delivery within a 15 km radius of the pharmacy. The owner requires some information on the time it takes for delivery. For a sample of 20 deliveries, he determined the following information regarding the amount of time (in minutes) spent on each delivery, displayed on the box-and-whisker plot below:

    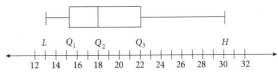

    a. Approximately how many deliveries took less than 15 minutes?

    b. Approximately what percent of the deliveries took more than 18 minutes?

    c. Comment on the skewness and shape of these data, based on the box-and-whisker plot.

6. A walk-in clinic's records indicate the number of patients seen each day over a five-day week.

44	29	38	42	47

    a. Determine the mean number of patients seen at the clinic during the week.

    b. Determine the mean absolute deviation.

7. A patient records her blood pressure (in mmHg) daily and creates the following chart:

	Systolic	Diastolic
Monday	146	92
Tuesday	132	84
Wednesday	154	102
Thursday	128	88
Friday	166	110
Saturday	140	96
Sunday	152	86

    a. Determine the range for both types of blood pressure.

    b. Using the Range Rule of Thumb, estimate the standard deviation for both types of blood pressure.

    c. Calculate the mean, variance, standard deviation, and coefficient of variation for both types of blood pressure using the exact data.

    d. Compare the standard deviation estimates in part (b) with the precise calculations in part (c).

    e. Which type of blood pressure is more stable (consistent) over the seven days, based on the coefficient of variation?

8. The members of a health club were observed on a randomly selected day. The average time they spent at the health club is 91.8 minutes with a standard deviation of 16.2 minutes. Using the Range Rule of Thumb, determine the minimum and maximum "typical" time spent at the club for the members.

9. Assume that college students' heights are bell shaped with a mean of 65.5 inches and a standard deviation of 4.36 inches. You plan to sell sweatsuits in the college bookstore. To minimize the start-up costs, you will not stock sweat suit sizes for the tallest 16% and the shortest 16% of students. Find the minimum and maximum heights of students for whom sweatsuits will be stocked.

10. For a set of 360 cholesterol measurements, the mean was found to be 172mg/100mL with a standard deviation of 4.5mg/100mL. Assuming the distribution is approximately bell-shaped,

   a. 99.7% of the 360 measurements fall within what values?

   b. How many of the measurements will be greater than 181mg/100mL?

   c. How many of the measurements will be greater than 167.5mg/100mL?

11. The recent starting salary of a massage therapist is $48,600 with a standard deviation of $1,600. Assuming that the salary follows a bell-curve, what percent of newly graduated massage therapists will have starting salaries below $53,400?

12. Birth weights display a bell-shaped distribution with a mean of 3,420 g and a standard deviation of 495 g. If a hospital wishes to set up special observation conditions for the lightest 2.5% of infants, determine the weight that separates the bottom 2.5% from the others.

13. The average biweekly amount contributed by the employees to the company's profit-sharing plan is $75.50, and the standard deviation is $8.45. Using Chebyshev's theorem, at least what percent of the contributions lies between $50.15 and $100.85?

14. The waiting time for patients seeking treatment at the emergency room has an unknown distribution with a mean of 90 minutes and a standard deviation of 15 minutes. Determine k such that a minimum of 96% of the waiting times are within k standard deviations of the mean. What is the range of values within k standard deviations of the mean?

15. The annual prices of stock offered by different pharmaceutical companies selling under $10 and over $50 are to be compared. The mean price of stocks selling for under $10 is $5.25 and the standard deviation $1.52. The mean price of stocks selling for over $50 is $92.50 and the standard deviation $5.28.

   a. To compare the dispersion in prices, why should the coefficient of variation be used?

   b. Calculate the coefficients of variation. What conclusion can you draw based on your calculations?

3 | Summary of Notation and Formulas

NOTATION

$P_k = k^{\text{th}}$ percentile

L = lowest value

Q_1 = first or lower quartile = P_{25}

Q_2 = second or middle quartile, or median = P_{50}

Q_3 = third or upper quartile = P_{75}

H = highest value

IQR = Interquartile Range

MAD = Mean Absolute Deviation from the mean

N = total number of data values in a population

n = total number of data values in a sample

μ = population mean

$\bar{x}$ = sample mean

σ^2 = population variance

s^2 = sample variance

σ = population standard deviation

s = sample standard deviation

CV = Coefficient of Variation

FORMULAS

Location of the kth Percentile | 3.1-a

$$L_k = \frac{k}{100} \cdot (n + 1)$$

Range | 3.1-b

Range = Maximum Value – Minimum Value

Interquartile Range | 3.1-c

Interquartile Range (IQR) = Upper Quartile (Q_3) – Lower Quartile (Q_1)

Mean Absolute Deviation from the Mean | 3.2-a

Mean Absolute Deviation from the Mean (MAD) = $\dfrac{\sum |x - \bar{x}|}{n}$

Variance of a Population | 3.2-b

$$\sigma^2 = \frac{\sum (x - \mu)^2}{N}$$

Variance of a Sample | 3.2-c

$$s^2 = \frac{\sum (x - \bar{x})^2}{n - 1} \quad \textbf{or} \quad s^2 = \frac{n \cdot (\sum x^2) - (\sum x)^2}{n(n - 1)}$$

Standard Deviation of a Population | 3.2-d

$$\sigma = \sqrt{\frac{\sum (x - \mu)^2}{N}}$$

Standard Deviation of a Sample | 3.2-e

$$s = \sqrt{\frac{\sum (x - \bar{x})^2}{n - 1}} \quad \textbf{or} \quad s = \sqrt{\frac{n \cdot (\sum x^2) - (\sum x)^2}{n(n - 1)}}$$

Coefficient of Variation | 3.2-f

$$CV_{\text{population}} = \frac{\sigma}{\mu} \times 100\% \quad \textbf{or} \quad CV_{\text{sample}} = \frac{s}{\bar{x}} \times 100\%$$

4 LINEAR CORRELATION AND REGRESSION

LEARNING OBJECTIVES

- Differentiate between independent variables and dependent variables.
- Create a scatter plot and identify possible relationships between the two variables.
- Compute the linear regression equation (line of best fit) using the least squares method and plot it against a scatter plot of the data.
- Interpret the slope and y-intercept of the line and use the regression equation to predict the value of the dependent variable for a selected value of the independent variable.
- Calculate the Pearson linear coefficient of correlation (r) to explain the type of relationship and calculate the coefficient of determination (r^2) to explain the strength of the relationship.
- Construct a residual plot and identify the outliers from a scatter plot.
- Define the terms 'explained deviation', 'unexplained deviation', and 'total deviation', calculate their values for a given data set, and use them to compute the coefficient of determination (r^2).

CHAPTER OUTLINE

4.1 Scatter Plots and Correlation

4.2 Linear Regression

Introduction

In Chapter 1, we introduced methods of visually displaying data. In all the examples given, there was only one value recorded for each piece of data. However, there are many instances where we may wish to record values for several variables for each piece of data - for example, health information about a patient, including age, height, weight, blood pressure, resting heart rate, number of hours of intense exercise per week, number of alcoholic drinks consumed per week, etc. If this information for a sample group of patients is to be summarized and displayed using the methods examined in Chapter 1, we would need a different chart for each piece of information (age, height, weight, etc.).

Often, however, we wish to be able to compare the values for two or more variables for each individual in the data set (e.g., resting heart rate and the number of hours of intense exercise per week) to determine the relationship between the two variables. Consider the following example, referring to ten adult male patients between the ages of 40-65:

Patient Number	Resting Heart Rate (bpm)	Intense Exercise (hours/week)
1	68	3.5
2	86	1.2
3	62	5.0
4	75	2.3
5	64	3.8
6	59	4.5
7	51	7.5
8	70	1.7
9	93	0.5
10	72	2.0

Imagine that someone asked you to summarize and interpret this data. Immediately, two questions come to mind:

1. How can we display this data in such a way that both pieces of information are displayed together for each patient?

2. What inferences can we make about the relationship between a patient's resting heart rate and the number of hours per week that the patient spends exercising intensely?

This chapter is devoted to answering these two questions in detail.

4.1 | Scatter Plots and Correlation

Independent and Dependent Variables

In order to properly answer the above two questions, we need to understand the following distinction:

The independent variable may be thought of as the **input** value, and the dependent variable may be thought of as the **output** value.

- An **independent variable** is the variable used for prediction, and it can take on any value within a certain range of values.

- A **dependent variable** is a variable that may have its value affected or predicted by the value of the independent variable (i.e., the value of the dependent variable *depends* on the value of the independent variable).

In our example above, the independent variable would be the number of hours of intense exercise per week, as that value could be anything between 0 and 168 (which is 24 hours per day, 7 days per week), and the dependent variable would be the resting heart rate, which may be partially determined by the value of the independent variable.

| Example 4.1-a | Identifying Independent and Dependent Variables |

For each of the following pairs of variables, identify which is most likely the independent variable and which is most likely the dependent variable:

(i)   Height (in cm) and mass (in kg) for a sample of adult females, aged 20-29 years.

(ii)   Length (in cm) and age (in months) for a sample of male children under the age of 2 years.

(iii)   Test mark (out of 50) and the time spent studying (in hours) for a sample of college students in a statistics course.

(iv)   The time spent working (in hours per week) and the time spent in recreation (in hours per week) for a sample of Canadian adults, aged 30-39 years.

Solution

(i)   The height (in cm) is the independent variable, and the mass (in kg) is the dependent variable, as it is affected by the height of the woman.

(ii)   The age (in months) of the child is the independent variable, and the length (in cm) is the dependent variable, as it is affected by the age of the child.

(iii)   The time spent studying (in hours) for the test is the independent variable, and the test mark (out of 50) is the dependent variable, as it is affected by the time spent studying.

(iv)   It is more difficult to identify the independent and dependent variables in this situation; however, it seems more likely that the hours spent working per week would (in part) determine the hours spent in recreation per week, and not the other way around. As such, it seems most likely that the time spent working is the independent variable and recreation time is the dependent variable.

Constructing X-Y Scatter Plots

In order to construct an X-Y scatter plot for a sample of paired data, follow the steps below:

Step 1:   Identify the independent and dependent variables.

Step 2:   Assign a 2-dimensional coordinate (x, y) to each piece of data, with the value of the independent variable assigned to the x-coordinate and the value of the dependent variable assigned to the y-coordinate.

Step 3:   Plot the sample of 2-dimensional coordinates as points on an X-Y rectangular coordinate system.

Step 4:   Include a chart title; a common chart title for an X-Y scatter plot is ***independent variable*** **vs *dependent variable***, where *independent variable* and *dependent variable* are the names of the independent and dependent variables, respectively.

Step 5:   Label the X- and Y-axes, including both the variable names and the units.

Example 4.1-b **Constructing an X-Y Scatter Plot**

Construct an X-Y scatter plot to visually display the Resting Heart Rate and Intense Exercise data introduced above:

Patient Number	Resting Heart Rate (bpm)	Intense Exercise (hours/week)
1	68	3.5
2	86	1.2
3	62	5.0
4	75	2.3
5	64	3.8
6	59	4.5
7	51	7.5
8	70	1.7
9	93	0.5
10	72	2.0

Solution

Since the hours of Intense Exercise (per week) is the independent variable and the Resting Heart Rate is the dependent variable, we will re-draw the above table, switching the two columns for convenience so that the independent variable (i.e., the x-coordinate) is listed first. Then we will add a column with the (x, y) coordinate point:

Patient Number	Intense Exercise (hours/week)	Resting Heart Rate (bpm)	(x, y) Coordinate Point
1	3.5	68	(3.5, 68)
2	1.2	86	(1.2, 86)
3	5.0	62	(5.0, 62)
4	2.3	75	(2.3, 75)
5	3.8	64	(3.8, 64)
6	4.5	59	(4.5, 59)
7	7.5	51	(7.5, 51)
8	1.7	70	(1.7, 70)
9	0.5	93	(0.5, 93)
10	2.0	72	(2.0, 72)

Now we take the (x, y) coordinate points and plot them on an X-Y rectangular coordinate system to construct the X-Y scatter plot, ensuring to include both a title and axis labels (with units):

Solution
continued

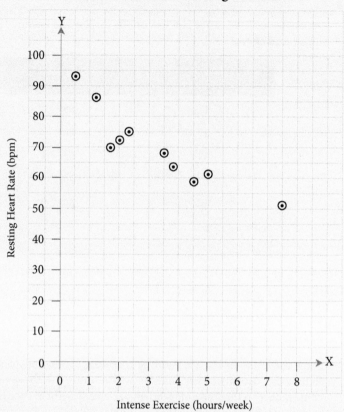

Intense Exercise vs Resting Heart Rate

Pearson's Linear Correlation Coefficient 'r'

The above scatter plot seems to indicate that there is a relationship between the number of hours of intense exercise an adult male performs each week and his resting heart rate. More specifically, it appears that as the number of hours of intense exercise performed each week increases, his resting heart rate decreases. However, this is not always true, as the three data points around two hours per week show a slight increase in resting heart rate as the number of hours of intense exercise increases - the opposite of the overall apparent trend. How then do we quantify this (non-perfect) downward relationship?

The English mathematician Karl Pearson came up with a value 'r' which would describe the strength of the **linear relationship** between two variables; this value is called **Pearson's Linear Correlation Coefficient** and is calculated by the following formula:

Formula 4.1	**Pearson's Linear Correlation Coefficient**

r essentially calculates the total "joint" deviation of the two variables and then normalizes that value as a proportion of the individual data sets' total deviations.

$$r = \frac{n\left(\sum xy\right) - \left(\sum x\right)\left(\sum y\right)}{\sqrt{n\left(\sum x^2\right) - \left(\sum x\right)^2} \cdot \sqrt{n\left(\sum y^2\right) - \left(\sum y\right)^2}}$$

Note: The correlation coefficient r is typically evaluated to a precision of three decimal places.

| Example 4.1-c | Calculating Pearson's Linear Correlation Coefficient |

Calculate Pearson's Linear Correlation Coefficient for the data set from Example 4.1-b.

Solution

In order to calculate the correlation coefficient, we first need to calculate the five summation values seen in the formula for r: Σx, Σx^2, Σy, Σy^2, and Σxy. This is most easily done by adding extra columns to the table and a summation row at the bottom:

Patient Number	x-values	y-values	x²-values	y²-values	xy-values
1	3.5	68	12.25	4,624	238
2	1.2	86	1.44	7,396	103.2
3	5.0	62	25	3,844	310
4	2.3	75	5.29	5,625	172.5
5	3.8	64	14.44	4,096	243.2
6	4.5	59	20.25	3,481	265.5
7	7.5	51	56.25	2,601	382.5
8	1.7	70	2.89	4,900	119
9	0.5	93	0.25	8,649	46.5
10	2.0	72	4	5,184	144
$n = 10$	$\Sigma x = 32$	$\Sigma y = 700$	$\Sigma x^2 = 142.06$	$\Sigma y^2 = 50,400$	$\Sigma xy = 2,024.4$

Using Formula 4.1,

$$r = \frac{n\left(\sum xy\right) - \left(\sum x\right)\left(\sum y\right)}{\sqrt{n\left(\sum x^2\right) - \left(\sum x\right)^2} \cdot \sqrt{n\left(\sum y^2\right) - \left(\sum y\right)^2}}$$

$$= \frac{10(2,024.4) - (32)(700)}{\sqrt{10(142.06) - (32)^2} \cdot \sqrt{10(50,400) - (700)^2}}$$

$$= \frac{-2,156}{\sqrt{396.6} \cdot \sqrt{14,000}}$$

$$= \frac{-2,156}{2,356.353114...}$$

$$= -0.914973... = -0.915$$

Therefore, $r = -0.915$.

Interpreting the Linear Correlation Coefficient

In order to understand the result of the r-value calculated above, we need to first understand what the correlation coefficient measures. As previously mentioned, r measures the total "joint" deviation:

- For a given point, if the x- and y-values both deviate from their respective means in the *same* direction (i.e., both above the mean or both below the mean), the joint deviation will be *positive*.

- For a given point, if the x- and y-values deviate from their respective means in the *opposite* directions (i.e., one above its mean and one below its mean), the joint deviation will be *negative*.

If most of the individual joint deviations are positive, the total joint deviation will be positive as well. Similarly, if most of the individual joint deviations are negative, the total joint deviation will be negative as well. If there is a fairly even mixture of positive and negative individual joint deviations, the total joint deviation will be 0. The total joint deviation is then divided by the total deviations of each of the two individual data sets.

Based on all the above information, the linear correlation coefficient r has the following properties:

- r is always a real number between –1 and +1 (inclusive); i.e., $-1 \leq r \leq 1$

- If r is positive, the correlation is positive (i.e., the data on the X-Y scatter plot would appear to have a positive slope); if it is equal to +1, the correlation is perfect and positive.

- If r is negative, the correlation is negative (i.e., the data on the X-Y scatter plot would appear to have a negative slope); if it is equal to –1, the correlation is perfect and negative.

- The closer the value of r is to +1 or –1, the stronger the linear correlation, which implies that there is a high likelihood of an actual linear relationship between the two variables.

  - An r-value with an absolute value greater than or equal to 0.7 is considered to imply **strong correlation**.

  - An r-value with an absolute value greater than or equal to 0.5 but less than 0.7 is considered to imply **moderate correlation**.

- The closer the value of r is to 0, the weaker the linear correlation, which implies that there is a low likelihood of an actual linear relationship between the two variables.

  - An r-value with an absolute value greater than or equal to 0.3 but less than 0.5 is considered to imply **weak correlation**.

  - An r-value with an absolute value less than 0.3 is considered to imply **very weak** to **no correlation**.

- r only measures the strength of a *linear* relationship; it does not indicate whether there are other relationships present between the two data sets.

- r does not distinguish between the independent and dependent variables, since x and y are interchangeable in the formula.

- r only measures *correlation*, **not** *causation;* since it does not distinguish between the independent and dependent variables, it cannot be used to conclude that a change in one variable *causes* a change in the other, only that the changes in variables are *related*.

We summarize these properties in the following table and diagram of some examples:

Table 4.1 Correlation Coefficient r and Strength of Relationship

Correlation Coefficient (r)	Strength of Relationship
$r = 1.0$	Perfect and Positive
$0.7 \leq r < 1.0$	Strong and Positive
$0.5 \leq r < 0.7$	Moderate and Positive
$0.3 \leq r < 0.5$	Weak and Positive
$0.1 \leq r < 0.3$	Very Weak and Positive
$r = -1.0$	Perfect and Negative
$-1.0 < r \leq -0.7$	Strong and Negative
$-0.7 < r \leq -0.5$	Moderate and Negative
$-0.5 < r \leq -0.3$	Weak and Negative
$-0.3 < r \leq -0.1$	Very Weak and Negative
$-0.1 < r < 0.1$	No Correlation

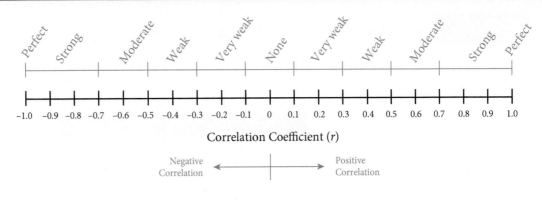

Correlation Coefficient (r)

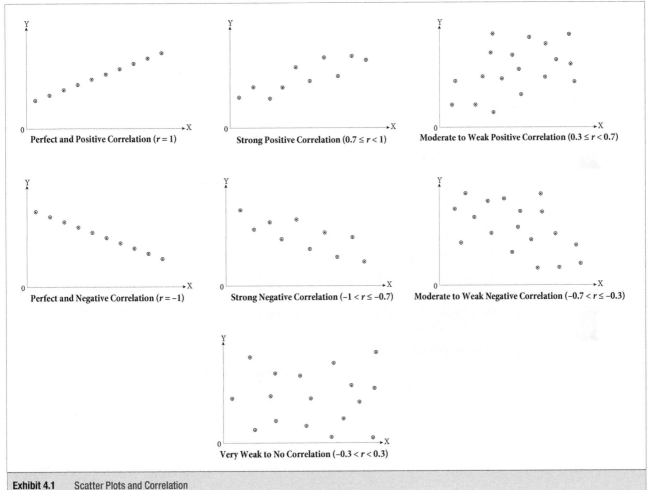

Exhibit 4.1   Scatter Plots and Correlation

Example 4.1-d   **Interpreting the Linear Correlation Coefficient**

Interpret the linear correlation coefficient calculated in Example 4.1-c and what that tells us about the data.

Solution

Recall, the value calculated for the linear correlation coefficient was $r = -0.915$. Since this value is negative and close to -1 (absolute value greater than 0.7), we can deduce that there is strong negative linear correlation present in the data. This implies that there is a high likelihood of a negative linear relationship between the number of hours of intense exercise per week for an adult male and his resting heart rate (i.e., a higher number of hours of intense exercise per week is very likely to be related to a lower resting heart rate).

Example 4.1-e	Using the Linear Correlation Coefficient to Analyze Paired Data

The monthly premium quoted by an insurance company for a 10-year-term, $100,000 critical illness policy was collected from a sample of twelve adult female non-smokers, between the ages of 25 and 55:

Age (in years)	Monthly Premium ($)
36	68
52	324
25	37
45	292
39	129
47	255
55	512
33	173
45	461
28	72
50	275
31	97

(i)   Plot this data on an X-Y scatter plot.

(ii)   Calculate the linear correlation coefficient (r) for this set of data.

(iii)   Interpret the meaning of r in the context of the data.

Solution

(i)   First, we identify the independent and dependent variables: in this case, Age is independent (x) and Monthly Premium is dependent (y).

Next, we plot the data on a scatter plot:

Age vs Monthly Critical Illness Insurance Premium

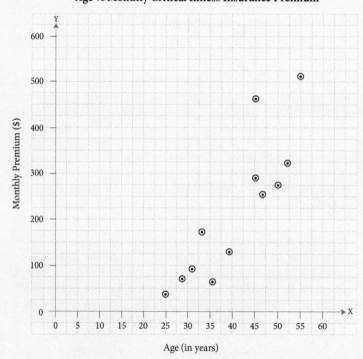

Age (in years)

(ii)   Fill in the table for x^2, y^2, and xy, and add a row at the bottom for the totals:

Data Number	Age (x)	Monthly Premium (y)	x^2	y^2	xy
1	36	68	1,296	4,624	2,448
2	52	324	2,704	104,976	16,848
3	25	37	625	1,369	925
4	45	292	2,025	85,264	13,140
5	39	129	1,521	16,641	5,031
6	47	255	2,209	65,025	11,985
7	55	512	3,025	262,144	28,160
8	33	173	1,089	29,929	5,709
9	45	461	2,025	212,521	20,745
10	28	72	784	5,184	2,016
11	50	275	2,500	75,625	13,750
12	31	97	961	9,409	3,007
$n = 12$	$\Sigma x = 486$	$\Sigma y = 2,695$	$\Sigma x^2 = 20,764$	$\Sigma y^2 = 872,711$	$\Sigma xy = 123,764$

Using Formula 4.1,

$$r = \frac{n\left(\sum xy\right) - \left(\sum x\right)\left(\sum y\right)}{\sqrt{n\left(\sum x^2\right) - \left(\sum x\right)^2} \cdot \sqrt{n\left(\sum y^2\right) - \left(\sum y\right)^2}}$$

$$= \frac{12(123,764) - (486)(2,695)}{\sqrt{12(20,764) - (486)^2} \cdot \sqrt{12(872,711) - (2,695)^2}}$$

$$= \frac{175,398}{\sqrt{12,972} \cdot \sqrt{3,209,507}}$$

$$= \frac{175,398}{204,043.4385\ldots}$$

$$= 0.859611\ldots = 0.860$$

Therefore, $r = 0.860$.

(iii)   This implies that there is a strong positive correlation between the age of the applicant and her monthly critical illness insurance premium (i.e., older age in females is highly likely to be related to higher critical illness insurance premiums).

4.1 | Exercises

Answers to odd-numbered problems are available at the end of the textbook.

For Problems 1 to 10, look at the scatterplot and identify the type of correlation (positive linear correlation, negative linear correlation, non-linear correlation, or no correlation) that is most likely present in the data. If linear correlation exists, identify whether it is perfect, strong, or moderate-weak.

1.

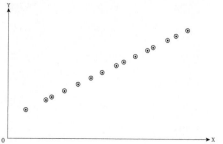

2.

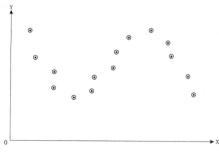

3.

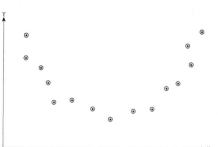

4.

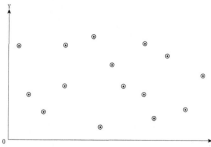

5.

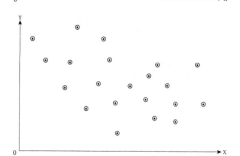

6.

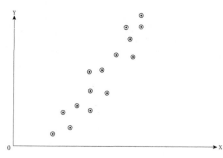

7.

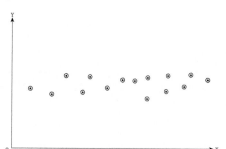

8.

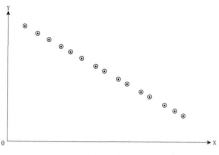

9.

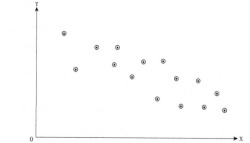

10.

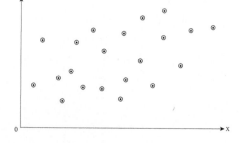

For Problems 11 to 18, complete the following instructions:

(i) Identify the independent and dependent variables.

(ii) Construct an X-Y scatterplot for the paired data. You may wish to use Excel or some other software.

(iii) Calculate and interpret the Pearson correlation coefficient r for the paired data. Be sure to indicate if the correlation is positive or negative, and whether it is strong, moderate, or weak, or if there does not appear to be any significant correlation.

11. A family physician compares the number of flu cases she diagnosed with the number of flu shots she administered each year for the last five years to see if there is a correlation between the data.

Number of flu cases diagnosed	Number of flu vaccinations administered
35	48
18	56
7	94
15	61
12	78

12. A family physician compares the price charged for a physician's note by six different clinics nearby and the number of notes requested in the last three months at each clinic to see if there is a correlation between the number of notes requested and the cost of the note. All six clinics see approximately the same number of patients each year.

Number of physician's notes issued in 3 months	Price of physician's note ($)
44	25
18	60
93	15
65	30
82	20
56	40

13. A researcher is trying to determine if the number of alcoholic drinks consumed at a social event affects the number of cigarettes smoked by smokers who desire to quit. She conducts a study whereby participants are asked to record the number of alcoholic drinks they consume over the course of seven social events, along with the number of cigarettes they smoke. One of the male participants records the following results:

Number of Alcoholic Drinks	Number of Cigarettes
2	1
5	3
3	0
5	5
4	2
7	5
4	3

14. The researcher in Problem 13 collects the results from a female participant in the study:

Number of Alcoholic Drinks	Number of Cigarettes
2	2
0	4
3	0
1	3
2	1
4	0
0	3

15. A physician records the LDL cholesterol level and the BMI for a sample of 10 of his overweight patients (BMI of 25 or more) to see if there is a correlation between the data:

Cholesterol Level (mg/dL)	BMI
89	27.5
106	31.2
135	34.8
182	30.9
117	29.6
205	37.0
94	32.5
76	28.8
128	26.2
144	31.3

16. In a study about the effectiveness of a new pain relief drug, 10 patients with similar medical conditions were given the ability to self-administer the new drug, but each with a different calibration for how much of the drug may be administered at one time (between 5 and 10 mg). The time between self-administered doses was recorded over a period of 24 hours, and the average time between doses was calculated for each patient and compared to the size of the dose given. All ten patients were approximately the same weight and with similar pain management needs.

Average time between doses (in hr)	Size of dose (in mg)
4.5	8.5
2.4	5.0
4.8	6.0
6.5	9.0
3.2	7.5
1.8	5.5
3.4	8.0
6.3	10.0
4.1	6.5
4.4	7.0

17. A nutritionist performs a study where a patient records the calories she consumed (as a percent of her baseline daily target) and the number of minutes she spent running on the treadmill every day over the course of two weeks to see if there is a correlation between the data.

Number of Minutes Running on Treadmill	% of Baseline Daily Calories Consumed
30	112
40	105
90	120
15	96
10	102
20	108
0	105
60	116
45	105
20	114
30	112
40	125
0	108
0	95

18. A nutrition researcher performs a study where 12 overweight adult males are each assigned a certain number of minutes of monitored treadmill running every day and their weight loss (in lb) after two weeks is recorded. All the participants were approximately the same weight to begin, were given a controlled diet to eat, and the speed of the treadmill was the same for all participants.

Number of minutes of running per day	Weight lost in 2 weeks (in lb)
30	4.6
40	5.4
25	2.8
15	0.6
10	2.4
20	1.4
25	7.2
30	3.0
45	5.6
20	2.4
30	5.2
35	4.0

19. A professor believes that there is a correlation between the number of homework questions a student completes and his/her mark on their final exam. At the end of the semester, he asks students to fill out a survey online answering the number of homework questions they completed and compares that to their final exam marks. A total of 10 students respond to the survey and the professor compares those responses to the final grades of those 10 students. He then calculates an r-value of 0.765, and concludes that there is strong positive correlation between the number of homework questions completed and the final exam mark. Identify three problems with this study that may have skewed his results.

20. A manager at a high-end restaurant claims that people who order expensive wine tip better. He takes a sample of 20 receipts from the end of the evening where the table ordered a bottle of wine, and compares the price of the bottle of wine to the amount of tip that was left. He notices that the results tend to match his hypothesis, with the exception of two obvious outliers, which are so far removed from the rest of the data that he discards them and uses the remaining 18 receipts. The correlation coefficient generated with the remaining 18 receipts is $r = 0.918$. Based on this result, he concludes there is strong positive correlation between people who buy expensive wine and people who tip well. Identify three problems with this study that may have skewed his results.

21. A researcher compares the cost of a certain medical procedure and the average salary of a nurse over the past 20 years and comes up with a correlation coefficient of $r = 0.825$. Based on this, she concludes that the rising costs associated with nurses' salaries have driven up the cost of the medical procedure. Identify at least two problems with this conclusion, and suggest a lurking variable that may have contributed to this result, which was not taken into consideration.

22. A physician compares the number of glasses of water that her patients consume per day and their body weight. Her study yields a correlation coefficient of $r = -0.636$, and so she concludes that drinking more water every day will cause a reduction in body weight. Identify at least two problems with this conclusion, and suggest a lurking variable that may have contributed to this result which, was not taken into consideration.

4.2 | Linear Regression

When there is significant linear correlation present in the data, it would be useful to be able to model the data using a graph and equation of a linear function. This linear model is known as the **least-squares regression line**, or simply the **line of best fit**, and it also allows us to make predictions about the dependent variable based on the value of the independent variable.

The Linear Regression Equation

The least-squares regression line for a set of paired data has the following equation:

$$\hat{y} = a + bx$$

where $\hat{y}$ (pronounced "y-hat") is the predicted value for y based on a given x-value, a is the y-intercept of the line, and b is the slope of the line. These values can be computed using the x- and y-values of the sample paired data:

Formula 4.2-a

Slope of the Least-Squares Regression Line

$$b = \frac{n\left(\sum xy\right) - \left(\sum x\right)\left(\sum y\right)}{n\left(\sum x^2\right) - \left(\sum x\right)^2}$$

Formula 4.2-b

y-intercept of the Least-Squares Regression Line

$$a = \bar{y} - b \cdot \bar{x}$$

where $\bar{x}$ and $\bar{y}$ are the sample means of the individual sets of data for the two variables x and y; i.e.,

$\bar{x} = \dfrac{\sum x}{n}$ and $\bar{y} = \dfrac{\sum y}{n}$.

Note: The formula for b is very similar to the formula for r, with one important difference: the denominator for b is only based on the total variation for x. As such, x and y are not interchangeable in this equation, and so correctly identifying the independent and dependent variables is very important.

Properties of the Regression Line

It is important to identify some important properties about the linear regression equation:

- Like the correlation coefficient, it only models a *linear* relationship.
- The linear regression equation is only useful for modelling data with significant linear correlation.
- The linear regression line always passes through the point $(\bar{x}, \bar{y})$.
- Unlike the correlation coefficient, the choice of independent and dependent variables matters; i.e., the values of a and b will be different if x and y are interchanged.
- The $\hat{y}$-value calculated for a particular x-value is the *predicted* value of the dependent variable, **not** the actual value.
- The linear regression equation will minimize the total squared deviation between the predicted values and actual values of y for a given value of x.

- Both b and r will have the same sign, since their numerators are identical and their denominators are always positive; i.e., if the correlation is positive, the slope of the regression line will be positive, and if the correlation is negative, the slope of the regression line will be negative.
- The regression coefficients a and b are typically rounded to three significant digits.
- The regression equation calculated above is based on *sample data* and, as such, it is only an **estimate** for the true population regression equation, given by the formula $\hat{y} = \alpha + \beta x$.

| Example 4.2-a | Finding the Least-Squares Regression Equation |

Find the equation of the least-squares regression line that best fits the Intense Exercise vs Resting Heart Rate data from Example 4.1-b:

Patient Number	Intense Exercise (hours/week) x-values	Resting Heart Rate (bpm) y-values
1	3.5	68
2	1.2	86
3	5.0	62
4	2.3	75
5	3.8	64
6	4.5	59
7	7.5	51
8	1.7	70
9	0.5	93
10	2.0	72

Solution

Recall the following table from Example 4.1-c when we computed r for this data set:

Patient Number	x-values	y-values	x^2-values	y^2-values	xy-values
1	3.5	68	12.25	4,624	238
2	1.2	86	1.44	7,396	103.2
3	5.0	62	25	3,844	310
4	2.3	75	5.29	5,625	172.5
5	3.8	64	14.44	4,096	243.2
6	4.5	59	20.25	3,481	265.5
7	7.5	51	56.25	2,601	382.5
8	1.7	70	2.89	4,900	119
9	0.5	93	0.25	8,649	46.5
10	2.0	72	4	5,184	144
$n = 10$	$\Sigma x = 32$	$\Sigma y = 700$	$\Sigma x^2 = 142.06$	$\Sigma y^2 = 50,400$	$\Sigma xy = 2,024.4$

Solution
continued

Using Formulas 4.2-a and 4.2-b,

$$b = \frac{n\left(\sum xy\right) - \left(\sum x\right)\left(\sum y\right)}{n\left(\sum x^2\right) - \left(\sum x\right)^2}$$

$$= \frac{10(2{,}024.4) - (32)(700)}{10(142.06) - (32)^2}$$

$$= \frac{-2{,}156}{396.6}$$

$$= -5.436207\ldots = -5.44$$

$$a = \bar{y} - b \cdot \bar{x}$$

$$= \left(\frac{700}{10}\right) - (-5.436207\ldots) \cdot \left(\frac{32}{10}\right)$$

$$= 70 + 17.395864\ldots$$

$$= 87.395864\ldots = 87.4$$

> Use the exact value of b when calculating a (i.e., not the value rounded to 3 significant digits).

Therefore, the least-squares regression equation that best fits the data is $\hat{y} = 87.4 - 5.44x$.

Graphing the Least-Squares Regression Line (Line of Best Fit)

Once we know the linear regression equation that best fits the data, we can plot it on a scatter plot of the data, as follows:

Step 1: Substitute the least x-value in the data (i.e., the x-value of the left-most point on the scatter plot), denoted x_1, into the regression equation to obtain a value for $\hat{y}_1$.

Step 2: Substitute the greatest x-value in the data (i.e., the x-value of the right-most point on the scatter plot), denoted x_2, into the regression equation to obtain a value for $\hat{y}_2$.

Drawing a linear graph requires only two points. However, at least three points will ensure that the formed line truly represents the given equation.

Step 3: Plot the two points calculated above, $(x_1, \hat{y}_1)$ and $(x_2, \hat{y}_2)$, onto the scatter plot and connect the points with a straight line.

Step 4: Substitute any value between the least and greatest x-values in the data, denoted x_3, into the linear regression equation to obtain a value for $\hat{y}_3$. Use this point as a checkpoint.

Note: Since we know the point $(\bar{x}, \bar{y})$ should lie on the regression line, we can use this as the checkpoint.

| Example 4.2-b | Graphing the Least-Squares Regression Line |

Graph the least-squares regression line using the regression equation calculated in Example 4.2-a onto a scatter plot of the data.

Solution

Recall, the linear regression equation calculated in Example 4.2-a is $\hat{y} = 87.4 - 5.44x$.

The least x-value in the data set is $x_1 = 0.5$ - substitute this value into the regression equation to obtain $\hat{y}_1$:

$$\hat{y}_1 = 87.4 - 5.44(0.5) \approx 84.7$$

The greatest x-value in the data set is $x_2 = 7.5$ - substitute this value into the regression equation to obtain $\hat{y}_2$:

$$\hat{y}_2 = 87.4 - 5.44(7.5) = 46.6$$

Now we plot these two points, $(0.5, 84.7)$ and $(7.5, 46.6)$, on the scatter plot of the data (constructed in Example 4.1-b) and connect the two points with a straight line, as shown below:

Solution
continued

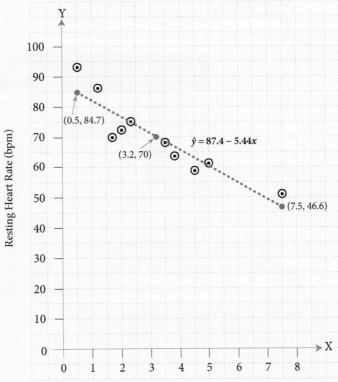

Intense Exercise vs Resting Heart Rate

(0.5, 84.7)

(3.2, 70)

$\hat{y} = 87.4 - 5.44x$

(7.5, 46.6)

Resting Heart Rate (bpm)

Intense Exercise (hours/week)

Finally, we calculate the point $(\bar{x}, \bar{y})$ as a checkpoint. Using the data from Example 4.2-a,

$$\bar{x} = \frac{\Sigma x}{n} = \frac{32}{10} = 3.2 \qquad \bar{y} = \frac{\Sigma y}{n} = \frac{700}{10} = 70$$

Plotting the point (3.2, 70) on the scatter plot, we see that it falls on our regression line.

Interpreting the Linear Regression Equation

The slope of the regression equation (b) is known as the marginal change and represents the predicted change in the dependent variable for a unit change in the independent variable. In other words, if x increases by 1 unit, y is expected to change by b units (increase if $b > 0$ and decrease if $b < 0$).

The y-intercept of the regression equation (a) is the predicted value for y if $x = 0$. In many situations, where $x = 0$ is not a reasonable value for the independent variable, this value does not have a practical meaning. For example, in a height vs. weight regression equation, a height of 0 cm is infeasible, so the value of a does not have a practical meaning in terms of weight (and may, in fact, be negative!)

| Example 4.2-c | Interpreting the Regression Equation |

Interpret the slope and y-intercept of the linear regression equation calculated in Example 4.2-a for the Exercise vs. Heart Rate data: $\hat{y} = 87.4 - 5.44x$. Be sure to state whether the y-intercept has a practical meaning in the context of the data.

Solution

The slope of the regression equation is −5.44, which means that for every increase of one hour of intense exercise per week, the resting heart rate of an adult male between the ages of 40-65 is expected to decrease by 5.44 bpm.

The y-intercept of the regression equation is 87.4, which means that an adult male between the ages of 40-65 who does no intense exercise (i.e., 0 hours/week) is expected to have a resting heart rate of 87.4 bpm. This value does indeed have a practical meaning, since it is possible for an adult male between the ages of 40-65 to do 0 hours of intense exercise per week.

| Example 4.2-d | Determining and Interpreting the Regression Equation |

Determine the regression equation for the Age vs Monthly Insurance Premium data from Example 4.1-e. Then interpret the values of the slope and y-intercept of the equation in context of the data.

Age (in years)	Monthly Premium ($)
36	68
52	324
25	37
45	292
39	129
47	255
55	512
33	173
45	461
28	72
50	275
31	97

Solution

Recall the completed table from the solution of Example 4.1-e:

Data Number	Age (x)	Monthly Premium (y)	x^2	y^2	xy
1	36	68	1,296	4,624	2,448
2	52	324	2,704	104,986	16,848
3	25	37	625	1,369	925
4	45	292	2,025	85,264	13,140
5	39	129	1,521	16,641	5,031
6	47	255	2,209	65,025	11,985
7	55	512	3,025	262,144	28,160
8	33	173	1,089	29,929	5,709
9	45	461	2,025	212,521	20,745
10	28	72	784	5,184	2,016
11	50	275	2,500	75,625	13,750
12	31	97	961	9,409	3,007
$n = 12$	$\Sigma x = 486$	$\Sigma y = 2,695$	$\Sigma x^2 = 20,764$	$\Sigma y^2 = 872,711$	$\Sigma xy = 123,764$

Using Formulas 4.2-a and 4.2-b,

$$b = \frac{n\left(\Sigma xy\right) - \left(\Sigma x\right)\left(\Sigma y\right)}{n\left(\Sigma x^2\right) - \left(\Sigma x\right)^2}$$

$$= \frac{12(123,764) - (486)(2,695)}{12(20,764) - (486)^2}$$

$$= \frac{175,398}{12,972}$$

$$= 13.521276\ldots = 13.5$$

$$a = \bar{y} - b \cdot \bar{x}$$

$$= \left(\frac{2,695}{12}\right) - (13.521276\ldots) \cdot \left(\frac{486}{12}\right)$$

$$= 224.583333\ldots - 547.611702\ldots$$

$$= -323.028368\ldots = -323$$

Therefore, the linear regression equation is $\hat{y} = -323 + 13.5x$.

The slope of the regression equation is 13.5, which means that for every increase of one year in age, the monthly insurance premium of an adult female non-smoker between the ages of 25 and 55 is expected to increase by $13.50.

The y-intercept of the regression equation is -323, which means that an adult female, age 0, will have a predicted monthly critical illness insurance premium of $-\$323$. This value does **not** have a practical meaning, as first of all, the data is only for adult females between the ages of 25-55, so it does not make sense to use this model to predict the monthly critical illness insurance premium for a newborn; and secondly, it is not possible to have a negative monthly insurance premium.

Making Predictions with the Linear Regression Equation

Now that we know how to calculate the regression equation and how to interpret it, we can use it to make predictions for the value of the dependent variable given a value for the independent variable.

Before we can make any predictions, however, we first need to ensure that there is significant linear correlation. The table below is used to measure an observed r-value against **critical r-values** in order to determine if there is significant linear correlation. If the value calculated for r for a given data set is larger than the corresponding critical value listed in the table based on the sample size, then the variables are said to have significant linear correlation at the **5% significance level**. This means that there is less than a 5% chance that there is actually no correlation between the variables and that the value for r was just a fluke. Put in a positive way, we can say that if the value for r exceeds the value in the table for the given sample size, we are **at least 95% confident** that there actually exists linear correlation between the two variables.

In order to use the table, first calculate the degrees of freedom (df), which in this case is ($n - 2$) (i.e., the sample size minus 2). Then compare the calculated value of r to the critical value listed beside the corresponding degrees of freedom.

| Table 4.2 | 5% Significance Table for r |

For r-values, there are ($n - 2$) degrees of freedom, because it measures the relationship between two variables.

df ($n - 2$)	r	df ($n - 2$)	r
1	0.997	16	0.468
2	0.950	17	0.456
3	0.878	18	0.444
4	0.811	19	0.433
5	0.754	20	0.423
6	0.707	21	0.413
7	0.666	22	0.404
8	0.632	23	0.396
9	0.602	24	0.388
10	0.576	25	0.381
11	0.553	26	0.374
12	0.532	27	0.367
13	0.514	28	0.361
14	0.497	29	0.355
15	0.482	30	0.349

- If the value for r **does not** indicate that linear correlation exists between the variables at the 5% significance level, the best prediction for y is $\bar{y}$ (the mean), regardless of the value for x.

- If the value for r **does** indicate that linear correlation exists between the variables at the 5% significance level, the best prediction for y is $\hat{y}$, when the value for x is substituted into the linear regression equation.

| Example 4.2-e | **Making Predictions using the Regression Equation** |

Using the regression equation $\hat{y} = -323 + 13.5x$, as computed for the Age vs Monthly Insurance Premium data in Example 4.2-d, predict the monthly critical illness insurance premium for a 40-year-old female applicant.

Solution

First of all, we recall that the correlation coefficient for this data was computed to be $r = 0.860$ in Example 4.1-e. Comparing to the critical value in the table for $df = 12 - 2 = 10$ (since $n = 12$) of 0.576, we see that the calculated r-value is greater than the critical value, which indicates significant linear correlation is present between the variables. As such, the best prediction for the monthly insurance premium for this applicant will come from substituting her age ($x = 40$) into the regression equation:

$$\hat{y} = -323 + 13.5(40) = 217$$

Therefore, we predict the 40-year-old female applicant will be quoted a monthly premium of $217 for her critical illness insurance.

Residuals

The linear regression equation is a good method of predicting the y-value given an x-value in situations where there is significant linear correlation between the two variables. However, it does not tell us what the *actual value* (y) of the dependent variable is - only the *predicted value* ($\hat{y}$). In fact, the actual y-value could be anything, though it is assumed that the distribution of possible y-values for a given x-value is bell-curved, symmetrical, and centred at the predicted value $\hat{y}$, meaning that the most-likely value for the dependent variable is the predicted value $\hat{y}$.

Despite the fact that $\hat{y}$ is the most-likely value for y given a value for x, most of the actual values for y will differ from those predicted by the regression equation, due to both randomness and the impact of other variables that are unaccounted for by the regression equation. The difference between the actual value of the dependent variable and the predicted value is known as a **residual**.

For example, consider the following graph of data with a linear regression equation of $\hat{y} = 0.9 + 2.5x$:

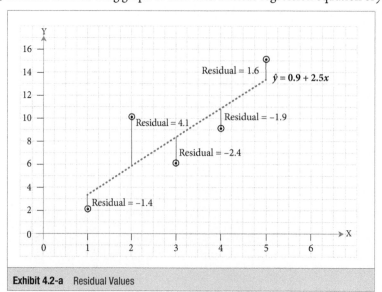

Exhibit 4.2-a   Residual Values

We can take the resulting residuals and plot them on their own chart, called a **Residual Plot**:

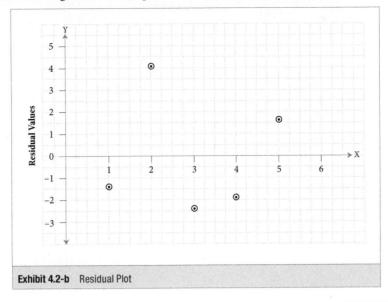

Exhibit 4.2-b   Residual Plot

Example 4.2-f   **Constructing a Residual Plot**

Construct a residual plot for the Age vs Monthly Insurance Premium data using the regression equation from Example 4.2-d: $\hat{y} = -323 + 13.5x$

Age (in years)	Monthly Premium ($)
36	68
52	324
25	37
45	292
39	129
47	255
55	512
33	173
45	461
28	72
50	275
31	97

Solution

We need to add two columns to the chart above: one for the predicted value $\hat{y}$ of the dependent variable, rounded to the nearest dollar (i.e., the same precision as the actual y-values), and one for the residual.

Age (*x*)	Monthly Premium (*y*)	Predicted Premium ($\hat{y}$)	Residual ($y - \hat{y}$)
36	68	$-323 + 13.5(36) = 163$	$68 - 163 = -95$
52	324	$-323 + 13.5(52) = 379$	$324 - 379 = -55$
25	37	$-323 + 13.5(25) \approx 15$	$37 - 15 = 22$
45	292	$-323 + 13.5(45) \approx 285$	$292 - 285 = 7$
39	129	$-323 + 13.5(39) \approx 204$	$129 - 204 = -75$
47	255	$-323 + 13.5(47) \approx 312$	$255 - 312 = -57$
55	512	$-323 + 13.5(55) \approx 420$	$512 - 420 = 92$
33	173	$-323 + 13.5(33) \approx 123$	$173 - 123 = 50$
45	461	$-323 + 13.5(45) \approx 285$	$461 - 285 = 176$
28	72	$-323 + 13.5(28) = 55$	$72 - 55 = 17$
50	275	$-323 + 13.5(50) = 352$	$275 - 352 = -77$
31	97	$-323 + 13.5(31) \approx 96$	$97 - 96 = 1$

Now we graph a residual plot using the data from the first (X) and last (Y) columns of the above table:

Residual Plot for Age vs Monthly Insurance Premiums

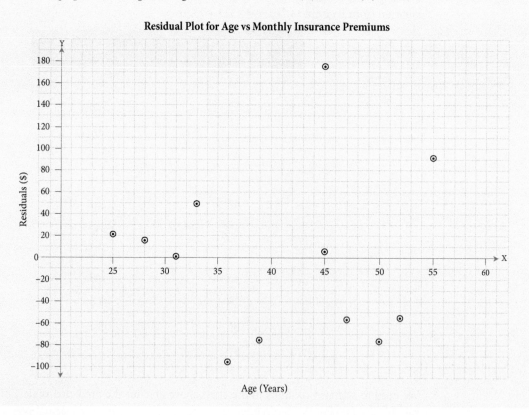

Outliers

Recall from previous chapters that an **outlier** is a value that is very different from the rest of the data set. On a scatter plot it can easily be identified as it is typically far removed from the rest of the data. For example, in the previous residual plot for Age vs Insurance Premiums, the point (45, 176) is an outlier.

Sometimes these outliers can significantly affect the regression line. Such outliers are called **influential points** and they can often skew the results of a regression analysis to the point of being worthless, especially when working with small samples.

Example 4.2-g	Identifying Outliers in a Scatter Plot

Consider the following data recorded by a high school math teacher for his class of 15 students, comparing the quiz mark received (out of 25) by each student to the number of homework questions completed (out of the 60 assigned):

Quiz Mark	24	23	20	24	20	14	10	17	24	17	15	22	20	17	17
Homework Questions Completed	54	50	41	53	50	58	28	39	60	44	34	56	10	38	45

Plot the data and regression line on a scatter plot, and identify any outliers present in the data.

Solution

First, we need to identify the independent and dependent variables.

In our example, it is reasonable to assume that the quiz mark would be dependent on the number of homework questions completed, which would be the independent variable. So our first row (quiz mark) represents the y-variable, and the second row (homework questions completed) represents the x-variable.

Using Formulas 4.2-a and 4.2-b (as previously shown), or inputting the values into Excel or some other statistical software, we can determine the regression equation to be:

$$\hat{y} = 12.8 + 0.139x$$

Inputting the least x-value, $x_1 = 10$, and greatest x-value, $x_2 = 60$, into the regression equation, we obtain the two end-points of the regression line: (10, 14.19) and (60, 21.14).

Plotting the data points and regression line on a scatter plot:

Checkpoint: the regression line passes through the point $(\bar{x}, \bar{y}) \approx (44, 18.9)$

Homework Questions Completed vs Quiz Mark

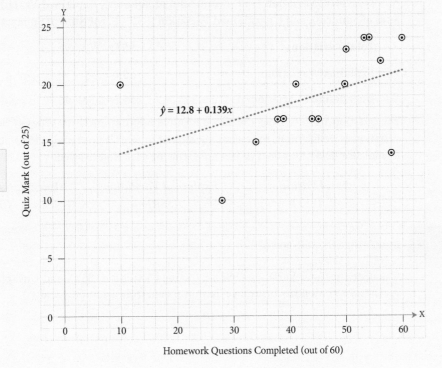

$\hat{y} = 12.8 + 0.139x$

Solution
continued

A positive, moderate-strong correlation is clearly visible between the number of homework questions completed and quiz mark received. However, the quiz mark received by the student who completed 10 homework questions is considerably higher than the trend would suggest, and the quiz mark received by the student who completed 58 questions is considerably lower. Therefore, the points (10, 20) and (58, 14) are outliers. These outlier values account for the reason that the regression line is less steep than the trend of the data may suggest.

Note: The point (10, 20) seems to especially affect the slope of the regression line, which suggests that it may be an influential point.

Explained vs Unexplained Variation

As mentioned previously, if there was no significant linear correlation between the two variables, our best prediction for an unknown y-value would be the mean $\bar{y}$.

- The difference between the actual value (y) and the mean value ($\bar{y}$) is called the **total deviation**: $y - \bar{y}$

However, if there is significant linear correlation between x and y, we can use the linear regression equation to explain some of that deviation:

- The difference between the predicted value ($\hat{y}$) and the mean value ($\bar{y}$) is called the **explained deviation**: $\hat{y} - \bar{y}$

- The remaining difference (i.e., the residual) between the actual value (y) and the predicted value ($\hat{y}$) is called the **unexplained deviation**: $y - \hat{y}$

It is fairly obvious to see that the following equation holds true:

$$\textit{Total Deviation} = \textit{Explained Deviation} + \textit{Unexplained Deviation}$$

If we were to sum up the total deviation for all y-values, the result would equal 0. So, in a manner similar to the calculation for variance, we square all the values and sum them, and refer to the results as **Total Variation (SST - Total Sum of Squares)**, **Explained Variation (SSR - Regression Sum of Squares)**, and **Unexplained Variation (SSE - Error Sum of Squares)** respectively:

Total Variation:	$SST = \Sigma(y - \bar{y})^2$
Explained Variation:	$SSR = \Sigma(\hat{y} - \bar{y})^2$
Unexplained Variation:	$SSE = \Sigma(y - \hat{y})^2$

The question now is "Does the above formula relating the three types of deviation hold true for variation as well?" While in general, the sum of squares is not equal to the square of sums, the above formula for deviations does in fact hold true for variations as well!

$$\begin{matrix} \textit{Total Variation} \\ \textit{(SST)} \end{matrix} = \begin{matrix} \textit{Explained Variation} \\ \textit{(SSR)} \end{matrix} + \begin{matrix} \textit{Unexplained Variation} \\ \textit{(SSE)} \end{matrix}$$

Example 4.2-h	Calculating SST, SSR, and SSE

Calculate the Total Variation (SST), Explained Variation (SSR), and Unexplained Variation (SSE) for the Age vs Monthly Insurance Premium data from Example 4.2-d:

Age (in years)	Monthly Premium ($)
36	68
52	324
25	37
45	292
39	129
47	255
55	512
33	173
45	461
28	72
50	275
31	97

Solution

We first add columns to the above table for $\bar{y}$, $\hat{y}$, $(y - \bar{y})$, $(\hat{y} - \bar{y})$, and $(y - \hat{y})$.

We can quickly calculate $\bar{y} = \dfrac{68 + 324 + 37 + ... + 97}{12} = 224.583333... \approx 225$

We can take the values for $\hat{y}$ from Example 4.2-f.

Note: We can use Excel to fill in the remaining columns to avoid tedious calculations and possible errors.

Age (x)	Monthly Premium (y)	$\bar{y}$	$\hat{y}$	$(y - \bar{y})$	$(\hat{y} - \bar{y})$	$(y - \hat{y})$
36	68	225	163	−157	−62	−95
52	324	225	379	99	154	−55
25	37	225	15	−188	−210	22
45	292	225	285	67	60	7
39	129	225	204	−96	−21	−75
47	255	225	312	30	87	−57
55	512	225	420	287	195	92
33	173	225	123	−52	−102	50
45	461	225	285	236	60	176
28	72	225	55	−153	−170	17
50	275	225	352	50	127	−77
31	97	225	96	−128	−129	1

Then we sum up the squares of all the values in the last three columns to obtain the following:

$$SST = \Sigma(y - \bar{y})^2 = (-157)^2 + (99)^2 + ... + (-128)^2 = 267,461$$

$$SSR = \Sigma(\hat{y} - \bar{y})^2 = (-62)^2 + (154)^2 + ... + (-129)^2 = 196,969$$

$$SSE = \Sigma(y - \hat{y})^2 = (-95)^2 + (-55)^2 + ... + (1)^2 = 69,616$$

The discrepancy between *SST* and *SSR* + *SSE* is a result of rounded values for $\bar{y}$ and $\hat{y}$.

Notice that $SSR + SSE = 196,969 + 69,616 = 266,585 \approx SST$, which validates our above claim.

The Coefficient of Determination

By now, it should be clear that there is a relationship between the strength of correlation in the data and how much of the variation is explained:

- Perfect correlation (i.e., $r = 1$) would imply zero residuals, which would imply zero unexplained variation (i.e., $SSE = 0$), which would imply that all variation is explained (i.e., $SSR = SST$).

- On the other hand, zero correlation (i.e., $r = 0$) would imply zero explained variation (i.e., $SSR = 0$), which would imply that all variation is unexplained (i.e., $SSE = SST$).

In fact, an incredible mathematical relationship exists between the correlation coefficient and the ratio of explained variation to the total variation:

*The square of the correlation coefficient (r^2) is called the **coefficient of determination** and is equal to the proportion of variation that is explained by the regression equation.*

Formula 4.2-c	**Coefficient of Determination**

$$r^2 = 1 - \frac{SSE}{SST} \qquad \text{or} \qquad r^2 = \frac{SSR}{SST}$$

The coefficient of determination is usually rounded to four decimal places.

Therefore, the coefficient of determination tells us the proportion of the variation in y that can be explained by the variation in x, as predicted by the linear regression equation.

Example 4.2-i	**Calculating and Interpreting the Coefficient of Determination**

Calculate the coefficient of determination (r^2) for the Age vs Monthly Insurance Premium data using the variation values calculated in Example 4.2-h. Then, compare the result to the square of the correlation coefficient calculated in Example 4.1-e. Finally, interpret the meaning of the coefficient of determination in context of this problem.

Solution

From Example 4.2-h, we have the following values: $SST = 267,461$; $SSR = 196,969$; $SSE = 69,616$.

$$r^2 = 1 - \frac{SSE}{SST} = 1 - \frac{69,616}{267,461} = 1 - 0.260284... = 0.739715... = 0.7397$$

The slight discrepancy between the two r^2 calculations is a result of rounded values.

From Example 4.1-e, we have the value of the correlation coefficient is $r = 0.860$.

$$r^2 = (0.860)^2 = 0.7396$$

We can see that both methods for computing r^2 yield (basically) the same result: 0.7397 using the variation values and 0.7396 using the correlation coefficient. This implies that approximately 74% of the variation in the monthly critical illness insurance premium (y) for females between the ages of 25-55 can be explained by variation in the age of the applicant (x) using the linear regression equation $\hat{y} = -323 + 13.5x$.

4.2 | Exercises

Answers to odd-numbered problems are available at the end of the textbook.

The scenarios in Problems 1 to 8 below have been copied from Problems 11 to 18, respectively, from Section 4.1. For each of these scenarios, complete the following instructions:

(i) *Determine the equation of the line of best fit and interpret the meaning of the slope.*

(ii) *Plot the line of best fit on the scatter plot of the data. You may wish to use Excel or some other software.*

(iii) *Construct a residual plot and identify any outliers present in the data. You may wish to use Excel or some other software.*

(iv) *Calculate the Total Variation (SST), Explained Variation (SSR), and Unexplained Variation (SSE).*

(v) *Based on your results from part (iv), calculate and interpret the coefficient of determination (r^2), and compare your result with the coefficient of correlation (r) calculated in the corresponding problem in 4.1.*

1. A family physician compares the number of flu cases she diagnosed with the number of flu shots she administered each year for the last five years to see if there is a correlation between the data. *Refer to Section 4.1, Problem 11.*

Number of flu cases diagnosed	Number of flu vaccinations administered
35	48
18	56
7	94
15	61
12	78

2. A family physician compares the price charged for a physician's note by six different clinics nearby and the number of notes requested in the last three months at each clinic to see if there is a correlation between the number of notes requested and the cost of the note. All six clinics see approximately the same number of patients each year. *Refer to Section 4.1, Problem 12.*

Number of physician's notes issued in 3 months	Price of physician's note ($)
44	25
18	60
93	15
65	30
82	20
56	40

3. A researcher is trying to determine if the number of alcoholic drinks consumed at a social event affects the number of cigarettes smoked by smokers who desire to quit. She conducts a study whereby participants are asked to record the number of alcoholic drinks they consume over the course of seven social events, along with the number of cigarettes they smoke. One of the male participants records the following results. *Refer to Section 4.1, Problem 13.*

Number of Alcoholic Drinks	Number of Cigarettes
2	1
5	3
3	0
5	5
4	2
7	5
4	3

4. The researcher in Problem 3 collects the results from a female participant in the study. *Refer to Section 4.1, Problem 14.*

Number of Alcoholic Drinks	Number of Cigarettes
2	2
0	4
3	0
1	3
2	1
4	0
0	3

5. A physician records the LDL cholesterol level and the BMI for a sample of 10 of his overweight patients (BMI of 25 or more) to see if there is a correlation between the data. *Refer to Section 4.1, Problem 15.*

Cholesterol Level (mg/dL)	BMI
89	27.5
106	31.2
135	34.8
182	30.9
117	29.6
205	37.0
94	32.5
76	28.8
128	26.2
144	31.3

6. In a study about the effectiveness of a new pain relief drug, 10 patients with similar medical conditions were given the ability to self-administer the new drug, but each with a different calibration for how much of the drug may be administered at one time (between 5 and 10 mg). The time between self-administered doses was recorded over a period of 24 hours, and the average time between doses was calculated for each patient and compared to the size of the dose given. All ten patients were approximately the same weight and with similar pain management needs. *Refer to Section 4.1, Problem 16.*

Average time between doses (in hr)	Size of dose (in mg)
4.5	8.5
2.4	5.0
4.8	6.0
6.5	9.0
3.2	7.5
1.8	5.5
3.4	8.0
6.3	10.0
4.1	6.5
4.4	7.0

7. A nutritionist performs a study where a patient records the calories she consumed (as a percent of her baseline daily target) and the number of minutes she spent running on the treadmill every day over the course of two weeks to see if there is a correlation between the data. *Refer to Section 4.1, Problem 17.*

Number of Minutes Running on Treadmill	% of Baseline Daily Calories Consumed
30	112
40	105
90	120
15	96
10	102
20	108
0	105
60	116
45	105
20	114
30	112
40	125
0	108
0	95

8. A nutrition researcher performs a study where 12 overweight adult males are each assigned a certain number of minutes of monitored treadmill running every day and their weight loss (in lb) after two weeks is recorded. All the participants were approximately the same weight to begin, were given a controlled diet to eat, and the speed of the treadmill was the same for all participants. *Refer to Section 4.1, Problem 18.*

Number of minutes of running per day	Weight lost in 2 weeks (in lb)
30	4.6
40	5.4
25	2.8
15	0.6
10	2.4
20	1.4
25	7.2
30	3.0
45	5.6
20	2.4
30	5.2
35	4.0

For Problems 9 to 20, determine if it is appropriate to use the linear regression equation to make the requested prediction for the value of the unknown variable. If so, state the predicted value of the unknown variable; if not, state the reason it is inappropriate.

9. The birth lengths in cm (X) and birth weights in kg (Y) of a sample of 50 newborn female babies are compared, yielding a correlation coefficient of $r = 0.578$ and a linear regression equation of $\hat{y} = -8.89 + 0.243x$. The babies all had lengths between 46.5 and 53.0 cm, and weights between 2.50 and 4.05 kg. Based on this, predict the birth weight of a newborn female baby with a birth length of 50.5 cm.

10. Based on the information from Problem 9, predict the birth weight of a newborn female baby with a birth length of 55.0 cm.

11. Based on the information from Problem 9, predict the birth length of a newborn female baby with a birth weight of 3.75 kg.

12. Based on the information from Problem 9, predict the birth weight of a newborn female baby with a birth length of 48.5 cm.

13. An administrator at a nursing home facility believes that patients who receive regular visits from family and friends tend to struggle less with depression. A sample of 20 residents are given a depression risk assessment, which assigns a risk value of 0-10 to the patient based on the questions they answer, where 0 indicates no risk of depression and 10 indicates imminent and severe risk of depression. Their scores on this assessment are compared to the number of visits from friends and family that were logged in the past six months (ranging from 0 to 25 visits), and a regression analysis was performed, yielding a regression equation of $\hat{y} = 9.28 - 0.352x$. Predict the depression risk value of a resident who had 15 visits in the past six months if the coefficient of correlation is $r = -0.549$.

14. Based on the information from Problem 13, predict the depression risk of a resident who had 18 visits in the past 6 months if the coefficient of correlation is $r = -0.216$.

15. Based on the information from Problem 13, predict the depression risk of a resident who had 24 visits in the past 6 months if the coefficient of correlation is $r = -0.381$.

16. Based on the information from Problem 13, predict the depression risk of a resident who had 12 visits in the past 6 months if the coefficient of correlation is $r = -0.487$.

17. A sample of 100 teenage male patients have their systolic (X) and diastolic (Y) blood pressures measured (in mmHg). The resulting correlation coefficient is $r = 0.939$ and the sample linear regression is $\hat{y} = -20.2 + 0.776x$. The systolic blood pressures ranged from 94 to 143, while the diastolic blood pressures ranged from 55 to 93. Based on this, predict the diastolic blood pressure of a teenage male patient with a systolic blood pressure of 120 mmHg.

18. Based on the information from Problem 17, predict the diastolic blood pressure of a teenage male patient with a systolic blood pressure of 130 mmHg.

19. Based on the information from Problem 17, predict the diastolic blood pressure of a teenage male patient with a systolic blood pressure of 160 mmHg.

20. Based on the information from Problem 17, predict the systolic blood pressure of a teenage male patient with a diastolic blood pressure of 80 mmHg.

For Problems 21 to 40, compute the missing value in the regression analysis.

21. Given the correlation coefficient –0.681 and the linear regression equation $\hat{y} = 181 - 6.35x$, compute the coefficient of determination.

22. Given the correlation coefficient 0.794 and the linear regression equation $\hat{y} = 16.4 + 1.58x$, compute the coefficient of determination.

23. Given the correlation coefficient 0.219 and the linear regression equation $\hat{y} = -2.68 + 0.977x$, compute the coefficient of determination.

24. Given the correlation coefficient –0.994 and the linear regression equation $\hat{y} = 212 - 1.81x$, compute the coefficient of determination.

25. Given the coefficient of determination 0.5762 and the linear regression equation $\hat{y} = 44.8 + 3.22x$, compute the correlation coefficient.

26. Given the coefficient of determination 0.7175 and the linear regression equation $\hat{y} = 5{,}750 - 845x$, compute the correlation coefficient.

27. Given the coefficient of determination 0.3957 and the linear regression equation $\hat{y} = 23.4 - 3.15x$, compute the correlation coefficient.

28. Given the coefficient of determination 0.1649 and the linear regression equation $\hat{y} = 75.1 + 5.62x$, compute the correlation coefficient.

29. Given $SST = 1{,}317.09$ and $SSE = 412.57$, compute r^2.

30. Given $SST = 14{,}865.21$ and $SSE = 2{,}571.39$, compute r^2.

31. Given $SSR = 849.05$ and $SSE = 1{,}473.62$, compute r^2.

32. Given $SSR = 7{,}296.14$ and $SSE = 285.07$, compute r^2.

33. Given $r^2 = 0.2245$ and $SST = 5{,}157.32$, compute SSR.

34. Given $r^2 = 0.4617$ and $SST = 8{,}451.77$, compute SSR.

35. Given $r^2 = 0.8320$ and $SST = 123.45$, compute SSE.

36. Given $r^2 = 0.0798$ and $SST = 769.54$, compute SSE.

37. Given $r^2 = 0.6233$ and $SSR = 413.57$, compute SST.

38. Given $r^2 = 0.3129$ and $SSR = 88.68$, compute SST.

39. Given $r^2 = 0.8572$ and $SSR = 9{,}836.35$, compute SSE.

40. Given $r^2 = 0.5105$ and $SSR = 7{,}442.98$, compute SSE.

4 | Review Exercises

For Problems 1 to 8, look at the scatter plot and identify the type of correlation (positive linear correlation, negative linear correlation, non-linear correlation, or no correlation) that is most likely present in the data. If linear correlation exists, identify whether it is perfect, strong, or moderate-weak.

1.

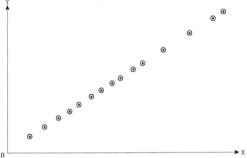

2.

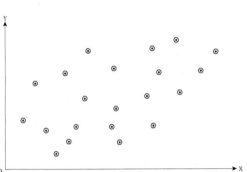

3.

4.

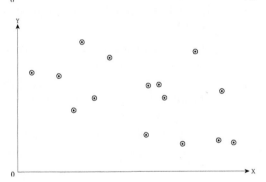

5.

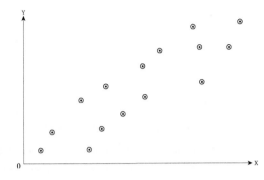

6.

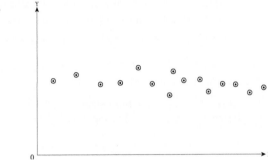

7.

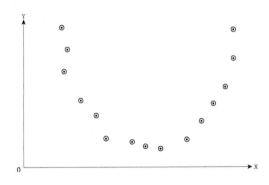

8.

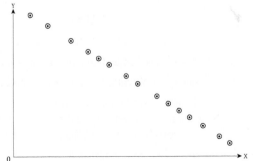

9. A student nurse conducts a study to determine whether there is a linear correlation between an individual's weight (in pounds) and daily water consumption (in ounces). The data are listed in the following table.

Weight (pounds)	Daily Water Consumption (ounces)
102	50
119	32
164	82
141	64
142	54
154	32
185	64
201	72
124	39

a. Identify the dependent and independent variables.

b. Create an X-Y scatter plot for the paired data.

c. Calculate and interpret the coefficient of correlation (r). Determine if there is significant linear correlation at the 5% significance level.

d. Identify two potential problems with this study.

10. The ages (in months) and the number of hours slept in a day by 15 infants were recorded:

Age (months)	Hours slept in a day
1	14.9
2	15.5
5	14.1
7	12.8
8	13.2
9	12.5
1	16.0
6	14.6
5	10.8
7	12.6
3	11.7
4	14.6
6	13.5
6	11.4
3	12.7

a. Identify the dependent and independent variables.

b. Create an X-Y scatter plot for the paired data.

c. Calculate and interpret the coefficient of correlation (r). Determine if there is significant linear correlation at the 5% significance level.

d. Identify two potential problems with this study.

11. A psychology researcher performed a study relating the age that infants were able to successfully crawl on their own (in weeks after birth) with the average outdoor temperature for that month (in °C). The sample results were recorded as follows:

Crawling on own (Weeks after birth)	Average Outdoor Temperature (°C)
32	15
34	10
29.5	22
33	4
29	19
28.5	27
31	7
27	12
33.5	0
35	2
30	25
35	9

a. Identify the dependent and independent variables.

b. Create an X-Y scatter plot for the paired data.

c. Calculate and interpret the coefficient of correlation (r). Determine if there is significant linear correlation at the 5% significance level.

d. Determine the equation of the line of best fit and interpret the slope.

e. Plot the line of best fit on the scatter plot from part (b).

f. Construct a residual plot and identify any outlier present in the data.

g. Calculate the Total Variation (SST), Explained Variation (SSR), and Unexplained Variation (SSE).

h. Calculate the coefficient of determination (r^2) using the results from part (c) and part (g). Compare the results and interpret its meaning.

12. The age (in years) of 10 men and their resting heart rates are recorded:

Age (years)	Resting Heart Rate (bpm)
16	69
25	52
29	70
57	75
22	81
39	66
45	72
64	85
70	92
49	78

a. Identify the dependent and independent variables.

b. Create an X-Y scatter plot for the paired data.

c. Calculate and interpret the coefficient of correlation (r). Determine if there is significant linear correlation at the 5% significance level.

d. Determine the equation of the line of best fit and interpret the slope.

e. Plot the line of best fit on the scatter plot from part (b).

f. Construct a residual plot and identify any outliers present in the data.

g. Calculate the Total Variation (SST), Explained Variation (SSR), and Unexplained Variation (SSE).

h. Calculate the coefficient of determination (r^2) using the results from part (c) and part (g). Compare the results and interpret its meaning.

For Problems 13 to 16, determine if it is appropriate to use the linear regression equation to make the requested prediction for the value of the unknown variable. If so, state the predicted value of the unknown variable; if not, state the reason it is inappropriate.

13. A college professor wants to demonstrate the relationship between class attendance (X) and final mark in a math course (Y). For a sample of 50 Pre-Health students, the professor recorded their attendance record (as a percent) for the whole term and final mark (as a percent) the students got in this course. The correlation coefficient (r) is found to be 0.964 and the line of best fit is $\hat{y} = 9.33 + 0.792x$. The percent of classes attended by the students sampled ranges from 25 to 100%, and the final mark in the course also ranges from 0 to 100%. Based on this, predict the final mark in the course if the percent of classes attended is 55%.

14. It is believed that age has an impact on a driver's ability to read road signs. A sample of 100 drivers were tested on the distance (in feet) that they can read road signs with respect to their age. The resulting correlation coefficient is $r = -0.705$ and the sample linear regression equation is $\hat{y} = 600 - 4.85x$. The sign legibility distance ranges from 300 to 600 feet and the driver age ranges from 16 to 70. Based on this, predict the sign legibility distance when the driver is 50 years old.

15. a. Predict the mark of a student who has attended no classes this semester using the regression equation from Problem 13, if it is appropriate to do so.

b. Predict the percent of classes attended by a student who received a final mark of 65% in the course using the regression equation from Problem 13, if it is appropriate to do so.

16. a. Predict the sign legibility distance (in feet) of a driver who is 80 years old using the regression equation from Problem 14, if it is appropriate to do so.

b. Predict the age of a driver who can read a road sign 520 feet away using the regression equation from Problem 14, if it is appropriate to do so.

17. Given the coefficient of determination 0.9405 and the linear regression equation $\hat{y} = 11.8 + 35.3x$, compute the correlation coefficient.

18. Given the coefficient of determination 0.3152 and the linear regression equation $\hat{y} = 5.12 - 3.55x$, compute the correlation coefficient.

19. Given $SST = 76.89$ and $SSR = 58.63$, compute SSE and r^2. If $\hat{y} = 112 - 24.5x$, compute r.

20. Given $SST = 5,126.88$ and $SSE = 2,257.88$, compute SSR and r^2. If $\hat{y} = 1.88 + 0.267x$, compute r.

21. Given $r^2 = 0.8045$ and $SSR = 1,276.09$, compute SST and SSE.

22. Given $r^2 = 0.6431$ and $SSE = 26.55$, compute SST and SSR.

4 | Self-Test Exercises

For Problems 1 to 4, look at the scatter plot and identify the type of correlation (positive linear correlation, negative linear correlation, non-linear correlation, or no correlation) that is most likely present in the data. If linear correlation exists, identify whether it is perfect, strong, or moderate-weak.

1.

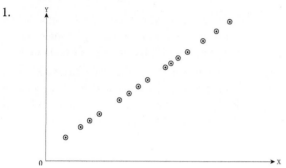

2.

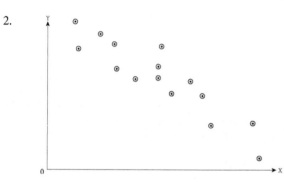

3.

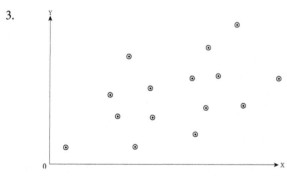

4.

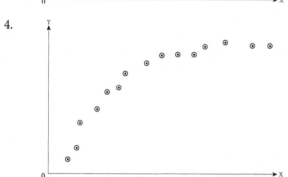

5. For each of the following situations, state the independent and dependent variables:

   a. The price of an electrical bill and the total electricity consumed during the month.

   b. The age of a patient and the number of cases of colon cancer per 100,000 patients of that age.

   c. The monthly extended health insurance premium charged by an insurance company and the age of the applicant.

   d. The number of family members living in a household and the average weekly grocery spending.

6. Recently, the annual number of driver deaths per 100,000 for the selected age groups were as follows:

Age (years)	Number of Driver Deaths per 100,000
16-25	38
26-35	36
36-45	24
46-55	19
56-65	20
66-75	18
76-85	28

Hint: You will need to calculate the class midpoints to complete this question.

   a. Identify the dependent and independent variables.

   b. Create an X-Y scatter plot for the paired data.

   c. Calculate and interpret the coefficient of correlation (r). Determine if there is significant linear correlation at the 5% significance level.

   d. Identify two potential problems with this study.

7. The following data presents the stress scores (out of 10, 10 being most stressed) before a math test and the math test scores (out of 100) for eight students:

Stress Score	Test Score
7	81
4	96
3	93
9	68
8	63
3	84
6	71
2	85

a. Identify the dependent and independent variables.

b. Create an X-Y scatter plot for the paired data.

c. Calculate and interpret the coefficient of correlation (r). Determine if there is significant linear correlation at the 5% significance level.

d. Determine the equation for the line of best fit and interpret the slope.

e. Plot the line of best fit on the scatter plot from part (b).

f. Construct a residual plot and identify any outliers present in the data.

g. Calculate the Total Variation (SST), Explained Variation (SSR), and Unexplained Variation (SSE).

h. Calculate the coefficient of determination (r^2) using the results from part (c) and part (g). Compare the results and interpret its meaning.

8. The following table presents data on Blood Alcohol Content (BAC) levels versus the amount of time (in hours) that it takes to become sober:

BAC level	Time (hours)
0.016	1
0.05	3.75
0.08	5
0.10	6.25
0.16	10
0.20	12.5
0.24	15

a. Identify the dependent and independent variables.

b. Create an X-Y scatter plot for the paired data.

c. Calculate and interpret the coefficient of correlation (r). Determine if there is significant linear correlation at the 5% significance level.

d. Determine the equation for the line of best fit and interpret the slope.

e. Plot the line of best fit on the scatter plot from part (b).

f. Construct a residual plot and identify any outliers present in the data.

g. Calculate the Total Variation (SST), Explained Variation (SSR), and Unexplained Variation (SSE).

h. Calculate the coefficient of determination (r^2) using the results from part (c) and part (g). Compare the results and interpret its meaning.

9. It is believed that age has an impact on body fat percentage. A sample of 18 adults aged between 23 and 61 years old were examined and their body fat percentages were recorded. The resulting correlation coefficient is $r = 0.825$, and the sample linear regression equation is $\hat{y} = 3.22 + 0.548x$.

a. Interpret the coefficients of the regression line.

b. Determine the strength of the linear correlation between the two data sets. Is it significant at the 5% level?

c. What is the coefficient of determination? Interpret its meaning.

For Problems 10 to 12, determine if it is appropriate to use the linear regression equation from Problem 9 to make the requested prediction for the value of the unknown variable. If so, state the predicted value of the unknown variable; if not, state the reason it is inappropriate.

10. Predict the body fat percentage of an adult who is 30 years old.

11. Predict the body fat percentage of an adult who is 85 years old.

12. Predict the age of the adult who has a body fat percentage of 35%.

13. Given the coefficient of determination 0.5468 and the linear regression equation $\hat{y} = 10.5 + 5.30x$, compute the correlation coefficient.

14. Given the coefficient of determination 0.8675 and the linear regression equation $\hat{y} = 4.51 - 0.550x$, compute the correlation coefficient.

15. Given $SST = 10.69$ and $SSR = 6.99$, compute SSE and r^2.

16. Given $r^2 = 0.9316$ and $SSE = 60.55$, compute SST and SSR.

4 | Summary of Notation and Formulas

NOTATION

n = total number of data values in a sample

r = Pearson's Linear Correlation Coefficient

$\bar{x}, \bar{y}$ = sample means of individual data sets x and y

$\hat{y}$ = the predicted value for y based on a given x-value, using the linear regression equation: $\hat{y} = a + bx$

df = degrees of freedom

SST = Total Sum of Squares = total variation

SSR = Regression Sum of Squares = explained variation

SSE = Error Sum of Squares = unexplained variation

r^2 = coefficient of determination

FORMULAS

Pearson's Linear Correlation Coefficient | 4.1

$$r = \frac{n\left(\sum xy\right) - \left(\sum x\right)\left(\sum y\right)}{\sqrt{n\left(\sum x^2\right) - \left(\sum x\right)^2} \cdot \sqrt{n\left(\sum y^2\right) - \left(\sum y\right)^2}}$$

Slope of the Least-Squares Regression Line | 4.2-a

$$b = \frac{n\left(\sum xy\right) - \left(\sum x\right)\left(\sum y\right)}{n\left(\sum x^2\right) - \left(\sum x\right)^2}$$

y-intercept of the Least-Squares Regression Line | 4.2-b

$$a = \bar{y} - b \cdot \bar{x}$$

Coefficient of Determination | 4.2-c

$$r^2 = 1 - \frac{SSE}{SST} \quad \text{or} \quad r^2 = \frac{SSR}{SST}$$

SUM OF SQUARES

Total Variation

$$SST = \Sigma(y - \bar{y})^2$$

Explained Variation

$$SSR = \Sigma(\hat{y} - \bar{y})^2$$

Unexplained Variation

$$SSE = \Sigma(y - \hat{y})^2$$

5% Significance Table for r | Table 4.2

df $(n - 2)$	r	df $(n - 2)$	r
1	0.997	16	0.468
2	0.950	17	0.456
3	0.878	18	0.444
4	0.811	19	0.433
5	0.754	20	0.423
6	0.707	21	0.413
7	0.666	22	0.404
8	0.632	23	0.396
9	0.602	24	0.388
10	0.576	25	0.381
11	0.553	26	0.374
12	0.532	27	0.367
13	0.514	28	0.361
14	0.497	29	0.355
15	0.482	30	0.349

5 ELEMENTARY PROBABILITY THEORY

LEARNING OBJECTIVES

- Distinguish between theoretical, empirical, and subjective approaches to probability.
- Determine the various outcomes and events for a given experiment.
- Use outcome tables, tree diagrams, and Venn diagrams to construct the sample space for an experiment.
- Distinguish between mutually exclusive and non-mutually exclusive events, as well as independent and dependent events.
- Calculate probabilities using a variety of approaches, including the general sample space approach, addition rule, multiplication rule, complementary event rule, and Bayes' Theorem.
- Calculate the odds against and the odds in favour of an event.
- Solve problems and calculate probabilities using a variety of counting rules, including the fundamental counting rules, factorial rules, permutations rule, and combinations rule.

CHAPTER OUTLINE

5.1 Fundamentals of Probability Theory

5.2 Compound Events

5.3 Counting Rules

Introduction

Towards the end of the last chapter, we began making predictions about the value of the dependent variable given the value of the independent variable. The question that you may have already asked yourself is *"How likely is that prediction to be correct?"* In order to answer that question, we need to introduce a concept known as probability, which we will study in-depth over the next several chapters.

Probability theory is the basis for statistical inference. The knowledge of probability is essential to make decisions about the population based on sample statistics. Probability involves the use of mathematics to describe the level of certainty (likelihood, chance, or possibility) that an event will occur. We hear about probabilities in everyday situations.

For example, it is easy to verify that the probability of rolling a "4" on a standard 6-sided die is $\frac{1}{6}$.

However, what is the probability of:

- rolling a "4" on the die, three times in a row?
- rolling an even number, three times in a row?
- rolling three unique numbers (i.e., no repetition of numbers) in three rolls?
- rolling three of one number and two of another number in five rolls (i.e., a full house)?

These are a just a few examples of questions that you will be able to answer by the end of this chapter.

5.1 | Fundamentals of Probability Theory

We begin our study of probability with some terms:

- An **experiment** (or **procedure**) is an action that produces measurable results.

  E.g., rolling a standard 6-sided die

- An **outcome** is a specific and unique result of an experiment.

  E.g., rolling a standard 6-sided die once has any one of 6 possible outcomes: 1, 2, 3, 4, 5, or 6

- An **event** is a collection of results of an experiment that possess some trait or characteristic.

  - A **simple event** is an event that has only one outcome.

    E.g., rolling a 4 on the die

  - A **compound event** is an event that has more than one outcome.

    E.g., rolling an even number on the die (i.e., either 2, 4, or 6)

- The **sample space** is the collection of all possible equally-likely outcomes of an experiment. We use *S* to denote the sample space.

We use the notation $P(A)$ to denote the probability of an event *A* occurring.

Example 5.1-a	Identifying Sample Space, Events, and Outcomes

Two coins are flipped.

(i)   Identify the sample space for this experiment.

(ii)   Identify the event and all possible outcomes if the results of both coins are Heads.

(iii)   Identify the event and all possible outcomes if the result of one coin is Heads and the other is Tails.

Solution

(i) $S = \{(H, H), (H, T), (T, H), (T, T)\}$, the set of all possible outcomes of the experiment

(ii)   **Event A:** 2 Heads

       Possible outcomes in A: (H, H) - since there is only a single outcome in which the results are 2 Heads, this is a simple event.

(iii) **Event B:** 1 Head and 1 Tail

       Possible outcomes in B: (H, T), (T, H) - since there are multiple outcomes in which the results are 1 Head and 1 Tail, this is a compound event.

Example 5.1-b   Understanding the Fundamentals of Probability

A pharmacy offers several different options for over-the-counter pain-killers: 6 different brands of acetaminophen, 4 different brands of ibuprofen, 3 different brands of aspirin, and 3 different brands of naproxen. Answer the following questions if one of the pain-killers is selected at random:

(i)   How many different outcomes are possible?

(ii)   What is the sample space for this experiment?

(iii) If the outcomes are grouped into events by medication type, how many different events are possible?

Solution

(i)   There are a total of 16 different outcomes possible:

       • 6 different acetaminophen outcomes

       • 4 different ibuprofen outcomes

       • 3 different aspirin outcomes

       • 3 different naproxen outcomes

(ii)   To construct the sample space, we need to assign a name to each of the 16 pain-killer outcomes. We will use the first two letters of the drug, with a subscript number to indicate the various outcomes:

$$S = \{Ac_1, Ac_2, Ac_3, Ac_4, Ac_5, Ac_6, Ib_1, Ib_2, Ib_3, Ib_4, As_1, As_2, As_3, Na_1, Na_2, Na_3\}$$

(iii) There are a total of 4 different events possible: acetaminophen, ibuprofen, aspirin, or naproxen.

Approaches for Calculating Probability

Depending on the situation we are analyzing, there are three different ways to calculate the probability of an event occurring:

1.   The **Theoretical Approach**, also known as the **Classical Approach**, which requires us to know all the outcomes in the sample space and that every outcome in the sample space has the same likelihood of occurring.

     • E.g., determining the likelihood of winning the lottery.

2.   The **Empirical Approach**, which uses results from identical (or as nearly-identical as is feasible) previous experiments that have been performed many times. It is more applicable in situations where the outcomes of an experiment are **not** all equally likely.

     • E.g., determining the likelihood of a certain complication of a surgical procedure.

3.   The **Subjective Approach**, which uses the knowledge of an expert who is able to analyze certain conditions and compare that to previous results where conditions were similar.

     • E.g., determining the likelihood of precipitation given certain weather conditions.

Approach 1: Theoretical Approach

Assume that the number of possible outcomes in the sample space S for a given experiment is denoted $n(S)$. If the number of ways an event A can occur in the sample space is counted and denoted $n(A)$, then the theoretical probability of event A occurring, $P(A)$, is calculated as follows:

Formula 5.1-a

Theoretical Approach to Probability

$$P(A) = \frac{\text{\# of ways event } A \text{ can occur}}{\text{total \# of outcomes in } S} = \frac{n(A)}{n(S)}$$

Example 5.1-c

Theoretical Approach to Probability

A 6-sided die is rolled once. Determine the probability of the following events:

(i)   Rolling the number 3.

(ii)   Rolling any number less than 4.

(iii)   Rolling a number 5 or more.

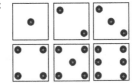

Solution

The die has 6 sides, and each number (outcome) is equally-likely to be rolled.

Therefore, using the theoretical approach to probability, $P(A) = \dfrac{n(A)}{n(S)}$, where $n(S) = 6$:

(i)   There is only one outcome for the event of rolling the number 3: $A = \{3\}$. Therefore, $n(A) = 1$.

$$P(A) = \frac{1}{6}$$

Therefore, the probability of rolling the number 3 is $\dfrac{1}{6}$.

(ii)   There are three outcomes for the event of rolling any number less than 4: $B = \{1, 2, 3\}$. Therefore, $n(B) = 3$.

$$P(B) = \frac{3}{6} = \frac{1}{2}$$

Therefore, the probability of rolling any number less than 4 is $\dfrac{1}{2}$.

(iii)   There are two outcomes for the event of rolling a number 5 or more: $C = \{5, 6\}$. Therefore, $n(C) = 2$.

$$P(C) = \frac{2}{6} = \frac{1}{3}$$

Therefore, the probability of rolling a number 5 or more is $\dfrac{1}{3}$.

Approach 2: Empirical Approach

Assume that the desired experiment E has already been conducted under (near-)identical circumstances in a large number of trials, denoted $n(E)$. In this case, the "sample space" is not all outcomes that are theoretically possible, but rather it is a listing of all the results from the trials of an actual experiment. If the number of occurrences of event A in those $n(E)$ trials is denoted $n(A)$, then the empirical probability of event A occurring, $P(A)$, is calculated as follows:

Formula 5.1-b

Empirical Approach to Probability

$$P(A) = \frac{\text{\# of ways event } A \text{ occurred}}{\text{total \# of trials}} = \frac{n(A)}{n(E)}$$

Example 5.1-d | Empirical Approach to Probability

Out of 150 calls received at a 911 call-center, 45 of them required an ambulance. Based on this, what is the probability that a call received at a 911 call-center will require an ambulance?

Solution

Using $P(A) = \dfrac{n(A)}{n(E)}$,

$$P(Ambulance) = \frac{45}{150} = \frac{3}{10}$$

Therefore, the probability of a call received at a 911 call-center requiring an ambulance is $\dfrac{3}{10}$.

*Note: The **Law of Large Numbers** states that if an experiment is repeated a large number of times, the empirical probability calculated will be approximately equal to the actual probability of the event occurring.*

Approach 3: Subjective Approach

Assume that past information about the likelihood of event A occurring under certain circumstances is known. Then an expert analyst may be able to approximate the likelihood of event A occurring in the future, based on the particular circumstances of the situation. However, there is no simple formula for calculating probability using the subjective approach.

Characteristics of Probability

Regardless of which approach is used to calculate the probability of an event occurring in a given situation, the probability of an event A will always be between 0 and 1 (inclusively). This is true because the number of outcomes where event A occurs (the numerator in the probability calculation) can never be less than 0 and can never be more than the total number of possible outcomes (the denominator in the probability calculation); hence, the fraction can never be less than 0 or more than 1.

We summarize this as follows: $0 \leq P(A) \leq 1$ for any event A.

The probability of an event cannot be negative or greater than 1.

- An event with a probability exactly equal to 0 is **impossible**.

- An event with a probability close to 0 is **unlikely**.

- An event with a probability exactly equal to 0.5 is equally likely to occur as it is to not occur - this is known as a **50-50 event**.

- An event with a probability close to 1 is **likely**.

- An event with a probability exactly equal to 1 is **certain**.

When calculating probability, we should always express the result as either a fraction (if it is a simple fraction like $\dfrac{1}{2}$ or $\dfrac{2}{3}$) or as a decimal with three significant digits (e.g., $\dfrac{47}{91} \approx 0.516$).

Example 5.1-e | Calculating Basic Probability using the Three Approaches

For the following three examples based on a clinical drug trial, identify which approach to probability is most appropriate and calculate the probability of the given events occurring using that approach (if possible):

(i) A clinical drug trial conducted at a hospital examines symptom relief of a new drug to treat symptoms in patients suffering from Multiple Sclerosis (MS). In the clinical trial of 200 patients, 50 patients are selected to form the control group, receiving a placebo instead of the drug. Prior to beginning the trial, each patient is informed of the probability that he/she will be part of the experimental group or the control group, and must consent to being in either group without the knowledge of which group they are in.

(ii) One of the doctors administering the trial answers a patient's questions about the likelihood of possible long-term side effects of the drug based on the chemical composition of the drug and the known long-term side effects of other similar drugs.

(iii) The results of the 150 patients receiving the actual drug are analyzed: 96 experienced significant improvements, 37 experienced mild/moderate improvements, and 17 did not experience any noticeable improvements. Based on these results, the probability of experiencing improvements on this drug is described to a new potential candidate for the drug.

Solution

(i) In this situation, there are 200 patients (outcomes) in the sample space, so $n(S) = 200$. Of those, 50 are in the control group ($n(C) = 50$) and 150 are in the experimental group ($n(E) = 150$). Every outcome in the sample space has the same likelihood of occurring.

Therefore, the **theoretical approach** should be used to calculate the probability that a randomly-selected patient will be in either the experimental group or the control group.

Using Formula 5.1-a, $\quad P(E) = \dfrac{150}{200} = 0.75, \quad$ and

$$P(C) = \dfrac{50}{200} = 0.25$$

(ii) In this situation, there is no data from previous experiments for the doctor to make his/her assessment from, so the doctor's expert knowledge of the drug's composition and the long-term side effects of other similar drugs are required in order to estimate the probability of long-term side effects. This is an example of the **subjective approach** to probability.

Therefore, it is not possible to calculate the probability of the given event.

(iii) In this situation, the results of the clinical trial are being used to provide probabilities to new patients who have not yet taken the drug. This is an example in which the **empirical approach** to probability is most appropriate.

Here, the total number of trials is $n = 150$, the number of outcomes that result in significant improvements is $n(SI) = 96$, the number of outcomes that result in mild/moderate improvements is $n(MMI) = 37$, and the number of outcomes that result in no improvements is $n(NI) = 17$.

Using Formula 5.1-b,

- Probability of Significant Improvements: $P(SI) = \dfrac{96}{150} = 0.64$

- Probability of Mild/Moderate Improvements: $P(MMI) = \dfrac{37}{150} \approx 0.247$

- Probability of No Improvements: $P(NI) = \dfrac{17}{150} \approx 0.113$

Determining the Sample Space

Most of the situations examined in this chapter will use the theoretical approach to probability. In order to calculate probability using this approach, it is first necessary to fully determine the outcomes in the **sample space** S (recall that the sample space is the set of all possible equally-likely outcomes that can occur for a given experiment).

Sometimes this is an easy task, as in the following situations:

- A fair coin is flipped and the result is recorded: $S = \{Heads, \ Tails\}$
- A single, 6-sided, fair die is rolled and the number showing is recorded: $S = \{1, 2, 3, 4, 5, 6\}$
- A baby is born and the sex is recorded: $S = \{Male, \ Female\}$

Sometimes, however, this task can be more complicated. Consider the following situations:

- Two 6-sided fair dice are rolled and the value of each die is recorded.
- A card is drawn from a standard deck of 52 cards and the suit and card value is recorded.
- Couples with four children are selected at random and the sex of each of their children is recorded.
- Out of the students in grade 12 at a given high school, some participate in drama, some participate in athletics, and some participate in leadership. A grade 12 student is selected at random, and his/her extracurricular activities are recorded.

In these situations, we will make use of diagrams to accurately determine the sample space.

Outcome Tables

In situations where there are two pieces of information to record for each outcome in the sample space, and where each of the results for each piece of information is equally-likely to occur, an **outcome table** can be used to identify the outcomes in the sample space. An outcome table has the results of one piece of information along the top row and the results of the other piece of information along the left-side column. The individual cells in the table represent the various outcomes in the sample space.

Consider the following example for twin baby births:

SEX OF FIRST TWIN BORN	SEX OF SECOND TWIN BORN	
	Female (F)	Male (M)
Female (F)	(F, F)	(F, M)
Male (M)	(M, F)	(M, M)

Example 5.1-f	Determining the Sample Space using an Outcome Table

Determine the sample spaces for the following scenarios:

(i)   Two 6-sided fair dice are rolled and the value of each die is recorded.

(ii)   A card is drawn from a standard deck of 52 cards and the suit and card value is recorded.

Solution

(i)   If two fair, standard, 6-sided dice are rolled, the outcomes for each die are 1, 2, 3, 4, 5, and 6.

DIE 1	DIE 2					
	1	2	3	4	5	6
1	(1, 1)	(1, 2)	(1, 3)	(1, 4)	(1, 5)	(1, 6)
2	(2, 1)	(2, 2)	(2, 3)	(2, 4)	(2, 5)	(2, 6)
3	(3, 1)	(3, 2)	(3, 3)	(3, 4)	(3, 5)	(3, 6)
4	(4, 1)	(4, 2)	(4, 3)	(4, 4)	(4, 5)	(4, 6)
5	(5, 1)	(5, 2)	(5, 3)	(5, 4)	(5, 5)	(5, 6)
6	(6, 1)	(6, 2)	(6, 3)	(6, 4)	(6, 5)	(6, 6)

Solution
continued

(ii) To solve probability problems involving cards, there are some basic facts about a deck of cards that need to be remembered:

1. A standard deck of playing cards consists of 4 suits, each with 13 cards, totaling 52 cards in the deck.

Spades	♠	Hearts	♥
Clubs	♣	Diamonds	♦

2. Two suits, Spades and Clubs, are black; i.e., there are 2 × 13 = 26 black cards.

3. Two suits, Hearts and Diamonds, are red; i.e., there are 2 × 13 = 26 red cards.

4. The 13 cards in each suit consist of: Ace (A), 2, 3, 4, 5, 6, 7, 8, 9, 10, Jack (J), Queen (Q), and King (K).

5. The Jack, Queen, and King cards from each suit are called face (or picture) cards; i.e., there are 3 × 4 = 12 face cards in the deck.

> "Ace" is not a face (or picture) card.

Therefore, using an outcome table to record the outcomes of the suit and value of the card:

SUIT	VALUE												
	A	2	3	4	5	6	7	8	9	10	J	Q	K
Spades (♠)	A(♠)	2(♠)	3(♠)	4(♠)	5(♠)	6(♠)	7(♠)	8(♠)	9(♠)	10(♠)	J(♠)	Q(♠)	K(♠)
Hearts (♥)	A(♥)	2(♥)	3(♥)	4(♥)	5(♥)	6(♥)	7(♥)	8(♥)	9(♥)	10(♥)	J(♥)	Q(♥)	K(♥)
Clubs (♣)	A(♣)	2(♣)	3(♣)	4(♣)	5(♣)	6(♣)	7(♣)	8(♣)	9(♣)	10(♣)	J(♣)	Q(♣)	K(♣)
Diamonds (♦)	A(♦)	2(♦)	3(♦)	4(♦)	5(♦)	6(♦)	7(♦)	8(♦)	9(♦)	10(♦)	J(♦)	Q(♦)	K(♦)

Tree Diagrams

When there are more than two pieces of information that need to be recorded, we cannot use outcome tables to identify all the outcomes, as we would need more than two dimensions in our table, making it infeasible or even impossible to write out. Another way to list out all the outcomes is to make use of a **tree diagram**.

In a tree diagram, each outcome is represented by a branch of a tree. Below is a tree diagram to demonstrate the possible outcomes of tossing a coin twice:

Step 1: When the coin is tossed once, there are two possible outcomes: Heads (*H*) and Tails (*T*). Therefore, start drawing two branches from a point and mark the end of one branch as *H* and the other as *T*.

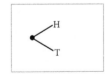

Step 2: When the coin is tossed a second time, there are two possible outcomes, *H* and *T*, as in the first toss. Draw two branches from the end point *H* (from Step 1) and mark the end of one branch as *H* and the other as *T*. This is to show the possible outcomes of a second toss when the outcome of the first toss is *H*.

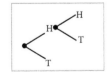

Step 3: Similarly, draw two branches from the end point *T* (from Step 1) and mark the end of one branch as *H* and the other as *T*. This is to show the possible outcomes of a second toss when the outcome of the first toss is *T*.

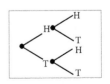

Step 4:   There are 4 end points marked *H, T, H,* and *T*. To identify the outcomes in the sample space, start from the original point and trace through the branches to the end point of each branch.

Therefore, the sample space, *S* = {*HH, HT, TH, TT*}.

Example 5.1-g	Determining the Sample Space for Tossing Three Coins using a Tree Diagram

Three coins are tossed. Draw a tree diagram and list the sample space.

Solution   The possible equally-likely outcomes for each coin toss are Heads (*H*) or Tails (*T*).

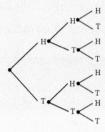

Therefore, the sample space, *S* = {*HHH, HHT, HTH, HTT, THH, THT, TTH, TTT*}.

Example 5.1-h	Determining the Sample Space for the Sexes of Four Children using a Tree Diagram

Couples with four children are selected at random and the sex of each of their children is recorded. Draw a tree diagram and list the sample space.

Solution   Given a couple with four children, the possible equally-likely outcomes for the sex of each child is either Male (*M*) or Female (*F*).

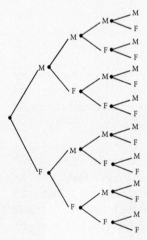

Therefore, the sample space is:

S = {*MMMM, MMMF, MMFM, MMFF, MFMM, MFMF, MFFM, MFFF, FMMM, FMMF, FMFM, FMFF, FFMM, FFMF, FFFM, FFFF*}

Venn Diagrams

In situations where the outcomes are grouped together by characteristics of the data into categories (with or without overlap), we can use a **Venn diagram** to determine the sample space. A Venn diagram consists of a large rectangle, which represents the entire sample space, containing smaller circles within, each representing a category of the data sharing a particular characteristic.

Consider a scenario where some grade 12 students participate in drama (D), some participate in athletics (A), and some participate in leadership (L); the Venn diagram to represent this scenario would be as follows:

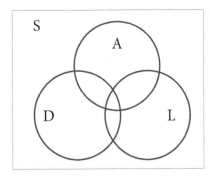

Example 5.1-i   Analyzing the Sample Space using a Venn Diagram

In the scenario above, a grade 12 student is selected at random, and his/her extracurricular activities are recorded.

Analyze the sample space for the scenario, given the following additional information:

- There are 150 students in grade 12

- 72 students are involved in Athletics (A)

- 58 students are involved in Drama (D)

- 49 students are involved in Leadership (L)

- 16 students are involved in Athletics **and** Drama (A and D)

- 27 students are involved in Athletics **and** Leadership (A and L)

- 23 students are involved in Drama **and** Leadership (D and L)

- 11 students are involved in all three (A, D, and L)

Solution

In order to analyze this sample space, we need to work from the inside of the Venn diagram (i.e., the overlap of all three circles) out:

- 11 students are involved in all three extracurricular activities (A, D, and L); this is the intersection of all three circles.

- 16 students are involved in Athletics **and** Drama, but of those, 11 are also involved in Leadership (i.e., all three); therefore, 16 – 11 = 5 are involved in Athletics **and** Drama (A and D) *only.*

  - Similarly, 27 – 11 = 16 are involved in Athletics **and** Leadership (A and L) *only.*

  - And, 23 – 11 = 12 are involved in Drama **and** Leadership (D and L) *only.*

Solution
continued

- 72 students are involved in Athletics, but of those, 5 are also involved in Drama, 16 are also involved in Leadership, and 11 are involved in all three; therefore, 72 – (5 + 16 + 11) = 40 are involved in Athletics (A) *only.*

  - Similarly, 58 – (5 + 12 + 11) = 30 are involved in Drama (D) *only.*

  - And, 49 – (16 + 12 + 11) = 10 are involved in Leadership (L) *only.*

- Therefore, there are 11 + 5 + 16 + 12 + 40 + 30 + 10 = 124 students involved in **at least one** extracurricular activity, which means 150 – 124 = 26 students are not involved in any.

We can summarize this information directly on the Venn diagram:

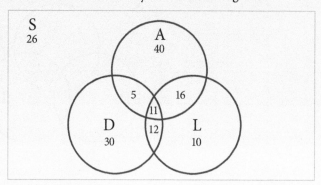

Complementary Events

Given an event A, the **complement of A**, denoted A^c (also A' or $\overline{A}$), is the set of all outcomes in the sample space for a given experiment that are not in A.

For example, if the experiment is rolling a standard 6-sided fair die, the sample space would be $S = \{1, 2, 3, 4, 5, 6\}$. So if event A is "Rolling an Odd Number" (i.e., $A = \{1, 3, 5\}$), then the complement of A is "Rolling an Even Number" (i.e., $A^c = \{2, 4, 6\}$).

This definition leads to the following conclusion:

- The number of outcomes in A^c is equal to the number of outcomes in the sample space S, minus the number of outcomes in A.

  i.e., $n(A^c) = n(S) - n(A)$

Dividing both sides of this equation by $n(S)$ results in the following:

$$\frac{n(A^c)}{n(S)} = \frac{n(S)}{n(S)} - \frac{n(A)}{n(S)}$$

$$P(A^c) = 1 - P(A)$$

i.e., the probability of A^c is equal to 1 minus the probability of event A.

Formula 5.1-c | **Probability of a Complementary Event**

$$P(A^c) = 1 - P(A)$$

Sometimes it is easier to find the probability of the complement of an event than the probability of the event itself.

For example, when a die is rolled, to calculate the probability of **not** rolling the number 2, we may determine the probability of rolling the number 2 and then subtract it from 1. That is, the event of rolling any of the numbers 1, 3, 4, 5, or 6 is the **complement** of the event of rolling the number 2.

Let A be the event of rolling the number 2. Then, A^c is the event of **not** rolling the number 2.

$$n(A) = 1 \text{ and } n(S) = 6$$

$$P(A) = \frac{n(A)}{n(S)} = \frac{1}{6} \text{ - i.e., the probability of rolling the number 2 is } \frac{1}{6}.$$

Using the complement rule,

$$P(A^c) = 1 - P(A) = 1 - \frac{1}{6} = \frac{5}{6}$$

Therefore, the probability of **not** rolling a 2 when a die is rolled is $\frac{5}{6}$.

Example 5.1-j	Calculating Probability using Complementary Events

Using the grade 12 student data from Example 5.1-i above, calculate the following:

(i) The probability that a randomly-selected grade 12 student is **not** involved in Athletics.

(ii) The probability that a randomly-selected grade 12 student is **not** involved in more than one extracurricular activity.

(iii) The probability that a randomly-selected grade 12 student is involved in **at least one** extracurricular activity.

Solution

(i) Let event A represent that the randomly-selected student is involved in Athletics. Then,

$$P(A) = \frac{72}{150} = 0.48$$

Therefore, A^c represents that the randomly-selected student is **not** involved in Athletics:

$$P(A^c) = 1 - 0.48 = 0.52$$

(ii) Let event B represent that the randomly-selected student is involved in more than one extracurricular activity. Then,

$$P(B) = \frac{16 + 12 + 5 + 11}{150} = \frac{44}{150} \approx 0.293$$

Therefore, B^c represents that the randomly-selected student is **not** involved in more than one extracurricular activity:

$$P(B^c) \approx 1 - 0.293 = 0.707$$

(iii) In this case, we first have to determine that the opposite of **at least one** is **none**. So, let event C represent that the randomly-selected student is involved in **no** extracurricular activities. Then,

$$P(C) = \frac{26}{150} \approx 0.173$$

Therefore, C^c represents that the randomly-selected student is involved in **at least one** extracurricular activity:

$$P(C^c) \approx 1 - 0.173 = 0.827$$

Odds

Quite often, we hear the phrase "the odds are..." when talking about probability. In reality, however, "odds" is not an interchangeable concept with "probability", though they are closely related:

- **Probability** is the proportion of outcomes that can occur that will result in event A, often expressed as a fraction, decimal, or percent.

- **Odds** is a ratio between the outcomes that will result in A and the outcomes that will not result in A, and it is almost always expressed as a ratio.

  - The **Odds Against** event A occurring is the ratio $n(A^c) : n(A)$, or $P(A^c) : P(A)$, expressed as a ratio in lowest terms.

  - The **Odds in Favour** of event A occurring is the ratio $n(A) : n(A^c)$, or $P(A) : P(A^c)$, expressed as a ratio in lowest terms.

The "Odds Against" are often used to determine a fair payout in a gambling situation. For example, if the odds against a certain event are $10 : 1$, then for every \$1 bet in favour of this event occurring, a fair payout would be \$10 (plus giving back the \$1 bet) if the event actually occurs.

Example 5.1-k | Calculating Odds Against and Odds in Favour

Using the definitions given above, calculate the following:

(i) In a standard deck of 52 cards, there are 12 face cards. What are the odds against and odds in favour of drawing a face card randomly out of a shuffled deck?

(ii) In a particular medical procedure, the probability of severe complications is approximately 4%. What are the odds against severe complications occurring as a result of this procedure?

Solution

(i) Let $A = \{drawing\ a\ face\ card\}$.

We know $n(A) = 12$ and $n(S) = 52$, so $n(A^c) = 52 - 12 = 40$. Therefore,

Odds Against $A = 40 : 12 = 10 : 3$

Odds in Favour of $A = 12 : 40 = 3 : 10$

(ii) Let $B = \{severe\ complications\ occur\}$.

We know $n(A) = 4\%$ and $n(S) = 100\%$, so $n(A^c) = 100\% - 4\% = 96\%$. Therefore,

Odds Against $B = 96\% : 4\% = 24 : 1$

Example 5.1-l | Odds vs Probability

A particular casino game states that for a particular bet, for every \$5 wagered, it pays out \$6 (and returns the \$5 wager).

(i) If this is a fair game, determine the probability of winning this bet.

(ii) If the house advantage is believed to be 5% (meaning that the house withholds approximately 5% of every bet for profit), determine the actual probability of winning.

Solution

(i) Let $C = \{winning\ the\ bet\}$. Then,

Odds Against $C = 6 : 5$

This means that for every $6 + 5 = 11$ outcomes, 5 of those will result in C occurring. Therefore,

$$P(C) = \frac{5}{11} \approx 0.455$$

Solution
continued

(ii)   If the house withholds 5% of every bet, then it is withholding 5% of $5 = $0.25 for every $5 bet. Then,

$$\text{Odds Against } C = 6.25 : 5$$

$$P(C) = \frac{5}{11.25} \approx 0.444$$

5.1 | Exercises

Answers to odd-numbered problems are available at the end of the textbook.

For Problems 1 to 6, analyze the scenarios and complete the following:

(i)   *Calculate the total number of outcomes.*

(ii)   *Construct the sample space by listing out all possible outcomes.*

(iii) *If the outcomes are grouped together by similar characteristics, how many different events are possible?*

1.   A doctor is explaining the post-surgical pain relief options to a patient and notes that there are 9 different prescription opioids, 5 different non-steroidal anti-inflammatory drugs (known as NSAIDs), and 1 over-the-counter (OTC) narcotic-acetaminophen.

2.   A pharmacist is explaining the OTC pain-relief options to a patient and notes that there are 12 different types of tablets, 8 different types of gel-caps, 7 different types of liquid oral suspensions, and 4 different types of chewable tablets.

3.   A consumer at a pharmacy is trying to decide what type of adhesive bandage to purchase. There are 10 different types of fabric bandages, 8 different types of plastic bandages, 4 different types of rubber/latex bandages, and 3 different types of liquid bandages.

4.   A consumer at a pharmacy is trying to decide what type of allergy medication to purchase. There are 4 different types of first-generation antihistamines, 6 different types of second-generation antihistamines, and 5 different types of third-generation antihistamines.

5.   A pregnant woman planning to have her baby delivered by Caesarian section (C-section) discusses the accommodation options after the birth with the charge nurse at her local hospital's maternity ward. She is told that there are 8 private rooms available with one bed in each, 6 semi-private rooms available with two beds in each, and 5 ward rooms with three beds in each.

6.   A patient in a hospital is given a choice for his meal: he can choose between 5 different types of sandwich, 4 different types of salad - each with 3 different choices of protein, or 3 different pasta options - each which can be made with regular pasta or gluten-free pasta.

For Problems 7 to 18, analyze the scenarios and complete the following:

(i)   *Determine what type of approach should be used to calculate the desired probability: theoretical, empirical, or subjective.*

(ii)   *Determine the probability of the desired event, if possible, rounded to 3 significant digits.*

7.   A clinical trial for a new pharmaceutical drug includes a sample of 500 randomly-selected patients. Of these patients, 83 experience mild side effects, including nausea and fatigue. Based on this, what is the probability that a patient will experience mild side effects while taking this new drug?

8.   Out of the 500 patients in Problem 7, 18 experienced serious side effects, including blurry vision and severe vomiting. Based on this, what is the probability that a patient will experience serious side effects while taking this new drug?

9.   In a hospital lottery, 2.5 million tickets are sold and there are 10 grand prizes of new homes worth approximately two million dollars. What is the probability of winning a grand prize in this lottery?

10.   In the lottery in Problem 9, there are 75 second prizes of cars valued between $30,000 and $50,000. What is the probability of winning a second prize in this lottery?

11.   A patient undergoing reconstructive knee surgery asks his surgeon about the probability of success for this operation. Based on the surgeon's experience and expert knowledge, what is the probability that the patient's surgery will be successful?

12. A patient with a form of terminal cancer asks her oncologist about the probability of surviving five or more years for patients receiving treatment for this type of cancer. Based on the oncologist's experience and expert knowledge, what is the probability that this patient will survive for five or more years?

13. During a quality control inspection of a sample of 1,250 pain-relief tablets, eight were found to be defective. Based on this, what is the probability that a randomly-selected tablet will be defective?

14. During a clinical placement, a nursing intern is supervised during her medication draws to ensure that they are done correctly and accurately. Out of the 82 times she draws medication, she makes an error three times (all three are subsequently caught by her supervisor, and so no patients were harmed in the making of this problem!). Based on this, what is the probability that the intern will make an error on her next medication draw?

15. Before writing a math test, a student in a pre-health program asks his math professor what she thinks the probability is that he will pass the test, based on the fact that he has come to every class and has done all of the homework. What will her answer be?

16. Another student from the program in Problem 15 who has done none of the homework and missed half of the classes asks the professor the same question. How will her answer change for this student?

17. A maternity ward in a hospital has 12 private rooms, 4 of which overlook the hospital gardens, and 3 of which look out onto the forest behind the hospital, while the rest overlook the parking lot. If a new mother is randomly assigned one of the private rooms, what is the probability that she will be assigned a room that overlooks the parking lot?

18. A nurse's schedule is based on a 9-day cycle of two 12-hour day shifts, followed by two 12-hour night shifts, followed by 5 days off in a row. Her friends are trying to decide on a date for a night out together, and she is free to attend any night except when she is scheduled to work the night shift. What is the probability that they will suggest a date that works for her?

For Problems 19 to 30, complete the following:

(i) *State which method should be used to best determine the sample space: an outcome table, a tree diagram, or a Venn diagram.*

(ii) *Calculate the probability of the desired event (assuming all outcomes are equally likely) using the method you decided upon in part (i), rounded to 3 significant digits as needed.*

19. A couple plans to have 4 children. What is the probability that they will have 2 boys and 2 girls?

20. A couple plans to have 4 children. What is the probability that they will have more boys than girls?

21. At a local hospital, there are 5 different obstetricians who deliver babies, 3 of whom are female doctors and the remaining 2 are male doctors. If a couple has 2 children, what is the probability that a female obstetrician will deliver both of their babies?

22. The blood type of a child is based on the blood types of his/her parents. The child's father has type A+ blood, meaning that the father could contribute A+, A−, O+, or O− antigens, and the child's mother has type B+ blood, meaning that the mother could contribute B+, B−, O+, or O− antigens. What is the probability that the child will have type O blood (i.e., will receive only O+ or O− antigens from both parents?)

23. A nursing student must register for 2 different practicum timeslots - one on Friday and one on Saturday. There are 5 timeslots available on both days - morning, midday, early afternoon, late afternoon, or early evening - and on Saturdays there is also a late evening timeslot. She is not a morning person and hopes that she will not be given any morning timeslots. If her timeslots are selected randomly, what is the probability that she will not have a morning practicum?

24. The same nursing student from Problem 23 is also registering for her 2 courses in the same semester, all of which run Monday to Thursday, so as not to conflict with the practicum timeslots. One course has 4 sections available, 2 of which are offered in the mornings; the other course has 7 sections available, 2 of which are offered in the mornings. None of the sections of either course run at the same time as any of the sections of the other course, so there is no chance of a conflict existing between the two classes the student is registered into. If her two sections are assigned randomly, what is the probability that she will not be assigned any morning classes?

25. A professor in a pre-health science class takes a poll of his 80 students and finds that 62 intend to go into nursing, 34 intend to pursue degrees, and 26 intend to pursue nursing degrees. Based on this, what is the probability that a randomly-selected student will pursue a non-degree credential in a non-nursing program?

26. A professor in a pre-health science class takes a poll of his 120 students and finds that 81 intend to go into nursing. Out of the 84 female students enrolled, 66 intend to go into nursing. Based on this, what is the probability that a randomly-selected student will not be female and will not be pursuing nursing as a career?

27. A pharmacy technician is required to take an online quiz as part of a workplace safety program. There are 15 questions on the quiz, all of which are True-False questions. He knows the answer to 10 of the questions, but he needs a score of 12 or better out of 15 to pass the quiz. What is the probability that he will pass the quiz by guessing randomly on the 5 questions he is unsure of?

28. A veterinary technician is required to take an online quiz as part of her ongoing professional development. There are 10 questions on the quiz, each with 3 possible answers, of which she knows the answer to 7. If she needs a score of 8 or better out of 10 to pass the quiz, what is the probability that she will pass the quiz by guessing randomly on the 3 questions she is unsure of?

29. There are 168 clients registered at a veterinarian clinic. Out of these clients, 105 own dogs, 82 own cats, and 45 own rodents. Within those groups, 53 own both a dog and a cat, 21 own a dog and a rodent, 11 own a cat and a rodent, and 7 own all three. What is the probability that a randomly-selected client registered at the clinic does not own any of these types of animal?

30. There are 96 patients on a wait list for a particular nursing home. Out of these patients, 72 are considered "high urgency" (i.e., they will need a bed in a nursing home in the next 3 months), 53 are considered "high priority" (i.e., they listed the nursing home as their first choice), and 48 are considered to be "high needs" (i.e., they require additional care and support at the home). Within those groups, 35 are both "high urgency" and "high priority", 37 are both "high urgency" and "high needs", 24 are both "high priority" and "high needs", and 15 are considered all three. What is the probability that a randomly-selected patient on the wait list is not in any of these three groups?

For Problems 31 to 42, complete the following:

(i) *Calculate the probability of the desired event, rounded to 3 significant digits as needed.*
(ii) *State the complementary event and calculate its probability.*
(iii) *Compute the odds against and odds in favour of the event.*

31. Flipping a coin 3 times and having it land "Heads" all 3 times.

32. Flipping a coin 4 times and having it land "Tails" all 4 times.

33. Drawing a card out of a standard deck and having it be a face card (Jack, Queen, or King).

34. Drawing a card out of a standard deck and having it be a heart.

35. Rolling a number greater than 16 on a 20-sided die.

36. Rolling a number less than 3 on a 12-sided die.

37. Being offered one of the 12 co-op jobs that you apply for and having it be one of your top 3 choices.

38. Being assigned one of 15 different elective courses and having it be one of your top 5 choices.

39. Randomly selecting one of the 288 out of 720 patients in a clinical drug trial selected to receive the placebo.

40. Randomly selecting one of the 360 out of 864 patients on a wait list for a family doctor selected to be assigned to a new family doctor at a medical clinic.

41. Randomly selecting one of the 17.6% of Canadians with hypertension (high blood pressure).

42. Randomly selecting one of the 9.5% of Canadians with diabetes.

5.2 | Compound Events

In the previous section, we examined ways to define and use the sample space for a given experiment to determine the probability of an event occurring. However, if there are a large number of outcomes (e.g., in most lotteries, there are several million different outcomes), it becomes infeasible to attempt to list all of them in the sample space.

Oftentimes these events are known as **compound events** - events that are made up of several simple events - and we can make use of shortcuts to calculate the probability of such, without needing to list out all the events in the sample space.

We will now examine several methods for calculating probabilities of compound events, and some of the situations in which they arise.

The Addition Rule

Consider that we are given two events A and B, and we want to know the probability that **at least one** of the two events occurs - i.e., the probability that either A **or** B occurs, denoted $P(A$ or $B)$.

*Note: In probability, the word **or** always refers to the "inclusive or", meaning that either A can occur or B can occur, or **both** A and B can occur.*

Addition Rule for Mutually Exclusive Events

Two or more events that have no outcomes in common are called mutually exclusive events.

The simplest example of calculating $P(A$ or $B)$ occurs when events A and B cannot occur simultaneously - i.e., the probability that both A and B can occur together is zero: $P(A$ and $B) = 0$. In this situation, we say that events A and B are **mutually exclusive**, as shown in Exhibit 5.2-a, and the probability that either A or B occurs is determined using the **Mutually Exclusive Addition Rule**:

$$P(A \text{ or } B) = P(A) + P(B)$$

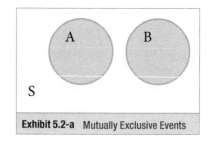

Exhibit 5.2-a   Mutually Exclusive Events

Example 5.2-a   Calculating Probability using the Mutually Exclusive Addition Rule

On the first day of a Statistics for Pre-Health Sciences class, the professor asks the 40 students in the class to indicate which **one** program they are planning to enrol in after graduation. The results show that there are 17 students who are planning to go into a Nursing program and 13 students who are planning to go into a Pharmacy program. If one student is selected at random, what is the probability that he/she is planning to go into a Nursing program or a Pharmacy program?

Solution

Since the students may only write down one choice of program, this tells us the two groups (those who are planning to enrol in a Nursing program and those who are planning to enrol in a Pharmacy program) are mutually exclusive. Hence,

$$P(Nursing \text{ or } Pharmacy) = P(Nursing) + P(Pharmacy)$$

Moreover, we know that $P(Nursing) = \dfrac{17}{40} = 0.425$ and $P(Pharmacy) = \dfrac{13}{40} = 0.325$. Therefore,

$$P(Nursing \text{ or } Pharmacy) = \frac{17}{40} + \frac{13}{40} = \frac{30}{40} = \frac{3}{4} = 0.75$$

This tells us that the probability that a randomly-selected student is interested in enrolling in a Nursing program or a Pharmacy program is 0.75.

Generalized Addition Rule

How do we calculate the probability of $P(A$ or $B)$ if the two events A and B are **not** mutually exclusive (i.e., they **can** occur together)? We can analyze this situation using a Venn diagram:

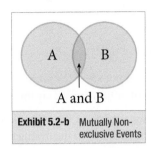

A and B

Exhibit 5.2-b Mutually Non-exclusive Events

In this diagram, if the circle with A represents $P(A)$, and the circle with B represents $P(B)$, then the probability of at least one of those two events occurring, denoted $P(A$ or $B)$, is still essentially the sum of the two individual probabilities. However, in this case, if we add the two probabilities together, we have double-counted the area represented by the overlap in the diagram, which is the probability that both A and B will occur, denoted $P(A$ and $B)$; hence, we need to subtract this value.

The formula to calculate the probability of either A or B occurring in this scenario is known as the **Generalized Addition Rule** and is given as follows:

Formula 5.2-a

Generalized Addition Rule for Probabilities

$$P(A \text{ or } B) = P(A) + P(B) - P(A \text{ and } B)$$

Note: This form of the Addition Rule still works in the case where A and B are mutually exclusive, as in that case, P(A and B) = 0, hence P(A or B) = P(A) + P(B) – 0 = P(A) + P(B). This is why it is known as the "Generalized" Addition Rule, because it works in every (general) case.

Example 5.2-b

Calculating Probability using the Generalized Addition Rule

The professor in Example 5.2-a decided instead to ask the students to write down the top **two** programs in which they were considering enrolling after graduating from the program. The results showed that 24 students listed Nursing, 19 students listed Pharmacy, and 6 students listed both. If one student is randomly selected from the class, what is the probability that he/she is interested in enrolling in a Nursing or Pharmacy program?

Solution

- $P(Nursing) = \dfrac{24}{40} = 0.6$

- $P(Pharmacy) = \dfrac{19}{40} = 0.475$

- $P(Nursing \text{ and } Pharmacy) = \dfrac{6}{40} = 0.15$

Therefore, using the Generalized Addition Rule,

$$P(Nursing \text{ or } Pharmacy) = \frac{24}{40} + \frac{19}{40} - \frac{6}{40} = \frac{37}{40} = 0.925$$

Hence, the probability that a randomly-selected student is interested in enrolling in a Nursing or Pharmacy program is 0.925.

The Multiplication Rule

The Addition Rule gave us a method to calculate the probability of event A **or** event B occurring. We now turn to a method for calculating the probability of event A **and** event B occurring, denoted $P(A \text{ and } B)$: the **Multiplication Rule**.

Multiplication Rule for Independent Events

If the occurrence of either of the two events A and B does not affect the probability of the occurrence of the other event, we say the two events are **independent**; otherwise, we say the events are **dependent**.

If two events A and B are independent (i.e., the occurrence of one event has no effect on the occurrence of the other event), then the probability of both events occurring simultaneously is the product of the probabilities of the individual events.

$$P(A \text{ and } B) = P(A) \cdot P(B)$$

In general, the word "and" in probability calculations indicates multiplication.

For example, if a coin is tossed and a die is rolled, the probability of flipping Heads and rolling 4 is as follows:

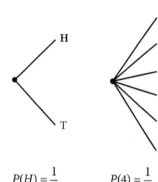

$$P(H \text{ and } 4) = P(H) \cdot P(4)$$
$$= \frac{1}{2} \cdot \frac{1}{6}$$
$$= \frac{1}{12}$$

$$P(H) = \frac{1}{2} \qquad P(4) = \frac{1}{6}$$

Example 5.2-c | Calculating Probability using the Multiplication Rule for Independent Events

A multiple-choice quiz consists of 10 questions, each with 4 possible answers. If a student who did not study guesses randomly on every question, what is the probability of the following events occurring?

(i) The student will correctly answer any given question.

(ii) The student will correctly answer the first two questions.

(iii) The student will correctly answer all 10 questions.

(iv) The student will not answer any questions correctly.

(v) The student will answer at least one question correctly.

Solution

(i) Since there are 4 possible answers for any given question, and there is only 1 correct answer, the probability of randomly answering a question correctly is $P(Correct) = \frac{1}{4} = 0.25$.

Since the correctness of the student's response on one question bears no impact on their probability of being correct on any subsequent question, we can use the multiplication rule for independent events for parts (ii), (iii), and (iv).

Solution
continued

(ii) $P(Correct\ and\ Correct) = \dfrac{1}{4} \cdot \dfrac{1}{4} = \dfrac{1}{16} = 0.0625$

(iii) $P(Correct\ on\ all\ 10\ Questions) = \dfrac{1}{4} \cdot \dfrac{1}{4} \cdot ... \cdot \dfrac{1}{4} = \left(\dfrac{1}{4}\right)^{10} = \dfrac{1}{1,048,576} \approx 0.000000954$

(iv) $P(Incorrect\ on\ all\ 10\ Questions) = \dfrac{3}{4} \cdot \dfrac{3}{4} \cdot ... \cdot \dfrac{3}{4} = \left(\dfrac{3}{4}\right)^{10} = \dfrac{59,049}{1,048,576} \approx 0.0563$

(v) Recall from Section 5.1 that $P(At\ least\ one) = 1 - P(None)$. Therefore,

$P(Correct\ on\ at\ least\ 1\ Question) = 1 - P(Incorrect\ on\ all\ 10\ Questions) \approx 1 - 0.0563 \approx 0.944$

Generalized Multiplication Rule

If two events A and B are **dependent** (i.e., the possible outcome of one event depends on the outcome of the other event), then the probability of obtaining both events, $P(A\ and\ B)$, must be calculated in a different way. Consider the following example:

Two marbles are drawn from a bag containing 6 red marbles and 3 white marbles, without replacement (i.e., the marbles are not put back into the bag after being drawn). What is the probability that the first marble is red and the second marble is white?

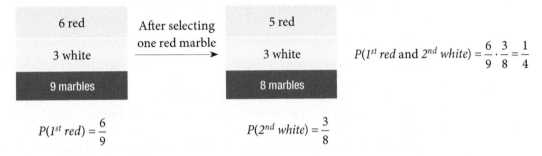

Notice that because we did not replace the first marble after drawing it, we have changed the probability that the second marble will be white. As such, we cannot simply use the multiplication rule we defined above, because the events are not independent.

The probability of selecting a white marble is $\dfrac{3}{8}$ because removing a red marble has reduced the total number of marbles in the bag from 9 to 8. This is known as **conditional probability**.

Conditional Probability

Conditional probability is the probability of event B occurring given that event A has already occurred. It is denoted $P(B|A)$ - the probability of B **given** A. In the previous example, the probability that the second marble is white **given** that the first marble is red would be written as $P(2^{nd}\ white|1^{st}\ red) = \dfrac{3}{8}$.

This brings us to the multiplication rule for dependent events:

$$P(A\ and\ B) = P(A) \cdot \underbrace{P(B|A)}$$

Probability of event B given
that event A has occurred

Conditional probability also gives us another way of determining if two events are independent:

$$P(B|A) = P(B)\ if\ and\ only\ if\ events\ A\ and\ B\ are\ independent$$
(i.e., the occurrence of A has no impact on the probability of the occurrence of B).

As such, if events A and B are independent, we can substitute $P(B|A)$ in for $P(B)$ in the multiplication rule for independent events:

$P(A \text{ and } B) = P(A) \cdot P(B)$ Substituting $P(B|A)$ in for $P(B)$, since A and B are independent,

$P(A \text{ and } B) = P(A) \cdot P(B|A)$ This is the multiplication rule for dependent events.

Therefore, the multiplication rule for dependent events is in fact a *generalized multiplication rule for probabilities*, since substituting $P(B|A) = P(B)$ has no effect on the formula when events A and B are independent.

Formula 5.2-b	**Generalized Multiplication Rule for Probabilities**

$$P(A \text{ and } B) = P(A) \cdot P(B|A)$$

Example 5.2-d	**Calculating Conditional Probability**

A deck of cards is shuffled and a card is drawn randomly and removed from the deck - it happens to be an Ace. The deck is reshuffled and another card is drawn from the deck; what is the probability that it is also an Ace? Is drawing the second Ace independent of drawing the first Ace?

Solution

Since there are 52 cards in the deck and 4 of them are Aces, the probability of drawing the first Ace out of the deck is $P(Ace1) = \dfrac{4}{52} \approx 0.0769$.

However, once that Ace is removed, there are now only 51 cards remaining, of which only 3 are Aces. Hence, the probability of drawing a second Ace is $P(Ace2 \mid Ace1) = \dfrac{3}{51} \approx 0.0588$.

Therefore, drawing the second Ace is not independent of drawing the first Ace, as the probabilities have changed as a result of the first Ace being drawn and removed from the deck.

Notice in the previous example, that if the first Ace was replaced (i.e., put back into the deck) and the deck was shuffled and **then** the second card was drawn, the probability of drawing a second Ace would be the same as drawing the first Ace: $\dfrac{4}{52} \approx 0.0769$, making the events independent.

This leads us to the following important conclusion:

- Drawing multiple cards from a deck **with** replacement represents **independent** events.
- Drawing multiple cards from a deck **without** replacement represents **dependent** events.

Example 5.2-e	**Calculating Probability using the Generalized Multiplication Rule**

If two cards are randomly drawn from a shuffled deck, without replacement, what is the probability of drawing the following:

(i) Two aces?

(ii) Two face cards?

(iii) An ace and a face card?

Solution

(i) There are 4 Aces in the deck, consisting of a total of 52 cards, so the probability that the first card drawn is an Ace is $P(Ace1) = \dfrac{4}{52}$.

After the first Ace is drawn, there are now 3 Aces remaining, in a deck now with only 51 cards, so the probability that the second card drawn is an Ace is $P(Ace2|Ace1) = \dfrac{3}{51}$.

Therefore, the probability that both cards drawn are Aces is as follows:

$$P(Ace1 \text{ and } Ace2) = P(Ace1) \cdot P(Ace2|Ace1) = \frac{4}{52} \cdot \frac{3}{51} = \frac{12}{2,652} = \frac{1}{221} \approx 0.00452$$

Solution
continued

(ii)   There are 12 Face cards in the deck, consisting of a total of 52 cards, so similar to part (i), the probability that the first card drawn is a Face card is $P(Face1) = \dfrac{12}{52}$, and the probability that the second card drawn is a Face card after the first one is drawn is $P(Face2|Face1) = \dfrac{11}{51}$. Therefore, the probability that both cards drawn are Face cards is as follows:

$$P(Face1 \text{ and } Face2) = P(Face1) \cdot P(Face2|Face1) = \frac{12}{52} \cdot \frac{11}{51} = \frac{132}{2,652} = \frac{11}{221} \approx 0.0498$$

(iii)   In order to draw both an Ace and a Face card, we could either draw the Ace first and the Face card second, or we could draw the Face card first and the Ace second, so we have to consider both cases. In both cases, there will be 4 Aces and 12 Face cards.

$$P(Ace1 \text{ and } Face2) = \frac{4}{52} \cdot \frac{12}{51} = \frac{48}{2,652} = \frac{4}{221} \approx 0.0181$$

$$P(Face1 \text{ and } Ace2) = \frac{12}{52} \cdot \frac{4}{51} = \frac{48}{2,652} = \frac{4}{221} \approx 0.0181$$

Therefore, the probability of drawing an Ace and a Face card in either order is as follows:

$$P(Ace \text{ and } Face) = P((Ace1 \text{ and } Face2) \text{ or } (Face1 \text{ and } Ace2))$$

And since these are mutually exclusive events, we can use the Mutually Exclusive Addition Rule:

$$P(Ace \text{ and } Face) = P(Ace1 \text{ and } Face2) + P(Face1 \text{ and } Ace2) = \frac{4}{221} + \frac{4}{221} = \frac{8}{221} \approx 0.0362$$

Bayes' Theorem

We have introduced the notion of conditional probability - when we are given the probability of one event occurring after another event has already occurred. However, many times in practical scenarios, the conditional probability that we are given is reversed from the one with which we need to make predictions.

For example, consider a doctor who suggests to all her female patients over 30 that they undergo a new screening for female reproductive system cancers as a preventative measure every few years. She informs her patients that this particular test reports back a positive result in 99% of all cases where the cancer is actually present (known as a 99% sensitivity) and reports back a negative result in 98% of all cases where the cancer is not actually present (known as a 98% specificity).

If a patient submits to the screening and receives a positive result, she may be convinced that there is a 99% chance that she does indeed have some form of reproductive system cancer. However, she is missing the information that, according to Statistics Canada, only about 0.058% of the female population actually have some form of reproductive system cancer, and that she was "randomly selected" to undergo the screening - that is, the doctor recommended this to all her female patients over 30 and had no reason to suggest the screening based on her symptoms. As such, the probability from which the patient is basing her assumption is the probability that she will test positive **given that she already has cancer**: $P(Test+|Cancer)$.

In fact, what the patient really needs to know is the probability that she has cancer **given that she tested positive**: $P(Cancer|Test+)$. How do we determine this "flipped" probability?

First, recall the Generalized Multiplication Rule:

$$P(A \text{ and } B) = P(A) \cdot P(B|A) \qquad \text{Equation (i)}$$

Rearranging this formula to solve for the conditional probability $P(B|A)$, we obtain:

$$P(B|A) = \frac{P(A \text{ and } B)}{P(A)} \qquad \text{Equation (ii)}$$

So, logically, if we wish to know $P(A|B)$, the formula would be as follows:

$$P(A|B) = \frac{P(A \text{ and } B)}{P(B)} \qquad \text{Equation (iii)}$$

Finally, substituting $P(A \text{ and } B) = P(A) \cdot P(B|A)$ from Equation (i) in for the numerator in Equation (iii):

$$P(A|B) = \frac{P(A) \cdot P(B|A)}{P(B)}$$

Thus, in order to calculate a flipped conditional probability, we need to know the reversed conditional probability, and the probability of each of the events occurring individually. However, in this (and many) situations, we do not know $P(B)$. Fortunately, an English mathematician by the name of Thomas Bayes came up with the following formula for determining $P(B)$ based on the information that would be readily available:

$$P(B) = P(B|A) \cdot P(A) + P(B|A^c) \cdot P(A^c)$$

(where A^c is the complement of event A).

Therefore, we can summarize the formula for the "flipped" conditional probability in the following way, which is formally known as Bayes' Theorem:

Formula 5.2-c — **Bayes' Theorem**

$$P(A|B) = \frac{P(B|A) \cdot P(A)}{P(B|A) \cdot P(A) + P(B|A^c) \cdot P(A^c)}$$

Example 5.2-f — **Calculating Bayesian Probability**

Calculate the probability that a randomly-selected patient in the example above who tests positive for female reproductive system cancer actually has cancer.

Solution

Let event A = "Has cancer" and event B = "Tests positive". This means that A^c = "No cancer" and B^c = "Tests negative".

Then the probability of testing positive given that the patient has cancer is $P(B|A) = 0.99$ and the probability of a randomly-selected female in the population having reproductive system cancer is $P(A) = 0.00058$.

> We always need to convert percents to decimals in our calculations.

We also know that the probability of testing negative given that the patient does not have cancer is $P(B^c|A^c) = 0.98$ and the probability of a randomly-selected female in the population not having reproductive system cancer is $P(A^c) = 1 - P(A) = 1 - 0.00058 = 0.99942$.

Finally, we need to know the probability of testing positive given that the patient does not have cancer, i.e., $P(B|A^c)$. This is the complement of testing negative given that the patient does not have cancer, so $P(B|A^c) = 1 - P(B^c|A^c) = 1 - 0.98 = 0.02$.

Now we have everything we need to evaluate Bayes' Theorem.

Using Formula 5.2-c,

$$P(A|B) = \frac{P(B|A) \cdot P(A)}{P(B|A) \cdot P(A) + P(B|A^c) \cdot P(A^c)}$$

$$= \frac{(0.99)(0.00058)}{(0.99)(0.00058) + (0.02)(0.99942)}$$

$$= \frac{0.0005742}{0.0005742 + 0.0199884}$$

$$= \frac{0.0005742}{0.0205626}$$

$$\approx 0.0279$$

Therefore, the patient who tests positive for a reproductive system cancer actually has less than a 3% chance of actually having cancer (much to the relief of the patient to be sure!).

The example above demonstrates the importance of not subjecting everyone in the population to medical screenings for certain diseases and conditions. As demonstrated in this example, even tests with a very high sensitivity (true positive rate) and specificity (true negative rate) can be very misleading if used over the entire population without any other information, especially if the likelihood of occurrence of the disease/condition in the general population is very low.

As such, it is important to only use these tests in instances where the doctor would have other information to indicate that the disease or condition may actually be present in the patient (or is at least more likely to be present in the patient). It is also a good idea to always double-check a positive result by performing another test before confirming the diagnosis and proceeding with treatment.

The example above also demonstrates that calculating the "flipped" conditional probability using Bayes' Theorem can be difficult to follow and even more difficult to work through. This indicates the need for a clearer way to display the information.

Contingency Tables

A **contingency table** is a method of displaying a summary of the values of two variables in a sample space: down the left-side column of the table, all the values of one variable are listed, and across the top row of the table, all the values of the other variable are listed. Then, in the body of the table, in each cell is listed the number of elements in the sample space that correspond to the values in the intersecting column and row.

Contingency tables are very useful in calculating the probability of compound events, as all the values in the sample space are clearly written out:

Event A Outcome	Event B Outcome		TOTAL PROBABILITY
	Positive (B)	Negative (B^c)	
Positive (A)	$P(A \text{ and } B)$	$P(A \text{ and } B^c)$	$P(A)$
Negative (A^c)	$P(A^c \text{ and } B)$	$P(A^c \text{ and } B^c)$	$P(A^c)$
TOTAL PROBABILITY	$P(B)$	$P(B^c)$	1.00

For the cancer test example above, the events would be as follows:

Let A = Patient Has Cancer - then, A^c = Patient Does Not Have Cancer

Let B = Positive Test Result - then, B^c = Negative Test Result

We know the following probabilities:

$P(Cancer) = P(A) = 0.00058$, which means $P(No\ Cancer) = P(A^c) = 1 - 0.00058 = 0.99942$

$P(Test+|Cancer) = P(B|A) = 0.99$, which means $P(Test-|Cancer) = P(B^c|A) = 0.01$

$P(Test-|No\ Cancer) = P(B^c|A^c) = 0.98$, which means $P(Test+|No\ Cancer) = P(B|A^c) = 0.02$

Using the Generalized Multiplication Rule, we can calculate the following joint probabilities for the table:

$P(A \text{ and } B) = P(A) \cdot P(B|A) = 0.00058(0.99) = 0.0005742$

$P(A \text{ and } B^c) = P(A) \cdot P(B^c|A) = 0.00058(0.01) = 0.0000058$

$P(A^c \text{ and } B) = P(A^c) \cdot P(B|A^c) = 0.99942(0.02) = 0.0199884$

$P(A^c \text{ and } B^c) = P(A^c) \cdot P(B^c|A^c) = 0.99942(0.98) = 0.9794316$

We now have all the values we need in order to fill in our contingency table:

Patient Condition	Test Result		TOTAL PROBABILITY
	Positive (B)	Negative (B^c)	
Has Cancer (A)	0.0005742	0.0000058	0.00058
Does Not Have Cancer (A^c)	0.0199884	0.9794316	0.99942
TOTAL PROBABILITY	0.0205626	0.9794374	1.00000

Hence, we can calculate the desired probability $P(Cancer|Test+)$ using the conditional probability formula:

$$P(A|B) = \frac{P(A \text{ and } B)}{P(B)} = \frac{0.0005742}{0.0205626} \approx 0.0279$$

We can also construct contingency tables for scenarios where we know the number of each type of outcome, usually from raw data that is collected. The contingency table gives us a way of summarizing the data and making probability calculations involving the data very straightforward.

Example 5.2-g	Calculating Probabilities with Contingency Tables

Assume 200 students graduating from a Pre-Health program are asked which program area they will be studying in next. The results are tallied and grouped by gender as well, and listed in a contingency table:

Program	Gender		TOTAL
	Male	Female	
Nursing	19	56	75
Pharmacy	24	18	42
Paramedics	18	10	28
Veterinary	8	12	20
Kinesiology	6	11	17
Athletic Therapy	3	8	11
Other	2	5	7
TOTAL	80	120	200

If a graduating student is selected at random from the population represented by the contingency table above, determine the following:

(i)   The probability that the student is female.

(ii)   The probability that the student is moving on to a Kinesiology program.

(iii)   The probability that the student is male and moving on to a Pharmacy program.

(iv)   The probability that the student is female given that the student is moving on to an Athletic Therapy program.

(v)   The probability that the student is moving on to a Paramedics program, given that the student is male.

(vi)   If two students are selected from those moving on to a Veterinary-related program to receive a special scholarship, what is the probability that both students are female?

(vii)   Based on the information above, is being female independent from moving on to a Nursing-related program?

(viii) Based on the information above, is being male independent from moving on to a Veterinary-related program?

Solution

(i) $P(Female) = \dfrac{120}{200} = 0.6$

(ii) $P(Kinesiology) = \dfrac{17}{200} = 0.085$

(iii) $P(Male \text{ and } Pharmacy) = \dfrac{24}{200} = 0.12$

(iv) $P(Female|Athletic\ Therapy) = \dfrac{8}{11} \approx 0.727$

(v) $P(Paramedics|Male) = \dfrac{18}{80} = 0.225$

(vi) $P(Female1|Veterinary) = \dfrac{12}{20} = 0.6$, and $P(Female2|Veterinary) = \dfrac{11}{19} \approx 0.579$

       Therefore, $P(Both\ Female|Veterinary) = \dfrac{12}{20} \cdot \dfrac{11}{19} = \dfrac{132}{380} \approx 0.347$

(vii) • $P(Female) = \dfrac{120}{200} = 0.6$

       • $P(Nursing) = \dfrac{75}{200} = 0.375$

       • $P(Female \text{ and } Nursing) = \dfrac{56}{200} = 0.28$

       • $P(Female) \cdot P(Nursing) = 0.6 \cdot 0.375 = 0.225$

Since $P(Female \text{ and } Nursing) \neq P(Female) \cdot P(Nursing)$, the two events (being female and going into a Nursing-related program) are **not** independent - i.e., being female changes the likelihood that the student will move on into a Nursing-related program. In fact, since the probability of the joint event is higher than the product of the individual probabilities, it tells us that female students are more-likely to go into a Nursing-related program.

(viii) • $P(Male) = \dfrac{80}{200} = 0.4$

       • $P(Veterinary) = \dfrac{20}{200} = 0.1$

       • $P(Male \text{ and } Veterinary) = \dfrac{8}{200} = 0.04$

       • $P(Male) \cdot P(Veterinary) = 0.4 \cdot 0.1 = 0.04$

Since $P(Male \text{ and } Veterinary) = P(Male) \cdot P(Veterinary)$, the two events (being male and going into a Veterinary-related program) **are** independent - i.e., being male does not impact the probability that the student will go into a Veterinary-related program. In fact, since the proportions of male and female students going into a Veterinary-related program is the same as the overall proportions of male and female students in the population, gender has no impact on the probability of a student going into a Veterinary-related program.

5.2 | Exercises

1. Calculate $P(A \text{ or } B)$ in the following scenarios:
   a. $P(A) = 0.45$, $P(B) = 0.2$; A and B *are mutually exclusive*
   b. $P(A) = 0.3$, $P(B) = 0.25$, $P(A \text{ and } B) = 0.1$
   c. $P(A) = 0.8$, $P(B) = 0.7$, $P(A \text{ and } B) = 0.65$

2. Calculate $P(A \text{ or } B)$ in the following scenarios:
   a. $P(A) = 0.5$, $P(B) = 0.35$; A and B *are mutually exclusive*
   b. $P(A) = 0.15$, $P(B) = 0.4$, $P(A \text{ and } B) = 0.05$
   c. $P(A) = 0.65$, $P(B) = 0.85$, $P(A \text{ and } B) = 0.55$

3. In a clinical drug trial of 150 patients, 26 experienced mild side effects, 11 experienced moderate side effects, and 5 experienced serious side effects. What is the probability that a randomly-selected patient experienced any side effects?

4. In a survey of 200 people about headache relief options, 85 said they usually took acetaminophen, 72 said they usually took ibuprofen, and 27 said they usually took aspirin, while the remainder said they did not take any medications. What is the probability that a randomly-selected patient takes some form of medication to deal with headache relief?

5. When asked to provide their height and weight, many Canadian patients gave their answers using US units of measurement. Out of a sample of 250 patients, 97 gave their height in feet and inches, 185 gave their weight in pounds, and 62 gave both their height and weight in US units. What is the probability that a randomly-selected patient gives his/her height or weight in US units?

6. In a recent study about the effects of obesity on blood pressure, 160 "at risk" patients were sampled, 108 of whom were obese, 75 of whom had high blood pressure (i.e., hypertension), and 41 of whom were obese with hypertension. What is the probability that a randomly-selected patient is obese or is diagnosed with hypertension?

7. Mothers with an Rh-negative blood type who deliver a baby with an Rh-positive blood type are at risk of developing antibodies from their baby's blood that crosses the placental barrier, causing a condition called "Rh-sensitization", which can pose significant threats to future pregnancies. A special injection called "Rho(D) immune globulin" is typically given to Rh-negative mothers who become pregnant with a child whose father does not have confirmed Rh-negative blood, or who deliver a baby with Rh-positive blood. In a sample of 124 mothers with Rh-negative blood, 113 had partners who did not for sure have Rh-negative blood, 108 gave birth to Rh-positive babies, and 104 met both criteria. If a mother has an Rh-negative blood type, what is the probability that she would be recommended for the Rho(D) immune globulin injection (i.e., has a partner who does not have confirmed Rh-negative blood or delivers a baby that is Rh-positive)?

8. Certain factors are known to put women at an increased risk of breast cancer - two of the most significant are family history and genetic conditions. In a sample of 75 women coming in for breast cancer screening, 42 had a family member who had breast cancer, 13 had genetic conditions that are related to an increased risk of breast cancer, and 7 had both. What is the probability that a randomly-selected woman from the sample will be at an increased risk of breast cancer?

9. In a survey that asked 60 people who admitted to over-eating to list the reasons why they overate, 42 said they overate when they were stressed, 37 said they overate when they were watching TV, and 28 said they did both.
   a. If a participant is randomly selected from the study, determine the probability that he/she overate because of stress **or** overate while watching TV.
   b. If a participant is randomly selected from the study, determine the probability that he/she overate for reasons not related to stress or watching TV.

10. In a survey that asked 80 people to indicate the reasons why they do not go to the gym, 54 responded that they were too busy, 27 said they felt too tired/lazy to go, and 19 said both.

    a. If a participant is randomly selected from the study, determine the probability that he/she does not go to the gym because he/she is too busy **or** because (s)he is too tired/lazy.

    b. If a participant is randomly selected from the study, determine the probability that he/she does not go to the gym for reasons not related to busyness or tiredness/laziness.

11. Calculate $P(A \text{ and } B)$ in the following scenarios:

    a. $P(A) = 0.65$, $P(B) = 0.2$; A and B *are independent*

    b. $P(A) = 0.4$, $P(B) = 0.7$, $P(B|A) = 0.6$

    c. $P(A) = 0.52$, $P(B) = 0.36$, $P(A|B) = 0.75$

12. Calculate $P(A \text{ and } B)$ in the following scenarios:

    a. $P(A) = 0.15$, $P(B) = 0.4$; A and B *are independent*

    b. $P(A) = 0.28$, $P(B) = 0.62$, $P(B|A) = 0.55$

    c. $P(A) = 0.45$, $P(B) = 0.8$, $P(A|B) = 0.55$

13. A box of 20 children's bandages have 4 different cartoon designs on them. The 4 designs are equally distributed - i.e., there are 5 bandages with each design.

    a. If a child really wants a specific design, what is the probability that the child will get that design on the first bandage chosen?

    b. What is the probability that the child will get the desired design on the fifth bandage if it did not already appear on the first four bandages chosen?

    c. What is the probability that the first five bandages chosen will all have the desired design?

14. Door prizes for a hospital charity golf tournament are given out by drawing 8 names from the registrations of the 144 golfers in the tournament. Golfers cannot win more than one prize.

    a. If there are 20 female golfers registered in the tournament, what is the probability that one of their names will be drawn for the first door prize?

    b. What is the probability that one of the female golfers will be chosen for the eighth (i.e., final) door prize if all male golfers were selected for the previous seven prizes?

    c. What is the probability that all eight of the door prizes will go to female golfers?

15. Approximately 32% of the adult population get a flu shot each year. Of this group, approximately 0.15% will still contract the flu virus.

    a. If a person is selected at random from the adult population, what is the probability that he/she had the flu shot and still contracted the flu virus?

    b. If approximately 1% of the population will contract the flu virus, what is the probability of a randomly-selected individual contracting the flu virus and having not had the flu shot?

    c. Based on your answer from part (b), what is the probability of a randomly-selected individual contracting the flu virus given that that person did not have the flu shot?

16. In a study about prescription drug abuse, it was revealed that approximately 10% of the population of youth ages 12-17 abused prescription drugs this past year, and approximately 23% of these youth were admitted to a hospital as a result of the drug abuse.

    a. If a person is selected at random from the youth population, what is the probability that he/she abused prescription drugs this past year and was admitted to a hospital as a result?

    b. If approximately 5% of the overall youth population were admitted to a hospital this past year, what is the probability of a randomly-selected youth being admitted to a hospital and not having abused prescription drugs?

    c. Based on your answer from part (b), what is the probability of a randomly-selected youth being admitted to a hospital given that that person did not abuse prescription drugs?

17. A pregnancy test returns a false negative approximately 3.5% of the time (meaning that approximately 3.5% of women who take the test who are actually pregnant will receive a negative result). However, due to the nature of the test, it is practically impossible to receive a false positive (i.e., it is practically impossible for a woman who is not pregnant to receive a positive test result). Typically, about 40% of women who are trying to become pregnant are successful in any given month where they were attempting to become pregnant with their partners.

   a. If a woman who is trying to get pregnant takes the test, what is the probability that she will be pregnant and that the test will display a false negative?

   b. What is the overall probability that a woman taking the test will receive a negative result?

   c. What is the probability that a woman who is trying to get pregnant and receives a negative test result is actually pregnant?

18. Repeat Problem 17, using an inferior test, with a 17.5% probability of a false negative.

19. A doctor runs some routine blood tests on a patient and one of the autoimmune tests comes back positive. The probability of this test being positive if the patient has lupus is 99.4%, and the probability that it will be negative if the patient does not have lupus is 96.5%. If approximately 0.08% of the population has lupus, determine the probability that this particular patient has lupus, given the positive test result. *Hint: use Bayes' Theorem.*

20. Repeat Problem 19, if the test is improved so that the probability of a negative result if the patient does not have lupus is increased to 98.5%, and the incidence rate of lupus in the population decreases to 0.06%.

For Problems 21 to 28, determine if the events A and B are mutually exclusive, independent, or neither.

21. $P(A) = 0.65$, $P(B) = 0.25$, $P(A \text{ and } B) = 0.1$

22. $P(A) = 0.45$, $P(B) = 0.4$, $P(A \text{ and } B) = 0.25$

23. $P(A) = 0.8$, $P(B) = 0.35$, $P(A \text{ or } B) = 0.87$

24. $P(A) = 0.32$, $P(B) = 0.15$, $P(A \text{ or } B) = 0.47$

25. $P(A) = 0.275$, $P(A \text{ or } B) = 0.445$, $P(A \text{ and } B) = 0$

26. $P(A) = 0.184$, $P(A \text{ or } B) = 0.625$, $P(A \text{ and } B) = 0.115$

27. $P(B) = \dfrac{2}{3}$, $P(A \text{ or } B) = \dfrac{3}{4}$, $P(A \text{ and } B) = \dfrac{1}{6}$

28. $P(B) = \dfrac{3}{8}$, $P(A \text{ or } B) = \dfrac{7}{12}$, $P(A \text{ and } B) = \dfrac{1}{8}$

For Problems 29 to 36, calculate the desired empirical probabilities (rounded to 3 significant digits) based on the blood type data from a sample of 300 patients, summarized in the following contingency table:

Blood Group vs Rh Antigen	Rh+	Rh–	TOTAL
O	116	19	135
A	109	20	129
B	15	6	21
AB	12	3	15
TOTAL	252	48	300

29.   a. $P(A)$
     b. $P(Rh+)$

30.   a. $P(B)$
     b. $P(Rh-)$

31.   a. $P(O \text{ and } Rh+)$
     b. $P(B \text{ and } Rh-)$

32.   a. $P(A \text{ and } Rh-)$
     b. $P(AB \text{ and } Rh+)$

33.   a. $P(AB \text{ or } Rh-)$
     b. $P(B \text{ or } Rh+)$

34.   a. $P(A \text{ or } Rh+)$
     b. $P(O \text{ or } Rh-)$

35.   a. $P(A | Rh+)$
     b. $P(Rh- | O)$

36.   a. $P(AB | Rh-)$
     b. $P(Rh+ | B)$

For Problems 37 to 44, calculate the desired empirical probabilities (rounded to 3 significant digits) based on the results of a sample of 400 trials of a new test designed to identify the presence of a certain disease that is believed to be present in 20% of the population. The results of the trials are summarized in the following contingency table:

Disease Presence vs Test Result	+ Result	– Result	TOTAL
Disease Present	73	7	80
NO Disease Present	12	308	320
TOTAL	85	315	400

37. a. The sensitivity of the test - i.e., $P(+Result|Disease)$
    b. The "false-positive" rate of the test - i.e., $P(+Result|No\ Disease)$

38. a. The specificity of the test - i.e. $P(-Result|No\ Disease)$
    b. The "false-negative" rate of the test - i.e., $P(-Result|Disease)$

39. a. The negative predictive value of the test - i.e., $P(No\ Disease|-Result)$
    b. The "false-scare" rate of the test - i.e., $P(No\ Disease|+Result)$

40. a. The positive predictive value of the test - i.e., $P(Disease|+Result)$
    b. The "false-safety" rate of the test - i.e., $P(Disease|-Result)$

41. a. Selecting 3 subjects in a row who all had the disease and had a positive test result.
    b. Selecting 3 subjects in a row who all had a "false-negative" test result.

42. a. Selecting 3 subjects in a row who did not have the disease and had a negative test result.
    b. Selecting 3 subjects in a row who all had a "false-positive" test result.

43. a. The probability that the 17th subject chosen does not have the disease, if the first 16 subjects chosen do have the disease.
    b. The probability that the 11th subject had a positive test result, if the first 10 subjects chosen had a negative test result.

44. a. The probability that the 26th subject chosen has the disease, if the first 25 subjects chosen do not have the disease.
    b. The probability that the 16th subject had a negative test result, if the first 15 subjects chosen had a positive test result.

5.3 | Counting Rules

There is another way to approach probability calculations for compound events, especially in very complex cases, when using the addition and multiplication rules for compound events can be quite challenging: using **counting rules** to determine $n(A)$ (i.e., the number of ways that event A can occur) and $n(S)$ (i.e., the number of outcomes in the sample space).

If we recall, the basic definition for (theoretical) probability is $P(A) = \dfrac{n(A)}{n(S)}$ and, when in doubt, we should always come back to this definition. As such, if we can develop some strategies for determining $n(A)$ and $n(S)$, we can calculate the probability of event A without needing to appeal to the probabilities of the individual events that make up the compound event.

Fundamental Counting Rules

We will start with the most basic counting rules, which are similar in concept to the Multiplication Rule for Probabilities of Independent Events from Section 5.2:

1. If procedure A has m outcomes and procedure B has n outcomes, then if procedures A and B are performed together, there will be a total of $m \cdot n$ outcomes (assuming that A and B are independent).

2. If procedure A has m outcomes and it is performed k times, then there will be a total of m^k outcomes (assuming each trial is independent).

Example 5.3-a	Using the Fundamental Counting Rules

(i)   If a (fair) 6-sided die is rolled and a (fair) coin is flipped at the same time, how many outcomes are possible?

(ii)   If five (fair) 6-sided dice are rolled, how many outcomes are possible?

Solution

(i)   Since procedure A (die) has 6 outcomes and procedure B (coin) has 2 outcomes, there is a total of $6 \cdot 2 = 12$ outcomes if they are performed together.

(ii)   Since procedure A (die) has 6 outcomes and is performed 5 times, there is a total of $6^5 = 7,776$ outcomes.

Factorial Notation

In the case where the outcomes of the procedures are **not** independent, we cannot simply multiply the number of outcomes of each procedure together to obtain the result. However, we can make use of another approach, similar in concept to the Generalized Multiplication Rule for Probabilities from Section 5.2: **factorial notation**.

For a given whole number n, we define $n!$ (read as "factorial of n" or "n factorial") as follows:

$$n! = n \cdot (n - 1) \cdot (n - 2) \cdot ... \cdot 3 \cdot 2 \cdot 1$$

For example, $8! = 8 \times 7 \times 6 \times 5 \times 4 \times 3 \times 2 \times 1 = 40,320$

$3! = 3 \times 2 \times 1 = 6$

$1! = 1$

*Note: By definition, $0! = 1$, **not** 0.*

Basic Factorial Rule

The **Basic Factorial Rule** is most useful when we want to determine how many arrangements of a group of unique items are possible:

If there are n unique items, there are $n!$ unique arrangements of those items.

If we have 5 unique items and want to know how many different arrangements of those items are possible, we first consider that we have 5 different options available for the first item. However, after the first item has been chosen, we only have 4 options left for the second item, 3 options for the third item, 2 options for the fourth item, and only 1 option for the fifth and final item. As such, there would be $5 \cdot 4 \cdot 3 \cdot 2 \cdot 1 = 120$ different arrangements of the items.

For example, the letters in the word MUSIC can be arranged in $5! = 5 \cdot 4 \cdot 3 \cdot 2 \cdot 1 = 120$ different ways.

Factorial Rule with Non-Unique (Repeated) Items

In the above example, we assumed that all 5 items were unique. If, however, two of the items were identical, then we would not be able to distinguish between different arrangements of those two items.

For example, the letters in the word STATS cannot be arranged in 5! = 120 different ways, because the two S's are indistinguishable, as are the two T's. So how many arrangements are possible? Well, if we consider that for each unique arrangement of the word, we have 2 options for the first S and 1 option for the second S (so 2! = 2 · 1 = 2 total options), as well as 2 options for the first T and 1 option for the second T (so 2! = 2 · 1 = 2 total options), we can see that the 120 non-unique arrangements can be partitioned into groups of 4 identical words (2 with the S's interchanged, times 2 with the T's interchanged). This leaves $\frac{5!}{(2!)(2!)} = \frac{120}{4} = 30$ groups of words that are all unique.

Therefore, for a group of n items that have a group of k_1 identical items, another group of k_2 identical items, another group of k_3 identical items, ... and a final group of k_m identical items, the total number of unique arrangements is given by the following formula:

Formula 5.3-a

Number of Arrangements with Repeated Items

$$\textbf{Number of Arrangements} = \frac{n!}{(k_1\,!)(k_2\,!)(k_3\,!)\,...\,(k_m\,!)}$$

Example 5.3-b

Counting with Factorial Rules

(i) Determine the number of arrangements of the letters in the word DUPLICATES.

(ii) Determine the number of arrangements of the letters in the word REARRANGE.

Solution

(i) Since there are no duplicated letters in the 10-letter word DUPLICATES (ironically!), there are 10! = 3,628,800 different arrangements of the letters.

(ii) Since there are 9 letters in the word REARRANGE, with the R repeated 3 times, and the E and A both repeated twice, there are $\frac{9!}{(3!)(2!)(2!)} = \frac{362,880}{(6)(2)(2)} = \frac{362,880}{24} = 15,120$ different arrangements of the letters.

Permutations

When we want to know how many arrangements of a subgroup of a set of unique items are possible, so the order of those items is important, we use the **Permutations Rule**:

In a group of n unique items, there are $_nP_r = \frac{n!}{(n-r)!}$ unique arrangements of a subgroup of r items.

Formula 5.3-b

Permutations

$$_nP_r = \frac{n!}{(n-r)!}$$

$_nP_r$ is read as "n pick r" or "n permute r".

For example, if we wanted to make a 4-letter "word" using the letters from the word DUPLICATES, there would be $\frac{10!}{(10-4)!} = \frac{10!}{6!} = \frac{3,628,800}{720} = 5,040$ different possible "words" we could make.

Note: In the above example, we define a "word" as any unique arrangement of letters, not necessarily as an English word that could be found in the dictionary. For example, LATE and PLCS would both be considered "words" in this context, even though only the former is actually a real English word.

This rule comes from an intuitive approach to the problem:

If we have n items and we want to arrange a subgroup of r items, we have n choices for the first item, $(n - 1)$ choices for the second item, $(n - 2)$ choices for the third item, ... and $(n - r + 1)$ choices for the final (r^{th}) item. Hence, the total number of arrangements of the subgroup is:

$$_nP_r = n \cdot (n - 1) \cdot (n - 2) \cdot ... \cdot (n - r + 1)$$

If we multiply and divide by $(n - r)!$ (which does not change the result), we get our formula:

$$_nP_r = \frac{n \cdot (n - 1) \cdot (n - 2) \cdot ... \cdot (n - r + 1)}{1} \cdot \frac{(n - r)!}{(n - r)!} = \frac{n!}{(n - r)!}$$

Example 5.3-c	**Counting with the Permutations Rule**

(i) How many unique 4-letter "words" can be made using the letters of the word MALNOURISHED?

(ii) If there are 20 patients in a given ward, and each nurse is assigned to a rotation of 5 patients (meaning there is an order for checking-in on the patients), how many different rotation assignments are possible for the first nurse?

(iii) In a race of 8 runners, how many different medal results (i.e., top-3 finishes: gold, silver, bronze) are possible?

Solution	

(i) There are no duplicated letters in the 12-letter word MALNOURISHED.

There are 12 options for the first letter, 11 options for the second letter, 10 options for the third letter, and 9 options for the final (fourth) letter; hence, there are a total of $12 \cdot 11 \cdot 10 \cdot 9$, or $_{12}P_4 = \dfrac{12!}{(12 - 4)!} = \dfrac{12!}{8!} = 11,880$ unique 4-letter "words" can be made using the letters of MALNOURISHED.

(ii) When preparing the rotation assignment for the first nurse, there are 20 options for the first patient, 19 options for the second patient, 18 options for the third patient, 17 options for the fourth patient, and 16 options for the final (fifth) patient; hence, there are a total of $20 \cdot 19 \cdot 18 \cdot 17 \cdot 16$, or $_{20}P_5 = \dfrac{20!}{(20 - 5)!} = \dfrac{20!}{15!} = 1,860,480$ unique rotations for the first nurse.

(iii) There are 8 options for 1st place (gold), 7 options for 2nd place (silver), and 6 options for 3rd place (bronze); hence, there are a total of $8 \cdot 7 \cdot 6$, or $_8P_3 = \dfrac{8!}{(8 - 3)!} = \dfrac{8!}{5!} = 336$ unique medal results.

Combinations

When we want to know how many subgroups of a set of unique items are possible, and the order (i.e., arrangement) of those items is irrelevant, we use the **Combinations Rule**:

In a group of n unique items, there are $_nC_r = \dfrac{n!}{(n - r)! \cdot r!}$ *unique subgroups of r items.*

Formula 5.3-c	**Combinations**

$$_nC_r = \frac{n!}{(n - r)! \cdot r!}$$

$_nC_r$ is read as "n choose r".

Again, if we start with the Permutations Rule, we can see that within that subgroup of r items, there are $r!$ arrangements of those items. Hence, if we do not care about the arrangement of the items, we consider all of those $r!$ arrangements of the same items as one subgroup, so we divide $_nP_r$ by $r!$ to get our formula for $_nC_r$:

$$_nC_r = {_nP_r} \div r! = \frac{n!}{(n-r)!} \div r! = \frac{n!}{(n-r)!} \cdot \frac{1}{r!} = \frac{n!}{(n-r)! \cdot r!}$$

Note: *The difference between permutations and combinations is whether or not the arrangement (i.e., the order) of the items in the subgroup matters. If the order is important, we use **permutations**; if the order is irrelevant, we use **combinations**.*

Example 5.3-d **Counting with the Combinations Rule**

(i)   From a standard deck of 52 cards, how many different 5-card poker "hands" are possible?

(ii)   In LOTTO-649, 6 winning numbers are randomly selected from 1-49 (order is irrelevant). How many different winning combinations are possible?

(iii) If 12 students apply to be on a 4-person yearbook committee, how many outcomes are possible?

Solution

(i)   In a game of cards, a "hand" always implies that the order of the cards dealt does not matter, as the player can pick them up and arrange them in his/her hand.

Since order is irrelevant, there are $_{52}C_5 = \dfrac{52!}{(52-5)! \cdot 5!} = \dfrac{52!}{47! \cdot 5!} = 2{,}598{,}960$ 5-card poker hands.

(ii)   Since order is irrelevant, there are $_{49}C_6 = \dfrac{49!}{(49-6)! \cdot 6!} = \dfrac{49!}{43! \cdot 6!} = 13{,}983{,}816$ unique possible winning combinations.

(iii) For the committee membership, the order in which the students are elected is irrelevant, so there are $_{12}C_4 = \dfrac{12!}{(12-4)! \cdot 4!} = \dfrac{12!}{8! \cdot 4!} = 495$ different possible committee membership outcomes.

The combination $_nC_r$ can also be expressed in the following, more common form: $\dbinom{n}{r}$.

For clarity, we restate Formula 5.3-c in this new form:

Formula 5.3-c **Combinations**

$$\binom{n}{r} = \frac{n!}{(n-r)! \cdot r!}$$

Note: *We will express combinations in this form throughout the remainder of the textbook. However, most calculators use the $_nC_r$ form. It is important to note that the two forms are interchangeable.*

Differentiating Between Counting Rules

It can be challenging to distinguish between when we should use each of the counting rules above. The following flowchart provides direction on determining the appropriate rule to use in a given situation:

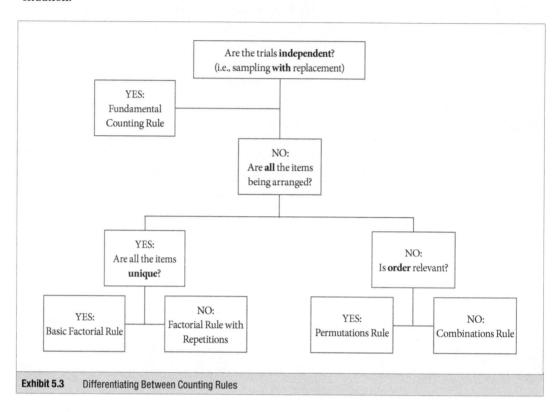

Exhibit 5.3   Differentiating Between Counting Rules

Example 5.3-e   Selecting the Appropriate Counting Rule

For the following examples, first select the appropriate counting rule. Then determine the number of outcomes in each situation:

(i)   A hospital administrator randomly selects the order in which she will review the 12 departments in the hospital. In how many ways can she do this?

(ii)   A College Student's Council Executive consisting of President, Vice President, Secretary, and Treasurer is selected from a group of 15 students on the council. How many different executives can be formed from the group?

(iii)   In a group of 20 finalists for a contest, each receives a prize randomly drawn from a bin containing 1 grand prize, 2 "gold" prizes, 5 "silver" prizes, and 12 "bronze" prizes. How many different distributions of the prizes are possible, assuming that the prizes in each category are all identical?

(iv)   In a certain lottery, 10 numbers from 1-30 are chosen at random. How many different winning combinations are possible, if order is irrelevant?

(v)   A typical combination lock consists of the numbers 0-39 and requires a sequence of 3 numbers to open it. If numbers may be chosen more than once, how many different combinations are possible?

Solution   (i)   Since there are 12 unique departments, and all are being reviewed without replacement, we use the Basic Factorial Rule.

Therefore, there are 12! = 479,001,600 different ways to review the 12 departments.

(ii)   Since there are 15 students being sampled from, without replacement (i.e., no student can hold two different roles) and there are 4 different roles to fill on the executive (so order is relevant), we use the Permutations Rule.

Therefore, there are $_{15}P_4 = \dfrac{15!}{(15-4)!} = 32{,}760$ different executives that can be formed.

(iii)   Since there are 20 different prizes to be sampled from, without replacement, and there are several repeated identical prizes, we use the Factorial Rule with Repetitions.

Therefore, there are $\dfrac{20!}{(12!)(5!)(2!)} = 21{,}162{,}960$ different prize distributions.

(iv)   Since there are 10 numbers to be chosen from 30 numbers without replacement, and order is irrelevant, we use the Combinations Rule.

Therefore, there are $\dbinom{30}{10} = \dfrac{30!}{(30-10)! \cdot 10!} = 30{,}045{,}015$ different winning number combinations.

(v)   Since there are 3 numbers to be chosen from 40 numbers (1 – 39, plus 0) **with** replacement, and order is important, we use the Fundamental Counting Rule.

Therefore, there are $40^3 = 64{,}000$ different lock combinations possible.

Counting Techniques and Probability

Now that we have these counting rules, we can apply them to our study of probability, as was our motivation at the beginning of this section:

If we are looking for the probability of an event A occurring, $P(A)$, we use the counting techniques discussed above to determine the number of ways A can occur, $n(A)$, as well as the number of outcomes in the sample space, $n(S)$.

Example 5.3-f	Calculating Probability using Counting Techniques

Determine the probability of the following events using appropriate counting techniques:

(i)   In a clinical drug trial of 100 participants, 50 receive the drug and 50 receive a placebo. If a group of 10 unique participants are selected at random, what is the probability that exactly half of them receive the drug and the other half receive the placebo?

(ii)   In the game of Yahtzee, 5 dice are rolled simultaneously. A full house occurs if only two values are showing on the 5 dice: exactly 3 of the dice all show one value and the other 2 dice both show the other value. What is the probability of rolling a full house?

(iii)   If a couple has 6 children, what is the probability that:

(a)   all of the children are girls?

(b)   they have the same number of girls as boys?

(c)   they will have at least one boy and at least one girl?

(iv)   A licence plate in Ontario is identified by a string of 4 letters chosen from the 21 allowable letters (excluding G, I, O, Q, and U) followed by a string of 3 numbers (from 0 – 9). If a licence plate is selected at random, what is the probability that it has no repeating letters or numbers?

Solution

(i) First of all, we note that we are sampling without replacement (a group of unique participants suggests the same person cannot be sampled twice), and order does not matter (it is a group, rather than an arrangement). Hence, we are using combinations:

- To determine $n(S)$, we note that there are 100 participants in the drug trial, from which we are choosing 10. Hence, $n(S) = \dbinom{100}{10}$

- To determine $n(5\ drug$ and $5\ placebo)$, we first calculate $n(5\ drug) = \dbinom{50}{5}$ and $n(5\ placebo) = \dbinom{50}{5}$ and use the Fundamental Counting Rule to obtain the following:

$$n(5\ drug\ \text{and}\ 5\ placebo) = \dbinom{50}{5} \cdot \dbinom{50}{5}$$

- Therefore, $P(5\ drug$ and $5\ placebo) = \dfrac{\dbinom{50}{5} \cdot \dbinom{50}{5}}{\dbinom{100}{10}} = \dfrac{2{,}118{,}760 \cdot 2{,}118{,}760}{1.731030946 \times 10^{13}} \approx 0.259$

Note: The denominator in the previous fraction is expressed in scientific notation, as most calculators cannot display numbers larger than 10 digits long.

(ii) Since the 5 dice being rolled are all independent of each other, we start by making use of the fundamental counting rule:

- To determine $n(S)$, we note that there are 5 dice, each with 6 possible outcomes. Hence, $n(S) = 6^5 = 7{,}776$

Even though all 5 dice are rolled simultaneously, it will be helpful in our calculations to think of them as being rolled one-at-a-time, and it will not impact the result:

- The first die rolled can be anything, so there are 6 outcomes; the second and third die would then have to be the same as the first, so there is only 1 outcome possible for each of those. The fourth die can be any of the remaining 5 numbers, so there are 5 outcomes; and the fifth die must be the same as the fourth, so there is 1 outcome. Hence, there are $6 \cdot 1 \cdot 1 \cdot 5 \cdot 1 = 30$ different outcomes.

However, since they can be rolled in any order, we need to multiply by the number of ways of arranging 5 dice, with 3 repetitions of one number and 2 repetitions of another number, which makes use of the Factorial Rule with Repetitions:

- $n(Full\ House) = 30 \cdot \dfrac{5!}{(3!)(2!)} = 30 \cdot \dfrac{120}{(6)(2)} = 300$

- Therefore, $P(Full\ House) = \dfrac{300}{7{,}776} \approx 0.0386$

(iii) As in the previous examples, we assume the outcome of the sex for each of the 6 children is independent of the outcomes of the sex for the other children (which, in light of modern medical evidence, may not in fact be true, but is a necessary assumption for our calculations). We also assume that both sex outcomes (male or female) are equally-likely to occur (another slightly-less-than-accurate assumption). Hence, $n(S) = 2^6 = 64$

- There is only 1 outcome in which all children are girls, so $P(All\ Girls) = \dfrac{1}{64} \approx 0.0156$

Solution
continued

- The easiest way to think of the number of outcomes where 3 children are boys and 3 children are girls is to think of the number of arrangements of the word BBBGGG, which uses the Factorial Rule with Repetitions:

  - $n(3\ Boys\ and\ 3\ Girls) = \dfrac{6!}{(3!)(3!)} = \dfrac{720}{(6)(6)} = 20$

  - Therefore, $P(3\ Boys\ and\ 3\ Girls) = \dfrac{20}{64} \approx 0.313$

- Having at least one child of each sex is the complement of having all girls or all boys.

  - We already know $P(All\ Girls) = \dfrac{1}{64} \approx 0.0156$

  - Similarly, $P(All\ Boys) = \dfrac{1}{64} \approx 0.0156$

  - Therefore, $P(\geq 1\ of\ each) = 1 - \left(\dfrac{1}{64} + \dfrac{1}{64}\right) = \dfrac{62}{64} \approx 0.969$

(iv)   In this example, there are 4 letters, each with 21 possible outcomes, followed by 3 numbers, each with 10 possible outcomes, and all the values are independent of each other. Therefore, we should use the Fundamental Counting Rule: hence, $n(S) = 21^4 \cdot 10^3 = 194{,}481{,}000$.

- To compute $n(No\ repetitions)$ we consider that now we are sampling without replacement, and that the order of the letters and numbers matters (i.e., it is an arrangement), so we use the Permutations Rule:

  $n(No\ repetitions) = (_{21}P_4)\ (_{10}P_3) = (143{,}640)\ (720) = 103{,}420{,}800$

- Therefore, $P(No\ repetitions) = \dfrac{103{,}420{,}800}{194{,}481{,}000} \approx 0.532$

5.3 | Exercises

Answers to odd-numbered problems are available at the end of the textbook.

For Problems 1 to 20, determine which counting method(s) to use and determine the number of outcomes for the desired event using that counting method(s).

1. A surgeon is deciding on a post-surgical pain-relief treatment plan for a patient. He must select one of four continuous-release pain relief medications and one of five quick-acting pain medications to combine for the treatment. How many different pain-relief treatment plans are possible, assuming that there are no contra-indications (i.e., restrictions due to negative interactions) between the various continuous-release and quick-acting drugs?

2. An oncologist is deciding on a treatment plan for a cancer patient that combines one of six methods of chemotherapy and one of three methods of radiation therapy. How many different cancer-treatment plans are possible?

3. The surgeon in Problem 1 has 6 different patients scheduled for surgery this week. Assuming that the same treatment options in Problem 1 are available for all 6 patients, how many different combinations of treatment plans could the surgeon recommend to his patients?

4. The oncologist in Problem 2 currently has 5 patients beginning treatment for cancer. Assuming that the same treatment options in Problem 2 are available for all 5 patients, how many different combinations of treatment plans could the oncologist recommend to her patients?

5. An obstetrics nurse practitioner helps to deliver 20 babies in one week. How many different combinations of sex outcomes are possible for the 20 babies that she delivered?

6. An E.R. triage nurse assesses incoming patients on a scale of 1-5, where 1 is the most severe triage level and 5 is the least severe triage level. If the nurse sees 10 patients before her first break, how many different combinations of triage results are possible for those patients?

7. A massage therapy clinic has 8 new patients and 8 RMTs. How many different ways can the patients be assigned to the RMTs so that each RMT takes on one new patient?

8. A veterinarian has 7 sick animals that are dropped off in the morning by their owners, to be treated throughout the day, and attempts to do so based on a combination of urgency and the owner's schedule as to when they would like to return to pick up their pet. In how many different orders can the veterinarian treat the animals?

9. In how many different ways can the letters of the word FARSIGHTED be arranged?

10. In how many different ways can the letters of the word HYPOGASTRIC be arranged?

11. In how many different ways can the letters of the words EXERCISE STRESS TEST be arranged?

12. In how many different ways can the letters of the words SEVERE SLEEPLESSNESS be arranged?

13. How many different four-letter "words" can be made from the letters of the word GRANULOCYTES?

14. How many different five-letter "words" can be made from the letters of the word CYTOPLASM?

15. A doctor's office is trying to schedule 15 patients in for an appointment every 30 minutes from 9:00 AM to 5:00 PM, based on the following restrictions:

   • 4 patients need to be seen as early in the morning as possible, so they should be seen first.

   • 3 patients need to be seen as late in the day as possible, so they should be seen last.

   • 2 physically-disabled patients have requested specific times at 12:00 PM and 2:30 PM, based on their transportation requirements.

   • The doctor prefers to take her lunch from 12:30 PM to 1:00 PM.

   How many different schedules are possible that accommodate all of the above restrictions?

16. A hospital is holding a charity dinner gala and is attempting to put together the head table seating arrangements. There are two tables of 8 on either side of the main podium on stage for the 16 guests of honour, with the following restrictions:

   • The M.C. and hospital president need to sit on either side of the podium, closest to the microphone.

   • The vice president needs to be seated beside the president and the remaining three members of the hospital executive board should sit on the other side, beside the M.C.

   • There are 2 couples that need to be seated together.

   How many different head table seating arrangements are possible that accommodate all of the above restrictions?

17. An ambulance paramedic receives a call to go to a serious automobile collision that is 5 blocks north and 6 blocks west from his current location.

   a. Assuming that the city is laid out in a grid, that the paramedic can take any route to get to the scene of the collision, and that he will only ever travel towards the collision, how many different routes are possible to the scene of the collision?

   b. If the intersection 2 blocks north and 2 blocks west of the paramedic's current location is closed due to construction, how many different routes are possible to the scene of the collision?

18. The ambulance paramedic from Problem 17 then has to transport the injured automobile driver to the hospital, which is 8 blocks east and 3 blocks north of the scene of the collision. How many different routes to the hospital are possible if:

   a. There are no restrictions?

   b. The intersection 1 block north and 3 blocks east of the scene of the collision is closed due to a water main break?

19. During a routine performance review of the nurses working in a certain hospital ward, a hospital administrator checks in with each patient in her ward to get a sense of their impressions of the nurses charged with their care. If there are 48 patients currently registered in the ward, and she would like to take a sample of 6 random patients, how many different combinations are possible?

20. A dental hygienist receives 4 weeks of vacation off every year, including the week between Christmas and New Year's. Out of the remaining 51 weeks of the year, how many different ways could she take her remaining 3 weeks of vacation?

For Problems 21 to 32, use appropriate counting techniques to determine the probability of the desired event.

21. Fraternal octuplets are an incredibly rare phenomenon, where eight babies are born in one pregnancy from eight different eggs being released simultaneously, successfully fertilized and implanted. What is the probability that the octuplets will consist of 4 boys and 4 girls?

22. A jury of 12 people is selected randomly from the population. What is the probability that the jury is comprised of 6 males and 6 females?

23. When women reach the age of 40, the probability of giving birth to a child with a chromosomal abnormality of any type is approximately 1.5%. If a woman has 3 children when she is around the age of 40, what is the probability that exactly one of them will have a chromosomal abnormality?

24. When women are between the ages of 35 and 40, the probability of a miscarriage is approximately 5.5%. If a woman gets pregnant 4 times between the ages of 35 and 40, what is the probability that exactly two of her pregnancies will be successful?

25. A hospital lottery sells scratch tickets: approximately 80% do not win anything, 15% win a small prize, 4% win a moderate prize, and 1% win a large prize. If a customer buys 5 tickets, what is the probability that she will win a prize from each of the three categories of prizes?

26. A veterinarian's practice consists of about 43% dogs, 36% cats, 13% rodents, 6% birds, and 2% other animals. If the veterinarian sees 6 animals on a given day, what is the probability of seeing 3 dogs, 1 cat, 1 rodent, and 1 bird?

27. A student committee is formed in the Health Sciences program at a local post-secondary institution, consisting of 10 students from the program. Committee members are selected randomly from applicants. If a group of 5 friends apply to be on the committee, what is the probability that all 5 will be selected, if 25 other students also apply to be on the committee?

28. In a sample of 450 blood donations, 32 are type O– blood. If 10 of the units of blood are randomly selected, what is the probability that exactly 3 are type O– blood?

29. A very popular professional athletic therapist agrees to take 12 co-op students from the four college athletic therapy programs in the region. He accepts 10 faculty-nominated student applications from each of the four colleges, and then selects the 12 co-op students from those 40 applications. What is the probability that exactly 3 students will be selected from each of the four colleges?

30. In a container of 75 children's vitamins of mixed flavours, 25 are grape flavour, 25 are orange flavour, and 25 are cherry flavour. In a family with six children, two of the children only like the grape flavour, one only likes the orange flavour, and the other three only like the cherry flavour. If 6 vitamins are randomly shaken out of the container, what is the probability that each of the six children will have their preferences met?

31. A physiotherapist orders a shipment of rubber physical therapy bands - 6 boxes of yellow (extra light resistance) bands, 10 boxes of green (light resistance) bands, 8 boxes of blue (medium resistance) bands, 4 boxes of black (heavy resistance) bands, and 2 boxes of red (extra heavy resistance) bands. Unfortunately, none of the boxes are labelled when she receives her shipment. If she randomly opens 5 boxes, what is the probability that:
   a. She opened one of each colour of physical therapy band?
   b. All five boxes are green-colour therapy bands?
   c. No heavy or extra heavy therapy bands are opened?

32. A pharmacist orders a shipment of four different types of cough medicine: 15 bottles of Brand A, 12 bottles of Brand B, 8 bottles of Brand C, and 5 bottles of Brand D. If 4 patients have a prescription for cough medicine, what is the probability that:
   a. Each patient receives a different brand of cough medicine?
   b. All four patients receive Brand A?
   c. None of the patients receive Brand B or Brand D?

5 | Review Exercises

For Problems 1 to 4, analyze the scenarios and complete the following:

(i) *Calculate the total number of outcomes.*

(ii) *Construct the sample space by listing out all possible outcomes.*

(iii) *If the outcomes are grouped together by similar characteristics, how many different events are possible?*

1. In a math class, an exam is randomly selected from a set of exams with the following grades: 4 A's, 6 B's, 5 C's, 3 D's, and 2 F's.

2. A survey is randomly selected from a group of Pre-Health graduates who have gone into the following industries within the health sciences: 5 in Pharmacy Technology, 2 in Paramedics, 5 in Athletic Therapy, 8 in Practical Nursing, 6 in Registered Nursing, and 4 in Veterinary Care.

3. A consumer at a pharmacy is trying to decide what type of vitamin to purchase. There are 8 types of Brand A, 4 types of Brand B, 7 types of Brand C, and 5 types of Brand D.

4. A consumer at a medical supply store is trying to decide what type of pillow to purchase. There are 10 memory foam pillows, 2 water-base pillows, and 4 cervical pillows.

For Problems 5 to 10, analyze the scenarios and complete the following:

(i) *Determine what type of approach should be used to calculate the desired probability: theoretical, empirical, or subjective.*

(ii) *Calculate the probability of the desired event, if possible, rounded to 3 significant digits.*

5. A survey of 1,250 employed people showed that 872 participated in a group health insurance plan where they worked. On the basis of this survey, what is the probability that an employed person participates in a group health insurance plan through work?

6. A patient is seeking advice from a lawyer about a medical malpractice claim against the hospital. This lawyer is specialized in lawsuits for medical negligence. After the discussion, the lawyer provides an estimate of the probability that the patient's case will be successful.

7. A nurse's schedule is based on a 7-day cycle of two 12-hour night shifts, followed by three 12-hour day shifts, followed by two days off. Her friends are trying to decide on a lunch date together, and she is free to attend any day except when she is scheduled to work the day shift. What is the probability that they will suggest a date that works for her?

8. 56 out of 2,391 obese patients died from weight loss bariatric surgery. Based on this, what is the probability that an obese patient will die following bariatric surgery?

9. A woman was successfully treated for breast cancer. She asks her doctor about the probability of local breast cancer reoccurrence. Based on the doctor's experience and expertise, he told her the percent of women who have had mastectomies who typically experience a recurrence.

10. With the Cancer Society VIP lottery, 600,000 tickets are sold and there are 5 grand prizes of "luxury car and cash package" worth between $50,000 to $90,000. What is the probability of winning a grand prize?

For Problems 11 to 18, complete the following:

(i) *State which method should be used to best determine the sample space: an outcome table, a tree diagram, or a Venn diagram.*

(ii) *Calculate the probability of the desired event (assuming all outcomes are equally likely) using the method you decided upon in part (i), rounded to 3 significant digits.*

11. Two parents with A+ blood can contribute one of the following four blood protein types to their child: A+, A−, O+, and O−. What is the probability that both parents will contribute the same type of blood proteins to their child?

12. A professor writes 2 multiple-choice questions for a quiz. There are 5 choices (a, b, c, d, or e) for both of the 2 questions. If the professor randomly chooses which question will have an answer of a, b, c, d, or e, what is the probability that the two correct answers on this quiz are both the same answer?

13. A nursing student is required to take an online quiz as part of her entrance assessment. There are 20 questions on the quiz, all of which are true or false questions, of which she knows the answers to 14. If she needs a score of 18 or better out of 20 to pass the quiz, what is the probability that she will pass the quiz by guessing randomly on the 6 questions she is unsure of?

14. A nursing student is required to take an online quiz as part of her ongoing training. There are 10 questions on the quiz, each with 3 possible answers, and she knows the answers to 6. If she needs a score of 8 or better out of 10 to pass the quiz, what is the probability that she will **not** pass the quiz by guessing randomly on the 4 questions she is unsure of?

15. A survey of 100 adults was taken. The results showed that 28 followed gluten-free diets, 15 followed lactose-free diets, and 10 followed both a gluten- and lactose-free diet. What is the probability that a randomly selected adult follows neither a gluten- nor lactose-free diet?

16. Of 400 college students, 120 were enrolled in Psychology, 220 were enrolled in Physics, and 55 were enrolled in both. What is the probability that a randomly selected student is enrolled in neither Psychology nor Physics?

17. 100 students studying in a Pre-Health program were asked if they liked Math, Chemistry, and Anatomy. Everyone answered that they liked at least one subject. 56 like Math; 43 like Chemistry; 35 like Anatomy; 18 like Math and Chemistry; 10 like Chemistry and Anatomy; 12 like Math and Anatomy; and 6 like all three subjects. What is the probability that a randomly selected student in the Pre-Health program likes only one subject?

18. "Poor quality medicines" is a term inclusive of counterfeit, substandard, and degraded medicines. In a study of 225 medications with questionable quality, the following data was obtained: 90 were found to be counterfeit, 80 were substandard, and 68 were degraded. 12 were also reported to be counterfeit and substandard, 10 were counterfeit and degraded, and 14 were substandard and degraded. There were 5 medications that had all three problems. What is the probability that a randomly selected medication in this study does not have any of these three problems?

For Problems 19 to 22, complete the following:

(i) *Calculate the probability of the desired event, rounded to 3 significant digits as needed.*

(ii) *State the complementary event and calculate its probability.*

(iii) *Compute the odds against and odds in favour of the event.*

19. Randomly selecting one of the 12 students who have a strong interest in math in a class of 40 students.

20. Randomly selecting one of the 49 patients who experience a side effect of nausea out of the 294 patients taking a prescription drug used to treat depression.

21. Randomly selecting one of the 32.5% of mothers who were between 30 and 34 years old when they had their first child.

22. Randomly selecting one of the 84% of all fractures in people 50+ caused by osteoporosis.

23. Calculate $P(A \text{ or } B)$ in the following scenarios:

    a. $P(A) = 0.38$, $P(B) = 0.24$; A and B are mutually exclusive

    b. $P(A) = 0.28$, $P(B) = 0.45$, $P(A \text{ and } B) = 0.23$

24. Calculate $P(A \text{ or } B)$ in the following scenarios:

    a. $P(A) = 0.17$, $P(B) = 0.05$; A and B are mutually exclusive

    b. $P(A) = 0.82$, $P(B) = 0.55$, $P(A \text{ and } B) = 0.42$

25. In a survey of 250 patients about their preference of toothpastes, 175 have used Brand A, 158 have used Brand B, and 93 have used both brands of toothpaste to brush their teeth. What is the probability that a randomly selected person uses either Brand A or Brand B toothpaste to brush their teeth?

26. In a survey of 150 people about their favourite beverages, 52 said that they usually drink coffee, 33 said that they drink green tea, and 10 of them drink both. What is probability that a randomly selected person drinks green tea or coffee?

27. Certain factors are known to put men at an increased risk of colon cancer - two of the factors are the presence of HNPCC (Lynch Syndrome) and FAP (Familial Adenomatous Polyposis). Research has shown that out of 225 men who have colon cancer, 126 carry HNPCC genes, 86 carry FAP genes, and 54 carry both.

   a. What is the probability that a randomly selected man from the study carries the HNPCC gene or the FAP gene?

   b. What is the probability that a randomly selected man from this study carries neither gene?

28. In a group of 2,500 people, 1,400 are under 30 years old, 600 are vegetarian, and 400 are under 30 years old and vegetarian.

   a. What is the probability that a randomly selected person from this group is under 30 or vegetarian?

   b. What is the probability that a randomly selected person from this group is neither under 30 nor vegetarian?

29. Calculate $P(A$ and $B)$ in the following scenarios:

   a. $P(A) = 0.82, P(B) = 0.55; A$ and B are independent

   b. $P(A) = 0.82, P(B) = 0.55, P(B|A) = 0.42$

30. Calculate $P(A$ and $B)$ in the following scenarios:

   a. $P(A) = 0.24, P(B) = 0.35; A$ and B are independent

   b. $P(A) = 0.24, P(B) = 0.35, P(A|B) = 0.62$

31. Mary is the quality control manager in a pharmaceutical company and audits the medical invoices for accuracy. In a group of 25 audits, she knows that 4 contain errors. If she randomly selects 3 audits without replacement, what is the probability that:

   a. all 3 audits will be correct?

   b. all 3 audits will contain errors?

   c. the last one will contain an error given that the first two did not contain errors?

32. In a survey of 50 college graduates, only 12 had the means to pay off their student loans within the first 6 months after graduation. If 4 graduates with student loans are randomly selected,

   a. What is the probability that all of them can pay off their student loan within 6 months of graduation?

   b. What is the probability that none of them can pay off their student loan within 6 months of graduation?

   c. What is the probability that the fourth student can pay off his/her student loans within 6 months of graduation if the first three students selected were not able to?

33. It is believed that a particular strain of the flu virus will affect 25% of the population this year. Of that group, approximately 96% will experience flu symptoms.

   a. If an individual is randomly selected from the population, what is the probability that the individual has contracted that particular strain of the flu virus and will show symptoms?

   b. If approximately 12% of those not infected by the flu still experience flu-like symptoms, what is the probability that a randomly-selected individual from the population will experience flu-like symptoms despite not actually having contracted the flu virus?

   c. Based on your answers from parts (a) and (b), what is the probability that a randomly selected individual has the flu virus if they show flu-like symptoms?

34. A certain virus infects 5% of the population. A test used to detect the virus in a person is positive 80% of the time if the person has the virus, and 10% of the time if the person does not have the virus.

   a. What is the probability that a randomly selected person tested positive and has the virus?

   b. What is the probability that a randomly selected person tested positive and does not have the virus?

   c. Based on your answers from parts (a) and (b), what is the probability that a randomly selected person has the virus given that they get a positive test result?

For Problems 35 to 40, determine if the events A and B are mutually exclusive, independent, or neither.

35. $P(A) = 0.82, P(B) = 0.7, P(A$ or $B) = 0.946$

36. $P(A) = 0.38, P(B) = 0.40, P(A$ or $B) = 0.78$

37. $P(A) = 0.45, P(B) = 0.60, P(A$ and $B) = 0$

38. $P(A) = 0.40, P(B) = 0.56, P(A$ and $B) = 0.16$

39. $P(A) = 0.45, P(A$ or $B) = 0.60, P(A$ and $B) = 0.27$

40. $P(A) = 0.65, P(A$ or $B) = 0.755, P(A$ and $B) = 0.195$

For Problems 41 and 42, calculate the desired empirical probabilities (rounded to 3 significant digits).

41. A pharmaceutical company manufactured depression drugs at three different manufacturing plants, Plant A, Plant B, and Plant C. The number of capsules produced in a day is listed by location in the following contingency table:

	Plant A	Plant B	Plant C	Total
Defective Capsules	10	30	25	65
Acceptable Capsules	290	370	475	1,135
Total	300	400	500	1,200

a. If one capsule is randomly selected from the daily production, what is the probability that it is acceptable?

b. If one capsule is randomly selected from the daily production, what is the probability that it is from Plant C?

c. If one capsule is randomly selected from the daily production, what is the probability that it is a defective capsule and it is from Plant B?

d. If one capsule is randomly selected from the daily production, what is the probability that it is acceptable or it is from Plant A?

e. Given that a capsule is selected from Plant C, what is the probability that it is a defect?

f. Given that a capsule is a defect, what is the probability that it is from Plant C?

g. If two capsules are randomly selected from the daily production (without replacement), what is the probability that they are both acceptable and that they are both from Plant B?

h. What is the probability that the tenth capsule inspected is defective, if the first nine capsules inspected are acceptable?

42. The following contingency table shows the pain-killer use in adults of three different age groups:

	No Pain-Killer	Over-The-Counter Pain-Killer	Prescription Pain-Killer	Total
Under 40	50	25	20	95
40-60	20	35	45	100
Over 60	10	45	80	135
Total	80	105	145	330

a. What is the probability that a randomly selected person is under 40?

b. What is the probability that a randomly selected person takes over-the-counter pain-killers?

c. If one person is randomly selected from this group, what is the probability that this person is under 40 and prefers not to use pain-killers?

d. If one person is randomly selected from this group, what is the probability that this person is between 40-60 or prefers to take prescription pain-killers?

e. Given that a person is over 60, what is the probability that this person prefers taking prescription pain-killers?

f. Given that a person prefers taking prescription pain-killers, what is the probability that this person is over 60?

g. If two people are randomly selected, what is the probability that they both typically use over-the-counter pain-killers?

h. If eight people are randomly selected, what is the probability that the eighth person chosen prefers to take prescription pain-killers when the first seven subjects chosen prefer to take over-the-counter pain-killers?

For Problems 43 to 50, determine which counting method(s) to use and determine the number of outcomes for the desired event using that counting method(s).

43. The access code for a medication cabinet consists of four digits. Each digit can be 0 through 9. How many access codes are possible if:

    a. each digit can be used only once and not repeated?

    b. each digit can be repeated?

44. To prevent fraud, health cards are appended with two random letters at the end of the patient ID number. How many letter combinations are possible if:

    a. each letter can be used only once and not repeated?

    b. each letter can be repeated?

45. Determine the number of arrangements of the letters in the word "PROBABILITY".

46. Determine the number of arrangements of the letters in the word "STATISTICS".

47. If there are 15 patients in a given wing, and each nurse is assigned to a rotation of 4 patients, how many different rotation assignments are possible for the first nurse?

48. The board of directors for a hospital has 12 members. One member is the president, another is the vice-president, another is the secretary, another is the treasurer, and another is the fundraising manager. How many different ways can these five positions be assigned?

49. The board of directors for a hospital has 12 members. A 5-person committee needs to be formed for a fundraising event. How many different ways can this committee be formed?

50. A hiring committee has developed 10 distinct questions designed to rate the performance of a head nurse candidate. The committee will select 5 of these questions. How many different groups of possible questions are there for the committee to ask?

For Problems 51 to 58, use appropriate counting techniques to determine the probability of the desired event.

51. In a group of 10 people, 4 have a type A personality and 6 have a type B personality. If 2 people are selected at random from this group, what is the probability that:

    a. the first of them has a type A personality and the second has type B personality?

    b. both have a type B personality?

52. In a group of 12 patients, 8 of them have never been to an ICU. If 2 patients are randomly selected from the group, what is the probability that:

    a. the first patient has never gone into ICU and the second patient has?

    b. both have never been to ICU?

53. 80% of open-heart surgeries are successful. What is the probability that in 4 randomly selected open-heart surgeries,

    a. all of them are successful?

    b. at least one surgery is successful?

54. 30% of patients are allergic to penicillin. If this drug is administered to 3 patients, what is the probability that:

    a. all 3 of them are allergic to it?

    b. at least one of them is not allergic to it?

55. In a sample of 20 blood donations, 8 are Type O blood, 8 are Type A blood, and 4 are Type B blood. If 6 of the units of blood are randomly selected, what is the probability that exactly 2 of each blood type are selected?

56. A student committee is formed at a college, consisting of 6 students from 3 different schools. Committee members are randomly selected from 5 student applications from each of the schools. What is the probability that exactly 2 students will be selected from each of the 3 schools?

57. The HR department of a hospital has filled 4 positions from 15 candidates which include 8 internal candidates and 7 external candidates. What is the probability that the hospital has hired:

    a. all 4 externally?

    b. 2 internal and 2 external candidates?

    c. at least one internal candidate?

58. A pharmacist orders a shipment of three different types of pain killers: 10 packs of acetaminophen, 12 packs of ibuprofen, and 15 packs of aspirin. If 3 patients each buy a pack of pain killers, what is the probability that:

    a. each patient buys a different brand of pain killer?

    b. all 3 the patients buy aspirin?

    c. at least one of the patients buy ibuprofen?

5 | Self-Test Exercises

1. A patient who has suffered a back injury is provided with a number of different referral options by his family doctor for treatment possibilities to choose from. There are 5 physiotherapists, 7 massage therapists, and 3 chiropractors in the region that the doctor can recommend to the patient.

   a. Calculate the total number of outcomes.

   b. Construct the sample space by listing out all possible outcomes.

   c. If the outcomes are grouped together by similar characteristics, how many different events are possible?

For Problems 2 to 4, analyze the scenarios and complete the following:

(i) *Determine what type of approach should be used to calculate the desired probability: theoretical, empirical, or subjective.*

(ii) *Calculate the probability of the desired event, if possible, rounded to 3 significant digits.*

2. A recent study of 412 patients at a local hospital indicated that 355 were either satisfied or very satisfied with the care they received while in the hospital. On the basis of this survey, what is the probability that a new patient will be satisfied or very satisfied with the care they receive at the hospital?

3. A blood-thirsty vampire living in a haunted house is allergic to the type-B blood protein. A group of 25 unsuspecting horror film enthusiasts from a local college decide to spend the weekend at the haunted house. 12 of the enthusiasts have type-O blood, 9 have type-A blood, 3 have type-B blood, and 1 has type-AB blood. If the vampire picks a student at random, what is the probability that he picks someone with a blood type he is allergic to?

4. A math professor believes that there is a strong relationship between class attendance and course grade. Based on her past experience, she predicts the probability that a student who attends all the classes will receive an "A" grade in the course.

For Problems 5 to 7, analyze the scenarios and complete the following:

(i) *State which method should be used to best determine the sample space: an outcome table, a tree diagram, or a Venn diagram.*

(ii) *Calculate the probability of the desired event (assuming all outcomes are equally likely) using the method you decided upon in part (i), rounded to 3 significant digits.*

5. 2 students are randomly selected from a statistics class and asked about their math anxiety level on a scale of 1-5, with 1 representing little to no anxiety and 5 representing extreme anxiety. If all 5 responses on the scale are equally likely to occur, what is the probability that both have a math anxiety of 3 or more?

6. Based on their blood types, a couple has a 50% chance of having a baby with O+ blood and a 50% chance of having a baby with O− blood. If the couple has 3 children, what is the probability that all three children will have the same blood type?

7. A survey of 100 grocery stores in a local community revealed that 40 stores had a pharmacy, 50 stores had a floral shop, and 70 stores had a deli. Of these stores, 30 stores have both a pharmacy and a deli, 25 stores have both a floral shop and a deli, 20 stores have both a pharmacy and a floral shop, and 10 stores have all three departments. What is the probability that a randomly selected store does not have any of these three departments?

8. In a group of 150 people, 70 know how to perform CPR, 90 know how to perform First Aid, and 60 know both.

   a. What is the probability that a randomly selected person from this group knows CPR or First Aid?

   b. What is the probability that a randomly selected person knows neither CPR nor First Aid?

9. Of 150 randomly selected open-heart surgery patients, 142 had a successful operation. Of the 120 patients in the group who were over the age of 40, 115 of them had a successful operation. What is the probability that a randomly selected patient from this group is 40 or younger and had an unsuccessful open-heart operation?

10. Percocet is a prescription drug used to treat pain. Of 320 randomly-selected patients taking this medication, 72 experienced side effects.

    a. Calculate the probability that a randomly selected patient from this group will experience side effects. Round to 3 significant digits as needed.

    b. State the complementary event and calculate its probability.

    c. Compute the odds against and odds in favour of the event.

11. In a survey of individuals in a city who were employed and married, 85% of them had health benefits through work, and 60% of them had partners who had health benefits through work. If 55% of respondents indicated that both partners had health benefits through work, determine the following probabilities for a randomly-selected individual in the city who is married and employed:

   a. either the individual or their partner has health benefits through work.

   b. neither of them have health benefits through work.

12. An insurance company survey shows that 90% of Ontario drivers wear seatbelts. For those who wear seatbelts, it is estimated that the probability of being seriously injured in a car accident is 2%, whereas those who do not wear seatbelts will have a 60% chance of being seriously injured in a car accident.

   a. What is the probability that a randomly-selected driver driver is wearing a seatbelt and suffers a serious injury in a car accident?

   b. What is the probability that a randomly-selected driver is not wearing a seatbelt and suffers a serious injury in a car accident?

   c. Based on your answers from parts (a) and (b), what is the probability that the driver was not wearing their seatbelt given they were seriously injured in a car accident?

13. The following contingency table shows the distribution of a sample of blood types in a city.

	A	B	AB	O	Total
Rh+	34	9	4	38	85
Rh–	6	2	1	6	15
Total	40	11	5	44	100

   a. If one person is randomly selected, what is the probability that the person will have type O blood?

   b. If one person is randomly selected, what is the probability that the person will be Rh+?

   c. If one person is randomly selected, what is the probability that the person will have type O blood and is Rh–?

   d. If one person is randomly selected, what is the probability that the person will have type B blood or is Rh+?

   e. Given that the person has type AB blood, what is the probability that the person is Rh+?

   f. Given that the person is Rh+, what is the probability that the person will have type AB blood?

   g. What is the probability that a married couple will both be Rh–?

   h. What is the probability that a married couple will both have type A blood?

14. Newer Ontario licence plates for commercial vehicles have two letters of the alphabet followed by a five-digit number.

   a. How many different licence plates are possible if all two-letter sequences are permitted and any five-digit number from 10001 to 99999 is allowed?

   b. A person witnessed a hit and run accident. He knows that the first letter on the licence plate of the offender's car was a B, the second letter was either an O or a Q, and that the last 3 numbers were 789. How many licence plates would fit this description?

15. Determine the number of arrangement of the letters in the following words:

   a. "NURSING"

   b. "PREHEALTH"

16. A foundation to assist people living with a certain disease decides to hold a lottery in which 5 unique numbers are chosen from the numbers 1-20. How many sets of numbers can be generated as tickets if:

   a. the order of the numbers matters?

   b. the order of the numbers does not matter?

17. The probability that a randomly-selected adult has ever experienced a migraine headache is 0.35. If 3 adults are randomly selected, what is the probability that:

   a. all three of them have experienced a migraine headache?

   b. none of them has ever experienced a migraine headache?

   c. at least 1 has experienced a migraine headache?

18. An optometrist office orders a shipment of four different types of contact lenses: 10 pairs of colour lenses, 20 pairs of daily lenses, 30 pairs of biweekly lenses, and 15 pairs of monthly lenses. If four patients each buy a pair of lenses, what is the probability that:

   a. Each patient buys a different type of contact lens?

   b. All 4 patients buy the biweekly lenses?

   c. None of the patients buy colour lenses?

5 | Summary of Notation and Formulas

NOTATION

S = sample space

$P(A)$ = the probability of event A occurring

$n(A)$ = # of ways event A can occur

$n(S)$ = total # of possible outcomes in S

A^c = the complement of event A

$P(B|A)$ = the probability of B given A

$n! = n \cdot (n-1) \cdot (n-2) \cdot \ldots \cdot 3 \cdot 2 \cdot 1$

$_nP_r$ = # of unique arrangements of a subgroup of r items in n unique items

$_nC_r = \binom{n}{r}$ = # of unique subgroups of r items in n unique items

FORMULAS

Theoretical Approach to Probability | 5.1-a

$$P(A) = \frac{\text{\# of ways event } A \text{ can occur}}{\text{total \# of outcomes in } S} = \frac{n(A)}{n(S)}$$

Empirical Approach to Probability | 5.1-b

$$P(A) = \frac{\text{\# of ways event } A \text{ occurred}}{\text{total \# of trials}} = \frac{n(A)}{n(E)}$$

Probability of a Complementary Event | 5.1-c

$$P(A^c) = 1 - P(A)$$

Generalized Addition Rule for Probabilities | 5.2-a

$$P(A \text{ or } B) = P(A) + P(B) - P(A \text{ and } B)$$

Generalized Multiplication Rule for Probabilities | 5.2-b

$$P(A \text{ and } B) = P(A) \cdot P(B|A)$$

Bayes' Theorem | 5.2-c

$$P(A|B) = \frac{P(B|A) \cdot P(A)}{P(B|A) \cdot P(A) + P(B|A^c) \cdot P(A^c)}$$

Number of Arrangements with Repeated Items | 5.3-a

$$\text{Number of Arrangements} = \frac{n!}{(k_1!)(k_2!)(k_3!) \ldots (k_m!)}$$

where $k_1, \ldots, k_m$ represent the sizes of each group of identical items in n items

Permutations | 5.3-b

$$_nP_r = \frac{n!}{(n-r)!}$$

Combinations | 5.3-c

$$_nC_r = \binom{n}{r} = \frac{n!}{(n-r)! \cdot r!}$$

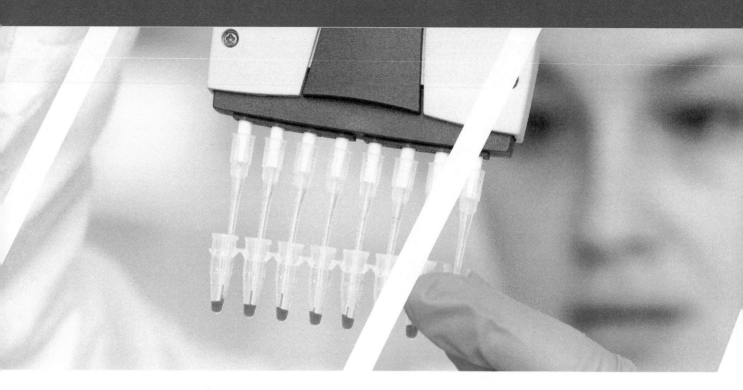

6

DISCRETE PROBABILITY DISTRIBUTIONS

LEARNING OBJECTIVES

- Differentiate between discrete random variables and continuous random variables.
- Construct probability distributions for discrete random variables.
- Calculate the expected value (mean), variance, and standard deviation of a discrete random variable using its probability distribution.
- State the properties of the binomial probability distribution.
- Interpret and apply the binomial formula to calculate probabilities for a binomial random variable.
- Calculate the expected value (mean), variance, and standard deviation of a binomial random variable.
- Calculate probabilities using the hypergeometric, geometric, and Poisson probability distributions.
- Calculate the expected value (mean), variance, and standard deviation of hypergeometric, geometric, and Poisson random variables.

CHAPTER OUTLINE

6.1 Discrete Random Variables and their Probability Distributions

6.2 The Binomial Distribution

6.3 Other Discrete Probability Distributions

Introduction

So far, we have analyzed probability using **sets** - that is, collections of results and outcomes of an experiment. For example, if our experiment is flipping a fair coin three times, then our sample space of all possible outcomes would be given by the set,

$$S = \{HHH, HHT, HTH, HTT, THH, THT, TTH, TTT\}$$

which could be constructed using a tree diagram or some other counting method discussed in Chapter 5. Furthermore, the event **"Exactly two (2) heads are flipped"** could be expressed using the set,

$$A = \{HHT, HTH, THH\}$$

However, for the sake of convenience and simplicity, it is often preferable to use numeric-variables like X and Y to describe the outcomes, as that allows us to apply concepts learned in arithmetic, algebra, geometry, trigonometry, and calculus to the study of probability. These variables are called **random variables**, and they are the focus of this chapter.

6.1 | Discrete Random Variables and their Probability Distributions

Overview of Random Variables

Random variables assign a numeric value to every outcome in the sample space. In the above example of flipping a fair coin three times, we can assign the random variable,

$$X = number\ of\ heads\ that\ are\ flipped$$

in which case, X can take on the values $x = 0$, 1, 2, or 3. The notation $X = x$, therefore, would represent the outcome(s) that are assigned to the value x for the random variable X.

Capital letters like X and Y are used to denote the random variables themselves, while lowercase letters like x and y are used to denote the values the respective variables can take on.

For example, the event **"Exactly two (2) heads are flipped"** could be described by $X = 2$, which would be assigned to three different outcomes: HHT, HTH, THH.

Now that we have established this convention of assigning random variables with numeric values to outcomes of an experiment, we are interested in determining the probability of those random variables taking on a certain value or range of values; however, before we can do this, we first need to classify random variables into two categories: discrete and continuous.

Discrete vs Continuous Random Variables

Depending on the nature of the values a random variable can take on, the way we analyze the probability distribution of that random variable will change. For instance, if we can list out all the values that X can take on, as we did in our coin-flipping example above, where X can only take on the values 0, 1, 2, or 3, we can count up the number of outcomes and write out the probability distribution for each value that X can take on, assuming that every other value has a probability of 0. Such cases are examples of **discrete random variables** - that is, the values that X can take on represent discrete data.

See Chapter 1 for a review of discrete vs continuous data.

However, what if X could take on any real number in a range of values? For example, let $X = the\ height$ $of\ a\ student\ in\ a\ statistics\ class$. In this situation, we cannot list out all possible outcomes, because X is a **continuous random variable** - that is, the values that X can take on represent continuous data.

Discrete Random Variables take on integer values that typically represent quantities. Some examples of discrete random variables include:

- The number of heads flipped in a repeated coin toss experiment.

- The number of patients processed in the E.R. in a day.

- The number of babies born in a week in a maternity ward.

- The number of pills in a bottle of medication.

Continuous Random Variables take on real-number values (within a given range of values) that typically represent measurements. Some examples of continuous random variables include:

- The diameter of a coin randomly selected for a coin toss experiment.

- The length of time a patient waits in the E.R.

- The weight of a baby born in a maternity ward.

- The volume of liquid medication in a bottle of medication.

Example 6.1-a	Identifying Discrete or Continuous Random Variables

Identify the following random variables as either discrete or continuous:

(i)   The mass of a benign tumour removed during an operation.

(ii)   The number of points a professional athlete scores during the course of a season.

(iii)   The angle of rotation of a joint in a patient with an injury.

(iv)   The distance travelled by a cyclist in one hour.

(v)   The number of each kind of animal a veterinarian sees during one week.

Solution

(i)   Since mass is a measurement with no smallest degree of precision, this is an example of a **continuous random variable**.

(ii)   Since the number of points scored can only take on whole number values, this is an example of a **discrete random variable**.

(iii)   Since the angle of rotation is a measurement with no smallest degree of precision, this is an example of a **continuous random variable**.

(iv)   Since distance is a measurement with no smallest degree of precision, this is an example of a **continuous random variable**.

(v)   Since the number of each kind of animal can only take on whole number values, this is an example of a **discrete random variable**.

Overview of Probability Distributions

In the previous chapter, we examined ways to define and use the sample space for a given procedure to determine the probability of an event occurring. However, if there are a large number of outcomes (e.g., in most lotteries, there are several million different outcomes), it becomes infeasible to attempt to list all of them in the sample space.

Oftentimes these events are known as **compound events** - events that are made up of several simple events - and we can make use of shortcuts to calculate the probability of such, without needing to list out all the events in the sample space.

Given a random variable X, the probability of the occurrence of a particular value x of the random variable would be denoted by $P(X = x)$, or often more informally as $P(x)$, meaning "the probability that X will take on the value x."

Recall that when three coins are flipped, there are eight possible outcomes: S = {*HHH, HHT, HTH, HTT, THH, THT, TTH, TTT*}. If X = *number of heads that are flipped* out of three coins, the probability of exactly two heads being flipped would be given by $P(X = 2)$, or simply $P(2)$, and can be calculated using methods from the previous chapter to be,

$$P(2) = \frac{3}{8}$$

If we went through each value that X could take on and calculated the probability of that value occurring, we would have what is known as a **probability distribution for X**, as given below:

# of heads (x)	0	1	2	3
$P(x)$	$\dfrac{1}{8}$	$\dfrac{3}{8}$	$\dfrac{3}{8}$	$\dfrac{1}{8}$

For any other values of x (e.g., x = 4, 5, etc.), the probability of X taking on that value is zero (i.e., $P(x) = 0$ for every $x \neq 0, 1, 2, 3$). As such, we can state the following two general properties, which are actually common to every probability distribution:

1. $0 \leq P(x) \leq 1$ for every x - i.e., the probability of X taking on a given value is always at least 0 and not greater than 1.

2. $\sum\limits_{all\ x} P(x) = 1$ - i.e., the sum of the probabilities of X taking on any given value is always 1.

E.g., in the example above, $\sum P(x) = \dfrac{1}{8} + \dfrac{3}{8} + \dfrac{3}{8} + \dfrac{1}{8} = \dfrac{8}{8} = 1$

Constructing Discrete Probability Distributions

The remainder of this chapter will focus on discrete probability distributions (continuous probability distributions will be studied more in depth in the next chapter).

To construct a probability distribution for a discrete random variable X, we need to list out all the possible values x that X can take on, and determine the probability of each of those values occurring (i.e., $P(X = x)$ for each x). The results are then listed in a table.

Example 6.1-b   **Constructing a Discrete Probability Distribution**

Two standard 6-sided dice are rolled and the sum of their values is recorded. Construct a probability distribution for the discrete random variable that models the outcomes of this experiment.

Solution

Let X = *the sum of two standard 6-sided dice.*

Recall the following outcome table of rolling two standard 6-sided dice from Chapter 5:

DIE 1	DIE 2					
	1	2	3	4	5	6
1	(1, 1)	(1, 2)	(1, 3)	(1, 4)	(1, 5)	(1, 6)
2	(2, 1)	(2, 2)	(2, 3)	(2, 4)	(2, 5)	(2, 6)
3	(3, 1)	(3, 2)	(3, 3)	(3, 4)	(3, 5)	(3, 6)
4	(4, 1)	(4, 2)	(4, 3)	(4, 4)	(4, 5)	(4, 6)
5	(5, 1)	(5, 2)	(5, 3)	(5, 4)	(5, 5)	(5, 6)
6	(6, 1)	(6, 2)	(6, 3)	(6, 4)	(6, 5)	(6, 6)

$x \in$ {*a set of values*} means that x is an element of the set; i.e., x can take on any of the values in the set.

By summing the two dice rolls from each outcome, we see $x \in$ {2, 3, 4, 5, 6, 7, 8, 9, 10, 11, 12}, and get the following probability distribution (probabilities left unreduced for clarity):

Solution
continued

x	2	3	4	5	6	7	8	9	10	11	12
P(x)	$\frac{1}{36}$	$\frac{2}{36}$	$\frac{3}{36}$	$\frac{4}{36}$	$\frac{5}{36}$	$\frac{6}{36}$	$\frac{5}{36}$	$\frac{4}{36}$	$\frac{3}{36}$	$\frac{2}{36}$	$\frac{1}{36}$

For every other value of x, $P(x) = 0$, which verifies the two properties of probability distributions that we identified earlier:

1. $0 \le P(x) \le 1$ for every x, and

2. $\sum_{\text{all } x} P(x) = \frac{1}{36} + \frac{2}{36} + \frac{3}{36} + \frac{4}{36} + \frac{5}{36} + \frac{6}{36} + \frac{5}{36} + \frac{4}{36} + \frac{3}{36} + \frac{2}{36} + \frac{1}{36} = \frac{36}{36} = 1$

Mean, Variance, and Standard Deviation of a Discrete Probability Distribution

Since we are now dealing with variables, we can perform a statistical analysis (including measures of centre and dispersion) of the data set comprised of the results of the variable.

For example, let the discrete random variable $X = $ *the sum of two standard 6-sided dice*. Assume two dice were rolled 10 times, and the following sample results were recorded:

$$X = 4, 7, 5, 10, 7, 3, 11, 9, 6, 7$$

If we perform a quick one-variable statistical analysis on this data, we get the following sample statistics:

Sample mean: $\bar{x} = \frac{\sum x}{n} = \frac{4 + 7 + 5 + \ldots + 7}{10} = 6.9$

It is easy to verify that this formula is the same as the following:

$$\bar{x} = \sum \left(x \cdot \frac{1}{n} \right)$$

$$= 4\left(\frac{1}{10}\right) + 7\left(\frac{1}{10}\right) + 5\left(\frac{1}{10}\right) + \ldots + 7\left(\frac{1}{10}\right) = 6.9$$

Sample variance: $s^2 = \frac{\sum (x - \bar{x})^2}{n - 1} = \frac{(4 - 6.9)^2 + (7 - 6.9)^2 + \ldots + (7 - 6.9)^2}{10 - 1} \approx 6.54$

Similarly, it is easy to verify that this formula is the same as the following:

$$s^2 = \sum \left((x - \bar{x})^2 \cdot \frac{1}{n - 1} \right)$$

$$= (4 - 6.9)^2 \left(\frac{1}{9}\right) + (7 - 6.9)^2 \left(\frac{1}{9}\right) + \ldots + (7 - 6.9)^2 \left(\frac{1}{9}\right) \approx 6.54$$

Sample standard deviation: $s = \sqrt{6.54} \approx 2.56$

However, how can we define population parameters in this situation? The population would be defined as "the sums of the face values of the two dice for **all** rolls of two standard 6-sided dice." But what does "all rolls" imply? Necessarily, this must be an infinite population, as there is no limit to how many times we could roll two standard 6-sided dice and record the outcome.

So how do we determine the mean and standard deviation in such a case, with an infinite number of data values? As it turns out, we can use the probability distribution - a beautiful overlap of statistical analysis and probability theory!

If we look at the above formulas, we only need to replace the following:

1. the sample data values with all the possible population values, and

2. the probability of occurrence of each data value x in the sample ($\frac{1}{n}$ in the sample mean formula and $\frac{1}{n-1}$ in the sample variance formula - corrected for the number of degrees of freedom) with the probability of occurrence of each data value x in the population: $P(x)$.

Expected Value (Mean), Variance, and Standard Deviation of Probability Distributions

Round expected value, variance, and standard deviation to 3 significant digits, unless otherwise indicated.

Replacing the sample probabilities with the population probabilities in the formulas above gives us the following formulas for the mean (also known as the **Expected Value** of the discrete probability distribution, as it is the most likely value to occur for the discrete random variable X), variance, and standard deviation for a discrete probability distribution:

Formula 6.1-a	**Expected Value (Mean) for a Discrete Probability Distribution**

$$E(X) = \mu = \sum_{\text{all } x} \left(x \cdot P(x) \right)$$

Formula 6.1-b	**Variance for a Discrete Probability Distribution**

$$Var(X) = \sigma^2 = \sum_{\text{all } x} \left((x - \mu)^2 \cdot P(x) \right) \quad \text{or} \quad Var(X) = \sigma^2 = \sum_{\text{all } x} \left(x^2 \cdot P(x) \right) - \mu^2$$

Formula 6.1-c	**Standard Deviation for a Discrete Probability Distribution**

$$SD(X) = \sigma = \sqrt{\sum_{\text{all } x} \left((x - \mu)^2 \cdot P(x) \right)} \quad \text{or} \quad SD(X) = \sigma = \sqrt{\sum_{\text{all } x} \left(x^2 \cdot P(x) \right) - \mu^2}$$

Note: The alternate forms of the variance and standard deviation formulas have been provided for ease of calculation.

Example 6.1-c	Calculating the Expected Value (Mean), Variance, and Standard Deviation of the Sum of Two Dice

Calculate the expected value (mean), variance, and standard deviation for the discrete probability distribution of the random variable X = *the sum of two standard 6-sided dice.*

Solution

x	$P(x)$	$x \cdot P(x)$	$(x - \mu)^2$	$(x - \mu)^2 \cdot P(x)$
2	$\dfrac{1}{36}$	$\dfrac{2}{36}$	$(2 - 7)^2 = 25$	$\dfrac{25}{36}$
3	$\dfrac{2}{36}$	$\dfrac{6}{36}$	$(3 - 7)^2 = 16$	$\dfrac{32}{36}$
4	$\dfrac{3}{36}$	$\dfrac{12}{36}$	$(4 - 7)^2 = 9$	$\dfrac{27}{36}$
5	$\dfrac{4}{36}$	$\dfrac{20}{36}$	$(5 - 7)^2 = 4$	$\dfrac{16}{36}$
6	$\dfrac{5}{36}$	$\dfrac{30}{36}$	$(6 - 7)^2 = 1$	$\dfrac{5}{36}$
7	$\dfrac{6}{36}$	$\dfrac{42}{36}$	$(7 - 7)^2 = 0$	0
8	$\dfrac{5}{36}$	$\dfrac{40}{36}$	$(8 - 7)^2 = 1$	$\dfrac{5}{36}$
9	$\dfrac{4}{36}$	$\dfrac{36}{36}$	$(9 - 7)^2 = 4$	$\dfrac{16}{36}$

Solution
continued

x	$P(x)$	$x \cdot P(x)$	$(x - \mu)^2$	$(x - \mu)^2 \cdot P(x)$
10	$\dfrac{3}{36}$	$\dfrac{30}{36}$	$(10 - 7)^2 = 9$	$\dfrac{27}{36}$
11	$\dfrac{2}{36}$	$\dfrac{22}{36}$	$(11 - 7)^2 = 16$	$\dfrac{32}{36}$
12	$\dfrac{1}{36}$	$\dfrac{12}{36}$	$(12 - 7)^2 = 25$	$\dfrac{25}{36}$
		$\begin{aligned} \mu &= \sum(x \cdot P(x)) \\ &= \dfrac{252}{36} = 7 \end{aligned}$		$\begin{aligned} \sigma^2 &= \sum((x - \mu)^2 \cdot P(x)) \\ &= \dfrac{210}{36} = \dfrac{35}{6} \approx 5.83 \end{aligned}$

Therefore, from the table,

$$E(X) = \mu = \sum(x \cdot P(x)) = 7$$

$$\sigma^2 = \sum((x - \mu)^2 \cdot P(x)) = \frac{35}{6} \approx 5.83$$

$$\sigma = \sqrt{\frac{35}{6}} \approx 2.42$$

Alternative Solution

x	$P(x)$	$x \cdot P(x)$	x^2	$x^2 \cdot P(x)$
2	$\dfrac{1}{36}$	$\dfrac{2}{36}$	4	$\dfrac{4}{36}$
3	$\dfrac{2}{36}$	$\dfrac{6}{36}$	9	$\dfrac{18}{36}$
4	$\dfrac{3}{36}$	$\dfrac{12}{36}$	16	$\dfrac{48}{36}$
5	$\dfrac{4}{36}$	$\dfrac{20}{36}$	25	$\dfrac{100}{36}$
6	$\dfrac{5}{36}$	$\dfrac{30}{36}$	36	$\dfrac{180}{36}$
7	$\dfrac{6}{36}$	$\dfrac{42}{36}$	49	$\dfrac{294}{36}$
8	$\dfrac{5}{36}$	$\dfrac{40}{36}$	64	$\dfrac{320}{36}$
9	$\dfrac{4}{36}$	$\dfrac{36}{36}$	81	$\dfrac{324}{36}$
10	$\dfrac{3}{36}$	$\dfrac{30}{36}$	100	$\dfrac{300}{36}$
11	$\dfrac{2}{36}$	$\dfrac{22}{36}$	121	$\dfrac{242}{36}$
12	$\dfrac{1}{36}$	$\dfrac{12}{36}$	144	$\dfrac{144}{36}$
		$\begin{aligned} \mu &= \sum(x \cdot P(x)) \\ &= \dfrac{252}{36} = 7 \end{aligned}$		$\sum(x^2 \cdot P(x)) = \dfrac{1,974}{36} = \dfrac{329}{6}$

Solution
continued

Therefore, from the table,

$$E(X) = \mu = \sum\left(x \cdot P(x)\right) = 7$$

$$\sigma^2 = \sum\left(x^2 \cdot P(x)\right) - \mu^2 = \frac{329}{6} - 7^2 = \frac{35}{6} \approx 5.83$$

$$\sigma = \sqrt{\frac{35}{6}} \approx 2.42$$

Example 6.1-d Calculating the Expected Value (Mean), Variance, and Standard Deviation of a Random Variable

For a hospital's charitable golf fundraiser, a 50-50 game is played in which 100 players each pay $20 for the opportunity to reach into a bag of tokens. 80 of the tokens have "Bogie" on them ($0 value), 12 tokens have "Par" on them ($25 value), 4 tokens have "Birdie" on them ($50 value), 3 tokens have "Eagle" on them ($100 value), and 1 token has "Hole in One" on it ($200 value).

(i) Create a discrete probability distribution table for this game and determine the expected value of a randomly-selected token.

(ii) Determine the standard deviation for this game.

For this problem, round monetary values to the nearest cent.

Solution (i)

x	$P(x)$	$x \cdot P(x)$
0	$\frac{80}{100} = 0.8$	$0(0.8) = 0$
25	$\frac{12}{100} = 0.12$	$25(0.12) = 3$
50	$\frac{4}{100} = 0.04$	$50(0.04) = 2$
100	$\frac{3}{100} = 0.03$	$100(0.03) = 3$
200	$\frac{1}{100} = 0.01$	$200(0.01) = 2$

$$\mu = \sum\left(x \cdot P(x)\right) = 10$$

From the probability distribution table,

$$E(X) = \mu = \sum\left(x \cdot P(x)\right) = 10$$

Therefore, the expected value of a randomly-selected token is $10.

This seems to make sense, given that the game costs $20 to play, and this is a 50-50 fundraiser, meaning that 50% of the funds are kept by the charity and the other 50% are given as prizes.

Solution
continued

(ii)   Extending our table from part (i),

x	P(x)	x · P(x)	(x − μ)²	(x − μ)² · P(x)
0	$\frac{80}{100} = 0.8$	$0(0.8) = 0$	$(0 - 10)^2 = 100$	$100(0.8) = 80$
25	$\frac{12}{100} = 0.12$	$25(0.12) = 3$	$(25 - 10)^2 = 225$	$225(0.12) = 27$
50	$\frac{4}{100} = 0.04$	$50(0.04) = 2$	$(50 - 10)^2 = 1{,}600$	$1{,}600(0.04) = 64$
100	$\frac{3}{100} = 0.03$	$100(0.03) = 3$	$(100 - 10)^2 = 8{,}100$	$8{,}100(0.03) = 243$
200	$\frac{1}{100} = 0.01$	$200(0.01) = 2$	$(200 - 10)^2 = 36{,}100$	$36{,}100(0.01) = 361$

$$\mu = \sum \left(x \cdot P(x) \right) = 10 \qquad \sigma^2 = \sum \left((x - \mu)^2 \cdot P(x) \right) = 775$$

From the probability distribution table,

$$\sigma^2 = \sum \left((x - \mu)^2 \cdot P(x) \right) = 775$$

$$\sigma = \sqrt{775} = 27.838821\ldots = \$27.84$$

Therefore, the standard deviation for this game is $27.84.

6.1 | Exercises

Answers to odd-numbered problems are available at the end of the textbook.

For Problems 1 to 12, determine if the random variables listed are continuous or discrete:

1. The number of children born to one mother.

2. The volume of a liquid suspension administered intravenously.

3. The percent body fat of a client at a nutrition clinic.

4. The number of cigarettes smoked in one day.

5. The angle formed by the legs during a particular stretch.

6. The average length of time spent running every day.

7. The total amount paid for a gym membership.

8. The number of puppies in a litter born at a veterinary clinic.

9. The length of time spent sleeping each night.

10. The number of tablets in a bottle of aspirin.

11. The year in which a patient was born.

12. The length of time a swimmer can hold his/her breath for.

For Problems 13 to 20, calculate the mean and standard deviation of the discrete probability distributions.

13.

x	0	1	2	3	4	5
P(x)	0.245	0.318	0.207	0.126	0.074	0.030

14.

x	0	1	2	3	4	5	6
P(x)	0.027	0.084	0.165	0.212	0.243	0.171	0.098

15.

x	0	10	20	30	40	50	60	70	80	90	100
P(x)	0.03	0.06	0.09	0.12	0.125	0.15	0.125	0.12	0.09	0.06	0.03

16.

x	0	5	10	15	20	25	30	35	40
P(x)	0.04	0.08	0.12	0.16	0.2	0.16	0.12	0.08	0.04

17.

x	15-19	20-24	25-29	30-34	35-39	40-44	45-49
P(x)	$\frac{7}{40}$	$\frac{17}{40}$	$\frac{8}{40}$	$\frac{5}{40}$	$\frac{2}{40}$	$\frac{0}{40}$	$\frac{1}{40}$

18.

x	3-4	5-6	7-8	9-10	11-12	13-14	15-16	17-18
P(x)	$\frac{1}{35}$	$\frac{0}{35}$	$\frac{3}{35}$	$\frac{4}{35}$	$\frac{5}{35}$	$\frac{7}{35}$	$\frac{9}{35}$	$\frac{6}{35}$

19.

x	0% to less than 20%	20% to less than 40%	40% to less than 60%	60% to less than 80%	80% to less than 100%
P(x)	0.156	0.318	0.244	0.202	0.080

20.

x	$0 to less than $5,000	$5,000 to less than $10,000	$10,000 to less than $15,000	$15,000 to less than $20,000	$20,000 to less than $25,000
P(x)	0.512	0.296	0.124	0.048	0.020

For Problems 21 to 28, analyze the scenarios and complete the following:

(i) *Construct a discrete probability distribution for the given variable.*

(ii) *Calculate the expected value and variance of the discrete probability distribution.*

21. The number of girls in a family with five children.

22. The number of patients in a ward room (i.e., with three patients in the room) who choose the first meal option when given a choice of 3 different meal options on the menu.

23. The value of a ticket in a small hospital lottery, in which 1,000 tickets are sold, with 1 grand prize of $1,000, 10 first prizes of $100, 20 second prizes of $50, and 40 third prizes of $25.

24. The value of a ticket in a small hospital lottery, in which 2,000 tickets are sold, with 1 grand prize of $2,500, 10 first prizes of $250, 20 second prizes of $100, and 60 third prizes of $50.

25. The number of complications arising from the three procedures that a physician performs in one day if the probability of complications arising on one procedure is 0.08.

26. The number of patients who will survive for five or more years, out of the four patients currently being treated by an oncologist for a certain type of cancer, if the 5-year survival rate is 0.85.

27. In response to growing concern about paramedical health insurance fraud, an insurance company calls a Registered Massage Therapist's (RMT's) office to randomly verify three claims submitted this past week. If, out of the 20 claims reported by patients of the RMT, 4 are fraudulent, determine the probability distribution for the number of fraudulent claims that were identified.

28. Out of 15 nurse practitioners who are on call on a given day, 3 are sick. If two on-call nurse practitioners are called in based on a random selection, determine the probability distribution for the number of sick nurse practitioners who are called in.

6.2 | The Binomial Distribution

We now turn our attention to a very specific and important discrete probability distribution known as the **Binomial Probability Distribution**. This type of discrete probability distribution is used to model experiments with two outcomes (or classes of outcomes): **successes** and **failures**. The number of trials of the experiment must be fixed (*n*), each trial must be independent of the other trials, and the trial must be repeated under identical conditions, with the probabilities of success and failure remaining constant for every trial. Such trials are known as **binomial experiments** or **Bernoulli trials**, named for Swiss mathematician Jacob Bernoulli (1655-1705), who did extensive work in the field of probability theory, and made significant contributions to the study of probability distributions and analysis.

The Binomial Formula

A **Binomial Random Variable** X is a random variable that measures the number of successes in n Bernoulli trials. We wish to develop a method to calculate $P(X = x)$, the probability of x successes in n Bernoulli trials.

Firstly, we can conclude that on n independent repeated trials, there are $\binom{n}{x}$ ways of getting x successes (and therefore, $(n - x)$ failures).

Furthermore, if the probability of a success on any one of those n trials is given by p, and therefore the probability of a failure on any one of the trials is given by $q = 1 - p$, then the probability of x successes and $(n - x)$ failures on any one of the $\binom{n}{x}$ combinations above would be $p^x \cdot q^{(n - x)}$.

Therefore, putting those two pieces together, we can deduce the following **Binomial Formula** for the probability of x successes on n Bernoulli trials:

Formula 6.2

Binomial Formula

$$P(x) = \binom{n}{x} p^x \cdot q^{(n - x)}$$

Example 6.2-a

Verifying the Binomial Formula

Using your knowledge of counting rules and your ability to calculate probability from the previous chapter, verify that the binomial formula holds in the following scenarios. Then, calculate the probabilities.

(i)   A fair coin is flipped 8 times. What is the probability of flipping exactly 3 heads?

(ii)   An unprepared student guesses on every one of the 10 questions of a multiple-choice statistics quiz. If each question has 5 possible answers, what is the probability that the student will guess exactly 5 correct (and therefore, pass the test)?

Solution

(i)   Let X represent the number of heads on 8 flips of the fair coin (so $p = 0.5$ and $q = 0.5$).

There are $\binom{8}{3}$ ways of flipping exactly 3 heads, and 2^8 total possible outcomes in the sample space. Therefore,

$$P(3) = \frac{\binom{8}{3}}{2^8} = \binom{8}{3} \cdot \left(\frac{1}{2}\right)^8 = \binom{8}{3}(0.5)^8 = \binom{8}{3}(0.5)^3(0.5)^5$$

> Recall exponent rule:
> $a^m \times a^n = a^{(m + n)}$

as the binomial formula predicts. Calculating the probability,

$$P(3) = \binom{8}{3}(0.5)^3(0.5)^5 \approx 0.219$$

Solution
continued

(ii) Let X represent the number of questions the student guessed correctly out of 10 questions. Since the answers for each question are independent of the other answers, the trials are independent and repeated; and since there are 5 possible answers for each question, the probability of guessing correctly on a given question is $p = \dfrac{1}{5} = 0.2$, and the probability of guessing incorrectly is $q = 1 - 0.2 = 0.8$.

There are $\dbinom{10}{5}$ ways of guessing exactly 5 questions correctly, and 4^5 options for the 5 questions that the student guessed incorrectly. There are a total of 5^{10} different possible outcomes for the multiple-choice quiz in the sample space. Therefore,

$$P(5) = \frac{\dbinom{10}{5} \cdot 4^5}{5^{10}} = \dbinom{10}{5} \cdot \frac{4^5}{5^{10}} = \dbinom{10}{5}\left(\frac{1}{5}\right)^5\left(\frac{4}{5}\right)^5 = \dbinom{10}{5}(0.2)^5(0.8)^5$$

as the binomial formula predicts. Calculating the probability,

$$P(5) = \dbinom{10}{5}(0.2)^5(0.8)^5 \approx 0.0264$$

Example 6.2-b | **Calculating Probability Using the Binomial Formula**

For the following scenarios, determine if they are binomial experiments, and if so, calculate the probability of the given event using the Binomial Formula.

(i) **Experiment:** 5 cards are drawn randomly from a shuffled deck **without** replacement.

   Event: 3 out of the 5 cards are face cards (Jack, Queen, or King).

(ii) **Experiment:** 5 cards are drawn randomly from a shuffled deck **with** replacement.

   Event: 3 out of the 5 cards are face cards (Jack, Queen, or King).

(iii) **Experiment:** 5 cards are drawn randomly from a shuffled deck **with** replacement.

   Event: At least 1 card out of each of the three face cards (Jack, Queen, King) are selected.

(iv) **Experiment:** A coin is flipped until it lands with Tails facing up.

   Event: The first Tails occurs on the 7th coin toss.

(v) **Experiment:** The number of calls to a local 911 call-center, which receives an average of 2 calls per minute, is recorded over a period of 5 minutes.

   Event: Exactly 10 calls are received during this period.

(vi) **Experiment:** 20 women receive positive test results on a certain pregnancy test that has a 95% accuracy rate (meaning 95% of all women who receive positive results are actually pregnant).

   Event: 19 out of the 20 women (i.e., 95% of the sample) are actually pregnant.

Solution

(i) Since the cards are selected without replacement, the trials are **not** independent, and therefore this does not represent a binomial experiment.

(ii) Since the cards are selected with replacement, the trials are independent and repeated 5 times, with fixed probabilities of success $p = \dfrac{12}{52} = \dfrac{3}{13}$ and failure $q = 1 - \dfrac{3}{13} = \dfrac{10}{13}$. Hence, this is a binomial experiment:

Using Formula 6.2, $\qquad P(x) = \dbinom{n}{x}p^x \cdot q^{(n-x)}$

$$P(3) = \dbinom{5}{3}\left(\frac{3}{13}\right)^3\left(\frac{10}{13}\right)^2 \approx 0.0727$$

(iii)   Though the trials are independent and the number of trials are fixed in this case, as they are in (ii), in this situation there are more than two outcomes (Jack, Queen, King). Therefore, this does not represent a binomial experiment.

(iv)   Since the number of coin tosses is not fixed, this does not represent a binomial experiment.

(v)   In this case, there are no "trials" to speak of - only a fixed length of time, during which the number of phone calls received can be anywhere from 0 to an unfixed, arbitrarily high value. There are also only successes. Hence, this does not represent a binomial experiment.

(vi)   In this case, the positive results of the pregnancy test are independent and repeated 20 times, with fixed probabilities of success (being pregnant) $p = 0.95$ and failure (not being pregnant) $q = 1 - 0.95 = 0.05$. Hence, this is a binomial experiment:

Using Formula 6.2, $P(x) = \begin{pmatrix} n \\ x \end{pmatrix} p^x \cdot q^{(n-x)}$

$$P(19) = \begin{pmatrix} 20 \\ 19 \end{pmatrix} (0.95)^{19}(0.05)^1 \approx 0.377$$

Properties of the Binomial Probability Distribution

Consider part (vi) in the previous example. Were you surprised by the result? In a sample of 20 pregnancy tests, with a 95% (i.e., $\frac{19}{20}$) success rate, we would **expect** 19 tests to be accurate and 1 test to be inaccurate. However, the solution to (vi) showed that there is only a probability of 0.377 (i.e., 37.7%) that this will, in fact, be the case. In order to understand this result, we need to dig a little deeper into the nature of the binomial distribution, including an analysis of the **expected value** and **variance** of the binomial distribution.

For simplicity's sake, let's consider a simpler example than the pregnancy test problem above:

Example 6.2-c	Understanding the Binomial Distribution

Consider a certain coffee chain that offers an annual promotion, whereby every cup of coffee purchased offers the chance to win a number of prizes. The coffee chain produces approximately 300 million cups in Canada for the promotion, with approximately 50 million of those cups containing prizes.

(i)   If an individual purchases 6 cups of coffee in a week, determine the probability that she will not win anything.

(ii)   Determine the probability that the same individual will win exactly 1 prize.

(iii)   Repeat your process in part (ii) to determine the probabilities that she will win exactly 2 prizes, 3 prizes, 4 prizes, 5 prizes, and 6 prizes.

(iv)   Discuss what your results from parts (i) to (iii) tell you about the distribution, and make a conclusion as to which event is most likely to occur.

For this problem, round probabilities to 4 decimal places.

Since there are 300 million coffee cups produced and 50 million cups contain prizes, the probability of winning a prize is $\frac{1}{6}$. Even though the coffee cups are sampled without replacement, since the number of coffee cups produced is so large, removing one cup will have a negligible impact on the probability of winning - hence, we may assume this represents a Bernoulli trial, with $n = 6$ trials, and outcomes of "Win" ($p = \frac{1}{6}$) and "Lose" ($q = 1 - \frac{1}{6} = \frac{5}{6}$).

Using Formula 6.2, $\qquad P(x) = \binom{n}{x} p^x \cdot q^{(n-x)}$

(i) $\qquad\qquad\qquad\qquad P(0) = \binom{6}{0}\left(\frac{1}{6}\right)^0 \left(\frac{5}{6}\right)^6 \approx 0.3349$

(ii) $\qquad\qquad\qquad\qquad P(1) = \binom{6}{1}\left(\frac{1}{6}\right)^1 \left(\frac{5}{6}\right)^5 \approx 0.4019$

(iii) $\qquad\qquad\qquad\qquad P(2) = \binom{6}{2}\left(\frac{1}{6}\right)^2 \left(\frac{5}{6}\right)^4 \approx 0.2009$

$\qquad\qquad\qquad\qquad\quad P(3) = \binom{6}{3}\left(\frac{1}{6}\right)^3 \left(\frac{5}{6}\right)^3 \approx 0.0536$

$\qquad\qquad\qquad\qquad\quad P(4) = \binom{6}{4}\left(\frac{1}{6}\right)^4 \left(\frac{5}{6}\right)^2 \approx 0.0080$

$\qquad\qquad\qquad\qquad\quad P(5) = \binom{6}{5}\left(\frac{1}{6}\right)^5 \left(\frac{5}{6}\right)^1 \approx 0.0006$

$\qquad\qquad\qquad\qquad\quad P(6) = \binom{6}{6}\left(\frac{1}{6}\right)^6 \left(\frac{5}{6}\right)^0 \approx 0.0001$

> $P(6)$ is actually equal to 0.0000 when rounded to 4 decimal places, but in order to have all the probabilities add up to 1, we round up to 0.0001.

(iv) To better understand the results of the probability distribution, we plot them on a bar graph:

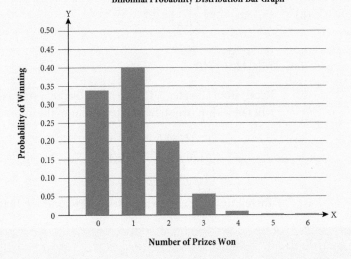

Binomial Probability Distribution Bar Graph

We can see from the graph that the most likely event to occur is 1 winning cup. This makes sense, given that the probability of winning on any individual trial is $p = \frac{1}{6}$.

However, it is still less likely for this event to actually occur (~0.40) than it is for another event to occur (~0.60). Such is the nature with **expected value** $E(X)$ - it is the single event that is **most likely** to occur, though it may be less likely to occur than all other events combined (i.e., $P(X = E(X)) < 0.5$).

Expected Value (Mean), Variance, and Standard Deviation of a Binomial Probability Distribution

To calculate the expected value (mean) of a binomial probability distribution, we simply multiply the number of trials (n) by the probability of success on any given trial (p):

Expected Value (Mean): $E(X) = \mu = np$

To calculate the variance of the binomial probability distribution, we multiply the expected value of the distribution by the probability of failure on any given trial ($q = 1 - p$):

Variance: $Var(X) = \sigma^2 = npq = np(1 - p)$

To calculate the standard deviation of the binomial distribution, we take the square root of the variance:

Standard Deviation: $SD(X) = \sigma = \sqrt{npq} = \sqrt{np(1 - p)}$

| Example 6.2-d | Calculating the Expected Value (Mean), Variance, and Standard Deviation of a Binomial Random Variable |

Consider the coffee promotion from the previous example (6.2-c). Assume that a regular coffee-drinker purchases 20 coffees during the promotion.

(i)   Determine the number of prizes he is expected to win.

(ii)   Calculate the variance and standard deviation for this binomial random variable.

(iii)   Use the standard deviation and Chebyshev's Theorem to predict a range of values that represent how many prizes he is expected to win, with a degree of accuracy of at least 75%.

For this problem, do not round your answers.

Solution

(i) $E(X) = np = 20\left(\dfrac{1}{6}\right) = 3.\overline{3}$

Therefore, he is expected to win approximately 3 prizes.

(ii) $\sigma^2 = npq = 20\left(\dfrac{1}{6}\right)\left(\dfrac{5}{6}\right) = 2.\overline{7}$

$\sigma = \sqrt{(2.\overline{7})} = 1.\overline{6}$

(iii)   Recall from Chapter 3, Chebyshev's Theorem states that 75% of the data of any distribution will fall within two standard deviations of the mean on either side:

$$\mu - 2\sigma < X < \mu + 2\sigma$$
$$3.\overline{3} - 2(1.\overline{6}) < X < 3.\overline{3} + 2(1.\overline{6})$$
$$0 < X < 6.\overline{6}$$

Therefore, we can say, with at least 75% accuracy, that he will win between 0 and 7 prizes.

6.2 | Exercises

Answers to odd-numbered problems are available at the end of the textbook.

For Problems 1 to 8, use the binomial formula to calculate the probability of the indicated event to 3 significant digits:

1. $n = 15, p = 0.2, P(X = 3)$

2. $n = 16, p = 0.25, P(X = 4)$

3. $n = 10, p = 0.7, P(X \geq 8)$

4. $n = 12, p = 0.8, P(X \geq 10)$

5. $n = 25, p = 0.1, P(X \leq 3)$

6. $n = 30, p = 0.05, P(X \leq 2)$

7. $n = 80, p = 0.15, P(10 \leq X \leq 15)$

8. $n = 120, p = 0.4, P(45 \leq X \leq 50)$

9. A mid-wife delivers 16 children in a month. What is the probability that half are boys and half are girls?

10. A veterinarian performs 24 operations to neuter/spay pets in a month. What is the probability that exactly half of the animals are male and half are female?

11. Approximately 8% of all males in the population have a form of Red-Green colour-blindness. In a sample of 50 males, what is the probability that exactly 8% of them will be diagnosed with a form of Red-Green colour-blindness?

12. A certain early response pregnancy test claims to be able to detect the pregnancy hormone in 76% of pregnant women, 5 days prior to their expected period. In a sample of 25 pregnant women who took the test 5 days before their period, what is the probability that exactly 76% of them saw a positive test result on their pregnancy test?

13. A laser-eye surgery clinic boasts that their procedure has a 90% success rate in eliminating the need for glasses or contact lenses. If 30 patients are seen in one week, what is the probability that at least 90% of them no longer need glasses or contact lenses?

14. A new prescription sleep-aid drug used to treat insomnia claims that 80% of the patients who take the drug experience no side effects at all. In a small study of 15 patients, what is the probability that at least 80% of the patients will experience no side effects?

15. Approximately 7% of the Canadian population have type O– blood and are considered "universal donors." A blood clinic receives donations from 72 people on a particular day.

    a. What is the probability that exactly 10 blood donors on that day are universal donors?

    b. What is the probability that at least 3 blood donors on that day are universal donors?

    c. How many universal donors are expected to be seen on that day?

    d. Using the Range Rule of Thumb, what is the approximate range of the number of universal donors that the clinic can expect to see on that day?

16. An oncologist performs a high-risk treatment on a very aggressive type of cancer for 26 different patients. The procedure has a success rate of only 35%.

    a. What is the probability that exactly half of the 26 treatments are successful?

    b. What is the probability that at least 5 of the treatments performed are successful?

    c. How many of the treatments should the oncologist expect to be successful?

    d. Using the Range Rule of Thumb, what is the approximate range of the number of treatments that the oncologist would expect to be successful?

17. Patients being admitted to a hospital must identify their next-of-kin, and their relationship: spouse, child, other family member, or no known next-of-kin. Approximately 41% of all adult patients admitted to a particular hospital identify their next-of-kin as their spouse. On a typical day, 22 new patients are admitted to this hospital.

    a. What is the probability that exactly half of the new patients admitted on a typical day indicate their spouse as their next-of-kin?

    b. What is the probability that at least 5 of the new patients admitted on a typical day identify their next-of-kin as someone other than their spouse?

    c. What is the expected number of new patients admitted on a typical day who indicate their spouse as their next-of-kin?

    d. Using the Range Rule of Thumb, what is the approximate range of the number of new patients that will identify their next-of-kin as their spouse?

18. Out of all patients being admitted to a particular ward of a hospital, approximately 15% choose a private room (at an additional cost) versus a semi-private or ward room. However, since there are a limited number of private rooms available, not all patients can have their requests honoured. Today, 14 patients are admitted to this ward, but there are only 3 private rooms available.

   a. What is the probability that exactly three patients will request a private room?

   b. What is the probability that a patient will not have his/her request for a private room honoured (i.e., at least four patients will request private rooms)?

   c. What is the expected number of patients that will request a private room today?

   d. Using the Range Rule of Thumb, what is the approximate range of the number of patients that will request a private room today?

19. During the quality control inspection process for a generic over-the-counter pain-relief tablet, approximately 0.8% of the tablets are defective. Each inspection batch contains 500 tablets.

   a. What is the probability that none of the tablets in the batch will be defective?

   b. What is the probability that at least one of the tablets in the batch will be defective?

   c. How many tablets in the batch are expected to be defective?

   d. What is the probability that exactly that many tablets (as calculated in part (c)) in the batch will be defective?

20. The needle used in a hypodermic syringe has to be produced according to very strict standards. As a result, approximately 2.5% of all the needles manufactured need to be discarded for defects and other imperfections. A batch of hypodermic needles contains 200 needles.

   a. What is the probability that none of the needles in a batch need to be discarded?

   b. What is the probability that at least one of the needles in the batch will be defective?

   c. How many needles are expected to be discarded due to imperfections?

   d. What is the probability that exactly that many needles (as calculated in part (c)) in a batch will need to be discarded?

The following contingency table details the sex and age distribution of the patients currently registered at a family physician's medical practice. If the doctor sees 18 patients per day, use the binomial formula and the information contained in the table to answer the questions in Problems 21 to 32:

SEX	AGE					
	Under 20	20 – 39	40 – 59	60 – 79	80 or over	TOTAL
Male	5.6%	12.8%	18.4%	14.4%	3.6%	54.8%
Female	2.8%	9.6%	13.2%	10.4%	9.2%	45.2%
TOTAL	8.4%	22.4%	31.6%	24.8%	12.8%	100.0%

21. What is the probability that exactly 10 of the patients seen in one day are male?

22. What is the probability that exactly 4 of the patients seen in one day are between the ages of 20 and 39?

23. What is the probability that at least two-thirds of the patients seen in a day are 40 years of age or over?

24. What is the probability that at most one-third of the patients seen in a day are female?

25. What is the probability that exactly 5 of the patients seen in a day are males under the age of 40?

26. What is the probability that exactly 3 of the patients seen in a day are females aged 60 or over?

27. What is the probability that the doctor sees at least one female patient under the age of 20 in a day?

28. What is the probability that the doctor sees at least one male patient aged 80 or over in a day?

29. If the doctor sees 12 male patients in a day, what is the probability that at least half of them are under 60?

30. If the doctor sees 8 female patients in a day, what is the probability that at least half of them are 60 years of age or over?

31. If the doctor sees 6 patients between the ages of 40 and 59, what is the probability that at least half are male?

32. If the doctor sees 6 patients between the ages of 60 and 79, what is the probability that at most half are female?

6.3 | Other Discrete Probability Distributions

We now turn our attention to other common discrete probability distributions that do not follow the binomial probability distribution.

The Hypergeometric Distribution

Consider part (i) from Example 6.2-b:

5 cards are drawn randomly from a shuffled deck without replacement.

In this case, the cards were drawn **without** replacement, so the trials were **not** independent, and the probabilities were not fixed; hence, it did not represent a binomial distribution. However, if we consider the repeated trials as **one** trial of drawing multiple cards from the deck of cards, this example can be classified as a **Hypergeometric Distribution**:

Given a collection of N objects, of which r are considered "successes" and $(N - r)$ are considered "failures", if n objects are sampled randomly without replacement and X represents the number of successes chosen out of the n objects sampled, then X is a discrete random variable that follows a hypergeometric distribution, with the following probability function:

Formula 6.3-a	**Hypergeometric Distribution**
	$$P(x) = \dfrac{\dbinom{r}{x} \cdot \dbinom{N-r}{n-x}}{\dbinom{N}{n}}$$

Rationale for the Hypergeometric Probability Distribution Function

- There are r successes available, so there are $\dbinom{r}{x}$ ways of choosing the desired x successes from the r objects available.

- There are $(N - r)$ failures available, so there are $\dbinom{N-r}{n-x}$ ways of choosing the desired $(n - x)$ failures out of the $(N - r)$ objects available.

- Since we want to choose exactly x successes (and therefore, $(n - x)$ failures), we multiply the two values to get $\dbinom{r}{x} \cdot \dbinom{N-r}{n-x}$, the number of ways of getting x successes and $(n - x)$ failures.

- There are a total of N objects available, so there are $\dbinom{N}{n}$ ways of choosing the desired n total objects for our sample out of the N objects available.

Expected Value (Mean), Variance, and Standard Deviation of a Hypergeometric Distribution

The expected value of this distribution is exactly the same as that of a binomial distribution - i.e., the probability of success prior to the first draw ($p = \dfrac{r}{N}$) multiplied by the number of trials:

Expected Value (Mean): $\qquad E(X) = \mu = np = n\left(\dfrac{r}{N}\right)$

The rationale for this is as follows:

- If a failure occurs, the probability of success on the next trial will increase (same number of successes to choose from in the numerator, but 1 less object in the denominator).

- If a success occurs, the probability of success on the next trial will decrease (both the numerator and denominator will decrease by 1, which decreases the proportion overall).

- The increase in the probability of success (if a failure occurs) multiplied by the probability of the failure occurring exactly equals the decrease in the probability of success (if a success occurs) multiplied by the probability of the success occurring.

The variance and standard deviation formulas for a random variable with a hypergeometric distribution are also similar to that of a binomial distribution, with $p = \dfrac{r}{N}$ representing the probability of success prior to the first draw, and $q = \dfrac{N - r}{N}$ representing the probability of failure prior to the first draw, but with a modification made for the changing probabilities as a sample of n objects are chosen from the population of N objects, given as follows:

Variance:
$$Var(X) = \sigma^2 = npq\left(\frac{N - n}{N - 1}\right) = n\left(\frac{r}{N}\right)\left(\frac{N - r}{N}\right)\left(\frac{N - n}{N - 1}\right)$$

Standard Deviation:
$$SD(X) = \sigma = \sqrt{npq\left(\frac{N - n}{N - 1}\right)} = \sqrt{n\left(\frac{r}{N}\right)\left(\frac{N - r}{N}\right)\left(\frac{N - n}{N - 1}\right)}$$

Example 6.3-a   **Calculating Probability for a Hypergeometric Distribution**

Recall Example 6.2-b(i):

Experiment: 5 cards are drawn randomly from a shuffled deck without replacement.

Event: 3 out of the 5 cards are face cards (Jack, Queen, or King).

(i)   Calculate the probability of the event occurring.

(ii)   Determine the expected value, variance, and standard deviation for this distribution.

Solution

(i)   There are $N = 52$ cards in the deck, of which $r = 12$ are face cards (4 Jacks, 4 Queens, 4 Kings). We randomly select $n = 5$ from the deck and want $x = 3$ of those to be face cards. Let X be a random variable representing the number of face cards chosen. Then X has a hypergeometric probability distribution and the probability that $X = 3$ is as follows:

Using Formula 6.3-a, $P(x) = \dfrac{\dbinom{r}{x} \cdot \dbinom{N - r}{n - x}}{\dbinom{N}{n}}$

$$P(3) = \frac{\dbinom{12}{3} \cdot \dbinom{40}{2}}{\dbinom{52}{5}} = \frac{(220)(780)}{2{,}598{,}960} \approx 0.0660$$

Solution
continued

(ii) $E(X) = n\left(\dfrac{r}{N}\right) = 5\left(\dfrac{12}{52}\right) \approx 1.15$

> Since $E(X) \approx 1.15$, we expect approximately 1 card to be a face card.

$\sigma^2 = n\left(\dfrac{r}{N}\right)\left(\dfrac{N-r}{N}\right)\left(\dfrac{N-n}{N-1}\right) = 5\left(\dfrac{12}{52}\right)\left(\dfrac{40}{52}\right)\left(\dfrac{47}{51}\right) \approx 0.818$

$\sigma = \sqrt{5\left(\dfrac{12}{52}\right)\left(\dfrac{40}{52}\right)\left(\dfrac{47}{51}\right)} \approx 0.904$

The Geometric Distribution

Consider part (iv) from Example 6.2-b:

A coin is flipped until it lands with Tails facing up.

In this case, the trials represented Bernoulli trials (independent, repeated, with two outcomes and fixed probabilities of success and failure), but the number of trials were **not** fixed; hence, it did not represent a binomial distribution. Instead, we were examining "how long it would take" (i.e., how many trials were needed) to see the first success. This example can be classified as a **Geometric Distribution**:

Given a sequence of Bernoulli trials - i.e., independent, repeated trials with two outcomes (success and failure) and fixed probabilities of success (p) and failure ($q = 1 - p$) - if X represents the number of trials needed for the first success to be observed, then X is a discrete random variable that follows a geometric distribution, with the following probability function:

Formula 6.3-b	**Geometric Distribution**

$$P(x) = q^{x-1} \cdot p = (1-p)^{x-1} \cdot p$$

Rationale for the Geometric Probability Distribution Function

- We wish to determine the probability of observing the first success on the xth trial, meaning we will observe ($x - 1$) failures in a row, followed by a success.
- Since the trials are independent, the probability of ($x - 1$) failures in a row is $q^{x-1} = (1-p)^{x-1}$
- The probability of success on any given trial is p.
- Hence, the probability of ($x - 1$) failures in a row, followed by success on the very next trial is $q^{x-1} \cdot p = (1-p)^{x-1} \cdot p$

Expected Value (Mean), Variance, and Standard Deviation of a Geometric Distribution

The expected value of this distribution is simply the reciprocal of the probability of success (p):

Expected Value (Mean): $E(X) = \mu = \dfrac{1}{p}$

The rationale for this is as follows:

- Since the trials are Bernoulli and the probability of success on a given trial (p) is fixed for each trial, we know, from the binomial distribution, that the number of successes on n trials is expected to be $n \cdot p$
- Since we wish to determine the number of trials needed to expect 1 success, we are looking to solve for n in the equation $n \cdot p = 1$
- Hence $n = \dfrac{1}{p}$ - the expected number of trials needed to see 1 success.

The variance and standard deviation formulas for a random variable with a geometric distribution are given as follows (without explanation for simplicity's sake):

Variance:
$$Var(X) = \sigma^2 = \frac{q}{p^2} = \frac{1-p}{p^2}$$

Standard Deviation:
$$SD(X) = \sigma = \sqrt{\frac{q}{p^2}} = \sqrt{\frac{1-p}{p^2}}$$

Example 6.3-b | Calculating Probability for a Geometric Distribution

Recall Example 6.2-b(iv):

Experiment: A coin is flipped until it lands with Tails facing up.

Event: The first Tails occurs on the 7th coin toss.

(i)   Calculate the probability of the event occurring.

(ii) Determine the expected value, variance, and standard deviation for this distribution.

Solution

(i)   Since we want to see Tails on the 7th coin toss, this means there will be 6 Heads (i.e., "Failures") in a row before the first Tails (i.e., "Success"). Let X be a random variable representing the number of trials needed until the first Tails is observed. Then X has a geometric probability distribution, and the probability that $X = 7$ is as follows:

Using Formula 6.3-b, $P(x) = (1-p)^{x-1} \cdot p$

$$P(7) = (1-0.5)^{7-1} \cdot (0.5) = (0.5)^6 \cdot (0.5) = (0.5)^7 \approx 0.00781$$

(ii) $E(X) = \dfrac{1}{p} = \dfrac{1}{0.5} = 2$

Since $E(X) = 2$, we expect to need 2 trials to observe 1 Tails.

$$\sigma^2 = \frac{1-p}{p^2} = \frac{0.5}{(0.5)^2} = 2$$

$$\sigma = \sqrt{2} \approx 1.41$$

Note: In this case, $Var(X) = E(X)$ since $q = p$, as shown below:

$$Var(X) = \frac{q}{p^2} = \frac{p}{p^2} = \frac{1}{p} = E(X)$$

The Poisson Distribution

Consider part (v) from Example 6.2-b:

The number of calls to a local 911 call-center, which receives an average of 2 calls per minute, is recorded over a period of 5 minutes.

In this case, there are no "trials" to speak of, just a fixed period of time, and while there are "successes" (the call center receives a 911 call), there are no identifiable "failures", as we cannot count the number of times that the call center did not receive a 911 call during the time period. Instead, we were examining the frequency of occurrence of an event (i.e., how often it occurs during a fixed time period). This example can be classified as a **Poisson Distribution**:

If X represents the number of occurrences of a certain event in a given interval of time or space, in which the events occur individually (i.e., no two events can occur at the same point in time or space) and independently of the occurrence of an event at another point in time or space, with a known average frequency of occurrence over the interval (λ), then X is a discrete random variable that follows a Poisson distribution, with the following probability function:

Formula 6.3-c	**Poisson Distribution**

$$P(x) = \frac{\lambda^x \cdot e^{-\lambda}}{x!}$$

Note: The rationale for the probability distribution function for the Poisson distribution is too complex to discuss in this textbook.

Expected Value (Mean), Variance, and Standard Deviation of a Poisson Distribution

Since the average frequency of occurrence in this distribution is given as λ, the expected value of this distribution is exactly λ. Even more incredibly, the variance is also given by λ.

Expected Value (Mean): $\qquad E(X) = \mu = \lambda$

Variance: $\qquad\qquad\quad Var(X) = \sigma^2 = \lambda$

Standard Deviation: $\qquad SD(X) = \sigma = \sqrt{\lambda}$

Example 6.3-c	**Calculating Probability for a Poisson Distribution**

Recall Example 6.2-b(v):

Experiment: The number of calls to a local 911 call-center, which receives an average of 2 calls per minute, is recorded over a period of 5 minutes.

Event: Exactly 10 calls are received during this period.

(i) Calculate the probability of the event occurring.

(ii) Determine the expected value, variance, and standard deviation for this distribution.

Solution

(i) Let X be a random variable representing the number of calls that a local 911 call-center received in a 5-minute period. The average number of calls received by this call center in a 5-minute period is $\lambda = 2(5) = 10$. Then X has a Poisson probability distribution, and the probability that $X = 10$ is as follows:

Using Formula 6.3-c, $\qquad P(x) = \frac{\lambda^x \cdot e^{-\lambda}}{x!}$

$$P(10) = \frac{10^{10} \cdot e^{-10}}{10!} \approx 0.125$$

(ii) $E(X) = \lambda = 10$

$\sigma^2 = \lambda = 10$

$\sigma = \sqrt{10} \approx 3.16$

> Since $E(X) = 10$, we expect to receive 10 calls in a 5 minute period.

6.3 | Exercises

Answers to odd-numbered problems are available at the end of the textbook.

For Problems 1 to 12, use the probability distribution identified to calculate the following:

(i) *The probability $P(x)$ for the indicated value(s) of x.*

(ii) *The mean and standard deviation of the distribution.*

1. A hypergeometric distribution with $N = 20$, $r = 8$, $n = 10$, $x = 5$

2. A hypergeometric distribution with $N = 25$, $r = 5$, $n = 6$, $x = 3$

3. A hypergeometric distribution with $N = 40$, $r = 15$, $n = 12$, $x \geq 3$

4. A hypergeometric distribution with $N = 52$, $r = 12$, $n = 5$, $x \le 2$

5. A geometric distribution with $p = 0.5$ and the first success on the $x = 4^{th}$ trial

6. A geometric distribution with $p = 0.4$ and the first success on the $x = 7^{th}$ trial

7. A geometric distribution with $p = 0.2$ and the first success on the $x = 9^{th}$ trial

8. A geometric distribution with $p = 0.8$ and the first success on the $x = 3^{rd}$ trial

9. A Poisson distribution with $\lambda = 8.4$ and $x = 10$

10. A Poisson distribution with $\lambda = 13.5$ and $x = 15$

11. A Poisson distribution with $\lambda = 3.8$ and $x \le 4$

12. A Poisson distribution with $\lambda = 5.7$ and $x \ge 5$

For Problems 13 to 28, analyze the following scenarios and complete the following instructions:

(i) *Determine which probability distribution (binomial, hypergeometric, geometric, or Poisson) should be used to model the scenario.*

(ii) *Calculate the probability of the indicated event.*

(iii) *Determine the expected value and variance of the random variable.*

13. A paramedic receives an average of 7.5 calls in a 12-hour night shift. What is the probability that the paramedic will receive 12 calls on a given 12-hour night shift?

14. A blood test for a certain autoimmune disease has a false-positive rate of approximately 3%. A sample of 25 patients who do not have the disease are tested for the disease using the blood test. What is the probability that at least two of them will test positive for the disease?

15. Out of the 16 patients currently in the maternity ward, 5 of them have just given birth for the first time. If 4 of the patients in the maternity ward are randomly selected, what is the probability that half of them have just given birth for the first time?

16. A dentist sees an average of 14.4 patients in his office every day. If the patients are typically evenly distributed throughout the day, determine the probability that he will see 10 patients in his office in the first half of the day tomorrow.

17. A college student is writing an aptitude exam to enter into a health sciences program. Each question has 4 multiple choice answers. If he guesses on every one, what is the probability that he will not get his first correct answer until the 10th question?

18. The evaluation at the end of a professional development training module is a quiz consisting of 10 true/false questions, which requires a grade of 80% or better to pass. What is the probability of passing the quiz by guessing on all the questions?

19. A box of multi-sized bandages contains 10 large bandages and 30 small bandages. There are 6 bandages left in the box. What is the probability that there is at least 1 large bandage left?

20. An obstetrician starts her residency in a hospital assisting the attending obstetricians in delivering babies. What is the probability that she will not deliver her first girl until the 8th baby she delivers?

21. What is the probability that a couple with 6 children will have more boys than girls?

22. Out of the 30 pets that are scheduled to see the veterinarian this week, 18 are dogs. If 6 of the animals have appointments on Monday, what is the probability that two-thirds are dogs?

23. An athletic therapist has an average of 27.6 patients at her clinic every day. If her clinic is open for 8 hours every day, and the patients are typically evenly distributed throughout the day, determine the probability that she will see 4 patients in her clinic in the first hour of the day tomorrow.

24. The probability of a baby being delivered still-born is approximately 0.625%. What is the probability that an obstetrics nurse will not have to witness a still-born birth until at least the 100th baby that is delivered?

25. A certain type of reconstructive shoulder surgery for athletes to repair the damage caused by frequent dislocations has a success rate of 85%, meaning that no further surgery is required to heal the shoulder, beyond the post-operative physiotherapy. If 30 athletes undergo this surgery, what is the probability that no more than 3 of them will have to undergo additional surgery?

26. An E.R. nurse typically sees an average of 37 patients in a 12-hour day shift. What is the probability that the nurse will see exactly 30 patients on a given 12-hour day shift?

27. A public health nurse knows that approximately 92% of individuals who come in to be tested for STIs have a negative test result. What is the probability that the nurse will not have to deliver the news of a positive result until at least the 20th individual who comes in for testing?

28. A business traveller packs 15 white acetaminophen tablets for pain relief and 10 pink antihistamine tablets for allergy relief with him in a small medicine bottle on a business trip. He develops a headache and wishes to take 2 acetaminophen tablets. If he pours out 5 tablets into his hand, what is the probability that there will be at least 2 acetaminophen tablets there?

6 | Review Exercises

Answers to odd-numbered problems are available at the end of the textbook.

For Problems 1 to 6, determine if the random variables listed are continuous or discrete.

1. The number of students enrolled in a Pre-health Math class.

2. The distance an orderly at a hospital walks during one day at work.

3. The average weight of a newborn baby.

4. The number of capsules in a pack of pills.

5. The time it takes to infuse 1,000 mL of normal saline.

6. The number of patients that were seen in a hospital's Emergency Department last month.

For Problems 7 to 10, calculate the mean and standard deviation of the discrete probability distributions.

7.

x	0	1	2	3	4
$P(x)$	0.1	0.2	0.3	0.3	0.1

8.

x	0	10	20	30	40	50	60
$P(x)$	0.315	0.211	0.178	0.113	0.089	0.050	0.044

9.

x	0-9	10-19	20-29	30-39	40-49	50-59
$P(x)$	$\frac{1}{36}$	$\frac{5}{36}$	$\frac{13}{36}$	$\frac{9}{36}$	$\frac{7}{36}$	$\frac{1}{36}$

10.

x	5-9	10-14	15-19	20-24	25-29
$P(x)$	$\frac{1}{15}$	$\frac{2}{15}$	$\frac{7}{15}$	$\frac{3}{15}$	$\frac{2}{15}$

11. The following data were collected by counting the number of operating rooms used each day at a large hospital over a 30-day period: on 5 of the days, only 1 operating room was used; on 7 of the days, 2 were used; on 10 of the days, 3 were used; and on the remaining days, all 4 of the hospital's operating rooms were used.

   a. Construct a discrete probability distribution for the number of operating rooms in use on any given day.

   b. Calculate the expected value, variance, and standard deviation of the discrete probability distribution.

12. The following data indicates the prize distribution for a small lottery of 500 tickets conducted at a local hospital: 50 tickets have a $50 prize, 25 tickets have a $100 prize, 5 tickets have a $500 prize, and 1 ticket has a $2,500 grand prize. The rest of the tickets do not win anything.

   a. Construct a discrete probability distribution for the prize amounts of a single ticket.

   b. Calculate the expected value, variance, and standard deviation of the discrete probability distribution.

13. According to a survey, 75% of all students at a college suffer from math anxiety. Two students are randomly selected from the college.

   a. Construct a discrete probability distribution for the number of students in this sample who suffer from math anxiety.

   b. Calculate the expected value, variance, and standard deviation of the discrete probability distribution.

14. According to a survey, 5% of motorists in a large city are uninsured. Three motorists are selected at random from the city.

    a. Construct a discrete probability distribution for the number of motorists in this sample who are uninsured.

    b. Calculate the expected value, variance, and standard deviation of the discrete probability distribution.

15. In a group of 15 people, 5 have a severe peanut allergy. Three people are randomly selected from this group.

    a. Construct a discrete probability distribution for the number of people with a severe peanut allergy in this sample.

    b. Calculate the expected value and standard deviation of the discrete probability distribution.

16. In a group of 12 people, 3 are left-handed. Two people are randomly selected from this group.

    a. Construct a discrete probability distribution for the number of left-handed people in this sample.

    b. Calculate the expected value and standard deviation of the discrete probability distribution.

For Problems 17 and 18, use the binomial formula to calculate the probability of the indicated events to 3 significant digits.

17. Given $n = 15$, $p = 0.75$:

    a. $P(X = 6)$

    b. $P(X > 12)$

    c. $P(X \leq 14)$

    d. $P(10 \leq X \leq 12)$

18. Given $n = 20$, $p = 0.2$:

    a. $P(X = 10)$

    b. $P(X \geq 1)$

    c. $P(X < 4)$

    d. $P(3 < X < 6)$

19. A doctor delivered 20 babies last month. What is the probability that half are boys and half are girls?

20. An online quiz has 10 True or False questions. What is the probability that a student got exactly half correct if they guessed on every question?

21. A pregnancy test claims to be 95% reliable in giving a "positive" result if the woman is indeed pregnant. In a sample of 40 pregnant women, what is the probability that exactly 95% receive a "positive" result from the test?

22. A new brand of drug-free nasal strip claims to be 90% effective in relieving nasal congestion to help you breathe and sleep better. In a sample of 50 patients, what is the probability that exactly 90% of the patients will find this nasal strip effective?

23. According to the Canada Obesity Network, one in four adult Canadians has clinical obesity. A sample of 32 adult Canadians is taken.

    a. What is the probability that exactly half of the 32 adults are obese?

    b. What is the probability that at least 3 are obese?

    c. How many patients are expected to be considered obese?

    d. What is the standard deviation of the number of obese Canadians in a sample of size 32?

    e. Using the Range Rule of Thumb, what is the approximate range of the number of obese patients one would expect to find in this sample?

24. Approximately 7 out of every 10 patients who undergo heart valve replacement surgery have a successful procedure with no complications. In the past month, there were 16 heart valve replacement surgeries performed at a hospital.

    a. What is the probability that exactly half of the 16 surgeries were successful?

    b. What is the probability that at most 13 surgeries were successful?

    c. How many surgeries are expected to be successful?

    d. What is the standard deviation of the success rate for this surgery in a sample of size 16?

    e. Using the Range Rule of Thumb, what is the approximate range of the number of surgeries one would expect to be successful in the past month?

25. Approximately 2% of the Canadian population has no health insurance. A random sample of 150 Canadians is taken.

    a. What is the probability that none of the Canadians sampled have any health insurance?

    b. What is the probability that at least 1 Canadian sampled has no health insurance?

    c. How many of the Canadians sampled are expected to have no health insurance?

    d. What is the probability that exactly that many Canadians (as calculated in part (c)) have no health insurance?

26. A manufacturer of I.V. tubes claims that only 0.5% of their products are defective. The manufacturer recently sold I.V. tubes in batches of 400 to a large local hospital.

    a. What is the probability that none of the I.V. tubes are defective in a batch?

    b. What is the probability that at least one I.V. tube is defective in a batch?

    c. How many defective I.V. tubes would you expect in a batch?

    d. What is the probability that exactly that many I.V. tubes (as calculated in part (c)) are defective?

The following contingency table details the smoking and age distribution of students currently attending a college. If 12 students are randomly selected from the college, use the binomial formula and the information contained in the table to answer Problems 27 to 36 (to 3 significant digits):

	Under 20	20 – 24	25 – 29	30 or Over	TOTAL
Smoker	7.8%	9.5%	12.2%	2.5%	32%
Non-Smoker	26.2%	20.5%	12.5%	8.8%	68%
TOTAL	34%	30%	24.7%	11.3%	100%

27. What is the probability that exactly 5 students are non-smokers?

28. What is the probability that exactly 4 students are between ages 20 and 24?

29. What is the probability that exactly 3 students are non-smokers under the age of 25?

30. What is the probability that exactly 2 students are smokers aged 20 or over?

31. What is the probability that at least 1 student is a smoker aged 30 or over?

32. What is the probability that at least 1 student is a non-smoker aged under 20?

33. If 9 out of the 12 students selected are under the age of 20, what is the probability that exactly one-third of them are smokers?

34. If 8 out of the 12 students selected are aged 30 or over, what is the probability that exactly three-quarters of them are non-smokers?

35. If 6 out of the 12 students selected are non-smokers, what is the probability that half of them are under the age of 30?

36. If 4 out of the 12 students selected are smokers, what is the probability that half of them are aged 25 or over?

37. Given a hypergeometric distribution with $N = 10$, $r = 4$, $n = 5$, determine the following:
   a. $P(X = 1)$
   b. $P(X \le 1)$
   c. The mean and standard deviation of the distribution.

38. Given a hypergeometric distribution with $N = 12$, $r = 3$, $n = 8$, determine the following:
   a. $P(X = 3)$
   b. $P(X > 1)$
   c. The mean and standard deviation of the distribution.

39. Given a geometric distribution with $p = 0.15$, determine the following:
   a. The probability that the first success is on the $x = 9^{th}$ trial.
   b. The mean and standard deviation of the distribution.

40. Given a geometric distribution with $p = 0.9$, determine the following:
   a. The probability that the first success is on the $x = 3^{rd}$ trial.
   b. The mean and standard deviation of the distribution.

41. Given a Poisson distribution with $\lambda = 4$, determine the following:
   a. $P(X = 3)$
   b. $P(X \le 3)$
   c. The mean and standard deviation of the distribution.

42. Given a Poisson distribution with $\lambda = 9$, determine the following:
   a. $P(X = 8)$
   b. $P(7 \le X \le 10)$
   c. The mean and standard deviation of the distribution.

For Problems 43 to 50, analyze the following scenarios and complete the following:

(i) Determine which probability distribution (binomial, hypergeometric, geometric, or Poisson) should be used to model the scenario.

(ii) Calculate the probability of the indicated event (to 3 significant digits).

(iii) Determine the expected value, variance, and standard deviation of the random variable.

43. An obstetrician starts her residency delivering babies in a hospital. What is the probability that she will not deliver her first boy until the 5th baby delivered?

44. A box of multi-sized I.V. tubing contains 8 large (10 gtt/mL) probability tubes and 10 small (60 mcgtt/mL) I.V. tubes. There are 9 I.V. tubes left in the box. What is the probability that there are at least 5 small (60 mcgtt/mL) I.V. tubes left?

45. A recent study revealed that 70% of student drivers do a rolling stop at a stop sign. A sample of 12 student drivers was selected. What is the probability that less than two-thirds of the sample will do a rolling stop at the stop sign?

46. A local 911 call-center receives an average of 10.7 calls per minute. What is the probability that the call center will receive 12 calls in a given minute?

47. A parent packs 10 white acetaminophen tablets for pain relief and 20 pink antihistamine tablets for allergy relief with her on a vacation. Her child, who has a mild peanut allergy, accidentally ate some food which contains peanuts. She needs to give 2 antihistamine tablets to her child. If she pours out 6 tablets into her hand, what is the probability that there will be at least 2 antihistamine tablets there?

48. A college student is writing an aptitude test to enter a health science program. Each question has 5 multiple choice answers with one correct answer. If he guesses on every one, what is the probability that he will not get a correct answer until the 10th question?

49. A chiropractor sees an average of 12 patients at his clinic every day. If his clinic is open for 8 hours every day, and the patients are typically evenly distributed throughout the day, determine the probability that he will see 3 patients in his clinic in the first hour of the day tomorrow.

50. A college student is writing a quiz consisting of 20 true or false questions, which requires a grade of 70% or better to pass. What is the probability of passing the quiz by guessing on all the questions?

6 | Self-Test Exercises

Answers to all problems are available at the end of the textbook.

For Problems 1 to 4, determine if the random variables listed are continuous or discrete.

1. The number of patients treated at a health clinic between 8:00 AM and 8:00 PM each day.

2. The distance between your home and the nearby hospital.

3. The time it takes to drive from home to the nearby hospital.

4. The number of doctors on-call at a local hospital on Thanksgiving night.

5. The following distribution gives the number of root canal surgeries performed by a dentist on a given day.

x	0	1	2	3	4	5
P(x)	0.13	0.28	0.30	0.17	0.08	0.04

   a. Calculate the mean and standard deviation of the discrete probability distribution.

   b. Interpret the meaning of the mean.

6. In a game of heads or tails, you flip a coin twice, and you win $2 if you throw two heads, you win $1 if you throw a head and a tail, and you lose $5 if you throw two tails. What is the expected winnings of this game? Is it advisable to play this game?

7. An auditor for an insurance company in Ontario reports that 70% of the policyholders 55 years or older submitted a claim during the last year. Three policyholders 55 years or older are randomly selected from company records.

   a. Construct a discrete probability distribution for the number of policyholders 55 years or older from the sample that have submitted a claim during the last year.

   b. Calculate the expected value, variance, and standard deviation of the discrete probability distribution.

8. In a group of 6 people, 4 have a severe peanut allergy. Two people are randomly selected from this group.

   a. Construct a discrete probability distribution for the number of people with severe peanut allergies in this sample.

   b. Calculate the expected value, variance, and standard deviation of the discrete probability distribution.

For Problems 9 to 11, use the Binomial Theorem to determine the desired probability. Round all answers to 4 decimal places.

9. An online quiz has 10 multiple choice questions. Each question has 4 possible answers with one correct answer. If the student guesses on every single question, what is the probability that:

   a. the student gets every question wrong?

   b. the student gets at least one question correct?

   c. the student passes the quiz (i.e., at least 5 correct)?

10. Heart disease is the second most prevalent cause of death for both women and men. Women are somewhat less likely than men to be diagnosed with heart disease. In the 45 to 64 age group, 4% of women have heart disease. In a sample of 50 women, what is the probability that:

   a. exactly 4% of the women will have heart disease?

   b. at most 4% of the women will have heart disease?

   c. at least 4% of the women will have heart disease?

11. In a recent survey, 2 out of every 3 of adult men aged 45-55 said that they would definitely consider a hair transplant if they could afford it. A random sample of 15 adult men aged 45-55 is taken.

   a. What is the probability that exactly 8 of the men would consider the hair transplant?

   b. What is the probability that less than half of the men would consider the hair transplant?

   c. What is the expected number of men that would consider the hair transplant?

   d. What is the standard deviation in the number of men who would consider the hair transplant in samples of size 15?

   e. Using the Range Rule of Thumb, what is the approximate range of the number of men that would consider the hair transplant?

12. The following contingency table details the cups of coffee consumed and packs of cigarettes smoked per day by an adult. If 10 adults are randomly selected, use the binomial formula and the information contained in the table to answer the following questions (round your answers to 3 significant digits):

Coffee (cups per day)	Smoking (packs per day)			
	0 (do not smoke)	1 pack or less	More than 1 pack	Total
0 (do not drink coffee)	8%	4%	3%	15%
1 - 3	42%	8%	2%	52%
Over 3	15%	10%	8%	33%
Total	65%	22%	13%	100%

   a. What is the probability that exactly 6 of the adults drink over 3 cups of coffee per day?

   b. What is the probability that exactly 3 of the adults smoke more than 1 pack per day?

   c. What is the probability that exactly 2 of the adults do not smoke and do not drink coffee?

   d. What is the probability that at least half of the adults drink 3 or less cups of coffee per day?

   e. What is the probability that at most 1 adult is a smoker?

   f. What is the probability that at least three-fifths of the adults will drink coffee?

   g. If 9 out of the 10 adults selected do not drink coffee, what is the probability that exactly one-third of them smoke?

   h. If 8 out of the 10 adults selected do not smoke, what is the probability that exactly three-quarters of them drink coffee?

For Problems 13 to 16, analyze the following scenarios and complete the following:

(i) *Determine which probability distribution (binomial, hypergeometric, geometric, or Poisson) should be used to model the scenario.*

(ii) *Calculate the probability of the indicated event (to 3 significant digits).*

(iii) *Determine the expected value, variance, and standard deviation of the random variable.*

13. According to a survey, 85% of employers believe that all college students should be required to perform a specified number of practical hours to graduate. A sample of 12 employers were selected. What is the probability that more than two-thirds of the employers will hold this view?

14. A dentist sees an average of 16.8 patients in his office every day. If the patients are typically evenly distributed throughout the day, determine the probability that he will see 7 patients in his office in the first half of the day tomorrow.

15. Out of the 12 patients in the palliative care ward of a local hospital, 7 have DNR (Do Not Resuscitate) orders, and the remaining 5 do not. If 3 out of 12 of these patients lose their vitals, what is the probability that the medical team will need to attempt to resuscitate at least one of the patients?

16. The probability of a newborn infant having severe jaundice is 0.85%. What is the probability that an obstetrician will not witness a newborn with severe jaundice until at least the 20th baby that is delivered?

6 | Summary of Notation and Formulas

FORMULAS

Expected Value (Mean) for a Discrete Probability Distribution | 6.1-a

$$E(X) = \mu = \sum_{all\ x} \left(x \cdot P(x) \right)$$

Variance for a Discrete Probability Distribution | 6.1-b

$$Var(X) = \sigma^2 = \sum_{all\ x} \left((x - \mu)^2 \cdot P(x) \right) \quad \text{or} \quad Var(X) = \sigma^2 = \sum_{all\ x} \left(x^2 \cdot P(x) \right) - \mu^2$$

Standard Deviation for a Discrete Probability Distribution | 6.1-c

$$SD(X) = \sigma = \sqrt{\sum_{all\ x} \left((x - \mu)^2 \cdot P(x) \right)} \quad \text{or} \quad SD(X) = \sigma = \sqrt{\sum_{all\ x} \left(x^2 \cdot P(x) \right) - \mu^2}$$

Binomial Formula | 6.2: $P(x) = \binom{n}{x} p^x \cdot q^{(n-x)}$

The probability of x successes in n Bernoulli trials, where p and q are the probabilities of success and failure on any one of the n trials, respectively.

Expected Value (Mean): $E(X) = \mu = np$

Variance: $Var(X) = \sigma^2 = npq = np(1 - p)$

Standard Deviation: $SD(X) = \sigma = \sqrt{npq} = \sqrt{np(1 - p)}$

Hypergeometric Distribution | 6.3-a: $P(x) = \dfrac{\binom{r}{x} \cdot \binom{N-r}{n-x}}{\binom{N}{n}}$

The probability of x successes if n objects are sampled randomly without replacement in a collection of N objects, of which r are considered "successes" and (N – r) are considered "failures".

Expected Value (Mean): $E(X) = \mu = np = n\left(\dfrac{r}{N}\right)$

Variance: $Var(X) = \sigma^2 = npq\left(\dfrac{N-n}{N-1}\right) = n\left(\dfrac{r}{N}\right)\left(\dfrac{N-r}{N}\right)\left(\dfrac{N-n}{N-1}\right)$

Standard Deviation: $SD(X) = \sigma = \sqrt{npq\left(\dfrac{N-n}{N-1}\right)} = \sqrt{n\left(\dfrac{r}{N}\right)\left(\dfrac{N-r}{N}\right)\left(\dfrac{N-n}{N-1}\right)}$

Geometric Distribution | 6.3-b: $P(x) = q^{x-1} \cdot p = (1-p)^{x-1} \cdot p$

The probability that it will take x Bernoulli trials for the first success to be observed, where p and q are the probabilities of success and failure of each trial, respectively.

Expected Value (Mean): $\qquad E(X) = \mu = \dfrac{1}{p}$

Variance: $\qquad Var(X) = \sigma^2 = \dfrac{q}{p^2} = \dfrac{1-p}{p^2}$

Standard Deviation: $\qquad SD(X) = \sigma = \sqrt{\dfrac{q}{p^2}} = \sqrt{\dfrac{1-p}{p^2}}$

Poisson Distribution | 6.3-c: $P(x) = \dfrac{\lambda^x \cdot e^{-\lambda}}{x!}$

The probability of x individual and independent occurrences of an event, where λ is the known average frequency of occurrence over the interval.

Expected Value (Mean): $\qquad E(X) = \mu = \lambda$

Variance: $\qquad Var(X) = \sigma^2 = \lambda$

Standard Deviation: $\qquad SD(X) = \sigma = \sqrt{\lambda}$

7 CONTINUOUS PROBABILITY DISTRIBUTIONS

LEARNING OBJECTIVES

- State the characteristics and the properties of a continuous probability distribution.
- Distinguish between the uniform and exponential continuous probability distributions.
- Calculate probabilities using the continuous uniform and exponential probability distributions, and solve application problems involving both distributions.
- Calculate the expected value (mean), variance, and standard deviation for uniform and exponential continuous random variables.
- Compare the properties of the normal distribution and standard normal distribution.
- Calculate the probabilities for the normal distribution by calculating the z-score and using the table of areas under the standard normal distribution curve and the Z-scores.
- Solve normal distribution problems corresponding to intervals above, below, or between given values.
- Convert raw X-scores to standardized Z-scores, and vice versa.
- Use the normal distribution to approximate the binomial probability distribution.

CHAPTER OUTLINE

Introduction

Recall from Chapter 1 that continuous variables are used to represent data that is obtained by measuring, such as length, weight, time, temperature, etc., and can take on any real number value, although usually rounded to a pre-defined level of precision (i.e., number of decimal places). Continuous variables do not have a smallest increment; between any two values a continuous variable can take on, there is another value in between that the variable could take on.

Just as with discrete random variables in the previous chapter, a **continuous random variable** assigns a numeric value to the outcome of a measurement of a randomly selected member of the population. Typically, all the possible outcomes will have measurements that fall within a finite range of values. However since there is no "smallest increment" in the measurement, there are (technically) infinitely-many possible outcomes within even a finite range of values. As such, it becomes very difficult, even impossible, to list out all the possible outcomes for a continuous random variable in a sample space. How then do we discuss probability for continuous random variables?

In this chapter, we will examine the concept of probability as it relates to continuous data.

7.1 | Continuous Random Variables and their Probability Distributions

Discrete vs Continuous Probability Distributions

Consider the following very simple discrete probability distribution for a randomly-selected, single-digit whole number (i.e., from 0 to 9), where each number has the same probability of being selected:

x	0	1	2	3	4	5	6	7	8	9
$P(x)$	0.1	0.1	0.1	0.1	0.1	0.1	0.1	0.1	0.1	0.1

We can express this probability distribution using a vertical bar graph:

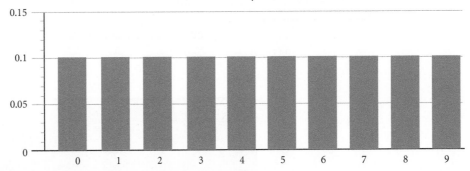

Discrete Probability Distribution

Now assume that we randomly generate a non-negative real number less than 10 (i.e., a real number from 0 up to, but not including, 10), allowing for any number of decimal places; how would that change our graph? We could group the data into a frequency table according to the whole number value of each measurement as follows:

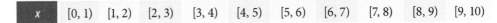

x	[0, 1)	[1, 2)	[2, 3)	[3, 4)	[4, 5)	[5, 6)	[6, 7)	[7, 8)	[8, 9)	[9, 10)

where $[a, b)$ denotes all real numbers from a up to, but not including, b.

What is the probability associated with each class? Since we have divided the range into 10 equal classes, and the number is selected randomly from the entire range, with no value more likely to occur than any other value, it is reasonable to say that the probability the randomly-selected value will fall in any of the 10 classes will be equal to $\frac{1}{10}$ or 0.1:

x	[0, 1)	[1, 2)	[2, 3)	[3, 4)	[4, 5)	[5, 6)	[6, 7)	[7, 8)	[8, 9)	[9, 10)
P(x)	0.1	0.1	0.1	0.1	0.1	0.1	0.1	0.1	0.1	0.1

We can express this using a histogram, since the data is continuous (i.e., there are no "gaps" between the adjacent classes):

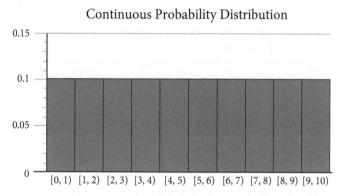

Notice that this corresponds exactly to the discrete example above, as there are still 10 possible whole-number values of any particular measurement: 0 to 9. As such, we can convert our continuous probability distribution back into a discrete probability distribution by recording only the whole-number portion of the measurement and ignoring the value of the measurement after the decimal point. Then we still have 10 outcomes (0 to 9), each with the same probability of occurrence: 0.1.

However, the difference between the discrete and continuous probability distributions is that, while the discrete probability distribution is represented by a bar graph, the continuous probability distribution is represented by a histogram. In fact, we could remove the dividing bars from the histogram above and see that the continuous probability distribution above can be represented as a graph of a straight line:

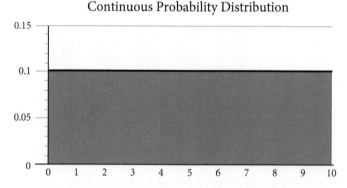

Notice that the area under the line is a rectangle with length 10 and width 0.1; hence, the total area is $10 \times 0.1 = 1.0$. Furthermore, the probability that a randomly-selected measurement will be between any two given values can be calculated by determining the area of the rectangle between those two values.

For example, to calculate the probability that a randomly-selected measurement will be at least 2, but less than 6 (i.e., in the range [2, 6)), we can multiply the length of the rectangle (6 − 2 = 4) by the width (0.1) to get a probability of 0.4. This value is verified by the probability distribution table above, by adding up the probabilities in the [2, 3), [3, 4), [4, 5) and [5, 6) classes: 0.1 + 0.1 + 0.1 + 0.1 = 0.4.

Properties of a Continuous Probability Distribution

A **continuous probability distribution** for a continuous random variable X is a graph in the XY-Cartesian system that has the following properties:

1. The Y-value is always at least 0 (i.e., never negative).

2. The total area under the curve (i.e., between the X-axis and the graph) is exactly equal to 1.

3. The area under the curve between any two X-values corresponds with the probability that the random variable X will take on a value in that range.

The above definition tells us that for a continuous random variable, the probability that it will be exactly equal to a certain real number is 0, since the area under the curve at a single point is a straight line (i.e., a rectangle with 0 width, hence 0 area). To verify this, imagine that you randomly generate a real number between 0 and 10 and you want to know the probability that it will be exactly equal to $\pi = 3.14159...$ The probability that the first digit is correct (i.e., 3) is 0.1; the probability the second digit is correct (i.e., 1) is 0.1; the probability that the third digit is correct (i.e., 4) is 0.1; etc. Hence, the probability that you will randomly select π gets smaller and smaller (by a factor of 0.1) for each additional digit of precision; for example, to randomly select 3.14159, the probability is 0.1^6, and to randomly select 3.14159265358979, the probability is 0.1^{15}. Therefore, the probability you will randomly select exactly π, correct to infinitely-many digits, is 0. This gives us the following fourth property of a continuous probability distribution:

4. $P(X = x) = 0$ for every real number x (i.e., the probability that X will be exactly equal to a particular real number is 0).

$P(X > a) = P(X \geq a)$

and

$P(X < b) = P(X \leq b)$

Therefore, when we are working with continuous random variables, we are not concerned with the probability that the variable will take on a particular value; rather, we determine the probability that the random variable will take on a value in a particular *range* of values.

We will now look at some specific examples of continuous probability distributions, and how to calculate probability for continuous random variables with those types of distributions.

The Continuous Uniform Distribution

A continuous random variable which can take on a value within a finite range of values, and in which every value has the same likelihood of being selected, has a **continuous uniform probability distribution**. The continuous uniform distribution has the following properties:

- Its graph is a straight horizontal line between two X-values: a and b.

- The Y-value of the horizontal line is equal to $\dfrac{1}{b-a}$

- Outside of the interval $[a, b]$, the graph has a Y-value of 0.

Consider the example from above, where X is a randomly-selected real number between 0 and 10, and determine the probability that X will be between 4.2 and 7.5:

Continuous Uniform Probability Distribution

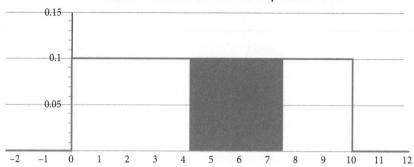

The probability that X will be between 4.2 and 7.5 is calculated by taking the rectangular area under the curve between those two values:

$$P(4.2 < X < 7.5) = l \cdot w = (7.5 - 4.2) \cdot (0.1) = 3.3(0.1) = 0.33$$

In general, for a continuous random variable X with a uniform probability distribution within the interval $[a, b]$, the probability that X will fall within the interval (c, d) is given as follows:

Formula 7.1-a

Continuous Uniform Distribution

$$P(c < X < d) = (d - c) \cdot \frac{1}{(b - a)} = \frac{(d - c)}{(b - a)}$$

Example 7.1-a Determining Probability using the Continuous Uniform Distribution

In the following examples, determine the desired probabilities, assuming that X is a continuous random variable with a uniform probability distribution:

(i) $P(1.5 < X < 3.2)$, given that X is selected randomly from the interval $[1, 5]$.

(ii) $P(X > 45)$, given that X is selected randomly from the interval $[10, 60]$.

(iii) $P(X < 0.86)$, given that X is selected randomly from the interval $[0, 1]$.

Solution

(i) $P(1.5 < X < 3.2) = \dfrac{3.2 - 1.5}{5 - 1} = \dfrac{1.7}{4} = 0.425$

(ii)   We are solving for $P(X > 45)$ on the interval $[10, 60]$, which means X cannot be greater than 60. Therefore, we are actually solving for $P(45 < X < 60)$.

$$P(X > 45) = \frac{60 - 45}{60 - 10} = \frac{15}{50} = 0.3$$

(iii) We are solving for $P(X < 0.86)$ on the interval $[0, 1]$, which means X cannot be less than 0. Therefore, we are actually solving for $P(0 < X < 0.86)$.

$$P(X < 0.86) = \frac{0.86 - 0}{1 - 0} = \frac{0.86}{1} = 0.86$$

Properties of the Continuous Uniform Distribution

We can very quickly determine that the expected value (mean) of the continuous uniform distribution will be halfway on the interval $[a, b]$, given that each value on that interval is equally-likely to occur, which means that for every value that occurs a certain distance above the halfway point, there is a value that same distance below the halfway point that is equally-likely to occur, averaging at exactly the halfway point. Hence,

Expected Value (Mean): $E(X) = \mu = \dfrac{a + b}{2}$

The variance, on the other hand, is more difficult to calculate (requiring calculus), and so will be stated without explanation:

Variance: $$Var(X) = \sigma^2 = \frac{(b-a)^2}{12}$$

Standard Deviation: $$SD(X) = \sigma = \sqrt{\frac{(b-a)^2}{12}} = \frac{(b-a)}{\sqrt{12}}$$

Example 7.1-b   Calculating the Expected Value and Variance of the Continuous Uniform Distribution

Calculate the expected value and variance (to 3 significant digits) for the three examples from 7.1-a above.

Solution

(i) $E(X) = \dfrac{a+b}{2} = \dfrac{1+5}{2} = 3$

(ii) $E(X) = \dfrac{a+b}{2} = \dfrac{10+60}{2} = 35$

$\sigma^2 = \dfrac{(b-a)^2}{12} = \dfrac{(5-1)^2}{12} = \dfrac{16}{12} \approx 1.33$

$\sigma^2 = \dfrac{(b-a)^2}{12} = \dfrac{(60-10)^2}{12} = \dfrac{2{,}500}{12} \approx 208$

(iii) $E(X) = \dfrac{a+b}{2} = \dfrac{0+1}{2} = 0.5$

$\sigma^2 = \dfrac{(b-a)^2}{12} = \dfrac{(1-0)^2}{12} = \dfrac{1}{12} \approx 0.0833$

Example 7.1-c   Solving Application Problems involving the Continuous Uniform Distribution

An I.V. line with replacement fluids is set to run continuously and at a consistent rate over the course of 6 hours, at which point the empty I.V. bag is removed and replaced with a full bag and the infusion is repeated. A shift change occurs at 7:00 AM, and it typically takes the new nurse about 30 minutes before he/she will have a chance to check-in on the patient.

(i) What is the probability the bag will need to be changed within the first 30 minutes of the shift change?

(ii) At what time would the nurse expect that the bag would need to be changed?

Solution

(i) Since the I.V. solution infuses continuously and consistently, the length of time remaining for the infusion can be modeled by a continuous random variable with a uniform probability distribution on the interval [0, 6]. Hence, the probability that the infusion will be completed in the next 30 minutes (i.e., 0.5 hours) can be calculated as follows:

Using Formula 7.1-a, $P(c < X < d) = \dfrac{(d-c)}{(b-a)}$

$$P(0 < X < 0.5) = \frac{0.5-0}{6-0} = \frac{0.5}{6} \approx 0.0833$$

(ii) The expected amount of time remaining on the infusion can be calculated as follows:

$$E(X) = \frac{a+b}{2} = \frac{0+6}{2} = 3 \text{ - i.e., 3 hours after the shift change}$$

Hence, the nurse would expect that the bag will need to be changed by 10:00 AM. However, he/she should check the chart to make sure and not make an assumption about this!

The Exponential Distribution

In the previous chapter, we examined both the geometric distribution, which analyzed the number of trials performed until the first success was recorded, and the Poisson distribution, which analyzed the number of successes that occur in a fixed period of time. Both of these were discrete probability distributions, as the geometric distribution counted the number of trials and the Poisson distribution counted the number of successes.

Imagine now that we wanted to know the length of time between two successes in a Poisson process. So instead of **counting** the number of successes in a fixed interval of time, we want to **measure** the interval of time between two successes. This will be represented by a continuous probability distribution known as the **Exponential Probability Distribution**.

The exponential distribution, which measures the time for a success to occur after a previous success, is the continuous version of the geometric distribution, which counts the number of trials needed for a success to occur after a previous success.

Since the exponential distribution is based on a Poisson process, it has only one parameter: λ - the average number of successes in a fixed interval of time.

The graph of the exponential probability distribution is given by the formula $y = \lambda e^{-\lambda t}$, where t represents the number of time periods since the last success. This graph will start at a y-intercept of λ and will decay continuously at a rate of λ per time period:

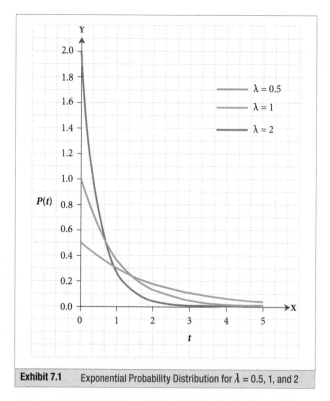

Exhibit 7.1   Exponential Probability Distribution for $\lambda = 0.5$, 1, and 2

Calculus tells us that the probability that the length of time between two successes (measured by the continuous random variable X) will be less than t time periods, greater than t time periods, or between two time periods t_1 and t_2, are given by the following formulas:

Formula 7.1-b   **Exponential Distribution**

$$P(X < t) = 1 - e^{-\lambda t} \qquad P(X > t) = e^{-\lambda t} \qquad P(t_1 < X < t_2) = e^{-\lambda t_1} - e^{-\lambda t_2}$$

Example 7.1-d **Determining Probability using the Exponential Distribution**

In the following examples, determine the desired probabilities, assuming that X is a continuous random variable with an exponential probability distribution:

(i) $P(X < 0.5)$, given that $\lambda = 3$

(ii) $P(X > 60)$, given that $\lambda = \dfrac{1}{15}$

(iii) $P(1.5 < X < 2.5)$, given that $\lambda = 0.08$

Solution

(i) $P(X < 0.5) = 1 - e^{-3(0.5)} \approx 0.777$

(ii) $P(X > 60) = e^{-\frac{1}{15}(60)} \approx 0.0183$

(iii) $P(1.5 < X < 2.5) = e^{-0.08(1.5)} - e^{-0.08(2.5)} \approx 0.0682$

Properties of the Exponential Distribution

As with the continuous uniform distribution, it is fairly simple to calculate the expected value or mean of the exponential distribution: since the average number of successes per time interval is λ, we would expect to wait, on average, $\dfrac{1}{\lambda}$ time periods to get our next success (e.g., at a rate of 2 successes per hour, we expect to wait approximately a $\dfrac{1}{2}$ hour - i.e., 30 minutes - between successes).

Expected Value (Mean): $E(X) = \mu = \dfrac{1}{\lambda}$

Also, as with the continuous uniform distribution, the variance is much more difficult to calculate, and so, again, it will be stated without explanation:

Variance: $Var(X) = \sigma^2 = \dfrac{1}{\lambda^2}$

Standard Deviation: $SD(X) = \sigma = \sqrt{\dfrac{1}{\lambda^2}} = \dfrac{1}{\lambda}$

Example 7.1-e **Calculating the Expected Value and Variance of the Exponential Distribution**

Calculate the expected value and variance (to 3 significant digits) for the three examples from 7.1-d above.

Solution

(i) $E(X) = \dfrac{1}{\lambda} = \dfrac{1}{3} \approx 0.333$

$\sigma^2 = \dfrac{1}{\lambda^2} = \dfrac{1}{3^2} = \dfrac{1}{9} \approx 0.111$

(ii) $E(X) = \dfrac{1}{\lambda} = \dfrac{1}{\left(\dfrac{1}{15}\right)} = 15$

$\sigma^2 = \dfrac{1}{\lambda^2} = \dfrac{1}{\left(\dfrac{1}{15}\right)^2} = \dfrac{1}{\left(\dfrac{1}{225}\right)} = 225$

(iii) $E(X) = \dfrac{1}{\lambda} = \dfrac{1}{0.08} = 12.5$

$\sigma^2 = \dfrac{1}{\lambda^2} = \dfrac{1}{0.08^2} = \dfrac{1}{0.0064} \approx 156$

Example 7.1-f | Solving Application Problems Involving the Exponential Distribution

A major city receives an average of 864 emergency 911 calls per day.

(i) Determine the length of time between 911 calls (in minutes) on any given day.

(ii) Calculate the probability that the length of time between two 911 calls will be less than 1 minute.

Solution

Since we are not given any information about specific time-of-day usage (e.g., peak periods), we assume that the 911 calls follow a Poisson process with $\lambda = 864$ calls per day.

(i) We let X be a continuous random variable representing the length of time (in minutes) between two consecutive 911 phone calls. Since our given λ represents the average number of calls per day, we need to convert that to calls per minute to use in the exponential distribution for X:

$$\lambda = \frac{864 \text{ calls}}{1 \text{ day}} \times \frac{1 \text{ day}}{24 \text{ hours}} \times \frac{1 \text{ hour}}{60 \text{ minutes}} = 0.6 \text{ calls/minute}$$

$$E(X) = \frac{1}{\lambda} = \frac{1}{0.6} \approx 1.67 \text{ minutes}$$

Therefore, the average length of time between two consecutive 911 calls is 1.67 minutes.

(ii) Using Formula 7.1-b, $\quad P(X < t) = 1 - e^{-\lambda t}$

$$P(X < 1) = 1 - e^{-0.6(1)} \approx 0.451$$

Therefore, the probability that two consecutive 911 calls occur within 1 minute of each other is 0.451.

7.1 | Exercises

Answers to odd-numbered problems are available at the end of the textbook.

For Problems 1 to 16, analyze the probability scenarios and complete the following:

(i) *Calculate the indicated probabilities (to 3 significant digits).*

(ii) *Determine the mean and standard deviation of the distribution (to 3 significant digits).*

1. $P(X < 2)$, given that X has a uniform probability distribution, and $0 < X < 6$.

2. $P(X < 5)$, given that X has a uniform probability distribution, and $0 < X < 8$.

3. $P(25 < X < 40)$, given that X has a uniform probability distribution, and $20 < X < 55$.

4. $P(9 < X < 12)$, given that X has a uniform probability distribution, and $5 < X < 18$.

5. $P(1.6 < X < 2.5)$, given that X has a uniform probability distribution, and $1.2 < X < 4.8$.

6. $P(8.5 < X < 13.9)$, given that X has a uniform probability distribution, and $2.4 < X < 18.6$.

7. $P(X > \frac{1}{3})$, given that X has a uniform probability distribution, and $0 < X < 1$.

8. $P(X > \frac{2}{5})$, given that X has a uniform probability distribution, and $0 < X < 1$.

9. $P(X < 0.4)$, given that X has an exponential probability distribution with $\lambda = 3.5$.

10. $P(X < 8.5)$, given that X has an exponential probability distribution with $\lambda = 0.25$.

11. $P(X > 12.6)$, given that X has an exponential probability distribution with $\lambda = 0.0625$.

12. $P(X > 1.25)$, given that X has an exponential probability distribution with $\lambda = 2.8$.

13. $P(1.88 < X < 3.12)$, given that X has an exponential probability distribution with $\lambda = 1.6$.

14. $P(5.05 < X < 10.10)$, given that X has an exponential probability distribution with $\lambda = 0.4$.

15. $P(3\frac{1}{3} < X < 6\frac{1}{4})$, given that X has an exponential probability distribution with $\lambda = \frac{1}{6}$.

16. $P\left(\frac{4}{15} < X < \frac{5}{6}\right)$, given that X has an exponential probability distribution with $\lambda = 1\frac{3}{4}$.

For Problems 17 to 32, determine which continuous probability distribution is appropriate to use - uniform or exponential - and then answer the questions using the properties of that distribution.

17. The average blood donor takes about 15 minutes to give 1 unit of blood. A registered nurse walks over to a donor who is in the middle of giving blood, not knowing how far along the blood donation process is. What is the probability that the process will be finished in the next 3 minutes? How long would the nurse expect the remainder of the blood donation to take?

18. A physiotherapist has a patient doing some slow jogging on a treadmill and sets the timer for 25 minutes. A little while later, the physiotherapist's assistant comes over to check on the patient, not knowing how much time is left on the treadmill. If the speed needs to be adjusted with 10 minutes left to go, what is the probability that the assistant will need to adjust the speed of the treadmill? How much time would the assistant expect to be remaining on the timer?

19. The blood clinic in Problem 17 sees approximately 30 donors every hour, spread out evenly. What is the probability that the next two donors will come in with less than 1 minute between them?

20. The physiotherapist in Problem 18 sees approximately 4 patients every hour, spread out evenly. What is the probability that the next two patients will come in more than 20 minutes apart?

21. During a busy time, a registered nurse working at a telephone health-care advice and referral service receives 8 calls from patients every hour. On average, what is the expected length of time between two calls received by this nurse? What is the probability that the length of time between two phone calls will be more than 10 minutes?

22. A walk-in clinic is busiest on a Saturday morning, when it typically sees an average of 18 patients every hour. On average, how much time elapses between patient arrivals at the clinic on Saturday mornings? What is the probability that the length of time between the next two patients arriving will be more than 5 minutes?

23. A patient requiring a 1,000 mL urinary catheter bag typically outputs 1,000 mL of urine every 12 hours, with the bag needing to be changed once it gets over 600 mL. If a nurse starting his shift comes in to check on the patient, what is the probability that the bag will need to be changed? What volume of urine would the nurse expect the bag to contain?

24. An anemic patient receives 150 mL of iron-in-saline solution over the course of an hour. If a nurse walks in to check on the patient, not knowing how much time is left in the infusion, what is the probability that there is less than 20 mL remaining? What volume of iron solution would the nurse expect the bag to contain?

25. A nurse working the night-shift receives an average of 18 calls from patients during the course of the 12-hour shift. If the nurse just responded to a call from a patient, what is the probability that she will have between a one- and two-hour break before the next call? How long of a break would she expect to have before she received the next call?

26. A Statistics for Health Sciences professor typically sees an average of 5 students during his 2 office hours every week. If the professor just saw one student at the start of his office hours, what is the probability he will not see another student for between 30 and 45 minutes? How much time would he expect to elapse before the next student comes to his office seeking assistance?

27. A pharmacy technician is asked to fill a prescription of a certain drug in a liquid suspension for a patient. The pharmacist instructs the technician to fill a bottle with 150 mL of the suspension from the 2.5 L bottle received from the distributor. If the bottle in use is only partially full, and the volume remaining is unknown, what is the probability that there will be enough of the medication in the large bottle to fill the prescription?

28. A personal trainer at a gym is preparing a protein shake for a client after a work-out. The protein shake requires a 30 g serving of protein powder, to be taken from the 1.2 kg tub. If the tub in use is only partially full, and the amount remaining is unknown, what is the probability that there is enough protein powder left in the tub to make the protein shake?

29. A home-care nurse is scheduled to arrive to visit a patient sometime between the hours of 11:00 AM and 3:30 PM. If the patient plans to eat lunch and watch a show on TV from 12:45 to 2:00 PM, what is the probability that the nurse will arrive during that period of time? When should the patient expect the nurse to arrive?

30. A pet owner told the vet that he would drop his pet off between the hours of 10:30 AM and 12:15 PM. The vet plans to take lunch from 11:30 AM to 12:00 PM. What is the probability that the owner will come during his lunch? When should he expect the owner to arrive?

31. A pharmacy typically fills 120 prescriptions over the course of the 8-hour afternoon shift.

   a. Determine how long, on average, the pharmacist would expect between patients filling prescriptions.

   b. What is the probability the next two patients will come less than 2 minutes apart?

   c. What is the probability that the next 8 patients will all arrive less than 2 minutes apart? (*Hint: Make sure you count the number of intervals between patients, rather than the number of patients themselves.*)

32. A paramedic typically receives approximately 15 calls in a 24-hour shift.

   a. If the paramedic just received a call, how much time would he expect to be able to complete this current call before he receives his next call?

   b. What is the probability that the next 2 calls will come less than 45 minutes apart?

   c. What is the probability that the next 5 calls will all come in less than 45 minutes apart? (*Hint: Make sure you count the number of intervals between phone calls, rather than the number of phone calls themselves.*)

7.2 | The Normal Distribution

A more in-depth analysis of probability for continuous random variables that arise in practical situations in the health sciences and in life in general reveals a fundamental flaw in the continuous uniform distribution: namely, the assumption that every value is equally-likely to occur. In reality, certain values (or ranges of values) are more likely to occur than others. Most commonly, the values in the middle are the most likely to occur, while extreme values on either side are less likely to occur.

Recall from Chapter 2 that probability distributions can be categorized in a variety of ways, including symmetrical or skewed, and "mound"-shaped or bimodal (i.e., two "mounds").

In this section, we will examine a special type of continuous probability distribution that is symmetrical and "mound"-shaped, called the **Normal Distribution**.

Properties of the Normal Distribution

The normal distribution has a graph that is given by the following function:

$$y = \frac{1}{\sqrt{2\pi\sigma^2}} \cdot e^{\frac{-(x-\mu)^2}{2\sigma^2}}$$

where μ is the mean of the distribution and σ^2 is the variance of the distribution. If X is a continuous random variable that follows a normal distribution with mean μ and variance σ^2, we say $X \sim N(\mu, \sigma^2)$.

Note: When using this notation, write the value of standard deviation raised to the power of 2, instead of the value of the variance; e.g., for $\mu = 100$ and $\sigma = 20$, write $X \sim N(100, 20^2)$, not $X \sim N(100, 400)$.

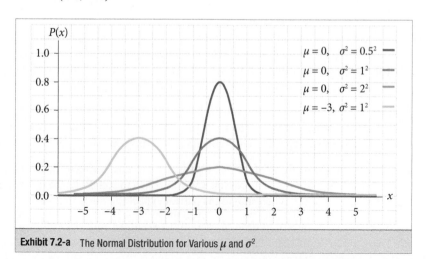

Exhibit 7.2-a The Normal Distribution for Various μ and σ^2

Notice that this graph is symmetrical about the mean, and that the size of the "mound" changes with the variance: as the variance increases, the mound gets shorter and wider, and as the variance decreases, the mound gets taller and narrower. It also decays exponentially to zero in both directions, which makes sense, given that the function is an exponential function with a negative exponent (decay) that is squared (so it will be the same in the negative direction as it is in the positive direction).

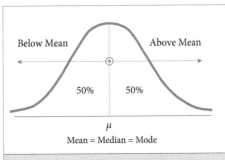

- "Mound"- or "bell"-shaped
- Symmetrical about the mean
- Mean = Median = Mode
- 50% of the data is above the mean and 50% of the data is below
- The curve approaches the X-axis but never touches it

Exhibit 7.2-b   Properties of the Normal Distribution

The normal distribution (or some approximation of it) arises quite frequently in practical scenarios in which we would like to analyze values of a continuous random variable, including measurements of living organisms and tissues, average monthly temperatures in a particular city on a given day of the year, expected lifespans of products for warranty-purposes, the magnitude of sampling errors present in experiments and studies such as drug trials and election polling, etc.

Unfortunately, calculus fails to provide a formula for the area under the curve of this particular function, which means that we do not have a formula for the probability of a continuous random variable with a normal distribution. This means that we cannot calculate probability in the vast number of situations where the normal distribution arises as simply as we did in the much-more-specific and narrowly-defined scenarios where the uniform or exponential distributions arise.

Fortunately, while there is no general probability formula for the normal distribution, calculus provides approximation methods that yield probabilities accurate to as many decimal places as we require. However, in order to do this, we first need to "standardize" this distribution - that is, we need a common mean and variance that we can use as a reference point for all other normal distributions.

The Standard Normal Distribution

First of all, in order to make the simplest possible normal distribution to use as the "standard", we want the middle (i.e., the mean) of the graph to create a natural symmetry - that is, the values on the right-side of the mean correspond in a natural way with the values on the left-side of the mean. Hence, the mean of this normal distribution should be 0.

Next, recall that the standard deviation is a standardized measure of distance from the mean, so we want a standard deviation that corresponds directly with the values of the variable - that is, the value of the variable is exactly the same as the number of standard deviations from the mean. Hence, the standard deviation of this normal distribution should be 1 (and thus, the variance will be 1 as well).

Therefore, the **Standard Normal Distribution** is a normal continuous probability distribution with a mean of 0 ($\mu = 0$) and variance of 1 ($\sigma^2 = 1$). Since the standard normal distribution is a special probability distribution, we use the variable Z to distinguish it from other probability distributions.

Hence, if Z is a continuous random variable with a standard normal distribution, then we say $Z \sim N(0, 1)$. The graph of the standard normal distribution for Z is as follows:

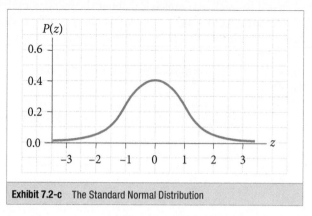

Exhibit 7.2-c   The Standard Normal Distribution

Note: We use the upper-case 'Z' to represent the continuous random variable for the standard normal distribution, and the lower-case 'z' to represent specific values that the random variable Z can take on.

The z-scores represent the number of standard deviations a value is from the mean, where positive z-scores represent values that are a certain number of standard deviations above the mean and negative z-scores represent values that are a certain number of standard deviations below the mean.

Calculating Probability for the Standard Normal Distribution

Now that we have a standardized normal distribution, we can look at how to calculate probability for this distribution. Recall from Chapter 3 the **Empirical Rule**, which states the following for a normal distribution:

- Approximately 68% of the data falls within 1 standard deviation on either side of the mean (i.e., between $z = -1$ and $z = +1$).

- Approximately 95% of the data falls within 2 standard deviations on either side of the mean (i.e., between $z = -2$ and $z = +2$).

- Approximately 99.7% of the data falls within 3 standard deviations on either side of the mean (i.e., between $z = -3$ and $z = +3$).

This is summarized in the following figure:

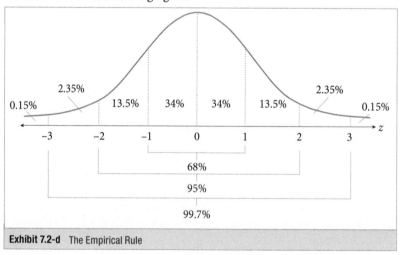

Exhibit 7.2-d   The Empirical Rule

The diagram above for the Empirical Rule provides the approximate area under the normal distribution graph between integer intervals of standard deviations. In other words, we can approximately calculate the probability that randomly-selected Z-scores will fall above, below, or between any two integer values from –3 to +3. However, we need values for the area above, below, and between Z-scores that are decimal numbers as well, and with a higher degree of precision than the Empirical Rule provides.

Mathematicians have calculated and recorded the areas (to 4 decimal places) under the standard normal distribution below all z-scores (to 2 decimal places), ranging from $z = -3.70$ to $z = +3.70$.

Using the Tables of Areas Under the Standard Normal Distribution

- **To find the probability that Z is *less than* a certain z-score (to 2 decimal places), $P(Z < z)$, look up the value in the z-table at the intersection of the row and column representing that z-score.**

    - For example, to find the probability that Z is less than −1.56, we look up the value at the intersection of the row with $z = -1.5$ in the left-side of the negative table, and the column with $z = 0.06$ at the top of the table (as highlighted in Table 7.2-a below): Hence, $P(Z < -1.56) = 0.0594$

    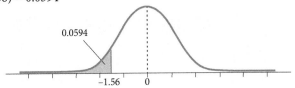

    - Similarly, to find the probability that Z is less than 0.90, we look up the value at the intersection of the row with $z = 0.9$ in the left-side of the positive table, and the column with $z = 0.00$ at the top of the table (as highlighted in Table 7.2-b below): Hence, $P(Z < 0.90) = 0.8159$

    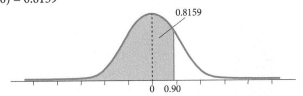

- **To find the probability that Z is *greater than* a certain z-score, look up the value corresponding with that z-score in the table and subtract it from 1, using the complementary events rule from Chapter 5: $P(Z > z) = 1 - P(Z < z)$**

    - For example, the probability that Z is greater than −1.56 is calculated as follows: $P(Z > -1.56) = 1 - P(Z < -1.56) = 1 - 0.0594 = 0.9406$

    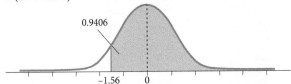

    - Similarly, the probability that Z is greater than 0.90 is calculated as follows: $P(Z > 0.90) = 1 - P(Z < 0.90) = 1 - 0.8159 = 0.1841$

    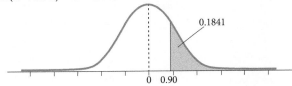

- **To find the probability that Z is *between* two z-scores (a and b), calculate the difference between the values corresponding with those z-scores in the z-table: $P(a < Z < b) = P(Z < b) - P(Z < a)$**

    - For example, the probability that Z is between −1.56 and 0.90 is calculated as follows: $P(-1.56 < Z < 0.90) = P(Z < 0.90) - P(Z < -1.56) = 0.8159 - 0.0594 = 0.7565$

    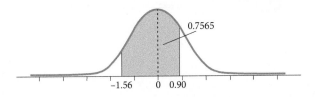

| Table 7.2-a | **Table of Areas under the Standard Normal Distribution below Negative z-scores** |

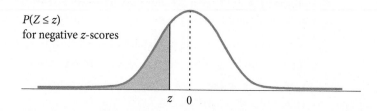

$P(Z \le z)$
for negative z-scores

These tables are also made available for reference in the Appendix on pages 402 and 403.

z	0.09	0.08	0.07	0.06	0.05	0.04	0.03	0.02	0.01	0.00
−3.6	0.0001	0.0001	0.0001	0.0001	0.0001	0.0001	0.0001	0.0001	0.0002	0.0002
−3.5	0.0002	0.0002	0.0002	0.0002	0.0002	0.0002	0.0002	0.0002	0.0002	0.0002
−3.4	0.0002	0.0003	0.0003	0.0003	0.0003	0.0003	0.0003	0.0003	0.0003	0.0003
−3.3	0.0003	0.0004	0.0004	0.0004	0.0004	0.0004	0.0004	0.0005	0.0005	0.0005
−3.2	0.0005	0.0005	0.0005	0.0006	0.0006	0.0006	0.0006	0.0006	0.0007	0.0007
−3.1	0.0007	0.0007	0.0008	0.0008	0.0008	0.0008	0.0009	0.0009	0.0009	0.0010
−3.0	0.0010	0.0010	0.0011	0.0011	0.0011	0.0012	0.0012	0.0013	0.0013	0.0013
−2.9	0.0014	0.0014	0.0015	0.0015	0.0016	0.0016	0.0017	0.0018	0.0018	0.0019
−2.8	0.0019	0.0020	0.0021	0.0021	0.0022	0.0023	0.0023	0.0024	0.0025	0.0026
−2.7	0.0026	0.0027	0.0028	0.0029	0.0030	0.0031	0.0032	0.0033	0.0034	0.0035
−2.6	0.0036	0.0037	0.0038	0.0039	0.0040	0.0041	0.0043	0.0044	0.0045	0.0047
−2.5	0.0048	0.0049	0.0051	0.0052	0.0054	0.0055	0.0057	0.0059	0.0060	0.0062
−2.4	0.0064	0.0066	0.0068	0.0069	0.0071	0.0073	0.0075	0.0078	0.0080	0.0082
−2.3	0.0084	0.0087	0.0089	0.0091	0.0094	0.0096	0.0099	0.0102	0.0104	0.0107
−2.2	0.0110	0.0113	0.0116	0.0119	0.0122	0.0125	0.0129	0.0132	0.0136	0.0139
−2.1	0.0143	0.0146	0.0150	0.0154	0.0158	0.0162	0.0166	0.0170	0.0174	0.0179
−2.0	0.0183	0.0188	0.0192	0.0197	0.0202	0.0207	0.0212	0.0217	0.0222	0.0228
−1.9	0.0233	0.0239	0.0244	0.0250	0.0256	0.0262	0.0268	0.0274	0.0281	0.0287
−1.8	0.0294	0.0301	0.0307	0.0314	0.0322	0.0329	0.0336	0.0344	0.0351	0.0359
−1.7	0.0367	0.0375	0.0384	0.0392	0.0401	0.0409	0.0418	0.0427	0.0436	0.0446
−1.6	0.0455	0.0465	0.0475	0.0485	0.0495	0.0505	0.0516	0.0526	0.0537	0.0548
−1.5	0.0559	0.0571	0.0582	0.0594	0.0606	0.0618	0.0630	0.0643	0.0655	0.0668
−1.4	0.0681	0.0694	0.0708	0.0721	0.0735	0.0749	0.0764	0.0778	0.0793	0.0808
−1.3	0.0823	0.0838	0.0853	0.0869	0.0885	0.0901	0.0918	0.0934	0.0951	0.0968
−1.2	0.0985	0.1003	0.1020	0.1038	0.1056	0.1075	0.1093	0.1112	0.1131	0.1151
−1.1	0.1170	0.1190	0.1210	0.1230	0.1251	0.1271	0.1292	0.1314	0.1335	0.1357
−1.0	0.1379	0.1401	0.1423	0.1446	0.1469	0.1492	0.1515	0.1539	0.1562	0.1587
−0.9	0.1611	0.1635	0.1660	0.1685	0.1711	0.1736	0.1762	0.1788	0.1814	0.1841
−0.8	0.1867	0.1894	0.1922	0.1949	0.1977	0.2005	0.2033	0.2061	0.2090	0.2119
−0.7	0.2148	0.2177	0.2206	0.2236	0.2266	0.2296	0.2327	0.2358	0.2389	0.2420
−0.6	0.2451	0.2483	0.2514	0.2546	0.2578	0.2611	0.2643	0.2676	0.2709	0.2743
−0.5	0.2776	0.2810	0.2843	0.2877	0.2912	0.2946	0.2981	0.3015	0.3050	0.3085
−0.4	0.3121	0.3156	0.3192	0.3228	0.3264	0.3300	0.3336	0.3372	0.3409	0.3446
−0.3	0.3483	0.3520	0.3557	0.3594	0.3632	0.3669	0.3707	0.3745	0.3783	0.3821
−0.2	0.3859	0.3897	0.3936	0.3974	0.4013	0.4052	0.4090	0.4129	0.4168	0.4207
−0.1	0.4247	0.4286	0.4325	0.4364	0.4404	0.4443	0.4483	0.4522	0.4562	0.4602
−0.0	0.4641	0.4681	0.4721	0.4761	0.4801	0.4840	0.4880	0.4920	0.4960	0.5000

The highlighted value shows the area under the standard normal distribution below z-score −1.56.

Note: For $z \le -3.70$, use $P(Z < z) \approx 0.0000$

Table 7.2-b · Table of Areas under the Standard Normal Distribution below Positive z-scores

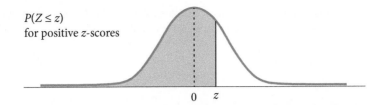

$P(Z \leq z)$
for positive z-scores

0   z

The highlighted value shows the area under the standard normal distribution below z-score 0.90.

z	0.00	0.01	0.02	0.03	0.04	0.05	0.06	0.07	0.08	0.09
0.0	0.5000	0.5040	0.5080	0.5120	0.5160	0.5199	0.5239	0.5279	0.5319	0.5359
0.1	0.5398	0.5438	0.5478	0.5517	0.5557	0.5596	0.5636	0.5675	0.5714	0.5753
0.2	0.5793	0.5832	0.5871	0.5910	0.5948	0.5987	0.6026	0.6064	0.6103	0.6141
0.3	0.6179	0.6217	0.6255	0.6293	0.6331	0.6368	0.6406	0.6443	0.6480	0.6517
0.4	0.6554	0.6591	0.6628	0.6664	0.6700	0.6736	0.6772	0.6808	0.6844	0.6879
0.5	0.6915	0.6950	0.6985	0.7019	0.7054	0.7088	0.7123	0.7157	0.7190	0.7224
0.6	0.7257	0.7291	0.7324	0.7357	0.7389	0.7422	0.7454	0.7486	0.7517	0.7549
0.7	0.7580	0.7611	0.7642	0.7673	0.7704	0.7734	0.7764	0.7794	0.7823	0.7852
0.8	0.7881	0.7910	0.7939	0.7967	0.7995	0.8023	0.8051	0.8078	0.8106	0.8133
0.9	0.8159	0.8186	0.8212	0.8238	0.8264	0.8289	0.8315	0.8340	0.8365	0.8389
1.0	0.8413	0.8438	0.8461	0.8485	0.8508	0.8531	0.8554	0.8577	0.8599	0.8621
1.1	0.8643	0.8665	0.8686	0.8708	0.8729	0.8749	0.8770	0.8790	0.8810	0.8830
1.2	0.8849	0.8869	0.8888	0.8907	0.8925	0.8944	0.8962	0.8980	0.8997	0.9015
1.3	0.9032	0.9049	0.9066	0.9082	0.9099	0.9115	0.9131	0.9147	0.9162	0.9177
1.4	0.9192	0.9207	0.9222	0.9236	0.9251	0.9265	0.9279	0.9292	0.9306	0.9319
1.5	0.9332	0.9345	0.9357	0.9370	0.9382	0.9394	0.9406	0.9418	0.9429	0.9441
1.6	0.9452	0.9463	0.9474	0.9484	0.9495	0.9505	0.9515	0.9525	0.9535	0.9545
1.7	0.9554	0.9564	0.9573	0.9582	0.9591	0.9599	0.9608	0.9616	0.9625	0.9633
1.8	0.9641	0.9649	0.9656	0.9664	0.9671	0.9678	0.9686	0.9693	0.9699	0.9706
1.9	0.9713	0.9719	0.9726	0.9732	0.9738	0.9744	0.9750	0.9756	0.9761	0.9767
2.0	0.9772	0.9778	0.9783	0.9788	0.9793	0.9798	0.9803	0.9808	0.9812	0.9817
2.1	0.9821	0.9826	0.9830	0.9834	0.9838	0.9842	0.9846	0.9850	0.9854	0.9857
2.2	0.9861	0.9864	0.9868	0.9871	0.9875	0.9878	0.9881	0.9884	0.9887	0.9890
2.3	0.9893	0.9896	0.9898	0.9901	0.9904	0.9906	0.9909	0.9911	0.9913	0.9916
2.4	0.9918	0.9920	0.9922	0.9925	0.9927	0.9929	0.9931	0.9932	0.9934	0.9936
2.5	0.9938	0.9940	0.9941	0.9943	0.9945	0.9946	0.9948	0.9949	0.9951	0.9952
2.6	0.9953	0.9955	0.9956	0.9957	0.9959	0.9960	0.9961	0.9962	0.9963	0.9964
2.7	0.9965	0.9966	0.9967	0.9968	0.9969	0.9970	0.9971	0.9972	0.9973	0.9974
2.8	0.9974	0.9975	0.9976	0.9977	0.9977	0.9978	0.9979	0.9979	0.9980	0.9981
2.9	0.9981	0.9982	0.9982	0.9983	0.9984	0.9984	0.9985	0.9985	0.9986	0.9986
3.0	0.9987	0.9987	0.9987	0.9988	0.9988	0.9989	0.9989	0.9989	0.9990	0.9990
3.1	0.9990	0.9991	0.9991	0.9991	0.9992	0.9992	0.9992	0.9992	0.9993	0.9993
3.2	0.9993	0.9993	0.9994	0.9994	0.9994	0.9994	0.9994	0.9995	0.9995	0.9995
3.3	0.9995	0.9995	0.9995	0.9996	0.9996	0.9996	0.9996	0.9996	0.9996	0.9997
3.4	0.9997	0.9997	0.9997	0.9997	0.9997	0.9997	0.9997	0.9997	0.9997	0.9998
3.5	0.9998	0.9998	0.9998	0.9998	0.9998	0.9998	0.9998	0.9998	0.9998	0.9998
3.6	0.9998	0.9998	0.9999	0.9999	0.9999	0.9999	0.9999	0.9999	0.9999	0.9999

Note: For $z \geq 3.70$, use $P(Z < z) \approx 1.0000$

Example 7.2-a   **Determining Probability using the Standard Normal Distribution Table**

If Z is a continuous random variable with a standard normal distribution, determine the following probabilities using the standard normal distribution table:

(i) $P(Z < 1.05)$

(ii) $P(Z < -2.16)$

(iii) $P(Z > -0.77)$

(iv) $P(Z > 0.09)$

(v) $P(0 < Z < 2.5)$

(vi) $P(-1.28 < Z < 4.33)$

(vii) $P(Z > \pi)$

Solution

(i)   Using the positive Standard Normal Distribution table, the area found at the intersection of the $z = 1.0$ row and the 0.05 column is 0.8531. Therefore,

$$P(Z < 1.05) = 0.8531$$

(ii)   Using the negative Standard Normal Distribution table, the area found at the intersection of the $z = -2.1$ row and the 0.06 column is 0.0154. Therefore,

$$P(Z < -2.16) = 0.0154$$

(iii)   Using the negative Standard Normal Distribution table, the area found at the intersection of the $z = -0.7$ row and the 0.07 column is 0.2206. Therefore,

$$P(Z > -0.77) = 1 - P(Z < -0.77) = 1 - 0.2206 = 0.7794$$

(iv)   Using the positive Standard Normal Distribution table, the area found at the intersection of the $z = 0.0$ row and the 0.09 column is 0.5359. Therefore,

$$P(Z > 0.09) = 1 - P(Z < 0.09) = 1 - 0.5359 = 0.4641$$

(v)   The area corresponding to $z = 0.00$ is 0.5000 (since the mean represents the middle of the data in a symmetrical distribution) and the area corresponding to $z = 2.50$ is 0.9938. Therefore,

$$P(0 < Z < 2.5) = P(Z < 2.5) - P(Z < 0) = 0.9938 - 0.5000 = 0.4938$$

(vi)   The area corresponding to $z = -1.28$ is 0.1003. Since $z = 4.33$ is outside of the range of z-scores provided in the chart, we use an area of 1.0000 for $z = 4.33$. Therefore,

$$P(-1.28 < Z < 4.33) = P(Z < 4.33) - P(Z < -1.28) = 1.0000 - 0.1003 = 0.8997$$

(vii)   Since the table only lists z-scores rounded to 2 decimal places, we first need to round $\pi \approx 3.14$. Next, we use the table to find the area corresponding to $z = 3.14$ is 0.9992. Therefore,

$$P(Z > \pi) = 1 - P(Z < \pi) \approx 1 - P(Z < 3.14) = 1 - 0.9992 = 0.0008$$

Determining Z-Scores Corresponding to Area

Sometimes, we may wish to know the value that corresponds to a given probability or percent of the data.

For example, in some standardized testing, the "pass/fail" line is not based on the actual mark the student achieved on the test, but rather is based on the student's ranking out of all the test scores. In these situations, typically a certain percentage of the top-ranked students pass the test, and the remaining students fail the test, regardless of their actual marks.

Another practical example of this occurs with warranties, where the company issuing the warranty would like to set a time-frame for the warranty so that there is only a small probability that the item (or part of the item) will fail during the warranty period. This helps to ensure that only defective items are being replaced under warranty, and not items that fail due to "wear and tear". In these cases, the warranty time is set so that the probability of needing to replace an item under warranty is approximately equal to the probability that the item is defective.

If we know a certain percentage of the data, or probability of occurrence, we can look that value up as an area in the Standard Normal Distribution table, and find the corresponding z-score for that area.

Example 7.2-b	Determining Z-Scores Given Percentages and Probabilities

(i) Determine the z-score that corresponds to the 20th percentile (i.e., the value that separates the bottom 20% of the data from the top 80% of the data).

(ii) Determine the z-score such that the probability that Z will be greater than that z-score is 0.05 (i.e., determine z such that $P(Z > z) = 0.05$).

(iii) Determine the z-scores between which the middle 50% of the data fall.

Solution

(i) The z-score that corresponds to the 20th percentile has a corresponding area of 0.2000.

> Use 0.2000 instead of 0.20 as a reminder that this is an area, not a z-score.

Looking up 0.2000 in the body of the negative table (since $0.2000 < 0.5$), we see that the closest area value is 0.2005, which results in a corresponding z-score of –0.84.

Therefore, $z = -0.84$ corresponds with the 20th percentile.

(ii) If we want the z-score such that $P(Z > z) = 0.05$, we need to rewrite this as $P(Z < z) = 1 - 0.05 = 0.95$, since our table gives us the area below the corresponding z-scores, not above.

Looking up 0.9500 in the body of the positive table (since $0.9500 > 0.5$), we see that the closest area values are 0.9495 and 0.9505, with corresponding z-scores of 1.64 and 1.65, respectively.

Since 0.9500 falls exactly between these two areas, we choose the z-score that is halfway between the two corresponding z-scores in the table:

> We only average z-scores when the desired area is *exactly* between two consecutive areas listed in the table.

$$z = \frac{1.64 + 1.65}{2} = 1.645$$

Therefore, $z = 1.645$ is the value such that $P(Z > z) = 0.05$.

(iii) The values between which the middle 50% of the data fall are shown on the following diagram:

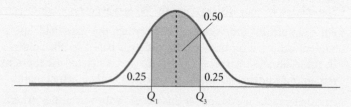

We know from Chapter 3 that the first quartile has 25% of the data below it, and the third quartile has 75% of the data below it. Hence, we are looking for the z-scores that correspond to the first and third quartiles (i.e., the values with corresponding areas of 0.2500 and 0.7500).

Q_1: Looking up 0.2500 in the body of the negative table, we see that the closest area value is 0.2514, which results in a corresponding z-score of −0.67.

Q_3: Looking up 0.7500 in the body of the positive table, we see that the closest area value is 0.7486, which results in a corresponding z-score of +0.67.

Therefore, the middle 50% of the data fall between the z-scores −0.67 and +0.67.

Note: The symmetry of the graph of the Standard Normal Distribution tells us that the z-scores corresponding to the same areas at the top and the bottom of the curve will have the same absolute value, but different signs (i.e., one positive, one negative).

Non-Standard Normal Distributions

Now that we know how to relate the values in a standard normal distribution with their corresponding area/probability/percentage values, we will study how to do the same for non-standard normal distributions (i.e., normal distributions with a mean that is not equal to 0 and/or a standard deviation that is not equal to 1).

Converting Raw X-Scores to Z-Scores

If we are given a raw x-score of a continuous random variable X with a normal distribution with mean $\mu \neq 0$ and standard deviation $\sigma \neq 1$, we can "standardize" the score by finding the corresponding z-score as follows:

Step 1: Determine how far away the raw x-score is from the mean μ by subtracting the mean from the x-score: $x - \mu$

Step 2: Determine the number of standard deviations this difference represents by dividing by the standard deviation σ.

This will give us our z-score:

Formula 7.2-a	**Converting Raw *X*-Scores to *Z*-Scores**

$$z = \frac{x - \mu}{\sigma}$$

Once we know the z-score, we can look it up in the Standard Normal Distribution table to find the corresponding area and proceed as we did previously.

| Example 7.2-c | **Determining Probability for Raw X-Scores of Normally-Distributed Variables** |

The life-expectancy for patients with a certain incurable disease who undergo treatment is normally-distributed with a mean of 5.7 years and a standard deviation of 1.8 years.

(i) Determine the probability that a patient with this diagnosis will live for at least 5 years.

(ii) Determine the probability that a patient with this diagnosis will not live for more than 10 years.

(iii) Determine the probability that a patient with this diagnosis will live between 4 and 8 years.

Solution

(i) First, we calculate the z-score corresponding to the raw x-score of 5:

$$z = \frac{x - \mu}{\sigma} = \frac{5 - 5.7}{1.8} = \frac{-0.7}{1.8} \approx -0.39$$

> z-scores are rounded to 2 decimal places.

Then, we look up $z = -0.39$ in the Standard Normal Distribution table and find the corresponding area to be 0.3483.

$$P(X > 5) = P(Z > -0.39) = 1 - P(Z < -0.39) = 1 - 0.3483 = 0.6517$$

Therefore, the probability that the patient will live for at least 5 years is 0.6517.

(ii) First, we calculate the z-score corresponding to the raw x-score of 10:

$$z = \frac{x - \mu}{\sigma} = \frac{10 - 5.7}{1.8} = \frac{4.3}{1.8} \approx 2.39$$

Then, we look up $z = 2.39$ in the Standard Normal Distribution table and find the corresponding area to be 0.9916.

$$P(X < 10) = P(Z < 2.39) = 0.9916$$

Therefore, the probability that the patient will not live for more than 10 years is 0.9916.

(iii) First, we calculate the z-scores corresponding to the raw x-scores of 4 and 8:

$$z = \frac{x - \mu}{\sigma} = \frac{4 - 5.7}{1.8} = \frac{-1.7}{1.8} \approx -0.94$$

$$z = \frac{x - \mu}{\sigma} = \frac{8 - 5.7}{1.8} = \frac{2.3}{1.8} \approx 1.28$$

Then, we look up $z = -0.94$ and $z = 1.28$ in the Standard Normal Distribution table and find the corresponding areas to be 0.1736 and 0.8997, respectively.

$$P(4 < X < 8) = P(-0.94 < Z < 1.28)$$
$$= P(Z < 1.28) - P(Z < -0.94)$$
$$= 0.8997 - 0.1736 = 0.7261$$

Therefore, the probability that the patient will live between 4 and 8 years is 0.7261.

Converting Z-Scores to Raw X-Scores

If we know the z-score corresponding to a particular data point or percentile, we can compute the raw x-score that corresponds to that z-score by rearranging Formula 7.2-a and solving for x:

$$z = \frac{x - \mu}{\sigma} \qquad \text{Multiplying both sides by } \sigma,$$

$$z \cdot \sigma = x - \mu \qquad \text{Adding } \mu \text{ to both sides and rearranging so } x \text{ is on the left,}$$

$$x = \mu + z \cdot \sigma$$

Formula 7.2-b	**Converting *Z*-Scores to Raw *X*-Scores**

$$x = \mu + z \cdot \sigma$$

Example 7.2-d	**Determining Raw *X*-Scores Given Percentages and Probabilities**

The scores of a certain standardized health-industry aptitude exam are approximately normally-distributed with a mean of 58.4 and a standard deviation of 11.7. Scores are calculated as percentages and rounded to the nearest tenth.

(i)   Determine the scores of the top 1% of applicants.

(ii)   Determine the scores of the bottom 25% of applicants.

(iii) If the top 40% of applicants pass the test, determine the minimum passing score.

Solution

(i)   To determine the scores of the top 1% of applicants, we must first find the *z*-score corresponding to the 99th percentile (since being in the top 1% means being greater than the 99th percentile). Hence, we look up an area of 0.9900 in the body of the positive Standard Normal Distribution table (since 0.9900 > 0.5) and find the closest value to be 0.9901, corresponding with a *z*-score of 2.33.

$$x = \mu + z \cdot \sigma = 58.4 + 2.33(11.7) = 85.661 = 85.7$$

Therefore, the top 1% of applicants have scores of 85.7 or better.

(ii)   To determine the scores of the bottom 25% of applicants, we must first find the *z*-score corresponding to the 25th percentile (since being in the bottom 25% means being less than the 25th percentile). Hence, we look up an area of 0.2500 in the body of the negative Standard Normal Distribution table (since 0.2500 < 0.5) and find the closest value to be 0.2514, corresponding with a *z*-score of –0.67.

$$x = \mu + z \cdot \sigma = 58.4 - 0.67(11.7) = 50.561 = 50.6$$

Therefore, the bottom 25% of applicants have scores of 50.6 or less.

(iii) To determine the scores of the top 40% of applicants, we must first find the *z*-score corresponding to the 60th percentile (since being in the top 40% means being greater than the 60th percentile). Hence, we look up an area of 0.6000 in the body of the positive Standard Normal Distribution table (since 0.6000 > 0.5) and find the closest value to be 0.5987, corresponding with a *z*-score of 0.25.

$$x = \mu + z \cdot \sigma = 58.4 + 0.25(11.7) = 61.325 = 61.4$$

Therefore, applicants need a minimum score of 61.4 to pass the exam.

> We round 61.325 **up** to 61.4 since we are calculating the **minimum** passing score.

7.2 | Exercises

Answers to odd-numbered problems are available at the end of the textbook.

For Problems 1 to 8, calculate the indicated probabilities, assuming that Z is a continuous random variable that follows a standard normal distribution:

1. a. $P(Z < 0.5)$ b. $P(Z > 1.2)$ c. $P(0.9 < Z < 2.7)$

2. a. $P(Z < 1.6)$ b. $P(Z > 0.8)$ c. $P(0.4 < Z < 2.2)$

3. a. $P(Z < -0.75)$ b. $P(Z > -1.64)$ c. $P(-1.28 < Z < -0.93)$

4. a. $P(Z < -1.48)$ b. $P(Z > -0.33)$ c. $P(-2.72 < Z < -1.17)$

5. a. $P(Z < 3.17)$ b. $P(Z > 2.92)$ c. $P(0 < Z < 1.85)$

6. a. $P(Z < -2.61)$ b. $P(Z > -3.03)$ c. $P(-2.23 < Z < 0)$

7.   a. $P(Z < -0.19)$ b. $P(Z > 2.62)$ c. $P(-0.19 < Z < 2.62)$

8.   a. $P(Z < -1.55)$ b. $P(Z > 1.36)$ c. $P(-1.55 < Z < 1.36)$

For Problems 9 to 16, find the z-values corresponding to the given measures of position, assuming that Z is a continuous random variable that follows a standard normal distribution:

9.   a. P_{55} - the 55th percentile   b.   The value that separates the bottom $\frac{1}{4}$ of the data from the top $\frac{3}{4}$

10. a. P_{15} - the 15th percentile   b.   The value that separates the top $\frac{1}{5}$ of the data from the bottom $\frac{4}{5}$

11. a. P_{30} - the 30th percentile   b.   The value that separates the top $\frac{1}{6}$ of the data from the bottom $\frac{5}{6}$

12. a. P_{60} - the 60th percentile   b.   The value that separates the bottom $\frac{1}{3}$ of the data from the top $\frac{2}{3}$

13. a.   The range of values of the bottom 33% of the data
     b.   The range of values of the middle 40% of the data

14. a.   The range of values of the bottom 28% of the data
     b.   The range of values of the middle 20% of the data

15. a.   The range of values of the top 14% of the data
     b.   The range of values of the middle 60% of the data

16. a.   The range of values of the top 9% of the data
     b.   The range of values of the middle 80% of the data

17. The weights of newborn baby girls are normally distributed with a mean of 3.23 kg and a standard deviation of 0.425 kg.
     a.   If a baby girl is born, determine the probability that her birth weight will be:
          (i)   Less than 2.75 kg
          (ii)   Greater than 3.55 kg
          (iii) Between 2.5 and 3.0 kg
     b.   Determine the weights of newborn baby girls that correspond to the:
          (i)   3rd percentile
          (ii)   97th percentile
          (iii) Middle 70% of newborn baby girl weights

18. The weights of newborn baby boys are normally distributed with a mean of 3.35 kg and a standard deviation of 0.463 kg.
     a.   If a baby boy is born, determine the probability that his birth weight will be:
          (i)   Less than 3.25 kg
          (ii)   Greater than 3.95 kg
          (iii) Between 3.0 and 3.5 kg
     b.   Determine the weights of newborn baby boys that correspond to the:
          (i)   2nd percentile
          (ii)   98th percentile
          (iii) Middle 50% of newborn baby boy weights

19. The lengths of newborn baby boys are normally distributed with a mean of 49.8 cm and a standard deviation of 1.96 cm.

   a. If a baby boy is born, determine the probability that his birth length will be:
      (i)   Less than 45 cm
      (ii) Greater than 52 cm
      (iii) Between 50 and 54 cm

   b. Determine the lengths of newborn baby boys that correspond to the:
      (i)   1st percentile
      (ii) 99th percentile
      (iii) Middle 60% of newborn baby boy lengths

20. The lengths of newborn baby girls are normally distributed with a mean of 49.3 cm and a standard deviation of 1.89 cm.

   a. If a baby girl is born, determine the probability that her birth length will be:
      (i)   Less than 50 cm
      (ii) Greater than 53 cm
      (iii) Between 45 and 49 cm

   b. Determine the lengths of newborn baby girls that correspond to the:
      (i)   4th percentile
      (ii) 96th percentile
      (iii) Middle 80% of newborn baby girl lengths

21. The concentration of blood hemoglobin in middle-aged adult males is normally distributed with a mean of 15.1 g/dL and a standard deviation of 0.92 g/dL.

   a. If a middle-aged adult male is randomly selected, determine the probability that his blood hemoglobin concentration will be:
      (i)   Less than 13.5 g/dL
      (ii) Greater than 16 g/dL
      (iii) Between 13.8 and 17.2 g/dL

   b. Determine the hemoglobin levels corresponding to the:
      (i)   5th percentile
      (ii) 95th percentile
      (iii) Middle 95% of middle-aged adult male hemoglobin levels

22. The concentration of blood hemoglobin in middle-aged adult females is normally distributed with a mean of 13.5 g/dL and a standard deviation of 0.86 g/dL.

   a. If a middle-aged adult female is randomly selected, determine the probability that her blood hemoglobin contentration will be:
      (i)   Less than 12 g/dL
      (ii) Greater than 14.5 g/dL
      (iii) Between 12.1 and 15.1 g/dL

   b. Determine the hemoglobin levels corresponding to the:
      (i)   10th percentile
      (ii) 90th percentile
      (iii) Middle 85% of middle-aged adult female hemoglobin levels

23. After surgery to repair a torn rotator cuff, the post-surgical recovery times until patients are released from physiotherapy are normally distributed with a mean of 24.3 weeks and a standard deviation of 2.4 weeks

   a. If a patient undergoing rotator cuff repair surgery is randomly selected, determine the probability that (s)he will have a post-surgical recovery time of:

      (i) Less than 20 weeks

      (ii) Greater than 26 weeks

      (iii) Between 22 and 24 weeks

   b. Determine the recovery time associated with the:

      (i) 15% of patients with the fastest recovery times

      (ii) 4% of patients with the slowest recovery times

      (iii) Middle 98% of post-surgical recovery times

24. After surgery to replace an arthritic hip joint, the short-term recovery times until the patient is able to walk without assistance or pain are normally distributed, with a mean of 34.5 days and a standard deviation of 5.8 days.

   a. If a patient receiving a new hip joint is randomly selected, determine the probability that (s)he will have a short-term recovery time of:

      (i) Less than 3 weeks (i.e., 21 days)

      (ii) Greater than 6 weeks (i.e., 42 days)

      (iii) Between 4 and 5 weeks (i.e., between 28 and 35 days)

   b. Determine the recovery time associated with the:

      (i) 20% of patients with the fastest recovery times

      (ii) 1% of patients with the slowest recovery times

      (iii) Middle 99% of short-term recovery times

25. A children's pain and fever relief medication comes in a liquid suspension with instructions to give 5 mL per dose. A study reveals that when asked to measure out the correct volume of medication, many parents approximate the volume using a spoon used for food instead of a proper measuring device, such as a measuring spoon, dosage cup, or oral syringe. The volume of medication poured in the study was normally distributed with a mean of 6.3 mL with a standard deviation of 1.1 mL.

   a. If a randomly-selected parent estimates one dose of the medication using a food spoon, calculate the probability that the volume of the dose will be:

      (i) Less than 5 mL

      (ii) Greater than 7.5 mL

      (iii) Between 4.75 and 5.25 mL (considered to be a correct dose)

   b. What volume separates the bottom 33% of doses from the top 67% of doses?

26. During a study about the general public's understanding of calorie density of certain foods, a large sample of participants were given the exact same meal, which contained 1,025 kCal. After the patients saw and ate the meal, they were asked to estimate how many calories were in the meal. Responses were normally distributed, with a mean of 788 kCal, and a standard deviation of 159 kCal.

   a. Calculate the probability that a randomly-selected participant will make a guess of:

      (i) Less than 500 kCal

      (ii) Greater than 900 kCal

      (iii) Between 1,000 kCal and 1,050 kCal (considered to be a correct guess)

   b. What calorie level separates the top 18% of responses from the bottom 82% of responses?

27. The lifespan of an artificial knee joint follows a normal distribution with a mean of 26.65 years and a standard deviation of 6.75 years.

   a. Calculate the probability that a randomly-selected patient who received a knee replacement will have their artificial knee fail and need to be replaced in:

   (i) Less than 15 years

   (ii) Greater than 30 years

   (iii) Between 20 and 25 years

   b. At what minimum age should an orthopedic surgeon recommend a knee replacement surgery if the surgeon wants to ensure that there is less than a 10% likelihood the knee will fail before the patient reaches the age of 75?

28. The lifespan of an X-ray tube used as part of an X-ray imaging machine follows a normal distribution with a mean of 6.25 years and a standard deviation of 1.65 years.

   a. Calculate the probability that a randomly-selected X-ray tube will have a lifespan of:

   (i) Less than 5 years

   (ii) Greater than 10 years

   (iii) Between 6 and 8 years

   b. What length warranty should be established on the X-ray tube so that no more than 2.5% of the units will need to be replaced under warranty?

29. Annual salaries of Registered Nurses (R.N.'s) are normally distributed with the middle 95% of nurses earning between $54,800 and $77,340.

   a. What is the mean and standard deviation of the annual salaries for R.N.'s?

   b. What is the probability that a randomly-selected R.N. will earn less than $60,000/year?

   c. What salary separates the top 1% of R.N.'s from the remaining 99% (to the nearest dollar)?

30. Annual salaries of pharmacists are normally distributed with the middle 95% of pharmacists earning between $85,200 and $109,700.

   a. What is the mean and standard deviation of the annual salaries for pharmacists?

   b. What is the probability that a randomly-selected pharmacist will earn more than $100,000/year?

   c. What salary separates the bottom 1% of pharmacists from the remaining 99% (to the nearest dollar)?

31. At the age of 1, the healthy weights of girls are roughly normally distributed. A girl weighing 7.92 kg corresponds to the 15th percentile, while a girl weighing 11.37 kg corresponds to the 97th percentile.

   a. What is the mean and standard deviation of the healthy weight of 1-year-old girls?

   b. What is the probability that a randomly-selected 1-year-old girl will weigh more than 10 kg?

   c. What weight separates the bottom 5% of 1-year-old girls from the remaining 95%?

32. At the age of 2, the normal heights of boys are roughly normally distributed. A boy who is 82 cm corresponds to the 3rd percentile, while a boy who is 91 cm corresponds to the 85th percentile.

   a. What is the mean and standard deviation of the normal height of 1-year-old boys?

   b. What is the probability that a randomly-selected 2-year-old boy will be shorter than 85 cm?

   c. What height separates the top 10% of 2-year-old boys from the remaining 90%?

7.3 | The Normal Approximation to the Binomial Distribution

In Chapter 6, we studied situations that involved the Binomial Distribution, such as the following example:

On a multiple choice quiz of 10 questions, with 5 possible answers for each question, what is the probability of passing the quiz (i.e., answering 5 or more questions correctly) by guessing randomly on all the questions?

We can use the Binomial Formula (Formula 6.2): $P(x) = \binom{n}{x} p^x \cdot q^{(n-x)}$, where $n = 10$, $p = \dfrac{1}{5} = 0.2$

(since there are 5 possible answers for each question), and $q = 1 - 0.2 = 0.8$ to construct the probability distribution for this scenario (probabilities rounded to three decimal places):

x	0	1	2	3	4	5	6	7	8	9	10
P(x)	0.107	0.268	0.302	0.201	0.088	0.026	0.006	0.001	0.000	0.000	0.000

We can compute the probability of passing the quiz (i.e., answering 5 or more questions correctly) as follows:

$$P(X \geq 5) = P(5) + P(6) + P(7) + P(8) + P(9) + P(10)$$

$$\approx 0.026 + 0.006 + 0.001 + 0 + 0 + 0 = 0.033$$

Now consider a similar situation, but it is an exam consisting of 100 questions, all True or False, and you need to answer 60 or more correctly to pass. What is the probability of passing by guessing randomly on all the questions?

This is another binomial experiment, with $n = 100$, $p = \dfrac{1}{2} = 0.5$ (since there are only 2 possible answers for each question) and $q = 1 - 0.5 = 0.5$, and we are looking for $P(X \geq 60)$. However, to compute this, we would need to determine the probability that $X = 60$, $X = 61$, $X = 62$, etc., all the way to $X = 100$ - an incredibly tedious task! What's more, even calculating just one of these values may prove to be difficult, as some calculators cannot handle numbers as large as $\binom{100}{60}$.

However, let's look at what happens when we generate these probabilities using a computer and plot the results:

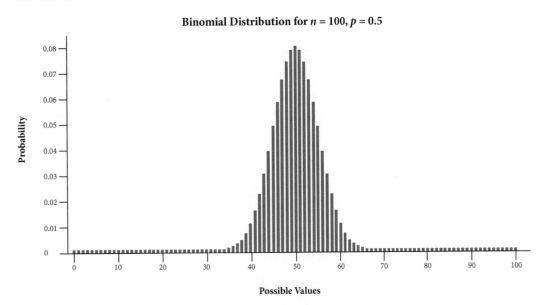

Binomial Distribution for *n* = 100, *p* = 0.5

What can we say about the shape of the resulting graph? It appears to be a normal distribution! In fact, as it turns out, the normal distribution is an excellent approximation to the binomial distribution, so long as the following criteria are met:

1. $n \geq 30$ (for values of $n < 30$, it is still reasonable to use the binomial distribution)

2. $p \geq 0.01$ (for very small values of p, the exponential distribution tends to be a better fit for the binomial distribution with large values of n)

3. $np > 5$ (this ensures that the graph of the distribution is not so right-skewed that the symmetrical nature of the normal curve does not well-approximate it)

4. $nq > 5$, or $n(1 - p) > 5$ (this ensures that the graph of the distribution is not so left-skewed that the symmetrical nature of the normal curve does not well-approximate it)

Notes:

- *While other texts may choose different minimum values for n, we have chosen 30 to be consistent with the Central Limit Theorem (which will be introduced in Chapter 8).*

- *Similarly, some texts suggest that np and nq should both be at least 10 to ensure a good fit. However, we will require that they only both be greater than 5, as this is more common.*

Example 7.3-a	When to Use the Normal Approximation to the Binomial Distribution

Determine in which of the following situations it would be appropriate to use the normal approximation to the binomial distribution:

(i) An experiment is performed 50 times, with all trials being independent and identical, and the probability of success on any given trial is 0.98.

(ii) A professor creates a 15-question multiple-choice quiz, with each question having 4 possible responses: A, B, C, or D. The responses are arranged randomly for each question so that the correct answer has the same probability of being A, B, C, or D for each of the 15 questions, independent of the other questions. The professor then runs a computer simulation to represent a student randomly guessing on all the questions on the quiz.

(iii) An event organizer runs a promotion in which the first 1,000 attendants are given a promotional scratch-ticket, of which 10 are winners. Tickets are given to attendants one-at-a-time as they enter the event and scratched immediately at the gate.

(iv) In a population, approximately 32% of individuals are expected to possess a certain antibody. A sample of 250 patients is collected and each patient is tested to see if they have the antibody.

Solution

(i) No, it is not appropriate to use the normal approximation to the binomial, since
$$n(1 - p) = 50(1 - 0.98) = 50(0.02) = 1 < 5.$$

(ii) No, it is not appropriate to use the normal approximation to the binomial, since $n = 15 < 30$ and $np = 15(0.25) = 3.75 < 5$.

(iii) No, it is not appropriate to use the normal approximation to the binomial, since the probability of success changes as each ticket is scratched, so this cannot be effectively modeled with a binomial distribution.

(iv) Yes, it is appropriate to use the normal approximation to the binomial, since the trials are independent and repeated, the probability of success $p = 0.32 > 0.01$ is sufficiently large and fixed, the sample size $n = 250 \geq 30$ is sufficiently large, and the approximation conditions are met: $np = 250(0.32) = 80 > 5$ and $n(1 - p) = 250(1 - 0.32) = 250(0.68) = 170 > 5$.

Parameters for the Normal Approximation to the Binomial Distribution

The parameters for the normal approximation to the binomial distribution are calculated using the formulas provided in Chapter 6 for the mean, variance, and standard deviation of the binomial distribution:

Expected Value (Mean): $\qquad\qquad E(X) = \mu = np$

Variance: $\qquad\qquad\qquad\quad Var(X) = \sigma^2 = npq = np(1-p)$

Standard Deviation: $\qquad\quad SD(X) = \sigma = \sqrt{npq} = \sqrt{np(1-p)}$

Therefore, if X is a discrete random variable with a binomial distribution, with n trials, probability of success p, and meeting the four conditions above, then X can be approximated with a normal distribution as follows: $X \sim N(np, npq)$.

So, for our 100-question, true-false exam example above, the random variable X can be approximated by the normal distribution as follows:

$$\mu = 100(0.5) = 50$$

$$\sigma^2 = 100(0.5)(0.5) = 25$$

$$\sigma = \sqrt{25} = 5$$

Therefore, $X \sim N(50, 5^2)$.

Example 7.3-b	How to Use the Normal Approximation to the Binomial Distribution

In each of the following examples, state the parameters needed to use the normal approximation to the binomial distribution (the approximation conditions are met in each of the examples, so you do not need to verify this). Round all values to 3 significant digits as needed.

(i) Over the course of a year, 132 patients undergo treatment for a certain disease that has a 65% probability of success.

(ii) In a pilot study for a new drug, 24% of patients experienced side effects. In the clinical trial for the drug, 500 patients receive the drug and the probability that patients will experience side effects is assumed to be the same as the pilot study.

(iii) In Canada, approximately 7% of the population are "universal donors" - i.e., they have type O-negative blood. A sample of 260 donors come in to give blood and their blood types are checked to see if they are universal donors.

Solution

(i) $n = 132$ and $p = 0.65$

- The mean is $\mu = 132(0.65) = 85.8$
- The variance is $\sigma^2 = 132(0.65)(1 - 0.65) \approx 30.0$
- Hence, the standard deviation is $\sigma = \sqrt{30.0} \approx 5.48$

Therefore, $X \sim N(85.8, 5.48^2)$

(ii) $n = 500$ and $p = 0.24$

- The mean is $\mu = 500(0.24) = 120$
- The variance is $\sigma^2 = 500(0.24)(1 - 0.24) = 91.2$
- Hence, the standard deviation is $\sigma = \sqrt{91.2} \approx 9.55$

Therefore, $X \sim N(120, 9.55^2)$

(iii) $n = 260$ and $p = 0.07$

- The mean is $\mu = 260(0.07) = 18.2$
- The variance is $\sigma^2 = 260(0.07)(1 - 0.07) \approx 16.9$
- Hence, the standard deviation is $\sigma = \sqrt{16.9} \approx 4.11$

Therefore, $X \sim N(18.2, 4.11^2)$

Correcting for Continuity

When we approximate the distribution of a discrete random variable with the distribution of a continuous random variable, there is a small error that occurs. This is because, unlike with a discrete variable, the probability that a continuous random variable will be *exactly* equal to a certain value in its domain is 0. As such, calculating the probability that a discrete random variable will be **at least** 60 (i.e., 60 or more), for example, is different than calculating the probability that it will be strictly **greater than** 60 (i.e., 61 or more); however, for a continuous random variable, at least 60 and greater than 60 mean the same thing. As such, the probability of "at least 60" in a continuous distribution like the normal distribution is not really the same thing as the probability of "at least 60" in a discrete distribution like the binomial distribution.

In order to understand how to correct for this error, it helps to think of rounding. When we round numbers, we are essentially converting a continuous variable to a discrete variable. If we want to use a continuous variable to approximate all numbers that are "at least 60" for the discrete variable, we need all numbers for the continuous variable that **round to at least 60** - i.e., all numbers greater than 59.5. Similarly, if we wanted "at most 60" (i.e., 60 or less) for the discrete variable, we would need all numbers less than 60.5 for the continuous variable.

Therefore, the correction made for using a continuous random variable to approximate a discrete random variable, called the **correction for continuity**, can be summarized as follows:

- If the value for the discrete variable is at the lower end of an interval of values (e.g., at least 12), use a half-value **below** for the continuous variable (e.g., at least 11.5).

- If the value for the discrete variable is at the upper end of an interval of values (e.g., at most 18), use a half-value **above** for the continuous variable (e.g., at most 18.5).

For example, to approximate the probability $P(12 \leq X \leq 18)$ in a binomial distribution, we would need to use $P(11.5 < X < 18.5)$ for the normal distribution.

Going back to our true-false exam example from above, to calculate the probability that a student would pass (i.e., 60 or more correct answers) by guessing randomly on the exam, we use a normal approximation to the binomial distribution, with the mean and standard deviation from above (50 and 5, respectively), and find $P(X > 59.5)$.

Finally, we convert the raw x-score of 59.5 to a z-score and use the Standard Normal Distribution table to calculate the approximate probability:

$$P(X > 59.5) = P\left(Z > \frac{59.5 - 50}{5}\right) = P(Z > 1.90) = 1 - P(Z < 1.90) = 1 - 0.9713 = 0.0287$$

Using the binomial formula (and a computer to help speed up the calculations), we can compute the actual probability to be 0.0284, which is off by less than one-thousandth. This example demonstrates that the normal approximation to the binomial is highly accurate and significantly more efficient than calculating the exact probability by repeatedly using the binomial formula.

Example 7.3-c	Calculating Probabilities using the Normal Approximation to the Binomial

The following examples are based on the scenarios from Example 7.3-b above. Refer to the solutions above for more information:

(i) Over the course of a year, 132 patients undergo treatment for a certain disease that has a 65% probability of success. What is the probability that at least 90 patients will have the disease successfully cured by the treatment?

(ii) In a pilot study for a new drug, 24% of patients experienced side effects. In the clinical trial for the drug, 500 patients receive the drug and the probability that patients will experience side effects is assumed to be the same as the pilot study. What is the probability that at most 100 patients in the clinical trial will experience side effects as a result of taking the drug?

(iii) In Canada, approximately 7% of the population are "universal donors" - i.e., they have type O-negative blood. A sample of 260 donors come in to give blood and their blood types are checked to see if they are universal donors. What is the probability that between 15 and 20 donors will have type O-negative blood?

Solution

(i) We wish to determine $P(X \geq 90)$. Using the normal approximation to the binomial from Example 7.3-b(i) above, $X \sim N(85.8, 5.48^2)$, and with the continuity correction, we wish to determine $P(X > 89.5)$, since 90 is at the lower-end of the range of values.

First, we calculate the z-score corresponding to the raw x-score of 89.5:

$$z = \frac{x - \mu}{\sigma} = \frac{89.5 - 85.8}{5.48} = \frac{3.7}{5.48} \approx 0.68$$

Then, we look up $z = 0.68$ in the Standard Normal Distribution table and find the corresponding area to be 0.7517.

$$P(X > 89.5) = P(Z > 0.68) = 1 - P(Z < 0.68) = 1 - 0.7517 = 0.2483$$

Therefore, the probability that at least 90 patients will have the disease successfully cured is approximately 0.2483.

(ii) We wish to determine $P(X \leq 100)$. Using the normal approximation to the binomial from Example 7.3-b(ii) above, $X \sim N(120, 9.55^2)$, and with the continuity correction, we wish to determine $P(X < 100.5)$, since 100 is at the upper-end of the range of values.

First, we calculate the z-score corresponding to the raw x-score of 100.5:

$$z = \frac{x - \mu}{\sigma} = \frac{100.5 - 120}{9.55} = \frac{-19.5}{9.55} \approx -2.04$$

Then, we look up $z = -2.04$ in the Standard Normal Distribution table and find the corresponding area to be 0.0207.

$$P(X < 100.5) = P(Z < -2.04) = 0.0207$$

Therefore, the probability that at most 100 patients will experience side effects is approximately 0.0207.

Solution
continued

(iii) We wish to determine $P(15 \leq X \leq 20)$. Using the normal approximation to the binomial from Example 7.3-b(iii) above, $X \sim N(18.2, 4.11^2)$, and with the continuity correction, we wish to determine $P(14.5 < X < 20.5)$, since 15 is at the lower-end of the range of values and 20 is at the upper-end.

First, we calculate the z-scores corresponding to the raw x-scores of 14.5 and 20.5:

$$z = \frac{x - \mu}{\sigma} = \frac{14.5 - 18.2}{4.11} = \frac{-3.7}{4.11} \approx -0.90$$

$$z = \frac{x - \mu}{\sigma} = \frac{20.5 - 18.2}{4.11} = \frac{2.3}{4.11} \approx 0.56$$

Then, we look up $z = -0.90$ and $z = 0.56$ in the Standard Normal Distribution table and find the corresponding areas to be 0.1841 and 0.7123, respectively.

$$P(14.5 < X < 20.5) = P(-0.90 < Z < 0.56)$$
$$= P(Z < 0.56) - P(Z < -0.90)$$
$$= 0.7123 - 0.1841 = 0.5282$$

Therefore, the probability that between 15 and 20 donors will have type O-negative blood (and are therefore considered to be "universal donors") is approximately 0.5282.

7.3 | Exercises

Answers to odd-numbered problems are available at the end of the textbook.

For Problems 1 to 12, if it is appropriate to do so, use the normal approximation to the binomial to calculate the indicated probabilities.

1. $n = 100, p = 0.25, P(X \geq 30)$

2. $n = 60, p = 0.40, P(X \leq 15)$

3. $n = 250, p = 0.01, P(X \geq 5)$

4. $n = 200, p = 0.98, P(X \leq 195)$

5. $n = 50, p = 0.60, P(25 \leq X \leq 35)$

6. $n = 80, p = 0.75, P(50 \leq X \leq 70)$

7. $n = 125, p = 0.20, P(X < 20)$

8. $n = 150, p = 0.30, P(X > 50)$

9. $n = 400, p = 0.99, P(390 \leq X \leq 400)$

10. $n = 300, p = 0.95, P(280 < X < 290)$

11. $n = 75, p = \dfrac{1}{6}, P(10 < X < 15)$

12. $n = 45, p = \dfrac{1}{12}, P(5 \leq X \leq 10)$

For Problems 13 to 28, use the normal approximation to the binomial to calculate the indicated probabilities, or explain why it is not appropriate to use the normal approximation to the binomial.

13. Out of all the calls a paramedic responds to, approximately 1 out of every 3 requires emergency transportation to the nearest hospital. In a given 24-hour shift, a paramedic responds to 18 calls. What is the probability that at least half of those require emergency transportation to the nearest hospital?

14. A blood test for a certain autoimmune disease has a false-positive rate of approximately 3%. A sample of 125 patients who do not have the disease are tested for the disease using the blood test. What is the probability that at least five of them will test positive for the disease?

15. Approximately 15% of the population has Rh– blood. Mothers who have Rh– blood are typically given a "Rho(D) immune globulin" injection to prevent complications that can arise from giving birth to a baby with an Rh+ blood type. Out of the 48 patients currently in the maternity ward, what is the probability that at least a quarter of them will require the injection?

16. A certain doctor's office has a tendency to make people wait longer than usual. In fact, 65% of all patients of this doctor have to wait in the waiting rooms for more than 30 minutes beyond their scheduled appointment time. If the office has 36 patients scheduled for that day, what is the probability that less than half of the patients that day have to wait for more than 30 minutes?

17. A college student is writing a multiple choice test with 30 questions, where each question has 4 possible answers to select from. If the student guesses on every one, what is the probability that (s)he will pass the test with a 50% or better?

18. The evaluation at the end of a professional development training module is a test consisting of 25 true/false questions, which requires a grade of 80% or better to pass. What is the probability of passing the test by guessing on all the questions?

19. An oncologist knows the success rate for a certain cancer treatment (defined as causing the cancer to go into remission) is approximately 85%. If the oncologist treats 96 patients with this treatment over the course of the year, what is the probability that less than 10 will not have a successful result from the treatment?

20. Approximately 42.5% of the pets registered at a certain veterinary clinic are cats. If the vet has 15 appointments scheduled for today, what is the probability that at least half are cats?

21. Approximately 1 in every 7 adults is infected with Herpes Simplex type 2 virus. If 100 adults are randomly selected and tested for the disease, what is the probability that between 15 and 20 (inclusive) of those adults tested are infected with the disease?

22. 1 in every 3 seniors taking 4 or more prescription drugs is at risk of an adverse reaction between the medications they are taking. If 35 seniors who take 4 or more prescription drugs every day are randomly selected, what is the probability that between 10 and 15 of them (inclusive) are taking combinations of prescription drugs that can cause an adverse reaction?

23. If an obstetrician delivers 12 babies today, what is the probability of delivering more boys than girls?

24. The probability of a baby being born with Trisomy 21 (i.e., Down syndrome) to a woman who is over 45 years old is approximately 3%. If 500 babies are born to mothers over the age of 45, what is the probability that less than 10 of them are born with Trisomy 21?

25. The defective rate of a pharmaceutical pain-relief tablet is approximately 1.2%. If 1,800 tablets are produced and inspected, what is the probability that at least 30 tablets (i.e., the amount packaged in one container of tablets) will be deemed defective and discarded?

26. The rejection rate for a transplanted organ within the first 12 months of the patient receiving the new organ is approximately 7.5%. If 250 patients receive new organs at a hospital this year, what is the probability that at most 15 of them will lose the organ due to their body rejecting it?

27. An athletic therapist knows that only 1 in 5 patients actually do their exercises at home between sessions. If she has 35 patients booked with appointments that day, what is the probability that more than 10 of them did their exercises at home since their last session?

28. A public health nurse knows that only 1 in 12 individuals who come in to be tested for STI's will receive a positive test result. If 156 patients are seen by the nurse over the course of a month, what is the probability that less than 12 of them will have a positive test result?

7 | Review Exercises

Answers to odd-numbered problems are available at the end of the textbook.

For Problems 1 to 16, analyze the probability scenarios and complete the following:

(i) Calculate the indicated probabilities (to 3 significant digits).

(ii) Determine the mean and standard deviation of the distribution (to 3 significant digits).

1. $P(X < 13.5)$, given that X has a uniform probability distribution, and $10 < X < 15$

2. $P(X < \frac{1}{4})$, given that X has a uniform probability distribution, and $0 < X < 1$

3. $P(X > \frac{4}{15})$, given that X has a uniform probability distribution, and $0 < X < 1$

4. $P(X > 2.6)$, given that X has a uniform probability distribution, and $1 < X < 5$

5. $P(32 < X < 48)$, given that X has a uniform probability distribution, and $30 < X < 50$

6. $P(17.5 < X < 24.8)$, given that X has a uniform probability distribution, and $10.2 < X < 42.8$

7. $P(\frac{3}{8} < X < \frac{4}{5})$, given that X has a uniform probability distribution, and $0 < X < 1$

8. $P(1\frac{3}{4} < X < 3\frac{1}{2})$, given that X has a uniform probability distribution, and $\frac{1}{2} < X < 5\frac{1}{4}$

9. $P(X < 0.5)$, given that X has an exponential probability distribution with $\lambda = 1.5$

10. $P(X < 3.2)$, given that X has an exponential probability distribution with $\lambda = 0.75$

11. $P(X > 18.4)$, given that X has an exponential probability distribution with $\lambda = 0.02$

12. $P(X > 1.2)$, given that X has an exponential probability distribution with $\lambda = 4.8$

13. $P(0.7 < X < 2.1)$, given that X has an exponential probability distribution with $\lambda = 1.8$

14. $P(10.25 < X < 15.50)$, given that X has an exponential probability distribution with $\lambda = 0.05$

15. $P(2\frac{3}{4} < X < 6\frac{1}{8})$, given that X has an exponential probability distribution with $\lambda = \frac{2}{5}$

16. $P(\frac{1}{6} < X < \frac{5}{12})$, given that X has an exponential probability distribution with $\lambda = 1\frac{1}{8}$

For Problems 17 to 24, determine which continuous probability distribution is appropriate to use - uniform or exponential - and then answer the questions using the properties of that distribution.

17. The average blood donor takes about 20 minutes to give 1 unit of blood. A registered nurse walks over to a donor who is in the middle of giving blood, not knowing how far along the blood donation process is. What is the probability that the process will be finished in the next 5 minutes? How long would the nurse expect the remainder of the blood donation to take?

18. A patient receives 500 mL of NS (normal saline) solution over the course of 4 hours. If a nurse walks in to check on the patient, not knowing how much time is left in the infusion, what is the probability that there is less than 100 mL remaining? What volume of NS solution would the nurse expect the bag to contain?

19. A registered nurse working at a telephone health-care referral service receives 12 calls from patients every hour. On average, what is the expected length of time between two calls received by this nurse? What is the probability that the length of time between the next two patients calling will be more than 8 minutes?

20. A nurse working the day shift receives an average of 20 calls from patients during the course of a 12-hour shift. If the nurse just responded to a call from a patient, what is the probability that she will have between a 30 minute and 45 minute break before the next call? How long of a break would she expect to have before she received the next call?

21. A home care nurse is scheduled to arrive to visit a patient sometime between the hours of 9:00 AM to 4:30 PM. If the patient plans to go out to do some errands from 1:00 PM to 2:30 PM, what is the probability that the nurse will arrive during that period of time? When should the patient expect the nurse to arrive?

22. An I.V. line with replacement fluids is set to run continuously and at a consistent rate over the course of 9 hours, at which point the empty I.V. bag is removed and replaced with a full bag and the infusion is repeated. A shift change occurs at 8:00 PM, and it typically takes the new nurse about 45 minutes before he/she will have a chance to check in on the patient. What is the probability the bag will need to be changed within the first 45 minutes after the shift change? At what time would the nurse expect that the bag would need to be changed?

23. A pharmacy typically fills 80 prescriptions over the course of the 8-hour shift.

    a. Determine how long, on average, the pharmacist would expect between patients filling prescriptions.

    b. What is the probability the next 2 patients will come less than 5 minutes apart?

    c. What is the probability the next 4 patients will all arrive less than 5 minutes apart from the previous patient?

24. A trauma surgeon can typically perform approximately 6 surgeries in an 8-hour day.

    a. If the surgeon just starts one surgery, how much time would he expect to be able to complete this current surgery before he is called upon for his next one?

    b. What is the probability that the next 2 surgeries will come less than an hour apart?

    c. What is the probability that the next 3 surgeries will all come less than an hour apart?

For Problems 25 and 26, calculate the indicated probabilities, assuming that Z is a continuous random variable that follows a standard normal distribution:

25.
   a. $P(Z < 1.65)$
   b. $P(Z < -2.28)$
   c. $P(Z > -1.42)$
   d. $P(Z > 2.15)$
   e. $P(0 < Z < 1)$
   f. $P(-0.2 < Z < 0)$
   g. $P(0.97 < Z < 2.50)$
   h. $P(-1.88 < Z < -1.38)$
   i. $P(-1.11 < Z < 2.31)$

26.
   a. $P(Z < 0.95)$
   b. $P(Z < -1.05)$
   c. $P(Z > -1.73)$
   d. $P(Z > 2.08)$
   e. $P(0 < Z < 3)$
   f. $P(-1.3 < Z < 0)$
   g. $P(2.12 < Z < 2.87)$
   h. $P(-1.54 < Z < -0.54)$
   i. $P(-0.09 < Z < 1.23)$

For Problems 27 and 28, find the z-values corresponding to the given measures of position, assuming that Z is a continuous random variable that follows a standard normal distribution:

27.
   a. P_{88} (the 88th percentile)
   b. The value that separates the bottom $\dfrac{3}{8}$ of the data from the top $\dfrac{5}{8}$
   c. The range of values of the bottom 15% of the data
   d. The range of values of the top 28% of the data
   e. The range of values of the middle 62% of the data

28.
   a. P_{45} (the 45th percentile)
   b. The value that separates the bottom $\dfrac{2}{3}$ of the data from the top $\dfrac{1}{3}$
   c. The range of values of the bottom 8% of the data
   d. The range of values of the top 5% of the data
   e. The range of values of the middle 34% of the data

29. For females aged 18-24, systolic blood pressures (in mmHg) are normally distributed with a mean of 114.8 and a standard deviation of 13.1.
   a. If a woman between the ages of 18-24 is randomly selected, calculate the probability that her systolic blood pressure will be:
      (i) Less than 105 mmHg
      (ii) Greater than 120 mmHg
      (iii) Between 118 and 132 mmHg
   b. Determine the systolic blood pressure(s) corresponding to the:
      (i) 90th percentile
      (ii) Middle 70% of all women aged 18-24

30. For males aged 18-24, systolic blood pressures (in mmHg) are normally distributed with a mean of 106.8 and a standard deviation of 12.5.
   a. If a man between the ages of 18-24 is randomly selected, calculate the probability that his systolic blood pressure will be:
      (i) Less than 100 mmHg
      (ii) Greater than 132 mmHg
      (iii) Between 95 and 105 mmHg
   b. Determine the systolic blood pressure(s) corresponding to the:
      (i) 22nd percentile
      (ii) middle 36% of all men aged 18-24

31. The recent average starting salaries for an entry-level registered nurse (RN) appear to be normally distributed with a mean of $52,500 and a standard deviation of $4,500.
   a. What is the probability of an entry-level RN receiving a salary less than $47,250?
   b. What is the probability of an entry-level RN receiving a salary more than $55,000?
   c. What is the probability of an entry-level RN receiving a salary between $50,000 and $55,000?

32. Human pregnancies of healthy singleton fetuses (i.e., excluding pregnancies with early-term complications or miscarriages, and multiple births) are normally distributed with a mean of 266 days and a standard deviation of 13 days.
   a. What is the probability that a baby is born between 250 and 275 days?
   b. If we stipulate that a baby is premature when born at least 3 weeks early, what is the probability a randomly selected baby is premature?
   c. If we stipulate that a baby is overdue when born more than 2 weeks after the expected date, what is the probability a randomly selected baby is overdue?

33. For a set of cholesterol measurements, the mean was found to be 180mg/100mL with a standard deviation of 3.5mg/100mL. Assuming the measurements follow a normal distribution, determine the following values:
   a. In a group of 265 patients, how many of their measurements could be expected to be less than 187mg/100mL?
   b. Above what value would measurements be considered to fall within the highest 10% of cholesterol levels?

34. The time needed to complete a midterm examination in a statistics course is normally distributed with a mean of 75 minutes and a standard deviation of 10 minutes.

    a. Assume that the class has 120 students and that the examination period is 90 minutes in length. How many students do you expect will be unable to complete the exam in the allotted time?

    b. What time separates the fastest 20% of students (i.e., those who finish the exam the earliest) from the remaining students?

35. The average annual MRI technologist salary is normally distributed. The lowest 10% of MRI technologist salaries are less than $56,280. The top 10% of MRI technologist salaries reach more than $83,340. *(Round all answers to the nearest ten dollars - i.e., four significant digits)*

    a. What is the mean and standard deviation of the annual salaries for MRI technologists?

    b. What is the probability that a randomly selected MRI technologists will earn more than $75,000?

    c. What salary separates the bottom 1% of MRI technologists salaries from the remaining 99%?

36. The average annual starting salary for students graduating from a particular health program is normally distributed. A starting salary of $30,430 corresponds to the 5th percentile, while a starting salary of $54,710 corresponds to the 95th percentile. *(Round all answers to the nearest ten dollars - i.e., four significant digits)*

    a. What is the mean and standard deviation of the annual starting salaries?

    b. What is the probability that a randomly selected new graduate from the program will earn a starting salary of less than $28,000?

    c. What salary separates the top 0.5% of annual starting salaries from the remaining 99%?

For Problems 37 to 46, if it is appropriate to do so, use the normal approximation to the binomial to calculate the indicated probabilities.

37. $n = 180$, $p = 0.35$, $P(X \geq 50)$

38. $n = 300$, $p = 0.01$, $P(X \geq 20)$

39. $n = 40$, $p = 0.95$, $P(X \leq 18)$

40. $n = 120$, $p = 0.15$, $P(X \leq 25)$

41. $n = 225$, $p = 0.25$, $P(40 < X < 70)$

42. $n = 70$, $p = 0.85$, $P(49 < X < 56)$

43. $n = 30$, $p = \dfrac{2}{3}$, $P(15 \leq X \leq 25)$

44. $n = 60$, $p = \dfrac{14}{15}$, $P(50 \leq X \leq 55)$

45. $n = 200$, $p = \dfrac{1}{50}$, $P(5 \leq X \leq 10)$

46. $n = 100$, $p = \dfrac{9}{25}$, $P(30 \leq X \leq 40)$

For Problems 47 to 54, use the normal approximation to the binomial to calculate the indicated probabilities, or explain why it is not appropriate to use the normal approximation to the binomial.

47. 1 in every 3 seniors have difficulty remembering whether they have taken their daily prescription drugs. If 36 seniors who need to take prescription drugs daily are randomly selected, what is the probability that between 6 and 12 (inclusive) of those patients have difficulty remembering to take their prescriptions?

48. A certain brand of pregnancy test has a false-positive rate of approximately 5%. A sample of 120 women who are not pregnant are tested using this brand of pregnancy test. What is the probability that between 6 and 9 (inclusive) of them will test positive for pregnancy?

49. A professor knows from past experience that only approximately 30% of her students actually do their readings and exercises at home before the next class. If she has 32 students, what is the probability that less than half of the class will have done their readings and exercises before the next class?

50. A college student is writing a multiple-choice test with 20 questions, where each question has 5 possible answers to select from. If the student guesses on all the questions, what is the probability that he/she will pass the test with a 50% or better?

51. If an obstetrician delivers 48 babies this month, what is the probability of delivering more girls than boys?

52. Out of all the 911 calls received, approximately 2 out of 3 require police involvement. In a given 24-hour shift, the 911 call center received 60 calls. What is the probability that at least three-quarters of them will involve the police?

53. A manufacturer of I.V. tubes claims that only 1.5% of their products are defective. The manufacturer recently sold I.V. tubes in batches of 250 to a large local hospital. What is the probability that at most 5 of the I.V. tubes are defective in a batch?

54. An oncologist knows that the success rate for a certain cancer treatment is approximately 83%. If the oncologist treats 72 patients with this treatment over the course of 6 months, what is the probability that less than 10 will **not** have a successful result from the treatment?

Round all probabilities to 3 significant digits, unless otherwise specified.

1. A patient receives 1,000 mL of D5NS (Dextrose 5% Normal Saline) solution over the course of 8 hours. If a nurse walks in to check on the patient, not knowing how much time is left in the infusion, what is the probability that there is less than 600 mL remaining? What volume of solution would the nurse expect the bag to contain?

2. A health care product is scheduled to be delivered some time between the hours of 1:00 PM to 6:00 PM. If the purchaser needs to go out between 2:30 PM to 3:00 PM, what is the probability that the delivery will arrive during that period of time? When should the purchaser expect the delivery to arrive?

3. A nurse working the night shift receives an average of 18 calls from patients during the course of the 12-hour shift. If the nurse just responded to a call from a patient, what is the probability that she will have between a 45 minute and 60 minute break before the next call? How long of a break would she expect to have before she received the next call?

4. An obstetrician typically delivers approximately 8 babies in a 24-hour day at a large hospital.

   a. If the obstetrician just starts to deliver one baby, how much time would she expect to be able to complete this current delivery before she is called upon for her next delivery?

   b. What is the probability that the next 2 babies will come less than an hour apart?

   c. What is the probability that the next 4 babies will all be delivered within an hour of the previous baby being delivered?

5. In a study of recovery from common colds, recovery time follows a normal distribution with a mean recovery time of 120 hours and a standard deviation of 18 hours. If a person has suffered from a common cold, calculate the probability that the recovery time will be:

   a. Less than 90 hours

   b. Greater than 130 hours

   c. Between 4 and 6 days

6. The distribution of healthy blood-glucose measurements is found to be normally distributed with a mean of 90mg/100mL and a standard deviation of 12.5mg/100mL. Determine the blood-glucose measurement (rounded to the nearest mg/100 mL) that corresponds to the:

   a. 24th percentile

   b. Middle 80% of all glucose measurements

7. Human pregnancies of healthy singleton fetuses are normally distributed with a mean of 266 days and a standard deviation of 13 days.

   a. What percent of probabilities will fall within 1 week of the due date on either side of the mean?

   b. Assuming the longest 5.5% of pregnancies are considered dangerous and require labour to be medically induced, determine the length (in days) of a pregnancy that a physician will require to be medically induced for health and safety reasons.

8. Replacement times for volumetric pumps are normally distributed with a mean of 5.2 years and a standard deviation of 1.1 years. If you want to provide a warranty so that only 5% of the volumetric pumps will be replaced before the warranty expires, what length of time would you recommend for the warranty?

9. The scores on a recent Statistics for Health Science test were normally distributed with a mean score of 72 and a standard deviation of 8.

   a. In a class of 40 students, how many of them would be expected to score less than 60?

   b. A competitive nursing program only accepts students in the top 1.5% of this class. What is the minimum test score a candidate needs to achieve to be considered for admission to the program?

10. The average annual occupational therapist salary is normally distributed. The lowest 15% of occupational therapist salaries are less than $59,800. The top 10% of occupational therapist salaries reach more than $76,620.

   a. What is the mean and standard deviation of the annual salaries for an occupational therapist?

   b. What is probability that a randomly selected occupational therapist will earn less than $55,000?

   c. What salary separates the top 3% of occupational therapists from the remaining 97%?

11. A public health nurse knows that only 1 in 15 individuals who come in to be tested for Hepatitis C will receive a positive test result. If 120 patients are seen by the nurse over the course of a month, what is the probability that at most 15 of them will have a positive result?

12. Approximately 40% of the patients who visit a walk-in clinic are children under the age of 10. If the clinic has 30 appointments scheduled for today, what is the probability that more than a third of them are children under the age of 10?

13. A certain doctor's office is known for the long waiting time; 70% of all patients have to wait at least an hour beyond their scheduled appointment time. If the office has 45 patients scheduled for today, what is the probability that less than half of the patients do not have to wait such a long time?

14. According to a recent study, 30% of large corporations offer maternity leave top-up payments. In a random sample of 125 large corporations, what is the probability that between 35 and 45 (inclusive) corporations offer such top-up payments?

15. A college student is writing a test that contains 30 true/false questions, which requires a grade of 70% or better to pass. What is the probability of passing this test by guessing on all the questions?

7 | Summary of Notation and Formulas

NOTATION

$X \sim N(\mu, \sigma^2)$ = X is a continuous random variable that follows a normal distribution with mean μ and variance σ^2.

$Z \sim N(0, 1)$ = Z is a continuous random variable that follows a standard normal distribution (with mean 0 and variance 1).

FORMULAS

Continuous Uniform Distribution | 7.1-a: $P(c < X < d) = (d - c) \cdot \dfrac{1}{(b - a)} = \dfrac{(d - c)}{(b - a)}$

The probability that a continuous random variable will take on a value between c and d, in which every value in range a to b has the same likelihood of being selected.

Expected Value (Mean): $E(X) = \mu = \dfrac{a + b}{2}$

Variance: $Var(X) = \sigma^2 = \dfrac{(b - a)^2}{12}$

Standard Deviation: $SD(X) = \sigma = \sqrt{\dfrac{(b - a)^2}{12}} = \dfrac{(b - a)}{\sqrt{12}}$

Exponential Distribution | 7.1-b: $P(X < t) = 1 - e^{-\lambda t}$ $P(X > t) = e^{-\lambda t}$ $P(t_1 < X < t_2) = e^{-\lambda t_1} - e^{-\lambda t_2}$

The probability that it will take less than time t , greater than time t, or between times t_1 and t_2 , respectively, for a "success" to occur after a previous success, where λ is the average number of successes in a fixed interval of time.

Expected Value (Mean): $E(X) = \mu = \dfrac{1}{\lambda}$

Variance: $Var(X) = \sigma^2 = \dfrac{1}{\lambda^2}$

Standard Deviation: $SD(X) = \sigma = \sqrt{\dfrac{1}{\lambda^2}} = \dfrac{1}{\lambda}$

Converting Raw X-Scores to Z-Scores | 7.2-a

$z = \dfrac{x - \mu}{\sigma}$

Converting Z-Scores to Raw X-Scores | 7.2-b

$x = \mu + z \cdot \sigma$

Table of Areas under the Standard Normal Distribution below Negative z-scores | Table 7.2-a

see Appendix I-a on page 402

Table of Areas under the Standard Normal Distribution below Positive z-scores | Table 7.2-b

see Appendix I-b on page 403

8

SAMPLING DISTRIBUTIONS AND THE CENTRAL LIMIT THEOREM

LEARNING OBJECTIVES

- Identify the characteristics of the sampling distributions of the sample means, sample proportions, and sample correlation coefficients for a random variable.
- Distinguish between the individual data values in a population distribution of a random variable and the grouped data values in a sampling distribution for that random variable.
- State the central limit theorem and use it to calculate the mean and standard error of the sampling distribution of sample means for a random variable.
- Define sampling error and standard errors and compute the standard error of the mean.
- Compute probabilities and predict ranges of values for the $\overline{X}$-distribution.
- Apply the finite population correction factor to correct the standard error of the mean.
- Compute the mean and standard error for the sampling distribution of sample proportions.
- Use the normal distribution to approximate the $\hat{p}$-distribution and predict a range of values for the $\hat{p}$-distribution.

CHAPTER OUTLINE

8.1 Population vs Sampling Distributions

8.2 Sampling Distribution of Sample Means

8.3 Sampling Distributions of Sample Proportions

Introduction

In the previous two chapters, we examined scenarios where we sampled individual values from the population and examined the probability that the results would be certain values or in a certain range of values. However, often we are less interested in individual data from within the population, as we are in grouped data from within the population, such as sample means or sample proportions.

For example, when travelling on vacation and trying to determine a hotel in which to stay, you would be less concerned with what one individual reviewer thought about the hotel as you would with what a group of reviewers thought about the hotel, such as the average rating the hotel received from a large group of reviewers, or the proportion of reviewers who would recommend the hotel.

In this chapter, we examine probability distributions for groups of values of a certain size randomly chosen from the population, rather than for individual values.

8.1 | Population vs Sampling Distributions

For a given sample size n, the distribution of values for the sample statistic for all possible random samples of size n drawn from the population is called a **sampling distribution**. For example:

- The **Sampling Distribution of Sample Means** is a distribution of the sample means of all samples of a particular sample size n.

- The **Sampling Distribution of Sample Proportions** is a distribution of the proportion of "successful" outcomes in a random sample of n repetitions of a binomial experiment.

The main difference between a population distribution and a sampling distribution is summarized in the following table:

Table 8.1   **Population vs Sampling Distributions**

	Population Distribution	Sampling Distribution
What is being sampled?	Individual elements drawn randomly from the population	Samples of a fixed size n, drawn randomly from the population
What data is being recorded?	Individual values of each of the elements drawn	Statistics from each of the samples drawn
What is the shape of the distribution (i.e., what does the distribution look like)?	Could be anything, based on all the possible individual outcomes of the population	As the sample size increases, the sampling distribution tends to approach a "nice" shape (e.g., a normal distribution curve)

Another way to understand the difference between the two kinds of distributions is with the following diagram:

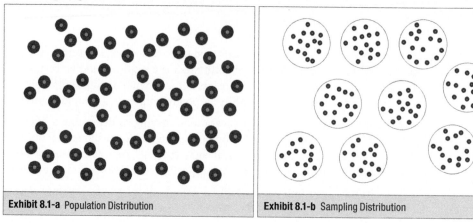

Exhibit 8.1-a Population Distribution

Exhibit 8.1-b Sampling Distribution

| Example 8.1 | **Constructing Sampling Distributions** |

A university researcher is collecting some information about the success of graduates from a particular program at the university. For each of the following desired pieces of information, a) discuss the nature of an individual value sampled from the population distribution for the data, and b) discuss the nature of a "group" value sampled from the sampling distribution for the data:

(i) The annual income of graduates from the program in the last five years.

(ii) The employment rate of graduates from the program in the last five years, in their vocational field, within six months of graduating from the program.

(iii) The relationship between the graduating average of the graduates from the program in the last five years and the starting annual income when they began their employment.

Solution

(i) A value from the population distribution is the annual income of an *individual* who graduated from the program in the last five years. It is continuous, quantitative data at the ratio level of measurement.

A value from the sampling distribution is the average annual income of a *group* of individuals sampled from those who graduated from the program in the last five years. It is continuous, quantitative data at the ratio level of measurement.

(ii) Data from the population distribution will have "Yes" or "No" values, based on whether or not an individual was employed in his/her vocational field within six months of graduating from the program. It is qualitative data at the nominal level of measurement.

A value from the sampling distribution is the proportion of graduates from each sample who were employed in their vocational fields within six months of graduating. It is continuous, quantitative data at the ratio level of measurement.

(iii) Individual data sampled from the population distribution will have two values for each graduate of the program in the last five years: the individual's graduating average and his/her starting annual income in his/her career. It is bivariate, paired continuous quantitative data, with the independent variable (graduating average) being at least interval (depending on the grading system used at the university), and the dependent variable (starting annual income) being at the ratio level of measurement.

A value from the sampling distribution is the Pearson correlation coefficient r between graduating average and starting income for each of those samples. It is continuous, quantitative data at the interval level of measurement.

Notice that in all the examples above, regardless of what the type of data was, the sampling distribution data was quantitative and continuous at either the interval or ratio level of measurement. This is one of the reasons why sampling distributions are often more beneficial than population distributions in analyzing the population and computing the probability of obtaining certain future results.

Sampling distributions are also more useful when we are more concerned about trends than we are about individual results - for example, when investing into RRSPs for your retirement or determining the effectiveness of a drug in treating a certain disease or symptom. Going back to the example at the beginning of the chapter about travelling and choosing a hotel, even while the information about your upcoming individual stay at a particular hotel is important, even more important is the quality of the information that the reviews will provide, on average, about all of your hotel stays - i.e., how trustworthy the reviews are overall in predicting the quality of your experiences.

8.1 | Exercises

Answers to odd-numbered problems are available at the end of the textbook.

For Problems 1 to 16, analyze the scenarios and discuss the nature of each of the following data values - including what the data value represents, whether the data is qualitative or quantitative, and what level of measurement can be used to classify the data - for:

(i)   *An individual data value sampled from the population.*

(ii)   *A grouped data value sampled from the sampling distribution.*

1. In a group of patients that undergo a specific procedure, the length of recovery time is measured for each individual patient to return to "normal activities" to determine the average length of recovery time for any patient undergoing the procedure.

2. In a group of physiotherapists, those who offer direct billing to a particular insurance company are recorded in order to determine the proportion of physiotherapists who offer direct billing to this particular insurance company.

3. In a group of families who are clients of a particular veterinarian clinic, the number of pets in each family is recorded to determine the proportion of clients at this clinic who own 2 or more pets.

4. In a group of patients who received a flu shot, each patient was asked one week after receiving the flu shot if they experienced any flu-like symptoms, in order to determine the proportion of those who receive the flu shot who experience flu-like symptoms afterwards.

5. In a group of blood donors, the blood type of each donor is recorded to determine the proportion of donors who are considered to be "universal donors" (i.e., with an O– blood type).

6. In a group of nurses, the number of hours of overtime worked by each nurse is recorded for the period of one month to determine the average number of overtime hours worked by nurses each month.

7. A sample of canned processed food is examined to determine how much the actual calories in the food deviated from the calories stated on the label, in order to determine the overall mean absolute percent deviation between the actual calories and the stated calories on the food label.

8. A sample of patients with high cholesterol have their LDL cholesterol levels measured before and after taking a prescription drug designed to lower their LDL cholesterol for 6 months, and the change in LDL cholesterol level is recorded to determine the average LDL cholesterol reduction by patients taking the prescription drug.

9. A group of newborn babies are sampled and the weight of each baby is recorded to establish the average weight of newborn babies.

10. A group of newborn babies are sampled and the weight of each baby is recorded along with the gestation length of the pregnancy in order to determine if there is a relationship between the newborn weight of the baby and the gestation length of the pregnancy.

11. A group of paramedics are asked to record for each 12-hour shift worked whether or not they received a break from their work, in order to determine the proportion of shifts that paramedics did not receive any breaks.

12. A group of paramedics are asked to record for each 12-hour shift worked the number of calls they received, in order to determine the average number of calls received in a 12-hour shift.

13. In a large batch of prescription drug tablets, each tablet is inspected to ensure that it is within guidelines established by the Canada Food and Drug Act, to determine the proportion of tablets that are considered to be "defective".

14. In a large batch of prescription drug tablets, the mass of the active drug is measured and the deviation between the actual mass of active drug and the mass stated on the drug label is recorded for each of the tablets to determine the mean absolute percent deviation between the actual mass of the drug and the stated mass of the drug on the drug label.

15. A study is done at the Emergency Room (E.R.) in a local hospital, where the number of doctors and nurses on staff each day and the average wait time of the patients seen at the E.R. are recorded every day for a month to determine if there is a relationship between the two sets of data.

16. A study is done at a local walk-in clinic, where the number of patients seen at the clinic every day is recorded for an entire month to determine the average number of patients seen by the clinic in a day in order to set funding and staffing requirements for the clinic.

8.2 | Sampling Distribution of Sample Means

The most common sampling distribution is the **Sampling Distribution of Sample Means** - that is, the probability distribution of the variable $\overline{X}$, i.e., the sample means of all possible random samples of a given sample size n.

The sampling distribution of sample means is common for two reasons:

1. The mean is the most commonly-desired statistical measure of a sample, as it represents a "group score" - that is, a numerical value in the centre of the original range of data values that can be assigned to an entire group - since it is the total group score of the sample divided equally amongst all the members of the sample.

2. The sampling distribution of sample means has some very desirable properties. We will now begin to examine some of these "desirable properties".

In the previous two chapters, we analyzed several different discrete and continuous probability distributions. Of all of these distributions, the normal distribution was the most common and the most convenient distribution, given its symmetrical properties, its relationship between standard deviation and probability, and the relative ease of computing the area under the curve between two values using the standard normal distribution table.

However, in many scenarios, the probability distribution that represents a certain data set is not normal - it may be skewed, or it may be bimodal, or it may have such a bizarre probability distribution that there is no formula to describe it! However, when we construct the sampling distribution of sample means for this same population, something amazing happens to the graph of the sampling distribution: as the size of the sample increases, it begins to look more and more like a normal distribution!

Consider, for example, the probability distribution of a standard 6-sided die - this has a uniform, discrete probability distribution, with outcomes of 1, 2, 3, 4, 5, and 6, which are all equally-likely to occur. The probability distribution is as follows:

Uniform Probability Distribution of a Standard 6-Sided Die

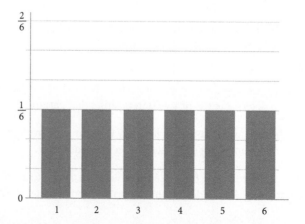

Using the formulas for expected value and variance of a discrete probability distribution from Chapter 6.1, we can compute the mean and the standard deviation of this probability distribution as follows:

$$\mu = \sum \left(x \cdot P(x) \right) = 1\left(\frac{1}{6}\right) + 2\left(\frac{1}{6}\right) + 3\left(\frac{1}{6}\right) + 4\left(\frac{1}{6}\right) + 5\left(\frac{1}{6}\right) + 6\left(\frac{1}{6}\right) = 3.5$$

$$\sigma^2 = \sum \left((x - \mu)^2 \cdot P(x) \right) = (1 - 3.5)^2 \left(\frac{1}{6}\right) + (2 - 3.5)^2 \left(\frac{1}{6}\right) + ... + (6 - 3.5)^2 \left(\frac{1}{6}\right) \approx 2.92$$

$$\sigma = \sqrt{2.92} \approx 1.71$$

Now consider what happens if two standard 6-sided dice are rolled, and the sample means of the values on the two dice are recorded. Then the sampling distribution of sample means for this scenario would be as follows:

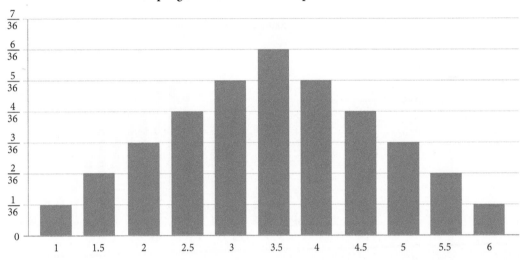

Sampling Distribution of the Sample Means - 2 Dice

This corresponds exactly with the probability distribution of the sums of the values on the two dice from Chapter 6, with the one difference being that the values on the horizontal axis represent *averages* rather than *sums*. It is important to note that the domain of the sample means in the sampling distribution has the same bounds as the domain of the original values in the population distribution (i.e., $1 \le x \le 6$).

Using the same methods as above, we can compute the mean and standard deviation for this distribution as follows:

$$\mu = \left(\sum x \cdot P(x) \right) = 1\left(\frac{1}{36}\right) + 1.5\left(\frac{2}{36}\right) + 2\left(\frac{3}{36}\right) + 2.5\left(\frac{4}{36}\right) + ... + 6\left(\frac{1}{36}\right) = 3.5$$

$$\sigma^2 = \sum \left((x - \mu)^2 \cdot P(x) \right) = (1 - 3.5)^2 \left(\frac{1}{36}\right) + (1.5 - 3.5)^2 \left(\frac{2}{36}\right) + ... + (6 - 3.5)^2 \left(\frac{1}{36}\right) \approx 1.46$$

$$\sigma = \sqrt{1.46} \approx 1.21$$

If we repeat this procedure for 4 dice and again for 6 dice, we get the following results:

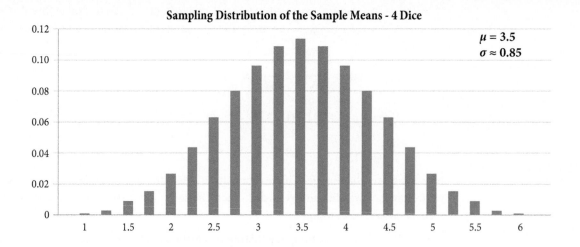

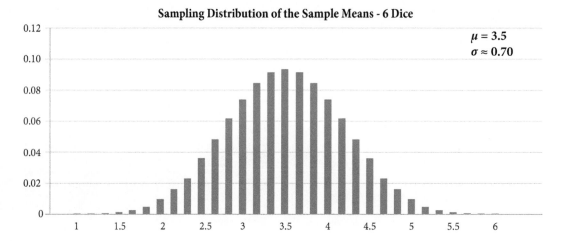

We can draw three conclusions from these sampling distributions:

- As the size of the sample n increases, the sampling distribution of sample means begins to look like a normal distribution.

- As the size of the sample n increases, the mean of the sample means remains constant at 3.5 - the population mean.

- As the size of the sample n increases, the variance and standard deviation of the sample means decrease - specifically, the variance is decreasing by a factor equal to the sample size, n, hence the standard deviation is decreasing by a factor of the square root of the sample size, $\sqrt{n}$.

In fact, the above three conclusions are true for *any sampling distribution of sample means*, regardless of the original population distribution! This is summarized in one of the most important theorems in statistics: the Central Limit Theorem.

The Central Limit Theorem

The **Central Limit Theorem** is one of the most powerful and useful theorems in all of statistics. It states, that for any random variable X that has some continuous distribution (not necessarily normal) with a mean of μ and a standard deviation of σ, if a sample of n values are randomly selected for X, then the distribution of the sample means $\overline{X}$ will approach a normal distribution as the sample size n increases; more specifically, if $n \geq 30$, then the sampling distribution of sample means is reasonably approximated by a normal distribution. The following observations about the sampling distribution of sample means are also proven to be true by the Central Limit Theorem:

- If the underlying distribution for X is normal to begin with, then the sampling distribution of sample means $\overline{X}$ is normal for all sample sizes n.

- The mean of the sampling distribution of sample means, denoted $\mu_{\overline{x}}$, is the same as the underlying population mean μ.

We will discuss the standard error of the mean later in this section.

- The standard deviation of the sampling distribution of sample means, denoted $\sigma_{\overline{x}}$, is called the **standard error of the mean** and is equal to $\dfrac{\sigma}{\sqrt{n}}$.

Formula 8.2-a

Z-score for Sampling Distribution of Sample Means

$$z = \frac{\overline{x} - \mu_{\overline{x}}}{\sigma_{\overline{x}}} = \frac{\overline{x} - \mu}{\dfrac{\sigma}{\sqrt{n}}}$$

The implications of the Central Limit Theorem are much more astonishing and far-reaching than a simple reading of the statement above would seem to indicate. In essence, the Central Limit Theorem states that, regardless of how complicated or indeterminate the underlying population distribution is, the normal distribution can be used to make very concrete statements about the sampling distribution of sample means, which allows us to draw conclusions about the entire population from a reasonably-sized sample ($n \geq 30$). This idea is at the very core of inferential statistics and will form the basis for the next two chapters, which examine how to create estimates and evaluate hypotheses about the population mean based on a sample mean.

Example 8.2-a

Calculating Probability for Sampling Distributions of Unknown Distributions

The average systolic blood pressure of males aged 40-59 in Canada is approximately 118 mmHg, with a standard deviation of approximately 12 mmHg. Determine the probability that a random sample of 100 Canadian males between the ages of 40-59 will have an average blood pressure of 120 mmHg or more, assuming that the shape of the underlying probability distribution for this data is unknown.

Solution

Regardless of what the underlying probability distribution is for this data, the Central Limit Theorem tells us that the sampling distribution of the means of random samples of size $n = 100$ will be approximately normal. Hence, we can compute the z-score for the sampling distribution of sample means as follows, given $\mu = 118$, $\sigma = 12$, and $\overline{x} = 120$:

Using Formula 8.2-a, $\quad z = \dfrac{\overline{x} - \mu}{\dfrac{\sigma}{\sqrt{n}}} = \dfrac{120 - 118}{\dfrac{12}{\sqrt{100}}} = \dfrac{2}{1.2} \approx 1.67$

> z-scores are rounded to 2 decimal places.

Looking up this z-score in the standard normal distribution table gives a cumulative probability of 0.9525. Hence, the probability that the average systolic blood pressure for a random sample of 100 males between the ages of 40-59 is greater than 120 is calculated as follows:

$$P(\overline{x} > 120) = P(z > 1.67) = 1 - P(z < 1.67) = 1 - 0.9525 = 0.0475$$

Therefore, there is less than a 5% probability that the average blood pressure for a group of Canadian males between the ages of 40 and 59 will exceed 120.

Example 8.2-b **Calculating Probability for Sampling Distributions of a Normal Distribution**

The average total time spent by patients with minor conditions who come to the Emergency Room (E.R.) at a local hospital is normally distributed with a mean of 4.3 hours and a standard deviation of 0.9 hours.

(i)   What is the probability that a randomly-selected patient in the E.R. with a minor condition will spend more than 5 hours in the hospital?

(i)   What is the probability that a random sample of 25 patients will spend an average total time of less than 4 hours in the E.R., which is the provincial standard?

Solution

(i)   Since we are only selecting an **individual** from the population, we use the underlying distribution for this population, which we are told is normal.

Using Formula 7.2-a, $z = \dfrac{x - \mu}{\sigma} = \dfrac{5 - 4.3}{0.9} = \dfrac{0.7}{0.9} \approx 0.78$

Looking up this z-score in the standard normal distribution table gives a cumulative probability of 0.7823. Hence, the probability that the total time spent in the E.R. by a randomly-selected patient will be greater than 5 hours is calculated as follows:

$$P(x > 5) = P(z > 0.78) = 1 - P(z < 0.78) = 1 - 0.7823 = 0.2177$$

Therefore, the probability that the patient will spend more than 5 hours in the E.R. is 0.2177.

(ii)   In this example, we are selecting a random **sample** of 25 patients from the population; the data is already normally distributed, so we may apply the Central Limit Theorem to the sampling distribution of sample means, even though $n = 25 < 30$.

Using Formula 8.2-a, $z = \dfrac{\bar{x} - \mu}{\dfrac{\sigma}{\sqrt{n}}} = \dfrac{4 - 4.3}{\dfrac{0.9}{\sqrt{25}}} = \dfrac{-0.3}{0.18} \approx -1.67$

Looking up this z-score in the standard normal distribution table gives a cumulative probability of 0.0475. Hence, the probability that the average total time spent in the E.R. by a randomly-selected sample of 25 patients will be less than 4 hours is calculated as follows:

$$P(\bar{x} < 4) = P(z < -1.67) = 0.0475$$

Therefore, the probability that the sample of 25 patients will spend, on average, less than 4 hours in the E.R. is 0.0475.

Sampling Error and Standard Error

When we collect a sufficiently-large random sample and compute a sample mean from it, we expect that sample mean to reasonably approximate the population mean, since it is an unbiased estimator.

For example, if we collect a sample of 120 obese patients on a strictly-regulated weight-loss program and determine the average weight loss in 10 weeks to be 30 lb, we expect that the average weight loss for all such obese patients on the same weight-loss program will be approximately 30 lb as well. If this is not the case, we refer to whatever difference exists between the sample and population means as "error" rather than simply as "deviation", because we expect the sample mean of 30 lb to be an unbiased estimate of the population mean.

As discussed in Chapter 1, the reasons why this error may occur are classified into two categories:

Non-sampling Error	Sampling Error
• the sample may have been collected improperly, the measurements may have been taken or recorded incorrectly, the researchers may have introduced their own biases, and/or there may have been an error made when the calculations were performed	• the difference between the sample mean and the population mean is entirely a result of the random nature of the sample and may occur even if the design of the study is flawless and all the measurements and calculations are totally accurate
• this type of error can be identified and avoided by using a proper study design to ensure proper sampling methods, blinding and double-blinding where appropriate to eliminate bias, and a rigorous procedure for verifying the accuracy and precision of measurements and calculations	• this type of error cannot be avoided
• data collected in a study in which this type of error exists must be discarded and cannot be used to make any inferences or hypotheses about the larger population	• we can calculate the probability that such an error will occur using the Central Limit Theorem

The Central Limit Theorem tells us how much of an error we should expect between a randomly-selected sample mean and the population mean, called the **Standard Error of the Mean**, based on two factors: the standard deviation of the underlying distribution and the size of the sample.

Obviously, a larger standard deviation in the population increases the size of the error that we would expect, as there is more variation inherent in the data being collected. The standard deviation is approximately the expected difference between the population mean and an individual value selected from the population (i.e., a sample of size 1).

The Central Limit Theorem also tells us that as the size of the sample increases, the size of the expected error decreases, proportional to the square root of the sample size. For example, if we take a sample of size 4, the expected error will decrease by a factor of $\frac{1}{2}$; if we take a sample of size 100, the expected error will decrease by a factor of $\frac{1}{10}$.

Hence, the standard error of the mean, $\sigma_{\bar{x}} = \frac{\sigma}{\sqrt{n}}$, represents the standard deviation of the sampling distribution of sample means, which is normal for sufficiently-large samples ($n \geq 30$). This provides us with a method for computing and restricting the probability of getting a sampling error outside of a pre-defined accepted margin of error. We will study this idea in more detail in Chapter 9.

Example 8.2-c	Using the Standard Error of the Mean to Compute and Limit Sampling Error

Recall, from Example 8.2-a, that the average systolic blood pressure of males aged 40-59 in Canada is approximately 118 mmHg, with a standard deviation of approximately 12 mmHg, but the underlying probability distribution for this data is not known.

(i)   If samples of size 100 are selected randomly, what upper bound can be established on the sample mean, such that the probability that the sampling error being greater than the upper bound is restricted to only 0.01?

(ii)   Suppose we want the upper bound on the sample means to be set at 120, with a probability of at most 0.01 that the sampling error will exceed this bound. What size samples must be collected to accomplish this upper bound?

Solution

(i)   In this example, we are given $\mu = 118$, $\sigma = 12$, and $n = 100$, and are asked to determine $\bar{x}$ such that $P(\overline{X} > \bar{x}) = 0.01$; i.e., $P(\overline{X} < \bar{x}) = 1 - 0.01 = 0.99$.

First, we look up the area of 0.9900 in the standard normal distribution table, and find the corresponding z-score to be 2.33 (the area in the table with the closest value is 0.9901).

Next, we compute the standard error: $\sigma_{\bar{x}} = \dfrac{\sigma}{\sqrt{n}} = \dfrac{12}{\sqrt{100}} = 1.2$

Finally, we rearrange the formula for the z-score for a sampling distribution of sample means (Formula 8.2-a) to solve for $\bar{x}$:

$$z = \frac{\bar{x} - \mu_{\bar{x}}}{\sigma_{\bar{x}}} \qquad \text{Rearranging and solving for } \bar{x},$$

$$\bar{x} = \mu_{\bar{x}} + z \cdot \sigma_{\bar{x}} \qquad \text{Substituting in the known values for } z, \sigma_{\bar{x}} \text{ and } \mu_{\bar{x}},$$

Recall:
$\mu_{\bar{x}} = \mu$

$$\bar{x} = 118 + 2.33 \cdot 1.2 \approx 120.8$$

Therefore, we can reasonably expect the upper bound of the mean for samples of size 100 to be less than 120.8, with only a 0.01 probability that the sampling error will be greater than this.

(ii)   Now we want to adjust the sample size n so that the upper bound for 99% of the sample means will be 120. It stands to reason that, since this upper bound is closer to the population mean of 118 than the upper bound we calculated in part (i), we will need a larger sample size.

Since we are still looking for the upper bound for 99% of the sample means (i.e., a probability of only 0.01 that the sample means will exceed this value), we can use the same z-score of 2.33 from part (i).

First, we rearrange the z-score formula for a sampling distribution of sample means (Formula 8.2-a) to solve for the standard error $\sigma_{\bar{x}}$:

$$z = \frac{\bar{x} - \mu_{\bar{x}}}{\sigma_{\bar{x}}} \qquad \text{Rearranging and solving for } \sigma_{\bar{x}},$$

$$\sigma_{\bar{x}} = \frac{\bar{x} - \mu_{\bar{x}}}{z} \qquad \text{Substituting in the known values for } z, \bar{x}, \text{ and } \mu_{\bar{x}},$$

$$\sigma_{\bar{x}} = \frac{120 - 118}{2.33} = 0.858369...$$

Next, we rearrange the formula for the standard error, $\sigma_{\bar{x}} = \dfrac{\sigma}{\sqrt{n}}$, to solve for n:

$$\sigma_{\bar{x}} = \frac{\sigma}{\sqrt{n}} \qquad \text{Rearranging and solving for } n,$$

$$n = \left[\frac{\sigma}{\sigma_{\bar{x}}} \right]^2 \qquad \text{Substituting in the known values for } \sigma_{\bar{x}} \text{ and } \sigma,$$

$$n = \left[\frac{12}{0.858369...} \right]^2 = 195.4404$$

Since our sample size must be a whole number, we **round up** the computed value of n to the next largest integer. This is because if we only take a sample of size 195, the probability that the sample mean will exceed 120 will be *slightly more than* 0.01. By rounding up, we guarantee that the probability will be *at most* 0.01, as desired.

Therefore, a sample of 196 patients must be collected.

| Example 8.2-d | Predicting a Range of Values for a Sample Mean |

For the same hospital in Example 8.2-b, the average length of time that patients with severe or complex conditions spent in the E.R. is normally distributed with a mean of 7.7 hours and a standard deviation of 1.2 hours.

(i)   Within what range of times will the middle 95% of all patients with severe/complex conditions spend in the E.R. of this hospital?

(ii)   If approximately 50 patients with severe/complex conditions are seen each day in this E.R., within what range will the middle 95% of all daily average times spent in the E.R. fall?

Solution

(i)   Since we are only selecting an **individual** from the population, we use the underlying distribution for this population, which we are told is normal. Since we are looking for the middle 95% of all E.R. times, we want to find the z-scores that separate the bottom and top 2.5% of the data from the middle 95%, as in the following diagram:

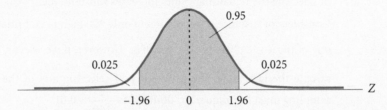

Looking up 0.0250 and 0.9750 in the body of the standard normal distribution table gives us the following z-scores: $z = \pm 1.96$. Using Formula 7.2-b,

$$x = \mu + z \cdot \sigma$$

$$x_{lower} = \mu + z_{lower} \cdot \sigma = 7.7 - 1.96(1.2) \approx 5.3$$

$$x_{upper} = \mu + z_{upper} \cdot \sigma = 7.7 + 1.96(1.2) \approx 10.1$$

> We round the boundary-values of the range to the same degree of precision as the values given, which in this case, is tenths.

Therefore, the middle 95% of all patients with severe/complex conditions will spend between 5.3 and 10.1 hours in the E.R.

(ii)   In this example, we are selecting a random **sample** of 50 patients from the population; we will use the same z-scores, but applying the Central Limit Theorem, we use the standard error of the mean instead of the standard deviation:

$$\bar{x}_{lower} = \mu_{\bar{x}} + z_{lower}\left(\frac{\sigma}{\sqrt{n}}\right) = 7.7 - 1.96\left(\frac{1.2}{\sqrt{50}}\right) \approx 7.4$$

$$\bar{x}_{upper} = \mu_{\bar{x}} + z_{upper}\left(\frac{\sigma}{\sqrt{n}}\right) = 7.7 + 1.96\left(\frac{1.2}{\sqrt{50}}\right) \approx 8.0$$

Therefore, the middle 95% of all daily average times spent in the E.R. by a sample of 50 patients with severe/complex conditions will be between 7.4 hours and 8.0 hours.

In the above example, we established a bound on the sampling error for 95% of all samples, referred to as the **maximal margin of error, E**. This means that, in 95% of all samples, the maximum difference between the sample mean and the population mean will be E; that is,

$$|\mu - \bar{x}| < E \quad \text{or} \quad \mu - E < \bar{x} < \mu + E$$

Note: We will discuss the maximal margin of error E in more detail in Chapter 9.

Correcting for a Finite Population

So far, we have assumed that the population was infinite or essentially infinite (i.e., so large that it would be practically impossible to gather the entire population) in order for the sampling to be independent (i.e., the probability of selecting any value does not change as a result of the previous selection), while still guaranteeing that no element of the population is selected more than once in the sample.

Put another way, we require the probability of choosing each value to be constant (independent), and at the same time, require the probability of selecting the same value more than once to be 0. This is only the case when the probability of choosing any particular value in the first place is 0 (or so small that it is essentially 0) - a situation that only arises in an infinite (or essentially infinite) population.

However, in some cases, the population may be small enough that as we start to take larger and larger samples, the probability of re-selecting a value that has already been sampled increases. If we restrict our sampling to require unique values only, then as the sample size increases, the probability of selecting the remaining values increases substantially.

Consider, for instance, a population of only 200 members. Initially, the probability of choosing any one of those members is $\frac{1}{200} = 0.005$. However, if we select a sample of size 100, by the time we sample the last value, the probability of selecting any of the remaining values (assuming our sampling must be unique) has **doubled** to $\frac{1}{100} = 0.01$.

As a result, as the sample size approaches the population size, the sampling error between our sample mean and our population mean will, in fact, decrease until the entire population is sampled (which is possible for a small, finite population), at which time the sampling error will be exactly 0, as the sample mean at that point will be exactly equal to the population mean.

We can still use the Central Limit Theorem in these situations, but we require a correction factor for the standard error of the mean to reflect that as the sample size increases, the standard error will decrease, until the entire population is sampled, at which time the standard error will be exactly 0.

For a finite (and relatively small) population, the standard error of the mean must be multiplied by the following Finite Population Correction (FPC) factor:

Formula 8.2-b	**Finite Population Correction (FPC) Factor**
	$$FPC = \sqrt{\frac{N-n}{N-1}}$$

Formula 8.2-c	**Corrected Standard Error of the Mean using the FPC Factor**
	$$\sigma_{\bar{x}} = \frac{\sigma}{\sqrt{n}} \cdot FPC = \frac{\sigma}{\sqrt{n}} \cdot \sqrt{\frac{N-n}{N-1}}$$

The following are important properties of the FPC factor:

1. For samples of size $n = 1$ (i.e., individual values selected from the underlying population), the FPC is 1, which does not change the standard error of the mean. This is because the sampling probability for a finite population changes only *after* the first value has been sampled.

2. For samples of size $n = N$ (i.e., the entire population is being sampled), the FPC is 0, which in turn makes the corrected standard error of the mean equal to 0 as well.

3. For very large values of N and very small values of n (i.e., large population, small sample), the FPC factor will be so close to 1 that it will have almost no effect on the standard error. As such, the FPC factor is typically only used when the *sample is greater than 5% of the population*:

i.e., **Use the Corrected Standard Error of the Mean when $n > 0.05N$**

Example 8.2-e   Applying the FPC Factor to a Sampling Distribution of Sample Means

In Major League Baseball (MLB), a team's record of games won is expressed as a decimal number between 0 and 1, rounded to 3 digits. For example, a team with a record of 0.000 has lost all their games, a team with a record of 1.000 has won all their games, and a team with a record of 0.527 has won 52.7% of their games. Since there are no ties in baseball (the game is played into extra innings until one team wins), the population mean for the records of the 30 teams in the league is always exactly 0.500, but the standard deviation will vary and the data may or may not be normally distributed, based on how the teams are playing each year. If the current season's standings yield a standard deviation of 0.075, and an approximately normal distribution, determine the probability that a random sample of 10 teams will have an average record between 0.525 and 0.550.

Solution

In this example, the data is already normally distributed, so we may apply the Central Limit Theorem to the sampling distribution of sample means, even though $n = 10 < 30$. However, in years where the data is not normally distributed, we would not be able to apply the CLT, since there will never be a big enough sample to justify it (since the population size is only 30).

In this case, we are sampling more than 5% of the population (since $n = 10 > 0.05(30) = 1.5$), so we must use the FPC factor to correct the standard error of the mean:

Using Formula 8.2-c, $\sigma_{\bar{x}} = \dfrac{\sigma}{\sqrt{n}} \cdot \sqrt{\dfrac{N-n}{N-1}} = \dfrac{0.075}{\sqrt{10}} \cdot \sqrt{\dfrac{30-10}{30-1}} \approx 0.0197$

Next, we compute the z-scores for the bounds on the sample mean of 0.525 and 0.550, using the corrected standard error:

Using Formula 8.2-a, $z_1 = \dfrac{\bar{x} - \mu_{\bar{x}}}{\sigma_{\bar{x}}} = \dfrac{0.525 - 0.500}{0.0197} = \dfrac{0.025}{0.0197} \approx 1.27$

$z_2 = \dfrac{\bar{x} - \mu_{\bar{x}}}{\sigma_{\bar{x}}} = \dfrac{0.550 - 0.500}{0.0197} = \dfrac{0.050}{0.0197} \approx 2.54$

Looking up these two z-scores in the standard normal distribution table gives cumulative probabilities of 0.8980 and 0.9945, respectively. Hence, the probability that the average record for a random sample of 10 teams is calculated as follows:

$P(0.525 < \bar{x} < 0.550) = P(1.27 < z < 2.54)$

$= P(z < 2.54) - P(z < 1.27)$

$= 0.9945 - 0.8980$

$= 0.0965$

Therefore, the probability that the average record is between 0.525 and 0.550 for the 10 teams is 0.0965.

8.2 | Exercises

For Problems 1 to 8, assume the population data is normally distributed.

1. A doctor samples the fasting blood-glucose level of a patient that is suspected to have diabetes. The mean fasting blood glucose levels of a non-diabetic person is 85 mg/dL, with a standard deviation of 8.8 mg/dL.

    a. What is the probability that someone without diabetes will have a fasting blood glucose level of over 100 mg/dL, which is indicative of diabetes?

    b. The doctor performs 5 different tests of the patient's fasting blood-glucose level on different days to ensure an accurate result. What is the probability that this patient's mean fasting blood-glucose level for the 5 test results will be above 100 mg/dL if they do not have diabetes? What can we conclude about such a result?

2. The mean white blood cell count of a healthy person is 7,000 cells per microlitre (mcL) of blood, with a standard deviation of 1,750 cells/mcL of blood.

    a. What is the probability that a healthy person will have a white blood cell count over 10,000 cells/mcL, which could indicate the presence of a disease the body is attempting to fight off?

    b. The doctor performs 8 different tests of the patient's blood in order to ensure an accurate result. What is the probability that this patient's mean white blood cell count for the 7 test results will be above 10,000 cells/mcL of blood if they are, in fact, healthy? What can we conclude about such a result?

3. A person with "normal" blood pressure has a systolic measurement of 110 mmHg, and a standard deviation of 7.5 mmHg.

    a. What is the probability that a person with "normal" blood pressure will get a systolic result of over 120 mmHg, indicating the possibility of pre-hypertension?

    b. Since blood pressure results can vary from test to test based on a variety of factors, one way to ensure the accuracy of the test result is to monitor results daily over the course of a period of time. If a patient takes their blood pressure every day for a week, what is the probability of getting an average systolic blood pressure result of over 120 mmHg, assuming the patient has normal blood pressure? What can we conclude about such a result?

4. A person with "normal" blood pressure has a diastolic measurement of 75 mmHg, and a standard deviation of 4.5 mmHg.

    a. What is the probability that a person with "normal" blood pressure will get a diastolic result of over 80 mmHg, indicating the possibility of pre-hypertension?

    b. If a patient takes their blood pressure every day for 10 days, what is the probability of getting an average diastolic blood pressure result of over 80 mmHg, assuming the patient has normal blood pressure? What can we conclude about such a result?

5. An EMT receives an average of 15 emergency response calls in a 24-hour shift, with a standard deviation of 4.5 calls.

    a. What is the probability that an EMT will have a shift with less than 10 calls?

    b. If the EMT works 8 shifts in a month, what is the probability he/she will receive between 100 and 125 calls over the course of the month?

6. A drug comes in the form of a liquid suspension with a mean concentration of 32 mg/mL. However, the concentration of the suspension is not completely uniform, having a standard deviation of 1.5 mg/mL, based on the random distribution of the drug particles suspended in the liquid solution.

    a. If one mL of the suspension is randomly drawn out of the bottle, what is the probability that the concentration is less than 30 mg/mL?

    b. If a tsp (i.e., 5 mL) of the suspension is randomly drawn out of the bottle, what is the probability that the amount of active drug in the suspension will be between 150 mg and 165 mg?

7. The average weight of a triplet at birth is 1,820 g, with a standard deviation of 150 g.

    a. What is the probability that a randomly-selected triplet had a birth weight between 1,800 and 2,000 g?

    b. What is the probability that a set of three triplets had a total birth weight between 5 kg and 5.5 kg?

8. The average weight of a quadruplet at birth is 1,410 g, with a standard deviation of 120 g.

   a. What is the probability that a randomly-selected quadruplet had a birth weight between 1,200 and 1,500 g?

   b. What is the probability that a set of four quadruplets had a total birth weight between 5.5 kg and 6 kg?

For Problems 9 to 16, use the Central Limit Theorem to find the probability of the indicated event, assuming that the distribution of the population data is unknown.

9. Across the province, nurses work an average of 18.2 hours of overtime every month, with a standard deviation of 7.8 hours. What is the probability that the average number of hours of overtime worked last month at a local hospital with 130 nurses on staff exceeds 20 hours?

10. Based on the information from Problem 9, what is the probability that the average number of hours of overtime worked last month at a local hospital with 160 nurses on staff is less than 16 hours?

11. The average wait time before a patient is seen by a doctor at a particular walk-in clinic on Saturdays is 69 minutes, with a standard deviation of 33 minutes. What is the probability that the average wait time for a group of 70 patients on a particular Saturday is under an hour?

12. Based on the information from Problem 11, what is the probability that the average wait time for a group of 90 patients on a particular Saturday is over 75 minutes?

13. An athletic therapist performs an arm rotation test to determine the range of motion of an athlete's shoulder joint. The average rotation for an athlete is 48.7°, with a standard deviation of 13.6°. What is the probability that a group of 50 athletes will have an average rotation of between 45° and 50°?

14. Based on the information from Problem 13, what is the probability that the same group of 50 athletes will instead have an average rotation of between 50° and 55°?

15. The average age of puppies brought to a veterinarian clinic for their first visit is 18.6 weeks, with a standard deviation of 7.3 weeks. Over the course of a year, the veterinarian sees 64 new puppies at her clinic. What is the probability that the age of these puppies on their first visit to the clinic is:

   a. Over 20 weeks old?

   b. Under 16 weeks old?

   c. Between 16 and 20 weeks old?

16. The average age of kittens brought to a veterinarian clinic for their first visit is 14.2 weeks, with a standard deviation of 5.1 weeks. Over the course of a year, the veterinarian sees 36 new kittens at his clinic. What is the probability that the age of these kittens on their first visit to the clinic is:

   a. Over 15 weeks old?

   b. Under 12 weeks old?

   c. Between 12 and 15 weeks old?

17. The average time spent by a triage nurse with each patient at the E.R. in a hospital is 4.5 minutes with a standard deviation of 1.8 minutes. If a triage nurse sees 56 patients during a shift, within what range of values are the middle 90% of average triage times expected to fall?

18. The average wait time for patients using a telephone health referral and advisement service to speak with a public health nurse is 52 minutes with a standard deviation of 19 minutes. If a sample of 80 patients who contacted the telephone health service on a given day are randomly selected and their wait time is recorded, within what range of values would the middle 80% of wait times be expected to fall?

19. If the average annual out-of-pocket medical costs for elderly patients in a particular region is approximately $5,340, with a standard deviation of $2,010, what is the range of expected values for the middle 99% of average annual out-of-pocket medical costs in a retirement home with 112 residents?

20. If the average prescription co-pay for patients at a pharmacy is $19.50 with a standard deviation of $12.75, what is the range of expected values for the middle 95% of prescription co-pay costs for a group of 93 patients who fill prescriptions at that pharmacy on a given day?

21. A homecare nurse is assigned to 32 patients, and the length of time that the nurse typically spends with each of these patients is normally distributed with a mean of 48 minutes and a standard deviation of 12 minutes, based on the patient's individual needs. The nurse is scheduled to visit with 6 of the patients today.

    a. What is the probability that the nurse will spend an average of less than 40 minutes with each patient?

    b. What is the probability that the nurse will spend a total of more than 5 hours with all 6 of the patients?

    c. Within what range of values will the middle 96% of average times spent with each of the 6 patients fall?

    d. What is the maximum total length of time the nurse would expect to spend with all 6 patients today, with a probability of 0.90?

22. A physiotherapist currently has 85 patients, and the length of time that the physiotherapist typically spends with each of these patients is normally distributed with a mean of 25 minutes and a standard deviation of 8 minutes, based on the patient's individual needs. The physiotherapist is scheduled to see 9 patients today.

    a. What is the probability that the physiotherapist will spend an average of more than 30 minutes with each patient?

    b. What is the probability that the physiotherapist will spend a total of less than 4 hours with all 9 of the patients?

    c. Within what range of values will the middle 95% of average times spent with each of the 9 patients fall?

    d. What is the minimum total length of time the physiotherapist would expect to spend with all 9 patients today, with a probability of 0.99?

23. An athletic therapist is assigned to a team of 40 baseball players. The length of time that the therapist typically spends with each player is normally distributed, and trainer spent an average of 56.2 minutes per day with each player he saw, with a standard deviation of 19.4 minutes. The athletic therapist is scheduled to work with 8 players tomorrow.

    a. What is the probability that the therapist will spend an average of more than 50 minutes with each player?

    b. What is the probability that the therapist will spend a total of less than 8 hours with all 8 of the players?

    c. Within what range of values will the middle 98% of average times spent with each of the 8 patients fall?

    d. What is the minimum total length of time the therapist would expect to spend with all 8 players today, with a probability of 0.95?

24. A hospital administrator is assigned to conduct performance reviews of the 44 nurses in the department, and the length of time that the administrator typically spends doing each of these performance reviews is normally distributed with a mean of 65.4 minutes and a standard deviation of 16.7 minutes. The administrator is scheduled to meet with 7 nurses today.

    a. What is the probability that the administrator will spend an average of less than one hour with each of the nurses?

    b. What is the probability that the administrator will spend a total of more than 7.5 hours with all 7 of the nurses?

    c. Within what range of values will the middle 99% of average times spent with each of the 7 nurses fall?

    d. What is the maximum total length of time the nurse would expect to spend with all 7 patients today, with a probability of 0.98?

8.3 | Sampling Distribution of Sample Proportions

Another sample statistic commonly used as an estimator for a population parameter is the **sample proportion** - that is, the proportion of the sample that meets a certain criteria. This statistic is used by polling companies during election campaigns to try to determine the candidate/party that will win the election, by pharmaceutical companies during clinical trials to try to determine the success rate of a given drug/treatment, and by quality control technicians during the production process of certain goods to determine the proportion of goods produced that are defective.

The random variable $\hat{p}$ is used to represent the proportion of "favourable" or "successful" outcomes in a sample of n trials:

$$\hat{p} = \frac{\text{number of favourable outcomes}}{\text{number of trials in the sample}} = \frac{x}{n}$$

Parameters of the $\hat{p}$-distribution

We can see that the $\hat{p}$-distribution is closely related to the binomial distribution (both are discrete probability distributions, with a fixed number of independent trials and a constant probability of success), with one key difference: where the binomial distribution represents the *total* number of successes for a fixed number of trials, the $\hat{p}$-distribution represents the *average* number of successes per trial.

Therefore, to compute the mean and standard error for the sampling distribution of sample proportions, we start with the mean and standard deviation for the binomial distribution, and divide both by n (the number of trials) to convert the "total successes" to "average successes".

Recall: p is the population proportion of successes and $q = 1 - p$ is the population proportion of failures.

$$\mu_{\hat{p}} = \frac{np}{n} = p$$

$$\sigma_{\hat{p}} = \frac{\sqrt{npq}}{n} = \sqrt{\frac{pq}{n}} = \sqrt{\frac{p(1-p)}{n}}$$

Example 8.3-a — Determining the Parameters of the $\hat{p}$-distribution

In a clinical drug trial of 600 patients taking the new drug, 492 had favourable results, while the remaining patients did not. Determine the parameters of the $\hat{p}$-distribution for samples of size 36.

Solution

The sample size, $n = 36$, and the population proportion of successes, $p = \frac{492}{600} = 0.82$.

Therefore, calculating the mean and standard error of the $\hat{p}$-distribution using the formulas above:

$$\mu_{\hat{p}} = p = 0.82$$

$$\sigma_{\hat{p}} = \sqrt{\frac{p(1-p)}{n}} = \sqrt{\frac{0.82(0.18)}{36}} = \sqrt{0.0041} \approx 0.0640$$

Normal Approximation to the $\hat{p}$-distribution

Just as the normal distribution can be used to approximate the binomial distribution, in the same way, the normal distribution can also be used to approximate the $\hat{p}$-distribution, so long as the following conditions are met:

1. n is sufficiently large (as we introduced in Chapter 7, we require $n \geq 30$).

2. $np > 5$ and $nq > 5$

Formula 8.3	**Z-score for Sampling Distribution of Sample Proportions**
	$$z = \frac{\hat{p} - \mu_{\hat{p}}}{\sigma_{\hat{p}}} = \frac{\hat{p} - p}{\sqrt{\dfrac{p(1-p)}{n}}}$$

Example 8.3-b	**Computing Probability for the $\hat{p}$-distribution**

Consider the clinical drug trial scenario from Example 8.3-a above, in which 82% of patients had favourable results from the drug treatment. If a random sample of 36 patients taking the drug is selected, what is the probability that at least 80% of them will have favourable outcomes?

Solution

In this case, $n = 36 \geq 30$, $np = 36(0.82) = 29.52 > 5$, and $nq = 36(0.18) = 6.48 > 5$, so all the criteria for the normal approximation to the $\hat{p}$-distribution are met.

Using the parameters of $\mu_{\hat{p}} = 0.82$ and $\sigma_{\hat{p}} = 0.0640$ as calculated in Example 8.3-a, we compute the z-score to use for the normal approximation to the $\hat{p}$-distribution.

Using Formula 8.3, $\quad z = \dfrac{\hat{p} - \mu_{\hat{p}}}{\sigma_{\hat{p}}} = \dfrac{0.80 - 0.82}{0.0640} = \dfrac{-0.02}{0.0640} \approx -0.31$

Looking that z-score up in the standard normal distribution table yields a cumulative area of 0.3783. Hence the probability that $\hat{p}$ will be at least 0.80 is computed as follows:

$P(\hat{p} > 0.80) = P(z > -0.31) = 1 - P(z < -0.31) = 1 - 0.3783 = 0.6217$

Therefore, there is a probability of 0.6217 that at least 80% of the patients in a random sample of 36 patients will experience favourable results from the drug treatment.

Example 8.3-c	**Predicting a Range of Values for the $\hat{p}$-distribution**

Consider the clinical drug trial scenario from Example 8.3-a above, in which 82% of patients had favourable results from the drug treatment. If a series of follow-up studies are conducted, each consisting of 75 patients, determine the range of values that the proportions of favourable results from the middle 90% of the follow-up studies will fall within.

Solution

In this case, $n = 75 \geq 30$, $np = 75(0.82) = 61.5 > 5$ and $nq = 75(0.18) = 13.5 > 5$, so all the criteria for the normal approximation to the $\hat{p}$-distribution are met.

We use the parameter of $\mu_{\hat{p}} = 0.82$ as calculated in Example 8.3-a, and since the size of the sample has changed, we recalculate $\sigma_{\hat{p}}$:

$$\sigma_{\hat{p}} = \sqrt{\frac{p(1-p)}{n}} = \sqrt{\frac{0.82(0.18)}{75}} = \sqrt{0.001968} \approx 0.0444$$

We now determine the z-scores that correspond to the middle 90%, i.e., the top and bottom 5%, as per the following diagram:

Solution
continued

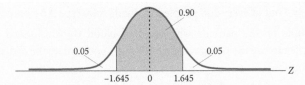

Looking up 0.0500 and 0.9500 in the body of the standard normal distribution table gives us the following z-scores: $z = \pm 1.645$. Hence,

$$\hat{P}_{lower} = \mu_{\hat{p}} + z_{lower} \cdot \sigma_{\hat{p}} = 0.82 - 1.645(0.0444) \approx 0.75$$

$$\hat{P}_{upper} = \mu_{\hat{p}} + z_{upper} \cdot \sigma_{\hat{p}} = 0.82 + 1.645(0.0444) \approx 0.89$$

> The desired probabilities fall **exactly** between the probabilities in the z-table for ± 1.64 and ± 1.65, so we use the values exactly halfway between these z-scores: $z = \pm 1.645$

Therefore, the proportion of favourable results of the middle 90% of all follow-up studies of 75 patients is expected to fall within the range of 0.75 and 0.89.

8.3 | Exercises

Answers to odd-numbered problems are available at the end of the textbook.

For Problems 1 to 12, if it is appropriate to do so, use the normal approximation to the $\hat{p}$-distribution to calculate the indicated probabilities.

1. $n = 50$, $p = 0.25$, $P(\hat{p} > 0.20)$

2. $n = 60$, $p = 0.40$, $P(\hat{p} < 0.50)$

3. $n = 150$, $p = 0.02$, $P(\hat{p} < 0.05)$

4. $n = 160$, $p = 0.99$, $P(\hat{p} > 0.96)$

5. $n = 70$, $p = 0.587$, $P(\hat{p} < 0.55)$

6. $n = 80$, $p = 0.715$, $P(\hat{p} > 0.75)$

7. $n = 125$, $p = 0.291$, $P(0.25 < \hat{p} < 0.30)$

8. $n = 120$, $p = 0.364$, $P(0.35 < \hat{p} < 0.40)$

9. $n = 15$, $p = 0.75$, $P(0.50 < \hat{p} < 0.60)$

10. $n = 12$, $p = 0.65$, $P(0.60 < \hat{p} < 0.70)$

11. $n = 90$, $p = \dfrac{1}{6}$, $P(0.10 < \hat{p} < 0.15)$

12. $n = 105$, $p = \dfrac{4}{15}$, $P(0.20 \leq \hat{p} \leq 0.25)$

13. A Canadian study in 2017 found that approximately 1 in every 3 paramedics had a positive screening for an anxiety disorder. A random sample of 64 paramedics is collected.

   a. What is the probability that more than 40% had a positive screening for an anxiety disorder?

   b. What is the probability that less than 25% had a positive screening for an anxiety disorder?

   c. What is the probability that between 30% and 35% had a positive screening for an anxiety disorder?

14. A provincial study in 2015 found that approximately 17 out of every 20 nurses had been verbally assaulted by a patient. A random sample of 81 nurses is collected.

   a. What is the probability that more than 90% of them have been verbally assaulted by a patient?

   b. What is the probability that less than 75% of them have been verbally assaulted by a patient?

   c. What is the probability that between 80% and 85% of them have been verbally assaulted by a patient?

15. An athletic therapist finds that approximately 3 out of every 20 of the athletes she works with who have shoulder injuries require surgery to fix the problem. The athletic therapist has 40 patients who have shoulder injuries this year.

   a. What is the probability that none of them will require shoulder surgery?

   b. What is the probability that between 10% and 20% will require shoulder surgery?

   c. What is the probability that more than 25% of them will require shoulder surgery?

   d. Within what range of values is the proportion of those 40 patients who will require shoulder surgery 95% likely to fall?

16. A study finds that approximately 1 out of every 10 Canadians do not take their prescription medication because they cannot afford the cost (known as "cost-related nonadherence"). A sample of 60 patients who have ongoing prescription medications is collected.

   a. What is the probability that none of them will experience cost-related nonadherence?

   b. What is the probability that between 12% and 15% will experience cost-related nonadherence?

   c. What is the probability that more than 20% of them will experience cost-related nonadherence?

   d. Within what range of values will the proportion of those 40 patients who will require shoulder surgery be 95% likely to fall?

17. Approximately 5 out of every 200 people in Canada have type AB+ blood and are considered universal blood recipients.

    a. If a sample of 250 patients who received blood transfusions is collected from a major urban hospital, is it appropriate to use the normal distribution to approximate the $\hat{p}$-distribution? If so, what are the parameters of the $\hat{p}$-distribution?

    b. If a sample of 150 patients who received blood transfusions is collected from a major urban hospital, is it appropriate to use the normal distribution to approximate the $\hat{p}$-distribution? If so, what are the parameters of the $\hat{p}$-distribution?

18. Approximately 7 out of every 100 people in Canada have type O– blood and are considered universal blood donors.

    a. If a sample of 80 donors is collected at a local blood donation drive, is it appropriate to use the normal distribution to approximate the $\hat{p}$-distribution? If so, what are the parameters of the $\hat{p}$-distribution?

    b. If a sample of 60 donors is collected at a local blood donation drive, is it appropriate to use the normal distribution to approximate the $\hat{p}$-distribution? If so, what are the parameters of the $\hat{p}$-distribution?

19. According to a recent study, 34.3% of adults in Canada received the flu vaccine shot last year.

    a. If a sample of 125 Canadian adults is collected, what is the probability that at least 40% of them received the flu shot last year?

    b. If approximately 90% of those who received the flu shot last year will receive it again this year, and approximately 30% of those who did not receive the flu shot last year will receive it this year, what is the expected proportion of adults in Canada who will receive the flu shot this year?

20. According to a recent study, approximately 13.2% of detected pregnancies result in miscarriage.

    a. In a sample of 200 women who have had pregnancies that are detected via a positive pregnancy tests, what is the probability that at least 20% will end in miscarriage?

    b. If approximately 25% of all pregnancies are undetected (all of which end in miscarriage before being detected), what is the expected proportion of all pregnancies (both detected and undetected) that will ultimately end in miscarriage?

21. A hospital lottery is run to raise funds for the hospital's expansion project. Break-open tickets are sold for $2 each and one in every eight tickets is a winner.

    a. How many tickets would have to be purchased in order to analyze the distribution of the proportion of winning tickets using the normal approximation to the $\hat{p}$-distribution?

    b. If a patient purchases 50 tickets, what is the probability that at least 20% of them will win?

    c. If the patient purchases 100 tickets instead of 50, will the probability increase or decrease from part (b)? Explain.

    d. If a patient purchases 50 tickets, what is the probability that between 10% and 15% of the tickets will win?

    e. If the patient purchases 100 tickets instead of 50, will the probability increase or decrease from part (d)? Explain.

22. As part of a fundraising drive, a hospital calls all of the people who have previously donated to the hospital. From past fund drives, it is known that approximately five out of every twelve past donors will donate again (known as donor retention).

    a. How many past donors would have to be called in order to analyze the distribution of the proportion of donor retention using the normal approximation to the $\hat{p}$-distribution?

    b. If a volunteer calls 30 past donors, what is the probability that at least 50% of them will donate again?

    c. If the volunteer calls 60 past donors instead of 30, will the probability increase or decrease from part (b)? Explain.

    d. If a volunteer calls 30 past donors, what is the probability that at between 40% and 45% of them will donate again?

    e. If the volunteer calls 60 past donors instead of 30, will the probability increase or decrease from part (d)? Explain.

23. Approximately two-thirds of Canadians have some form of privately-covered extended health insurance. If random groups of 120 Canadians are sampled, find the range of values that the proportion of those with extended health insurance are 75% likely to fall within.

24. Approximately one-third of Canadians have some form of privately-covered long-term disability insurance. If random groups of 150 Canadians are sampled, find the range of values that the proportion of those with long-term disability health insurance are 80% likely to fall within.

8 | Review Exercises

For Problems 1 to 6, analyze the scenario and discuss the nature of each of the following data values - including what the data value represents, whether the data is qualitative or quantitative, and what level of measurement can be used to classify the data - for:

(i) *An individual data value sampled from the population.*

(ii) *A grouped data value sampled from the sampling distribution.*

1. A factory produces pieces that may be defective. A group of pieces is randomly selected from those produced on a particular day and defective pieces are counted in order to determine the proportion of defective pieces.

2. A study is done involving college students to determine the relationship between their BMI and the average number of hours they spend being physically active during the week.

3. In a group of patients undergoing chemotherapy, hemoglobin values are measured before and after chemotherapy to determine the average reduction.

4. In a clinical trial, patients undergo an experimental therapy. A group of patients is randomly selected among those who participated in the trial in order to determine the proportion of patients who positively respond to the therapy.

5. A group of pregnant women followed in a hospital are tested to determine the relationship between weight and age of onset of gestational diabetes.

6. A culture of infectious bacteria are being analyzed in a biohazard lab to determine the average lifespan of the bacteria.

For Problems 7 to 10, assume the population data is normally distributed.

7. The average final exam score for students enrolled in a Statistics for Health Sciences course is 68, with a standard deviation of 16.

   a. What is the probability that a student will have a score over 80?

   b. What is the probability that a random sample of 16 students enrolled students will receive an average score of over 80?

8. The average number of calls received by an EMT over the course of a month is 120 with a standard deviation of 10.

   a. What is the probability that an EMT receives more than 130 calls over a particular month?

   b. What is the probability that an EMT receives a total of more than 520 calls over 4 consecutive months?

9. A healthy person with "normal" blood pressure has an average systolic measurement of 110 mmHg, and a standard deviation of 7.5 mmHg.

   a. What is the probability that a person with "normal" blood pressure will get a systolic result under 95 mmHg **or** over 120 mmHg?

   b. If a patient takes their blood pressure every day for a week, what is the probability of getting an average systolic blood pressure result of under 95 mmHg **or** over 120 mmHg, assuming the patient has normal blood pressure?

10. The average length of time spent recovering after an outpatient surgery is 4.75 hours, with a standard deviation of 1.05 hours.

    a. What is the probability that a randomly-selected patient who underwent outpatient surgery will recover in the hospital for less than 3 hours **or** more than 6 hours?

    b. What is the probability that 5 consecutive patients who undergo outpatient surgery will recover in the hospital for less than 3 hours **or** more than 6 hours?

For Problems 11 to 20, use the Central Limit Theorem to find the probability of the indicated event, assuming that the distribution of the population data is unknown.

11. The lifespan of the battery of a pacemaker is 5 years with a standard deviation of 6 months.

    a. If the hospital purchases 5 batteries, is it possible to calculate the probability that the average lifespan of the 5 batteries is less than 4 years and 6 months without knowing the distribution of battery lifespan? Why?

    b. Is it possible to calculate the probability that the average lifespan of the 5 batteries is less than 4 years and 6 months knowing that the lifespan of the batteries is normally distributed? If so, what is the probability?

12. A teacher observes that the average score of students on an exam is 77 with a standard deviation of 10.

    a. Is it possible to calculate the probability that a group of 20 students will get an average score of over 80 without knowing the distribution of the scores? Why?

    b. Is it possible to calculate the probability that a group of 20 students will get an average score over 80 knowing that the exam score is normally distributed? If so, what is the probability?

13. Across the province, pharmacies earn, on average, $108 per day on the sale of aspirin, with a standard deviation of $18.

    a. What is the probability that a randomly selected group of 40 pharmacies will earn, on average, more than $800 from the sale of aspirin in a week?

    b. What is the range of values in which the middle 90% of average total weekly sales is likely to fall?

    c. How would your answers in parts a. and b. change if the study included more than 40 pharmacies?

14. The average length of time a physiotherapist spends with a patient each day is 27 minutes, with a standard deviation of 9.5 minutes.

    a. If the physiotherapist has a total of 60 patients booked for appointments this week, what is the probability that she will need to spend a total of more than 30 hours with her patients this week?

    b. What is the range of values in which the middle 80% of average total weekly hours spent with patients is likely to fall?

    c. How would your answers in parts a. and b. change if the study included less than 60 patients?

15. A professor in a nursing program at a college knows that the average student spends 2.9 minutes per question on a test, with a standard deviation of 0.85 minutes.

    a. If the test consists of 50 questions, and the exam is 2.5 hours long, what proportion of students would be expected to complete the exam in time?

    b. If the professor wanted to ensure that 95% of students completed the exam in time, how long would the professor need to provide the students for the exam?

    c. If, instead of increasing the length of time scheduled for the exam, the professor chose to eliminate 2 questions from the exam, would this bring the percent of students who complete the exam in the time allotted inside the professor's desired parameters?

16. A hospital administrator is scheduling the O.R. and knows that the average surgery takes 2.65 hours with a standard deviation of 1.08 hours.

    a. If there are 35 surgeries that need to be booked this week, and the O.R. can be booked for a maximum of 98 hours over the course of the week, what is the probability that all the surgeries will be able to be completed this week?

    b. If the administrator wanted the probability that the surgeries will need to be cancelled on the day of to be reduced to less than 1%, how many hours would she need to book the O.R. for?

    c. If, instead of increasing the length of time scheduled in the O.R., the administrator decided to postpone 3 surgeries that were lower on the priority list, would this bring the probability of cancelling a surgery on the day of within the administrator's desired parameters?

17. A pediatrician observes that his newborn patients sleep on average 12.8 hours a day with a standard deviation of 2.2 hours.

    a. What is the probability that the average number of hours of sleep in a group of 75 newborn patients is between 12.5 and 13 hours?

    b. What values separate the top and bottom 1% of average sleep times in a sample of 75 newborns?

    c. How would your answers in parts a. and b. change if the number of newborns included in the study was decreased?

18. A surgeon observes that the average recovery time from a particular in-patient procedure she performs is 6.5 days with a standard deviation of 2.3 days.

    a. What is the probability that a group of 40 patients undergoing this procedure this year have an average recovery time between 6 and 8 days?

    b. What values separate the top and bottom 5% of average recovery times in a sample of 40 patients?

    c. How would your answers in parts a. and b. change if the number of patients included in the study was increased?

19. The average length of time the 145 residents of a nursing home have lived at the home for is 874 days, with a standard deviation of 352 days. A sample of 64 residents is selected to determine the overall quality and patient satisfaction at the nursing home.

    a. What is the probability that the average length of time the residents included in the sample have lived at the home for is less than 2 years (i.e., 730 days)?

    b. What is the probability that the average length of time the residents included in the sample have lived at the home for is more than 2.5 years (i.e., 912.5 days)?

    c. What is the range of values in which the average length of time lived at the home is 95% likely to fall?

20. A professor has 65 students in his statistics class, and the average final grade in the class was 62.4%, with a standard deviation of 13.7%. A random sample of 16 of his students is collected to take part in a program review.

    a. What is the probability that the average final grade for the sample is over 70%?

    b. What is the probability that the average final grade for the sample is under 60%?

    c. What is the range of values in which the average final grade for the sample is 99% likely to fall?

For Problems 21 to 26, use the normal approximation to the $\hat{p}$-distribution to calculate the desired probabilities, if appropriate; otherwise, explain why it is not appropriate to do so.

21. The success rate for a hip replacement 20 years after the surgery is 85%. A surgeon performs hip replacements surgeries on a sample of 80 patients.

    a. What is the probability that at least 90% of the replacement hips will still be useful in 20 years?

    b. What is the probability that between 75% and 80% of the hips will still be useful in 20 years?

    c. Within what range of values is the actual proportion of hip replacements still useful after 20 years 98% likely to fall?

22. The success rate for a hip replacement 10 years after the surgery is significantly greater, at 95%. For the sample of 80 patients from Problem 21, determine the following:

    a. What is the probability that at least 98% of the replacement hips will still be useful in 10 years?

    b. What is the probability that between 90% and 95% of the hips will still be useful in 10 years?

    c. Within what range of values is the actual proportion of hip replacements still useful after 10 years 95% likely to fall?

23. Approximately 6% of the general population has an allergy to natural latex. For a random sample of 55 patients seen by an E.R. doctor in one day, determine the following:

    a. What is the probability that more than 5% of the patients will have a latex allergy?

    b. What is the probability that between 8% and 10% of the patients will have a latex allergy?

    c. Within what range of values is the middle 99% of sample proportions of patients with latex allergies likely to fall?

24. Because of the overuse of natural latex gloves, the number of healthcare workers who have developed latex sensitivities is significantly higher than the general population at 16%. If there are 66 healthcare workers in the E.R., determine the following:

    a. What is the probability that more than 20% of the healthcare workers in the E.R. will have a latex allergy?

    b. What is the probability that between 12% and 15% of the healthcare workers in the E.R. will have a latex allergy?

    c. Within what range of values is the middle 90% of sample proportions of healthcare workers in the E.R. with latex allergies likely to fall?

25. Among the participants of a study, the proportion of smokers is $\frac{1}{5}$. A random sample of 50 of the participants is collected.

    a. What is the probability that more than 25% are smokers?

    b. What is the probability that there are between 5 and 15 smokers?

26. Among nurses in a hospital, the proportion of nurses that work more than 10 hours of overtime in a week is $\frac{1}{4}$. A random sample of 30 nurses is collected.

    a. What is the probability that over 30% of the nurses worked more than 10 hours of overtime last week?

    b. What is the probability that between 4 and 8 nurses worked more than 10 hours of overtime last week?

8 | Self-Test Exercises

Answers to all problems are available at the end of the textbook.

For Problems 1 to 3, analyze the scenarios and discuss the nature of each of the following data values - including what the data value represents, whether the data is qualitative or quantitative, and what level of measurement can be used to classify the data - for:
(i) An individual data value sampled from the population.
(ii) A grouped data value sampled from the sampling distribution.

1. In a group of psychologists, those who have an ABA certification are recorded to determine the proportion of psychologists who are currently qualified to conduct studies on behavioural analysis.

2. A study was completed to determine if there was a correlation between the wait times in an E.R. ward and the length of nurses' shifts.

3. The heights of children of age 3 who were born prematurely are recorded to determine the average height of 3-year-old children who were born prematurely.

4. A person with a "normal" cholesterol level has a measurement of 200 mg/dL and standard deviation of 23.2 mg/dL. Assume the population data in this scenario is normally distributed.

    a. What is the probability that a person with "normal" cholesterol levels will get a result of greater than 215 mg/dL (considered borderline-high)?

    b. If a patient having "normal" cholesterol levels is measured every day for the next 25 days, what is the probability of getting an average result of greater than 215 mg/dL?

5. The length of times typically required for a pharmaceutical manufacturer to complete a batch of pills is normally distributed with a mean of 15.9 minutes and a standard deviation of 3.1 minutes. A sample of 12 batches is collected.

   a. What is the probability that the average time to complete a single batch in the sample will be less 13 minutes?

   b. What is the probability that average time to complete all 12 batches will be over 3 hours and 24 minutes?

   c. Within what range of values will the middle 95% of average times to complete all 12 batches fall?

   d. What is the minimum length of time for all 12 batches to be completed, with a probability of 0.99?

6. A study finds that the average length of time it takes for babies to reach double their birth weight is 117 days, with a standard deviation of 15.2 days. A pediatrician is monitoring the growth in weight of a sample of 52 new babies.

   a. What is the probability that the average length of time it takes the babies to double their birth-weight is more than 17 weeks?

   b. What is the probability that the average length of time it takes the babies to double their birth-weight is between 16 and 18 weeks?

   c. Within what range of values are the middle 96% of average lengths of time required for the babies to double their birth weight likely to fall?

7. In order to be properly vaccinated against Hepatitis A, two vaccination shots are required. The average length of time between vaccination shots is 192 days, with a standard deviation of 8 days, and follows a normal distribution. If 10 patients who have received the first vaccination shot are randomly selected, what is the probability that the average length of time until those 10 patients get their second shot will be:

   a. Greater than 195 days?

   b. Between 27 and 28 weeks?

   c. Less than half a year (assume 365 days in a year)?

8. A psychiatrist finds that the lengths of time needed for anorexic patients to complete therapy and become fully self-sustainable are normally distributed with a mean of 49 months and a standard deviation of 7.8 months.

   a. What is the probability that a sample of 15 patients will have an average complete rehabilitation time of less than 4 years?

   b. What is the probability that the same sample will have an average complete rehabilitation time of between 50 and 55 months?

   c. What range of values will the middle 98% of all average complete rehabilitation times for a sample of 15 patients fall within?

   d. What minimum sample size is need in order to ensure, with a 99% accuracy, that the average complete rehabilitation time is between 48 and 50 months?

9. The average annual income for the 82 therapists employed at the multiple locations of a paramedical health association is $71,250 per year, with a standard deviation of $13,490.

   a. If a random sample of 16 therapists is collected, what is the probability that the average annual income is more than $75,000?

   b. If a random sample of 25 therapists is collected, what is the probability that the average annual income is between $65,000 and $70,000?

   c. Within what range of values would we expect the middle 85% of all average annual incomes for samples of 36 therapists to fall?

10. The average proportion of domesticated dogs with kennel cough at a veterinarian clinic in the region is approximately 5.3%. If the current number of dogs at a particular clinic is 150 and the population distribution is unknown, determine the following:

   a. What is the probability that less than 5% of the dogs at the clinic have kennel cough?

   b. What is the probability that between 7-10% of the dogs at the clinic have kennel cough?

   c. What is the middle 95% range of proportions that the actual proportion of dogs with kennel cough at the clinic is likely to fall within?

11. A doctor performing a study on short-term memory finds that of the 100 chosen words, the patient is able to remember 56 of them.

   a. Determine the parameters of the $\hat{p}$-distribution for samples of 30 words and deduce why the normal approximation to the $\hat{p}$-distribution can be used to calculate the probability of an event occurring. (*Hint: you will need to correct the standard error using the Finite Population Correction Factor.*)

   b. If a sample of 30 of the 100 words is taken, what is the probability that the patient was able to remember at least 60% of them?

   c. If a sample of 30 of the 100 words is taken, what is the probability that the patient was unable to remember more than 45% of them?

12. Approximately 22.5% of patients admitted to a hospital develop nosocomial infections that lead to prolonged hospitalizations.

    a. How many patients must be tested to analyze the distribution of the infected proportion of patients using the normal approximation to the $\hat{p}$-distribution?

    b. If the hospital has a total of 280 patients, what is the probability of at least 30% being infected?

    c. Without recalculating your answer, determine if the number of patients increased to 400, whether the probability from part (b) will increase or decrease. Explain your answer.

    d. If the hospital has a total of 280 patients, what is the probability that between 15% and 25% of patients will be infected?

    e. Without recalculating your answer, determine if the number of patients increased to 400, whether the probability from part (d) will increase or decrease. Explain your answer.

8 | Summary of Notation and Formulas

NOTATION

N = total number of data values in a population

n = total number of data values in a sample

μ = population mean

$\bar{x}$ = sample mean

σ^2 = population variance

σ = population standard deviation

p = population proportion of successes

q = population proportion of failures = $1 - p$

$\bar{X}$ = sample mean of a random sample of size n

$\mu_{\bar{x}}$ = mean of the sampling distribution of sample means = μ

$\sigma_{\bar{x}}$ = standard error of the mean = $\dfrac{\sigma}{\sqrt{n}}$

$\hat{p}$ = proportion of successes in a sample of n trials

$\mu_{\hat{p}}$ = mean of the sampling distribution of sample proportions = p

$\sigma_{\hat{p}}$ = standard error of the proportion = $\sqrt{\dfrac{p(1-p)}{n}}$

FORMULAS

Z-score for Sampling Distribution of Sample Means | 8.2-a

$$z = \frac{\bar{x} - \mu_{\bar{x}}}{\sigma_{\bar{x}}} = \frac{\bar{x} - \mu}{\dfrac{\sigma}{\sqrt{n}}}$$

Finite Population Correction (FPC) Factor | 8.2-b

$$FPC = \sqrt{\frac{N-n}{N-1}}$$

Corrected Standard Error of the Mean using the FPC Factor | 8.2-c

$$\sigma_{\bar{x}} = \frac{\sigma}{\sqrt{n}} \cdot FPC = \frac{\sigma}{\sqrt{n}} \cdot \sqrt{\frac{N-n}{N-1}}$$

Z-score for Sampling Distribution of Sample Proportions | 8.3

$$z = \frac{\hat{p} - \mu_{\hat{p}}}{\sigma_{\hat{p}}} = \frac{\hat{p} - p}{\sqrt{\dfrac{p(1-p)}{n}}}$$

9 ESTIMATION AND CONFIDENCE INTERVALS

LEARNING OBJECTIVES

- Define inferential statistics, population parameters, and biased and unbiased estimators.
- Differentiate between point estimates and range (or interval) estimates.
- Identify the appropriate population parameter based on the sample data and the estimator for that parameter.
- Define and interpret confidence level, level of significance, and margin of error.
- Construct confidence intervals for the population mean when the population standard deviation is known, using the normal Z-distribution.
- Compare accuracy and precision of confidence intervals and determine the sample size required for a given accuracy and precision.
- State the characteristics and properties of the Student's t-distribution.
- Construct confidence intervals for the population mean when the population standard deviation is unknown, using the Student's t-distribution.
- Construct confidence intervals for population proportions.

CHAPTER OUTLINE

9.1 Inferential Statistics and Estimation

9.2 Confidence Intervals for μ when σ is Known

9.3 Confidence Intervals for μ when σ is Unknown

9.4 Confidence Intervals for p

Introduction

So far, in most of the scenarios we have examined in our study of probability, we assumed that we had information about the entire population: either we had the sample space with all elements in the population listed out, or we had population parameters such as the mean μ and standard deviation σ.

However, in reality, this is often not the case. Consider the example of the clinical drug trial briefly discussed in the opening section of Chapter 5, in which, out of 150 patients receiving the drug, a certain number experienced significant improvements and this proportion was used as a preliminary probability that future patients would experience significant improvements from the use of the drug. This example was used to introduce us to the concept of **empirical probability**, which allows us to approximate the probability that an event will occur when information about the entire population is not readily available. Empirical probability goes hand-in-hand with the **law of large numbers**, which says that as the size of our sample increases, our probability estimate approaches the true probability of the event occurring in the population.

In this chapter and the next chapter, we will formalize the relationship between sample statistics and population parameters by examining scenarios in which the population information is not (or cannot be) known, and in which we will use our knowledge of probability and probability distributions to make inferences about the population based on information extracted from sample data.

9.1 | Inferential Statistics and Estimation

Recall from Chapter 1 that there are two major classifications of statistics: descriptive and inferential. Descriptive statistics, which were covered extensively in Chapters 2 to 4, provide summary information about sample data collected from a population. Conversely, **inferential statistics** use the sample data to draw conclusions about the population data. Along with probability, descriptive statistics and inferential statistics form the three fundamental branches of statistics. We can understand how probability, descriptive statistics, and inferential statistics relate a population to a sample collected from within the population via the following diagram, known as the "Central Dogma of Statistics" (Akey, 2008):

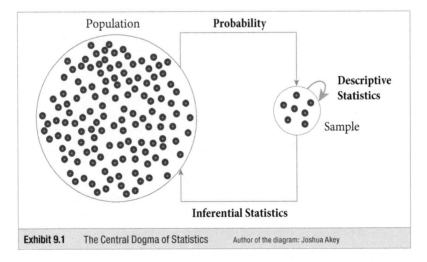

Exhibit 9.1   The Central Dogma of Statistics   Author of the diagram: Joshua Akey

We can see from this diagram that probability helps us to understand what kind of sample we will obtain from a population, descriptive statistics help us to understand characteristics of the sample obtained, and inferential statistics tell us how to use those characteristics to learn about the corresponding characteristics of the entire population.

Sampling and Estimators

The use of inferential statistics is most important when the population is too large or too challenging to measure those attributes directly (e.g., every person who lives in Canada, every instance of lung cancer, every time a certain crime is committed, etc.); in these situations, we must rely on samples that we collect to tell us about the population. As such, we need to make sure we understand the concepts in Chapter 1 that discuss how to collect a good sample, because without a good sample, none of the ideas or techniques discussed in this and the following chapter will be valid!

Note: If the sample data is not obtained using proper methods, or if bias is allowed to influence the selection of the sample, we cannot use the sample to make any claims about the population. The sample data must be discarded, and new sample data must be collected, using proper sampling methods, randomization techniques, and blinding strategies to eliminate bias, as needed.

Once we have collected a valid random sample according to the principles, strategies, and techniques discussed in Chapter 1, we then need to compute some descriptive statistics for the sample, as discussed in Chapters 2, 3, and 4 - such as the sample mean ($\bar{x}$), sample standard deviation (s), sample proportion (p), sample correlation coefficient (r), etc. - based on what we wish to know about the population. Finally, we need to learn how these sample statistics can be interpreted within the context of the entire population, and the information they give us about the population.

Sample statistics, such as the ones mentioned above, are called **estimators** of population parameters. The **bias** of an estimator is the difference between the actual value of a population parameter and the expected value (or average) of the results of the estimator for all possible samples of a given size drawn from a population.

Estimators are called **unbiased estimators** if they tend to well-approximate the desired population parameter (i.e., the expected or average difference between the population parameter and the estimator is zero); estimators that tend to consistently over- or under-approximate the desired population parameter are called **biased estimators**.

For example, the sample mean ($\bar{x}$) of a random sample is an unbiased estimator of the population mean (μ). On the other hand, the sample Pearson correlation coefficient (r) is a biased estimator for small samples, as it tends to under-approximate the population correlation coefficient (ρ - pronounced "rho"); however, for large samples, the sample correlation coefficient r is a reasonably unbiased estimator of ρ.

Note: We have so far learned about the sample correlation coefficient, r, in Chapter 4. We will learn more about the population correlation coefficient, ρ, in Chapter 10.

Another example of a biased estimator is the Mean Squared Error of a sample, $MSE = \dfrac{\sum (x - \bar{x})^2}{n}$, which also consistently under-approximates the population variance (σ^2). However, the sample variance, $s^2 = \dfrac{\sum (x - \bar{x})^2}{n - 1}$, with a corrected factor of ($n - 1$) in the denominator instead of n, is an unbiased estimator of the population variance. Using the factor of ($n - 1$) is known as Bessel's Correction, and can be explained by the notion of degrees of freedom, as discussed in Chapter 3.

Example 9.1-a	Estimators of Population Parameters

Recall Example 8.1 from the last chapter, where a university researcher is collecting some information about the success of graduates from a particular program at the university. For each of the following pieces of information, state the desired population parameter and determine an appropriate estimator to use for that parameter:

(i)   The annual income of graduates from the program in the last five years.

(ii)   The employment rate of graduates from the program in the last five years, in their vocational field, within six months of graduating from the program.

(iii)   The relationship between the graduating average of the graduates from the program in the last five years and the starting annual income when they began their employment.

(i) The desired population parameter is μ - the mean annual income of all graduates from the program in the last five years. An appropriate estimator for μ would be $\bar{x}$ - the mean annual income of a sample of n graduates from the program in the last five years.

(ii) The desired population parameter is p - the proportion of all graduates from the program in the last five years who were employed in their field within six months of graduating. An appropriate estimator for p would be $\hat{p}$ - the proportion of those in a random sample of n graduates from the program who were employed in their field within six months of graduating.

(iii) The desired population parameter is ρ - the correlation coefficient between the graduating average and the starting annual income for every graduate from the program in the last five years. An appropriate estimator for ρ would be r - the correlation coefficient between the graduating average and the starting annual income for a sample of n graduates from the program. However, in order to be an unbiased estimator, the sample size must be sufficiently large.

Confidence Intervals

Even if we use an unbiased estimator to estimate the value of a population parameter, known as the **point estimate**, the likelihood that the value of that estimator will be **exactly equal** to the value of the population parameter is very low; in fact, since the values that a population parameter can take are continuous, the probability the estimator will be equal to the parameter is essentially zero!

However, we can make use of the concepts and strategies introduced in the last chapter about sampling distributions to establish a range of values around our point estimate, known as a **range estimate**, that has a high probability of including the true value of the population parameter. This range estimate is called a **confidence interval**, and the remainder of this chapter will focus on constructing and interpreting confidence intervals for two of the population parameters discussed above: the population mean (μ) and the population proportion (p).

Note: The construction of a confidence interval for the population correlation coefficient ρ requires much more complex calculations, and is beyond the scope of this textbook.

In the last chapter, we saw how, given the population mean and standard error of sample means or sample proportions, we can determine a maximal error E that we would expect between a sample statistic and the corresponding population parameter, for a certain percent of the data.

For example, for a given set of data, we can compute the maximal sampling error E between the population mean (or proportion) and the sample mean (or proportion) for 95% of all samples collected. Hence, if we were to calculate a sample statistic $\bar{x}$ or $\hat{p}$, without knowing the value of the corresponding population parameter μ or p, we would still be able to say that we are 95% confident that our sample statistic will fall within the maximal margin of error E of the population parameter - i.e., $|\mu - \bar{x}| < E$ in the case of sample means, or $|p - \hat{p}| < E$ in the case of sample proportions.

In the previous chapter, we used the above inequalities to give us a bound on our sample statistics, given the value of the population parameter; however, now we can use these same inequalities to establish a bound on the population parameters, given the value of a sample statistic.

The confidence interval of the population parameter for the mean is: $\qquad \bar{x} - E < \mu < \bar{x} + E$

The confidence interval of the population parameter for a proportion is: $\quad \hat{p} - E < p < \hat{p} + E$

The level of confidence is the likelihood that our range of values will actually contain the true value of the population parameter, and is equal to the percent of the data that we expect to fall within the margin of error E, assuming the sampling distribution is normally distributed (which the Central Limit Theorem essentially guarantees, given a large enough sample size).

Example 9.1-b Establishing a Confidence Interval for the Population Mean

A sample of 95 patients undergoing a certain out-patient surgery have a mean post-operative recovery time of 5.2 hours. The margin of error at the 5% level of significance is computed to be 0.35 hours.

(i) Establish the 95% confidence interval for the true population mean post-operative recovery time for all patients undergoing this out-patient surgery.

(ii) Would the margin of error at the 1% level of significance be greater or lesser than 0.35 hours?

Solution

(i) The sample mean is $\bar{x}$ = 5.2 hours and the margin of error at the 5% level of significance is E = 0.35 hours. Hence, we are 100% – 5% = 95% confident that the population mean will fall within the following interval:

$$\bar{x} - E < \mu < \bar{x} + E$$
$$5.2 - 0.35 < \mu < 5.2 + 0.35$$
$$4.85 < \mu < 5.55 \text{ hours}$$

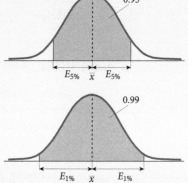

(ii) Since the probability that the population mean will not be contained within this range is only 1% (99% confidence interval), which is less than the original probability of 5% (95% confidence interval), the margin of error at the 1% level of significance must be **greater than** 0.35 hours.

Example 9.1-c Establishing a Confidence Interval for the Population Proportion

Of the 95 patients in the sample above, 74 were cleared to resume work/school after their 1 week follow-up appointment with the surgeon.

(i) Establish the 99% confidence interval for the true proportion of all patients who will be cleared to resume work/school after their 1 week follow-up appointment, if the margin of error is 0.11 at the 1% level of significance.

(ii) Would the margin of error at the 10% level of significance be greater or lesser than 0.11?

Solution

(i) The sample proportion is $\hat{p} = \dfrac{74}{95} \approx 0.78$ and the margin of error at the 1% level of significance

is E = 0.11. Hence, we are 100% – 1% = 99% confident that the population proportion will fall within the following interval:

$$\hat{p} - E < p < \hat{p} + E$$
$$0.78 - 0.11 < p < 0.78 + 0.11$$
$$0.67 < p < 0.89$$

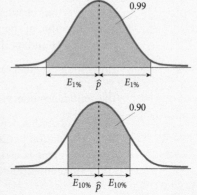

(ii) Since the probability that the population proportion will not be contained within this range is as high as 10% (90% confidence interval), which is much greater than the original probability of 1% (99% confidence interval), the margin of error at the 10% level of significance must be **less than** 0.11.

In the next three sections, we will look at how to calculate the margin of error, given the sample information for both population means and population proportions.

For Problems 1 to 6, a sample of 50 patients undergoing a new type of chemotherapy is collected and analyzed, using properly randomized sampling techniques and properly blinded observation techniques. Identify the following for each scenario presented:

(i)   *The sample statistic being used to estimate the desired population parameter.*

(ii) *The confidence level of the range estimate being used.*

(iii) *The confidence interval for the desired population parameter based on the estimator.*

1.   The average tumor size of patients undergoing treatment was 3.8 cm, which is accurate to within a margin of 0.4 cm, 19 times out of 20.

2.   The proportion of patients who went into remission after the treatment was 0.78, which is accurate to within a margin of 0.032, 9 times out of 10.

3.   The correlation between the duration of treatment and the reduction in the tumor size was given by a coefficient of 0.514, which is accurate to within a margin of 0.067, 9 times out of 10.

4.   The average percent reduction in the size of the tumor was 48.5%, which is accurate to within a margin of 7.3%, 99 times out of 100.

5.   The proportion of patients who were recommended surgery to remove the tumor after undergoing treatment was 0.64, which is accurate to within a margin of 0.045, 99 times out of 100.

6.   The correlation between the size of the tumor after treatment that was estimated by an MRI and the actual size of the tumor for those who underwent surgery was 0.818, which is accurate to within a margin of 0.040, 19 times out of 20.

For Problems 7 to 12, a sample of 80 clinically obese patients on a strict diet and exercise plan to reduce body fat and improve cardiovascular health is collected and analyzed, using properly randomized sampling techniques and properly blinded observation techniques. Identify the following for each scenario presented:

(i)   *The sample statistic being used to estimate the desired population parameter.*

(ii) *The confidence level of the range estimate being used.*

(iii) *The confidence interval for the desired population parameter based on the estimator.*

7.   The proportion of patients who began treatment with high LDL cholesterol levels ($\geq$160 mg/dL) was 0.775, and the margin of error at the 10% level of significance is computed to be 0.036.

8.   The average change in LDL cholesterol level from week 0 to week 8 of the treatment plan was 17.6 mg/dL, and the margin of error at the 5% level of significance is computed to be 2.9 mg/dL.

9.   The correlation between the percent body fat lost and the number of minutes spent on the treadmill every day was 0.388, and the margin of error at the 1% level of significance is computed to be 0.052.

10. The correlation between the percent body fat lost and the average number of calories consumed per day was -0.627, and the margin of error at the 10% level of significance is computed to be 0.049.

11. The average change in resting heart rate from week 0 to week 8 of the treatment plan was 18.6 bpm, and the margin of error at the 5% level of significance is computed to be 4.1 bpm.

12. The proportion of patients who experienced a significant change in their blood pressure after 8 weeks of treatment was 0.589, and the margin of error at the 1% level of significance is computed to be 0.016.

For Problems 13 to 16, determine what will happen to the resulting confidence interval for the given scenario, if the proposed changes are made (assume each change is made independently to the original scenario):

In order to estimate a population mean, a sample mean of 34.2 is collected from a sample of size $n = 60$, and the margin of error is computed to be 2.9 at the 5% level of significance. The resulting confidence interval for the population mean is $31.3 < \mu < 37.1$.

13. a.   The level of significance is decreased to 1%   b.   The sample size is increased to $n = 70$

14. a.   The level of significance is increased to 10%   b.   The sample size is decreased to $n = 50$

15. a. The sample mean is recalculated to be 35.6   b. The margin of error is recalculated to be 3.3

16. a. The sample mean is recalculated to be 32.4   b. The margin of error is recalculated to be 2.7

For Problems 17 to 20, determine what will happen to the resulting confidence interval for the given scenario, if the proposed changes are made (assume each change is made independently to the original scenario):

In order to estimate a population proportion, a sample proportion of 0.285 is collected from a sample of size $n = 150$, and the margin of error is computed to be 0.013 at the 2% level of significance. The resulting confidence interval for the population proportion is $0.272 < p < 0.298$.

17. a. The level of significance is increased to 5%   b. The sample size is decreased to $n = 120$

18. a. The level of significance is decreased to 1%   b. The sample size is increased to $n = 180$

19. a. The sample proportion is recalculated to be 0.263   b. The margin of error is recalculated to be 0.011

20. a. The sample proportion is recalculated to be 0.298   b. The margin of error is recalculated to be 0.016

9.2 | Confidence Intervals for μ when σ is Known

We start by determining the method to calculate the margin of error for the population mean when the population standard deviation is known. This may seem highly unrealistic, since calculating the population standard deviation requires the knowledge of the population mean, and in fact, it *is* highly unrealistic. However, in order to understand how to calculate the margin of error, and hence to construct a confidence interval, we first need to make the assumption that σ is known.

Note: In the next section, we will examine the more realistic cases where σ is also unknown.

Calculating the Margin of Error for μ when σ is Known

If we refer back to Chapter 8, we can see that, given the population mean of the sampling distribution of sample means, a random sample mean is expected to fall within the following range of values:

$$\mu_{\bar{x}} - z \cdot \sigma_{\bar{x}} < \bar{x} < \mu_{\bar{x}} + z \cdot \sigma_{\bar{x}}$$

The level of **confidence** is the probability that our range contains the value of interest.

The level of **significance** is the probability that our range **does not** contain the value of interest.

Confidence = 1 – Significance

We can see that the maximal margin of error E is simply the product of the standard error $\sigma_{\bar{x}}$ and the z-score corresponding to the percent of the sampling distribution data we are looking to capture, which corresponds with the desired confidence level, denoted $(1 - \alpha)$. For example, if we want to capture 95% of the sampling distribution data (i.e., establish a 95% confidence interval), then $1 - \alpha = 0.95$. Solving for α gives us $\alpha = 0.05$. This is known as the **level of significance**, and is the probability that our sample mean will fall outside our boundaries.

In the case of a confidence interval, this probability is split into the two "tails" on either side of the normal distribution curve, which we refer to as $\alpha/2$ - the probability that a sample mean will fall above the upper boundary, and the probability that it will fall below the lower boundary. For example, if we are looking to capture the middle 95% of the sample means, then the 5% of the sample means that we miss will be split into the bottom 2.5% and the top 2.5%. We call the z-score that separates those tails the **critical z-value** and denote it as $z_{\alpha/2}$.

Hence, the margin of error is calculated as follows:

Formula 9.2-a	**Maximal Margin of Error between μ and $\bar{x}$**

$$E = z_{\alpha/2} \cdot \sigma_{\bar{x}} = z_{\alpha/2} \cdot \frac{\sigma}{\sqrt{n}}$$

We can use the z-table to determine our critical z-value for any confidence level by computing the level of significance α, splitting it into two tails, and then determining the z-scores (both will have the same absolute value, one being positive and the other being negative) that separate those tails from the body of data in the middle of the curve.

Example 9.2-a   Calculating Critical Z-Values

Compute the critical z-values for the following confidence intervals:

(i)   75% confidence interval

(ii)   80% confidence interval

(iii)   92% confidence interval

Solution

(i)   For a 75% confidence interval, the level of significance is $\alpha = 1 - 0.75 = 0.25$. Hence,

$$\alpha/2 = \frac{0.25}{2} = 0.125$$

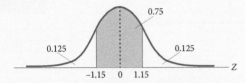

Looking up 0.1250 (bottom 12.5%) and 0.8750 (top 12.5%) in the z-table gives critical z-values of $z_{\alpha/2} = \pm 1.15$ (the closest values in the z-table are 0.1251 and 0.8749, respectively).

(ii)   For an 80% confidence interval, the level of significance is $\alpha = 1 - 0.80 = 0.20$. Hence,

$$\alpha/2 = \frac{0.20}{2} = 0.10$$

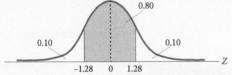

Looking up 0.1000 (bottom 10%) and 0.9000 (top 10%) in the z-table gives critical z-values of $z_{\alpha/2} = \pm 1.28$ (the closest values in the z-table are 0.1003 and 0.8997, respectively).

(iii)   For a 92% confidence interval, the level of significance is $\alpha = 1 - 0.92 = 0.08$. Hence,

$$\alpha/2 = \frac{0.08}{2} = 0.04$$

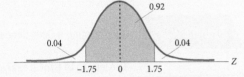

Looking up 0.0400 (bottom 4%) and 0.9600 (top 4%) in the z-table gives critical z-values of $z_{\alpha/2} = \pm 1.75$ (the closest values in the z-table are 0.0401 and 0.9599, respectively).

Example 9.2-b   Calculating the Margin of Error when σ is Known

Compute the maximal margin of error E for each of the following confidence intervals (round your answers to 3 significant digits):

(i)   75% confidence interval, $\sigma = 12.1$, $n = 30$

(ii)   80% confidence interval, $\sigma = 105$, $n = 75$

(iii)   92% confidence interval, $\sigma = 0.452$, $n = 240$

Solution

(i)   For a 75% confidence interval, we have determined the critical z-values are $z_{\alpha/2} = \pm 1.15$.

Using Formula 9.2-a, $E = z_{\alpha/2} \cdot \dfrac{\sigma}{\sqrt{n}} = 1.15 \cdot \dfrac{12.1}{\sqrt{30}} \approx 2.54$

(ii)   For an 80% confidence interval, we have determined the critical z-values are $z_{\alpha/2} = \pm 1.28$.

Using Formula 9.2-a, $E = z_{\alpha/2} \cdot \dfrac{\sigma}{\sqrt{n}} = 1.28 \cdot \dfrac{105}{\sqrt{75}} \approx 15.5$

(iii)   For a 92% confidence interval, we have determined the critical z-values are $z_{\alpha/2} = \pm 1.75$.

Using Formula 9.2-a, $E = z_{\alpha/2} \cdot \dfrac{\sigma}{\sqrt{n}} = 1.75 \cdot \dfrac{0.452}{\sqrt{240}} \approx 0.0511$

Although we can use the z-table to look up the critical z-values for any confidence interval, we list the critical z-values for the most common confidence intervals below, for convenience (rounded to 3 decimal places, instead of the usual 2, to provide a higher degree of accuracy):

Table 9.2

Critical z–values ($z_{\alpha/2}$) for Various Confidence Levels

Confidence Level	Critical z-value ($z_{\alpha/2}$)
80%	1.282
90%	1.645
95%	1.960
98%	2.326
99%	2.576

Once we have computed the maximal margin of error, E, we set up our confidence interval for μ as follows:

Formula 9.2-b

Confidence Interval for μ

$$\bar{x} - E < \mu < \bar{x} + E$$

Example 9.2-c

Constructing a Confidence Interval for μ when σ is Known

The length of time it takes the team of pharmacists to fill prescriptions at a local drug store is normally distributed with a mean of 21.2 minutes and a standard deviation of 3.5 minutes. A new system is implemented which is expected to improve the speed at which prescriptions are filled, to get the average time required to fill a prescription under the pharmacy's stated goal of 20 minutes. A sample of 25 prescriptions is taken, with a mean time required to fill the prescription of 18.9 minutes, with no noticeable change in the standard deviation (it is assumed to be independent of the system change).

(i)   Construct a 95% confidence interval for the true mean time required to fill a prescription under the new system.

(ii)   Discuss whether or not the pharmacy can claim they have met their stated goal.

Solution

(i)   We gather the following required information from the question:

$\bar{x} = 18.9$

$\sigma = 3.5$

$n = 25$

For a 95% confidence interval, we use a critical z-value of $z_{\alpha/2} = 1.960$, as from Table 9.2 above. From the above information, we can compute the margin of error:

Using Formula 9.2-a, $E = z_{\alpha/2} \cdot \dfrac{\sigma}{\sqrt{n}} = 1.960 \cdot \dfrac{3.5}{\sqrt{25}} \approx 1.37$

Hence, we are 95% confident that the population mean time required for a prescription to be filled is within the following interval:

Using Formula 9.2-b, $\bar{x} - E < \mu < \bar{x} + E$

$18.9 - 1.37 < \mu < 18.9 + 1.37$

$17.53 < \mu < 20.27$ minutes

Solution
continued

(ii)   While there is some evidence to back up the pharmacy's claim that they have met their goal of getting the average time required to fill a prescription under 20 minutes, there is not enough evidence to support this claim at the 95% confidence level, since the upper bound of the confidence interval for μ is 20.27 minutes. The pharmacy should take a larger sample size, and if their average time truly is under 20 minutes, they will be able to construct a confidence interval with an upper bound below 20 minutes.

Accuracy vs Precision of Confidence Intervals

When we construct a confidence interval for the population mean, we are estimating the value of μ, within a certain margin of error. We have two goals for our range estimate for μ:

1.   That the range estimate would be **accurate** - i.e., that there is a high probability that the true value for μ would actually be contained within our estimated range of values.

2.   That the range estimate would be **precise** - i.e., that the range of values is small enough to give us a close approximation of μ.

If we cannot reasonably accomplish both of the above stated goals, our range estimate is useless:

- A range that is too small will be unlikely to contain the actual value of μ, so we cannot trust the estimate.

- A range that is too large does not provide us with a close estimate for the actual value of μ, so we cannot use the estimate.

The problem, of course, is that increasing the accuracy (i.e., increasing the confidence interval) causes the precision to decrease, and increasing the precision (i.e., decreasing the confidence interval) causes the accuracy to decrease. So how do we accomplish both goals simultaneously? The answer, as is often the case in statistics, is to take a larger sample!

Determining the Sample Size Required for a Given Accuracy and Precision

The desired confidence level gives us the degree of accuracy and the maximal bound on the margin of error gives us the degree of precision we would like to establish with our range estimate. If we also know the population standard deviation σ, we can compute the minimum sample size that we require in order to achieve the desired confidence interval, by solving for n in Formula 9.2-a above:

Formula 9.2-c	**Sample Size for μ**

$$n = \left(\frac{z_{\alpha/2} \cdot \sigma}{E} \right)^2$$

*Note: Since n is the minimal sample size required, the final answer should be **rounded up** to the next whole number.*

Example 9.2-d	Determining the Sample Size Required for a Confidence Interval for μ

Assume that in Example 9.2-c above, the maximal margin of error that the pharmacy wanted to establish on their mean time required to fill a prescription, at the 95% confidence level, was 0.5 minutes. What size sample would they need to select in order to achieve this goal?

Recall the population standard deviation is assumed to be 3.5 minutes.

Solution

In order to establish a maximal margin of error of $E = 0.5$ at the 95% confidence level (with a critical z-value of $z_{\alpha/2} = 1.960$), we can calculate the minimum required sample size as follows:

Using Formula 9.2-c, $n = \left(\frac{z_{\alpha/2} \cdot \sigma}{E} \right)^2 = \left(\frac{1.960 \cdot 3.5}{0.5} \right)^2 = 13.72^2 = 188.2384$

188.2384 is **rounded up** to 189 since n is the **minimal** sample size required.

Therefore, the pharmacy would need to collect a sample of **at least** 189 prescriptions and determine the sample mean time taken to fill those prescriptions, in order to construct a confidence interval for the true mean time at their desired levels of accuracy and precision.

9.2 | Exercises

For Problems 1 to 8, calculate the margin of error and construct the confidence interval for the population mean (you may assume the population data is normally distributed):

1. a. $\bar{x} = 36.7$, $n = 45$, $\sigma = 0.64$, $\alpha = 0.05$ b. $\bar{x} = 74.5$, $n = 62$, $\sigma = 15.6$, $\alpha = 0.01$

2. a. $\bar{x} = 99.4$, $n = 70$, $\sigma = 1.25$, $\alpha = 0.10$ b. $\bar{x} = 51.3$, $n = 96$, $\sigma = 12.6$, $\alpha = 0.05$

3. a. $\bar{x} = 7.12$, $n = 128$, $\sigma = 1.79$, $\alpha = 0.02$ b. $\bar{x} = 4.63$, $n = 156$, $\sigma = 1.36$, $\alpha = 0.10$

4. a. $\bar{x} = 9.55$, $n = 136$, $\sigma = 0.89$, $\alpha = 0.01$ b. $\bar{x} = 3.24$, $n = 175$, $\sigma = 0.58$, $\alpha = 0.02$

5. a. $\bar{x} = 183.4$, $n = 20$, $\sigma = 17.8$, $\alpha = 0.20$ b. $\bar{x} = 0.255$, $n = 36$, $\sigma = 0.083$, $\alpha = 0.05$

6. a. $\bar{x} = 202.5$, $n = 25$, $\sigma = 19.6$, $\alpha = 0.20$ b. $\bar{x} = 0.477$, $n = 32$, $\sigma = 0.102$, $\alpha = 0.10$

7. a. $\bar{x} = 5.915$, $n = 240$, $\sigma = 0.787$, $\alpha = 0.01$ b. $\bar{x} = 13.28$, $n = 500$, $\sigma = 2.67$, $\alpha = 0.02$

8. a. $\bar{x} = 6.138$, $n = 316$, $\sigma = 0.941$, $\alpha = 0.05$ b. $\bar{x} = 17.63$, $n = 625$, $\sigma = 3.44$, $\alpha = 0.01$

9. A government initiative is implemented to reduce the average annual out-of-pocket medical costs for senior citizens. It is known from previous data that under the old system, the population mean annual cost in a particular region was $5,340 and the population standard deviation was $2,010. After the new program is implemented, the annual out-of-pocket medical costs are recorded for a sample of 75 senior citizens, and the resulting sample mean is $4,820. Calculate the margin of error and construct the 99% confidence interval for the new population mean, assuming that the population standard deviation remains unchanged. Does the result seem to support the government's claim that the new program has reduced the annual out-of-pocket cost to seniors?

10. A pharmacy restructures its fees in order to charge patients a smaller co-pay on prescription drugs. It is known from previous data that the population mean prescription co-pay was $19.50 and the population standard deviation was $12.75. After the new program is implemented, the average prescription co-pay for a sample of 55 patients was $15.25. Calculate the margin of error and construct the 90% confidence interval for the new population mean, assuming that the population standard deviation remains unchanged. Does the result seem to support the pharmacy's claim that the new program has reduced the average prescription co-pay?

11. The effects of a cholesterol-reducing drug is being clinically tested on a group of 140 patients with high cholesterol. Combined with a specific treatment plan, those using the drug experienced an average cholesterol reduction of 42.8 mg/dL more than those who were not using the drug. It is known from previous clinical trials that the standard deviation of the reduction in cholesterol levels as a result of using the drug is 17.5 mg/dL. Calculate the margin of error and construct the 90% confidence interval for the true mean cholesterol-level reduction caused by the drug.

12. The effects of an iron supplement in increasing hemoglobin levels is being clinically tested on a group of 160 patients suffering from anemia (low iron). Combined with a specific dietary plan, those using the supplement experienced an average hemoglobin increase of 6.8 g/dL. It is known from previous clinical trials that the standard deviation of the increase in hemoglobin levels as a result of using the supplement is 2.9 g/dL. Calculate the margin of error and construct the 99% confidence interval for the true mean hemoglobin-level increase caused by the supplement.

13. A patient with suspected high blood pressure measures his blood pressure using an automated test at a pharmacy every day for 30 days. The results of the blood pressure samples reveal a sample mean systolic blood pressure of 128.3 mmHg. If it is known that the standard deviation between systolic blood pressure measurements for the average person is 15.2 mmHg, calculate the margin of error and construct the 95% confidence interval for the population mean systolic blood pressure for this patient.

14. The blood pressure tests for the patient in Problem 13 reveal a sample mean diastolic blood pressure of 85.7 mmHg. If the standard deviation between diastolic blood pressure measurements for the average person is 9.6 mmHg, calculate the margin of error and construct the 95% confidence interval for the population mean diastolic blood pressure for this patient.

15. One of the side effects of a drug used to treat symptoms of Multiple Sclerosis (MS) is weight gain, especially in women. Previously, the weight gain of women who used the drug was normally distributed with a mean of 18.5 lb and a standard deviation of 7.25 lb. The pharmaceutical company makes some changes to the drug to try to reduce the weight-gain side effect. It is tested on a sample of 20 women with MS, and the sample mean weight-gain over the course of the drug treatment is 15.4 lb. Calculate the margin of error and construct a 98% confidence interval for the true mean weight gain for women with MS who use this drug, assuming that the standard deviation remains unchanged from the previous version of the drug. Does this result tell us that the weight gain effects of the drug have been improved significantly or not?

16. The study in Problem 15 was repeated a few years later with another modification made to the drug. This time, the clinical trial consisted of a larger sample of 40 women with MS, and the sample mean weight-gain over the course of the drug treatment was 13.8 lb. Calculate the margin of error and construct a 98% confidence interval for the true mean weight gain for women with MS who use this drug, assuming that the standard deviation remains unchanged from the original version of the drug. Does this result tell us that the weight gain effects of the drug have been improved significantly or not?

For Problems 17 to 20, we may assume that the sample standard deviation s is an accurate approximation of the population standard deviation σ (i.e., s ≈ σ), given that the sample size is so large (n > 200).

17. Scored tablets are used when pill-splitting is commonly needed to give half-doses of the drug. However, there is always concern that the masses of the pill halves will not be equal. A sample of 500 tablets, each with a mass of 500 mg, are split and the sample mean absolute difference between the masses of the two halves is computed to be 19.8 mg, with a standard deviation of 11.6 mg. Calculate the margin of error and construct the 95% confidence interval for the true population mean difference between the masses of the split halves of scored tablets.

18. Liquid suspensions are commonly used in children's medications. There is a concern about liquid suspensions around incorrect dosing, due to the imprecise nature of measuring out a dose. A sample of 300 parents are asked to pour out one dose (5 mL) of the medication in their usual way, and the amounts are measured. The sample mean is 6.2 mL, with a standard deviation of 0.75 mL. Calculate the margin of error and construct the 90% confidence interval for the true population mean difference between the masses of the split halves of scored tablets.

19. The mean annual salary of a sample of 256 Registered Nurses is $81,750 with a standard deviation of $11,490. Calculate the margin of error and construct the 99% confidence interval for the true population mean annual salary for Registered Nurses.

20. The mean annual salary of a sample of 225 Opticians is $49,870 with a standard deviation of $7,960. Calculate the margin of error and construct the 98% confidence interval for the true population mean annual salary for Opticians.

For Problems 21 to 28, determine the minimal sample size required to estimate the mean within the desired margin of error at the given level of significance.

21. A doctor is measuring uric acid levels in a patient's bloodstream via regular urine tests. If the population standard deviation of uric acid levels is 0.95 mg/dL, determine the number of tests the doctor will need to perform in order to ensure that this patient's mean uric acid level is accurate to within 0.5 mg/dL at the 2% level of significance?

22. A doctor is measuring glucose levels in a patient's bloodstream via regular finger-prick tests. If the population standard deviation of blood glucose levels is 23 mg/dL, determine the number of tests the doctor will need to perform in order to ensure that this patient's mean blood glucose level is accurate to within 10 mg/dL at the 10% level of significance?

23. If the doctor in Problem 21 made some changes to the parameters of the desired confidence interval, how would these affect the sample size required:
    a. Using half the level of significance - i.e., the 1% level of significance?
    b. Using half the margin of error - i.e., a margin of error of 0.25 mg/dL?
    (Note: use the original 2% level of significance)
    c. Based on your results from parts (a) and (b), which has more of an effect on the sample size - changing the level of significance or changing the margin of error?

24. If the doctor in Problem 22 made some changes to the parameters of the desired confidence interval, how would these affect the sample size required:

    a. Using half the level of significance - i.e., the 5% level of significance?

    b. Using half the margin of error - i.e., a margin of error of 5 mg/dL?
       (Note: use the original 10% level of significance)

    c. Based on your results from parts (a) and (b), which has more of an effect on the sample size - changing the level of significance or changing the margin of error?

25. The pharmaceutical company that produced the cholesterol-reducing drug from Problem 11 wishes to establish the mean LDL cholesterol-level reduction of the drug to within 2 mg/dL. If it is known from previous studies that the standard deviation in the reduction of LDL cholesterol levels as a result of using the drug is 17.5 mg/dL, what size sample will be needed to achieve the desired accuracy at the 10% level of significance?

26. The pharmaceutical company that produced the iron supplement from Problem 12 wishes to establish the mean hemoglobin-level increase of the supplement to within 0.5 g/dL. If it is known from previous studies that the standard deviation in the increase of hemoglobin levels as a result of using the supplement is 2.9 g/dL, what size sample will be needed to achieve the desired accuracy at the 1% level of significance?

27. A hospital administrator concerned with the wait times experienced by patients in the E.R. to see a triage nurse decides to conduct a study to measure the average wait time, accurate to within 1 minute. If it is known from previous studies that the standard deviation in wait times is approximately 4.25 minutes, how many patients will need to be sampled to achieve the desired accuracy at the 5% level of significance?

28. A pharmacy administrator concerned with the wait times experienced by patients ordering prescriptions at the pharmacy decides to conduct a study to measure the average wait time, accurate to within 0.5 minutes. If it is known from previous studies that the standard deviation in wait times is approximately 1.85 minutes, how many patients will need to be sampled to achieve the desired accuracy at the 2% level of significance?

9.3 | Confidence Intervals for μ when σ is Unknown

The confidence intervals constructed in the previous section relied on the knowledge of the population standard deviation. However, as previously stated, if we do not know the population mean, it is very unlikely that we would know the population standard deviation, especially since the population mean is required in order to calculate the population standard deviation.

In the absence of any information about the population standard deviation σ, we need to use the sample standard deviation s as an estimate for σ. As a result, the resulting sampling distribution is not necessarily well-approximated by a normal distribution, especially for small values of n. However, in some cases it is similar to a normal distribution, with some important distinguishing characteristics.

In the early 1900's, an English mathematician named William Gosset studied such distributions extensively, calling them t-distributions, in contrast to the normal z-distribution. However, as he was working for the Guinness brewery at the time, he was not allowed to publish his results. Gosset decided to publish his results anyways, but under the pseudonym "Student". As such, to this day, Gosset's distribution is known as the **Student's t-distribution** and is a very important distribution used to estimate an unknown population mean with a confidence interval constructed using the mean and standard deviation of a *sample*.

Student's *t*-Distribution

The Student's *t*-value is calculated in a very similar manner to the standard normal *z*-value:

Formula 9.3-a

Student's *t*-value

$$t = \frac{\bar{x} - \mu}{\frac{s}{\sqrt{n}}}$$

Note: We do not use the above formula to calculate t-statistics until Chapter 10, but it is introduced here to explain the nature of the t-distribution.

The Student's *t*-distribution is a sampling distribution of sample means with the following properties:

- The underlying population distribution for the variable *x must be normal.*

- The shape of the *t*-distribution is symmetrical and bell-curved, but flatter and wider than the standard normal *z*-distribution, the extent of which depends entirely on the size of the sample *n*.

- The *t*-distribution approaches a standard normal *z*-distribution as $n \to \infty$.

- The *t*-distribution has $(n - 1)$ degrees of freedom - i.e., $df = n - 1$, since the sample standard deviation is being used to approximate the population standard deviation.

Exhibit 9.3 shows how the *t*-distribution approaches the standard normal distribution as $n \to \infty$.

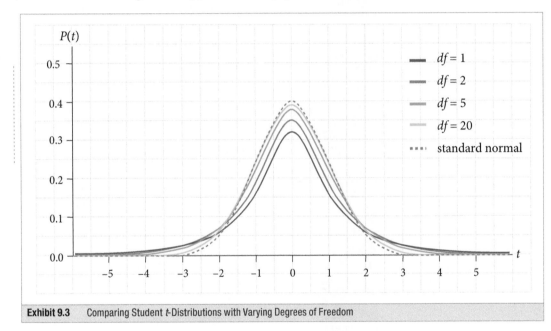

Exhibit 9.3 Comparing Student *t*-Distributions with Varying Degrees of Freedom

The critical values for the *t*-distribution, denoted $t_{\alpha/2}$, for a significance level α depend entirely on the size of the sample *n*, as summarized in the Student's *t*-distribution table on the next page.

Table 9.3 | Student's *t*-Distribution Table

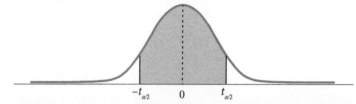

This table is also made available for reference in the Appendix on page 404.

df	80% confidence $\alpha = 0.20$ $\alpha/2 = 0.10$	90% confidence $\alpha = 0.10$ $\alpha/2 = 0.05$	95% confidence $\alpha = 0.05$ $\alpha/2 = 0.025$	98% confidence $\alpha = 0.02$ $\alpha/2 = 0.01$	99% confidence $\alpha = 0.01$ $\alpha/2 = 0.005$
1	3.078	6.314	12.706	31.820	63.657
2	1.886	2.920	4.303	6.965	9.925
3	1.638	2.353	3.182	4.541	5.841
4	1.533	2.132	2.776	3.747	4.604
5	1.476	2.015	2.571	3.365	4.032
6	1.440	1.943	2.447	3.143	3.707
7	1.415	1.895	2.365	2.998	3.499
8	1.397	1.860	2.306	2.897	3.355
9	1.383	1.833	2.262	2.821	3.250
10	1.372	1.812	2.228	2.764	3.169
11	1.363	1.796	2.201	2.718	3.106
12	1.356	1.782	2.179	2.681	3.055
13	1.350	1.771	2.160	2.650	3.012
14	1.345	1.761	2.145	2.625	2.977
15	1.341	1.753	2.131	2.602	2.947
16	1.337	1.746	2.120	2.584	2.921
17	1.333	1.740	2.110	2.567	2.898
18	1.330	1.734	2.101	2.552	2.878
19	1.328	1.729	2.093	2.539	2.861
20	1.325	1.725	2.086	2.528	2.845
21	1.323	1.721	2.080	2.518	2.831
22	1.321	1.717	2.074	2.508	2.819
23	1.319	1.714	2.069	2.500	2.807
24	1.318	1.711	2.064	2.492	2.797
25	1.316	1.708	2.060	2.485	2.787
26	1.315	1.706	2.056	2.479	2.779
27	1.314	1.703	2.052	2.473	2.771
28	1.313	1.701	2.048	2.467	2.763
29	1.311	1.699	2.045	2.462	2.756
30	1.310	1.697	2.042	2.457	2.750
35	1.306	1.690	2.030	2.438	2.724
40	1.303	1.684	2.021	2.423	2.704
45	1.301	1.679	2.014	2.412	2.690
50	1.299	1.676	2.009	2.403	2.678
60	1.296	1.671	2.000	2.390	2.660
70	1.294	1.667	1.994	2.381	2.648
80	1.292	1.664	1.990	2.374	2.639
90	1.291	1.662	1.987	2.369	2.632
100	1.290	1.660	1.984	2.364	2.626
120	1.289	1.658	1.980	2.358	2.617
150	1.287	1.655	1.976	2.351	2.609
200	1.286	1.652	1.972	2.345	2.601
∞ $(z_{\alpha/2})$	1.282	1.645	1.960	2.326	2.576

The highlighted value shows the critical *t*-value at the 95% confidence level ($\alpha/2 = 0.025$) for a sample with 50 degrees of freedom.

To use the *t*-table, follow these steps:

Step 1: Determine the number of degrees of freedom using $df = n - 1$, where n is the size of the sample, and round **down** to the closest value for *df* listed in the left-most column of the table.

For example, if the size of your sample is 57, then $df = 57 - 1 = 56$. Since 56 is not on the *t*-table, we round down to the closest value: 50.

Step 2: Look up the value in the body of the table at the intersection of the row corresponding to the degrees of freedom and the column representing the desired confidence level. This value is the **critical *t*-value** $t_{\alpha/2}$.

For example, for $df = 50$, at a 95% confidence interval (i.e., $\alpha/2 = 0.025$), $t_{\alpha/2} = 2.009$, as illustrated in Table 9.3 above.

Once we have determined the critical *t*-value $t_{\alpha/2}$ using the *t*-table, we can substitute it into the formula below to determine the maximal margin of error (similar to as we did with the critical *z*-value $z_{\alpha/2}$ in the previous section):

Formula 9.3-b	**Maximal Margin of Error for the Student's *t*-distribution**

$$E = t_{\alpha/2} \cdot \frac{s}{\sqrt{n}}$$

Example 9.3-a	**Determining which Sampling Distribution to Use**

In the following scenarios, determine if it is appropriate to use the Standard Normal Distribution, the Student's *t*-Distribution, or neither:

(i)   A sample of 15 is taken from a population that is approximately normal, and the sample mean of 12.1 and sample standard deviation of 2.72 are used to construct the 90% confidence interval for μ.

(ii) A sample of 72 is taken from a population whose distribution is unknown, and for which the standard deviation is known to be 15.6, and the sample mean of 72.5 is used to construct the 95% confidence interval for μ.

(iii) A sample of 24 is taken from a population whose distribution is unknown, and the sample mean of 0.875 and sample standard deviation of 0.0644 are used to construct the 99% confidence interval for μ.

Solution	

(i)   Since the population distribution is normal, but the population standard deviation is not known, we can use the Student's *t*-distribution to construct the confidence interval.

(ii) Since the population standard deviation is known and the sample size is relatively large ($n > 30$), we can use the standard normal *z*-distribution to construct the confidence interval.

(iii) Since the population distribution is unknown, we cannot use the *t*-distribution; since the population standard deviation is not known and the sample size is small ($n < 30$), the Central Limit Theorem does not apply, and so we cannot use the *z*-distribution.

Therefore, neither the standard normal distribution nor the student's *t*-distribution is appropriate to construct the confidence interval.

Example 9.3-b	**Constructing a Confidence Interval for μ when σ is Unknown**

A sample of the masses of 125 acetaminophen tablets yields a sample mean of 647.25 mg with a sample standard deviation of 8.78 mg. The data appears to be normally distributed.

(i)   Construct a 98% confidence interval for the mean mass for all such acetaminophen tablets.

(ii) If the pharmaceutical company claims that the average mass of their acetaminophen tablets is 650 mg, what do your results tell you about their claim?

Solution

(i) We are given in the question that $\bar{x} = 647.25$ and $s = 8.78$.

Looking up the critical t-value in Table 9.3 corresponding with $df = 125 - 1 = 124$, rounded down to $df = 120$, and a confidence level of 98% (i.e., $\alpha/2 = 0.01$), gives us $t_{\alpha/2} = 2.358$.

We can therefore compute the maximal margin of error:

Using Formula 9.3-b, $\qquad E = t_{\alpha/2} \cdot \dfrac{s}{\sqrt{n}} = 2.358 \cdot \dfrac{8.78}{\sqrt{125}} \approx 1.85$

Therefore, we are 98% confident that μ is within the following interval:

Using Formula 9.2-b, $\qquad \bar{x} - E < \mu < \bar{x} + E$

$$647.25 - 1.85 < \mu < 647.25 + 1.85$$

$$645.40 < \mu < 649.10$$

(ii) Since the upper bound of the confidence interval, 649.10, is less than 650, it is very unlikely (< 0.01) that the true mean mass of the acetaminophen tablets is equal to 650 mg.

Example 9.3-c Constructing a Confidence Interval for μ from Raw Data

A physician, studying the correlation between diastolic blood pressure and cardiac disease, takes the diastolic blood pressure from a sample of 15 male patients and records the results:

$$80 \quad 85 \quad 108 \quad 90 \quad 80 \quad 87 \quad 113 \quad 95 \quad 75 \quad 69 \quad 81 \quad 82 \quad 78 \quad 97 \quad 73$$

(i) Calculate the sample mean and sample standard deviation.

(ii) Construct the 90% confidence interval for the true population mean diastolic blood pressure of all male patients at his medical practice.

Solution

(i) $\qquad \bar{x} = \dfrac{80 + 85 + 108 + \ldots + 97 + 73}{15} = \dfrac{1{,}293}{15} = 86.2$

$$s = \sqrt{\dfrac{(80 - 86.2)^2 + (85 - 86.2)^2 + (108 - 86.2)^2 + \ldots + (97 - 86.2)^2 + (73 - 86.2)^2}{15 - 1}}$$

$$= \sqrt{\dfrac{2{,}188.4}{14}} \approx 12.5$$

(ii) Constructing a frequency distribution for this data indicates that it appears to be normally distributed, so we can use the Student's t-distribution.

Looking up the critical t-value in Table 9.3 corresponding with $df = 15 - 1 = 14$ and a confidence level of 90% (i.e., $\alpha/2 = 0.05$), gives us $t_{\alpha/2} = 1.761$.

We can therefore compute the maximal margin of error:

Using Formula 9.3-b, $\qquad E = t_{\alpha/2} \cdot \dfrac{s}{\sqrt{n}} = 1.761 \cdot \dfrac{12.5}{\sqrt{15}} \approx 5.68$

Therefore, we are 90% confident that μ is within the following interval:

Using Formula 9.2-b, $\qquad \bar{x} - E < \mu < \bar{x} + E$

$$86.2 - 5.68 < \mu < 86.2 + 5.68$$

$$80.52 < \mu < 91.88$$

9.3 | Exercises

For Problems 1 to 8, calculate the margin of error and construct the confidence interval for the population mean using the Student's t-distribution (you may assume the population data is normally distributed):

1. a. $\bar{x} = 48.2, n = 36, s = 22.5, \alpha = 0.05$ b. $\bar{x} = 66.5, n = 75, s = 19.7, \alpha = 0.01$

2. a. $\bar{x} = 85.5, n = 64, s = 13.5, \alpha = 0.10$ b. $\bar{x} = 34.7, n = 42, s = 18.2, \alpha = 0.05$

3. a. $\bar{x} = 7.66, n = 133, s = 1.84, \alpha = 0.02$ b. $\bar{x} = 3.81, n = 105, s = 0.66, \alpha = 0.10$

4. a. $\bar{x} = 9.15, n = 92, s = 2.31, \alpha = 0.01$ b. $\bar{x} = 4.24, n = 128, s = 1.12, \alpha = 0.02$

5. a. $\bar{x} = 168.5, n = 24, s = 10.8, \alpha = 0.20$ b. $\bar{x} = 0.316, n = 16, s = 0.125, \alpha = 0.05$

6. a. $\bar{x} = 142.9, n = 12, s = 15.3, \alpha = 0.02$ b. $\bar{x} = 0.144, n = 25, s = 0.061, \alpha = 0.20$

7. a. $\bar{x} = 2.814, n = 185, s = 0.786, \alpha = 0.01$ b. $\bar{x} = 21.45, n = 300, s = 6.53, \alpha = 0.02$

8. a. $\bar{x} = 1.957, n = 196, s = 0.466, \alpha = 0.05$ b. $\bar{x} = 17.86, n = 425, s = 5.77, \alpha = 0.01$

9. A sample of 88 pre-operative patients is collected and the patients' body temperatures are recorded. The average temperature is 36.5 °C, with a standard deviation of 0.74 °C. Calculate the margin of error and construct the 95% confidence interval for the population mean pre-operative body temperature.

10. A sample of 96 post-operative patients is collected and the patients' urine outputs are recorded. The average output in the first 8 hours is 375 mL, with a standard deviation of 96 mL. Calculate the margin of error and construct the 90% confidence interval for the population mean post-operative urine output.

11. A sample of 44 patients at a walk-in clinic have an average wait time of 48.5 minutes before seeing a doctor, with a standard deviation of 16.4 minutes. Calculate the margin of error and construct the 99% confidence interval for the population mean total time spent in the E.R. for patients with minor conditions.

12. A sample of 52 patients who come to the E.R. with minor conditions are required to spend an average total of 4.27 hours in the hospital before being discharged, with a standard deviation of 1.12 hours. Calculate the margin of error and construct the 95% confidence interval for the population mean wait time at the walk-in clinic.

13. An athletic trainer has his client run for as long as he can at a sprinting speed on a treadmill and enters the results into a tracking software 5 days a week for 3 weeks to measure his progress. The distribution of the lengths of time the patient can run at that speed on the treadmill appear to be normally distributed, with a sample mean of 4.83 minutes and a standard deviation of 1.27 minutes. Calculate the margin of error and construct the 90% confidence interval for the true mean time that the client can run on the treadmill.

14. The athletic trainer in Problem 13 also measures the maximum weight the patient can leg press over the 3 weeks, but only takes 4 measurements every week. The distribution of maximum weights the patient can leg press appear to be normally distributed, with a sample mean of 198.2 lb and a standard deviation of 16.5 lb. Calculate the margin of error and construct the 99% confidence interval for the true mean maximum weight that the client can leg press.

For Problems 15 to 20, you may assume that the data is approximately normally distributed. This can be easily verified by constructing a frequency distribution for the data.

15. A veterinarian records the weights of 8-week-old puppies of a certain breed (measured in kg):

    | 5.78 | 8.71 | 3.07 | 3.35 | 5.97 | 5.02 | 4.24 | 6.32 |
    | 5.40 | 2.87 | 6.91 | 5.58 | 5.64 | 4.86 | 4.18 | 3.10 |

    a. Calculate the sample mean and standard deviation.

    b. Construct the 95% confidence interval for the mean 8-week-old weight for all puppies of this breed.

16. A pediatrician records the weights of 1-month-old baby girls (measured in kg):

    | 4.79 | 3.56 | 4.47 | 4.65 | 3.57 | 4.13 | 3.52 |
    | 4.35 | 4.04 | 5.04 | 4.65 | 4.02 | 4.20 | 3.78 |

    a. Calculate the sample mean and standard deviation.

    b. Construct the 99% confidence interval for the mean 1-month-old weight of all baby girls.

17. A health insurance broker records the monthly extended health and dental insurance premiums for 20 non-smoking male clients between the ages of 41 and 50 (measured in $):

73	166	89	67	56	92	171	145	99	52
181	123	105	121	59	81	141	101	96	78

a. Calculate the sample mean and standard deviation.

b. Construct the 99% confidence interval for the mean monthly insurance premium for all non-smoking males between the ages of 41 and 50.

18. A health insurance broker records the monthly extended health and dental insurance premiums for 18 non-smoking female clients between the ages of 31 and 40 (measured in $):

112	56	89	121	103	48	82	121	99
127	87	125	151	60	115	89	113	67

a. Calculate the sample mean and standard deviation.

b. Construct the 98% confidence interval for the mean monthly insurance premium for all non-smoking females between the ages of 31 and 40.

19. A physiotherapist measures the improvement in the angle of external rotation of the shoulder for 9 patients over the course of the first 6 weeks of treatment (measured in degrees of rotation):

33	13	22	10	27	31	27	40	15

a. Calculate the sample mean and standard deviation.

b. Construct the 90% confidence interval for the mean improvement in external rotation of the shoulder for all patients over the course of the first 6 weeks of treatment.

20. An oncologist records the decrease in the size of the tumor of 12 different breast-cancer patients after a full round of chemotherapy (measured in % decrease from the initial diameter):

25	55	53	13	62	78	37	28	66	35	50	46

a. Calculate the sample mean and standard deviation.

b. Construct the 95% confidence interval for the mean reduction in tumor size for all breast-cancer patients after a full round of chemotherapy.

For Problems 21 to 24, determine the sample mean and sample standard deviation based on the confidence interval for the population mean:

21. a. $n = 25$, 95% confidence interval: $5.77 < \mu < 6.73$

    b. $n = 18$, 90% confidence interval: $26.6 < \mu < 38.2$

22. a. $n = 16$, 99% confidence interval: $6.90 < \mu < 8.78$

    b. $n = 30$, 95% confidence interval: $39.4 < \mu < 49.0$

23. a. $n = 10$, 98% confidence interval: $0.606 < \mu < 0.824$

    b. $n = 36$, 99% confidence interval: $165 < \mu < 187$

24. a. $n = 12$, 90% confidence interval: $0.565 < \mu < 0.719$

    b. $n = 81$, 98% confidence interval: $206 < \mu < 224$

9.4 | Confidence Intervals for p

We conclude the chapter by constructing range estimates for the true population proportion of successes in a binomial distribution, based on a sample proportion of successes. This section relies heavily on the content from Section 9.2, as well as that from Section 7.3 (The Normal Approximation to the Binomial Distribution), and Section 8.3 (Sampling Distribution of Sample Proportions).

In order to make use of the normal approximation to the $\hat{p}$-distribution, we need to ensure that the "sufficiently large sample" conditions are met:

1. The sample size is sufficiently large - i.e., $n \geq 30$.

2. The sample number of successes and failures are both greater than 5 - i.e., $n\hat{p} > 5$ and $n\hat{q} > 5$.

If those conditions hold true, then the normal curve is a reasonable approximation to the $\hat{p}$-distribution, and the sample data provides reasonable estimates for the parameters:

$$\hat{p} = \frac{x}{n}$$

is the best point estimate for p - the population proportion of successes - where x is the number of successful outcomes in n trials of a binomial experiment.

$$\hat{q} = 1 - \hat{p}$$

is the best point estimate for q - the population proportion of failures.

$$s_{\hat{p}} = \sqrt{\frac{\hat{p} \cdot \hat{q}}{n}}$$

is a good approximation of $\sigma_{\hat{p}}$ - the population standard error of the $\hat{p}$-distribution.

Hence, we can use the z-distribution to determine the critical values needed to construct the confidence interval for p:

Formula 9.4-a	**Maximal Margin of Error between p and $\hat{p}$**

$$E = z_{\alpha/2} \cdot \sigma_{\hat{p}} \approx z_{\alpha/2} \cdot \sqrt{\frac{\hat{p} \cdot \hat{q}}{n}}$$

Here, E is the maximal margin of error expected between p and $\hat{p}$ with a level of significance equal to α, which we can then use to determine the confidence interval for the true population proportion p, as follows:

Formula 9.4-b	**Confidence Interval for p**

$$\hat{p} - E < p < \hat{p} + E$$

Example 9.4-a	**Constructing a Confidence Interval for p**

In a clinical trial of a new antibiotic, 481 out of 520 patients had their infection completely healed within the indicated treatment time without any unexpected side effects (considered a "successful" treatment). Based on the results from this clinical study, construct a 99% confidence interval for the true proportion of patients that will have their infection successfully treated by this new antibiotic.

Solution

Before attempting to make any estimates for the population proportion, we first need to check that the conditions for the normal approximation to the $\hat{p}$-distribution are met:

- The sample size is 520, which is much larger than 30.

- The number of successes is 481 and the number of failures is $520 - 481 = 39$, both of which are much greater than 5.

Hence, we are able to use the normal (i.e., z-distribution) approximation to the $\hat{p}$-distribution. We compute the sample values for the $\hat{p}$-distribution:

$$\hat{p} = \frac{481}{520} = 0.925, \qquad \hat{q} = 1 - 0.925 = 0.075, \qquad n = 520$$

For a 99% confidence interval, we use a critical z-value of $z_{\alpha/2} = 2.576$ (as from Table 9.2).

Using Formula 9.4-a, $\qquad E = z_{\alpha/2} \cdot \sqrt{\dfrac{\hat{p} \cdot \hat{q}}{n}} = 2.576 \cdot \sqrt{\dfrac{0.925 \cdot 0.075}{520}} \approx 0.0298$

Therefore, we are 99% confident that the population proportion of successful treatments is within the following interval:

Using Formula 9.4-b, $\qquad \hat{p} - E < p < \hat{p} + E$

$$0.925 - 0.0298 < p < 0.925 + 0.0298$$

$$0.8952 < p < 0.9548$$

Example 9.4-b | **Interpreting a Confidence Interval for p**

A polling company conducts a poll leading up to a federal election to determine the percent of the voters in the country who still approve of the prime minister. The survey asks voters to rank their approval of the prime minister on a scale of 1-5, where 1 is "strongly disapprove", 2 is "disapprove", 3 is "neutral", 4 is "approve", and 5 is "strongly approve". A sample of 1,000 voters are surveyed, and the results of the poll show that 32.4% of the voters approve or strongly approve of the prime minister. The polling company states that the poll is "accurate within 3 percentage points, 19 times out of 20". Using the language of confidence intervals, interpret the meaning of the polling company's statement, and verify its accuracy.

Solution

The statement that the poll is accurate within 3 percentage points indicates that the maximal margin of error for p is 0.03 from $\hat{p} = 0.324$. That is, $0.294 < p < 0.354$.

The statement that the poll is accurate 19 times out of 20 indicates a confidence level of $\dfrac{19}{20} = 95\%$.

Based on the information provided in the question, $\hat{p} = 0.324$, $\hat{q} = 1 - 0.324 = 0.676$, and $n = 1{,}000$.

Therefore, the standard error is $\sigma_{\hat{p}} = \sqrt{\dfrac{\hat{p} \cdot \hat{q}}{n}} = \sqrt{\dfrac{0.324 \cdot 0.676}{1{,}000}} \approx 0.0148$.

Since the polling company is using a 95% confidence interval, the critical z-value is $z_{\alpha/2} = 1.960$.

Hence, the maximal margin of error is $E = z_{\alpha/2} \cdot \sigma_{\hat{p}} = 1.960 \cdot 0.0148 \approx 0.0290$, which is inside the stated maximal margin of error of 0.03; therefore, the results of the poll are stated correctly.

In order to obtain a confidence interval for the population proportion with a desired level of accuracy (i.e., confidence level) and precision (i.e., margin of error), we can compute the minimum required sample size, just as we did for a confidence interval for the population mean.

Formula 9.4-c | **Sample Size for p**

$$n = \hat{p} \cdot \hat{q} \cdot \left(\frac{z_{\alpha/2}}{E} \right)^2$$

---

*Note: Since n is the minimal sample size required, the final answer should be **rounded up** to the next whole number.*

Notice that in this formula, unlike for a confidence interval for the population mean, we do not need to know the standard deviation to compute n; we can simply use preliminary estimates for $\hat{p}$ and $\hat{q}$. If we do not have preliminary estimates for $\hat{p}$ and $\hat{q}$, we can use $\hat{p} = \hat{q} = 0.5$, since that will give us the largest possible sample size needed.

Note: You can prove that $\hat{p} = \hat{q} = 0.5$ will give the largest possible sample size needed by using quadratic equations - or even trial and error - to determine what value of $\hat{p}$ will maximize the equation $M = \hat{p}(1 - \hat{p})$.

Example 9.4-c | **Determining the Sample Size Required for a Confidence Interval for p**

If the polling company in Example 9.4-b wanted to ensure that every survey they conducted would be "accurate within 3 percentage points, 19 times out of 20", regardless of the proportion of population support for the prime minister, determine the sample size they would need to collect for every survey.

Solution

Without an estimate for $\hat{p}$ and $\hat{q}$, we use $\hat{p} = \hat{q} = 0.5$. We also know that $E = 0.03$, and since this is a 95% confidence interval, the critical z-value is $z_{\alpha/2} = 1.960$. Hence, we can calculate the minimum required sample size as follows:

Using Formula 9.4-c, $\quad n = \hat{p} \cdot \hat{q} \cdot \left(\dfrac{z_{\alpha/2}}{E} \right)^2$

$$= (0.5)(0.5)\left(\frac{1.960}{0.03} \right)^2$$

$$= (0.25)(65.333333\ldots)^2$$

$$= 1{,}067.\overline{1}$$

> $1{,}067.\overline{1}$ is **rounded up to 1,068** since n is the **minimal sample size required.**

Therefore, the polling company would need to conduct a survey from a sample of **at least** 1,068 voters.

9.4 | Exercises

Answers to odd-numbered problems are available at the end of the textbook.

For Problems 1 to 8, calculate the sample proportion and the margin of error and construct the confidence interval for the population proportion using the normal approximation to the $\hat{p}$-distribution (if it is appropriate to do so):

1. a. $x = 12$, $n = 40$, $\alpha = 0.05$ b. $x = 52$, $n = 80$, $\alpha = 0.01$

2. a. $x = 19$, $n = 50$, $\alpha = 0.10$ b. $x = 36$, $n = 75$, $\alpha = 0.05$

3. a. $x = 111$, $n = 150$, $\alpha = 0.02$ b. $x = 63$, $n = 180$, $\alpha = 0.10$

4. a. $x = 128$, $n = 160$, $\alpha = 0.01$ b. $x = 45$, $n = 120$, $\alpha = 0.02$

5. a. $x = 363$, $n = 400$, $\alpha = 0.20$ b. $x = 4$, $n = 250$, $\alpha = 0.05$

6. a. $x = 297$, $n = 300$, $\alpha = 0.02$ b. $x = 21$, $n = 350$, $\alpha = 0.20$

7. a. $x = 9$, $n = 18$, $\alpha = 0.01$ b. $x = 28$, $n = 42$, $\alpha = 0.02$

8. a. $x = 6$, $n = 36$, $\alpha = 0.05$ b. $x = 8$, $n = 16$, $\alpha = 0.01$

9. In a study to determine the prevalence of undiagnosed diabetes and prediabetes in the population, a sample of 400 people who had not been previously diagnosed with diabetes or prediabetes had their fasting blood glucose measured to determine if they were at risk. Out of this sample, 14 people had fasting blood glucose levels that indicated they were diabetic. Based on this result, construct the 99% confidence interval for the true proportion of undiagnosed diabetes in the general population.

10. In the study in Problem 9, out of the 400 people that were sampled, 52 had a fasting blood glucose level that indicated they were prediabetic. Based on this result, construct the 95% confidence interval for the true proportion of undiagnosed prediabetes in the general population.

11. A study was conducted to analyze the appearance of surgical site infections that occur in patients who have undergone surgery. In a random sample of 1,000 patients who had undergone surgery, 112 developed surgical site infections afterwards. Based on this result, construct the 98% confidence interval for the true proportion of patients that have undergone surgery who develop a surgical site infection afterwards.

12. Out of the 112 patients who developed surgical site infections in Problem 11, 78 of those patients developed their infection after they were discharged from the hospital. Based on this result, construct the 90% confidence interval for the true proportion of surgical site infections that develop after the patient has been discharged from the hospital.

13. A survey was conducted at a local hospital to determine patient satisfaction with the care provided. The survey consisted of several questions on a 5-point scale, where 1 was extremely unsatisfied and 5 was extremely satisfied, and where a response of 4 (satisfied) or 5 (extremely satisfied) is considered to be a success in the hospital's ability to provide an appropriate standard of care. Out of the 520 patients who were sampled, 424 responded with either a 4 or 5 to the overall care provided by the nursing team. Calculate the margin of error of this result at the 5% level of significance, and construct the corresponding confidence interval for the true proportion of patients who felt the nursing team succeeded in providing an appropriate standard of care.

14. The data collected from the survey in Problem 13 indicated that 368 out of the 520 patients surveyed responded with either a 4 or a 5 to the overall care provided by the attending physician(s). Calculate the margin of error of this result at the 2% level of significance, and construct the corresponding confidence interval for the true proportion of patients who felt the physician(s) succeeded in providing an appropriate standard of care.

15. A study is being conducted by a group of veterinarians to analyze the decisions of pet owners who do not have pet insurance who would opt for medical treatment for their pet if the cost of the treatment exceeded $1,000. A random stratified sample of 150 pet owners without pet insurance was collected, and out of those sampled, 78 said they would opt for treatment when presented with the choice if the treatment would cost over $1,000 in total. Calculate the margin of error for this result at the 1% level of significance, and construct the corresponding confidence interval for the true proportion of pet owners that do not have pet insurance who would be willing to pay over $1,000 for medical treatment for their pet.

16. A study conducted in Problem 15 was revised to study how the result changed when the cost of treatment increased to over $5,000. This time, only 33 out of the 150 pet owners surveyed said they would opt for treatment when presented with the choice if the treatment would cost over $5,000 in total. Calculate the margin of error for this result at the 5% level of significance, and construct the corresponding confidence interval for the true proportion of pet owners that do not have pet insurance who would be willing to pay over $5,000 for medical treatment for their pet.

17. A group of athletic therapists conduct a study of the effectiveness of a new type of therapy used to treat injured athletes. A sample of 102 injured athletes who were expected to remain on the disabled list for an entire season as a result of their injuries had their injuries treated using the new type of therapy. Of those athletes, 87 were cleared to return to training earlier than expected. Calculate the margin of error for this result at the 10% level of significance, and construct the corresponding confidence interval for the true proportion of athletes treated using the new type of therapy who will be cleared to return to training earlier than expected.

18. Out of the 102 injured athletes in Problem 17 who were treated using the new type of therapy, 28 were cleared to return to playing without restrictions earlier than expected. Calculate the margin of error for this result at the 10% level of significance, and construct the corresponding confidence interval for the true proportion of athletes treated using the new type of therapy who will be cleared to return to playing without restrictions earlier than expected.

For Problems 19 to 24, interpret the results of the study using the language of confidence intervals and verify the results. If the results are incorrect, modify the statement made so that the results are stated correctly.

19. Prior to an election, a polling company conducts a stratified national survey of 1,000 registered voters and states that results show that the proportion of voters who plan to vote for the current government party is 28.7%, accurate within 3 percentage points, 19 times out of 20.

20. The polling company in Problem 19 states that the results of the sample of 1,000 voters claim that the proportion of voters who plan to vote for the current opposition party is 35.2%, accurate within 3 percentage points, 19 times out of 20.

21. An oncologist providing information to a patient with cancer quotes a study of 500 people with the same type of cancer, in which the treatment combination of chemotherapy and radiation successfully caused the cancer to go into remission in 64.6% of the cases. The study claims to be accurate within 5 percentage points, 99 times out of 100.

22. On a second opinion, the patient from Problem 21 is encouraged to try another type of treatment that, although riskier, has a higher rate of success at 79.7%. However, the study only included 200 patients and claims to be accurate within 5 percentage points only 9 times out of 10.

23. A new pharmaceutical drug claims to relieve symptoms within 1 hour in 95% of the patients who use it. The study was conducted on a sample of 750 patients and claims to be accurate within 2 percentage points, 49 times out of 50.

24. The pharmaceutical drug in Problem 23 claims to relieve symptoms within 15 minutes in 70% of the patients who use it, based on the same sample of 750 patients, and also claims to be accurate within 2 percentage points, 49 times out of 50.

For Problems 25 to 32, determine the minimal sample size required to estimate the population proportion within the desired margin of error at the given level of significance.

25. A researcher believes that when a couple has a second child, there is a higher probability that the child will be the same sex as the first child. To study this, the researcher wishes to collect a sample of couples with exactly two biological children and record the proportion of those whose children are both the same sex (statistically speaking, if sex is an independent characteristic for each child, then the proportion of couples with two children of the same sex should be 0.50). What size sample will need to be collected in order to estimate the true proportion of couples with two children, both of the same sex, accurate to within 0.03 at the 5% level of significance?

26. The researcher in Problem 25 wishes to examine if the same trend of a higher-than-expected proportion of couples having children of all the same sex holds true for couples with three children as well (statistically speaking, if sex is an independent characteristic for each child, then the proportion of couples with three children of the same sex should be 0.25). What size sample will need to be collected in order to estimate the true proportion of couples with three children, all of the same sex, accurate to within 0.03 at the 1% level of significance?

27. A pharmaceutical company wishes to conduct a sample to determine the proportion of tablets produced that are considered defective, within a margin of error of 0.01 at the 10% level of significance. If the pharmaceutical company knows for sure that no more than 5% of all tablets produced are defective, how many tablets need to be sampled in order to estimate the true proportion at the desired level of accuracy?

28. If the pharmaceutical company in Problem 27 knows that in fact the proportion of defective tablets is no more than 2%, how would this change the size of the sample needed to estimate the true proportion of defective tablets within a margin of error of 0.01 at the 10% level of significance.

29. An orthopedic surgeon would like to know the proportion of patients who undergo reconstructive shoulder surgery that have a totally successful surgery with no further issues with their shoulder for at least 5 years afterwards. How big a sample would the surgeon need to collect in order to estimate the true proportion within 0.05 at the 1% level of significance, if she estimates the proportion to be at least 0.75?

30. A dentist wishes to know what proportion of the adult population in his region have had their wisdom teeth removed within 0.04 at the 2% level of significance. How big a sample must he collect, if he estimates the true proportion to be at least 0.60?

31. An EMT wishes to determine the proportion of 911 calls that EMTs respond to that are false alarms. How big a sample would the EMT need to collect in order to estimate the true proportion within 0.08 at the 2% level of significance, if he has no preliminary notion of the true proportion?

32. A nurse administrator wishes to know the proportion of nurses that are currently using a very costly benefit to determine if it is still considered to be valuable by the nursing staff. If the administrator has no preliminary notion of the proportion of nurses using the benefit, how big a sample must she collect to be accurate within 0.10 at the 1% level of significance?

9 | Review Exercises

For Problems 1 to 4, a sample of 270 doses of a liquid suspension fever-reducing medication is collected and analyzed, using properly randomized sampling techniques and properly blinded observation techniques. Identify the following for each scenario presented:

(i) *The sample statistic being used to estimate the desired population parameter.*

(ii) *The confidence level of the range estimate being used.*

(iii) *The confidence interval for the desired population parameter based on the estimator.*

1. The correlation between the volume of medication measured out and the amount of drug in the dose is given by a correlation coefficient of 0.996, accurate to within a margin of 0.003, 99 times out of 100.

2. The average concentration of the liquid suspension is 31.8 mg/mL, which is accurate to within a margin of 0.25 mg/mL, 19 times out of 20.

3. The average measured dose of the liquid suspension was 9.7 mL, which is accurate to within 0.8 mL, 9 times out of 10.

4. The proportion of doses containing contaminants was 0.015, which is accurate to within 0.004, 49 times out of 50.

For Problems 5 to 8, determine what will happen to the resulting confidence interval for the given scenario, if the proposed changes are made (assume each change is made independently to the original scenario):

In order to estimate a population proportion, a sample proportion of 0.3 is collected from a sample of size of $n = 500$, and the margin of error is computed to be 0.04 at the 5% level of significance. The resulting confidence interval for the population proportion is $0.26 < p < 0.34$.

5. a. The level of significance is increased to 10%
    b. The sample size is decreased to 200

6. a. The level of significance is decreased to 2%
    b. The sample size is increased to 450

7. a. The sample proportion is recalculated to be 0.42
    b. The margin of error is recalculated to be 0.035

8. a. The sample proportion is recalculated to be 0.24
    b. The margin of error is recalculated to be 0.044

For Problems 9 and 10, calculate the margin of error and construct the confidence interval for the population mean (you may assume the population data is normally distributed):

9. a. $\bar{x} = 151.2$, $n = 278$, $\sigma = 23.3$, $\alpha = 0.05$
    b. $\bar{x} = 35.4$, $n = 25$, $\sigma = 5.1$, $\alpha = 0.01$

10. a. $\bar{x} = 2.45$, $n = 50$, $\sigma = 0.8$, $\alpha = 0.20$
    b. $\bar{x} = 501.5$, $n = 361$, $\sigma = 16.8$, $\alpha = 0.10$

11. The average number of LDL-reducing medication tablets produced at a pharmaceutical company in a given hour is 3,500 with a standard deviation of 160. After a recent equipment upgrade, a sample of 64 hourly production times were recorded, and the sample mean number of pills produced per hour increased to 3,592. Calculate the margin of error and construct the 95% confidence interval for the population mean, assuming the standard deviation remains unchanged. Does the result seem to support the claim that the number of pills produced has increased using the new equipment?

12. The average number of patients seen and treated in an E.R. ward of a hospital over an 8-hour shift is 320 with a standard deviation of 60. After the implementation of a new queuing system, a sample of 36 8-hour shifts was taken, and the sample mean number of patients seen and treated is 343. Calculate the margin of error and construct the 95% confidence interval for the population mean, assuming the standard deviation remains unchanged. Does the result seem to support the claim that the efficiency of the E.R. has increased after adding the queuing system?

For Problems 13 and 14, we may assume that the sample standard deviation s is an accurate approximation of the population standard deviation σ (i.e., $s \approx \sigma$), given that the sample size is so large ($n > 200$).

13. During aerobic exercise, the heart rate can increase up to 200 bpm or more. A sample of 289 participants were asked to sprint 200 metres and record their maximum heart rates. The sample mean is 174.3 bpm with a standard deviation of 28.56 bpm. Calculate the margin of error and construct the 99% confidence interval for the true population mean bpm for heart rates during aerobic exercise.

14. The mean annual salary of a sample of 400 paediatricians is $215,620 with a standard deviation of $38,790. Calculate the margin of error and construct the 98% confidence interval for the true population mean salary for paediatricians.

For Problems 15 and 16, determine the minimal sample size required to estimate the mean within the desired margin of error at the given level of significance.

15. A pharmaceutical company manufacturing diabetes medication wishes to test the mean concentration of metformin in each of its pills, accurate to within 0.5 mg. From an earlier test, the company knows that the standard deviation is 2.75 mg. What sample size will be needed to achieve the desired accuracy at the 5% significance level?

16. Scientists experimenting with cancerous cells wish to control the number of T-cells in a petri dish, with a standard deviation of 500 cells. Determine the number of tests that the scientists will need to perform in order to ensure that population mean number of T-cells is accurate to within 100 cells, at the 1% significance level.

For Problems 17 and 18, calculate the margin of error and construct the confidence interval for the population mean using the Student's t-distribution (you may assume the population data is normally distributed):

17. a. $\bar{x} = 24.57$, $n = 144$, $s = 8.3$, $\alpha = 0.02$

    b. $\bar{x} = 0.95$, $n = 36$, $s = 0.08$, $\alpha = 0.10$

18. a. $\bar{x} = 12.85$, $n = 49$, $s = 1.78$, $\alpha = 0.05$

    b. $\bar{x} = 240$, $n = 196$, $s = 10.5$, $\alpha = 0.01$

19. A sample of 100 pills being developed to treat obesity is taken. The result of the sample show a mean statin concentration of 60 mg per pill with a sample standard deviation of 4.5 mg. Use the Student's t-distribution to calculate the margin of error and construct the 99% confidence interval for the population mean concentration of statin in the pill.

20. A patient has his systolic blood pressure monitored daily over the course of 3 months (i.e., 90 days), with an average of 130 mmHg and a standard deviation of 6.9 mmHg. Use the Student's t-distribution to calculate the margin of error and construct the 90% confidence interval for the patient's true mean systolic blood pressure.

For Problems 21 and 22, you may assume that the data is approximately normally distributed.

21. An equestrian surgeon records the number of open heart surgeries that she performs per month, over the course of one year:

    | 13 | 20 | 15 | 19 | 15 | 9 |
    | 8 | 10 | 12 | 24 | 18 | 14 |

    a. Calculate the sample mean and standard deviation.

    b. Construct the 95% confidence interval for the mean number of open heart surgeries the surgeon performs in a month.

22. An athletic therapist and sports trainer records the maximum weight (in lb) her patient can squat press every day for a week:

    | 80 | 75 | 90 | 95 | 85 | 90 | 100 |

    a. Calculate the sample mean and standard deviation.

    b. Construct the 80% confidence interval for the true mean maximum weight the patient can squat press.

For Problems 23 and 24, determine the sample mean and sample standard deviation based on the confidence interval for the population mean:

23. a. $n = 36$, 98% confidence interval: $23.45 < \mu < 27.97$

    b. $n = 19$, 90% confidence interval: $0.89 < \mu < 1.17$

24. a. $n = 25$, 80% confidence interval: $403.7 < \mu < 453.9$

    b. $n = 40$, 95% confidence interval: $0.892 < \mu < 0.928$

For Problems 25 and 26, calculate the sample proportion and the margin of error and construct the confidence interval for the population proportion using the normal approximation to the $\hat{p}$-distribution (if it is appropriate to do so):

25. a. $x = 27$, $n = 64$, $\alpha = 0.10$

    b. $x = 250$, $n = 900$, $\alpha = 0.01$

26. a. $x = 324$, $n = 400$, $\alpha = 0.05$

    b. $x = 7$, $n = 25$, $\alpha = 0.20$

27. A study is being done by a group of paediatricians to determine the probability that their patients experience physical symptoms of chicken pox within three days after contracting the disease. A sample of 500 children showed that 375 experienced physical symptoms by the third day. Construct the 95% confidence interval for the true proportion of children who experience chicken pox symptoms within three days of contracting the disease.

28. After experiencing anaphylactic shock, an epinephrine auto-injector is punctured into the thigh muscle to release an adrenaline solution into the bloodstream. Sometimes, a second puncture needs to be administered due to poor body response. In a recent survey of 640 patients, 144 of those patients required a second dose. Calculate the margin of error of this result at the 5% level of significance, and construct the corresponding confidence interval for the true proportion of patients who require a second dose of epinephrine to treat anaphylaxis.

For Problems 29 and 30, determine the minimal sample size required to estimate the population proportion within the desired margin of error at the given level of significance.

29. A dentist believes that approximately 60% of the clients that come to her for a regular cleaning have at least one cavity. What size sample will be needed to estimate the true proportion of clients with cavities, accurate to within 0.03 at the 1% level of significance?

30. A pharmaceutical company wants to test what proportion of their insulin monitoring units are defective. If they want the true proportion to be within a margin of error of 0.005 at a 5% level of significance, what size sample should be collected?

9 | Self-Test Exercises

1. Health care administrators use a sample of 196 women in the maternity ward over the course of a month to determine if the average duration of a pregnancy is correlated to the baby's weight. They determine the correlation is 0.672, which is accurate to within a margin of 0.068, 4 times out of 5. Identify the following for the scenario presented:

    a. The sample statistic being used to estimate the desired population parameter.

    b. The confidence level of the range estimate being used.

    c. The confidence interval for the desired population parameter based on the estimator.

For Problems 2 and 3, determine what will happen to the resulting confidence interval for the given scenario, if the proposed changes are made (assume each change is made independently to the original scenario):

In order to estimate a population proportion, a sample proportion of 0.58 is collected from a sample of size of $n = 200$, and the margin of error is computed to be 0.06 at the 10% level of significance. The resulting confidence interval for the population proportion of $0.52 < p < 0.64$.

2. a. The level of significance is decreased to 2%

    b. The sample size is decreased to $n = 100$

3. a. The sample proportion is recalculated to be 0.54

    b. The margin of error is recalculated to be 0.05

4. Based on the following information, and assuming the population data is normally distributed, calculate the margin of error and construct the confidence interval for the population mean:

    a. $\bar{x} = 56.3$, $n = 365$, $\sigma = 14.1$, $\alpha = 0.01$

    b. $\bar{x} = 37.0$, $n = 20$, $\sigma = 10.6$, $\alpha = 0.02$

    c. $\bar{x} = 8.314$, $n = 400$, $\sigma = 2.523$, $\alpha = 0.10$

    d. $\bar{x} = 12.84$, $n = 175$, $\sigma = 1.69$, $\alpha = 0.05$

5. An optometry technician measures the visual acuity of a sample of 75 patients who have had corrective laser eye surgery using a linear scale known as the LOGMAR scale (compared to the traditional exponential 20/XX scale), where 0.00 on the scale is "normal vision", positive values represent poorer than normal vision, and negative values represent better than normal vision. The average visual acuity score of the sample is –0.054. If it is known that the standard deviation in visual acuity is 0.234, calculate the margin of error and construct a 99% confidence interval for the true mean visual acuity score after the procedure. Based on this result, can the optometry technician claim that the procedure definitively results in better than normal vision for patients at the 1% level of significance?

6. The number of waitlisted kidney transplants in Ontario have greatly increased in the past decade. In a recent Statistics Canada report, wait lists had a mean of 531 days and a standard deviation of 58.7 days. After introducing a new legislative policy, a study tested the result with a sample of 250 accommodating hospitals across Ontario with a sample mean of 490 days. Calculate the margin of error and construct a 98% confidence interval for the true mean waitlisted time of kidney transplants under the new policy, assuming that the standard deviation remains unchanged. Does this result tell us that the waitlist time has decreased significantly or not at the 5% level of significance?

For Problems 7 and 8, we may assume that the sample standard deviation s is an accurate approximation of the population standard deviation σ (i.e., s ≈ σ), given that the sample size is so large (n > 200).

7. The average tumour size in a sample of 5,000 patients who have had brain tumours removed is 4.25 cm with a standard deviation of 1.88 cm. Calculate the margin of error and construct the 90% confidence interval for the true population mean tumour size.

8. The mean annual salary of a sample of 325 oncologists is $320,590 with a standard deviation of $44,730. Calculate the margin of error and construct the 80% confidence interval for the true population mean salary of oncologists.

9. A team of doctors would like to compile a report measuring diastolic blood pressure in their patients. If the patients' population standard deviation for diastolic blood pressure is known to be 12.4 mmHg, determine the number of patients the doctors require to ensure that the report's mean diastolic blood pressure is accurate to within 2.0 mmHg at the 5% level of significance.

For Problems 10 and 11, you may assume that the data is approximately normally distributed.

10. A pharmaceutical company tests the weight of 12 finasteride pills in milligrams:

27	32	39	25	29	35
37	39	41	29	32	30

    a. Calculate the sample mean and standard deviation.

    b. Construct the 99% confidence interval for the mean weight of finasteride pills at this company.

11. The daily number of patients in an E.R. ward are recorded for two weeks:

83	89	65	76	78	79	71
94	80	79	69	73	87	83

    a. Calculate the sample mean and standard deviation.

    b. Construct the 95% confidence interval for the mean number of patients in the E.R. ward.

12. Determine the sample mean and sample standard deviation based on the confidence interval for the population mean:

    a. $n = 49$, 99% confidence interval: $56.32 < \mu < 67.80$

    b. $n = 81$, 98% confidence interval: $0.815 < \mu < 0.939$

13. Calculate the sample proportion and the margin of error and construct the confidence interval for the population proportion using the normal approximation to the $\hat{p}$-distribution (if it is appropriate to do so):

    a. $x = 182$, $n = 400$, $\alpha = 0.10$

    b. $x = 12$, $n = 38$, $\alpha = 0.20$

14. A pharmacist taking a sample of 400 metformin pills claims that 78% of the pills are underweight. The pharmacist claims to be accurate within 3 percentage points, 49 times out of 50. Interpret the results of the study using the language of confidence intervals and verify the results. If the results are incorrect, modify the statement made so that the results are stated correctly.

15. An optometrist wishes to know the proportion of patients who undergo laser eye surgery who end up with 20/20 vision or better following the surgery. If the optometrist wishes to achieve an accuracy within 0.02 at the 5% level of significance, what size sample is required if there is no preliminary notion of the true proportion for this study?

16. A sample of patients are tested to determine if they have any hospital borne infections. How large of a sample must be collected to be accurate within 0.01 at the 1% level of significance, if the hospital estimates the true proportion of patients infected is 0.045?

9 | Summary of Notation and Formulas

NOTATION

n = total number of data values in a sample

μ = population mean

$\bar{x}$ = sample mean

σ = population standard deviation

s = sample standard deviation

p = population proportion of successes

q = population proportion of failures = $1 - p$

$\hat{p}$ = sample proportion of successes

$\hat{q}$ = sample proportion of failures = $1 - \hat{p}$

E = maximal margin of error

$(1 - \alpha)$ = confidence level

α = level of significance

$z_{\alpha/2}$ = critical z-value

$t_{\alpha/2}$ = critical t-value

$\sigma_{\bar{x}}$ = standard error of the mean

$\sigma_{\hat{p}}$ = standard error of the proportion

FORMULAS

Maximal Margin of Error between μ and $\bar{x}$ | 9.2-a

$$E = z_{\alpha/2} \cdot \sigma_{\bar{x}} = z_{\alpha/2} \cdot \frac{\sigma}{\sqrt{n}}$$

Confidence Interval for μ | 9.2-b

$$\bar{x} - E < \mu < \bar{x} + E$$

Sample Size for μ | 9.2-c

$$n = \left(\frac{z_{\alpha/2} \cdot \sigma}{E} \right)^2$$

Student's t-value | 9.3-a

$$t = \frac{\bar{x} - \mu}{\frac{s}{\sqrt{n}}}$$

Maximal Margin of Error for the Student's t-distribution | 9.3-b

$$E = t_{\alpha/2} \cdot \frac{s}{\sqrt{n}}$$

Maximal Margin of Error between p and $\hat{p}$ | 9.4-a

$$E = z_{\alpha/2} \cdot \sigma_{\hat{p}} \approx z_{\alpha/2} \cdot \sqrt{\frac{\hat{p} \cdot \hat{q}}{n}}$$

Confidence Interval for p | 9.4-b

$$\hat{p} - E < p < \hat{p} + E$$

Sample Size for p | 9.4-c

$$n = \hat{p} \cdot \hat{q} \cdot \left(\frac{z_{\alpha/2}}{E} \right)^2$$

Critical z-values ($z_{\alpha/2}$) for Various Confidence Levels | Table 9.2

Confidence Level	Critical z-value ($z_{\alpha/2}$)
80%	1.282
90%	1.645
95%	1.960
98%	2.326
99%	2.576

Student's t-Distribution Table | Table 9.3

see Appendix II on page 404

10 HYPOTHESIS TESTING

LEARNING OBJECTIVES

- Define the terms used in hypothesis testing, including null and alternative hypotheses, one- and two-tailed tests, test statistic, p-value, level of significance, and type I and type II errors.
- State the procedure for evaluating hypotheses using the 5 steps for formal hypothesis testing.
- Conduct and evaluate hypothesis tests of a population mean using the normal Z-distribution when the population standard deviation is known (or a large sample size is used).
- Conduct and evaluate hypothesis tests of a population mean using the Student's t-distribution when the population standard deviation is unknown.
- Conduct and evaluate hypothesis tests of a population proportion using the normal Z-distribution.
- Conduct and evaluate hypothesis tests for the linear correlation coefficient using the test statistic approach and the critical r-value approach.

CHAPTER OUTLINE

Introduction

In the previous chapter, we examined how to make use of sample statistics to estimate population parameters, such as using the average weight loss of a sample of patients on a medical diet program to predict the true average weight loss of all patients on that diet program, or using the proportion of patients who experience side effects during the clinical trials of a new drug therapy to predict the proportion of all patients who will experience side effects from the drug therapy. However, there is another important use of estimators: testing a claim about a population parameter.

Consider the well-known claim that "normal" human body temperature is 37 °C. Most people assume that this is the average healthy human body temperature (i.e., a population mean), but is this, in fact, true? In order to determine the truth of this claim, we would have to collect the body temperatures of the more than 7 billion humans alive on the planet today, ensuring that each one is healthy when sampled; this is not only a difficult task, but an impossible one when we also factor in the number of people who are dying or being born at any given minute.

However, instead, we can collect a (large) sample of healthy individuals and measure their body temperature, and use that result to test the claim about the true mean healthy body temperature. Obviously, we cannot use the exact value of the sample mean to determine the true population mean, as the sample statistic is only that: a statistic. However, we can use the ideas discussed in the previous chapter to establish a range of values within which we would reasonably expect the sample statistic to fall, **assuming the claim about the population parameter is true**. This is known as **hypothesis testing**.

10.1 | Concept and Approach to Hypothesis Testing

The Informal Hypothesis Test

Consider a scenario from our society in which you are selected to serve on a jury for a criminal case:

*You are a juror in a criminal case that you know nothing about - the details of the crime, the identity of the accused, etc., are all unknown to you prior to the trial. The accused has pled "Not Guilty" to the crime, and you do not know anything about whether the accused is actually innocent or guilty of committing this crime. However, the law requires that you assume the accused is innocent of the crime until otherwise proven guilty, **beyond a reasonable doubt**.*

In essence, you are being asked to test the hypothesis that the accused is innocent against the evidence that will be presented. Your default assumption is that the hypothesis of innocence is **correct**, but there is only a certain amount of condemning evidence against the accused that you are willing to accept before you become convinced that the hypothesis is too unlikely to be true in light of all the evidence.

After all the evidence is presented, you will return with one of two verdicts: "Guilty" - in which case you reject the hypothesis of innocence, beyond a reasonable doubt, in light of the overwhelming evidence; or "Not Guilty" - in which case there is not sufficient evidence to reject the hypothesis of innocence, beyond a reasonable doubt.

Notice that you do not have the choice between "Guilty" and "Innocent" verdicts - instead the choices are "Guilty" or "Not Guilty". This is because your default assumption that the hypothesis of innocence is correct does not need to be proven - instead, there is either enough evidence to suggest it is false, or not. Let's look back at that scenario again:

The first piece of evidence introduced is circumstantial - the fingerprints of the accused were found at the crime-scene and on items associated with the crime.

At this point, it is still very possible that the hypothesis that the accused is innocent is true, and there are other reasons for the fingerprints being at the crime-scene and on the associated items.

The second piece of evidence is an eye-witness who claims to have witnessed the accused going into the crime-scene moments before the crime and coming out moments afterwards.

Now there is a significant amount of evidence to indicate that the accused is actually guilty. In fact, it may even be *more* likely that the accused is guilty than innocent. However, you are not being asked to weigh the two options, but instead to test the claim that the accused is innocent, and to only reject it if there is enough evidence to warrant it. As such, if the evidence were to stop here, you would likely need to return a "Not Guilty" verdict, as we only know the accused was **at the scene of the crime**, but cannot prove, beyond a reasonable doubt, that the accused **committed the crime**.

> *Finally, a video surveillance tape is shown which clearly depicts the accused actually committing the crime.*

At this point, the evidence seems overwhelmingly in opposition to the hypothesis of innocence. Of course, while it is possible that the fingerprints may have been planted and the eye-witness may have been bribed and the video could have been tampered with, the probability of all these things occurring together is so unlikely that it is far more reasonable to conclude that our assumption was incorrect and that the accused is, in fact, guilty of committing the alleged crime.

The Null and Alternative Hypotheses

In the scenario above, there were actually two hypotheses being presented: the hypothesis of the accused's innocence, which the law requires to be the default assumption, and the hypothesis of the accused's guilt, which is being presented by the prosecution. As a juror, you are not being asked to weigh these two options and select the more likely one - instead you are being told to assume the hypothesis of innocence is correct, until there is enough evidence for you to believe it is false, at which point the only other option (in an ideal, simplistic scenario) is for you to accept the prosecution's hypothesis instead: if the accused is not innocent, then he/she must be guilty!

In statistics, the default hypothesis - the one which is assumed from the start - is called the **null hypothesis**, denoted H_0, and the opposite assumption is called the **alternative hypothesis**, denoted H_1. In the criminal trial example above, the two hypotheses would be stated as follows:

$$H_0: \text{the accused is innocent}$$

$$H_1: \text{the accused is guilty}$$

In statistical hypothesis testing, the hypotheses are always statements about the numerical value of a population parameter, such as the population mean μ, the population proportion p, or the population correlation coefficient ρ ("rho" - the Greek letter "r", not to be confused with p). The null hypothesis is always a statement of equality about the population parameter - i.e., we will always test a single hypothesized value for the population parameter, not a range of values. The alternative hypothesis, on the other hand, is one of three statements of inequality about the population parameter: that it is less than ($<$), greater than ($>$), or simply not equal to ($\neq$) the hypothesized value.

For example, in the healthy body temperature example, the null hypothesis would be stated as follows:

$$H_0: \mu = 37.0$$

The alternative hypothesis, therefore, could be any **one** of the following three statements:

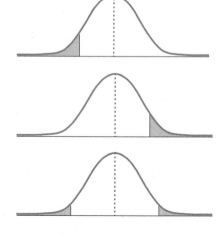

1. $H_1: \mu < 37.0$ - known as a **left-tailed** hypothesis

2. $H_1: \mu > 37.0$ - known as a **right-tailed** hypothesis

3. $H_1: \mu \neq 37.0$ - known as a **two-tailed** hypothesis

One- and Two-Tailed Hypothesis Tests

In most scenarios, we will assume a two-tailed hypothesis test, unless otherwise specified. This is because in most scenarios, we simply wish to know if the claim about the population parameter is true or false - i.e., whether the true value is higher or lower than the claimed value is irrelevant; all that matters is whether the claimed value is correct or incorrect.

However, in some scenarios, there is reason to only consider one side of the inequality. For example, when offering warranties, manufacturers are only concerned with items that do not last for as long as expected (known as "defective items"), and do not care about items that last much longer than expected. As such, manufacturers trying to establish an appropriate warranty period would conduct a left-tailed hypothesis test against their hypothesized average life span, as they are only concerned if the average life span is *less than* expected.

On the other hand, when donated blood samples are tested for diseases (known as "tainted samples"), the proportion of tainted samples allowed to be given to patients must be as low as possible. Therefore, the method used to test the samples must undergo strict quality control to ensure that tainted samples are not given to patients. As such, health officials trying to establish a proper testing procedure would want to use a right-tailed test against the proportion of tainted samples allowed to pass (known as "false negatives"), as they are only concerned if the proportion of false negatives is *higher than* tolerated.

In any case, the null hypothesis is **always a statement of equality**, and never a statement of inequality, as we must always be testing the evidence against a specific hypothesized value, and not a range of values, or it would be difficult (or even impossible) to disprove the hypothesis.

*Note: Sometimes the stated claim that we wish to test is a statement of inequality. In these scenarios, the stated claim is actually the **alternative hypothesis**, and the null hypothesis is therefore the opposing claim of equality.*

Example 10.1-a	Null and Alternative Hypotheses

In the following scenarios, first establish the null hypothesis. Then determine if the hypothesis is a left-tailed, right-tailed, or two-tailed test, and based on this decision, establish the alternative hypothesis.

(i) A certain pharmaceutical drug tablet is under investigation for recall for having an incorrect amount of medication contained in the drug. The label states that the tablets each contain 30 mg of the drug.

(ii) A therapist claims that only 20% of patients who complete an addiction treatment program she developed will revert back to their addiction again.

(iii) The producers of a new transdermal patch to continuously administer insulin to diabetic patients claim that the average fasting blood glucose level of patients using the patch is less than 108 mg/dL, which is considered to be "normal".

(iv) A clinical researcher is attempting to determine if there is any correlation between UDL cholesterol levels and dollars spent monthly on fast food. The researcher wishes to test his hypothesis that there is a positive correlation between the two variables - i.e., the more money spent every month on fast food, the higher the person's UDL cholesterol levels will be.

Solution

(i) In this scenario, the claim is about the population mean amount of medication contained in each tablet, denoted by μ, and the null hypothesis is $H_0 : \mu = 30$.

Since the tablets must contain the **exact** amount of drug stated (too much or too little can be dangerous), this is a two-tailed test, and the alternative hypothesis is $H_1 : \mu \neq 30$.

(ii) In this scenario, the claim is about the population proportion of those who complete the treatment program that will revert back to addictive behaviour, denoted by p, and the null hypothesis is $H_0 : p = 0.20$.

On the surface, this may appear to be a two-tailed hypothesis test, but upon further reflection, we note that a lower proportion of reversion to addictive behaviours would still be considered successful. The only way to reject this claim is to prove the average proportion is **greater than** 0.20. Hence, this is a right-tailed hypothesis test, and the alternative hypothesis is $H_1 : p > 0.20$.

Solution
continued

(iii)   In this scenario, the claim is about the population mean fasting blood glucose level of patients using the new transdermal patch, denoted by μ. However, in this case, the stated claim that $\mu < 108$ does not contain a statement of equality, which means it must be the alternative hypothesis - i.e., $H_1 : \mu < 108$. Hence, the null hypothesis is $H_0 : \mu = 108$, and this is a left-tailed hypothesis test.

(iv)   In this scenario, the claim is about the population correlation coefficient, denoted by ρ (i.e., "rho") between the amount spent every month on fast food and the person's UDL cholesterol level. However, as with part (iii), the stated claim that positive correlation exists between the two variables is expressed as $\rho > 0$, which does not contain a statement of equality. Therefore, it must be the alternative hypothesis - i.e., $H_1 : \rho > 0$ - which means that the null hypothesis is $H_0 : \rho = 0$, and this is a right-tailed hypothesis test.

Testing the Hypotheses

Once we have established the null and alternative hypotheses, we then need to actually test the claim using the sample data collected (i.e., the "evidence" we will use to challenge the claim). It is important to note that we are actually testing the evidence *against* the null hypothesis, since the null hypothesis is assumed to be true. Therefore, in essence, we are trying to ascertain if the alternative hypothesis is true by challenging the assumption that the null hypothesis is true using the sample evidence selected. We cannot ever prove the truth of the null hypothesis, just as we cannot (and do not need to) prove the innocence of an individual accused of a crime. The two conclusions available are to either:

1.   reject the null hypothesis, and therefore conclude that the alternative hypothesis is correct, or,

2.   fail to reject the null hypothesis, in which case we cannot say anything about the truth of *either* hypothesis.

In order to actually perform a statistical hypothesis test, we first need to establish a number of parameters that will form the basis for our test. These are the level of significance, the test statistic, and the p-value.

Level of Significance

In order to test the claim, we first need to determine what level of significance we will require for the test. The **level of significance**, denoted α, was introduced in the previous chapter: it is the probability that we will end up with a sample statistic that does **not** provide a reasonable range estimate for the population parameter. Put another way, the level of significance is the complement (i.e., the opposite) of the confidence level - for example, if we have a 95% confidence level, we are using a 5% level of significance ($\alpha = 1 - 0.95 = 0.05$).

In terms of hypothesis testing, the level of significance is the probability that our null hypothesis is actually correct, but our sample statistic will be so far from the hypothesized value as to cause us to reject the null hypothesis and (incorrectly) conclude that the alternative hypothesis is true instead. In other words, the level of significance is the area in the tail(s) under the probability distribution curve. In the case of a one-tailed hypothesis test, the entire area (α) will be contained in one tail, either to the left or to the right, depending on the type of test. In the case of a two-tailed test, the area will be split equally between the two tails: half of the area ($\alpha/2$) in the left tail, and the other half in the right tail.

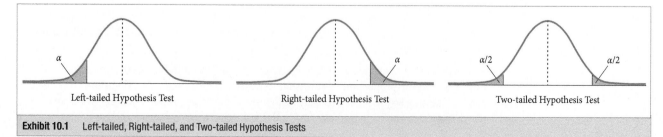

| Left-tailed Hypothesis Test | Right-tailed Hypothesis Test | Two-tailed Hypothesis Test |

Exhibit 10.1   Left-tailed, Right-tailed, and Two-tailed Hypothesis Tests

The most common levels of significance are 20%, 10%, 5%, 2%, and 1%; of these, the three most common are 10%, 5%, and 1%. In order to select an appropriate level of significance, there are many factors to consider, including the size of the sample (smaller samples usually require lower levels of significance in order to be considered statistically valid), the nature of the claim being tested, and the risk priorities of the decision-maker.

For instance, if it is very important to not wrongly reject a true null hypothesis, as is the case in the "innocent until proven guilty beyond a reasonable doubt" scenario above, then we would want to use a low level of significance, such as 1%. In fact, this is known as **Blackstone's Formulation**, based on the works of British judge Sir William Blackstone, which states "It is better that ten guilty persons go free than one innocent person should suffer", and was later emphasized and exaggerated by Benjamin Franklin, to state "It is better that 100 guilty persons go free than one innocent person should suffer."

However, if it was instead more important to ensure that we don't fail to reject a false null hypotheses, as is the case with the blood sample testing example above, we may want to use a higher level of significance, like 10%. In this case, it would be much better to throw out a blood sample that is, in fact, acceptable than it is to use a blood sample that has been tainted by some disease.

For most hypothesis tests, though, a 5% level of significance is a good balance between the two priorities, and tends to be the default level of significance for any test, unless otherwise specified.

Computing Test Statistics

Once we know what level of significance we are going to use, we need to determine the value of our **test statistic**. This is most often a z-value or a t-value (depending on what parameter is being tested and whether or not σ is known), but it could also be an r-value (for correlation) or some other standardized statistic. We use the information collected from the sample, as well as any information known about the population (if any) to determine the value of our test statistic.

Example 10.1-b Calculating the Value of a One-Tailed Test Statistic for a z-Distribution

Determine the value of the test statistic for the following hypothesis test:

$H_0 : \mu = 625$ mg   Sample mean: $\bar{x} = 623.3$ mg

$H_1 : \mu < 625$ mg   Known population standard deviation: $\sigma = 5.8$ mg

Level of significance: $\alpha = 0.01$ Unknown distribution of population data

Sample size: $n = 100$

Solution

Since we know the population standard deviation, and our sample size is sufficiently large ($n = 100 > 30$), we can assume, by the Central Limit Theorem, that the sampling distribution of sample means is approximately normal, which means that it follows a z-distribution. Hence, we compute a z-score for our test statistic, based on the information given, assuming the null hypothesis to be true:

Using Formula 8.2-a, $z = \dfrac{\bar{x} - \mu}{\dfrac{\sigma}{\sqrt{n}}} = \dfrac{623.3 - 625}{\dfrac{5.8}{\sqrt{100}}} = \dfrac{-1.7}{0.58} \approx -2.93$

> z-scores are rounded to 2 decimal places to match the values in the z-table.

Therefore, our test statistic is $z = -2.93$.

Example 10.1-c Calculating the Value of a Two-Tailed Test Statistic for a z-Distribution

Determine the value of the test statistic for the following hypothesis test:

$H_0 : \mu = 37$ °C   Sample mean: $\bar{x} = 36.79$ °C

$H_1 : \mu \neq 37$ °C   Known population standard deviation: $\sigma = 0.55$ °C

Level of significance: $\alpha = 0.05$ Data appears to be normally distributed

Sample size: $n = 25$

Since we know the population standard deviation, we can assume, by the Central Limit Theorem, that the sampling distribution of sample means follows a normal distribution, even though we are dealing with a small sample, since the population data appears to be normally distributed. Hence, we compute a z-score for our test statistic, based on the information given, assuming the null hypothesis to be true:

Using Formula 8.2-a, $\quad z = \dfrac{\bar{x} - \mu}{\dfrac{\sigma}{\sqrt{n}}} = \dfrac{36.79 - 37}{\dfrac{0.55}{\sqrt{25}}} = \dfrac{-0.21}{0.11} \approx -1.91$

Therefore, our test statistic is $z = -1.91$.

Determining p-values

Once we have computed the test statistic (i.e., our "evidence"), we need to compare that to our established level of significance (i.e., our "reasonable doubt threshold") to determine whether or not we should reject the null hypothesis. In order to accomplish this, we use what's known as a p-value.

A **p-value** is the probability of getting a result at least as extreme as the test statistic that we computed - i.e., it is the area under the curve of the probability distribution in the tail defined by the test statistic. For a test statistic that follows a z-distribution, we calculate the p-value as follows:

- If we are performing a left-tailed test, the p-value is equal to the probability $P(Z < z)$ found by looking up the z-score in the z-table.

- If we are performing a right-tailed test, the p-value is equal to the probability $P(Z > z)$ found by looking up the z-score in the z-table, and subtracting it from 1, since $P(Z > z) = 1 - P(Z < z)$.

- If we are performing a two-tailed test, the p-value is equal to **double** the probability $P(Z < z)$ if the test z-score is negative, or **double** the probability $P(Z > z)$ if the test z-score is positive , since the test statistic could fall in the tail on **either side** of the mean.

Once we have determined the p-value, we compare it to the level of significance (α). If the p-value is less than or equal to the desired level of significance, then we reject the null hypothesis and adopt the alternative hypothesis instead; otherwise, if it is greater than α, we fail to reject the null hypothesis.

*Note: It is very important that we set the level of significance **before** selecting any samples, based on the risk priorities of our study. If we change our level of significance after selecting the sample and calculating the test statistic, we would be in danger of manipulating the results of the study in order to arrive at the conclusion we desire, which would invalidate the entire study!*

Interpreting p-values

Unfortunately, p-values are one of the most commonly misunderstood statistical values in all of inferential statistics. Since p-values are calculated based on the assumption that the null hypothesis is correct, we cannot ever interpret them as the probability that our null hypothesis is correct, or the probability that we will reject a true null hypothesis (known as a Type I error, which will be discussed later in this section). In fact, p-values actually tell us very little about our hypotheses, except whether or not there is statistically significant evidence to support changing our assumption from the null hypothesis to the alternative hypothesis, based on our pre-determined level of significance.

Moreover, p-values should be only one of many tools used before making any changes to policies or procedures as the result of a hypothesis test. For example, consider a new cholesterol medication that claims to lower the cholesterol of patients better than another medication, and there is a statistically significantly small p-value to support this. Our analysis would tell us to adopt the new medication instead of the old medication, but if the new medication lowers cholesterol only slightly and costs ten times more than the old medication, it may be better for patients to keep using the less expensive medication.

Another example would be at a casino, if a player gets five blackjacks in a row, the p-value of that event would be so small as to make us reject the hypothesis that the player and dealer are both playing fairly and instead adopt the hypothesis that one of them is cheating. However, given how difficult it would be to cheat at a casino game, it is far more likely to conclude that this is just a random anomaly, and that both player and dealer are still playing fairly (though it may warrant some monitoring!)

To fully understand p-values and how to interpret them, we need something called Bayesian Analysis, which is beyond the scope of this textbook. For the purposes of this book, then, we can consider p-values as tools to help us make decisions, by following these "Do's" and "Don'ts" of p-values:

DO:

- use a p-value to determine if there is statistically significant evidence to warrant changing your assumption from the null hypothesis to the alternative hypothesis, based on the predetermined level of significance chosen

- see the p-value as a tool to help you make a decision

- recognize the p-value is specific only to that sample

- consider how that p-value relates to other information available about the decision

DON'T:

- use a p-value to try to calculate the probability that the null hypothesis is correct or incorrect

- use a p-value to try to calculate the probability that the alternative hypothesis is correct or incorrect

- use a p-value to try to calculate the probability that we will mistakenly reject the null hypothesis when it is, in fact, true

- use a p-value to try to determine how likely we are to make a correct or incorrect decision about which hypothesis is correct

- use a p-value to establish what level of significance would allow you to reject the null hypothesis, as the level of significance must be established **before** the study is conducted

- use a p-value to try to infer anything about the population

---

Example 10.1-d | **Determining p-values**

Compute the p-value for Examples 10.1-b and 10.1-c above, and determine whether or not to reject the null hypothesis.

Solution

Example 10.1-b: Recall: $H_0 : \mu = 625$ mg, $H_1 : \mu < 625$ mg, $\alpha = 0.01$, $z = -2.93$

Looking up the probability $P(Z < -2.93)$ in the z-table, we get a value of 0.0017. Since this is a left-tailed test, our p-value is therefore equal to 0.0017. Since the p-value is less than the level of significance $\alpha = 0.01$, we reject the null hypothesis $\mu = 625$ mg and adopt the alternative hypothesis $\mu < 625$ mg.

Example 10.1-c: Recall: $H_0 : \mu = 37\,°C$, $H_1 : \mu \neq 37\,°C$, $\alpha = 0.05$, $z = -1.91$

Looking up the probability $P(Z < -1.91)$ in the z-table, we get a value of 0.0281. However, since this is a two-tailed test, we need to multiply the probability by 2 to get a p-value of 0.0562. Since the p-value is greater than the level of significance $\alpha = 0.05$, we fail to reject the null hypothesis $\mu = 37\,°C$.

Drawing Conclusions from the Hypothesis Test

It is vitally important to remember that we arrive at only one of two conclusions: reject the null hypothesis (in which case, we accept the alternative hypothesis), or fail to reject the null hypothesis (in which case, we cannot evaluate the validity of either the null hypothesis or the alternative hypothesis). Notice that in no scenario can we ever prove the null hypothesis to be true, as it is assumed to be true to begin with; neither can we fully prove the null hypothesis to be false, because there is always some probability, however small it may be, that our conclusion is wrong based on random sampling error.

The following table is a summary of our two possible conclusions based on the result of the p-value:

Table 10.1-a	Drawing Conclusions from the Hypothesis Test

RESULT	CONCLUSION
The p-value is less than or equal to the significance level ($p \leq \alpha$)	There is sufficient evidence to reject the assumption that the null hypothesis is true, and to instead support the claim that the alternative hypothesis is true.
The p-value is greater than the significance level ($p > \alpha$)	There is **not** sufficient evidence to reject the assumption that the null hypothesis is true; hence, the evidence is insufficient to support the claim that the alternative hypothesis is true.

It is for this reason that, most often, if there is a claim that we wish to "prove", it is stated as an alternative hypothesis rather than as a null hypothesis. This is because it is impossible to prove that a population parameter is equal to a value; however, we may be able to support a claim that a population parameter is not equal to a certain value, given strong enough evidence. Still, even then, we cannot fully "prove" the alternative hypothesis to be true - rather, we can only statistically support the alternative hypothesis as more likely than the null hypothesis, based on the evidence provided. This is why the words "beyond a reasonable doubt" are added to the end of the legal phrase "innocent until proven guilty"; otherwise, it would be practically impossible to ever prove someone to be guilty.

The Formal Hypothesis Test

Now that we understand the basic concepts of the statistical hypothesis test, we will formalize the procedure for evaluating hypotheses using rigorous, mathematically-proven, statistical methods:

Step 1: State the null and alternative hypotheses (H_0 and H_1, respectively) and determine whether it is a one-tailed or two-tailed test.

Step 2: Determine a significance level (α) to be used to test the claims. If unsure, use a 5% significance level.

Step 3: Compute a test statistic based on the sample data collected, and any population information known.

Step 4: Look up the p-value associated with the computed test statistic and compare to the level of significance (α).

Step 5: Draw a conclusion about the null and alternative hypotheses and state your conclusion in context of the specific claim being tested.

Example 10.1-e	Conducting a Formal Hypothesis Test

A government official with the ministry of health wishes to test the claim that the average wait time in Ontario emergency rooms for patients with minor conditions is no longer than 4 hours. He collects a random sample of 500 E.R. patients with minor conditions from various hospitals across the province, using multi-stage sampling techniques. The sample mean is 4.15 hours and the standard deviation is 1.38 hours. Test the claim that the average wait time is no more than 4 hours at the 5% significance level and interpret your results.

Solution

Step 1: The population parameter being tested is the population mean wait time for minor conditions at E.R.'s across Ontario, denoted by μ, and the null hypothesis is $H_0 : \mu = 4$. Since anything under 4 hours would still be a success, the alternative hypothesis is $H_1 : \mu > 4$, making this a right-tailed test.

Step 2: We are instructed in this problem to use the standard 5% significance level (i.e., $\alpha = 0.05$).

Step 3: Since we do not know the population standard deviation, the sampling distribution of sample mean wait times technically follows the Student's t-distribution. However, given that our sample size is so large ($n = 500$), we may assume that the sampling distribution is approximately normal (i.e., it follows a z-distribution) - we will discuss this more in the next section:

> Recall from Chapter 9: the t-distribution approaches the standard normal distribution as $n \to \infty$.

Using Formula 8.2-a, $\quad z = \dfrac{\overline{x} - \mu}{\dfrac{\sigma}{\sqrt{n}}} = \dfrac{4.15 - 4}{\dfrac{1.38}{\sqrt{500}}} = \dfrac{0.15}{0.061715...} \approx 2.43$

Step 4: Looking up $z = 2.43$ in the z-table, we get $P(Z < 2.43) = 0.9925$.

Since this is a right-tailed test,

$p = P(Z > 2.43) = 1 - P(Z < 2.43) = 1 - 0.9925 = 0.0075$

Therefore, our p-value is less than the critical significance level of $\alpha = 0.05$.

> Alternatively, we can look up the **negative** z-value in the table, as the p-value corresponds to the area in the tail of the normal curve:
>
> $p = P(Z < -2.43) = 0.0075$

Step 5: We reject the null hypothesis that the average wait time is no more than 4 hours, and instead conclude that the evidence supports the alternative hypothesis that the average wait time at emergency rooms in Ontario hospitals for patients with minor conditions is greater than 4 hours.

Type I and II Errors in Hypothesis Testing

As we have already emphasized, there are only two possible decisions we can make at the conclusion of a hypothesis test: to reject the null hypothesis and therefore support the alternative hypothesis, or to fail to reject the null hypothesis. Similarly, there are only two possible truth states for the hypotheses, regardless of the decision we make: either that the null hypothesis is true, or that it is false and the alternative hypothesis is true. Summarizing these decisions and truth states in a table shows four possible outcomes:

Table 10.1-b   **Hypothesis Test Decision Outcomes**

TRUTH STATE	DECISION	
	REJECT H_0	FAIL TO REJECT H_0
H_0 IS TRUE	TYPE I ERROR (probability is equal to α, the significance level chosen)	CORRECT DECISION
H_0 IS FALSE (H_1 IS TRUE)	CORRECT DECISION	TYPE II ERROR (probability is equal to β, which is not covered in this book)

Type I Error: H_0 is true but rejected.

Type II Error: H_0 is false but not rejected.

Two of the four possible decision outcomes are the correct decision. However, there are two scenarios where we made an error - rejecting a true null hypothesis (called a **Type I Error**), or failing to reject a false null hypothesis (called a **Type II Error**).

The probability of a Type I error is exactly equal to the established level of significance, α. A hypothesis test with a low probability of a Type I error is said to have **high specificity**. To decrease the probability of a Type I error (i.e., to increase the specificity), we need only reduce the level of significance. A Type I error is the only error possible if we decide to reject the null hypothesis.

The probability of a Type II error is denoted using the Greek letter β (beta), and is much more difficult to calculate, as it depends on the actual true value of the population parameter that we are testing, which we do not (and often cannot) know. However, we do know that increasing the value of the significance level α will increase the likelihood of rejecting the null hypothesis, and therefore decrease the likelihood of a Type II error, which is failing to reject a false null hypothesis. A hypothesis test with a low probability of a Type II error is said to have **high sensitivity**. A Type II error is the only error possible if we fail to reject the null hypothesis. When β - the probability of a Type II error - is decreased, this increases what is known as the **power of the test**, which is the overall likelihood that the alternative hypothesis will be accepted.

Limiting the Two Types of Errors

When testing hypotheses, ideally we want to limit the probability of making either type of error to being as small as possible, within the restrictions of feasibility and acceptable risks, depending on the situation. As we discussed above, according to the charter of human rights and freedoms, it is considered unacceptable to convict someone who is innocent. In this case, we seek to limit a Type I error, and we can do this by restricting the level of significance α to be quite small, such as $\alpha = 0.01$.

However, what if we are trying to limit a Type II error? We know that we need to somehow limit β, but we do not even know how to calculate β, let alone minimize it. Fortunately, while we cannot calculate β exactly without knowing the true value of the population parameter that we are testing, we do know that there is a relationship between α, β, and the sample size n:

- For a fixed sample size n, an increase in α results in a decrease in β, and vice versa.

- For a fixed level of significance α, an increase in the sample size results in a decrease in β, and vice versa.

Hence, if we want to restrict both α and β, we can choose a low level of significance and a large sample.

Example 10.1-f	**Possible Decision Error Type**

Determine the possible decision errors that could have been made in Examples 10.1-b, 10.1-c, and 10.1-e, and calculate the probability (if possible) that these errors will occur.

Solution

Example 10.1-b: Recall: we rejected the null hypothesis $\mu = 625$ mg and instead adopted the alternative hypothesis $\mu < 625$ mg.

The only possible decision error is a Type I error, which has a probability of occurrence of $\alpha = 0.01$.

Example 10.1-c: Recall: we failed to reject the null hypothesis $\mu = 37\ °C$.

The only possible decision error is a Type II error. It is not possible to calculate the exact probability of making a Type II error in this scenario without knowing the true value of the population mean.

Example 10.1-e: Recall: we rejected the null hypothesis $\mu = 4$ hr and instead adopted the alternative hypothesis $\mu > 4$ hr.

The only possible decision error is a Type I error, which has a probability of occurrence of $\alpha = 0.05$.

10.1 | Exercises

For Problems 1 to 10, perform the following:

(i)   *Determine what population parameter is being tested.*

(ii) *State the null and alternative hypotheses and determine if it is a left-tailed, right-tailed, or two-tailed test.*

(iii) *Determine the most appropriate level of significance to use: 1%, 5%, or 10%.*

1. According to Stats Canada, the average age of women when they gave birth to their first child was 28.5 years old in 2011. An obstetrician believes this number has decreased since then. A large random sample of first-time mothers is selected to test the obstetrician's claim.

2. According to Stats Canada, the average weight of a baby born in Canada in 2013 was 3.35 kg. A pediatrician believes this number has increased since then. A large random sample of newborn babies is selected to test the pediatrician's claim.

3. The Canadian Cancer Society projects that prostate cancer will account for 20.7% of all new cancer cases in Canadian men in 2017. A large random sample of male patients with newly-developed cancers in 2017 is selected to test this claim.

4. The Canadian Cancer Society projects that breast cancer will account for 25.5% of all new cancer cases in Canadian women in 2017. A large random sample of female patients with newly-developed cancers in 2017 is selected to test this claim.

5. A new chemotherapy drug is being tested on drug-resistant cancer cells in rats. The average tumor size before treatment is 12.8 mm, and the pharmaceutical company claims the new drug will result in a significant decrease to the tumor size after three weeks of treatment. There are no known additional side effects or drawbacks to this drug, and the potential benefits of the drug to patients with drug-resistant cancers are a high priority.

6. The average nurse spends 1.25 hours on paperwork during every 8-hour shift. A new procedure is implemented with the hopes of reducing this time. However, given the high cost of changing procedures, the administration wants to be as certain as possible that the new system will actually reduce the time spent on paperwork before making the change.

7. The established success rate of a particular treatment is 85%. A physician believes that his success rate is higher than this, so he tests this claim using a large random sample of his patients who have had the treatment in the past three years. However, he does not wish to claim that his patients experience more success than average unless he is as certain as he possibly can be.

8. A dentist in a small town is considering relocating his office to a building with a substantially cheaper rent, but it is significantly further away from the downtown area. He does a cost-benefit analysis and determines he will still save money with the move so long as no more than 20% of his patients will leave his practice as a result. He is confident that he won't lose more than 20% of his patients, but given that he does not want to have to rebuild his practice, decides to give an anonymous survey to a random sample of his patients, just to be totally sure before he moves.

9. A medical professional is interested in testing the correlation between the weight gained by a mother during pregnancy and the weight of her child at birth. The medical professional believes, based on past evidence, that positive correlation exists between the two data sets, but wishes to demonstrate this using a statistically valid study and a formal hypothesis tests.

10. A researcher is interested in testing the relationship between wealth and healthy-eating habits, by seeing if there is any correlation between monthly income and the amount spent on fast food each month. If correlation exists, the researcher has no prior knowledge whether the correlation will be positive or negative.

For Problems 11 to 20, perform the following:

(i)   *Compute the value of the test statistic and its corresponding p-value.*

(ii)   *Conclude whether to reject the null hypothesis or not based on the p-value.*

(iii) *State the decision error type that is possible.*

11. H_0: $\mu = 350$ mg
     H_1: $\mu \neq 350$ mg
     Level of significance: $\alpha = 0.05$
     Sample size: $n = 80$
     Sample mean: $\bar{x} = 348.6$ mg
     Known population standard deviation: $\sigma = 7.5$ mg
     Unknown distribution of population data

12. H_0: $\mu = 2.7$ hr
     H_1: $\mu < 2.7$ hr
     Level of significance: $\alpha = 0.01$
     Sample size: $n = 65$
     Sample mean: $\bar{x} = 2.64$ hr
     Known population standard deviation: $\sigma = 0.24$ hr
     Unknown distribution of population data

13. H_0: $\mu = 45.2$ mm
     H_1: $\mu > 45.2$ mm
     Level of significance: $\alpha = 0.10$
     Sample size: $n = 120$
     Sample mean: $\bar{x} = 46.8$ mm
     Known population standard deviation: $\sigma = 8.15$ mm
     Unknown distribution of population data

14. H_0: $\mu = 212$ °F
     H_1: $\mu \neq 212$ °F
     Level of significance: $\alpha = 0.05$
     Sample size: $n = 150$
     Sample mean: $\bar{x} = 210.6$ °F
     Known population standard deviation: $\sigma = 4.8$ °F
     Unknown distribution of population data

15. H_0: $\mu = \$4{,}200$
     H_1: $\mu < \$4{,}200$
     Level of significance: $\alpha = 0.01$
     Sample size: $n = 18$
     Sample mean: $\bar{x} = \$3{,}925$
     Known population standard deviation: $\sigma = \$645$
     Distribution of population data appears normal

16. H_0: $\mu = \$37{,}700$
     H_1: $\mu > \$37{,}700$
     Level of significance: $\alpha = 0.05$
     Sample size: $n = 24$
     Sample mean: $\bar{x} = \$40{,}350$
     Known population standard deviation: $\sigma = \$8{,}200$
     Distribution of population data appears normal

17. H_0: $\mu = 250$ mcg
     H_1: $\mu \neq 250$ mcg
     Level of significance: $\alpha = 0.10$
     Sample size: $n = 40$
     Sample mean: $\bar{x} = 251.6$ mcg
     Known population standard deviation: $\sigma = 5.4$ mcg
     Unknown distribution of population data

18. H_0: $\mu = 15$ kg
     H_1: $\mu > 15$ kg
     Level of significance: $\alpha = 0.10$
     Sample size: $n = 36$
     Sample mean: $\bar{x} = 15.4$ kg
     Known population standard deviation: $\sigma = 1.8$ kg
     Distribution of population data appears normal

19. H_0: $\mu = 13.8$ yr
     H_1: $\mu > 13.8$ yr
     Level of significance: $\alpha = 0.05$
     Sample size: $n = 400$
     Sample mean: $\bar{x} = 14.1$ yr
     Sample standard deviation: $s = 2.3$ yr
     Distribution of population data appears normal

20. H_0: $\mu = 60.00$ s
     H_1: $\mu \neq 60.00$ s
     Level of significance: $\alpha = 0.01$
     Sample size: $n = 1{,}000$
     Sample mean: $\bar{x} = 59.992$ s
     Sample standard deviation: $s = 0.105$ s
     Distribution of population data appears normal

For Problems 21 to 24, conduct a full formal hypothesis test on the claims made.

21.   A drug company is performing quality control on their epinephrine injectors. The injectable solution is labelled to contain 100 mcg of epinephrine per 1 mL of solution. Since too much or too little of the drug can be dangerous during an allergic reaction, the standard deviation for the process is only 2.5 mcg/mL. The solutions from a sample of 40 injectors are tested with a mean concentration of 98.9 mcg/mL. Test the claim that the mean concentration is 100 mcg/mL at the 5% level of significance.

22.   A drug company is performing quality control on their injectable solutions of fentanyl for anesthesia. The solution is labelled to contain 50 mcg of fentanyl per 1 mL of solution. Due to the dangers of overdose if the patient is given too high a dose, and the dangers of the patient waking up prematurely if given too low a dose, extra steps must be taken to ensure that the doses are accurate. As such, the standard deviation of the process is only 1.8 mcg/mL. A sample of 75 vials is tested to ensure quality control and dose accuracy, and reveals a mean of 50.4 mcg/mL. Test the claim that the mean concentration is 50 mcg/mL at the 10% level of significance.

23. A patient with pre-hypertension (moderately high blood pressure) has his blood pressure monitored three times a day over the course of 14 days. The average systolic pressure of the patient was 142.4 mmHg. Stage 1 hypertension is considered to be anything over 140 mmHg. If the standard deviation in blood pressure readings for the average person is 13.6 mmHg, determine if there is enough evidence to support the claim that the patient's condition has worsened to Stage 1 hypertension at the 10% level of significance.

24. A female patient with anemia (iron deficiency) has her hemoglobin levels measured once a month for 3 years, as her physician wants to monitor her condition. The patient's mean hemoglobin concentration over the 3 years is 7.6 g per dL of blood. The physician informs the patient that her condition has progressed to severe anemia, which is characterized by hemoglobin levels of less than 8 g/dL. If the standard deviation for hemoglobin levels for women is 0.75 g/dL, test the physician's claim that the patient's condition has progressed to severe anemia at the 1% level of significance.

10.2 | Testing a Hypothesis about a Population Mean

For the remainder of the chapter, we will focus on how to test hypotheses about specific population parameters, and the similarities and differences between the tests of the various claims. We will start by examining the process for testing claims about two common population parameters: the population mean and the population proportion. We will see that the procedures used for both are very similar, with some specific differences when it comes to setting up the test statistic.

In this section we will examine how to test a hypothesis about a population mean.

Steps for Testing a Hypothesis about a Population Mean

In order to test a hypothesis about a population mean, we follow the five steps of the Formal Hypothesis Test, described in Section 10.1, ensuring that our hypotheses, test statistics, and conclusions all relate to the calculation of a mean:

Step 1: State the null and alternative hypotheses (H_0 and H_1, respectively) in terms of the population mean μ and determine whether it is a one-tailed or two-tailed test.

Step 2: Determine a significance level (α) to be used to test the claims. If unsure, use a 5% significance level.

Step 3: Compute a test statistic based on the sample mean $\bar{x}$, and either the population standard deviation σ (if it is known) or the sample standard deviation s. The sample statistic should either be a z-score (if σ is known or the sample is large) or a t-score (if σ is unknown and the sample is small):

$$z = \frac{\bar{x} - \mu}{\frac{\sigma}{\sqrt{n}}} \qquad \textbf{or} \qquad t = \frac{\bar{x} - \mu}{\frac{s}{\sqrt{n}}}$$

Step 4: Look-up the p-value associated with the computed test statistic and compare to the level of significance (α). There are different ways of doing this if you are working with a z-score or a t-score, and they will each be discussed in detail in this section.

- If the test statistic is a z-score, the p-value is equal to the probability corresponding to the **negative** z-score in the z-table, regardless of whether z is negative or positive. This is true because the p-value represents the probability of getting a value *at least as extreme as z* - i.e., the area in the corresponding tail.

- If the test statistic is a t-score, the p-value cannot be determined exactly, but we can give a range of values the p-value will fall within. We will discuss this further, later in the section.

Step 5: Draw a conclusion about the null and alternative hypotheses and state your conclusion in context of the specific claim about the population mean that is being tested.

Hypothesis Testing for μ using the Normal z-Distribution (σ is Known or n is Large)

As mentioned in Chapter 9, it is not very common to know the population standard deviation σ without knowing the population mean μ. However, there are times when we might have an accurate estimate of σ and yet not know μ, such as when a process with a known population mean and standard deviation is changed so that the mean will either increase or decrease. Though we don't know for certain the standard deviation of the new process, we can assume it would be fairly close to the original, since the only thing being changed is the mean.

Alternatively, if we have a large enough sample, the Student's t-distribution will closely approximate the normal distribution, and we may assume, therefore, that the sample standard deviation s is a good approximation of the population standard deviation σ, i.e., $s \cong \sigma$. In most circumstances, this approximation is considered "good enough" when $n \geq 30$. However, since we have t-values for up to 200 degrees of freedom in our t-table, we will only use the normal approximation to the t-distribution when $n > 201$ (i.e., when $df > 200$).

Example 10.2-a	Testing a Hypothesis about μ when σ is Known

A drug company produces over-the-counter pain relief tablets with a mean mass of 600 mg and a standard deviation of 3.5 mg. Suppose that the company wishes to change the process so that the mean mass will be 625 mg instead. A sample of 80 tablets is selected with a sample mean mass of 623.7 mg. We can reasonably assume that the standard deviation of the process has remained the same at 3.5 mg. Test the claim that the new mean mass has, in fact, been increased to 625 mg at the 5% level of significance.

Solution

Step 1: $H_0 : \mu = 625$ mg

               $H_1 : \mu \neq 625$ mg

               Since, prior to the collection of the sample, we do not know whether the new process will have over-estimated or under-estimated the new mean weight, we must set up a two-tailed hypothesis test.

Step 2:   We will use a significance level of 5% - i.e., $\alpha = 0.05$.

Step 3:   Since we know the population standard deviation $\sigma = 3.5$ mg, we compute a test z-statistic, using the sample mean of $\bar{x} = 623.7$ mg and a sample size of $n = 80$:

$$z = \frac{\bar{x} - \mu}{\dfrac{\sigma}{\sqrt{n}}} = \frac{623.7 - 625}{\dfrac{3.5}{\sqrt{80}}} = \frac{-1.3}{0.391311\ldots} \approx -3.32$$

Step 4:   In the z-table, we look up the probability $P(Z < -3.32) = 0.0005$. Since we are working with a two-tailed hypothesis test, we double this probability to get our p-value:

               $p = 2(0.0005) = 0.0010 < 0.05 = \alpha$

Step 5:   Since $p < \alpha$, there is sufficient evidence to reject the null hypothesis that the mean mass has been increased to 625 mg. The drug company must revisit the process, as it appears that the new mass is too low.

Example 10.2-b	Testing a Hypothesis about μ when n is Large

Assume the drug company from Example 10.2-a decides to change their process entirely, purchasing brand new equipment to replace their current aging equipment. As such, the population standard deviation is not known. A sample of 250 tablets is taken with a sample mean mass of 625.5 mg and a sample standard deviation of 5.2 mg. Since the equipment is new, the drug company wants to ensure that the equipment is properly calibrated so that the true mean of the tablets will be 625 mg, and they want to minimize the probability of allowing under- or over-weight tablets to be produced.

(i) Determine which type of error the drug company is trying to avoid and what to set the significance level at in order to minimize that type of error.

(ii) Test the claim that the new mean mass is equal to 625 mg.

Solution

(i) The null hypothesis in this case is $H_0 : \mu = 625$ mg. Since the drug company wants to ensure that they don't accidentally allow the production of tablets with a different mean (i.e., when H_0 is false), they are trying to minimize the probability of failing to reject a false null hypothesis - a Type II error. Since the sample size is already set at 250 tablets, the only way to minimize a Type II error is to make α as large as possible. Hence, the company will test the claim at a 10% level of significance - i.e., $\alpha = 0.10$.

(ii) Step 1: $H_0 : \mu = 625$ mg

$H_1 : \mu \neq 625$ mg

Since, prior to the collection of the sample, we do not know whether the new process will have over-estimated or under-estimated the new mean weight, we must set up a two-tailed hypothesis test.

Step 2: We have established that we will use a significance level of 10% - i.e., $\alpha = 0.10$.

Step 3: In this case, we do not know the population standard deviation σ, but since we are using such a large sample, we can approximate σ using the sample standard deviation $s = 5.2$ mg and compute a test z-statistic, using the sample mean of $\overline{x} = 625.5$ mg and a sample size of $n = 250$:

$$z = \frac{\overline{x} - \mu}{\frac{\sigma}{\sqrt{n}}} = \frac{625.5 - 625}{\frac{5.2}{\sqrt{250}}} = \frac{0.5}{0.328876\ldots} \approx 1.52$$

Step 4: Since the p-value corresponds to the area in the tail of the z-table, we look up the probability that z will be less than the **negative** z-value computed: $P(Z < -1.52) = 0.0643$. Since we are working with a two-tailed hypothesis test, we double this probability to get our p-value:

$$p = 2(0.0643) = 0.1286 > 0.10 = \alpha$$

Step 5: Since p > α, there is not sufficient evidence to reject the null hypothesis that the mean mass has been increased to 625 mg. The drug company can, therefore, reasonably assume that the new equipment has been properly calibrated and they can begin production of their new pain relief tablets.

Hypothesis Testing for μ Using the Student's t-Distribution (σ is Unknown)

In reality, most hypothesis tests for an unknown population mean require the use of the Student's t-distribution, as the population standard deviation is unknown, and the sample size isn't large enough for an accurate estimate using the normal distribution. There are only two differences between the procedures for hypothesis testing using the normal z-distribution and the Student's t-distribution:

1. The test statistic will be a *t*-statistic (denoted t_{test}) involving *s*, instead of a *z*-statistic involving σ.

2. The p-value cannot be determined exactly using the *t*-table - we can only calculate a *range of values* that the p-value can fall within. However, this isn't a problem, as the range of values will always be between critical values, so we will always be able to determine if $p < \alpha$ or $p \geq \alpha$, which is all that really matters anyways.

Determining p-values for *t*-tests

To determine the p-value of the test statistic for a *t*-distribution, follow the steps below. The following example is provided as a guide:

$$t_{\text{test}} = 2.245, n = 25$$

Remember:
If $n > 201$ (i.e., $df > 200$), we can use a *z*-test even if σ is unknown.

Step 1: First, determine the degrees of freedom, $df = n - 1$, and look up the corresponding row in the *t*-table (if *df* is not found in the table, round **down** to the nearest *df* value in the table).

$$df = n - 1 = 25 - 1 = 24$$

Step 2: Compare the **absolute value** of the test *t*-statistic (t_{test}) that you calculated to the *t*-values listed in the corresponding row for the degrees of freedom from Step 1. Find the two consecutive values that your test *t*-statistic falls between in that row, and call them t_{lower} and t_{upper}, as they are the lower and upper bounds for your test *t*-statistic.

$t_{\text{test}} = 2.245$; therefore:

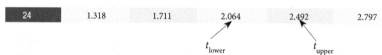

| 24 | 1.318 | 1.711 | 2.064 | 2.492 | 2.797 |

t_{lower} (pointing to 2.064) $\quad$ t_{upper} (pointing to 2.492)

Step 3: The boundaries for the critical p-value are the values of α (two-tailed test) or $\alpha/2$ (one-tailed test) in the top row of the *t*-table corresponding to the t_{lower} and t_{upper} values from Step 2.

df	$\alpha = 0.20$ $\alpha/2 = 0.10$	$\alpha = 0.10$ $\alpha/2 = 0.05$	$\alpha = 0.05$ $\alpha/2 = 0.025$	$\alpha = 0.02$ $\alpha/2 = 0.01$	$\alpha = 0.01$ $\alpha/2 = 0.005$
...					
24	1.318	1.711	2.064	2.492	2.797

Therefore,

- For a two-tailed test: $0.02 < p < 0.05$
- For a one-tailed test: $0.01 < p < 0.025$

Notes:

- t_{lower} *corresponds with the upper bound for* p *and* t_{upper} *corresponds with the lower bound for* p*, because higher t-values are further away from the mean, which correspond to lower p-values.*

- *If the value of* t_{test} *is less than the lowest t-value in that row, the* p*-value is* **greater** *than* $\alpha = 0.20$ *(two-tailed test) or* $\alpha/2 = 0.10$ *(one-tailed test).*

- *If the value of* t_{test} *is greater than the highest t-value in that row, the* p*-value is* **less** *than* $\alpha = 0.01$ *(two-tailed test) or* $\alpha/2 = 0.005$ *(one-tailed test).*

Example 10.2-c   Determining the p-value for *t*-tests

Determine the range of p-values for the following test *t*-statistics:

(i) $t_{\text{test}} = 2.575$, $n = 15$,   two-tailed

(ii) $t_{\text{test}} = 3.119$, $n = 10$,   right-tailed

(iii) $t_{\text{test}} = 1.628$, $n = 30$,   left-tailed

Solution

(i) $df = 15 - 1 = 14$

Looking up row 14 of the t-table, we see that the two consecutive values that $t_{test} = 2.575$ fall between are 2.145 and 2.625. Therefore,

$t_{lower} = 2.145$, so for a two-tailed test, the upper bound for p is $\alpha = 0.05$

$t_{upper} = 2.625$, so for a two-tailed test, the lower bound for p is $\alpha = 0.02$

Hence, $0.02 < p < 0.05$.

(ii) $df = 10 - 1 = 9$

Looking up row 9 of the t-table, we see that the two consecutive values that $t_{test} = 3.119$ fall between are 2.821 and 3.250. Therefore,

$t_{lower} = 2.821$, so for a one-tailed test, the upper bound for p is $\alpha/2 = 0.01$

$t_{upper} = 3.250$, so for a one-tailed test, the lower bound for p is $\alpha/2 = 0.005$

Hence, $0.005 < p < 0.01$.

(iii) $df = 30 - 1 = 29$

Looking up row 29 of the t-table, we see that the two consecutive values that $t_{test} = 1.628$ fall between are 1.311 and 1.699. Therefore,

$t_{lower} = 1.311$, so for a one-tailed test, the upper bound for p is $\alpha/2 = 0.10$

$t_{upper} = 1.699$, so for a one-tailed test, the lower bound for p is $\alpha/2 = 0.05$

Hence, $0.05 < p < 0.10$.

Example 10.2-d   **Testing a Hypothesis about μ when σ is Unknown and n is Small**

A veterinarian is testing the claims of a pet insurance company, which states the average annual veterinarian costs for dog owners is \$3,051. The veterinarian believes the cost is lower than this. She pulls the bills from the previous year for 20 randomly-selected families with dogs that she provides veterinary care for and records the total annual invoice amounts:

\$5,210	\$1,963	\$3,764	\$4,202	\$2,504	\$3,056	\$1,824	\$4,784
\$869	\$2,589	\$2,562	\$2,253	\$2,502	\$1,379	\$3,615	\$2,830
\$3,323	\$2,175	\$3,111	\$1,617				

Note: The data appears to be approximately normally distributed.

Test the hypothesis that the average annual veterinarian costs for dog owners is \$3,051 at the 5% significance level.

Solution

The use of a statistical calculator or software such as Excel is recommended for these calculations, rather than performing by hand.

First, we need to calculate the sample mean and standard deviation:

$$\bar{x} = \frac{5,210.00 + 1,963.00 + 3,764.00 + ... + 3,111.00 + 1,617.00}{20} = \$2,806.60$$

$$s = \sqrt{\frac{(5,210.00 - 2,806.60)^2 + (1,963.00 - 2,806.60)^2 + ... + (1,617.00 - 2,806.60)^2}{20 - 1}} \approx \$1,112.31$$

Now we have all the components we need to test the hypothesis that $\mu = \$3,051$:

Step 1: $H_0 : \mu = \$3,051$

$H_1 : \mu < \$3,051$

Since the veterinarian believes that the actual population mean is less than \$3,051, this is a left-tailed hypothesis test.

Solution
continued

Step 2: We will use a significance level of 5% - i.e., $\alpha = 0.05$.

Step 3: In this case, since we do not know the population standard deviation σ, $n \leq 30$, and the population data appears to approximately follow a normal distribution, we will use the Student's t-distribution, with a sample mean of $\bar{x} = \$2,806.60$, a sample standard deviation of $s = \$1,112.31$, and a sample size of $n = 20$:

$$t = \frac{\bar{x} - \mu}{\frac{s}{\sqrt{n}}} = \frac{2,806.60 - 3,051.00}{\frac{1,112.31}{\sqrt{20}}} = \frac{-244.40}{248.720077...} \approx -0.983$$

Since the test t-statistic is always positive (i.e., the absolute value), we use $t_{test} = 0.983$.

Step 4: Looking up the row with $df = 20 - 1 = 19$ in the t-table, we see that $t_{test} = 0.983$ is less than the lowest critical t-value of 1.328.

Therefore, our one-tailed p-value is greater than $\alpha/2 = 0.10$ - i.e., p > 0.10.

Step 5: Since $p > \alpha = 0.05$, there is not sufficient evidence to reject the hypothesis that the mean annual cost is \$3,051. The veterinarian's data set is not large enough, and the sample standard deviation is too high to support her claim that $\mu < \$3,051$.

10.2 | Exercises

Answers to odd-numbered problems are available at the end of the textbook.

For Problems 1 to 8, calculate the test statistic, determine the p-value of the test statistic for the hypothesis test, and use that to decide whether there is sufficient evidence to reject the null hypothesis or not at the given level of significance.

1. $H_0 : \mu = 7.25$
   $H_1 : \mu \neq 7.25$
   $\bar{x} = 6.88$
   $\sigma = 1.43$
   $n = 52$
   $\alpha = 0.05$

2. $H_0 : \mu = 420$
   $H_1 : \mu \neq 420$
   $\bar{x} = 452.3$
   $\sigma = 116.5$
   $n = 96$
   $\alpha = 0.01$

3. $H_0 : \mu = 28$
   $H_1 : \mu < 28$
   $\bar{x} = 26.3$
   $s = 2.57$
   $n = 12$
   $\alpha = 0.10$

4. $H_0 : \mu = 12.5$
   $H_1 : \mu > 12.5$
   $\bar{x} = 13.76$
   $s = 3.12$
   $n = 18$
   $\alpha = 0.05$

5. $H_0 : \mu = 37,500$
   $H_1 : \mu \neq 37,500$
   $\bar{x} = 41,260$
   $s = 7,943$
   $n = 32$
   $\alpha = 0.01$

6. $H_0 : \mu = 9,480$
   $H_1 : \mu < 9,480$
   $\bar{x} = 9,235$
   $s = 1,238$
   $n = 63$
   $\alpha = 0.10$

7. $H_0 : \mu = 0$
   $H_1 : \mu > 0$
   $\bar{x} = 1.71$
   $s = 8.56$
   $n = 225$
   $\alpha = 0.05$

8. $H_0 : \mu = 40$
   $H_1 : \mu \neq 40$
   $\bar{x} = 39.57$
   $s = 2.14$
   $n = 256$
   $\alpha = 0.05$

For Problems 9 to 20, decide whether to use a z-distribution or a t-distribution to set up the hypothesis test. Then perform a full formal hypothesis test on the claim.

9. Test the claim that the average nurse's salary is \$69,450 if a sample of 225 nurses' salaries are collected, with a sample mean of \$67,880 and a sample standard deviation of \$11,440. Use a 5% level of significance.

10. Test the claim that the average dose of a certain liquid cold medication taken at home is equal to the indicated dose of 10 mL, if 219 patients are sampled and asked to pour out one dose of medicine, resulting in a sample mean of 10.7 mL, with a sample standard deviation of 3.9 mL. Use a 10% level of significance.

11. Test the claim that the average length of time a prescription pain-killer will be effective is at least 12 hours (measured by when the patient asks for another dose), if 24 patients are randomly selected, and the sample mean time between requested doses is 10.75 hours, with a sample standard deviation of 2.92 hours. The data appears normally distributed. Use a 1% level of significance.

12. Test the claim that the average weight loss of patients on a certain weight-loss program in 3 months is at least 20 lbs, if 15 patients are randomly selected and the sample mean weight loss is 18.2 lbs, with a sample standard deviation of 5.4 lbs. The data appears normally distributed. Use a 10% level of significance.

13. Test the claim that the average cost of a certain medical procedure is $15,000, if a sample of 36 procedures is collected, with a sample mean of $17,190 and a sample standard deviation of $4,680. Use a 1% level of significance.

14. Test the claim that the average recovery time for a certain operation is 4 weeks (measured by when the patient can fully return to normal daily activities), if a sample of 64 patient recovery times are collected, with a sample mean of 4.45 weeks and a sample standard deviation of 1.32 weeks. Use a 5% level of significance.

15. Assume that it is known that the average female baby weighs 3,350 g at birth, with a standard deviation of 570 g. Test the claim that the average weight of newborn male babies is greater than the average weight of newborn female babies, if a sample of 48 male birth weights are collected, with a sample mean of 3,520 g, assuming the standard deviation for males is the same as the standard deviation for females. Use a 10% level of significance.

16. Assume that it is known that the length of time it takes for a local pharmacy to fill a prescription is 18.2 minutes, with a standard deviation of 4.7 minutes. Test the claim that a new procedure significantly reduces this time, if a sample of the times taken to fill 132 prescriptions is collected, with a sample mean of 15.5 minutes, assuming the standard deviation remains the same. Use a 5% level of significance.

17. A doctor believes that a female patient of hers may be mildly anemic, that is, with hemoglobin counts of less than 12 mg/dL of blood. The doctor runs a series of 10 blood tests to confirm her suspected diagnosis. The hemoglobin levels in the tests are as follows (in mg/dL):

    | 10.5 | 10.2 | 11.8 | 13.3 | 9.6 | 12.0 | 10.1 | 11.4 | 12.9 | 10.2 |

    Note: The data appears to be approximately normally distributed.

    Based on the blood test results above, test the doctor's hypothesis that the patient is anemic (i.e., the average hemoglobin level is less than 12 mg/dL) at the 10% level of significance.

18. A nurse is monitoring the bilirubin levels in an elderly patient who appears to be jaundiced (in mg/dL):

    | 3.1 | 3.5 | 2.8 | 3.3 | 2.6 | 3.4 | 2.7 | 2.4 | 2.9 | 3.2 | 3.3 | 3.0 |

    Note: The data appears to be approximately normally distributed.

    Patients with bilirubin levels above 3 mg/dL are considered to be jaundiced, which can be pose a serious health problem. Test the claim that this patient is jaundiced at the 5% level of significance.

19. An older male patient tests his blood pressure every time he goes to the pharmacy to ensure that his blood pressure is still within "normal" range (i.e., a systolic blood pressure of at most 120 mmHg and a diastolic blood pressure of at most 80 mmHg). He records his systolic pressure during his visits to the pharmacy over the course of 3 months (in mmHg):

    | 116 | 125 | 119 | 112 | 128 | 135 | 126 | 118 | 120 | 124 | 130 | 116 | 126 | 121 |

    Note: The data appears to be approximately normally distributed.

    Test the patient's claim that his systolic blood pressure is within the "normal" range at the 1% level of significance.

20. The patient from Problem 19 also records his diastolic blood pressure during that 3-month period (in mmHg):

    | 76 | 79 | 78 | 76 | 84 | 91 | 82 | 84 | 79 | 86 | 88 | 78 | 81 | 80 |

    Note: The data appears to be approximately normally distributed.

    Test the patient's claim that his diastolic blood pressure is within the "normal" range at the 1% level of significance.

10.3 | Testing a Hypothesis about a Population Proportion

Now we turn our attention to the study of how to test a hypothesis about a population proportion that has a specific characteristic. In this section, we must be working with a large sample in order for the normal approximation to the binomial principles discussed in the previous chapters to apply.

Hypothesis Testing for p using the Normal z-Distribution

These are the conditions required to use the normal approximation to the binomial distribution, as discussed in previous chapters.

In order to test a claim about the population proportion p, the following conditions must be met:

- A binomial experiment (independent trials, each with two outcomes - success or failure - with constant probabilities for each outcome) must be repeated n times.

- n must be large enough so that all the following are true: $n \geq 30$, $np > 5$, and $nq > 5$.

- $\hat{p} = \dfrac{x}{n}$, where x is the number of successes observed in the n trials of the experiment, is the sample proportion of successes, and it is the best point estimate for the population proportion p.

- The standard deviation of the p-distribution is calculated by $\sigma = \sqrt{npq}$, where p and q are the hypothesized population proportions of successes and failures, respectively (i.e., $q = 1 - p$).

  - Hence, the standard error of the $\hat{p}$-distribution is given by $\sigma_{\hat{p}} = \sqrt{\dfrac{pq}{n}}$

Therefore, the test z-statistic for a population proportion is given by the following formula:

$$z = \frac{\hat{p} - p}{\sqrt{\dfrac{pq}{n}}}$$

Steps for Testing a Hypothesis about a Population Proportion

In order to test a hypothesis about a population proportion, we follow the five steps of the Formal Hypothesis Test, described in Section 10.1, ensuring that our hypotheses, test statistics, and conclusions all relate to the calculation of a proportion:

Step 1: State the null and alternative hypotheses (H_0 and H_1, respectively) in terms of the population proportion p and determine whether it is a one-tailed or two-tailed test.

Step 2: Determine a significance level (α) to be used to test the claims. If unsure, use a 5% significance level.

Step 3: Compute a test statistic based on the sample proportion $\hat{p}$. Since n is large, we can assume the sampling distribution is approximately normal; therefore, the sample test statistic is a z-score:

$$z = \frac{\hat{p} - p}{\sqrt{\dfrac{pq}{n}}}$$

Step 4: Look-up the p-value associated with the computed test z-statistic (as in Section 10.2) and compare to the level of significance (α).

*Note: Remember to always look up the **negative** z-score in the z-table!*

Step 5: Draw a conclusion about the null and alternative hypotheses and state your conclusion in context of the specific claim about the population proportion that is being tested.

Example 10.3-a	Testing a Hypothesis about p

A researcher believes that people living in the GTA are at a higher risk of diabetes than the general population in Canada. A random sample of 400 residents of the GTA is collected, of which 43 have diabetes. Test the researcher's claim at the 10% level of significance if the proportion of all Canadians who have been diagnosed with diabetes is 0.093.

Solution

Step 1: $H_0 : p = 0.093$

$H_1 : p > 0.093$

The null hypothesis in this case is that the proportion of residents with diabetes in the GTA is the same as the national proportion, making the researcher's claim that it is more than the national proportion the alternative hypothesis - hence, this is a right-tailed test.

Step 2: We will use a significance level of 10% - i.e., $\alpha = 0.10$.

Step 3: First we ensure that we can use the normal approximation to the binomial by checking that $n = 400 \geq 30$, $np = 400(0.093) = 37.2 > 5$, and $nq = 400(1 - 0.093) = 362.8 > 5$.

Then we compute the sample proportion $\hat{p} = \dfrac{43}{400} = 0.1075$ and use that to calculate the test z-statistic:

$$z = \frac{\hat{p} - p}{\sqrt{\dfrac{pq}{n}}} = \frac{0.1075 - 0.093}{\sqrt{\dfrac{0.093(1 - 0.093)}{400}}} = \frac{0.0145}{0.014521...} \approx 1.00$$

Step 4: Since the p-value corresponds to the area in the tail of the z-table, we look up the probability that z will be less than the negative z-value computed: $P(Z < -1.00) = 0.1587$. Since we are working with a one-tailed hypothesis test, this is our p-value:

$p = 0.1587 > 0.10 = \alpha$

Step 5: Since $p > \alpha$, there is not sufficient evidence to reject the null hypothesis that the proportion of residents of the GTA is the same as the national proportion. Hence, the researcher cannot conclude that the prevalence of diabetes in the GTA is any higher than it is in Canada.

Example 10.3-b	Testing a Hypothesis about p from Raw Data

A blood donor clinic in a certain town is always in need of O+ and O– type blood, as they are considered to be the most universal blood types, since O+ blood can be received by any + blood type, and O– can be received by any blood type at all. However, despite type-O bloods being the most common blood types, together accounting for 46% of all Canadians, this town seems to always be in short supply. One of the nurses at the blood clinic hypothesizes that the town has a lower proportion of type-O blood donors than the rest of the country, and she records the blood types of 100 donors to test this claim:

O–	A+	O+	A–	O+	A+	B+	A+	A+	A+
A+	O+	A+	A+	A+	A+	A+	A+	A–	B+
A+	B+	O+	O+	A+	O+	A–	O+	B–	O+
A+	A+	A+	A+	O+	A+	O+	A+	O+	O+
AB–	A+	O+	O+	B+	A+	AB+	B+	AB+	AB–
A+	B+	B–	A+	A+	B+	O+	A+	A+	A+
A+	O+	A+	A+	O+	A–	A+	A+	O+	B+
A+	A+	A+	A+	A+	O–	O+	A+	A+	A+
A–	O+	A+	B+	O+	A+	A+	O+	A+	A+
O+	A+	A+	B+	A+	O+	A+	B+	O–	O+

Test the nurse's claim.

Solution

Step 1: $H_0 : p = 0.46$

$H_1 : p < 0.46$

The null hypothesis in this case is that the proportion of type-O blood in the small town is the same as the national proportion, making the nurse's claim that it is less than the national proportion the alternative hypothesis - hence, this is a left-tailed test.

Step 2: Since we are given no information, we will use a standard significance level of 5% - i.e., $\alpha = 0.05$.

Step 3: First we ensure that we can use the normal approximation to the binomial by checking that $n = 100 \geq 30$, $np = 100(0.46) = 46 > 5$, and $nq = 100(1 - 0.46) = 54 > 5$.

Next we count the number of type-O blood donors; there are 25 O+ and 3 O−, a total of 28.

Then we compute the sample proportion $\hat{p} = \dfrac{28}{100} = 0.28$, and use that to calculate the test z-statistic:

$$z = \frac{\hat{p} - p}{\sqrt{\dfrac{pq}{n}}} = \frac{0.28 - 0.46}{\sqrt{\dfrac{0.46(1 - 0.46)}{100}}} = \frac{-0.18}{0.049839\ldots} \approx -3.61$$

Step 4: In the z-table, we look up the probability $P(Z < -3.61) = 0.0002$. Since we are working with a one-tailed hypothesis test, this is our p-value:

$$p = 0.0002 < 0.05 = \alpha$$

Step 5: Since $p < \alpha$, there is sufficient evidence to reject the null hypothesis that the proportion of type-O blood donors in the small town is the same as the national proportion. Therefore, the sample evidence supports the nurse's claim that the town has a lower proportion of type-O blood than the rest of the county.

10.3 | Exercises

Answers to odd-numbered problems are available at the end of the textbook.

For Problems 1 to 8, first determine if the conditions required for the normal approximation to the binomial are met. Then calculate the test statistic, determine the p-value of the test statistic for the hypothesis test, and use that to decide whether there is sufficient evidence to reject the null hypothesis or not at the given level of significance.

1. $H_0 : p = 0.725$
$H_1 : p \neq 0.725$
$\hat{p} = 0.817$
$n = 60$
$\alpha = 0.10$

2. $H_0 : p = 0.85$
$H_1 : p \neq 0.85$
$\hat{p} = 0.784$
$n = 125$
$\alpha = 0.05$

3. $H_0 : p = 0.033$
$H_1 : p \neq 0.033$
$\hat{p} = 0.075$
$n = 40$
$\alpha = 0.05$

4. $H_0 : p = 0.96$
$H_1 : p \neq 0.96$
$\hat{p} = 0.875$
$n = 80$
$\alpha = 0.01$

5. $H_0 : p = 0.24$
$H_1 : p < 0.24$
$x = 43$
$n = 250$
$\alpha = 0.01$

6. $H_0 : p = 0.333$
$H_1 : p > 0.333$
$x = 61$
$n = 150$
$\alpha = 0.10$

7. $H_0 : p = 0.167$
$H_1 : p > 0.167$
$x = 16$
$n = 75$
$\alpha = 0.05$

8. $H_0 : p = 0.139$
$H_1 : p < 0.139$
$x = 5$
$n = 72$
$\alpha = 0.01$

For Problems 9 to 12, a random binomial process is repeated several times, in an attempt to see if the process is fair - i.e., the actual probability of the event occurring matches the expected probability. In order to test if the process is fair, first determine if the conditions required for the normal approximation to the binomial are met. Then state the null and alternative hypotheses, calculate the test statistic, determine the p-value of the test statistic for the hypothesis test, and use that to decide whether there is sufficient evidence to reject the null hypothesis or not at the 5% level of significance.

9. A coin is flipped 15 times, and results in heads facing up 9 times.

10. A 6-sided die is rolled 50 times, and results in a "6" facing up 15 times.

11. Two 6-sided dice are rolled 60 times, and results in a sum of "7" a total of 5 times.

12. 40 digital playing cards are "drawn" randomly from a digital deck of 52 cards using a computer program, and results in a King being drawn 4 times.

For Problems 13 to 24, determine if the conditions required for the normal approximation to the binomial are met. Then perform a full formal hypothesis test on the claim.

13. A pharmaceutical company that produces a sleep-aid pill claims that less than 5% of patients taking the pill experience any side effects. To test this claim, a research conducts a study involving 500 people taking the drug and records that 36 patients experienced side effects. Test the pharmaceutical company's claim at the 5% level of significance.

14. A new "quit smoking" aid manufacturer claims that more than 90% of all smokers who use their product have quit smoking after 3 months of continuous use. In a study to test this claim, 200 smokers were given the product to use continuously for a 3-month period, and then were asked to live their lives normally for 3 months, after which they were to come back and indicate if they had smoked any tobacco in the 3 months after they stopped using the product. 172 indicated they were still "smoke-free" after the 3 months. Test the manufacturer's claim at the 10% level of significance.

15. A massage therapist is considering increasing her rate for massage therapy by $10 per hour, but she is afraid that she will lose patients as a result. She typically sees around 120 patients each month, and is willing to accept a loss of no more than 10% of her patients. She pilots the price increase and in the subsequent month, she only saw 102 patients. Test the claim that she lost more than 10% of her patients at the 1% level of significance.

16. A doctor's office is piloting a new "no-show" fee to attempt to deter some of the numerous patients each month that do not show up for their scheduled appointments. In a typical month, they average about 36 no-shows and are trying to reduce that number by more than 50%. They send the information about the new fee to all their patients over a 3-month period. In the first month that the new cancellation fee is implemented, they only have 12 no-shows. Test the claim that the no-show fee successfully deterred more than 50% of no-shows each month at the 5% level of significance.

17. A doctor working in the Emergency Room of a local hospital during a night shift claims that only 10% of all the patients she sees in the E.R. during her shift have serious medical concerns that need immediate attention. Her colleague decides to test this claim one night, and records that out of the 42 patients that came into the E.R. during her shift, 11 had serious medical concerns that needed immediate attention. Test the doctor's claim at the 5% level of significance.

18. A medical website claims that approximately 3% of all babies born have some sort of birth defect. An obstetrician decides to test that claim. Out of the 120 babies that he delivers in a month, only 2 have birth defects. Using this data, test the website's claim at the 1% level of significance.

19. According to MADD Canada, 58.8% of all fatalities resulting from traffic accidents in 2012 involved drivers who had drugs or alcohol in their system at the time of the crash. A researcher believes that the percentage has changed since then, and decides to test this claim. He takes a random sample of 85 traffic-related fatalities, and of these, 43 of the crashes involved drivers with drugs or alcohol in their system. Test the researcher's claim at the 10% level of significance.

20. In a pre-health statistics course, approximately 25% of the students fail the test on hypothesis testing. A professor implements a new method for teaching the material and wishes to test whether this method significantly changes the number of students who fail the test. She uses the new method in all three of her classes, and gives the same test to all 105 students across her three sections of the course, of which 18 fail the test. Test the professor's claim at the 5% level of significance.

21. A naturopath hypothesizes that less than 25% of people eat the recommended minimum 5 servings of fruits and vegetables, even 5 days a week. He decides to test this claim by giving a survey to 100 of his patients, asking them to record how many days they ate at least 5 servings of fruits and vegetables over the course of 2 weeks, and received the following results:

3	5	9	2	13	3	4	12	14	3
10	4	8	2	14	2	7	1	6	3
4	9	6	12	7	11	6	5	2	14
4	6	3	7	4	5	9	6	4	6
10	8	4	9	3	0	5	5	2	5
6	2	2	7	4	7	2	2	8	9
4	7	3	6	5	10	12	11	3	6
5	5	2	9	5	3	11	7	6	14
1	4	9	3	11	1	6	1	10	7
2	4	11	9	4	4	8	0	7	5

Test the naturopath's claim at the 5% level of significance.

22. The naturopath from Problem 21 believes that less than 20% of people exercise for at least 30 minutes a day, at least 5 days a week. So he also asks his patients to record the number of days where they exercised for 30 minutes or more over the 2 week period. The following are the results:

2	3	10	4	2	3	8	4	8	10
5	0	6	3	9	13	6	3	12	5
3	3	5	1	5	9	8	5	8	2
6	4	4	2	12	1	3	3	2	12
7	3	14	2	8	5	2	6	1	5
6	9	6	8	10	1	11	3	2	1
5	4	1	2	3	13	7	4	8	3
7	4	3	2	10	3	1	7	11	8
4	7	6	7	8	11	7	6	3	2
5	0	4	6	5	12	2	10	1	2

Test the naturopath's claim at the 5% level of significance.

23. An athletic therapist believes that she sees more male patients to treat a sports injury than she does female patients. She takes a random sample of 48 patients and records their gender:

M	M	F	M	M	M	F	M	M	F	M	F
F	F	M	M	M	F	F	M	M	M	M	M
M	F	M	M	F	F	M	M	F	M	M	F
F	M	M	F	F	M	M	M	M	F	M	F

Test the athletic therapist's claim that she sees more male patients than female patients at the 1% level of significance.

24. A professor believes that the majority of students at the college are in favour of having more private health-care options available, so long as the public health-care system doesn't decrease or diminish in any way. He takes a poll of 60 randomly-selected students at the college, asking the following question: "Are you in favour of more private health-care options, if the current public health-care system is not decreased or diminished in any way?" The results are recorded below:

N	Y	Y	Y	Y	N	N	N	Y	Y	Y	N
N	N	Y	Y	N	Y	Y	Y	Y	N	N	Y
Y	N	Y	N	Y	N	Y	Y	Y	Y	N	Y
Y	Y	N	Y	Y	N	Y	Y	Y	N	N	N
Y	Y	Y	Y	Y	N	N	Y	Y	Y	Y	N

Test the professor's claim that the majority of students are in favour of more private health-care options available at the 1% level of significance.

10.4 | Testing a Hypothesis about Linear Correlation

We conclude the chapter (and the book!) with a look back to Chapter 4, where we first introduced the notion of **linear correlation**:

> *Recall that two variables are said to be linearly correlated if the variation in one variable affects the variation in the other variable by a constant rate. The linear correlation between the two variables is measured by Pearson's correlation coefficient r.*

This *r*-value, however, only represents the correlation present in a sample of data, and does not necessarily reflect the relationship between the two variables overall. In Chapter 4, we discussed the notion that random variation could lead to an *r*-value that indicated some correlation between two variables when, in fact, there was none. As the sample size increased, the value of *r* that could arise between two unrelated variables based only on random variation decreased. As a result, for a given sample size, if we computed a large-enough *r*-value, we were confident (at a 5% level of significance) that the large value for *r* indicated that significant linear correlation actually existed between the two variables. We didn't know it then, but we were essentially testing the hypothesis that there existed significant linear correlation between the two variables! We will now formalize this concept using the language of hypothesis tests learned in this chapter.

Testing a Hypothesis about the Linear Correlation Coefficient

Establishing a Population Parameter for Linear Correlation

In order to establish a formal hypothesis test for the linear correlation coefficient, we need to establish a variable to use for the population parameter. Since we used μ - "mu", the Greek letter "m" - to represent the population **m**ean and σ - "sigma", the Greek letter "s" - for the population **s**tandard deviation, it seems only logical that we would use ρ - "rho", the Greek letter "r" - to represent the population *r*-value.

Determining the Null and Alternative Hypotheses

Unlike hypothesis tests for the population mean and proportions, where the null hypothesis values can be anything, the null hypothesis when testing if two variables are linearly correlated or not is always the same: we assume that there is no significant correlation between the two variables:

$$H_0 : \rho = 0$$

The alternative hypothesis, therefore, may be any one of the following three statements, depending on whether there is any known information about the relationship between the two variables, if it exists:

$$H_1 : \rho \neq 0 \qquad\qquad H_1 : \rho < 0 \qquad\qquad H_1 : \rho > 0$$

Two-tailed   **Left-tailed**   **Right-tailed**

Calculating the Test Statistic

The test statistic used to test a correlation coefficient is actually a *t*-statistic! Hence, it has the same form as a *t*-statistic for a sampling distribution:

$$t = \frac{r - \mu_r}{s_r}$$

where μ_r is the population mean of all sample *r*-values, and s_r is the sample standard error of sample *r*-values.

Since we always assume that there is no correlation between the two variables (i.e., $\rho = 0$), it stands to reason, therefore, that $\mu_r = 0$.

The formula for the standard error is too complex to calculate for the purposes of this book, and so

it will simply be stated without explanation: $s_r = \sqrt{\dfrac{1 - r^2}{n - 2}}$

Note: From this formula, we note that the degrees of freedom when working with r-values is actually (n – 2), instead of the typical (n – 1). This will be important when looking up our test t-statistics to determine the corresponding p-values.

Therefore, we can state the formula for the test *t*-statistic as follows:

$$t = \frac{r}{\sqrt{\dfrac{1 - r^2}{n - 2}}}$$

Now we have everything we need in order to test whether or not there is significant linear correlation present between two variables or not, by following the usual 5-step formal hypothesis method.

Example 10.4-a	Testing if Significant Linear Correlation Exists (Two-tails)

A doctor decides to test the claims of a natural, herb-based diet supplement for its weight-loss properties, which claims that the more you take of it, the more weight you will lose. While he believes that the herb is safe, he also believes that there is no correlation between taking the herb and weight loss, but decides to perform a double-blinded scientific study between the amount of the herb taken and the amount of weight lost by each of the participants to determine if there is any correlation between the two variables.

The study involves 40 participants over the course of 8 weeks, and the resulting *r*-value is 0.192. Test the researcher's claim that there is no correlation between the variables at the 5% level of significance.

Solution   Step 1: $H_0 : \rho = 0$

                        $H_1 : \rho \neq 0$

                        The null hypothesis in this case is that the correlation coefficient is 0 (i.e., there is no correlation between the variables), and the alternative hypothesis is that the correlation is not 0 (i.e., there does exist some significant correlation between the variables).

     Step 2:   We are instructed to use a standard significance level of 5%- i.e., $\alpha = 0.05$.

Solution
continued

Step 3: We use the sample r-value of 0.192 to calculate the test t-statistic:

$$t = \frac{r}{\sqrt{\dfrac{1-r^2}{n-2}}} = \frac{0.192}{\sqrt{\dfrac{1-0.192^2}{40-2}}} = \frac{0.192}{0.159203\ldots} \approx 1.206$$

Therefore, $t_{\text{test}} = 1.206$.

Step 4: There is no row in the t-table with $df = 40 - 2 = 38$, so we will look up our test t-statistic in the row with $df = 35$. Looking up $t_{\text{test}} = 1.206$ in that row, we see that it is less than the lowest critical t-value of 1.306.

Therefore, our two-tailed p-value is greater than $\alpha = 0.20$ - i.e., $p > 0.20$.

Step 5: Since $p > \alpha = 0.05$, there is not sufficient evidence to reject the null hypothesis that there is no correlation between the amount of herb taken and the weight loss experienced. However, this does not prove the researcher's claim that there is no correlation between the variables.

Example 10.4-b	Testing if Significant Linear Correlation Exists (One-tail)

The producer of the herbal diet supplement from Example 10.4-a reads the published results of the physician's study and decides to conduct their own study to show that their diet supplement is actually effective by showing there is a positive correlation between the amount of the supplement taken and the amount of weight lost. They collect a sample of 30 dieters who have used their supplement for 8 weeks and reported their weight loss, and they compare the amount of the supplement taken by each dieter and the amount of weight lost and determine the r-value to be 0.286.

(i) Perform a hypothesis test on the manufacturer's claim that there is positive correlation between the amount of supplement taken and the amount of weight lost at the 10% significance level.

(ii) Explain some of the reasons why we would end up with a different conclusion than we did in Example 10.4-a.

Solution

(i) Step 1: $H_0 : \rho = 0$

$H_1 : \rho > 0$

As with all linear correlation hypothesis tests, the null hypothesis is that the correlation coefficient is 0 (i.e., there is no correlation between the variables) and, in this case, the alternative hypothesis is the manufacturer's claim that there is positive linear correlation between the two variables (i.e., $\rho > 0$).

Step 2: We are instructed to use a significance level of 10% - i.e., $\alpha = 0.10$.

Step 3: We use the sample r-value of 0.286 to calculate the test t-statistic:

$$t = \frac{r}{\sqrt{\dfrac{1-r^2}{n-2}}} = \frac{0.286}{\sqrt{\dfrac{1-0.286^2}{30-2}}} = \frac{0.286}{0.181088\ldots} \approx 1.579$$

Therefore, $t_{\text{test}} = 1.579$.

Step 4: Looking up the row with $df = 30 - 2 = 28$, we see that $t_{\text{lower}} = 1.313$ and $t_{\text{upper}} = 1.701$. Therefore, our one-tailed p-value is less than $\alpha/2 = 0.10$ and greater than $\alpha/2 = 0.05$ - i.e., $0.05 < p < 0.10$.

Step 5: Since p $< \alpha = 0.10$, there is sufficient evidence to reject the hypothesis that there is no correlation between the amount of herb taken and the weight loss experienced, and therefore to adopt the claim that there is positive correlation between the two variables.

(ii) There are several problems with this second study that would explain the different result from 10.4-a:

- The manufacturer has a clear bias in this study.

- The information used for the study is self-reported by the dieters and has not been independently verified, so it cannot be trusted (it is highly-likely that the results may have been exaggerated).

- There were no apparent attempts made to randomize or blind the study, or to control any of the lurking variables.

- A smaller sample was used, indicating a higher likelihood of sampling error.

- A higher significance level was used, making it more likely that a Type I error would be committed - i.e., rejecting the true null hypothesis that there is, in fact, no correlation between the variables.

- A one-tailed test was used instead of a two-tailed test, which increases the power of the test - i.e., decreases β - which, in turn, results in a higher likelihood of a Type I error being committed.

The Critical Value Approach to Hypothesis Testing

Another method for testing hypotheses that was not covered in this book is known as the "Critical Value Approach". This approach makes use of the same principles learned to test a hypothesis using p-values, but instead of calculating the p-value and comparing it to the level of significance, a maximum and/or minimum acceptable test statistic value, known as a **critical value**, is calculated for the given level of significance. If the test statistic lies beyond that critical value (i.e., in the tail), then the null hypothesis is rejected; otherwise, the null hypothesis is not rejected.

The Critical Value Approach is very similar to the way the upper and lower bounds of the confidence intervals in Chapter 9 were computed, creating a sort of "reverse confidence interval" for reasonable sample test statistics if the population parameter is the value claimed in the null hypothesis. Any test statistic falling outside that range suggests that the null hypothesis may, in fact, be incorrect, and therefore provides support for the alternative hypothesis being correct instead.

The "critical *r*-values" presented in Table 4.2 in Chapter 4 were computed using this approach, assuming a 5% level of significance and a two-tailed hypothesis test. These values are presented again below as a reference:

Table 10.4	**5% Significance Table for r**

df $(n-2)$	r	df $(n-2)$	r
1	0.997	16	0.468
2	0.950	17	0.456
3	0.878	18	0.444
4	0.811	19	0.433
5	0.754	20	0.423
6	0.707	21	0.413
7	0.666	22	0.404
8	0.632	23	0.396
9	0.602	24	0.388
10	0.576	25	0.381
11	0.553	26	0.374
12	0.532	27	0.367
13	0.514	28	0.361
14	0.497	29	0.355
15	0.482	30	0.349

To conduct a two-tailed hypothesis test if significant linear correlation is present between two variables at the 5% level of significance using the Critical Value Approach, simply compute the sample r-value and compare its absolute value to the critical r-value in the table above:

- If the absolute sample r-value is greater than the critical r-value, reject the null hypothesis, and adopt the alternative hypothesis instead.

- If the absolute sample r-value is less than or equal to the critical r-value, fail to reject the null hypothesis.

We will now revisit an example that we covered in Chapter 4, now that we have a better understanding of the concepts of hypothesis testing and how we define significant linear correlation.

Example 10.4-c	**Testing if Significant Linear Correlation Exists Using Critical r-Values**

The monthly premium quoted by an insurance company for a 10-year-term, $100,000 critical illness policy was collected from a sample of twelve adult female non-smokers, between the ages of 25 and 55:

Age	36	52	25	45	39	47	55	33	45	28	50	31
Premium	$68	$324	$37	$292	$129	$255	$512	$173	$461	$72	$275	$97

Use this data to test whether there is a linear correlation between the two variables at the 5% level of significance.

Solution	Step 1:	$H_0 : \rho = 0$
		$H_1 : \rho \neq 0$

The null hypothesis in this case is that the correlation coefficient is 0 (i.e., there is no correlation between the variables), and the alternative hypothesis is that the correlation is not 0 (i.e., there does exist some significant correlation between the variables).

Step 2: We are instructed to use a significance level of 5%: $\alpha = 0.05$.

Step 3: We compute the sample r-value using the formula learned in Chapter 4.1, or statistical software like Excel, and come up with the value $r_{test} = 0.860$.

Step 4: Looking up $df = 12 - 2 = 10$ in the Critical r-value Table 10.4, we find a critical r-value of 0.576, which our test r-statistic of 0.860 is greater than.

Step 5: Since $r_{test} > 0.576$, there is sufficient evidence to reject the null hypothesis that there is no correlation between the age and the cost of the insurance premium, and instead adopt the alternative hypothesis that the two variables are linearly correlated.

10.4 | Exercises

Answers to odd-numbered problems are available at the end of the textbook.

For Problems 1 to 8, calculate the test statistic, determine the p-value of the test statistic for the hypothesis test, and use that to decide whether there is sufficient evidence to reject the null hypothesis or not at the given level of significance.

1.	$H_0 : \rho = 0$	2.	$H_0 : \rho = 0$	3.	$H_0 : \rho = 0$	4.	$H_0 : \rho = 0$
	$H_1 : \rho \neq 0$		$H_1 : \rho \neq 0$		$H_1 : \rho < 0$		$H_1 : \rho > 0$
	$r = 0.341$		$r = -0.296$		$r = -0.638$		$r = 0.574$
	$n = 37$		$n = 52$		$n = 12$		$n = 15$
	$\alpha = 0.05$		$\alpha = 0.05$		$\alpha = 0.01$		$\alpha = 0.01$

5.	$H_0 : \rho = 0$	6.	$H_0 : \rho = 0$	7.	$H_0 : \rho = 0$	8.	$H_0 : \rho = 0$
	$H_1 : \rho > 0$		$H_1 : \rho \neq 0$		$H_1 : \rho \neq 0$		$H_1 : \rho < 0$
	$r = 0.135$		$r = 0.196$		$r = -0.489$		$r = -0.373$
	$n = 230$		$n = 260$		$n = 28$		$n = 22$
	$\alpha = 0.05$		$\alpha = 0.01$		$\alpha = 0.01$		$\alpha = 0.05$

For Problems 9 to 16, determine whether or not there is significant linear correlation present at the 5% significance level, based on the r-value and sample size, using the Critical Value Approach.

9.	$r = 0.588$	10.	$r = 0.512$	11.	$r = -0.493$	12.	$r = -0.345$
	$n = 10$		$n = 16$		$n = 17$		$n = 32$

13.	$r = 0.850$	14.	$r = -0.914$	15.	$r = -0.291$	16.	$r = 0.463$
	$n = 6$		$n = 4$		$n = 26$		$n = 21$

For Problems 17 to 24, determine if there is evidence for significant linear correlation by performing a full formal hypothesis test on the claim that there is no linear correlation, clearly stating the null and alternative hypotheses. You may use either the test statistic approach or the critical values approach.

17. A nutritionist does a study comparing the BMI of an individual and the number of sugary drinks they consumed in a week. The study consisted of 72 participants and yielded a sample $r = 0.411$. Test the claim that there is no linear correlation at the 1% level of significance.

18. The nutritionist from Problem 17 repeated the study with a different sample of 72 participants, this time comparing the BMI of each individual and the number of glasses of water they consumed in a week. The study yielded a sample $r = -0.275$. Test the claim that there is no linear correlation at the 1% level of significance.

19. A pediatrician does a study comparing the birth weight of 24 babies and the number of weeks gestation they were when they were born. The study yielded a sample $r = 0.372$. Test the claim that there is no linear correlation at the 5% level of significance.

20. A nurse practitioner in the child-birth ward at a hospital does a study comparing the birth length and birth weight of 20 newborn babies. The study yielded a sample $r = 0.718$. Test the claim that there is no linear correlation at the 5% level of significance.

21. A health-care practitioner does a study comparing the number of hours of sleep and performance on a test of focus, spatial awareness, and short-term memory. The practitioner believes that the more hours a person sleeps the night before, the higher they will score on the test. He takes a random sample of 50 participants, conducts the test and records the results, which yield a sample $r = 0.506$. Test the practitioner's claim at the 1% level of significance.

22. A university health-care worker and community activist who is working to prevent impaired driving has people perform a focus and reflexes test after having consumed alcohol. The participants' test scores are compared to their BAC (Blood-Alcohol-Content), and the health-care worker believes that the higher the BAC, the lower the score the participant will receive, so she performs a study to test this hypothesis. She conducts the study at the on-campus bar, randomly sampling 35 participants who have been drinking to take the reflexes and focus test, along with a Breathalyzer test. She compiles the results and the study reveals a sample $r = -0.492$. Test her claim at the 1% level of significance.

23. An oncologist does a study involving patients with terminal cancer who refuse treatment to compare the size of the tumour when discovered and the length of time the patients live after the diagnosis. She believes the larger the tumour, the shorter the life-span of the patient. Based on the strict parameters for the study, the doctor gathers a sample over the course of 2 years. However, she still is only able to gather a relatively small sample of 14 patients, and compiles the results, with a sample $r = -0.368$. Test the doctor's claim at the 5% significance level.

24. A college professor teaching statistics for health sciences conducts a study of his 27 students, comparing the number of homework exercises completed and the score on the final exam, claiming that the more exercises a student completes, the higher his/her mark will be on the exam. His study yields a sample $r = 0.915$. Test the professor's claim at a 1% significance level.

10 | Review Exercises

Answers to odd-numbered problems are available at the end of the textbook.

For Problems 1 to 4, determine the null and alternative hypotheses for the following scenarios. State whether the test is left-, right-, or two-tailed.

1. A hospital hypothesizes that 43% of their diabetic patients are qualified to try the new metformin drug. A large sample size of 785 diabetic patients is used to test this claim.

2. A researcher does not believe that the average human body temperature is 37 °C, and conducts a study with 1,000 patients to test the claim.

3. A pharmaceutical company claims that a certain skin disease can be cured with a new medical ointment in less than 10 days.

4. Pediatricians claim that children need more than 3 weeks to recover from a nosocomial infection.

For Problems 5 to 10, perform the following:

(i) Compute the value of the test static and its corresponding p-value.

(ii) Conclude whether to reject the null hypothesis or not based on the p-value.

(iii) State the decision error type that is possible.

5. $H_0 : \mu = 25$ mg
$H_1 : \mu > 25$ mg
Level of significance: $\alpha = 0.01$
Sample size: $n = 100$
Sample mean: $\bar{x} = 27.1$ mg
Known population standard deviation: $\sigma = 10.4$ mg

6. $H_0 : \mu = 20°$
$H_1 : \mu \neq 20°$
Level of significance: $\alpha = 0.01$
Sample size: $n = 144$
Sample mean: $\bar{x} = 19.1°$
Known population standard deviation: $\sigma = 3.6°$

7. $H_0 : \mu = 4$ hours
$H_1 : \mu \neq 4$ hours
Level of significance: $\alpha = 0.05$
Sample size: $n = 625$
Sample mean: $\bar{x} = 3.95$ hours
Sample standard deviation: $s = 0.38$ hours

8. $H_0 : \mu = 130$ mmHg

$H_1 : \mu < 130$ mmHg

Level of significance: $\alpha = 0.05$

Sample size: $n = 900$

Sample mean: $\bar{x} = 129.5$ mmHg

Sample standard deviation: $s = 6.9$ mmHg

9. $H_0 : \mu = 34.2$

$H_1 : \mu < 34.2$

Level of significance: $\alpha = 0.10$

Sample size: $n = 40$

Sample mean: $\bar{x} = 32.0$

Sample standard deviation: $s = 4.1$

10. $H_0 : \mu = 592$

$H_1 : \mu > 592$

Level of significance: $\alpha = 0.05$

Sample size: $n = 55$

Sample mean: $\bar{x} = 596$

Sample standard deviation: $s = 18.75$

For Problems 11 to 16, decide whether to use a z-distribution or a t-distribution to set up the hypothesis test. Then perform a full formal hypothesis test on the claim.

11. A study suggests that high potassium levels (over 5.0 mmol/L) are correlated with diabetes. An endocrinologist believes that the average potassium level of his diabetic patients is less than 4.9 mmol/L. He measures the levels of potassium of 400 patients, and finds the mean is 4.85 mmol/L, with a standard deviation of 0.25 mmol/L. Test the endocrinologist's claim that the average potassium level of a diabetic is less than 4.9 mmol/L at the 5% level of significance.

12. Statistics Canada states that the average time to process an E.R. patient is 4 hours. 300 randomly-selected E.R. patients were timed, and the mean process time was found to be 4.1 hours with a standard deviation of 1 hour. Test the claim that the average time to process an E.R. patient is greater than 4 hours at the 10% level of significance.

13. A Toronto heroin clinic administers an average of 6.98 mg of naloxone to 50 addicted persons to reverse the effects of an overdose. If too high a dose is given, the patient may experience severe symptoms, and if too little is given, then the person may relapse. The sample standard deviation is 0.1 mg. If the required dosage amount is 7 mg, test the claim that the appropriate dosage amount is given at the 1% level of significance.

14. A certain sedative is expected to last for 120 minutes. To test this claim, 30 patients were randomly selected, and the mean time was found to be 115 minutes with a sample standard deviation of 9 minutes. Test the claim that the average length of time that the sedative lasts for is 120 minutes at the 2% level of significance.

15. A nurse checks the hypoglycemic levels (in mmol/L) of a diabetic patient every month for a year.

5.2	4.7	5.4	4.8	5.6	6.1
4.3	5.7	5.3	5.1	5.2	6.2

Note: The data appears to be approximately normally distributed.

Test the claim that the average hypoglycemic level for this patient is greater than 5 mmol/L at the 10% level of significance.

16. A pharmaceutical company quality tests a random sample of 10 ibuprofen pills. The required dose for each pill is 200 mg, and the actual doses for a sample of 10 pills is recorded (in mg):

206	205	197	199	202
210	199	195	202	208

Note: The data appears to be approximately normally distributed.

Test the claim that the average pill dose is 200 mg at the 1% level of significance.

For Problems 17 and 18, first determine if the conditions required for the normal approximation to the binomial are met. Then calculate the test statistic, determine the p-value of the test statistic for the hypothesis test, and use that to decide whether there is sufficient evidence to reject the null hypothesis or not at the given level of significance.

17. $H_0 : p = 0.85$

$H_1 : p \neq 0.85$

$\hat{p} = 0.76$

$n = 70$

$\alpha = 0.05$

18. $H_0 : p = 0.43$

$H_1 : p > 0.43$

$\hat{p} = 0.475$

$n = 150$

$\alpha = 0.01$

For Problems 19 and 20, determine if the conditions required for the normal approximation to the binomial are met. Then, perform a full formal hypothesis test on the claim at the 5% significance level.

19. A chiropractor claims that more than half of her patients prefer appointments of 60-minutes in length, and decides to test this claim by recording the length of her sessions for two weeks:

60	75	60	45	90	60	75
60	60	90	60	120	75	60
60	105	60	75	90	60	60
105	60	60	75	60	60	60
90	105	60	60	120	60	90
45	90	60	75	60	60	60
60	60	60	60	75	60	90
60	45	60	60	90	105	120
60	75	90	60	90	120	60
45	60	60				

20. Following arthroscopic shoulder surgery, patients are given prescriptions for a 10-day supply of powerful opioid pain-killers. A surgeon believes the prescriptions should only be given for 8 days, in order to help patients to ween themselves as quickly as possible to avoid creating dependency. The physician claims that more than 80% of patients don't use the pain-killers after 8 days anyways, and that can lead to abuse of prescription medications. She performs a study with 30 of her patients after 10 days to determine how long they took the prescription pain-killers for. The results are recorded below:

6	4	8	7	3	5	6
6	4	8	8	9	7	4
8	10	6	5	8	9	7
8	8	5	8	6	7	4
9	8					

For Problems 21 and 22, calculate the test statistic, determine the p-value of the test statistic for the hypothesis test, and use that to decide whether there is sufficient evidence to reject the null hypothesis or not at the given level of significance.

21. $H_0 : \rho = 0$
$H_1 : \rho < 0$
$r = -0.298$
$n = 80$
$\alpha = 0.05$

22. $H_0 : \rho = 0$
$H_1 : \rho \neq 0$
$r = 0.375$
$n = 40$
$\alpha = 0.01$

For Problems 23 and 24, determine whether or not there is significant linear correlation at the 5% level, based on the r-value and the sample size, using the Critical Value Approach.

23. $r = 0.609$; $n = 10$

24. $r = -0.452$; $n = 25$

For Problems 25 and 26, determine if there is evidence for significant linear correlation by performing a full formal hypothesis test on the claim that there is no linear correlation, clearly stating the null and alternative hypotheses.

25. A psychologist does a study comparing the number of hours of sleep 70 participants had each night against the number of calories they consumed the following day. This study yielded a sample correlation coefficient of $r = -0.332$. Test the claim that there is no linear correlation at the 1% level of significance.

26. A college statistics professor assigns homework questions online, but doesn't assign any marks for their completion. However, the tests are created using **very similar** examples to the homework questions the professor assigns (seriously folks, we actually do this!). At the end of the semester the professor compares the final grades of the 30 students in the class to the number of homework questions completed online and finds a correlation coefficient of $r = 0.769$. Test the claim that there is no linear correlation at the 5% level of significance.

10 | Self-Test Exercises

Answers to all problems are available at the end of the textbook.

1. A drug company is under scrutiny for producing pills having less than 500 mg per pill, which is the strength labelled on the pill bottle. A team of scientists test this claim.

   a. Determine the population parameter that is being tested.

   b. State the null and alternative hypotheses and determine if it is a left-tailed, right-tailed, or two-tailed test.

   c. Determine the most appropriate level of significance to use: 1%, 5%, or 10%.

For Problems 2 to 4, perform the following:
(i) *Compute the value of the test statistic and its corresponding p-value.*
(ii) *Conclude whether to reject the null hypothesis or not based on the p-value.*
(iii) *State the decision error type that is possible.*

2. $H_0 : \mu = 71$ seconds
$H_1 : \mu \neq 71$ seconds
Level of significance: $\alpha = 0.01$
Sample size: $n = 196$
Sample mean: $\bar{x} = 72.7$ seconds
Known population standard deviation: $\sigma = 8.8$ seconds

3. $H_0 : \mu = 501$ hours
$H_1 : \mu > 501$ hours
Level of significance: $\alpha = 0.10$
Sample size: $n = 640$
Sample mean: $\bar{x} = 505$ hours
Sample standard deviation: $s = 82.9$ hours

4. $H_0 : \mu = 29$ cm
$H_1 : \mu < 29$ cm
Level of significance: $\alpha = 0.05$
Sample size: $n = 56$
Sample mean: $\bar{x} = 27.7$ cm
Sample standard deviation: $s = 4.3$ cm

For Problems 5 to 9, decide whether to use a z-distribution or a t-distribution to set up the hypothesis test. Then perform a full formal hypothesis test on the claim.

5. A pharmaceutical rep claims that a new anti-inflammatory drug delivers 50 mg of ibuprofen. From a sample of 75 pills, the average concentration was 49.8 mg with a standard deviation of 1.32 mg. Test this claim at the 5% level of significance.

6. The average weight of a baby boy at birth is believed to be 3,530 g with a standard deviation of 56 g. Conduct a two-tailed test to test this claim if a sample of 96 male babies have a mean weight of 3,545 g. Use a 10% level of significance.

7. A claim is made that the average salary of a nurse in Canada is $84,590. A random sample of 25 nurses' salaries across the country revealed a distribution that looked approximately normal, with a sample mean of $81,250 and a standard deviation of $12,870. Based on this sample, test the claim that the average Canadian nurse's salary is less than $84,590 at the 1% level of significance.

8. The claim that the average wait time at a private clinic is 45 minutes was tested using a sample of 400 patients. The mean time was 46.4 minutes with a standard deviation of 10 minutes. Test the claim that wait times are greater than 45 minutes at the 1% level of significance.

9. It is widely believed that the average gestational length of a human fetus from conception to birth is 266 days. The gestational lengths of a sample of 16 pregnancies are recorded below (pregnancy length is measured from start of last menstrual cycle to birth, and then 14 days is subtracted to compute gestational length from conception to birth):

    256 267 269 265 263 262 269 252
    260 255 268 280 256 259 258 269

    Based on this sample data, test the claim that the average gestational length of a human fetus is 266 days at the 5% level of signficance.

10. In response to recent legislation that provides first responders with more access to treatment for Post-Traumatic Stress Disorder (PTSD) that excluded nurses, the president of a local nurse's union decides to conduct a study to support the claim that nurses experience PTSD at a rate significantly higher than the general population. The highest published proportion of PTSD in the general population is 0.104 and the president of the local nurses' union claims that the proportion of nurses who fit the diagnostic criteria for PTSD is significantly higher than that. He conducts a study of nurses from across the province and out of the 250 nurses randomly sampled, 45 fit the diagnostic criteria for PTSD. Test the local union president's claim at the 1% level of significance.

11. A health sciences program at a local university publishes that over 75% of its graduates have jobs in the health industry within 1 year of graduation. To test this claim, an alumnus conducted a sample of 100 graduates, with the following results:
    *   28 in nursing or medicine
    *   15 in pharmacy
    *   12 in athletic or physiotherapy
    *   10 in business or marketing
    *   8 in dentistry
    *   7 in paramedical services
    *   5 in retail services
    *   5 in veterinary medicine
    *   3 in optometry
    *   3 in other health-related fields
    *   2 in other non-health-related fields
    *   2 without jobs

    Test the university's claim at the 5% level of significance.

For Problems 12 and 13, determine if there is evidence for significant linear correlation by performing a full formal hypothesis test on the claim that there is no linear correlation, clearly stating the null and alternative hypotheses. You may use either the test statistic approach or the critical values approach.

12. A dietician conducts a test on her 15 clients to examine if there is a correlation between a client's weight and the frequency of their visits using a 5% level of significance. The r-value is 0.483.

13. A new study claims that increasing the dosage of a certain oral contraceptive leads to lower levels of natural estrogen in young women. With a significance level of 1%, the manufacturing company of the contraceptives test this by collecting a sample of 66 women who take increasing doses for 6 months and recording their levels before and after the study. They determine that the r-value is –0.280.

10 | Summary of Notation and Formulas

NOTATION

H_0 = the null hypothesis

H_1 = the alternative hypothesis

α = level of significance

p = probability of getting a result at least as extreme as the test statistic

df = degrees of freedom

n = total number of data values in a sample

μ = population mean

$\bar{x}$ = sample mean

σ = population standard deviation

s = sample standard deviation

p = population proportion of successes

q = population proportion of failures = $1 - p$

$\hat{p}$ = sample proportion of successes

$\hat{q}$ = sample proportion of failures = $1 - \hat{p}$

ρ = population correlation coefficient

r = sample correlation coefficient

FORMULAS

Test Statistic for μ when σ is known or n is large ($n > 201$)

$$z = \frac{\bar{x} - \mu}{\frac{\sigma}{\sqrt{n}}}$$

Test Statistic for μ when σ is unknown

$$t = \frac{\bar{x} - \mu}{\frac{s}{\sqrt{n}}}$$

Test Statistic for p

$$z = \frac{\hat{p} - p}{\sqrt{\frac{pq}{n}}}$$

Test Statistic for ρ

$$t = \frac{r}{\sqrt{\frac{1 - r^2}{n - 2}}}$$

5% Significance Table for r | Table 10.4

df $(n - 2)$	r	df $(n - 2)$	r
1	0.997	16	0.468
2	0.950	17	0.456
3	0.878	18	0.444
4	0.811	19	0.433
5	0.754	20	0.423
6	0.707	21	0.413
7	0.666	22	0.404
8	0.632	23	0.396
9	0.602	24	0.388
10	0.576	25	0.381
11	0.553	26	0.374
12	0.532	27	0.367
13	0.514	28	0.361
14	0.497	29	0.355
15	0.482	30	0.349

Answer Key

Chapter 1

Exercises 1.1

1. a. Stratified Random Sampling

   b. Multi-stage Random Sampling

   c. Convenience Sampling

   d. Systematic Sampling

3. a. Observational Study

   b. Observational Study

   c. Experiment

   d. Survey

5. a. Quantitative   b. Qualitative

   c. Quantitative   d. Qualitative

7. a. Continuous   b. Discrete

   c. Continuous   d. Discrete

9. a. Nominal   b. Ratio

   c. Interval   d. Ordinal

Exercises 1.2

1.

Subject	Tally	Frequency(f)
Math (M)	⦀⦀⦀ ⦀⦀⦀ ||||	14
Biology (B)	⦀⦀⦀ ⦀⦀⦀ |	11
Chemistry (C)	⦀⦀⦀ ||||	9
Physics (P)	⦀⦀⦀ |	6

3. a.

Rating	Tally	Frequency(f)
Outstanding (O)	⦀⦀⦀ ⦀⦀⦀ ⦀⦀⦀ |	16
Very Good (V)	⦀⦀⦀ ⦀⦀⦀ ||	12
Good (G)	⦀⦀⦀ ⦀⦀⦀	10
Average (A)	⦀⦀⦀ |	6
Poor (P)	||||	4

b. 48   c. Outstanding

5.

Subject	Tally	Frequency(f)	Relative Frequency
Math (M)	⦀⦀⦀ ⦀⦀⦀ ||||	14	$\frac{14}{40} = 35\%$
Biology (B)	⦀⦀⦀ ⦀⦀⦀ |	11	$\frac{11}{40} = 27.5\%$
Chemistry (C)	⦀⦀⦀ ||||	9	$\frac{9}{40} = 22.5\%$
Physics (P)	⦀⦀⦀ |	6	$\frac{6}{40} = 15\%$
	Total	40	100%

7. a.

Rating	Tally	Frequency(f)	Relative Frequency
Outstanding (O)	⦀⦀⦀ ⦀⦀⦀ ⦀⦀⦀ |	16	$\frac{16}{48} \approx 33.33\%$
Very Good (V)	⦀⦀⦀ ⦀⦀⦀ ||	12	$\frac{12}{48} = 25\%$
Good (G)	⦀⦀⦀ ⦀⦀⦀	10	$\frac{10}{48} \approx 20.83\%$
Average (A)	⦀⦀⦀ |	6	$\frac{6}{48} = 12.5\%$
Poor (P)	||||	4	$\frac{4}{48} \approx 8.33\%$
	Total	48	*99.99%

*discrepancy due to rounding

    b. 58.33%   c. 4 : 1

9. a.

Grade	Number of Students	Percent	Angle
A+	24	12%	43.2°
A	30	15%	54°
B	36	18%	64.8°
C	52	26%	93.6°
D	42	21%	75.6°
F	16	8%	28.8°
Total	200	100%	360°

b.

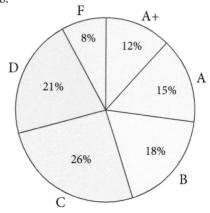

11. a. Middle-Aged Adults   b. 7 : 5

   c. 82%   d. 300

13.

Bar Chart of Number of Volunteers vs Starting Time

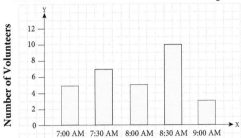

15. a.

Pareto Chart of Number of Volunteers vs Starting Times

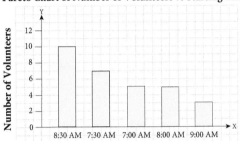

   b. 8:30

   c. It does not make sense to put this set in a Pareto chart since the data are ordinal, not nominal.

17. a.

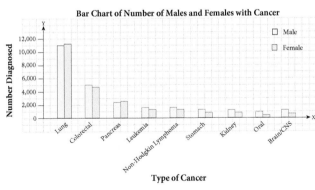

   b. Brain/CNS   c. 54 : 29

19. a. 810   b. 63 : 46   c. 117 : 85

Exercises 1.3

1.

Stem	Leaf
1	3 8 9 9
2	1 5 7 8 9
3	1 1 2 4 7 8 9
4	3 4

3.

Stem	Leaf
14	5 8
15	1 2 5 9
16	4 5 9
17	0 3 5 7 8
18	0 1 1 2 4 5 8
19	2 5 7

5. a. 30   b. 99, 34   c. 16

7.

Number of Babies	Tally	Frequency(f)
0					3
1						4
2							5
3									7
4						4
5						4
6					3

   b. 3, 7   c. 11   d. 3

9.

Data	Tally	Frequency(f)
13-19	||||	4
20-26	||	2
27-33	|||||		6
34-40	||||	4
41-47	||	2

11.

Heights	Tally	Frequency(f)
145-155	|||||	5
156-166	|||	3
167-177	|||||	5
178-188	||||| |||	8
189-199	|||	3

13. a.

Number of I.V. Tubes	Tally	Frequency(f)
140-148	||	2
149-157	||||| ||	7
158-166	|||	3
167-175			1
176-184	|||||		6
185-193			1

   b.

Histogram and Frequency Polygon for I.V. Tube Production

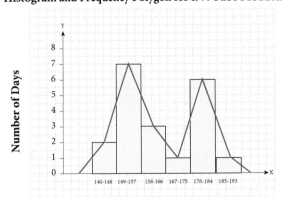

Number of I.V. Tubes

15. a.

Histogram and Frequency Polygon for Years of Teaching

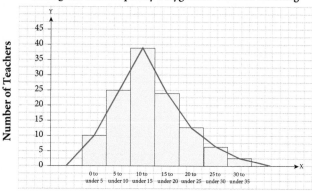

b.

Years of Teaching	Class Boundaries	Class Midpoint
0 to under 5	0	2.5
	5	
5 to under 10		7.5
	10	
10 to under 15		12.5
	15	
15 to under 20		17.5
	20	
20 to under 25		22.5
	25	
25 to under 30		27.5
	30	
30 to under 35		32.5
	35	

17.

Histogram and Frequency Polygon for Weight of Male Clients

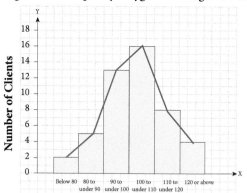

19.

Number of I.V. Tubes	Tally	Frequency(f)	Relative Frequency	Cumulative Frequency	Relative Cumulative Frequency
140-148	||	2	10%	2	10%
149-157	||||| ||	7	35%	9	45%
158-166	|||	3	15%	12	60%
167-175			1	5%	13	65%
176-184	|||||		6	30%	19	95%
185-193			1	5%	20	100%

Relative cumulative frequency of I.V. Tube Production

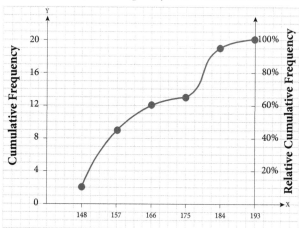

Number of I.V. Tubes

21.

Years of Teaching	Frequency	Relative Frequency	Cumulative Frequency	Relative Cumulative Frequency
0 to under 5	10	8.33%	10	8.33%
5 to under 10	25	20.83%	35	29.16%
10 to under 15	39	32.5%	74	61.66%
15 to under 20	24	20%	98	81.66%
20 to under 25	13	10.83%	111	92.49%
25 to under 30	7	5.83%	118	98.32%
30 to under 35	2	1.67%	120	*99.99%

*discrepancy due to rounding

Relative cumulative frequency of Years Teaching

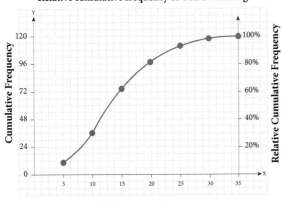

Number of Years Taught

23.

Line Graph of Sales ($ Thousands)

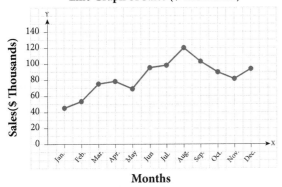

Months

25.

ASIR for Prostate and Breast Cancers in Canada

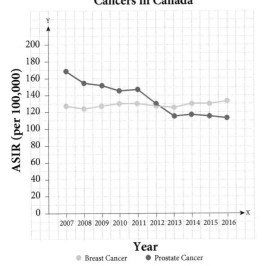

27. a. The trend of prostate cancer incidence is decreasing, with a strong decrease between 2011 and 2013.

b. The trend of breast cancer incidence is fairly constant.

c. 2.34%   d. 32.74%

Chapter 1 Review Exercises

1. a. Convenience Sampling

   b. Cluster Sampling

   c. Systematic Sampling

   d. Stratified Sampling

3. a. Qualitative

   b. Quantitative Discrete

   c. Qualitative

   d. Quantitative Continuous

5. a. Ordinal   b. Ratio

   c. Nominal   d. Ordinal

7. a.

   b. 27%   c. 5 : 2

9. a.

Referral	Tally	Frequency(f)
Emergency Room	⦀⦀ |	6
Inpatient Department	||||	4
Orthopedic Surgeon	⦀⦀	5
Family Physician	|||	3

   b.

Pareto Chart of Referrals to a Fracture and Orthopaedic Clinic

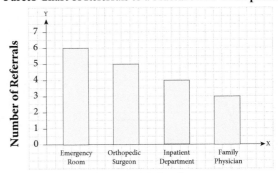

Source of Referral

   c. Emergency Room   d. 44.44%

11. a.

Stem	Leaf
4	7
5	0 2
6	0 5 8
7	1 1 1 2 6 7 9
8	0 0 1 1 1 5 6 7 9
9	0 2 3 3 5 6 8 9

b. 3   c. 12

13. a.

Number of Orders	Tally	Frequency(*f*)
20-29	||||	4
30-39	₶ ₶ |||	13
40-49	₶ ||||	9
50-59	||||	4

b. 30-39 orders   c. 43.33%

15. a. Quantitative Continuous

b., c., d., e.

Years of Service	Frequency(*f*)	Relative Frequency	Cumulative Frequency	Relative Cumulative Frequency
6 to under 11	5	20.83%	5	20.83%
11 to under 16	8	33.33%	13	54.16%
16 to under 21	5	20.83%	18	74.99%
21 to under 26	3	12.5%	21	87.49%
26 to under 31	3	12.5%	24	*99.99%

*discrepancy due to rounding

f.

Histogram and Frequency Polygon of Nurses' Years of Service

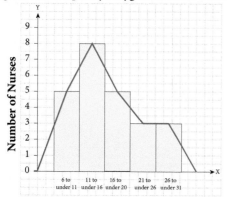

g.

Cumulative Frequency and Relative Cumulative Frequency vs Years of Service

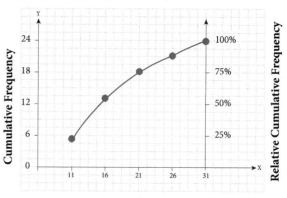

h. (i) 8   (ii) 13   (iii) 6

17.

Time (in minutes)	Frequency(*f*)	Relative Frequency	Cumulative Frequency	Relative Cumulative Frequency
Below 30	2	8%	2	8%
30 to under 40	4	16%	6	24%
40 to under 50	3	12%	9	36%
51 to under 60	10	40%	19	76%
60 and above	6	24%	25	100%

Histogram and Frequency Polygon of Statistics Test Completion

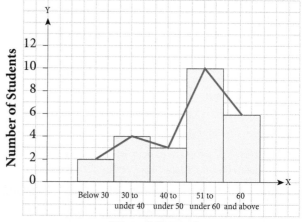

19. a.

Canadian Teenagers with Meningitis Vaccine

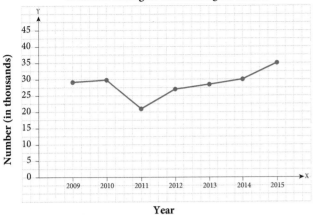

b. 2010 - 2011   c. 22.73%

21. a.

Multiline Graph Monthly Rainfall in Edmonton and Vancouver

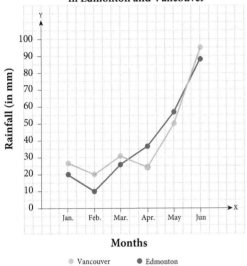

b. April

c. Vancouver had more rain 4 out of the 6 months recorded

d. May and June by 31 mm

e. May and June by 7 mm

Chapter 1 Self Test Exercises

1. a. Women whose mothers did take the drug during pregnancy, and women whose mothers did not take the drug during pregnancy

   b. Survey

2. a. Cluster Sampling   b. Systematic Sampling
   c. Convenience Sampling   d. Stratified Sampling

3. a. Quantitative Discrete   b. Quantitative Discrete
   c. Qualitative   d. Quantitative Continuous
   e. Qualitative

4. a. Interval   b. Nominal
   c. Ordinal   d. Ratio

   e. Ordinal

5. a. Cancer

   b. 302 : 197

   c. 10,616,000

6. a.

Stem	Leaf
3	3
4	1 6 6
5	0 0 5 8 9
6	1 5 6 7 7
7	0 1 5 6 7 8 8
8	0 1 1 2 7 8
9	0 2 7

b. 33   c. 9   d. 9

7. a. Quantitative Continuous

   b., c., d., e.

Cholesterol Levels (mg/dL)	Frequency(*f*)	Relative Frequency	Cumulative Frequency	Relative Cumulative Frequency
140 to under 160	5	25%	5	25%
160 to under 180	3	15%	8	40%
180 to under 200	4	20%	12	60%
200 to under 220	3	15%	15	75%
220 to under 240	3	15%	18	90%
240 to under 260	2	10%	20	100%

f.

Histogram and Frequency Polygon of Patients' Cholesterol Levels

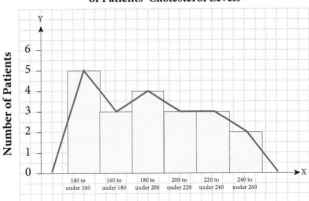

g.

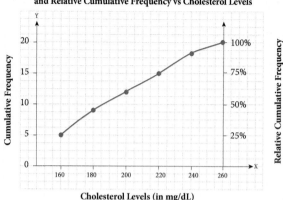

Cumulative Frequency
and Relative Cumulative Frequency vs Cholesterol Levels

Cholesterol Levels (in mg/dL)

h. (i) 9   (ii) 8   (iii) 4

8. a.

Continent	Tally	Frequency(f)
Asia	ⅢⅢ Ⅰ	6
Europe	ⅢⅢ	5
North America	ⅢⅢ Ⅰ	6
South America	‖‖	3

b.

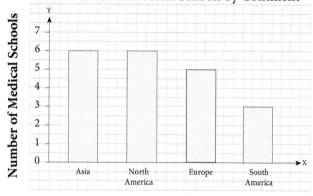

Pareto Chart of Medical Schools by Continent

Continent

c. Asia and North America   d. 30%

9. a. Smoking

b. Smoking, Inadequate Vegetable Intake, Alcohol Consumption

c. 8%   d. 9%   e. 4%

10. a. Bladder   b. Prostate

c. Lung and bronchus   d. 1992

Chapter 2

Exercises 2.1

1. 84.5   3. 92   5. 17.6

7. 75   9. $8,000   11. 50 kg

13. a. 51   b. 25   c. 26

15. a. 39.5   b. 14.5   c.78

17. a. 26   b. 25.5

19. a. no mode   b. 31   c. 36, 41

Exercises 2.2

1. a. 566.17   b. 268

3. a. 744.7   b. 777.125

5. 3.2   7. 71.67   9. $3,875

11. a. 12   b. 4   c.1.14

13. 5.19%   15. 80 km/h

Exercises 2.3

1. Mean: 2.72;   Median: 3;   Mode: 2

3. Mean: 7.37;   Median: 7.5;   Mode: 7

5. Mean: $16.02;   Median: $17;

Modal class: $16 to under $18

7. Mean: $268.67;   Median: $250;

Modal class: $200 to under $300

9. a. Mean: 113.5 mg/dL

Median: 115 mg/dL

Modal class: 100 to under 110

b. Diabetic:

Mean: 117.67 mg/dL

Median: 120 mg/dL

Modal class: 120 to under 130

Non-diabetic:

Mean: 109.33 mg/dL

Median: 105 mg/dL

Modal class: 80 to under 90 and 100 to under 110

Exercises 2.4

1. a. Mean: 55.65;   Median: 57.5;   Mode: 64

b. Skewness: Negatively Skewed;   Shape: Mound

3. a. Mean: $136.80;   Median: $90;

Modal class: $60 to under $120

b. Skewness: Positively Skewed;   Shape: Mound

5. Mode: 14;   Skewness: Positively Skewed

7. Mean: 18;   Skewness: Negatively Skewed

9. Median: 39.83;   Skewness: Positively Skewed

Chapter 2 Review Exercises

1. a. 2,335.57 mg   b. Yes

3. 23°C   5. 52.5 kg

7. a. Mean: 66.17;   Median: 66.5;   Mode: No Mode

b. Since the distribution of the data is symmetric without outliers, we can consider the mean as the best measure for approximate the data.

9. a. 23.375   b. 25.8

11. 96.5%   13. 5.23%   15. 1.36 m/s

17. a. Mean: 6.3

Median: 2.5

Modal class: 0 to under 5

b. Skewness: Positively Skewed

Shape: Mound

19. Mean: 124   Skewness: Negatively Skewed

Chapter 2 Self Test Exercises

1. a. 263 pairs   b. $223.55

2. $376   3. 30

4. a. Mean: 138.4;   Median: 137;

Mode: 127 and 144

b. 136.75

5. 70.05   7. 9.98 km/h

6. 13.79%

8. a. Mean: 25.7;   Median: 25;

Modal class: 20 to under 30

b. Skewness: Approximately symmetrical

Shape: Mound

9. a. Mean: 80.17;   Median: 82.5;   Mode: 85

b. Skewness: Negatively Skewed: Shape: Mound

10. $375.43; Approximately symmetrical

Chapter 3

Exercises 3.1

1. a. 76   b. 13   c. 13.2

3. a. $Q_1 = 6, Q_3 = 19.5$ b. $Q_1 = 123, Q_3 = 147$

5. a. $IQR = 13.5$, no outliers   b. $IQR = 24$, no outliers

7. a. $P_{10} = 2.5, P_{90} = 22.5, P_{90} - P_{10} = 20$

b. $P_{10} = 103.5, P_{90} = 163, P_{90} - P_{10} = 59.5$

9. a. 79   b. 23

11. a. $L = 24, Q_1 = 30, Q_2 = 39, Q_3 = 51, H = 62$

b. Between the median and the third quartile

c. $IQR = 21$

13. $P_{70} = 49$; Approx. 70% of the employees has age less than or equal to 49 years old.

15. Approximately 80% of the scores on this Biology test are lower than Mary's score. Mary did well in compared to her class. Only about 20% of the class did better than Mary.

17. If you receive a grade of 60% it means that you got 60% of the maximum score. If you score in approximately 60th percentile, it means that approximately 60% of the other students got a score lower than your score.

19.

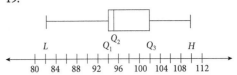

21. a. Median: 97   b. $Q_1 = 76, Q_3 = 100.5$

c. $IQR = 24.5$ d. No outliers

23.

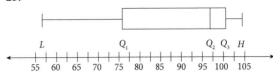

25.

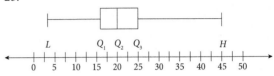

The outliers are: 3,45

27.

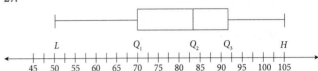

The median is closer to the right-side of the box and the right whisker is shorter than the left whisker, we can conclude that the distribution is negatively-skewed. The box is significantly shorter than the two whiskers combined, so the distribution is likely mound-shaped.

29. a. 30   b. 45   c. 25%

Exercises 3.2

1. 6

3. (b) has a bigger mean absolute deviation (a. 1.2, b. 4.56)

5. a. Variance: 2.5, Standard Deviation: 1.58

b. Variance: 32.7, Standard Deviation: 5.72

7. Variance: 4.44, Standard Deviation: 2.11

9. a. Mean: 81.2   b. Standard Deviation: 5.88

11. a. Mean: $79,600

b. Mean Absolute Deviation: $5,520

c. Variance: 50,300,000

d. Standard Deviation: $7,092.25

13. Approximate Standard Deviation: $4,500

15. a. Approximate minimum: $72,800,
Approximate maximum: $133,144

17. a. 68%   b. Between 300 and 700
c. Between 200 and 800

19. Approximate average weight: 800g,
Approximate Standard Deviation: 10g

21. Approximate minimum: 125,
Approximate maximum: 575

23. a. 95%   b. 6   c. 3,360

25. Less than 124 hours/week

27. a. Mean: 40.3, Standard Deviation: 8.93

b. 55.6%

c. $\dfrac{9}{10}$ = 90% of the data fall within the range

(26.91, 53.70), which is more than the guaranteed 55.6%.

29. 84%

31. a. 88.9%   b. 99.7%

c. The results vary by ~10%. Chebyshev's Rule guarantees getting a lower bound on the proportion of data for any distribution. Empirical rule only works with Bell shaped data.

33. $k = \sqrt{2}$, (57.86, 86.14)

35. $CV = 8.06\%$; The standard deviation represents 8.06% of the mean. A low coefficient of variation, as in this case, indicates that the data are fairly consistent.

37. a. Patient I Mean: 69.4, Standard Deviation: 6.23
Patient II Mean: 87.2, Standard Deviation: 6.30

b. Patient I has a slightly smaller standard deviation

c. Patient I $CV = 8.98\%$
Patient II $CV = 7.23\%$

d. The second patient has more consistent measurements.

39. Nurse A's hospital

Chapter 3 Review Exercises

1. a. $Q_1 = 52$, $Q_2 = 57$, $Q_3 = 66$ b. $IQR = 14$
c. 87   d. 31
e. No outliers

3. a. $P_{10} = 4.6$, $P_{90} = 9.45$ b. 4.85

5. a.

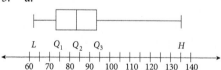

b. 135 is an outlier.

c. The left whisker is shorter than the right whisker, so the distribution is likely positively-skewed. The box is shorter than the two whiskers combined, so the distribution is mound-shaped.

7. Approximately 68% of men in his age group weight less than him.

9. Student A Mean: 78.6, Mean Absolute Deviation: 5.52, Standard Deviation: 7.50
Student B Mean: 71, Mean Absolute Deviation: 3.74, Standard Deviation: 5.83
Student A shows more variation.

11. a. Range First year students: 15, fourth year students: 7

b. Mean First year students: 7.92, fourth year students: 3.85

c. Standard Deviation First year students: 4.34, fourth year students: 1.95

d. Coefficient of Variation First year students: 54.78%, fourth year students: 50.73%

e. Fourth year students

13. Minimum: 14 days, maximum: 27 days

15. 29-65 years old

17. a. 84%   b. 5.1 inches

19. a. 44 - 137 minutes   b. 67%

21. a. Summer and winter have the same standard deviation value, and hence same variation.

b. CV for summer = 14.91%; CV for winter = 28.87%; Hence, summer month is more consistent.

Chapter 3 Self Test Exercises

1. a. $Q_1 = 8$, $Q_2 = 10.5$, $Q_3 = 12$ b. $IQR = 4$
c. 18   d. 2
e. No outliers

2. $P_{10} = 20.5$, $P_{90} = 43.5$, $P_{90} - P_{10} = 23$

3. Yes, it means that the approximately 92% of the class got a score less than her score.

4. a.

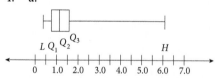

b. There are two outliers: 5.01, 6.05

5. a. 5 deliveries

b. 50%

c. The median is closer to the left-side of the box and the left whisker is shorter than the right whisker, we can conclude that the distribution is positively-skewed. The box is shorter than the two whiskers combined, so the distribution is likely mound-shaped.

6. a. 40   b. 5.2

7. a. Systolic range: 38, Diastolic range: 26

b. Approximate standard deviation for Systolic pressure: 9.5, approximate standard deviation for diastolic range: 6.5

c. Systolic pressure Mean: 145.43, Variance: 175.61, Standard Deviation: 13.25, *CV*: 9.11%

Diastolic pressure Mean: 94, Variance: 88 Standard Deviation: 9.38, *CV*: 9.98%

d. Range Rule of Thumb estimates were smaller than the precise calculations.

e. Systolic pressure has a smaller *CV*, therefore is more consistent.

8. Approximate minimum: 59.4 minutes,

approximate maximum: 124.2 minutes

9. Minimum height: 61.14 inches,

maximum height: 69.86 inches

10. a. 158.5 - 185.5 mg/100mL

b. 9   c. 302

11. 99.85%   12. 2,430 g

13. 89%

14. $k = 5$, the values ranges from 15 minutes to 165 minutes.

15. a. *CV* should be used since we are comparing two different sets of data with very different means.

b. *CV* for stocks under $10: 28.95%, *CV* for stocks over $50: 5.71%

Stocks prices over 50$ are more consistent.

Chapter 4

Exercises 4.1

1. Perfect positive linear correlation

3. Non-linear correlation

5. Moderate-weak negative linear correlation

7. No correlation

9. Strong negative linear correlation

11. (i) Independent: Number of flu vaccinations administered

Dependent: Number of flu cases diagnosed

(ii)

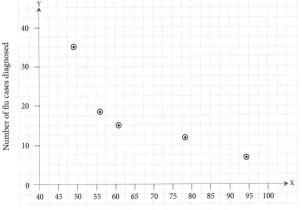

Number of flu vaccinations administered

(iii) $r = -0.847$, which appears to indicate strong negative correlation between the data: i.e. as the number of flu vaccinations increases, the number of flu cases decreases.

13. (i) Independent: Number of alcoholic drinks consumed

Dependent: Number of cigarettes smoked

(ii)

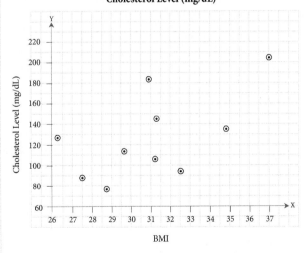

(iii) $r = 0.856$, which appears to indicate strong positive correlation between the data: i.e., as the number of alcoholic drinks consumed, the number of cigarettes smoked also increases.

15. (i) Independent: BMI

Dependent: Cholesterol Level

(ii)

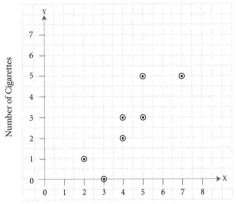

(iii) $r = 0.583$, which appears to indicate moderate positive correlation between the data: i.e., as the patient's BMI increases, his cholesterol level also increases.

17. (i) Independent: Number of Minutes Running on Treadmill

Dependent: % of Baseline Daily Calories Consumed

(ii)

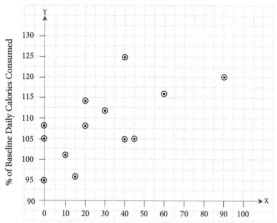

Number of Minutes Running on Treadmill
vs
% of Baseline Daily Calories Consumed

Number of Minutes Running on Treadmill

(iii) $r = 0.639$, which appears to indicate moderate positive correlation between the data: i.e. as the number of minutes spent running on the treadmill increases, the percent of the patient's daily baseline calories consumed also increases.

19. • Self-selected sample

• Small sample size: $n = 10$

• Unreliable results - no way to verify the values, which were likely estimations

21. • Correlation does not necessarily imply causation.

• The study hasn't isolated the variables to ensure no other variables will confound the results.

• One possible lurking variable could be the annual rising costs of living due to inflation that tend to affect all prices: goods, services, and wages. The study should account for this by first adjusting all the numbers for inflation.

Exercises 4.2

1. (i) $\hat{y} = 50.3 - 0.488x$. The slope of -0.488 indicates that for every 1 additional vaccination administered, it is predicted that approximately 0.488 fewer patients will be diagnosed with the flu.

(ii)

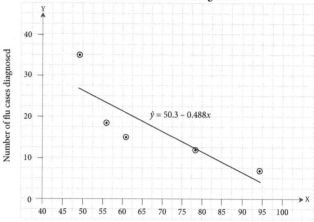

Number of Flu Vaccinations Administered
vs
Number of Flu Cases Diagnosed

$\hat{y} = 50.3 - 0.488x$

Number of flu vaccinations administered

(iii)

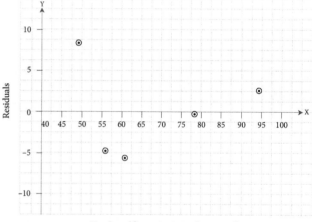

Residual Plot for Flu Vaccinations Administered
vs Flu Cases Diagnosed

Number of flu vaccinations administered

(iv) $SST = 453.2$, $SSR = 325.2$, $SSE = 128.0$

(v) $r^2 = \dfrac{325.2}{453.2} \approx 0.7176$, which means that approximately 71.76% of the variation in the number of flu cases the doctor diagnoses can be explained by variation in the number of flu vaccinations administered. This is consistent with the r-value of -0.847 calculated in 4.1, as $r^2 = (-0.847)^2 = 0.7174$ (the slight difference in values can be attributed to rounding errors).

3. (i) $\hat{y} = -1.61 + 1.01x$. The slope of 1.01 indicates that for every 1 additional alcoholic drink consumed in a social setting by this smoker who is trying to quit, it is predicted that he will smoke approximately 1.01 additional cigarettes.

(ii)

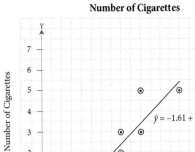
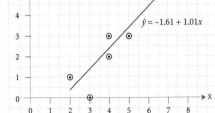

Number of Alcoholic Drinks vs Number of Cigarettes

$\hat{y} = -1.61 + 1.01x$

(iii)

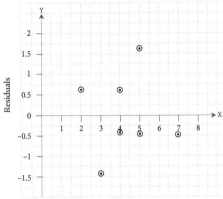

Residual Plot for Alcoholic Drinks vs Cigarettes

(iv) $SST = 21.43$, $SSR = 15.72$, $SSE = 5.71$

(v) $r^2 = \dfrac{15.72}{21.43} \approx 0.7336$, which means that approximately 73.36% of the variation in the number of cigarettes smoked in a social setting by smokers who desire to quit can be explained by the number of alcoholic drinks consumed. This is consistent with the r-value of 0.856 calculated in 4.1, as $r^2 = (0.856)^2 = 0.7327$ (the slight difference in values can be attributed to rounding errors).

5. (i) $\hat{y} = -100.5 + 7.36x$. The slope of 7.36 indicates that for every increase by 1 point to the patient's BMI, the patient's LDL cholesterol is predicted to increase by 7.36 mg/dL.

(ii)

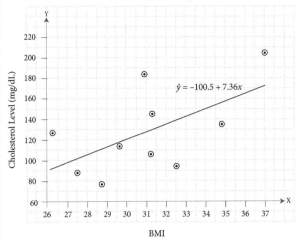

BMI vs Cholesterol Level (mg/dL)

$\hat{y} = -100.5 + 7.36x$

(iii)

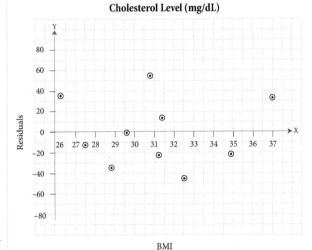

Residual Plot for BMI vs Cholesterol Level (mg/dL)

(iv) $SST = 15{,}134.4$, $SSR = 5{,}145.1$, $SSE = 9{,}989.3$

(v) $r^2 = \dfrac{5145.1}{15134.4} \approx 0.3400$, which means that approximately 34.00% of the variation in the LDL cholesterol levels of the patient can be explained by variation in the patient's BMI. This is consistent with the r-value of 0.583 calculated in 4.1, as $r^2 = (0.583)^2 = 0.3399$ (the slight difference in values can be attributed to rounding errors).

7. (i) $\hat{y} = 102.7 + 0.213x$. The slope of 0.213 indicates that for every 1 additional minute the patient spends on the treadmill running each day, she will consume an additional 0.213% of her baseline daily calories.

(ii)

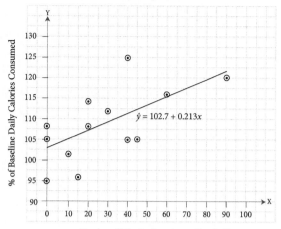

Number of Minutes Running on Treadmill
vs
% of Baseline Daily Calories Consumed

$\hat{y} = 102.7 + 0.213x$

Number of Minutes Running on Treadmill

(iii)

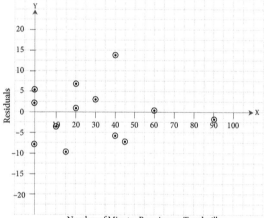

Residual Plot for Minutes Running on Treadmill
vs Baseline Daily Calories Consumed

Number of Minutes Running on Treadmill

(iv) $SST = 932.4$, $SSR = 380.8$, $SSE = 551.6$

(v) $r^2 = \dfrac{380.8}{932.4} \approx 0.4084$, which means that approximately 40.84% of the variation in the percent of the patient's daily baseline calories consumed can be explained by variation in the number of minutes she spends running on the treadmill each day. This is consistent with the r-value of 0.639 calculated in 4.1, as $r^2 = (0.639)^2 = 0.4083$ (the slight difference in values can be attributed to rounding errors).

9. Predicted birth weight = 3.38 kg

11. Can't use the regression equation to make predictions about the independent variable.

13. Predicted depression risk score = 4.0

15. Since the absolute value of the correlation coefficient is less than the critical r-value of 0.444 for $df = 18$ ($n = 20$), there is not enough evidence to suggest there is significant linear correlation. Hence we should not use the regression equation to make predictions about the variables.

17. Predicted diastolic blood pressure = 73 mmHg

19. We should not use the regression equation to make a prediction for the diastolic blood pressure based on a systolic blood pressure of 160 mmHg, as it is outside the range of systolic blood pressure values used to construct the regression equation.

21. $r^2 = 0.4638$ 23. $r^2 = 0.0480$

25. $r = 0.759$ 27. $r = -0.629$

29. $r^2 = 0.6868$ 31. $r^2 = 0.3655$

33. $SSR = 1,157.82$ 35. $SSE = 20.74$

37. $SST = 663.52$ 39. $SSE = 1,638.63$

Chapter 4 Review Exercises

1. Perfect positive linear correlation

3. Moderate-weak negative linear correlation

5. Strong positive linear correlation

7. Non-linear correlation

9. a. Independent: weight,
   Dependent: daily water consumption

   b.

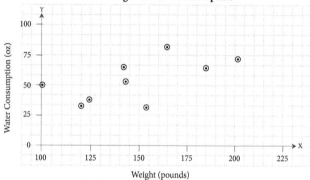

Weight vs Water Consumption

   c. $r = 0.610$ (moderate positive);

   $|r| < 0.666$ ($n = 9$, $df = 7$), so no significant correlation at the 5% level of significance.

   d. Small study, Possible confounding variables (e.g., sex, age, height, level of activity, etc.)

11. a. Independent: Average outdoor temperature
    Dependent: Crawling on own

    b.

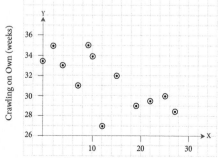

Average Outdoor Temperature vs Crawling on Own

Average Outdoor Temperature (°C)

c. $r = -0.693$;

$|r| > 0.576$ ($n = 12$, $df = 10$), so there is significant correlation at the 5% level of significance

d. $\hat{y} = 34.1 - 0.206x$. The slope of -0.206 indicates that for every 1 degree the average outdoor temperature increases, the age that a baby learns to crawl on their own decreases by 0.206 weeks.

e.

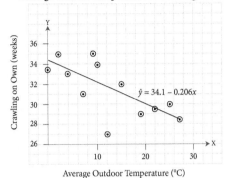

Average Outdoor Temperature vs Crawling on Own

f.

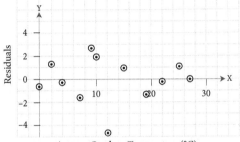

Residual Plot for Average Outdoor Temperature vs Crawling on Own

g. $SST = 79.2$; $SSR = 37.9$; $SSE = 41.2$

h. $r^2 = (-0.693)^2 = 0.4802$ and $r^2 = \dfrac{37.9}{79.2} = 0.4785$. The slight differences between these two values can be explained by rounding errors. This implies that approximately 48% of the variation in the age a baby starts crawling on his/her own can be explained by variation in the average outdoor temperature for that month.

13. 53%

15. a. Not appropriate - outside domain of input values

b. Not appropriate - cannot use regression equation "in reverse"

17. $r = 0.970$

19. $SSE = 18.26$, $r^2 = 0.7625$, $r = -0.873$

21. $SST = 1,586.19$, $SSE = 310.10$

Chapter 4 Self Test Exercises

1. Perfect positive linear correlation

2. Strong negative linear correlation

3. Moderate-weak positive linear correlation

4. Non-linear correlation

5. a. Independent: monthly consumption
   Dependent: price of the electrical bill

   b. Independent: age of patients
   Dependent: number of cases of colon cancer per 100,000 patients

   c. Independent: age of the applicant
   Dependent: medical insurance premiums

   d. Independent: number of family members in the household
   Dependent: amount of weekly grocery spending

6. a. Independent: age group of the drivers
   Dependent: number of driver deaths per 100,000

   b

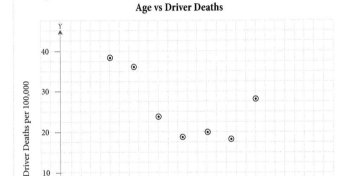

Age vs Driver Deaths

   c. $r = -0.661$ (moderate negative correlation); $|r| < 0.754$ ($n = 7$, $df = 5$), so no significant correlation at the 5% level of significance.

   d. Small sample, since the data is grouped into relatively large classes; no information about how many drivers in each group; no indicated control of confounding variables

7. a. Independent: stress score,
   Dependent: test score

   b

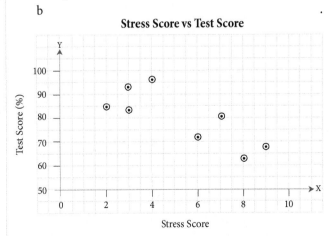

Stress Score vs Test Score

   c. $r = -0.793$ (strong negative correlation); $|r| > 0.707$ ($n = 8$, $df = 6$), so there is significant correlation at the 5% level of significance.

d. $\hat{y} = 99.1 - 3.61x$; the slope of -3.61 means that for every increase of 1 on the student's stress score, the student can expect a decrease of 3.61 marks on their test.

e.

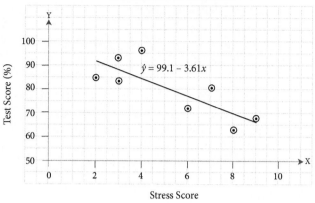

Stress Score vs Test Score

f.

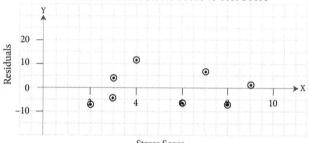

Residual Plot for Stress Score vs Test Score

g. $SST = 980.9$, $SSR = 617.4$, $SSE = 363.5$

h. $r^2 = (-0.793)^2 = 0.6288$ and $r^2 = SSR/SST = 0.6294$. The slight differences between these two values can be explained by rounding errors. This implies that approximately 63% of the variation in a student's math test score can be explained by variation in his/her stress test score.

8. a. Independent: BAC
Dependent: time (in hours) until sober

b.

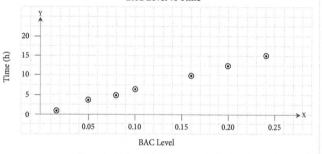

BAC Level vs Time

c. $r = 0.999$ (near perfect positive correlation); $|r| > 0.754$ ($n = 7$, $df = 5$), so there is significant correlation at the 5% level of significance.

d. $\hat{y} = 0.223 + 61.4x$; the slope of 61.4 means that for every increase of 1.00 in the person's BAC, it will take

an extra 61.4 hours to sober up (more realistically, then, for every increase of 0.01 in the person's BAC, it will take an extra 0.614 hours to sober up).

e.

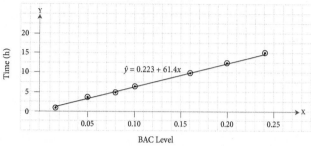

BAC Level vs Time

f.

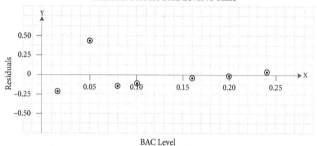

Residual Plot for BAC Level vs Time

g. $SST = 151.5$, $SSR = 151.2$, $SSE = 0.3$

h. $r^2 = (0.999)^2 = 0.9980$ and $r^2 = SSR/SST = 0.9980$. This implies that approximately 99.8% of the variation in the time it takes for a person to get sober can be explained by variation in the person's Blood Alcohol Content.

9. a. y-intercept: 3.22 - the percent body fat of someone who is 0 years old - not useful in this context, since the study only sampled adults between the ages of 23 and 61 years old.

slope: 0.548 - for every additional 1 year the person ages, his/her body fat will increase by 0.548%.

b. $r = 0.825$ indicates strong positive correlation; $|r| > 0.468$ ($n = 18$, $df = 16$), so there is significant correlation at the 5% level of significance.

c. $r^2 = 0.6806$, which means that approximately 68% of the variation in the percent body fat of an adult can be explained by variation in the adult's age.

10. Okay to use the regression equation to predict - $\hat{y} = 19.66$

11. Not appropriate - outside domain of input values

12. Not appropriate - cannot use regression equation "in reverse"

13. $r = 0.739$

14. $r = -0.931$

15. $SSE = 3.70$ and $r^2 = 0.6539$

16. $SST = 885.23$ and $SSR = 824.68$

Chapter 5

Exercises 5.1

1. (i) There are 15 outcomes – 9 prescription opioids + 5 NSAIDs + 1 OTC narcotic

 (ii) $S = \{Op_1,\ Op_2,\ Op_3,\ Op_4,\ Op_5,\ Op_6,\ Op_7,\ Op_8,\ Op_9,\ NS_1,\ NS_2,\ NS_3,\ NS_4,\ NS_5,\ Acetaminophen\}$

 (iii) There are 3 events – prescription opioid, NSAID, or OTC narcotic

3. (i) There are 25 outcomes – 10 fabric bandages + 8 plastic bandages + 4 rubber/latex bandages + 3 liquid bandages

 (ii) $S = \{F_1, F_2, F_3, F_4, F_5, F_6, F_7, F_8, F_9, F_{10}, P_1, P_2, P_3, P_4, P_5, P_6, P_7, P_8, RL_1, RL_2, RL_3, RL_4, L_1, L_2, L_3\}$

 (iii) There are 4 events – fabric bandage, plastic bandage, rubber/latex bandage, liquid bandage

5. (i) There are 35 outcomes – 8 beds in private rooms + 12 beds in a semi-private rooms + 15 beds in ward rooms

 (ii) $S = \{P_1, P_2, P_3, P_4, P_5, P_6, P_7, P_8, S_{1A}, S_{1B}, S_{2A}, S_{2B}, S_{3A}, S_{3B}, S_{4A}, S_{4B}, S_{5A}, S_{5B}, S_{6A}, S_{6B}, W_{1A}, W_{1B}, W_{1C}, W_{2A}, W_{2B}, W_{2C}, W_{3A}, W_{3B}, W_{3C}, W_{4A}, W_{4B}, W_{4C}, W_{5A}, W_{5B}, W_{5C}\}$

 (iii) There are 3 events – private room, semi-private room, ward room

7. (i) Empirical

 (ii) $P(Mild\ SE) = \dfrac{83}{500} = 0.166$

9. (i) Theoretical

 (ii) $P(Grand\ Prize) = \dfrac{10}{2,500,000} = 0.000004$

11. (i) Subjective

 (ii) Cannot calculate $P(Success)$ based on information given

13. (i) Empirical

 (ii) $P(Defective) = \dfrac{8}{1,250} = 0.0064$

15. (i) Subjective

 (ii) Cannot calculate $P(Pass)$ based on information given

17. (i) Theoretical

 (ii) $P(Parking\ Lot) = \dfrac{5}{12} \approx 0.417$

19. (i) Tree diagram

 (ii) $P(2G, 2B) = \dfrac{6}{16} = 0.375$

21. (i) Outcome table

 (ii) $P(Both\ Females) = \dfrac{9}{25} = 0.36$

23. (i) Outcome table

 (ii) $P(No\ mornings) = \dfrac{20}{30} \approx 0.667$

25. (i) Venn diagram

 (ii) $P(Non\text{-}degree,\ Non\text{-}nursing) = \dfrac{10}{80} = 0.125$

27. (i) Tree diagram

 (ii) $P(\geq 2\ Correct\ out\ of\ 5) = \dfrac{26}{32} \approx 0.813$

29. (i) Venn diagram

 (ii) $P(No\ dog,\ no\ cat,\ no\ rodent) = \dfrac{14}{168} \approx 0.0833$

31. (i) $P(All\ 3\ Heads) = \dfrac{1}{8} = 0.125$

 (ii) Complementary Event is "At least 1 Tails"; $P(At\ least\ 1\ Tails) = 0.875$

 (iii) Odds against "All 3 Heads" are 7 : 1; Odds in favour of "All 3 Heads" are 1 : 7

33. (i) $P(Face\ Card) = \dfrac{12}{52} \approx 0.231$

 (ii) Complementary Event is "Non-Face Card"; $P(Non\text{-}Face\ Card) = 0.769$

 (iii) Odds against "Face Card" are 10 : 3; Odds in favour of "All 3 Heads" are 3 : 10

35. (i) $P(> 16) = \dfrac{4}{20} = 0.2$

 (ii) Complementary Event is "Less than or equal to 16"; $P(\leq 16) = 0.8$

 (iii) Odds against "Greater than 16" are 4 : 1; Odds in favour of "Greater than 16" are 1 : 4

37. (i) $P(Top\ 3) = \dfrac{3}{12} = 0.25$

 (ii) Complementary Event is "Bottom 9"; $P(Bottom\ 9) = 0.75$

 (iii) Odds against "Top 3" are 3 : 1; Odds in favour of "Top 3" are 1 : 3

39. (i) $P(Placebo) = \dfrac{288}{720} = 0.4$

 (ii) Complementary Event is "Treatment"; $P(Treatment) = 0.6$

 (iii) Odds against "Placebo" are 3 : 2; Odds in favour of "Placebo" are 2 : 3

41. (i) $P(Hypertension) = 0.176$

 (ii) Complementary Event is "No hypertension"; $P(No\ hypertension) = 0.824$

 (iii) Odds against "Hypertension" are 103 : 22; Odds in favour of "Hypertension" are 22 : 103

Exercises 5.2

1. a. $P(A\ or\ B) = 0.65$

 b. $P(A\ or\ B) = 0.45$

 c. $P(A\ or\ B) = 0.85$

3. $P(Side\ Effects) = \dfrac{42}{150} = 0.28$

5. $P(US\ Units) = \dfrac{220}{250} = 0.88$

7. $P(Injection) = \dfrac{117}{124} \approx 0.944$

9. a. $P(Stress \text{ or } TV) = \dfrac{51}{60} = 0.85$

    b. $P(Other\ reasons) = 0.15$

11. a. $P(A \text{ and } B) = 0.13$

    b. $P(A \text{ and } B) = 0.24$

    c. $P(A \text{ and } B) = 0.27$

13. a. $P(Success \text{ on } 1^{st}\ choice) = \dfrac{5}{20} = 0.25$

    b. $P(Success \text{ on } 5^{th}\ choice \mid No\ Success \text{ on } 1^{st}\ to\ 4^{th})$
$= \dfrac{5}{16} \approx 0.313$

    c. $P(Succes \text{ on first 5 choices}) \approx 0.0000645$

15. a. $P(Flu \text{ and } Flu\ Shot) = 0.00048$

    b. $P(Flu \text{ and } NO\ Flu\ Shot) = 0.00952$

    c. $P(Flu \mid No\ Flu\ Shot) = 0.014$

17. a. $P(Pregnant \text{ and } Negative\ Test) = 0.014$

    b. $P(Negative\ Test) = 0.614$

    c. $P(Pregnant \mid Negative\ Test) \approx 0.0228$

19. $P(Lupus \mid + Test) \approx 0.0222$

21. Neither   23. Independent

25. Mutually Exclusive   27. Independent

29. a. $P(A) = \dfrac{129}{300} = 0.43$

    b. $P(Rh+) = \dfrac{252}{300} = 0.84$

31. a. $P(O \text{ and } Rh+) = \dfrac{116}{300} \approx 0.387$

    b. $P(B \text{ and } Rh-) = \dfrac{6}{300} = 0.02$

33. a. $P(AB \text{ or } Rh-) = \dfrac{60}{300} = 0.2$

    b. $P(B \text{ or } Rh+) = \dfrac{258}{300} = 0.86$

35. a. $P(A \mid Rh+) = \dfrac{109}{252} \approx 0.433$

    b. $P(Rh- \mid O) = \dfrac{19}{135} \approx 0.141$

37. a. $P(+Result \mid Disease) = \dfrac{73}{80} = 0.913$

    b. $P(+Result \mid No\ Disease) = \dfrac{12}{320} = 0.0375$

39. a. $P(No\ Disease \mid -Result) = \dfrac{308}{315} \approx 0.978$

    b. $P(No\ Disease \mid +Result) = \dfrac{12}{85} \approx 0.141$

41. a. $P(3 \text{ with Disease and } +Result) = 0.00587$

    b. $P(3 \text{ with Disease and } -Result) = 0.00000331$

43. $P(17^{th} \text{ with No Disease}) = \dfrac{320}{384} \approx 0.833$

    $P(11^{th} \text{ with } +Result) = \dfrac{85}{390} \approx 0.218$

Exercises 5.3

1. 20   3. 64,000,000

5. 1,048,576   7. 40,320

9. 3,628,800   11. 37,050,773,760

13. 11,880   15. 103,680

17. a. 462   b. 252

19. 12,271,512   21. 0.273   23. 0.0437

25. 0.0023   27. 0.000842   29. 0.0371

31. a. 0.0269   b. 0.00177   c. 0.298

Chapter 5 Review Exercises

1. (i) 20 outcomes

    (ii) $S = \{A_1, A_2, A_3, A_4, B_1, B_2, B_3, B_4, B_5, B_6, C_1, C_2, C_3, C_4,$
       $C_5, D_1, D_2, D_3, F_1, F_2\}$

    (iii) 5 events – A, B, C, D, F

3. (i) 24 outcomes

    (ii) $S = \{A_1, A_2, A_3, A_4, A_5, A_6, A_7, A_8, B_1, B_2, B_3, B_4, C_1,$
       $C_2, C_3, C_4, C_5, C_6, C_7, D_1, D_2, D_3, D_4, D_5\}$

    (iii) 4 events – Brand A, Brand B, Brand C, Brand D

5. (i) Empirical   (ii) $\dfrac{872}{1,250} \approx 0.698$

7. (i) Theoretical (Classical)   (ii) $\dfrac{4}{7} \approx 0.571$

9. (i) Subjective

    (ii) Can't determine probability based on information given

11. (i) Outcome table   (ii) $\dfrac{4}{16} = 0.25$

13. (i) Tree diagram   (ii) $\dfrac{22}{64} \approx 0.344$

15. (i) Venn diagram   (ii) $\dfrac{67}{100} = 0.67$

17. (i) Venn diagram

    (ii) $P(\text{One subject only}) = 0.72$

19. (i) $\dfrac{3}{10} = 0.3$

    (ii) No strong interest in math; 0.7

    (iii) 7 : 3 (Odds against) and 3 : 7 (Odds in favour)

21. (i) 0.325

    (ii) Mother's not between 30 and 34 years old when first child was born; 0.675

    (iii) 27 : 13 (Odds against) and 13 : 27 (Odds in favour)

23. a. 0.62   b. 0.50

25. $P(A \text{ or } B) = \dfrac{240}{250} = 0.96$

27. a. $P(H \text{ or } F) = \dfrac{158}{225} \approx 0.702$

    b. $P(\text{Neither}) = 0.298$

29. a. 0.451   b. 0.344

31. a. 0.00174   b. 0.578   c. 0.913

33. a. 0.24   b. 0.09   c. 0.727

35. Independent   37. Mutually Exclusive

39. Neither

41. a. 0.946   b. 0.417

    c. 0.025   d. 0.954

    e. 0.05   f. 0.385

    g. 0.0949   h. 0.0546

43. a. 5,040   b. 10,000

45. 9,979,200   47. 32,760

49. 792

51. a. 0.267   b. 0.333

53. a. 0.410   b. 0.998

55. 0.121

57. a. 0.0256   b. 0.431   c. 0.974

Chapter 5 Self Test Exercises

1. a. 15 outcomes

    b. $S = \{P_1, P_2, P_3, P_4, P_5, M_1, M_2, M_3, M_4, M_5, M_6, M_7, C_1, C_2, C_3\}$

    c. 3 events – Physiotherapy, Massage Therapy, or Chiropractic Care

2. (i) Empirical   (ii) $\dfrac{355}{412} \approx 0.862$

3. (i) Theoretical (Classical)   (ii) $\dfrac{4}{25} = 0.16$

4. (i) Subjective

    (ii) Can't determine probability based on information given

5. (i) Outcome table   (ii) 0.36

6. (i) Tree diagram   (ii) $\dfrac{2}{8} = 0.25$

7. (i) Venn diagram   (ii) $\dfrac{5}{100} = 0.05$

8. a. $P(CPR \text{ or } FA) = \dfrac{100}{150} \approx 0.667$

    b. $P(\text{Neither}) = 0.333$

9. $P(\text{Successful and Under 40}) = 0.9$

10. a. $P(\text{Side Effects}) = \dfrac{72}{320} \approx 0.225$

    b. $P(\text{No Side Effects}) = \dfrac{248}{320} \approx 0.775$

    c. 31 : 9 (Odds Against); 9 : 31 (Odds in Favour)

11. a. $P(\text{Either partner has benefits through work}) = 0.90$

    b. $P(\text{Neither partner has benefits through work}) = 0.10$

12. a. $P(\text{Seatbelt and Serious Injury}) = 0.018$

    b. $P(\text{No Seatbelt and Serious Injury}) = 0.06$

    c. $P(\text{No Seatbelt} \mid \text{Serious Injury}) = 0.769$

13. a. 0.44   b. 0.85   c. 0.06

    d. 0.87   e. 0.80   f. 0.0471

    g. 0.0225   h. 0.16

14. a. 60,839,324   b. 180

15. a. 5,040   b. 90,720

16. a. 1,860,480   b. 15,504

17. a. 0.0429   b. 0.275   c. 0.725

18. a. 0.0740   b. 0.0225   c. 0.557

Chapter 6

Exercises 6.1

1. Discrete   3. Continuous

5. Continuous   7. Discrete

9. Continuous   11. Discrete

13. $\mu = 1.556, \sigma = 1.339$ 15. $\mu = 50, \sigma = 25$

17. $\mu = 24.75, \sigma = 6.418$ 19. $\mu = 44.64, \sigma = 23.60$

21. (i) Probability Distribution:

x	0	1	2	3	4	5
$P(x)$	0.03125	0.15625	0.3125	0.3125	0.15625	0.03125

    (ii) $E(X) = 2.5$, $Var(X) = 1.25$

23. (i) Probability Distribution:

x	\$1,000	\$100	\$50	\$25	\$0
$P(x)$	0.001	0.01	0.02	0.04	0.929

    (ii) $E(X) = \$4$, $Var(X) = 1,159$

25. (i) Probability Distribution:

x	0	1	2	3
$P(x)$	0.7787	0.2031	0.0177	0.0005

    (ii) $E(X) = 0.24$, $Var(X) = 0.2208$

27. (i) Probability Distribution:

x	0	1	2	3
$P(x)$	0.4912	0.4211	0.0842	0.0035

    (ii) $E(X) = 0.6$, $Var(X) = 0.4295$

Exercises 6.2

1. $P(X = 3) = 0.250$ 3. $P(X \geq 8) = 0.383$

5. $P(X \leq 3) = 0.764$ 7. $P(10 \leq X \leq 15) = 0.641$

9. $n = 16$ $p = 0.5$ $P(X = 8) = 0.196$

11. $n = 50$ $p = 0.08$ $P(X = 4) = 0.204$

13. $n = 30$ $p = 0.9$ $P(X \geq 27) = 0.647$

15. a. $n = 72$ $p = 0.07$ $P(X = 10) = 0.0168$

   b. $P(X \geq 3) = 1 - P(X \leq 2) = 0.888$

   c. $E(X) = 5.04$ - therefore, approximately 5 universal donors are expected that day.

   d. $0.71 \leq x \leq 9.37$

   Therefore, between 1 and 9 universal blood donors can reasonably be expected that day.

17. a. $n = 22$ $p = 0.41$ $P(X = 11) = 0.117$

   b. $P(X \geq 5) = 0.979$

   c. $E(X) = 9.02$ - therefore, approximately 9 patients are expected to identify their spouse as their next-of-kin.

   d. $4.406 \leq x \leq 13.634$

   Therefore, between 4 and 14 patients can reasonably be expected to identify their spouse as their next-of-kin.

19. a. $n = 500$ $p = 0.008$ $P(X = 0) = 0.0180$

   b. $P(X \geq 1) = 1 - P(X = 0) = 0.982$

   c. $E(X) = 4$ - therefore, approximately 4 tablets are expected to be defective per batch.

   d. $P(X = 4) = 0.196$

21. $n = 18$ $p = 0.548$ $P(X = 10) = 0.186$

23. $n = 18$ $p = 0.692$ $P(X \geq 12) = 0.696$

25. $n = 18$ $p = 0.184$ $P(X = 5) = 0.129$

27. $n = 18$ $p = 0.028$ $P(X \geq 1) = 0.400$

29. $n = 12$ $p = \dfrac{0.184 + 0.128 + 0.056}{0.548} \approx 0.6715$

   $P(X \geq 6) = 0.938$

31. $n = 6$ $p = \dfrac{0.184}{0.316} \approx 0.5823$ $P(X \geq 3) = 0.795$

Exercises 6.3

1. (i) $P(X = 5) = 0.240$ (ii) $\mu = 4, \sigma = 1.12$

3. (i) $P(X \geq 3) = 0.926$ (ii) $\mu = 4.5, \sigma = 1.42$

5. (i) $P(X = 4) = 0.0625$ (ii) $\mu = 2, \sigma = 1.41$

7. (i) $P(X = 9) = 0.0335$ (ii) $\mu = 5, \sigma = 4.47$

9. (i) $P(X = 10) = 0.108$ (ii) $\mu = 8.4, \sigma = 2.90$

11. (i) $P(X \leq 4) = 0.668$ (ii) $\mu = 3.8, \sigma = 1.95$

13. (i) Poisson, with $\lambda = 7.5$ and $x = 12$

   (ii) $P(X = 12) = 0.0366$

   (iii) $E(X) = 7.5, Var(X) = 7.5$

15. (i) Hypergeometric, with $N = 16$, $r = 5$, $n = 4$ and $x = 2$

   (ii) $P(X = 2) = 0.302$

   (iii) $E(X) = 1.25, Var(X) = 0.6875$

17. (i) Geometric, with $p = 0.25$ and $x = 10$

   (ii) $P(X = 10) = 0.0188$

   (iii) $E(X) = 4, Var(X) = 12$

19. (i) Hypergeometric, with $N = 40$, $r = 10$, $n = 6$ and $x \geq 1$

   (ii) $P(X \geq 1) = 0.845$

   (iii) $E(X) = 1.5, Var(X) = 0.9808$

21. (i) Binomial, with $n = 6$, $p = 0.5$ and $x \geq 4$

   (ii) $P(X \geq 4) = 0.344$

   (iii) $E(X) = 3, Var(X) = 1.5$

23. (i) Poisson, with $\lambda = \dfrac{27.6}{8} = 3.45$ and $x = 4$

   (ii) $P(X = 4) = 0.187$

   (iii) $E(X) = 3.45, Var(X) = 3.45$

25. (i) Binomial, with $n = 30$, $p = 1 - 0.85 = 0.15$ and $x \leq 3$

   (ii) $P(X \leq 3) = 0.322$

   (iii) $E(X) = 4.5, Var(X) = 3.825$

27. (i) Geometric, with $p = 1 - 0.92 = 0.08$ and $x \geq 20$

   (ii) $P(X \geq 20) = 0.21$

   (iii) $E(X) = 12.5, Var(X) = 143.75$

Chapter 6 Review Exercises

1. Discrete   3. Continuous

5. Continuous   7. $\mu = 2.1, \sigma = 1.14$

9. $\mu = 29.78, \sigma = 11.18$

11. a.

x	1	2	3	4
$P(x)$	$\dfrac{5}{30}$	$\dfrac{7}{30}$	$\dfrac{10}{30}$	$\dfrac{8}{30}$

   b. $E(X) = 2.7, Var(X) = 1.08, SD(X) = 1.04$

13. a.

x	0	1	2
$P(x)$	0.0625	0.375	0.5625

   b. $E(X) = 1.5, Var(X) = 0.375, SD(X) = 0.612$

15. a.

x	0	1	2	3
$P(x)$	$\dfrac{120}{455} \approx 0.264$	$\dfrac{225}{455} \approx 0.495$	$\dfrac{100}{455} \approx 0.220$	$\dfrac{10}{455} \approx 0.022$

   b. $E(X) = 1, Var(X) = 0.571, SD(X) = 0.756$

17. a. 0.00340   b. 0.236

   c. 0.987   d. 0.615

19. 0.176   21. 0.278

23. a. 0.00140   b. 0.993   c. 8

   d. 2.45   e. Approximately 3 to 13 obese patients.

25. a. 0.0483   b. 0.952

    c. 3   d. 0.226

27. 0.0396   29. 0.0778

31. 0.262   33. 0.212

35. 0.0286

37. a. 0.238   b. 0.262   c. $\mu = 2$, $\sigma = 0.816$

39. a. 0.0409   b. $\mu = 6.67$, $\sigma = 6.15$

41. a. 0.195   b. 0.433   c. $\mu = 4$, $\sigma = 2$

43. (i) Geometric

    (ii) $P(X = 5) = 0.0313$

    (iii) $E(X) = 2$, $Var(X) = 2$, $SD(X) = 1.41$

45. (i) Binomial

    (ii) $P(X < 8) = 0.276$

    (iii) $E(X) = 8.4$, $Var(X) = 2.52$, $SD(X) = 1.59$

47. (i) Hypergeometric

    (ii) $P(X \geq 2) = 0.969$

    (iii) $E(X) = 4$, $Var(X) = 1.10$, $SD(X) = 1.05$

49. (i) Poisson

    (ii) $P(X = 3) = 0.126$

    (iii) $E(X) = 1.5$, $Var(X) = 1.5$, $SD(X) = 1.22$

Chapter 6 Self Test Exercises

1. Discrete   2. Continuous

3. Continuous   4. Discrete

5. a. $\mu = 1.91$, $\sigma = 1.28$

    b. On average, the dentist performs 1.91 root canal surgeries per day. In other words, over the course of 100 days, the dentist is expected to perform approximately 191 root canal surgeries.

6. $E(X) = -\$0.25$

    Since the expected value of the game is negative, it is not advisable to play the game, as it is expected that the player will lose money over time the longer he/she plays the game.

7. a.

x	0	1	2	3
$P(x)$	0.027	0.189	0.441	0.343

    b. $E(X) = 2.1$ $Var(X) = 0.63$ $SD(X) = 0.794$

8. a.

x	0	1	2
$P(x)$	$\frac{1}{15} \approx 0.067$	$\frac{8}{15} \approx 0.533$	$\frac{6}{15} = 0.4$

    b. $E(X) = 1.33$ $Var(X) = 0.356$ $SD(X) = 0.596$

9. a. $P(X = 0) = 0.0563$

    b. $P(X \geq 1) = 0.9437$

    c. $P(X \geq 5) = 0.0781$

10. a. $P(X = 2) = 0.2762$

    b. $P(X \leq 2) = 0.6767$

    c. $P(X \geq 2) = 0.5995$

11. a. $P(X = 8) = 0.1148$

    b. $P(X \geq 7) = 0.0882$

    c. 10   d. 1.8257

    e. Approximately 6-14 men would consider the hair transplant

12. a. 0.0547   b. 0.0995   c. 0.148

    d. 0.927   e. 0.0860   f. 0.990

    g. 0.196   h. 0.193

13. (i) Binomial

    (ii) $P(X > 8) = 0.908$

    (iii) $E(X) = 10.2$, $Var(X) = 1.53$, $SD(X) = 1.24$

14. (i) Poisson

    (ii) $P(X = 7) = 0.132$

    (iii) $E(X) = 8.4$, $Var(X) = 8.4$, $SD(X) = 2.90$

15. (i) Hypergeometric

    (ii) $P(X \geq 1) = 0.636$

    (iii) $E(X) = 1.25$, $Var(X) = 0.597$, $SD(X) = 0.772$

16. (i) Geometric

    (ii) $P(X \geq 20) = 0.850$

    (iii) $E(X) = 118$, $Var(X) = 13,723$, $SD(X) = 117$

Chapter 7

Exercises 7.1

1. (i) $P(X < 2) = \frac{1}{3} \approx 0.333$

    (ii) $\mu = 3$, $\sigma \approx 1.73$

3. (i) $P(25 < X < 40) = \frac{3}{7} \approx 0.429$

    (ii) $\mu = 37.5$, $\sigma \approx 10.10$

5. (i) $P(1.6 < X < 2.5) = \frac{1}{4} = 0.25$

    (ii) $\mu = 3.0$, $\sigma \approx 1.04$

7. (i) $P(X > \frac{1}{3}) = \frac{2}{3} \approx 0.667$

    (ii) $\mu = 0.5$, $\sigma \approx 0.289$

9. (i) $P(X < 0.4) \approx 0.753$

    (ii) $\mu = \sigma \approx 0.286$

11. (i) $P(X > 12.6) \approx 0.455$

    (ii) $\mu = \sigma = 16$

13. (i) $P(1.88 < X < 3.12) = 0.0426$ (ii) $\mu = \sigma = 0.625$

15. (i) $P(3\frac{1}{3} < X < 6\frac{1}{4}) = 0.221$

    (ii) $\mu = \sigma = 6$

17. X follows a Uniform distribution, with $0 < X < 15$; $P(X < 3) = 0.2$; $E(X) = 7.5$ minutes

19. X follows an Exponential distribution, with $\lambda = \dfrac{30}{60} = 0.5$; $P(X < 1) \approx 0.393$

21. X follows an Exponential distribution, with $\lambda = 8$; $E(X) = 0.125$ hours or 7.5 minutes; $P(X > 10) \approx 0.264$

23. X follows a Uniform distribution, with $0 < X < 1,000$; $P(X > 600) = 0.4$; $E(X) = 500$ mL

25. X follows an Exponential distribution, with $\lambda = \dfrac{18}{12} = 1.5$; $P(1 < X < 2) = 0.173$; $E(X) = 40$ minutes

27. X follows a Uniform distribution, with $0 < X < 2,500$; $P(X > 150) = 0.94$

29. X follows a Uniform distribution, with $11 < X < 15.5$ (times expressed as decimal hours on a 24-hour clock); $P(12.75 < X < 14) \approx 0.278$; $E(X) = 13{:}25$ h or 1:15 PM

31. a. 4 minutes   b. 0.528   c. 0.0114

Exercises 7.2

1. a. 0.6915   b. 0.1151   c. 0.1806
3. a. 0.2266   b. 0.9495   c. 0.0759
5. a. 0.9992   b. 0.0018   c. 0.4678
7. a. 0.4247   b. 0.0044   c. 0.5709
9. a. $Z = 0.13$ b. $Z = -0.67$
11. a. $Z = -0.52$ b. $Z = 0.97$
13. a. $Z < -0.44$ b. $-0.52 < Z < 0.52$
15. a. $Z > 1.08$ b. $-0.84 < Z < 0.84$
17. a. (i) $P(X < 2.75) = P(Z < -1.13) = 0.1292$
    (ii) $P(X > 3.55) = P(Z > 0.75) = 0.2266$
    (iii) $P(2.5 < X < 3.0) = P(-1.72 < Z < -0.54) = 0.2519$
    b. (i) $P_3 = 2.43$ kg
    (ii) $P_{97} = 4.03$ kg
    (iii) Middle 70% = P_{15} to P_{85} = 2.79 to 3.67 kg
19. a. (i) $P(X < 45) = P(Z < -2.45) = 0.0071$
    (ii) $P(X > 52) = P(Z > 1.12) = 0.1314$
    (iii) $P(50 < X < 54) = P(0.10 < Z < 2.14) = 0.4440$
    b. (i) $P_1 = 45.2$ cm
    (ii) $P_{99} = 54.4$ cm
    (iii) Middle 60% = P_{20} to P_{80} = 48.2 to 51.4 cm
21. a. (i) $P(X < 13.5) = P(Z < -1.74) = 0.0409$
    (ii) $P(X > 16) = P(Z > 0.98) = 0.1635$
    (iii) $P(13.8 < X < 17.2) = P(-1.41 < Z < 2.28) = 0.9094$
    b. (i) $P_5 = 13.6$ g/dL
    (ii) $P_{95} = 16.6$ g/dL
    (iii) Middle 95% = $P_{2.5}$ to $P_{97.5}$ = 13.3 to 16.9 g/dL

23. a. (i) $P(X < 20) = P(Z < -1.79) = 0.0367$
    (ii) $P(X > 26) = P(Z > 0.71) = 0.2389$
    (iii) $P(22 < X < 24) = P(-0.96 < Z < -0.13) = 0.2798$
    b. (i) $P_{15} = 21.8$ weeks and less
    (ii) $P_{96} = 28.5$ weeks and more
    (iii) Middle 98% = P_1 to P_{99} = 18.7 to 29.9 weeks
25. a. (i) $P(X < 5) = P(Z < -1.18) = 0.1190$
    (ii) $P(X > 7.5) = P(Z > 1.09) = 0.1379$
    (iii) $P(4.75 < X < 5.25) = P(-1.41 < Z < -0.95) = 0.0918$
    b. $P_{33} = 5.8$ mL
27. a. (i) $P(X < 15) = P(Z < -1.73) = 0.0418$
    (ii) $P(X > 30) = P(Z > 0.50) = 0.3085$
    (iii) $P(20 < X < 25) = P(-0.99 < Z < -0.24) = 0.2441$
    b. $P_{10} \approx 18$ years, so the surgeon should recommend the patient be a minimum age of 57 years old before having the knee replacement surgery.
29. a. $\mu = \$66{,}070$, $\sigma = \$5{,}750$
    b. $P(X < 60{,}000) = P(Z < -1.06) = 0.1446$
    c. $P_{99} = \$79{,}468$
31. a. $\mu = 9.15$ kg, $\sigma = 1.18$ kg
    b. $P(X > 10) = P(Z > 0.72) = 0.2358$
    c. $P_5 = 7.21$ kg

Exercises 7.3

1. $\mu = 25$, $\sigma \approx 4.33$
   $P(X \geq 30) = P(X > 29.5) = P(Z > 1.04) = 0.1492$
3. Can't use the Normal Approximation to the Binomial, since $np = 2.5 < 5$.
5. $\mu = 30$, $\sigma \approx 3.46$
   $P(25 \leq X \leq 35) = 0.8882$
7. $\mu = 25$, $\sigma \approx 4.47$
   $P(X < 20) = 0.1093$
9. Can't use the Normal Approximation to the Binomial, since $n(1 - p) = 4 < 5$.
11. $\mu = 12.5$, $\sigma \approx 3.23$
    $P(10 < X < 15) = 0.4648$
13. $n = 18$, $p = \dfrac{1}{3}$
    Can't use the Normal Approximation to the Binomial, since $n = 18 < 30$
15. $n = 48$, $p = 0.15$
    $\mu = 7.2$, $\sigma \approx 2.47$
    $P(X \geq 12) = P(X > 11.5) = P(Z > 1.74) = 0.0409$

17. $n = 30, p = \dfrac{1}{4}$

 $\mu = 7.5, \sigma \approx 2.37$

 $P(X \geq 15) = P(X > 14.5) = P(Z > 2.95) = 0.0016$

19. $n = 96, p = 0.85$

 $\mu = 81.6, \sigma \approx 3.50$

 Since the question gives the probability of success, less than 10 with no success is equivalent to more than 85 with equipment failure.

 $P(X > 85) = P(X > 84.5) = P(Z > 0.83) = 0.2033$

21. $n = 100, p = \dfrac{1}{7}$

 $\mu \approx 14.3, \sigma \approx 3.50$

 $P(15 \leq X \leq 20) = P(14.5 < X < 20.5) = P(0.06 < Z < 1.77)$
 $= 0.4377$

23. $n = 12, p = 0.5$

 Can't use the Normal Approximation to the Binomial, since $n = 12 < 20$.

25. $n = 1,800, p = 0.012$

 $\mu = 21.6, \sigma \approx 4.62$

 $P(X \geq 30) = P(X > 29.5) = P(Z > 1.71) = 0.0436$

27. $n = 35, p = \dfrac{1}{5}$

 $\mu = 7, \sigma \approx 2.37$

 $P(X > 10) = P(X > 10.5) = P(Z > 1.48) = 0.0694$

Chapter 7 Review Exercises

1. (i) $\dfrac{3.5}{5} = 0.7$ (ii) $\mu = 12.5, \sigma \approx 1.44$

3. (i) $\dfrac{11}{15} \approx 0.733$ (ii) $\mu = 0.5, \sigma \approx 0.289$

5. (i) $\dfrac{16}{20} = 0.8$ (ii) $\mu = 40, \sigma \approx 5.77$

7. (i) $\dfrac{17}{40} = 0.425$ (ii) $\mu = 0.5, \sigma \approx 0.289$

9. (i) 0.528   (ii) $\mu = \sigma \approx 0.667$

11. (i) 0.692   (ii) $\mu = \sigma = 50$

13. (i) 0.261   (ii) $\mu = \sigma \approx 0.556$

15. (i) 0.247   (ii) $\mu = \sigma = 2.5$

17. Uniform; $P(X < 5) = \dfrac{5}{20} = 0.25; E(X) = 10$ min

19. Exponential ($\lambda = \dfrac{12}{60} = 0.2$ calls/min); $E(X) = 5$ min;

 $P(X > 8) \approx 0.202$

21. Uniform ($X = $ number of hours after 9:00 AM);
 $P(4 < X < 5.5) = \dfrac{1.5}{7.5} = 0.2; E(X) = 3.75$ (12:45 PM)

23. Exponential ($\lambda = \dfrac{1}{6}$ prescriptions/min)

 a. $E(X) = 6$ min

 b. $P(X < 5) \approx 0.565$

 c. P(Next 4 patients are all within 5 minutes of previous patient) $= P(X < 5)^3 \approx 0.181$

25. a. 0.9505   b. 0.0113

 c. 0.9222   d. 0.0158

 e. 0.3413   f. 0.0793

 g. 0.1598   h. 0.0537

 i. 0.8561

27. a. $Z = 1.175$

 b. $Z = -0.32$

 c. $Z = -1.04$

 d. $Z = 0.58$

 e. $-0.88 < Z < 0.88$

29. a. (i) $P(X < 105) = P(Z < -0.75) = 0.2266$

  (ii) $P(X > 120) = P(Z > 0.40) = 0.3446$

  (iii) $P(118 < X < 132) = P(0.24 < Z < 1.31) = 0.3101$

 b. (i) $X \approx 131.6$ mmHg

  (ii) $101.2 < X < 128.4$ mmHg

31. a. $P(X < 47,250) = P(Z < -1.17) = 0.1210$

 b. $P(X > 55,000) = P(Z > 0.56) = 0.2877$

 c. $P(50,000 < X < 55,000) = P(-0.56 < Z < 0.56) = 0.4246$

33. a. 259 patients

 b. $X = 184.5$ mg/100mL

35. a. $\mu = \$69,810, \sigma = \$10,570$

 b. $P(X > 75,000) = P(Z > 0.49) = 0.3121$

 c. $X = \$45,180$

37. $\mu = 63, \sigma = 6.40\ P(X \geq 50) = P(X > 49.5) = P(Z > -2.11) = 0.9826$

39. Can't use the Normal approximation, since $nq = 4 < 5$

41. $\mu = 56.25, \sigma = 6.50, P(40 < X < 70)$
 $= P(40.5 < X < 69.5) = P(-2.42 < Z < 2.04) = 0.9715$

43. $\mu = 20, \sigma = 2.58, P(15 \leq X \leq 25)$
 $= P(14.5 < X < 25.5) = P(-2.13 < Z < 2.13) = 0.9668$

45. Can't use the Normal approximation, since $np = 4 < 5$

47. $\mu = 12, \sigma = 2.83, P(6 \leq X \leq 12)$
 $= P(5.5 < X < 12.5) = P(-2.30 < Z < 0.18) = 0.5607$

49. $\mu = 9.6, \sigma = 2.59, P(X < 16)$
 $= P(X < 15.5) = P(Z < 2.28) = 0.9887$

51. $\mu = 24, \sigma = 3.46, P(X > 24) = P(X > 24.5)$
 $= P(Z > 0.14) = 0.4443$

53. Can't use the Normal approximation, since $np = 3.75 < 5$

Chapter 7 Self Test Exercises

1. Uniform distribution; $P(X < 600) = \dfrac{600}{1,000} = 0.6$;

 $E(X) = 500$ mL

2. Uniform distribution ($X = $ hours after 1:00 PM);
 $P(1.5 < X < 2) = \dfrac{0.5}{5} = 0.1; E(X) = 2.5$ (3:30 PM)

3. Exponential distribution ($\lambda = 1.5$ calls/hr);
 $P(0.75 < X < 1) \approx 0.102; E(X) = 40$ min

4. Exponential distribution ($\lambda = \frac{1}{3}$ babies/hr)

    a. $E(X) = 3$ hours

    b. $P(X < 1) \approx 0.283$

    c. P(Next 4 babies delivered within 1 hour of previous baby) $= P(X < 1)^3 \approx 0.0228$

5.   a. $P(X < 90) = P(Z < -1.67) = 0.0475$

    b. $P(X > 130) = P(Z > 0.56) = 0.2877$

    c. $P(96 < X < 144) = P(-1.33 < Z < 1.33) = 0.8164$

6.   a. 81 mg/100 mL

    b. Between 74 mg/100 mL and 106 mg/100 mL

7.   a. $P(259 < X < 273) = P(-0.54 < Z < 0.54) = 0.4108$

    b. 287 days

8.   3.4 years

9.   a. 3 students

    b. $X = 89.36\%$; He/she needs a minimum score of approximately 90% to be considered for admission

10. a. $\sigma = \$7{,}250$, $\mu = \$67{,}340$

    b. $P(X < \$55{,}000) = P(Z < -1.70) = 0.0446$

    c. $X = \$80{,}970$

11. $\mu = 8$, $\sigma \approx 2.73$, $P(X \le 15) = P(X < 15.5) = P(Z < 2.75) = 0.9970$

12. $\mu = 12$, $\sigma \approx 2.68$, $P(X \ge 10) = P(X > 9.5) = P(Z > -0.93) = 0.8238$

13. $\mu = 31.5$, $\sigma \approx 3.07$, $P(X \le 22) = P(X < 22.5) = P(Z < -2.93) = 0.0017$

14. $\mu = 37.5$, $\sigma \approx 5.12$, $P(35 \le X \le 45) = P(34.5 < X < 45.5) = P(-0.59 < Z < 1.56) = 0.6630$

15. $\mu = 15$, $\sigma \approx 2.74$, $P(X \ge 21) = P(X > 20.5) = P(Z > 2.01) = 0.0222$

Chapter 8

Exercises 8.1

1. (i) The individual data represents an individual's recovery time from the procedure.

    It is quantitative data at the ratio level of measurement.

  (ii) The grouped data represents the sample mean recovery time from the procedure.

    It is also quantitative data at the ratio level of measurement.

3. (i) The individual data represents the number of pets each family has.

    It is quantitative data at the ratio level of measurement.

  (ii) The grouped data represents the sample proportion of families who own 2 or more pets.

    It is also quantitative data at the ratio level of measurement.

5. (i) The individual data represents the blood type of each blood donor.

    It is qualitative data at the nominal level of measurement.

  (ii) The grouped data represents the sample proportion of "Universal Donors" (i.e., O– blood type).

    It is quantitative data at the ratio level of measurement.

7. (i) The individual data represents the total deviation between the calories listed on the label of the can and the actual amount of calories contained by the food in the can.

    It is quantitative data at the ratio level of measurement.

  (ii) The grouped data represents the sample mean deviation between the calories listed on the label of the can and the actual amount of calories contained by the food in the can.

    It is also quantitative data at the ratio level of measurement.

9. (i) The individual data represents the birth weight of each newborn baby.

    It is quantitative data at the ratio level of measurement.

  (ii) The grouped data represents the sample mean birth weight of a group of newborn babies.

    It is also quantitative data at the ratio level of measurement.

11. (i) The individual data is Yes or No data representing whether each paramedic received a break on that particular shift or not.

    It is qualitative data at the nominal level of measurement.

  (ii) The grouped data represents the sample proportion of paramedics' shifts in which the paramedic did not receive a break.

    It is quantitative data at the ratio level of measurement.

13. (i) The individual data is Yes or No data representing whether each tablet is defective or not.

    It is qualitative data at the nominal level of measurement.

  (ii) The grouped data represents the sample proportion of defective tablets in a batch.

    It is quantitative data at the ratio level of measurement.

15. (i) There are two sets of data being recorded, representing the number of staffed medical professionals on duty in the E.R. on a given day, and the average wait time for patients in the E.R. that day.

    It is bivariate, quantitative data, with both data sets at the ratio level of measurement.

  (ii) The grouped data represents the sample correlation coefficient between the two data sets.

    It is quantitative data whose absolute value is at the interval level of measurement.

Exercises 8.2

1. a. $P(X > 100) = P(Z > 1.70) = 0.0446$

   b. $P(\overline{X} > 100) = P(Z > 3.81) = 0.0000$

   Therefore, since it's practically impossible to get such a result if the patient does not have diabetes, we can conclude that the patient very likely does, in fact, have diabetes.

3. a. $P(X > 120) = P(Z > 1.33) = 0.0918$

   b. $P(\overline{X} > 120) = P(Z > 3.53) = 0.0002$

   Therefore, since it's so unlikely to get such a result if the patient does not have hypertension, we can conclude that the patient very likely does, in fact, have hypertension.

5. a. $P(X < 10) = P(Z < -1.11) = 0.1335$

   b. $P(12.5 < \overline{X} < 15.625) = P(-1.57 < Z < 0.39) = 0.5935$

7. a. $P(1800 < X < 2000) = P(-0.13 < Z < 1.20) = 0.4366$

   b. $P(1666.7 < \overline{X} < 1833.3) = P(-1.02 < Z < 0.09) = 0.3820$

9. $P(\overline{X} > 20) = P(Z > 2.63) = 0.0043$

11. $P(\overline{X} < 60) = P(Z < -2.28) = 0.0113$

13. $P(45 < \overline{X} < 50) = P(-1.92 < Z < 0.68) = 0.7243$

15. a. $P(\overline{X} > 20) = P(Z > 1.53) = 0.0630$

    b. $P(\overline{X} < 16) = P(Z < -2.85) = 0.0022$

    c. $P(16 < \overline{X} < 20) = P(-2.85 < Z < 1.53) = 0.9348$

17. 4.1 minutes $< \overline{X} < 4.9$ minutes

19. $\$4,850 < \overline{X} < \$5,830$

21. a. $P(\overline{X} < 40) = P(Z < -1.78) = 0.0375$

    b. $P(\overline{X} > 50) = P(Z > 0.45) = 0.3264$

    c. 38.8 minutes $< \overline{X} < 57.2$ minutes

    d. $\overline{X} < 53.7$ minutes

23. a. $P(\overline{X} > 50) = P(Z > -1.00) = 0.8413$

    b. $P(\overline{X} < 60) = P(Z < 0.61) = 0.7291$

    c. 41.7 minutes $< \overline{X} < 70.7$ minutes

    d. $\overline{X} > 66.4$ minutes

Exercises 8.3

1. $P(\hat{p} > 0.20) = P(Z > -0.82) = 0.7939$

3. Can't use the Normal Approximation to the Binomial, since $np = 3 < 5$.

5. $P(\hat{p} < 0.55) = P(Z < -0.63) = 0.2643$

7. $P(0.25 < \hat{p} < 0.30) = P(-1.01 < Z < 0.22) = 0.4309$

9. Can't use the Normal Approximation to the Binomial, since $n < 30$ and $n(1 - p) = 3.75 < 5$.

11. $P(0.10 < \hat{p} < 0.15) = P(-1.70 < Z < -0.42) = 0.2710$

13. $p = \dfrac{1}{3} = 0.\overline{3}$

    a. $P(\hat{p} > 0.40) > P(Z > 1.13) = 0.1292$

    b. $P(\hat{p} < 0.25) > P(Z < -1.41) = 0.0793$

    c. $P(0.30 < \hat{p} < 0.35) = P(-0.57 < Z < 0.28) = 0.3260$

15. $p = \dfrac{3}{20} = 0.15$

    a. Binomial (discrete, not continuous): $P(X = 0) = 0.85^{40} = 0.00150$

    b. $P(0.10 < \hat{p} < 0.20) = P(-0.89 < Z < 0.89) = 0.6266$

    c. $P(\hat{p} > 0.25) = P(Z > 1.77) = 0.0384$

    d. $0.04 < \hat{p} < 0.26$

17. a. Yes, since $n > 30$, $np > 5$, and $n(1 - p) > 5$.

    $\mu_{\hat{p}} = \dfrac{5}{200} = 0.025$ and $\sigma_{\hat{p}} = 0.0099$

    b. No, since $np = 3.75 < 5$

19. a. $P(\hat{p} > 0.40) = P(Z > 1.34) = 0.0901$

    b. $\hat{p} = 0.5058$

21. a. $n > 40$ tickets would need to be sold, so that $np > 5$.

    b. $P(\hat{p} > 0.20) = P(Z > 1.60) = 0.0548$

    c. The probability will decrease, since an increase in the size of the sample will increase the absolute Z-value, thereby decreasing the probability in the tail beyond that Z-value.

    d. $P(0.10 < \hat{p} < 0.15) = P(-0.53 < Z < 0.53) = 0.4038$

    e. The probability will increase, since an increase in the size of the sample will increase the absolute Z-value, thereby increasing the probability in the middle between the Z-values.

23. $n = 120$, $p = \dfrac{2}{3} = 0.\overline{6}$

    Therefore, the range of values containing the middle 75% of proportions of Canadians in groups of 120 that have private extended health insurance, is between $0.617 < \hat{p} < 0.716$.

Chapter 8 Review Exercises

1. (i) Individual – Defective or Not Defective; Qualitative Nominal Data

   (ii) Grouped – Proportion of defective items; Continuous Quantitative Ratio Data

3. (i) Individual – Hemoglobin level reduction; Continuous Quantitative Ratio Data

   (ii) Grouped – Average hemoglobin level reduction in sample; Continuous Quantitative Ratio Data

5. (i) Individual – Weight and age of onset of a pregnant woman; Paired Continuous Quantitative Data, both at the Ratio level of measurement

   (ii) Grouped – Correlation coefficient between paired data; Continuous Quantitative Interval Data

7. a. $P(X > 80) = P(Z > 0.75) = 0.2266$

    b. $P(\overline{X} > 80) = P(Z > 3) = 0.0013$

9. a. $P(X < 95$ or $X > 120) = P(X < 95) + P(> 120)$
    $= P(Z < -2) + P(Z > 1.33) = 0.1146$

    b. $P(\overline{X} < 95$ or $\overline{X} > 120) = P(\overline{X} < 95) + P(\overline{X} > 120)$
    $= P(Z < -5.67) + P(Z > 3.78) = 0.0000$

11. a. No, it is not possible to calculate probability for the average of the 5 batteries, since the CLT only applies if the sample size is at least 30. Since the sample size is only 5, we cannot assume that the sampling distribution of sample means is normal (or even approximately normal).

    b. Yes, since the population distribution is known to be normal, the CLT tells us the sampling distribution of sample means is also normal, with standard error of $\dfrac{\sigma}{\sqrt{n}}$.

    $P(\overline{X} < 4.5) = P(Z < -2.24) = 0.0125$

13. a. $P(\overline{X} > \$114.29) = P(Z > 2.21) = 0.0136$

    b. Total weekly sales will fall within ($723, $789).

    c. If the number of pharmacies increased, the standard error would decrease, shrinking the probability in the tail in part a, as well as shrinking the range of values in part b.

15. a. $P(\overline{X} < 3$ min$) = P(Z < 0.83) = 0.7967$

    b. He should give 3 hr and 5 min.

    c. $P(\overline{X} < 3.125) = P(Z < 1.87) = 0.9693$. Yes, this will accomplish the desired goal of ensuring more than 95% of students finish the exam in time.

17. a. $P(12.5 < \overline{X} < 13) = P(-1.18 < Z < 0.79) = 0.6662$

    b. Top 1%: 13.4 hours; Bottom 1%: 12.2 hours

    c. If the number of newborns in the sample decreased, the standard error would increase, shrinking the area in the middle of the distribution in part a. and stretching out the values separating the top and bottom 1% tails in part b.

19. a. $FPC = 0.75$;
    $P(\overline{X} < 730) = P(Z < -2.45) = 0.0071$

    b. $P(\overline{X} > 912.5) = P(Z > 0.66) = 0.2546$

    c. 759 days $< \overline{X} <$ 989 days

21. a. $P(\hat{p} > 0.90) = P(Z > 1.25) = 0.1056$

    b. $P(0.75 < \hat{p} < 0.80) = P(-2.50 < Z < -1.25) = 0.0994$

    c. $0.757 < \hat{p} < 0.943$

23. Cannot use the Normal approximation to the $\hat{p}$-distribution, since $np = 3.3 < 5$

25. a. $P(\hat{p} > 0.25) = P(Z > 0.88) = 0.1894$

    b. $P(5 < X < 15) = P(0.10 < \hat{p} < 0.30) = P(-1.77 < Z < 1.77)$
    $= 0.9232$

Chapter 8 Self Test Exercises

1. (i) Individual – ABA Certified or Not ABA Certified; Qualitative Nominal Data

    (ii) Grouped – Proportion of psychologists who are ABA certified; Continuous Quantitative Ratio Data

2. (i) Individual– Wait times in E.R. and Length of E.R. nurses' shifts; Paired Continuous Quantitative Data, both at the ratio levels of measurement

    (ii) Grouped – Correlation coefficient between paired data; Continuous Quantitative Interval Data

3. (i) Individual – Height of 3-year old child born prematurely; Continuous Quantitative Ratio Data

    (ii) Grouped – Average height of a sample of 3-year olds born prematurely; Continuous Quantitative Ratio Data

4. a. $P(X > 215) = P(Z > 0.65) = 0.2578$

    b. $P(\overline{X} > 215) = P(Z > 3.23) = 0.0006$

5. a. $P(X < 13) = P(Z < -0.94) = 0.0475$

    b. $P(\overline{X} > 17) = P(Z > 3.46) = 0.0003$

    c. $14.15 < \overline{X} < 17.65$

    d. $\overline{X} > 13.8$ minutes

6. a. $P(\overline{X} > 119) = P(Z > 0.95) = 0.1711$

    b. $P(112 < \overline{X} < 126) = P(-2.37 < Z < 4.27) = 0.9911$

    c. $112.7 < \overline{X} < 121.3$

7. a. $P(\overline{X} > 195) = P(Z > 1.19) = 0.1170$

    b. $P(189 < \overline{X} < 196) = P(-1.19 < Z < 1.58) = 0.8259$

    c. $P(\overline{X} < 182.5) = P(Z < -3.76) = 0.0000$

8. a. $P(\overline{X} < 48) = P(Z < -0.50) = 0.3085$

    b. $P(50 < \overline{X} < 55) = P(0.50 < Z < 2.98) = 0.3071$

    c. $44.3 < \overline{X} < 53.7$

    d. 404 patients

9. a. $P(\overline{X} > 75,000) = P(Z > 1.11) = 0.1335$

    b. $P(65,000 < \overline{X} < 70,000) = P(-2.32 < Z < -0.46) = 0.3126$

    c. $\$68,012 < \overline{X} < \$74,488$

10. a. $P(\hat{p} < 0.05) = P(Z < -0.16) = 0.4364$

    b. $P(0.07 < \hat{p} < 0.10) = P(0.93 < Z < 2.57) = 0.1711$

    c. $0.017 < \hat{p} < 0.089$

11. a. $\mu_{\hat{p}} = 0.56$,

$\sigma_{\hat{p}} \approx 0.0762$

b. $P(\hat{p} > 0.60) = P(Z > 0.52) = 0.3015$

c. $P(\hat{p} < 0.45) = P(Z < -1.44) = 0.0749$

12. a. $n \geq 30$

b. $P(\hat{p} > 0.30) = P(Z > 3.01) = 0.0013$

c. If $n = 400$, the standard error will decrease, which will cause the distribution to become narrower and the area in the tails to decrease, thereby decreasing the probability in part b.

d. $P(0.15 < \hat{p} < 0.25) = P(-3.01 < Z < 1.00) = 0.8400$

e. If $n = 400$, the standard error will decrease, which will cause the distribution to become narrower, which causes the area in the middle to increase, thereby increasing the probability in part d.

Chapter 9

Exercises 9.1

1. (i) Estimator: $\bar{x}$ - the sample mean tumor size

(ii) Confidence level: 95%

(iii) Confidence interval: $3.4 < \mu < 4.2$

3. (i) Estimator: r - the sample correlation coefficient between treatment duration and tumor reduction

(ii) Confidence level: 90%

(iii) Confidence interval: $0.447 < \rho < 0.581$

5. (i) Estimator: $\hat{p}$ - the sample proportion of patients who were recommended surgery

(ii) Confidence level: 99%

(iii) Confidence interval: $0.595 < p < 0.685$

7. (i) Estimator: $\hat{p}$ - the sample proportion of patients who began with high LDL cholesterol levels

(ii) Confidence level: 90%

(iii) Confidence interval: $0.739 < p < 0.811$

9. (i) Estimator: r - the sample correlation coefficient between percent body fat lost and time on treadmill

(ii) Confidence level: 99%

(iii) Confidence interval: $0.336 < \rho < 0.440$

11. (i) Sample statistic: $\bar{x}$ - the sample mean change in resting heart rate over 8 weeks of treatment

(ii) Confidence level: 95%

(iii) Confidence interval: $14.5 < \mu < 22.7$

13. a. The margin of error will increase, creating a larger confidence interval around $\bar{x} = 34.2$

b. The margin of error will decrease, creating a smaller confidence interval around $\bar{x} = 34.2$

15. a. The confidence interval will shift up by 1.4, to $32.7 < \mu < 38.5$

b. The confidence interval will expand by 0.4 at each end, to $30.9 < \mu < 37.5$

17. a. The margin of error will decrease, creating a smaller confidence interval around $\hat{p} = 0.285$

b. The margin of error will increase, creating a larger confidence interval around $\hat{p} = 0.285$

19. a. The confidence interval will shift down by 0.022, to $0.250 < p < 0.276$

b. The confidence interval will shrink by 0.002 at each end, to $0.274 < p < 0.296$

Exercises 9.2

1. a. $E = 0.19$, $36.51 < \mu < 36.89$

b. $E = 5.1$, $69.4 < \mu < 79.6$

3. a. $E = 0.37$, $6.75 < \mu < 7.49$

b. $E = 0.18$, $4.45 < \mu < 4.81$

5. a. $E = 5.1$, $178.3 < \mu < 188.5$

b. $E = 0.027$, $0.228 < \mu < 0.282$

7. a. $E = 0.131$, $5.784 < \mu < 6.046$

b. $E = 0.28$, $13.00 < \mu < 13.56$

9. $E = \$598$, $\$4,222 < \mu < \$5,418$

The previous mean of $5,340 is still within the 99% confidence interval for the new mean, which implies that there may not have been any change between the old mean and the new mean.

11. $E = 2.4$ mg/dL, $40.4 < \mu < 45.2$ mg/dL

13. $E = 5.4$ mmHg, $122.9 < \mu < 133.7$ mmHg

15. $E = 3.8$ lb, $11.6 < \mu < 19.2$ lb

17. $E = 1.0$ mg, $18.8 < \mu < 20.8$ mg

19. $E = \$1,850$, $\$79,900 < \mu < \$83,600$

21. $n \geq 20$

23. a. $n \geq 24$ b. $n \geq 79$

c. The margin of error has a greater effect on the sample size required than the significance level

25. $n \geq 208$ 27. $n \geq 70$

Exercises 9.3

1. a. $E = 7.6$, $40.6 < \mu < 55.8$

b. $E = 6.0$, $60.5 < \mu < 72.5$

3. a. $E = 0.38$, $7.28 < \mu < 8.04$

b. $E = 0.11$, $3.70 < \mu < 3.92$

5. a. $E = 2.9$, $165.6 < \mu < 171.4$

b. $E = 0.067$, $0.249 < \mu < 0.383$

7. a. $E = 0.151$, $2.663 < \mu < 2.965$

b. $E = 0.88$, $20.57 < \mu < 22.33$

9. $E = 0.16$ °C, $36.34 < \mu < 36.66$ °C

11. $E = 6.7$ min, $41.8 < \mu < 55.2$ min

13. $E = 0.58$ min, $4.25 < \mu < 5.41$ min

15. a. $\bar{x} = 5.06$, $s = 1.58$

    b. $n = 16$ ($df = 15$), $\alpha = 0.05$

    $t_{\alpha/2} = 2.131$, $E = 0.84$

    $4.22 < \mu < 5.90$

17. a. $\bar{x} = 104.8$, $s = 39.06$

    b. $n = 20$ ($df = 19$), $\alpha = 0.01$

    $t_{\alpha/2} = 2.861$, $E = 25.0$

    $79.8 < \mu < 129.8$

19. a. $\bar{x} = 24.2$, $s = 10.0$

    b. $n = 9$ ($df = 8$), $\alpha = 0.10$

    $t_{\alpha/2} = 1.860$, $E = 6.2$

    $18.0 < \mu < 30.4$

21. a. $\bar{x} = 6.25$, $s = 1.16$ b. $\bar{x} = 32.4$, $s = 14.1$

23. a. $\bar{x} = 0.715$, $s = 0.122$ b. $\bar{x} = 176$, $s = 24$

Exercises 9.4

1. a. $\hat{p} = \dfrac{12}{40} = 0.30$, $E = 0.142$, $0.158 < p < 0.442$

   b. $\hat{p} = \dfrac{52}{80} = 0.65$, $E = 0.137$, $0.513 < p < 0.787$

3. a. $\hat{p} = \dfrac{111}{150} = 0.74$, $E = 0.083$, $0.657 < p < 0.823$

   b. $\hat{p} = \dfrac{63}{180} = 0.35$, $E = 0.058$, $0.292 < p < 0.408$

5. a. $\hat{p} = \dfrac{363}{400} = 0.9075$, $E = 0.0186$, $0.8889 < p < 0.9261$

   b. Can't use the Normal approximation to the $\hat{p}$-distribution since $x = np < 5$.

7. a. Can't use the Normal approximation to the $\hat{p}$-distribution since $n < 30$.

   b. $\hat{p} = \dfrac{28}{42} = 0.667$, $E = 0.169$, $0.497 < p < 0.836$

9. $\hat{p} = \dfrac{14}{400} = 0.035$, $E = 0.024$, $0.011 < p < 0.059$

11. $\hat{p} = \dfrac{112}{1,000} = 0.112$, $E = 0.023$, $0.089 < p < 0.135$

13. $\hat{p} = \dfrac{424}{520} = 0.815$, $E = 0.033$, $0.782 < p < 0.848$

15. $\hat{p} = \dfrac{78}{150} = 0.520$, $E = 0.105$, $0.415 < p < 0.625$

17. $\hat{p} = \dfrac{28}{42} = 0.853$, $E = 0.058$, $0.795 < p < 0.911$

19. The results state that the 95% confidence interval for the population proportion who plan to vote for the government party in the next election is $0.257 < p < 0.317$. Based on a sample size of $n = 1,000$ and a sample proportion of $\hat{p} = 0.287$, we compute the margin of error at the 5% level of significance to be $E = 0.028$, which is within the stated margin of error of 0.03, so the results of the study are interpreted and stated correctly.

21. The results state that the 99% confidence interval for the true proportion of cancer patients whose cancer goes into remission after treatment is completed is $0.596 < p < 0.696$. Based on a sample size of $n = 500$ and a sample proportion of $\hat{p} = 0.646$, we compute the margin of error at the 1% level of significance to be $E = 0.055$, which is NOT within the stated margin of error of 0.05, so the results of the study are not interpreted and stated correctly.

23. The results state that the 98% confidence interval for the true proportion of patients who experience symptom relief in under 1 hour is $0.93 < p < 0.97$. Based on a sample size of $n = 750$ and a sample proportion of $\hat{p} = 0.95$, we compute the margin of error at the 2% level of significance to be $E = 0.019$, which is within the stated margin of error of 0.02, so the results of the study are interpreted and stated correctly.

25. $\hat{p} = 0.50$, $n = 1068$

27. $\hat{p} = 0.05$, $n = 1286$

29. $\hat{p} = 0.75$, $n = 498$

31. $\hat{p} = 0.50$ (since we have no preliminary estimate for $\hat{p}$), $n = 212$

Chapter 9 Review Exercises

1. (i) correlation coefficient

   (ii) 99%

   (iii) $CI: 0.993 < r < 0.999$

3. (i) mean measured dose

   (ii) 90%

   (iii) $CI: 8.9 < \mu < 10.5$ mL

5. a. E will decrease, CI will narrow

   b. E will increase, CI will widen

7. a. CI will shift to $0.38 < p < 0.46$

   b. CI will narrow to $0.265 < p < 0.335$

9. a. $E = 2.74$ $CI: 148.46 < \mu < 153.94$

   b. $E = 2.63$ $CI: 32.77 < \mu < 38.03$

11. $E = 39.2$ $CI: 3,552.8 < \mu < 3,631.2$

    Yes, since 3,500 falls outside of the confidence interval.

13. $E = 4.33$ $CI: 169.97 < \mu < 178.63$ bpm

15. 117 people

17. a. $E = 1.63$ $CI: 22.94 < \mu < 26.20$

    b. $E = 0.022$ $CI: 0.927 < \mu < 0.973$

19. $E = 1.18$ $CI: 58.82 < \mu < 61.18$ mg

21. a. $\bar{x} = 14.75$ $s = 4.81$

    b. $E = 3.06$ $CI: 11.69 < \mu < 17.81$

23. a. $\bar{x} = 25.71$ $s = 5.56$

    b. $\bar{x} = 1.03$ $s = 0.352$

25. a. $\hat{p} = 0.422$ $E = 0.102$ $CI: 0.320 < p < 0.524$

    b. $\hat{p} = 0.278$ $E = 0.038$ $CI: 0.240 < p < 0.316$

27. $\hat{p} = 0.75$ $E = 0.038$

$CI : 0.712 < p < 0.788$

29. 1,770 people

Chapter 9 Self Test Exercises

1. a. correlation coefficient - r

   b. 80%   c. $0.604 < r < 0.740$

2. a. E will increase, CI will widen

   b. E will decrease, CI will shrink

3. a. CI will shift to $0.48 < p < 0.60$

   b. CI will narrow to $0.53 < p < 0.63$

4. a. $E = 1.9$ $CI : 54.4 < \mu < 58.2$

   b. $E = 5.5$ $CI : 31.5 < \mu < 42.5$

   c. $E = 0.208$ $CI : 8.106 < \mu < 8.522$

   d. $E = 0.25$ $CI : 12.59 < \mu < 13.09$

5. $E = 0.07$ $CI : -0.124 < \mu < 0.016$

   No, since 0.00 is still within the confidence interval

6. $E = 8.6$ $CI : 481.4 < \mu < 498.6$ days

   Yes, since 531 days is outside of the confidence interval

7. $E = 0.044$ $CI : 4.206 < \mu < 4.294$

8. $E = \$3,181$ $CI : 317,409 < \mu < 323,771$

9. 148 people

10. a. $\bar{x} = 32.92$ $s = 5.21$

    b. $E = 4.67$ $CI : 28.25 < \mu < 37.59$

11. a. $\bar{x} = 79$ $s = 7.98$

    b. $E = 4.61$ $CI : 74.39 < \mu < 83.61$

12. a. $\bar{x} = 62.06$ $s = 14.94$

    b. $\bar{x} = 0.877$ $s = 0.235$

13. a. $\hat{p} = 0.455$ $E = 0.041$ $CI : 0.414 < p < 0.496$

    b. $\hat{p} = 0.316$ $E = 0.097$ $CI : 0.219 < p < 0.413$

14. The pharmacist is suggesting that the 98% confidence interval for the true population proportion of underweight pills is $0.75 < p < 0.81$. However, the actual margin of error is computed to be $E = 0.048$, which is greater than the pharmacist's claim. The correct 98% confidence interval for the true proportion of underweight pills is $0.732 < p < 0.828$.

15. 2,401 people   16. 2,852 patients

Chapter 10

Exercises 10.1

1. (i) The population mean μ

   (ii) $H_0 : \mu = 28.5$ yrs $H_1 : \mu < 28.5$ yrs

   (iii) No information is given, so the 5% level of significance ($\alpha = 0.05$) is used by default.

3. (i) The population proportion p

   (ii) $H_0 : p = 0.207$ $H_1 : p \neq 0.207$

   (iii) No information is given, so the 5% level of significance ($\alpha = 0.05$) is used by default.

5. (i) The population mean μ

   (ii) $H_0 : \mu = 12.8$ mm $H_1 : \mu < 12.8$ mm

   (iii) Since there are no additional risks of using the drug even if it's not effective (i.e., no concern about a type I error), and the benefits for the patient are a high priority, a 10% level of significance ($\alpha = 0.10$) should be used to reduce the possibility of a type II error.

7. (i) The population proportion p

   (ii) $H_0 : p = 0.85$ $H_1 : p > 0.85$

   (iii) Since the physician wants to be as confident in his claim of the alternative hypothesis as possible before actually adopting it, he should use a 1% level of significance ($\alpha = 0.01$) in order to make the probability of a type I error as low as possible.

9. (i) The population correlation coefficient ρ

   (ii) $H_0 : \rho = 0$ $H_1 : \rho > 0$

   (iii) No information is given, so the 5% level of significance ($\alpha = 0.05$) is used by default.

11. (i) $z = 1.67$ $p = 2(0.0475) = 0.095$

    (ii) Since $p = 0.095 > 0.05 = \alpha$, we fail to reject the null hypothesis.

    (iii) A type II error is possible (failing to reject a false null hypothesis)

13. (i) $z = 2.15$ $p = 0.0158$

    (ii) Since $p = 0.0158 < 0.10 = \alpha$, we reject the null hypothesis.

    (iii) A type I error is possible (rejecting a true null hypothesis)

15. (i) $z = -1.81$ $p = 0.0351$

    (ii) Since $p = 0.0351 > 0.01 = \alpha$, we fail to reject the null hypothesis.

    (iii) A type II error is possible (failing to reject a false null hypothesis)

17. (i) $z = 1.87$ $p = 2(0.0307) = 0.0614$

    (ii) Since $p = 0.0614 < 0.10 = \alpha$, we reject the null hypothesis.

    (iii) A type I error is possible (rejecting a true null hypothesis)

19. (i) $z = 2.61$ $p = 0.0045$

    (ii) Since $p = 0.0045 < 0.05 = \alpha$, we reject the null hypothesis.

    (iii) A type I error is possible (rejecting a true null hypothesis)

21. (i) $H_0 : \mu = 100$ mcg/mL $H_1 : \mu \neq 100$ mcg/mL
    (ii) $\alpha = 0.05$ (iii) $z = -2.78$
    (iv) p = 2(0.0027) = 0.0054
    (v) Since p = 0.0045 < 0.05 = α, we reject the null hypothesis that the mean concentration is 100 mcg/mL. Hence, there is enough evidence to support the alternative hypothesis that the mean concentration is not 100 mcg/mL, as labelled.

23. (i) $H_0 : \mu = 140$ mmHg $H_1 : \mu > 140$ mmHg
    (ii) $\alpha = 0.10$ (iii) $z = 1.14$
    (iv) p = 0.1271
    (v) Since p = 0.1271 > 0.10 = α, we fail to reject the null hypothesis that the patient's blood pressure is 140 mmHg. Hence, there is not enough evidence to support the alternative hypothesis that the patient's condition has worsened to Stage 1 hypertension.

Exercises 10.2

1. $z = -1.87$, p = 2(0.0307) = 0.0614, fail to reject
3. $t = -2.291$, $df = 11$, $0.01 < p < 0.025$, reject
5. $t = 2.678$, $df = 31$ (rounded down to 30), $0.01 < p < 0.02$, fail to reject
7. $z = 3.00$, p = 0.0013, reject
9. Z-test, $H_0 = 69450$, $H_1 \neq 69450$, $z = -2.06$, p = 2(0.0197) = 0.0394, reject.
11. t-test, $H_0 = 12$ hours, $H_1 < 12$ hours, $t = 2.097$, $df = 23$, $t_l = 2.069$, $t_u = 2.500$, $0.01 < p < 0.025$, fail to reject.
13. t-test, $H_0 = 15{,}000$, $H_1 \neq 15{,}000$, $t = 2.808$, $df = 35$, $t_l = 2.724$, $p < 0.01$ (2-tailed), reject.
15. Z-test, $H_0 = 3350$g, $H_1 > 3350$g, $z = 2.07$, p = 0.0192 < 0.10, reject.
17. t-test, $H_0 = 12$, $H_1 < 12$, $\bar{x} = 11.2$, $s = 1.274$, $t = -1.986$, $df = 9$, $t_l = 1.833$, $t_u = 2.262$, $0.025 < p < 0.05$ (1-tailed), reject.
19. t-test, $H_0 = 120$, $H_1 > 120$, $\bar{x} = 122.3$, $s = 6.651$, $t = 1.294$, $df = 13$, $t_u = 1.350$, $p > 0.10$ (1-tailed), fail to reject.

Exercises 10.3

1. $z = 1.60$, p = 2(0.0548) = 0.1096, fail to reject
3. Since $np < 5$, we cannot use the Normal Approximation to the Binomial
5. $\hat{p} = 0.172$, $z = -2.52$, p = 0.0059, reject
7. $\hat{p} = 0.213$, $z = 1.07$, p = 0.1423, fail to reject
9. Since $n < 30$, we cannot use the Normal Approximation to the Binomial
11. $H_0 = \dfrac{6}{36} = 0.167$, $H_1 = 0.833$, $\hat{p} = 0.083$, $z = -1.74$, p = 2(0.0409) = 0.0818, fail to reject
13. $H_0 = 0.05$, $H_1 < 0.05$, $\hat{p} = 0.072$, $z = 2.26$, p = 0.0119, reject

15. $H_0 = 0.10$, $H_1 > 0.10$, $\hat{p} = 0.15$, $z = 1.83$, p = 0.0336, fail to reject
17. Since $np < 5$, we cannot use the Normal Approximation to the Binomial
19. $H_0 = 0.588$, $H_1 \neq 0.588$, $\hat{p} = 0.506$, $z = -1.54$, p = 2(0.0618) = 0.1236, fail to reject
21. $H_0 = 0.25$, $H_1 < 25$, $\hat{p} = 0.17$, $z = -1.85$, p = 0.0322, reject
23. $H_0 = 0.5$, $H_1 > 0.5$, $\hat{p} = 0.625$, $z = 1.73$, p = 0.0418, fail to reject

Exercises 10.4

1. $t = 2.146$, $df = 35$, $0.02 < p < 0.05$ (two-tails), reject
3. $t = -2.620$, $df = 10$, $0.01 < p < 0.025$ (one-tail), fail to reject
5. Since $n > 202$ (i.e., $df > 200$), we may use z: $z = 2.06$, p = 0.0197 (one-tail), reject
7. $t = 2.858$, $df = 26$, $p < 0.01$ (two-tails), reject
9. $df = 8$, $r_c = 0.632$, fail to reject
11. $df = 15$, $r_c = 0.482$, reject
13. $df = 4$, $r_c = 0.811$, reject
15. $df = 24$, $r_c = 0.388$, fail to reject
17. $H_0 = 0$, $H_1 \neq 0$, $t = 3.772$, $p < 0.01$ (two-tailed), reject.
19. $df = 22$, $r_c = 0.404$, fail to reject
21. $H_0 = 0$, $H_1 > 0$, $t = 4.064$, $p < 0.005$ (one-tailed), reject.
23. $H_0 = 0$, $H_1 < 0$, $t = -1.371$, $0.10 < p < 0.20$ (one-tailed), fail to reject.

Chapter 10 Review Exercises

1. $H_0 : p = 0.43$ $H_1 : p \neq 0.43$ 2-tailed
3. $H_0 : \mu = 10$ days $H_1 : \mu < 10$ days   left-tailed
5. (i) $z = 2.02$ p = 0.0434
   (ii) $p > 0.01$ fail to reject H_0
   (iii) Type II
7. (i) $z = -3.29$ p = 0.0010
   (ii) $p < 0.05$ reject H_0
   (iii) Type I
9. (i) $t = -3.394$ $p < 0.01$
   (ii) $p < 0.10$ reject H_0
   (iii) Type I
11. $H_0 : \mu = 4.9$ $H_1 : \mu < 4.9$ left-tailed
    $\alpha = 0.05$ $z = -4$
    $p = 0$ $p < 0.05$ reject H_0
13. $H_0 : \mu = 7$ $H_1 : \mu \neq 7$ 2 tailed
    $\alpha = 0.01$ $t = -1.414$
    $0.10 < p < 0.20$ $p > 0.01$ fail to reject H_0

15. $H_0 : \mu = 5$ $\qquad$ $H_1 : \mu > 5$ right-tailed

$\alpha = 0.10$ $\qquad$ $\bar{x} = 5.3$

$s = 0.554$ $\qquad$ $t = 1.875$

$0.025 < p < 0.05$ $\qquad$ $p < 0.10$ reject H_0

17. $z = -2.11$ $\qquad$ $p = 0.0348$

$p < 0.05$ reject H_0

19. $\hat{p} = 0.545$ $\qquad$ $z = 0.74$ $p = 0.2296$

$p > 0.05$ fail to reject H_0

21. $t = -2.757$

$p < 0.01$ $\qquad$ $p < 0.05$ reject H_0

23. $r = 0.609 < 0.632$ fail to reject

25. $H_0 : \rho = 0$ $\qquad$ $H_1 : \rho \neq 0$ 2-tailed

$\alpha = 0.01$ $\qquad$ $t = 2.902$

$p < 0.01$ reject H_0

Chapter 10 Self Test Exercises

1. a. mean dosage per pill

   b. $H_0 : \mu = 500$ mg $H_1 : \mu < 500$ mg left-tailed

   c. With no specific instructions given and no concerns stated about a type I or type II error, a 5% significance level should be used to balance the likelihood of the two types of error.

2. (i) $z = 2.70$, $p = 0.0070$

   (ii) $p < 0.01$ reject H_0 $\qquad$ (iii) Possible type I error

3. (i) $z = 1.22$, $p = 0.1112$

   (ii) $p > 0.10$ fail to reject H_0

   (iii) Possible type II error

4. (i) $t = -2.262$, $n = 56$, left-tailed $0.01 < p < 0.025$

   (ii) $p < 0.05$ reject H_0

   (iii) Possible type I error

5. $H_0 : \mu = 50$ mg $\qquad$ $H_1 : \mu \neq 50$ mg 2-tailed

   $\alpha = 0.05$

   $t = -1.312$, $0.10 < p < 0.20$

   $p > 0.05$ fail to reject H_0

6. $H_0 : \mu = 3{,}530$ g $\qquad$ $H_1 : \mu \neq 3{,}530$ g 2-tailed

   $\alpha = 0.10$

   $z = 2.62$ $p = 0.0088$

   $p < 0.10$ reject H_0

7. $H_0 : \mu = 84{,}590$ $\qquad$ $H_1 : \mu < 84{,}590$ left-tailed

   $\alpha = 0.01$

   $t = -1.298$, $p > 0.10$

   $p > 0.01$ fail to reject H_0

8. $H_0 : \mu = 45$ min $\qquad$ $H_1 : \mu > 45$ min right-tailed

   $\alpha = 0.01$

   $z = 2.8$ $p = 0.0026$ $\qquad$ $p < 0.01$ reject H_0

9. $H_0 : \mu = 266$ $\qquad$ $H_1 : \mu \neq 266$ 2-tailed

   $\alpha = 0.05$

   $\bar{x} = 263$, $s = 7.19$ $t = -1.669$, $\qquad$ $0.10 < p < 0.20$

   $p > 0.05$ fail to reject H_0

10. $H_0 : p = 0.104$ $\qquad$ $H_1 : p > 0.104$ right-tailed

    $\alpha = 0.01$

    $\hat{p} = 0.18$ $\qquad$ $z = 3.94$ $\qquad$ $p < 0.0001$ (≈ 0.0000)

    $p < 0.01$ reject H_0

11. $H_0 : p = 0.75$ $\qquad$ $H_1 : p > 0.75$ right-tailed

    $\alpha = 0.05$

    $\hat{p} = 0.81$ $\qquad$ $z = 1.39$, $p = 0.0823$

    $p > 0.05$ fail to reject H_0

12. $H_0 : \rho = 0$ $\qquad$ $H_1 : \rho \neq 0$ 2-tailed

    $\alpha = 0.05$

    $n = 15$, $d_f = 13$, Critical r-value $= 0.514$

    $r = 0.483 < 0.514$ fail to reject H_0

13. $H_0 : \rho = 0$ $\qquad$ $H_1 : \rho < 0$ left-tailed

    $\alpha = 0.05$

    $t = -2.333$ $\qquad$ $0.01 < p < 0.025$

    $p > 0.01$ fail to reject H_0

Glossary

50-50 event is an event with a probability exactly equal to 0.5, which is as equally likely to occur as it is to not occur.

Absolute Deviation is the amount by which a value in a data set differs from the mean, irrespective of its sign.

Attribute is a characteristic of the data that can be observed, measured, or categorized.

Basic Factorial Rule is most useful when we want to determine how many arrangements of a group of unique items are possible: If there are n unique items, there are $n!$ unique arrangements of those items.

Bias of an estimator is the difference between the actual value of a population parameter and the expected value (or average) of the results of the estimator for all possible samples of a given size drawn from a population.

Bi-modal data set is a data set with two modes.

Binomial Probability Distribution is the type of discrete probability distribution used to model experiments with two outcomes (or classes of outcomes): successes and failures.

Certain event is an event with a probability exactly equal to 1 is.

Chart is a method of displaying data in a graph, constructed of plotted points, lines, bars, or slices.

Clusters can be thought of as "mini-populations", and so selecting a sample requires only randomly selecting a sufficient number of these clusters and then sampling every element of the selected clusters.

Coefficient of Determination is the proportion of variation that is explained by the regression line.

Combinations are the number of unique subgroups of a set of unique objects when the order (i.e., arrangement) is irrelevant.

Complementary events given an event A, the complement of A, denoted A^c (also A' or A), is the set of all outcomes in the sample space for a given procedure that are not in A.

Compound event is an event that has more than one outcome.

Conditional probability is the probability of event B occurring given that event A has already occurred.

Confidence Interval is the range of values around an estimator that has a high probability of including the true value of the population parameter.

Contingency table is a method of displaying a summary of the values of two variables in a sample space: down the left-side column of the table, all the values of one variable are listed, and across the top row of the table, all the values of the other variable are listed.

Continuous random variable assigns a numeric value to the outcome of a measurement of a randomly selected member of the population.

Continuous uniform probability distribution is continuous random variable which can take on a value within a finite range of values, and in which every value has the same likelihood of being selected.

Continuous variables represent data that are obtained by measuring, such as measurements of length, weight, time, temperature, etc.

Convenience sampling is a method that is sometimes used to collect a sample by selecting elements of the population who are readily available and willing to participate.

Correlation coefficient (r) describes the strength of the linear relationship between two variables.

Dependent variable is a variable that may have its value affected or predicted by the value of the independent variable.

Descriptive Statistics deals with the organizing, presenting, and summarizing of raw data to provide meaningful information about the data and the group from which it was collected.

Discrete random variables take on integer values that typically represent quantities.

Discrete variables represent data that are either obtained by counting or that can only take on specific values, such as the number of students in a class, the year an event took place, the number on a die roll, etc.

Empirical Approach is an approach to calculate the probability of an event occurring, which uses results from identical (or as nearly-identical as is feasible) previous experiments that have been performed many times. It is more applicable to situations where the outcomes of an experiment are not all equally likely.

Estimators are sample statistics used to approximate population parameters.

Event is a collection of results of a procedure that possess some trait or characteristic.

Experiment (or procedure) is an action that produces measurable results.

Experimental studies, or simply experiments, involve manipulating the value of a particular variable - called a **treatment** - to determine the impact on another variable - called the **response**.

Exponential Probability Distribution is a type of continuous probability distribution that measures the time for a success to occur after a previous success.

Geometric Probability Distribution is the type of discrete probability distribution used to model experiments where the number of trials is not fixed; i.e., number of trials required to reach the first success.

Hypergeometric Probability Distribution is a type of discrete probability distribution used to model experiments where the trials are not independent; i.e., cards drawn without replacement.

Hypothesis testing is when you establish a range of values within which we would reasonably expect the sample statistic to fall, assuming the claim about the population parameter is true.

Impossible event is an event with a probability exactly equal to 0.

Independent variable is the variable used for prediction, and it can take on any value within a certain range of values.

Inferential Statistics deals with the analysis of a smaller sample drawn from a larger population to develop meaningful conclusions about the population based on sample results.

Influential points are outliers that can significantly affect (skew) the regression line.

Law of Large Numbers states that as size of sample increases, our probability estimate approaches the true probability of the event occurring in the population.

Level of Confidence is the likelihood that our range of values (confidence interval) will actually contain the true value of the population parameter.

Level of Measurement of a variable indicates what limitations (if any) exist in how the variable can be analyzed.

Level of Significance is the probability that our range (confidence interval) does not contain the value of interest.

Likely event is an event with a probability close to 1.

Maximal Margin of Error is the maximum difference between the sample statistic and the population parameter.

Mean indicates the central position of the frequency distribution; average of values in data set; measure of central tendency.

Measures of Deviation analyse the spread between data values in the set and the centre value, usually the mean.

Measures of Dispersion provide information on how the data in the data set vary from each other and/or from the central number.

Measures of Position and Range analyse the relative position of data values in the set and the spread between those values.

Median is the middle value in a data set when the terms are arranged in ascending or descending order.

Mode is the most frequently observed value in a data set.

Multi-modal is a data set with more than 2 modes.

Mutually exclusive events are two or more events that have no outcomes in common.

Non-sampling error is the result of an error in the study, such as poor sampling or data collection techniques, incorrect measurements or calculations, or researcher bias in the study.

Null Hypothesis is the default hypothesis assumed true from the start; always a statement of equality.

Observational study is a study in which researchers observe and measure the results of a particular variable in a sample of the population, without attempting to influence or manipulate the variable in any way.

Odds is a ratio between the outcomes that will result in A and the outcomes that will not result in A.

Outcome is the result observed and recorded from a simple trial of a procedure.

Outcome table can be used to identify the outcomes in the sample space in situations where there are two pieces of information to record for each outcome in the sample space, and where each of the results for each piece of information is equally-likely to occur.

Outlier is a value that is very different from the rest of the data set.

Parameter is a value that summarizes a certain variable for an entire population.

Percentiles are the data values below which a certain percentage of the ranked values lie.

Permutations are the number of unique arrangements of a subgroup of a set of unique objects when the order is important.

Placebo effect is the effect where patients seem to experience improvement, despite the treatment actually having no effect.

Poisson Distribution is the type of discrete probability distribution used to model the frequency of an occurrence of an event.

Population refers to a set of all possible individuals, objects, or measurements of items of interest.

Power of a test is the overall likelihood that the alternative hypothesis will be accepted.

Probability is the proportion of outcomes that can occur that will result in event A, often expressed as a fraction, decimal, or percent.

p-value is the probability of getting a result at least as extreme as the test statistic that we computed.

Qualitative variables represent non-numeric data that can neither be measured nor counted.

Quantitative variables represent numeric data that can be measured or counted.

Random variables assign a numeric value to every outcome in the sample space.

Randomization is a sampling method where every element in the population has an equal chance of being selected for the sample.

Range is the difference between the highest value and lowest value in a data set.

Residual is the difference between the actual value of the dependent variable and the predicted value.

Sample refers to a subset drawn from the population, meaning a portion or part of the population.

Sample Proportion is the proportion of a sample that meets a certain criteria.

Sample space is the collection of all possible equally-likely outcomes of a procedure. We use S to denote the sample space.

Sampling Distribution is the distribution of values for the sample statistic for all possible random samples of size n drawn from the population; more useful when more concerned about trends than individual results.

Sampling Distribution of Sample Means is a distribution of the sample means of all samples of a particular sample size n.

Sampling Distribution of Sample Proportions is a distribution of the proportion of "successful" outcomes in a random sample of n repetitions of a binomial experiment.

Sampling error is the difference between an observed sample statistic and actual population parameter is known.

Simple event is an event that has only one outcome.

Slope of the regression equation is the predictable change in the dependent variable for a unit change in the independent variable.

Standard deviation is the extent to which scores deviate from the mean.

Standard Error of Mean is the standard deviation of the sampling distribution of sample means.

Standard Normal Distribution is a normal continuous probability distribution with a mean of 0 ($\mu = 0$) and variance of 1 ($\sigma^2 = 1$).

Statistic is a value that summarizes a certain variable for a sample.

Statistical studies are conducted when researchers desire to know the value of a particular variable in a population.

Statistics is a branch of both mathematics and science that helps researchers to develop a set of procedures to collect, organize, present, analyze, and interpret data for the purposes of drawing conclusions and/or making a decision.

Student's t-distribution is used to estimate an unknown population mean with a confidence interval constructed using the mean and standard deviation of a sample.

Subjective Approach is an approach to calculate the probability of an event occurring which uses the knowledge of an expert who is able to analyze certain conditions and compare that to previous results where conditions were similar.

Survey is one of the main types of statistical study. In a survey, respondents are asked questions and they are responsible for providing the information about themselves to researchers through their answers.

Table is a method of displaying data in a 2-dimensional grid, organized into rows and columns.

Theoretical Approach, also known as the Classical Approach, is an approach to calculate the probability of an event occurring, which requires us to know all the outcomes in the sample space and that every outcome in the sample space has the same likelihood of occurring.

Tree diagram is a method to list out all the outcomes in an experiment.

Trimmed mean is a simple arithmetic mean of the middle values in the data set after a certain percent of highest and lowest values are removed from the data set.

Type I Error is rejecting a true null hypothesis.

Type II Error is failing to reject a false null hypothesis.

Unlikely event is an event with a probability close to 0.

Variable represents the value of an attribute.

Variance is the mean of the squared deviations from each data value to the mean.

Venn diagram is used to determine the sample space in situations where the outcomes are grouped together by characteristics of the data into categories (with or without overlap).

Index

Summary of Formulas

Measures of Central Tendency

Mean of a Sample | 2.1-a

$$\bar{x} = \frac{Sum\ of\ All\ the\ Values\ of\ the\ Terms}{Number\ of\ Terms} = \frac{\sum x}{n}$$

Location of the Median | 2.1-c

$$L_m = \frac{(n+1)}{2}$$

Geometric Mean | 2.2-b

$$G = \sqrt[n]{\prod x} = \left(\prod x\right)^{\frac{1}{n}}$$

Mean of a Population | 2.1-b

$$\mu = \frac{Sum\ of\ All\ the\ Values\ of\ the\ Terms}{Number\ of\ Terms} = \frac{\sum x}{N}$$

Weighted Arithmetic Mean | 2.2-a

$$\bar{x} = \frac{Sum\ of\ All\ the\ Weighted\ Data\ Values}{Sum\ of\ All\ the\ Weights} = \frac{\sum(w \cdot x)}{\sum w}$$

Harmonic Mean | 2.2-c

$$H = \frac{n}{\sum\left(\frac{1}{x}\right)}$$

Measures of Dispersion

Location of the kth Percentile | 3.1-a

$$L_k = \frac{k}{100} \cdot (n+1)$$

Range | 3.1-b

$$Range = Maximum\ Value - Minimum\ Value$$

Interquartile Range | 3.1-c

$$Interquartile\ Range\ (IQR) = Upper\ Quartile\ (Q_3) - Lower\ Quartile\ (Q_1)$$

Mean Absolute Deviation from the Mean | 3.2-a

$$Mean\ Absolute\ Deviation\ from\ the\ Mean\ (MAD) = \frac{\sum|x - \bar{x}|}{n}$$

Variance of a Population | 3.2-b

$$\sigma^2 = \frac{\sum(x - \mu)^2}{N}$$

Variance of a Sample | 3.2-c

$$s^2 = \frac{\sum(x - \bar{x})^2}{n-1} \quad \textbf{or} \quad s^2 = \frac{n \cdot (\sum x^2) - (\sum x)^2}{n(n-1)}$$

Standard Deviation of a Population | 3.2-d

$$\sigma = \sqrt{\frac{\sum(x - \mu)^2}{N}}$$

Standard Deviation of a Sample | 3.2-e

$$s = \sqrt{\frac{\sum(x - \bar{x})^2}{n-1}} \quad \textbf{or} \quad s = \sqrt{\frac{n \cdot (\sum x^2) - (\sum x)^2}{n(n-1)}}$$

Coefficient of Variation | 3.2-f

$$CV_{population} = \frac{\sigma}{\mu} \times 100\% \quad \textbf{or} \quad CV_{sample} = \frac{s}{\bar{x}} \times 100\%$$

Linear Correlation and Regression

Pearson's Linear Correlation Coefficient | 4.1

$$r = \frac{n\left(\sum xy\right) - \left(\sum x\right)\left(\sum y\right)}{\sqrt{n\left(\sum x^2\right) - \left(\sum x\right)^2} \cdot \sqrt{n\left(\sum y^2\right) - \left(\sum y\right)^2}}$$

Slope of the Least-Squares Regression Line | 4.2-a

$$b = \frac{n\left(\sum xy\right) - \left(\sum x\right)\left(\sum y\right)}{n\left(\sum x^2\right) - \left(\sum x\right)^2}$$

y-intercept of the Least-Squares Regression Line | 4.2-b

$$a = \bar{y} - b \cdot \bar{x}$$

Coefficient of Determination | 4.2-c

$$r^2 = 1 - \frac{SSE}{SST} \quad \textbf{or} \quad r^2 = \frac{SSR}{SST}$$

SUM OF SQUARES

Total Variation

$$SST = \Sigma(y - \bar{y})^2$$

Explained Variation

$$SSR = \Sigma(\hat{y} - \bar{y})^2$$

Unexplained Variation

$$SSE = \Sigma(y - \hat{y})^2$$

Elementary Probability Theory

Theoretical Approach to Probability | 5.1-a

$$P(A) = \frac{\text{\# of ways event } A \text{ can occur}}{\text{total \# of outcomes in } S} = \frac{n(A)}{n(S)}$$

Empirical Approach to Probability | 5.1-b

$$P(A) = \frac{\text{\# of ways event } A \text{ occurred}}{\text{total \# of trials}} = \frac{n(A)}{n(E)}$$

Probability of a Complementary Event | 5.1-c

$$P(A^c) = 1 - P(A)$$

Generalized Addition Rule for Probabilities | 5.2-a

$$P(A \text{ or } B) = P(A) + P(B) - P(A \text{ and } B)$$

Generalized Multiplication Rule for Probabilities | 5.2-b

$$P(A \text{ and } B) = P(A) \cdot P(B|A)$$

Bayes' Theorem | 5.2-c

$$P(A|B) = \frac{P(B|A) \cdot P(A)}{P(B|A) \cdot P(A) + P(B|A^c) \cdot P(A^c)}$$

Number of Arrangements with Repeated Items | 5.3-a

$$\text{Number of Arrangements} = \frac{n!}{(k_1!)(k_2!)(k_3!) \dots (k_m!)}$$

where $k_1, \dots, k_m$ represent the sizes of each group of identical items in n items

Permutations | 5.3-b

$$_nP_r = \frac{n!}{(n - r)!}$$

Combinations | 5.3-c

$$_nC_r = \binom{n}{r} = \frac{n!}{(n - r)! \cdot r!}$$

Discrete Probability Distributions

Expected Value (Mean) for a Discrete Probability Distribution | 6.1-a

$$E(X) = \mu = \sum_{\text{all } x} \left(x \cdot P(x)\right)$$

Variance for a Discrete Probability Distribution | 6.1-b

$$Var(X) = \sigma^2 = \sum_{\text{all } x} \left((x - \mu)^2 \cdot P(x)\right) \quad \textbf{or}$$

$$Var(X) = \sigma^2 = \sum_{\text{all } x} \left(x^2 \cdot P(x)\right) - \mu^2$$

Standard Deviation for a Discrete Probability Distribution | 6.1-c

$$SD(X) = \sigma = \sqrt{\sum_{\text{all } x} \left((x - \mu)^2 \cdot P(x)\right)} \quad \textbf{or}$$

$$SD(X) = \sigma = \sqrt{\sum_{\text{all } x} \left(x^2 \cdot P(x)\right) - \mu^2}$$

Binomial Formula | 6.2

$$P(x) = \binom{n}{x} p^x \cdot q^{(n-x)}$$

Hypergeometric Distribution | 6.3-a

$$P(x) = \frac{\binom{r}{x} \cdot \binom{N-r}{n-x}}{\binom{N}{n}}$$

Geometric Distribution | 6.3-b

$$P(x) = q^{x-1} \cdot p = (1-p)^{x-1} \cdot p$$

Poisson Distribution | 6.3-c

$$P(x) = \frac{\lambda^x \cdot e^{-\lambda}}{x!}$$

Continuous Probability Distributions

Continuous Uniform Distribution | 7.1-a

$$P(c < X < d) = (d-c) \cdot \frac{1}{(b-a)} = \frac{(d-c)}{(b-a)}$$

Exponential Distribution | 7.1-b

$$P(X < t) = 1 - e^{-\lambda t} \qquad P(X > t) = e^{-\lambda t} \qquad P(t_1 < X < t_2) = e^{-\lambda t_1} - e^{-\lambda t_2}$$

Converting Raw X-Scores to Z-Scores | 7.2-a

$$z = \frac{x - \mu}{\sigma}$$

Converting Z-Scores to Raw X-Scores | 7.2-b

$$x = \mu + z \cdot \sigma$$

Sampling Distributions and the Central Limit Theorem

Z-score for Sampling Distribution of Sample Means | 8.2-a

$$z = \frac{\bar{x} - \mu_{\bar{x}}}{\sigma_{\bar{x}}} = \frac{\bar{x} - \mu}{\frac{\sigma}{\sqrt{n}}}$$

Finite Population Correction (FPC) Factor | 8.2-b

$$FPC = \sqrt{\frac{N-n}{N-1}}$$

Corrected Standard Error of the Mean using the FPC Factor | 8.2-c

$$\sigma_{\bar{x}} = \frac{\sigma}{\sqrt{n}} \cdot FPC = \frac{\sigma}{\sqrt{n}} \cdot \sqrt{\frac{N-n}{N-1}}$$

Z-score for Sampling Distribution of Sample Proportions | 8.3

$$z = \frac{\hat{p} - \mu_{\hat{p}}}{\sigma_{\hat{p}}} = \frac{\hat{p} - p}{\sqrt{\frac{p(1-p)}{n}}}$$

Estimation and Confidence Intervals

Maximal Margin of Error between μ and $\bar{x}$ | 9.2-a

$$E = z_{\alpha/2} \cdot \sigma_{\bar{x}} = z_{\alpha/2} \cdot \frac{\sigma}{\sqrt{n}}$$

Confidence Interval for μ | 9.2-b

$$\bar{x} - E < \mu < \bar{x} + E$$

Sample Size for μ | 9.2-c

$$n = \left(\frac{z_{\alpha/2} \cdot \sigma}{E} \right)^2$$

Student's t-value | 9.3-a

$$t = \frac{\bar{x} - \mu}{\frac{s}{\sqrt{n}}}$$

Maximal Margin of Error for the Student's t-distribution | 9.3-b

$$E = t_{\alpha/2} \cdot \frac{s}{\sqrt{n}}$$

Maximal Margin of Error between p and $\hat{p}$ | 9.4-a

$$E = z_{\alpha/2} \cdot \sigma_{\hat{p}} \approx z_{\alpha/2} \cdot \sqrt{\frac{\hat{p} \cdot \hat{q}}{n}}$$

Confidence Interval for p | 9.4-b

$$\hat{p} - E < p < \hat{p} + E$$

Sample Size for p | 9.4-c

$$n = \hat{p} \cdot \hat{q} \cdot \left(\frac{z_{\alpha/2}}{E}\right)^2$$

Hypothesis Testing

Test Statistic for μ when σ is known or n is large ($n > 201$)

$$z = \frac{\bar{x} - \mu}{\frac{\sigma}{\sqrt{n}}}$$

Test Statistic for μ when σ is unknown

$$t = \frac{\bar{x} - \mu}{\frac{s}{\sqrt{n}}}$$

Test Statistic for p

$$z = \frac{\hat{p} - p}{\sqrt{\frac{pq}{n}}}$$

Test Statistic for ρ

$$t = \frac{r}{\sqrt{\frac{1 - r^2}{n - 2}}}$$

Appendices

Appendix I-a: Table of Areas under the Standard Normal Distribution below Negative z-scores

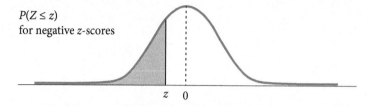

$P(Z \leq z)$
for negative z-scores

z	0.09	0.08	0.07	0.06	0.05	0.04	0.03	0.02	0.01	0.00
−3.6	0.0001	0.0001	0.0001	0.0001	0.0001	0.0001	0.0001	0.0001	0.0002	0.0002
−3.5	0.0002	0.0002	0.0002	0.0002	0.0002	0.0002	0.0002	0.0002	0.0002	0.0002
−3.4	0.0002	0.0003	0.0003	0.0003	0.0003	0.0003	0.0003	0.0003	0.0003	0.0003
−3.3	0.0003	0.0004	0.0004	0.0004	0.0004	0.0004	0.0004	0.0005	0.0005	0.0005
−3.2	0.0005	0.0005	0.0005	0.0006	0.0006	0.0006	0.0006	0.0006	0.0007	0.0007
−3.1	0.0007	0.0007	0.0008	0.0008	0.0008	0.0008	0.0009	0.0009	0.0009	0.0010
−3.0	0.0010	0.0010	0.0011	0.0011	0.0011	0.0012	0.0012	0.0013	0.0013	0.0013
−2.9	0.0014	0.0014	0.0015	0.0015	0.0016	0.0016	0.0017	0.0018	0.0018	0.0019
−2.8	0.0019	0.0020	0.0021	0.0021	0.0022	0.0023	0.0023	0.0024	0.0025	0.0026
−2.7	0.0026	0.0027	0.0028	0.0029	0.0030	0.0031	0.0032	0.0033	0.0034	0.0035
−2.6	0.0036	0.0037	0.0038	0.0039	0.0040	0.0041	0.0043	0.0044	0.0045	0.0047
−2.5	0.0048	0.0049	0.0051	0.0052	0.0054	0.0055	0.0057	0.0059	0.0060	0.0062
−2.4	0.0064	0.0066	0.0068	0.0069	0.0071	0.0073	0.0075	0.0078	0.0080	0.0082
−2.3	0.0084	0.0087	0.0089	0.0091	0.0094	0.0096	0.0099	0.0102	0.0104	0.0107
−2.2	0.0110	0.0113	0.0116	0.0119	0.0122	0.0125	0.0129	0.0132	0.0136	0.0139
−2.1	0.0143	0.0146	0.0150	0.0154	0.0158	0.0162	0.0166	0.0170	0.0174	0.0179
−2.0	0.0183	0.0188	0.0192	0.0197	0.0202	0.0207	0.0212	0.0217	0.0222	0.0228
−1.9	0.0233	0.0239	0.0244	0.0250	0.0256	0.0262	0.0268	0.0274	0.0281	0.0287
−1.8	0.0294	0.0301	0.0307	0.0314	0.0322	0.0329	0.0336	0.0344	0.0351	0.0359
−1.7	0.0367	0.0375	0.0384	0.0392	0.0401	0.0409	0.0418	0.0427	0.0436	0.0446
−1.6	0.0455	0.0465	0.0475	0.0485	0.0495	0.0505	0.0516	0.0526	0.0537	0.0548
−1.5	0.0559	0.0571	0.0582	0.0594	0.0606	0.0618	0.0630	0.0643	0.0655	0.0668
−1.4	0.0681	0.0694	0.0708	0.0721	0.0735	0.0749	0.0764	0.0778	0.0793	0.0808
−1.3	0.0823	0.0838	0.0853	0.0869	0.0885	0.0901	0.0918	0.0934	0.0951	0.0968
−1.2	0.0985	0.1003	0.1020	0.1038	0.1056	0.1075	0.1093	0.1112	0.1131	0.1151
−1.1	0.1170	0.1190	0.1210	0.1230	0.1251	0.1271	0.1292	0.1314	0.1335	0.1357
−1.0	0.1379	0.1401	0.1423	0.1446	0.1469	0.1492	0.1515	0.1539	0.1562	0.1587
−0.9	0.1611	0.1635	0.1660	0.1685	0.1711	0.1736	0.1762	0.1788	0.1814	0.1841
−0.8	0.1867	0.1894	0.1922	0.1949	0.1977	0.2005	0.2033	0.2061	0.2090	0.2119
−0.7	0.2148	0.2177	0.2206	0.2236	0.2266	0.2296	0.2327	0.2358	0.2389	0.2420
−0.6	0.2451	0.2483	0.2514	0.2546	0.2578	0.2611	0.2643	0.2676	0.2709	0.2743
−0.5	0.2776	0.2810	0.2843	0.2877	0.2912	0.2946	0.2981	0.3015	0.3050	0.3085
−0.4	0.3121	0.3156	0.3192	0.3228	0.3264	0.3300	0.3336	0.3372	0.3409	0.3446
−0.3	0.3483	0.3520	0.3557	0.3594	0.3632	0.3669	0.3707	0.3745	0.3783	0.3821
−0.2	0.3859	0.3897	0.3936	0.3974	0.4013	0.4052	0.4090	0.4129	0.4168	0.4207
−0.1	0.4247	0.4286	0.4325	0.4364	0.4404	0.4443	0.4483	0.4522	0.4562	0.4602
−0.0	0.4641	0.4681	0.4721	0.4761	0.4801	0.4840	0.4880	0.4920	0.4960	0.5000

Appendix I-b: Table of Areas under the Standard Normal Distribution below Positive z-scores

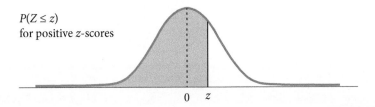

$P(Z \leq z)$
for positive z-scores

z	0.00	0.01	0.02	0.03	0.04	0.05	0.06	0.07	0.08	0.09
0.0	0.5000	0.5040	0.5080	0.5120	0.5160	0.5199	0.5239	0.5279	0.5319	0.5359
0.1	0.5398	0.5438	0.5478	0.5517	0.5557	0.5596	0.5636	0.5675	0.5714	0.5753
0.2	0.5793	0.5832	0.5871	0.5910	0.5948	0.5987	0.6026	0.6064	0.6103	0.6141
0.3	0.6179	0.6217	0.6255	0.6293	0.6331	0.6368	0.6406	0.6443	0.6480	0.6517
0.4	0.6554	0.6591	0.6628	0.6664	0.6700	0.6736	0.6772	0.6808	0.6844	0.6879
0.5	0.6915	0.6950	0.6985	0.7019	0.7054	0.7088	0.7123	0.7157	0.7190	0.7224
0.6	0.7257	0.7291	0.7324	0.7357	0.7389	0.7422	0.7454	0.7486	0.7517	0.7549
0.7	0.7580	0.7611	0.7642	0.7673	0.7704	0.7734	0.7764	0.7794	0.7823	0.7852
0.8	0.7881	0.7910	0.7939	0.7967	0.7995	0.8023	0.8051	0.8078	0.8106	0.8133
0.9	0.8159	0.8186	0.8212	0.8238	0.8264	0.8289	0.8315	0.8340	0.8365	0.8389
1.0	0.8413	0.8438	0.8461	0.8485	0.8508	0.8531	0.8554	0.8577	0.8599	0.8621
1.1	0.8643	0.8665	0.8686	0.8708	0.8729	0.8749	0.8770	0.8790	0.8810	0.8830
1.2	0.8849	0.8869	0.8888	0.8907	0.8925	0.8944	0.8962	0.8980	0.8997	0.9015
1.3	0.9032	0.9049	0.9066	0.9082	0.9099	0.9115	0.9131	0.9147	0.9162	0.9177
1.4	0.9192	0.9207	0.9222	0.9236	0.9251	0.9265	0.9279	0.9292	0.9306	0.9319
1.5	0.9332	0.9345	0.9357	0.9370	0.9382	0.9394	0.9406	0.9418	0.9429	0.9441
1.6	0.9452	0.9463	0.9474	0.9484	0.9495	0.9505	0.9515	0.9525	0.9535	0.9545
1.7	0.9554	0.9564	0.9573	0.9582	0.9591	0.9599	0.9608	0.9616	0.9625	0.9633
1.8	0.9641	0.9649	0.9656	0.9664	0.9671	0.9678	0.9686	0.9693	0.9699	0.9706
1.9	0.9713	0.9719	0.9726	0.9732	0.9738	0.9744	0.9750	0.9756	0.9761	0.9767
2.0	0.9772	0.9778	0.9783	0.9788	0.9793	0.9798	0.9803	0.9808	0.9812	0.9817
2.1	0.9821	0.9826	0.9830	0.9834	0.9838	0.9842	0.9846	0.9850	0.9854	0.9857
2.2	0.9861	0.9864	0.9868	0.9871	0.9875	0.9878	0.9881	0.9884	0.9887	0.9890
2.3	0.9893	0.9896	0.9898	0.9901	0.9904	0.9906	0.9909	0.9911	0.9913	0.9916
2.4	0.9918	0.9920	0.9922	0.9925	0.9927	0.9929	0.9931	0.9932	0.9934	0.9936
2.5	0.9938	0.9940	0.9941	0.9943	0.9945	0.9946	0.9948	0.9949	0.9951	0.9952
2.6	0.9953	0.9955	0.9956	0.9957	0.9959	0.9960	0.9961	0.9962	0.9963	0.9964
2.7	0.9965	0.9966	0.9967	0.9968	0.9969	0.9970	0.9971	0.9972	0.9973	0.9974
2.8	0.9974	0.9975	0.9976	0.9977	0.9977	0.9978	0.9979	0.9979	0.9980	0.9981
2.9	0.9981	0.9982	0.9982	0.9983	0.9984	0.9984	0.9985	0.9985	0.9986	0.9986
3.0	0.9987	0.9987	0.9987	0.9988	0.9988	0.9989	0.9989	0.9989	0.9990	0.9990
3.1	0.9990	0.9991	0.9991	0.9991	0.9992	0.9992	0.9992	0.9992	0.9993	0.9993
3.2	0.9993	0.9993	0.9994	0.9994	0.9994	0.9994	0.9994	0.9995	0.9995	0.9995
3.3	0.9995	0.9995	0.9995	0.9996	0.9996	0.9996	0.9996	0.9996	0.9996	0.9997
3.4	0.9997	0.9997	0.9997	0.9997	0.9997	0.9997	0.9997	0.9997	0.9997	0.9998
3.5	0.9998	0.9998	0.9998	0.9998	0.9998	0.9998	0.9998	0.9998	0.9998	0.9998
3.6	0.9998	0.9998	0.9999	0.9999	0.9999	0.9999	0.9999	0.9999	0.9999	0.9999

Appendix II: Student's *t*-Distribution Table

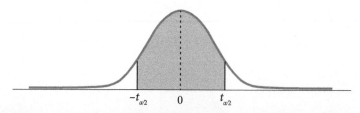

df	80% confidence $\alpha = 0.20$ $\alpha/2 = 0.10$	90% confidence $\alpha = 0.10$ $\alpha/2 = 0.05$	95% confidence $\alpha = 0.05$ $\alpha/2 = 0.025$	98% confidence $\alpha = 0.02$ $\alpha/2 = 0.01$	99% confidence $\alpha = 0.01$ $\alpha/2 = 0.005$
1	3.078	6.314	12.706	31.820	63.657
2	1.886	2.920	4.303	6.965	9.925
3	1.638	2.353	3.182	4.541	5.841
4	1.533	2.132	2.776	3.747	4.604
5	1.476	2.015	2.571	3.365	4.032
6	1.440	1.943	2.447	3.143	3.707
7	1.415	1.895	2.365	2.998	3.499
8	1.397	1.860	2.306	2.897	3.355
9	1.383	1.833	2.262	2.821	3.250
10	1.372	1.812	2.228	2.764	3.169
11	1.363	1.796	2.201	2.718	3.106
12	1.356	1.782	2.179	2.681	3.055
13	1.350	1.771	2.160	2.650	3.012
14	1.345	1.761	2.145	2.625	2.977
15	1.341	1.753	2.131	2.602	2.947
16	1.337	1.746	2.120	2.584	2.921
17	1.333	1.740	2.110	2.567	2.898
18	1.330	1.734	2.101	2.552	2.878
19	1.328	1.729	2.093	2.539	2.861
20	1.325	1.725	2.086	2.528	2.845
21	1.323	1.721	2.080	2.518	2.831
22	1.321	1.717	2.074	2.508	2.819
23	1.319	1.714	2.069	2.500	2.807
24	1.318	1.711	2.064	2.492	2.797
25	1.316	1.708	2.060	2.485	2.787
26	1.315	1.706	2.056	2.479	2.779
27	1.314	1.703	2.052	2.473	2.771
28	1.313	1.701	2.048	2.467	2.763
29	1.311	1.699	2.045	2.462	2.756
30	1.310	1.697	2.042	2.457	2.750
35	1.306	1.690	2.030	2.438	2.724
40	1.303	1.684	2.021	2.423	2.704
45	1.301	1.679	2.014	2.412	2.690
50	1.299	1.676	2.009	2.403	2.678
60	1.296	1.671	2.000	2.390	2.660
70	1.294	1.667	1.994	2.381	2.648
80	1.292	1.664	1.990	2.374	2.639
90	1.291	1.662	1.987	2.369	2.632
100	1.290	1.660	1.984	2.364	2.626
120	1.289	1.658	1.980	2.358	2.617
150	1.287	1.655	1.976	2.351	2.609
200	1.286	1.652	1.972	2.345	2.601
$\infty\,(z_{\alpha/2})$	1.282	1.645	1.960	2.326	2.576

Appendix III: Critical z–values ($z_{\alpha/2}$) for Various Confidence Levels

Confidence Level	Critical z-value ($z_{\alpha/2}$)
80%	1.282
90%	1.645
95%	1.960
98%	2.326
99%	2.576

Appendix IV-a: Correlation Coefficient r and Strength of Relationship

Correlation Coefficient (r)	Strength of Relationship
$r = 1.0$	Perfect and Positive
$0.7 \leq r < 1.0$	Strong and Positive
$0.5 \leq r < 0.7$	Moderate and Positive
$0.3 \leq r < 0.5$	Weak and Positive
$0.1 \leq r < 0.3$	Very Weak and Positive
$r = -1.0$	Perfect and Negative
$-1.0 < r \leq -0.7$	Strong and Negative
$-0.7 < r \leq -0.5$	Moderate and Negative
$-0.5 < r \leq -0.3$	Weak and Negative
$-0.3 < r \leq -0.1$	Very Weak and Negative
$-0.1 < r < 0.1$	No Correlation

Appendix IV-b: 5% Significance Table for r

df $(n-2)$	r	df $(n-2)$	r
1	0.997	16	0.468
2	0.950	17	0.456
3	0.878	18	0.444
4	0.811	19	0.433
5	0.754	20	0.423
6	0.707	21	0.413
7	0.666	22	0.404
8	0.632	23	0.396
9	0.602	24	0.388
10	0.576	25	0.381
11	0.553	26	0.374
12	0.532	27	0.367
13	0.514	28	0.361
14	0.497	29	0.355
15	0.482	30	0.349